THE JUDICIAL PROCESS

LAW, COURTS, AND JUDICIAL POLITICS

Second Edition

CHRISTOPHER P. BANKS
KENT STATE UNIVERSITY

DAVID M. O'BRIEN
THE LATE LEONE REAVES AND GEORGE W. SPICER PROFESSOR
UNIVERSITY OF VIRGINIA

WEST
ACADEMIC
PUBLISHING

© 2021 LEG, Inc. d/b/a West Academic
    444 Cedar Street, Suite 700
    St. Paul, MN 55101
    1-877-888-1330

West, West Academic Publishing, and West Academic are trademarks of West Publishing Corporation, used under license.

Printed in the United States of America

ISBN: 978-1-64242-255-9

From Christopher P. Banks:

To the memory of my parents, Richard and Frances Banks, and my mentor, co-author and friend, David M. O'Brien.

From the family of David M. O'Brien:

To the memory of our beloved dad and husband, David M. O'Brien.

Tables and Figures

Figures

Preface

The Judicial Process: Law, Courts, and Judicial Politics introduces students to the nature and significance of the judicial process in the United States and across the globe. It is written from a unique interdisciplinary perspective that combines political science research with scholarship that is centered in traditional legal studies. At its core, the textbook is an introduction to civil and criminal law, jurisprudence, judicial organization and judicial selection, the legal profession, the criminal and civil judicial process, and the scope and limitations of judicial policymaking. It is designed for a wide range of courses in the legal academy, political science and sociology. All instructors teaching law or law-related courses will find it attractive because it contains an in-depth analysis of legal theory and political jurisprudence, topics that are frequently absent from other textbooks. Moreover, unlike most textbooks, it focuses not only on U.S. courts, but also to comparative courts and judicial politics. In addition, this book highlights contemporary controversies and debates over the role of courts in American society and elsewhere. Overall, these features will engage and challenge students to learn about the law and the politics underlying the judicial process.

Key Features

The Judicial Process: Law, Courts, and Judicial Politics' unique legal and social science perspective is complemented by several useful pedagogical tools that facilitate student learning. The book's **"Contemporary Controversies over Courts"** boxes offer unique insight into cutting-edge and highly relevant issues of law, courts, and judicial politics, such as problem-solving courts, the "hardball politics" of judicial selection, "pay as you go" justice, animal rights, plea bargaining trends, the law of precedent, judicial decisions limiting the availability of class actions, and the role of courts in making social policy, among others. The **"In Comparative Perspective"** boxes acquaint students with a range of topics, including the significance of major global legal systems, comparative perspectives on law and morality, constitutional courts in Europe and the European Court of Justice, as well as the roles lawyers, juries, and alternative dispute-resolution techniques play in the United States and throughout the world. In addition to containing numerous visual and descriptive aids for students, including easy to comprehend **charts** and **figures** on all aspects of the judicial process, each chapter has a **chapter summary, key questions for review and critical analysis, web links,** and **selected readings**. These features highlight poignant issues relating to the study of the judicial process, law, courts, and judicial politics. The **Glossary** is a key resource for understanding the complexities of legal terminology. In addition, **Appendix A** gives students the "nuts and bolts" of how to conduct legal research and writing. Finally, **Appendix B** is a useful resource listing the historical and contemporary membership of the Supreme Court of the United States, the most important judicial forum in the United States.

Instructor Resources

For this textbook, instructor resources are available at West Academic's web page at westacademic.com. These include:

- A **test bank** that provides a diverse range of pre-written questions as well as the opportunity to edit any question and/or insert personalized questions to effectively assess students' progress and understanding.

- Editable, chapter-specific **PowerPoint slides** that offer complete flexibility for creating a multimedia presentation for the course.

- **Moot court hypotheticals** that give instructors the flexibility to edit for application to contemporary, cutting-edge issues in constitutional law and politics.

- **Edited U.S. Supreme Court and other key federal or state judicial opinions** that are referred to in the textbook or of current interest to academics and court watchers.

Overview

Part I focuses on the nature of law and its relationship to judicial politics in society. **Chapter One** analyzes legal systems, the sources of public and private law, and the role courts play in resolving legal disputes and defending personal freedoms. **Chapter Two** addresses classical and contemporary legal theories, or political jurisprudence ranging from natural law to critical legal studies, and how those theories affect law and policy.

Part II considers judicial organization and administration. **Chapter Three** describes the origin and structure of state and federal courts, as well as the politics of judicial reform. **Chapter Four** builds on that discussion by explaining how judges become political actors as they are socialized in the various ways they are recruited, retained, and removed from office.

Part III turns to access to courts and how formal and informal barriers affect judicial decision-making and access to justice. Adversarial civil and criminal judicial processes are analyzed. In **Chapter Five**, the role legal culture and lawyers play in delivering legal services and providing access to justice is discussed. Access to courts in terms of formal and informal barriers of justiciability (legal standing, mootness, and similar doctrines of judicial restraint or abstention) is the subject of **Chapter Six**, along with the different strategies interest groups employ to effectuate policy change during litigation. Chapters Seven and Eight analyze the adversarial system and the differences between criminal procedure and civil litigation at the trial level. In **Chapter Seven**, the key role prosecutors play in charging defendants and negotiating plea bargains, as well as the significance of juries and the politics underlying sentencing practices, is detailed. In contrast, **Chapter Eight** considers civil litigation, liability trends, and the process of seeking monetary compensation for personal injuries, along with tort reform and alternative dispute-resolution methods.

Part IV explores judicial policymaking and the scope and limits of judicial power in appellate courts. **Chapter Nine** details the appellate judicial process, including how scholars generally study judicial behavior, and how courts establish law and public policy in setting their agendas and writing judicial opinions. **Chapter Ten**, then, concludes with a consideration of controversies over the role and impact of appellate courts, with particular attention to the legal and political debate over public school financing, abortion, capital punishment, school desegregation, and LGBT rights and same-sex marriage cases in state and federal courts. The different types of internal and external constraints on judicial power, along with the policymaking impact of courts, are thoroughly considered in the context of those areas of law, along with the important issue of race, equality, and school desegregation.

This second edition updates the chapter introductions, the content, and the contemporary controversies and comparative perspective boxes. It adds new perspectives that incorporate the unique impact that the Trump administration has on law and courts, and the judicial process, including his appointments to the lower federal courts as well as to the Supreme Court by way of the confirmations of Justices Neil Gorsuch and Brett Kavanaugh. It blends recent Supreme Court cases, and the impact of the Covid 19 pandemic, and the civil unrest generated by George Floyd's killing by a white police officer and ongoing racial tensions, into its analyses of the judicial process. It has several new boxes that address cutting edge issues, such as the politicization of the Foreign Intelligence Surveillance Court, the impact of veterans' problem-solving courts, Title IX sexual assaults on campus, European Constitutional Courts, the role of the Federalist Society in judicial selection, legal education and lawyers in Western democracies, the right to counsel and "pay as you go" criminal justice, justiciability in animal rights' cases, global legal trends in plea bargaining, the global impact of jury systems and alternative dispute resolution methods, the dispute pyramid, class actions, constitutional interpretation, the significance of the doctrine of *stare decisis* and the law of precedent, the European Court of Justice, and the judicial role in creating major social change. Also new to this edition are the pedagogical tools of moot court hypotheticals, which will aid instructors in teaching students about critical legal reasoning and advocacy skills with respect of U.S. Supreme Court jurisprudence, and edited U.S. Supreme Court and other key federal or state judicial opinions that are referred to in the textbook or of current interest to academics and court watchers. Some of the features of the new edition include:

- Analyses of the political and jurisprudential implications of the impeachment hearings initiated against President Donald Trump.

- Detailed overviews of the President Trump's and Senate Republicans to transform the ideological direction of the Supreme Court and lower federal courts through a hardline court packing strategy that departs from longstanding Senate procedures and norms and emphasizes the role that the Federalist Society plays in judicial selection.

- Discussions of recent Supreme Court decisions affecting or restricting immigration, abortion rights, defendant freedoms relative to capital punishment, same-sex and transgender liberties, partisan gerrymandering, and unanimous jury verdicts in state felony trials.

- Comprehensive narratives surveying the growing impact that special interest group advocacy and unregulated political money has on judicial campaigns in state supreme court elections.

- New coverage of the lack of diversity and representation on federal and states courts, leading to the institutionalization of a professional, "career" judiciary.

- Expanded discussion of the critical role lawyers, and BigLaw, play in the judicial process and highly specialized and stratified legal profession that creates multiple challenges in fully providing for access to justice to politically marginalized litigants.

- Fresh analyzes of justiciability and procedural doctrines and their application to key areas of the law, such as animal rights and Second Amendment gun rights.

- Focused treatment of the strengths and weaknesses of the criminal and civil adversarial process and the implications of new legislative initiatives, such as the First Step Act, and the politics of tort reform.

- New coverage on understanding judicial behavior theories and the role of appellate courts in altering precedent to achieve political preferences and forging social policy change in controversial areas of the law, including capital punishment, abortion, school educational financing, racial discrimination, and LGBT/same-sex marriage cases.

Acknowledgments

The undergraduate and graduate students taught at the University of Virginia, the University of Akron, and Kent State University remain an inspiration. Numerous faculty colleagues and graduate students have contributed to the research and writing process, but Lisa Hager and Kevin White, among others, were especially helpful in creating and refining the chapters and the data contained in the tables, graphs, and figures. A particular dose of gratitude is extended to the library staff (and colleagues) at Kent State University, who went beyond the call of duty in allowing access to books and articles during the Covid 19 pandemic and University shutdown in March 2020: namely, Kara Robinson, Thomas Warren and Cynthia Kristof, among others. The textbook could not have been written without the extraordinary efforts and confidence shown in the project from the editors from West Academic Press: Elizabeth Eisenhart and Ryan Pfeiffer. We are also grateful to Monica Eckman, Sam Rosenberg, Sarah Cabali and Natalie Kopinski, and the rest of the staff at Sage/CQ Press, for their efforts in helping us publish the first edition. During the production process at West Academic, the expertise and assistance from Laura Holle, Whitney Esson, Greg Olson and several others were essential to getting the textbook published. We would also like to thank the following reviewers for their valuable insight and suggestions:

J. Michael Bitzer, Catawba College

Paul Chen, Western Washington University

Michelle D. Deardorff, University of Tennessee at Chattanooga

John Gruhl, University of Nebraska-Lincoln

Kim Seckler, New Mexico State University

Steven Tauber, University of South Florida

Laurie A. Walsh, Daemen College

Yvonne Wollenberg, Rutgers University

A Note on Authorship

This book could not have been published without my late mentor, colleague and friend, David M. O'Brien. He first introduced the possibility of me pursing a doctoral degree at the University of Virginia, and later joining on to write a judicial process textbook many years ago at an American Political Science Association convention after inviting me to lunch with him. I had no idea he was approached to do such a project, and I was flattered that he asked. But that was typical David—generous with his time and expertise, to a fault perhaps, and always willing to allow others to succeed when there was little possibility to do so. David was very accessible, but, at times, a difficult taskmaster. He did not demand perfection, but he always expected excellent quality and plenty of hard work to generate it. Admittedly, one had to have a bit of thick skin to absorb some of his criticisms and suggestions; but I am forever grateful that he took the time and effort to offer them. It did not hurt, either, that most of the time he was right.

Sadly he passed away unexpectedly, and quickly, as we neared the task of completing this second edition. While I finished the project without him, I am comforted by knowing that the pages we wrote together are a reflection of his spirit and professionalism. I hope that I can only pass on some of what he taught me to the students I have met at the University of Akron and Kent State University, and to future students. He will be sorely missed but never forgotten.

—Chris Banks

April 2020

Summary of Contents

PART I. LAW AND POLITICAL JURISPRUDENCE
IN A GLOBALIZED SOCIETY

PART II. JUDICIAL ORGANIZATION AND
ADMINISTRATIVE PROCESSES

PART III. ACCESS TO COURTS AND
JUDICIAL DECISION-MAKING

Table of Contents

PART I. LAW AND POLITICAL JURISPRUDENCE
IN A GLOBALIZED SOCIETY

PART IV. JUDICIAL POLICYMAKING

Table of Cases

THE JUDICIAL PROCESS

Law, Courts, and Judicial Politics

Second Edition

Law and Political Jurisprudence in a Globalized Society

CHAPTER 1

The Politics of Law and Courts in Society

In many countries, the law permits adult citizens to make basic choices about how they want to live their life. Such personal decisions include who to marry, what type of career to pursue, or making travel arrangements. One exercising these choices would often reasonably expect that the government will pass laws to regulate these activities without fear of facing legal sanctions. In some countries, however, segments of the population are governed by laws that interfere, and sometimes punish harshly, ordinary activities are taken for granted in other countries. Until recently, for example, women in Saudi Arabia were deprived of the right to vote and faced criminal penalties if they chose to drive a car. Before the ban on driving was lifted, a Saudi female, Shaimaa Ghassaneya, was sentenced to ten lashings for operating a motor vehicle. In other instances, a sixty-seven year old Saudi widowed mother needed written permission from her twenty-seven year old son to board a plane and a thirty-six year old Saudi woman could not renew her passport after she separated from her husband.[1]

Notably, the discriminatory treatment of Saudi women originates from a single passage of the Qur'an, the Islamic religious text that is a basis for the Saudi Arabian theocratic legal system and social governance. The passage, Sura 4 Verse 34 declares that "Men are the protectors and maintainers of women, because Allah has given the one more (strength) than the other, and because they support them from their means." Although this religious precept is not codified in Saudi Arabian Basic Law (its foundational law, enacted in 1992), it established a system of male guardianship over women. Under that system, it is customary to subordinate all women under the control of their closest male relative, who becomes their official guardian, or *wali al-amr*. A male *wali al-amr* takes all decision-making away from the woman who must get consent to go to school, get a job, get married, or seek medical treatment. At times, such control is not merely inconvenient, but also life-threatening. In 2006, an abusive husband, who shot his wife three different times

3

and who later died, escaped prosecution because the Saudi police refused to intervene unless her husband filed an official complaint, which he obviously did not do.[2]

Numerous other events across the globe illustrate the role law and judicial systems play in maintaining social control and ensuring that cultural norms remain intact. In 2020, Indian courts upheld the hanging execution of four men for the rape and murder of young student on a New Delhi bus, a sentence that was condemned by Amnesty International India (who opposes capital punishment) but also one that helped galvanize political and public pressure to reform India's longstanding and antiquated system of criminal punishment that often gave little justice to female victims of sexual violence. In 2017, the Russian Supreme Court upheld the Russian justice ministry's decision to suspend the activities of Jehovah's Witnesses because they violated laws designed to stop extremism. By affirming a nationwide criminal ban on an independent religious minority group, the Court's ruling was immediately condemned as a violation of religious freedom by the European Union and other western democracies.[3]

In the United States, Donald Trump's nativist and populist rhetoric led to executive action that imposed travel bans on immigrants from countries with predominately Muslim populations, prompting a backlash in the lower federal courts that has mostly agreed with the criticism that he was abusing his powers by discriminating against disfavored religious minorities under the pretext of protecting the nation's borders. Still, in *Hawaii v. Trump* (2018),[4] the Supreme Court upheld President Trump's third executive order on statutory and constitutional grounds. But even before President Trump's election, several European countries, as well as parts of Canada, took similar action by enacting bans on the wearing of Muslim headscarves and veils that cover both the face (niqabs) and the full body (burqas), as well as legal edits on wearing other religious symbols, including Jewish yarmulkes, Sikh turbans, and large crucifixes, in public spaces and workplaces. Defenders of these types of prohibitions routinely claim they promote government neutrality, ensure national security, preserve national culture, and discourage separatist movements. Even so, such restrictions increasingly are met with judicial and public resistance. As a result, courts and judges throughout the world are often are called upon to resolve these controversies by trying to strike a balance between preserving public norms and individual rights.[5]

These examples illustrate how the practical application of law is greatly influenced by the historical evolution of cultural and political norms, social behavior patterns, and legal traditions within communities, societies, and countries. The different ways in which courts resolve disputes and maintain social control within a polity reflects the operation of legal systems.[6]

This chapter examines different kinds of legal systems around the world, and identifies the sources of law, as well as the roles courts play in contemporary societies.

LEGAL SYSTEMS

Given the so-called globalization of law, the differences among legal systems in the world should not be obscured. Every legal system is to a certain extent distinct, simply because each society and its legal norms vary. Yet, generalizations about what constitutes a legal system are still possible. A **legal system** refers to a set of institutional structures for applying the law, legal procedures for administering the law, and substantive legal rules.[7] No less important are how various elements of the legal system (conceptions of law, the legal profession, courts, and the citizenry) interact. Because there are numerous legal systems in the world, and many are of "mixed" character, scholars from various academic disciplines (comparative law, history, or legal philosophy) do not agree on how to classify legal systems or whether it is even possible to do so.[8]

Regardless, a common framework typically depicts legal systems as "families of law."[9] Although legal families evolve over time and may share certain structures, procedures, or rules, a distinguishing factor among legal systems is the law's origin. For example, civil law systems in the Romanic-Germanic family emphasize written civil codes constructed by legislatures, whereas the common law family—including the American legal system—concentrates on the administration of law by judges and lawyers. Before the fall of the Soviet Union in 1989, and in contrast to civil and common law systems, the socialist legal family derived law from Marxism political ideology. Other legal families are rooted in religious sources, as exemplified by the Muslim, Hindu, or Jewish legal systems. Some legal systems are strongly influenced by customary law (law based on social customs enforced by the community), or, as with "mixed" systems, the elements of more than one legal system may operate within a single jurisdiction (see "In Comparative Perspective: Major Global Legal Systems"). The rest of this section analyzes the major legal families by surveying the predominant legal systems and situating them in the global legal order and international law framework.

Civil Law

Most European countries have **civil law systems**. In the sixth century (A.D.), the emperor Justinian sought to restore the glory of Roman law by codifying portions of it into one source, the *Corpus Juris Civilis* (CJC)—consisting of Institutes (an introduction to basic principles), a Digest (a summary of past Roman scholarship), Codes (a compilation of past Roman legislation, edits, and other laws), and Novels (a section for future legislation after the Code and Digest were completed). After the fall of the Roman Empire, the CJC was rediscovered by scholars at the University of Bologna, Italy, in the eleventh century. The rediscovery coincided with the development of the canon law by the Catholic Church and the rise of commercial law—a set of rules governing commercial relationships across the European continent. In time, the CJC (Roman civil law), canon law, and commercial law helped to produce a common law, the *jus commune* ("law of the community"), which became part of the civil law that was later "received," or adapted, in one form or another by European states. This history shaped the basic codes found in civil law countries, namely, the civil code, the commercial code, the code of civil procedure, the penal code, and the code of criminal procedure.[10]

Two variations of what became the modern civil law system took hold in France and in Germany during the nineteenth century. The French Civil Code of 1804, or *Code Napoléon*, developed under the rule of the emperor Napoléon Bonaparte, eradicated all traces of aristocratic power in French nobility, clergy, and judiciary. It was built on three pillars—codes broadly protecting property, contract, and patriarchal family relationships—that formerly were under the domain of the church or the aristocracy. Since the law was based on universal ideas of natural justice (liberty and equality), it was crafted in simple terms, and it accordingly limited the need for lawyers and courts. The code was thus distinctly antifeudal and antijudicial because French judges were part of the aristocratic class that had too often abused power. The bias against the judiciary is important because it laid the foundation for a tradition that institutionally isolated courts from other branches of government and reduced judges to civil servants.

Whereas the French Civil Code was inspired by revolution and strived to protect rights universally, the German Civil Code of 1896 was more technical. Proponents of the German Historical School, led by Friedrich Carl von Savigny (1779–1861), argued that legal systems must be constructed from historically derived principles of legal science. Accordingly, the German Civil Code of 1896 was a self-contained body of written law: Lawyers or judges did not have to resort to extraneous social, economic, political, or moral values to apply it. Unlike the French code, the German code made clear that the science of law (rules, legislation, and the like) was left to the realm of the lawyer and the judge, not to the common person. Hence, the German Civil Code was detailed, precise, and logical. Definitions and elaborate cross-references (to other parts of the code) contained pragmatic guides for applying law that was virtually inaccessible except to legal experts.

The civil law tradition remains infused in legal systems throughout continental Europe, Asia, Latin America, South America, and parts of the Caribbean (see "In Comparative Perspective: Major Global Legal Systems"). Until recently, civil law systems did not provide for judicial review—the power to declare acts of the legislature or executive branch unconstitutional. The absence of judicial review is explained by the subordinate role courts play to legislatures. The nature of legal analysis in civil law systems also gives little discretion to courts in interpreting codes and legislation. In other words, modern civil codes are generally a systematic collection of general legal principles and laws enacted by legislative bodies. As one civil lawyer put it: "The Code. . .is a construction of the mind, designed to impose a rational and well-defined legal order on a particular society. It is the materialization of a legal philosophy at one point in time, as well as the solidification of a society's ever-changing morals into a fixed set of written rules."[11] For civil law judges, then, the civil code is both the starting and the ending point for legal analysis.

However, since the second half of the twentieth century, the traditional civil law model has been changing. After World War II, new constitutional courts, along with the power of judicial review, were introduced in Europe (see the "In Comparative Perspective: Constitutional Courts in Europe" box in Chapter Three). As a result, some European constitutional courts, like U.S. courts, are now playing a more dynamic role in interpreting law and making social policy.

Civil law systems are **inquisitorial** in operation and differ from **adversarial** systems used in common law jurisdictions like the United States (as further discussed in the next section). In inquisitorial systems, legal institutions and practices are structured to arrive at legal truths under a written code or by following specific legal procedures. Lawyers, who are trained as specialists in narrowly defined areas of law, earn a formal law degree at a university as undergraduates before they become eligible to practice. Judges are prepared to be civil servants who begin (and often end) their careers in a judicial bureaucracy. Finally, adjudication in inquisitorial civil law systems is proactive in the sense that all who play a role in litigation (especially judges) are active participants in, typically, a three-stage process that usually has a preliminary hearing, an evidence-taking stage, and a decision-making stage. Each stage is structured to engage litigants and judges in an active search for facts and evidence.[12] Except for select criminal cases, there is basically no "trial" process *per se*, and the presence of a lay jury is rare, because judges play the fact-finding role and determine the facts (evidence) before issuing a ruling. Some of the key differences between inquisitorial and adversarial systems are detailed in Table 1.1.

Table 1.1	Inquisitorial and Adversarial Systems	
Traits	**Inquisitorial (Civil Law)**	**Adversarial (Common Law)**
Facts investigation	Collaborative effort with prosecutor and judge discovering facts together	Litigants opposing each other separately discover facts without judge's help
Pretrial process	Less extensive	More extensive
Trial process	More disjointed and costlier	Singular event (after pretrial) and less costly
Judge's role	Active, engaged; more bureaucratic	Passive, neutral; less bureaucratic
Jury	Rarely used	Used often (especially in United States)
Bail	Rarely used	Used often (especially in United States)
Legal education	Undergraduate education	Professional (graduate) education
Attorney's role	More collaborative and less influential	Less collaborative and more influential
Plea bargaining or pretrial settlement	Unusual	Typical

Sources: Herbert M. Kritzer, ed., *Legal Systems of the World: A Political, Social and Cultural Encyclopedia,* Vol. 1 (Santa Barbara, Calif.: ABC-CLIO, 2002), 6–9; Christopher E. Smith, *Courts and Trials: A Reference Handbook* (Santa Barbara, Calif.: ABC-CLIO, 2003), 40–45.

In Comparative Perspective: Major Global Legal Systems

There are 221 different legal systems in the world today. The major legal systems consist of civil law and mixed legal systems, followed by common law, customary, and religious legal systems. As a result of the Soviet Union's collapse in 1989 the Socialist (ideological) legal family is not as pervasive, so it is excluded from analysis. Muslim law, and to a lesser degree, Talmudic law are identified separately from other religious-based systems because Muslim law is more permanent and widespread, whereas Talmudic law and Israel's mixed legal system are highly distinctive. Other initially religious legal systems are not as unique. As a result, many their defining characteristics have been blended into customary or state systems.

The sources of law for each legal system vary:

— *Civil law systems* use written codes created by legislatures

— *Common law systems* use judicial decisions by courts

— *Customary law systems* use social customs that are enforced by community sanction

— *Religious legal systems* are based on sacred religious texts, like the Koran

— *Mixed legal systems* are based on a combination of sources of law drawn off various other legal systems.

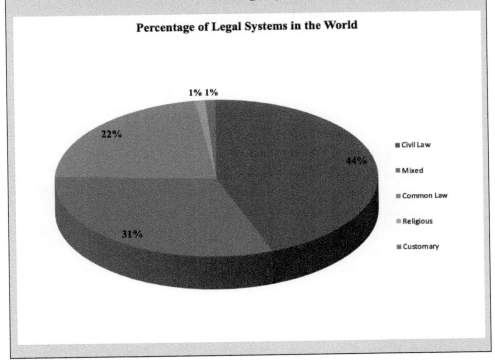

Percentage of Legal Systems in the World

Legal Systems Throughout the Globe	
Type of Legal System	*Examples*
Civil law systems	Brazil, Cuba, Denmark, France, Germany, Russia, Turkey
Common law systems	Australia, Canada, Ireland, United Kingdom, United States
Customary law systems	Andorra, Guernsey Island (U.K.), Jersey Island (U.K.)
Religious legal systems	Afghanistan, Saudi Arabia, Maldives Islands
Mixed legal systems	
• *Civil Law and Common Law*	Philippines, Scotland (U.K.), South Africa
• *Civil Law and Customary Law*	Chad, Japan, North and South Korea
• *Civil Law and Muslim Law*	Egypt, Iran, Iraq, Palestine
• *Civil Law, Religious (Muslim), and Customary Law*	Djibouti, Eritrea, Indonesia, Timor-Leste
• *Civil Law, Common Law and Customary Law*	Cameroun, Sri Lanka, Zimbabwe
• *Religious (Muslim), Common Law, Civil Law, and Customary*	Bahrain, Qatar, Somalia, Yemen
• *Religious (Talmudic and Muslim), Civil Law, Common Law*	Israel

Source: The University of Ottawa, "JuriGlobe—World Legal Systems" available from http://www.juriglobe.ca/eng/index.php (last retrieved January 29, 2020).

Common Law

Whereas civil law systems are based on the primacy of the legislature and a legal code, common law systems are based on the rule of judges. The origin of common law stems from the Norman conquest of the Anglo-Saxons in the Battle of Hastings in 1066 by King William I. After taking control, William I distributed the land only after the fee holders swore loyalty and promised to pay sums of money to the king. In short, William I solved the problem of maintaining order and earning tax revenue by creating a legal system for resolving private disputes among the landholders. Beginning in 1300, three central royal courts of justice—the Court of Exchequer, the Court of Common Pleas, and the Court of King's Bench—emerged in Westminster Hall, in London, and all were staffed by judges empowered to act in the king's absence. As agents for the king, royal judges had strict instructions on how to handle local legal disputes. Access was also a privilege instead of a right: Citizens had to ask permission from a royal judge to deliver a petition to have a court hearing. What developed was a highly procedural system of writs—or petitions requesting legal relief. For example, to remove a trespasser from land, a writ of ejectment was used. The emphasis on procedure meant that "where there is no remedy there is no wrong," and where there was no remedy there was no right.[13]

The writ system reinforced the king's power and simultaneously consolidated the royal judges' power to make unwritten law as the king's delegates. The judge was a **de facto** (in fact) gatekeeper of the judicial process. Over time, the process of determining the facts in disputes fell to juries, and the judge's role was only to apply the law. By the fifteenth century, common law evolved alongside the law of **equity**—a special set of rules permitting relief for those who suffered injustices because of the strict operation of the writs system. For example, if a legal remedy did not address an injury, then an equitable remedy might be available if that injury violated some sense of the king's fairness. There was a separate Court of Chancery to handle such cases.

Accordingly, the judge is the central figure in a common law system. The rulings of early common law judges were "unwritten" in the sense that written law did not exist to guide their discretion. Still, once a ruling was made, it became binding as a precedent for future cases. As more and more cases were decided, "a common law in the realm" emerged. Notably, whereas judges had the obligation to "declare" the law based on precedent, they also had the power to "make" law by creating new precedent if that was necessary to avoid an injustice for litigants. As Judge Benjamin Cardozo remarked, "The power to declare the law carries with it the power, and within limits the duty, to make law when none exists."[14] Striking the proper balance between declaring and making law was conditioned by the norm that the highest court of appeal was not bound by its own precedents and, hence, high courts could reject past decisions. In sum, precedent gives law stability and predictability but remains open to change. As explained further in Chapter Nine, the doctrine of precedent, or **stare decisis** ("let the decision stand"), is a key aspect of judicial behavior in the U.S. judicial system and elsewhere.

Apart from England, contemporary common law legal systems include the United States, Canada, Australia, and Ireland (see the "In Comparative Perspective" box on major global legal systems). In the United States, the common law was adopted in conjunction with each colony's distinctive legal heritage. The reception of common law was facilitated by the writings of Sir William Blackstone (1723–1780). Blackstone held the first professorship of English law at Oxford University, where he delivered a series of lectures later published as *Commentaries on the Laws of England* (1765–1769). The *Commentaries* received wide distribution and represented "the most ambitious and most successful effort ever made to reduce the disorderly overgrowth of English law to an intelligible and learnable system."[15] Blackstone's *Commentaries* were also influential in reinforcing an integral aspect of U.S. constitutionalism by emphasizing that judges are the "living oracle of the law," who only "declare" the law, not make it. Indeed, in a classic statement of judicial restraint, Alexander Hamilton asserted in *Federalist* No. 78 that courts have "neither FORCE nor WILL, but merely judgment."[16] However, Blackstone's **declaratory theory of law** was ultimately challenged in the late nineteenth century by judges and legal theorists who advanced a jurisprudence of American legal realism (as explained in Chapter Two).

The complexity of common law produced new pressures in the early nineteenth century to codify a U.S. version of the common law, principally in Massachusetts and then in New York. In 1811, Jeremy Bentham, a noted English legal reformer, went so far as to offer to write a code in a letter sent to President James Madison.[17] Even though Madison declined, the **codification movement**, led by the lawyer David Dudley Field, succeeded in enacting a Code of Civil Procedure in New York in 1848. Field's efforts met harsh resistance from the East Coast legal establishment; yet the Field Codes, as they were called, were adopted toward the end of the century in the Dakotas, Idaho, Louisiana, Montana, and California. Notably, the common law system ultimately survived the codification movement because support for codification waned by the onset of the twentieth century.

Unlike the civil law tradition, common law systems are **adversarial**, so lawyers have considerable power to shape and make the law through a competitive struggle to win a case. Former New York Judge Jerome Frank once referred to this process as the **fight theory** (its application to criminal and civil cases is analyzed in Chapters Seven and Eight). In Judge Frank's view, "The lawyer aims at victory, at winning in the fight, not at aiding the court to discover the facts." In other words, the lawyer "does not want the trial court to reach a sound educated guess, if it is likely to be contrary to his client's interest." As Frank concluded, "Our present trial method is thus the equivalent of throwing pepper in the eyes of a surgeon when he is performing an operation."[18] As a result, lawyers have more control and influence in common law systems, and judges ostensibly let attorneys "fight it out." In contrast to the civil law system, the common law system lets the litigants and their lawyers, instead of the government, carry the burden of developing facts and defending rights.

Historically, a common law attorney's training is also different. Unlike the training for a civil law practitioner, legal education in common law countries is generalist in scope and gained through a graduate degree after earning an undergraduate degree (legal training and its implications are discussed more fully in Chapter Five). Consequently, adversarial systems place great value on practical experience (i.e., apprenticeship and gaining professional experience through the "practice" of law), rather than undergraduate instruction followed by an examination and admission into a **career judiciary** (discussed more fully in Chapter Four). Judges also tend to be selected for service based on their professional accomplishments instead of their formal academic achievements. Thus, all the main protagonists in the common law drama—the lawyer, the judge, and even the jury—wield enormous authority to discover, apply, and "make" law through adjudication. Not only may common law attorneys manipulate precedents through their advocacy, but judges may embrace or reject an advocate's arguments because of the specific facts in a case, and thereby assert the power to make law. Moreover, juries are in a unique position to apply the law to facts as they see fit. The law's evolution in a common law system is therefore fluid, despite the constraints imposed by the doctrine of precedent.

Ideological Legal Systems

Before the fall of communism in central and eastern Europe, scholars generally agreed that socialist law ought to be considered an important third legal system. Although its origin began with the 1917 Bolshevik revolution in Russia, its impact did not become widespread until the end of World War II, when the Communist Party took control in Romania, Bulgaria, Albania, Poland, Hungary, Czechoslovakia, and eastern Germany. The People's Republic of China was also receptive, and it became a foundation for Mao Tse-tung's legal regime. Although the collapse of the Soviet Union in 1989 diminished its global significance, socialist law continues to influence the legal systems in China, Russia, North Korea, Vietnam, Laos, and some other countries.[19]

Socialist legal systems borrow heavily from the civil law system and use of codes. However, their defining characteristic is political ideology and the instrumental use of law in service of the socialist state. In this respect, socialist doctrine cannot embrace a Western conception of law. In this light, law in the Western sense is the foundation of liberal democracy because it limits the operation of government and is a safeguard for individual rights. Conversely, socialist legal ideology denies that law as understood in the West exists and, instead, contends that law is used to enslave the populace.

Accordingly, as it is based on Marxist political and economic principles, socialist ideology rejects outright Western liberal democratic thought. Marxist doctrine was espoused by Karl Marx (1818–1883) and inspired by Friedrich Engels (1820–1895). Marxist ideology theorizes that history is a series of alternating cycles of birth and destruction, in which one economic system is created, destroyed, and replaced by another. Feudalism, for example, was replaced by capitalism as new forms of production took hold. At the heart of socialist ideology is the belief that the wealthy elites in civil society (the bourgeoisie) capture the means of economic production from the working class (the proletariat) and deprive workers from enjoying the fruit of their labor. For socialists, Western law supports capitalist economic arrangements and promotes individuals' alienation by taking away personal liberty.

Marxist theory, therefore, seeks to eliminate the source of the class struggle, namely individual ownership of private property and the accumulation of wealth. Marx hypothesized that capitalism would be replaced after a revolution in which the proletariat overthrew the bourgeoisie and, ultimately, restored freedom through the collective ownership of the economic means of production. An ideal state would then emerge in which law and government would "whither away" because there would be no need for law to maintain social control.

Marxist theory, however, failed to be realized in socialist-influenced legal systems. Nonetheless, Marxism found expression in a principle of socialist legality. That is, the concept of law is meaningful only if it furthers the objectives of the underlying socialist ideology. In the former Soviet Union, the law's purpose was to ensure national security and educate the masses (by force, if necessary) to advance socialist economic development.[20]

Religious Legal Systems

Religion has influenced the development of law and legal systems throughout history. Roman Catholic canon law in continental Europe continues to loom large in the civil law tradition, and, likewise, Hinduism remains an important part of

Indian legal culture. The Bible inspired the development of Anglo-Saxon law. The Talmud, oral interpretations of scriptures committed to writing in Jewish law, helped shape Israel's "mixed" legal system of Talmudic, civil, common, and Muslim law. Muslim or Islamic law as expressed in the Koran, Islam's holy book, is the touchstone for "mixed" legal systems found in Pakistan, parts of Malaysia and Indonesia, northern and eastern Africa, and much of the Middle East.

Indeed, a large proportion of the world's population adheres to the tenets of Islamic religion. Although in its "pure" form it has ostensibly only been in place in Afghanistan (before the U.S.-coalition-led occupation after September 11, 2001), the Maldives Islands, and Saudi Arabia, many of the world's major legal systems embody Islamic law. A personal commitment to the Islamic faith is holistic, involving all aspects of life. "Islam," as has been said, "is a religion, a legal system, and a lifestyle all in one."[21] Islamic law is based on the word of Allah, as revealed to the Prophet Muhammad ibn Abdullah (570–632 C.E.) by the angel Gabriel. The revelations were compiled into Islam's most important sacred text, the Koran, which is supplemented by the Sunnah, which reports the teachings of the prophet Muhammad. Together, the Koran and the Sunnah constitute the basis for Islamic law, the Shariah. As divine law, the Shariah cannot be changed by man. It can be interpreted by scholars, but, by a command from Allah, anything less than total compliance is a violation of the whole Islamic community and subject to severe sanctions not only in this world but also in the next.

The Shariah identifies five pillars of personal responsibility (profession of faith, daily prayer, almsgiving, fasting, and pilgrimage to Mecca), and it provides guidelines for social relations involving family, criminal, contract, and international law. During the nineteenth and twentieth centuries, nations subscribing to Islamic law were greatly affected by their contacts with the West, and consequently many of them incorporated versions of Islamic law in accordance with the civil law tradition. Indeed, the demise of the Ottoman Empire in the early twentieth century helped spur on the emergence of secular codes and parallel court systems that displaced Shariah law in countries undergoing Western modernization. However, the assimilation process generated controversy, and secular Western norms increasingly clash with those of Islamic fundamentalists who advocate returning to a traditional form of Shariah.[22]

Notably, the region now known as the Kingdom of Saudi Arabia was not subjected to pressures other Muslim countries faced in adapting to Western values and secularism. This explains why Saudi Arabian courts have had difficulties in trying to modernize their operations while also attempting to follow the theory and practice of Shariah law. As a theocracy, Saudi Arabia's legal structures and procedures remain based on an orthodox version of Islamic law. The Basic Law of 1992, for example, is expected to conform to Shariah. Because there is no separation between political and religious life, the legal process aims to reveal religious truths rather than discover empirical facts. Shariah encourages reconciliation, and most disputes are resolved in this manner, rather than in courts. The concept of *sulh*, "compromise, settlement or agreement between the parties," is derived from the Koran. Indeed, one study reports that 99 percent of all civil cases are resolved in this fashion.[23] Lawyers and judges work to reach amicable solutions in an informal manner by emphasizing oral testimony instead of written documents or evidence. In this fashion, *kadi* justice—the law as delivered by judges construing religious doctrine—is neither adversarial (as in common law) nor investigative (as in civil law). Instead, the process is one of religious obligation, aimed at achieving a just result according to the word of Allah.

In 2007, Saudi Arabia enacted a series of legal reforms that underscore the tensions between its religious orientation and the growing influence of Western legal norms. By decree, King Abdullah bin Abdul-Aziz declared a new Law of the Judiciary, which transferred judicial powers from the Supreme Judicial Council to a newly formed Supreme Court; reorganized the old Shariah Review Court into a new court of appeals; authorized a new Judicial Supreme Council to set up specialized courts (previously under the Minister of Justice in the executive branch); and allowed the new Supreme Court to administer government decrees and state legislation. Since Shariah courts and judges have historically valued their autonomy to apply divine law without interference from the state, these reforms have created deep divisions over modernization. Significantly, the trend towards Western democratic modernization has accelerated under the rule of Saudi Crown Prince Mohammed bin Salman, who replaced King Abdullah after he died in 2015. Apart from letting women drive and vote, these reforms include limiting the powers of the religious police and establishing a new Global Center for Combatting Extremist Ideology, where hundreds of analysts monitor Arabic social media traffic for threats presented by extremist groups. The new Saudi Prince also took the bold step of cracking down on government corruption in late 2017 by arresting several hundred wealthy Saudis, some of which that were very prominent princes and cabinet officers and forced them to pay restitution before being released. Notably, the crackdown ended in March 2019, but not until the government received more than 106 billion dollars in settlement monies from senior princes, ministers, and influential business, mainly through forfeiture of real estate, companies, cash and other assets.[24]

Customary and "Mixed" Legal Systems

Although only a few countries base their legal systems on local customs, customary law, or those rules based on social customs and enforced by community sanctions, influences a considerable number of mixed legal systems. Historically, the strongest influences of customary law have been found in sub-Saharan Africa (Ethiopia, Somalia, the Congo, and Madagascar), where customs define social obligations and methods of dispute resolution. Typically, customs are recognized by consensus of the social group, or tribe, often through familial or kinship ties. Accordingly, it was not unusual for African customary courts to appeal to customs in reconciling the competing interests of disputants. However, customs often yielded to other legal traditions brought by the European colonization of Africa and, subsequently, African independence. For example, since achieving its independence from British rule in 1960, Nigeria's constitutional system has been organized around a mixture of common law, Islamic law, and customary law. As a result, Nigeria's judicial system has distinct courts with separate jurisdictions for handling civil disputes. The Shariah Court of Appeal applies Muslim law, whereas the Customary Court of Appeal uses customary law.[25]

The legal systems in China and Israel provide further illustrations of contemporary mixed legal systems. The legal tradition in China is rooted in *Confucianism*, a philosophy derived from the teachings from Master K'ong (Kung Fu-tse), or Confucius (551–479 B.C.). Confucius, a government official and teacher who helped restore order in the Chou Dynasty in the fifth century (B.C.), espoused the principle of social harmony, as expressed through the relativism of *li*—a moral code of socially accepted behavior in order to achieve a harmonious balance between nature and man. *Li* directs people to accept fault instead of assigning blame, which reinforces social harmony. *Li* stands in sharp opposition to law and formal sanctions (*fa*). Instead, *li* makes "law," as understood in the West, superfluous, and, hence, it is frowned upon to resort to courts and formal sanctions. When social harmony is disrupted, order is restored through persuasion and conciliation, rather than formal edicts that traditionally were perceived to serve the selfish aims of rulers.[26]

Such traditional customs inhibited the development of law and a legal profession in premodern China; but they were reinforced through political events that shaped China's legal system in the twentieth century. Whereas the West introduced the civil law system and the codification of law, the socialist legalist principle (borrowed from the Soviet Union) was infused into the country's government during the Cultural Revolution (1966–1976) under Chairman Mao Tse-tung after the creation of the People's Republic of China (in 1949). Under

Mao, political power was consolidated in the Chinese Communist Party, and law became an instrument of the state. Lawyers, who were bourgeois guardians of property rights, were banned from legal practice, and the judicial system was denigrated as well. But since 1979, the legal profession has slowly reemerged because of economic modernization under Deng Xiaoping, Mao's successor, and China's entry into the World Trade Organization in 2001.[27] Still, despite increasing modernization, China's mixed legal system is strongly influenced by cultural norms that tend to reject Western conceptions of law.

As a result, China's contemporary legal system is an amalgam of civil, customary, and socialist legal traditions. Although there has been state-led reform favoring Western-style adversarialism, the legal process remains inquisitorial in practice, and judges preside over trials in accordance with code law established by the National People's Congress. By some estimates, in a nation of over 1.3 billion, there are only approximately 230,000 lawyers and 210,000 judges, and the average number of cases handled by judges on an annual basis remains low (less than a hundred per year, in contrast to the thousands of cases U.S. judges adjudicate annually). Although graduate training is available, legal education is primarily based on the civil law model of university instruction, so traditionally most lawyers are trained to be "state legal workers" ("*guojia gongzuo renyuan*") or specialist bureaucrats. Yet China's trajectory toward market reform has grown, so Chinese lawyers have been able to diversify their legal practice into the private sector and become more independent "professionals serving society" ("*wei shehui fuwude zhiye renyuan*").[28]

In late 2013, leader Xi Jinping and the Chinese Communist Party announced a series of political, economic, and legal reforms designed to increase market prosperity and reduce party interference with legal institutions and human rights. The legal reforms, which included ending a state reeducation through labor program for criminal offenders and proposals to centralize court funding and judicial appointments to reduce local corruption, purport to improve judicial independence and promote the rule of law. Whether they ultimately have that effect is uncertain because the legal profession remains tightly regulated by the state and the political persecution of human rights' activists has not stopped since the reforms were proposed. In early 2018, the Chinese legislature instituted more sweeping reforms by approving major changes to the Chinese Constitution. These included the removal of term limits on leader Xi Jinping, thus allowing him to stay in office beyond 2023. Other amendments, moreover, created an anti-corruption agency that is infused with influence from the Communist Party's Central Commission for Discipline Inspection (with the power to investigate and detain suspects without access to lawyers), as well as inserting a statement of Xi's political theory ("Xi Jinping Thought on Socialism with Chinese Characteristics for a New Era") about how the Chinese government should operate, directly into the Constitution. For some global observers and critics, the revisions have further reinforced the Communist Party's and Xi's grip on the country and have muted efforts by political reformers to separate Party control from government structures. The historical evolution of the Chinese constitution and the different influences at work in its mixed legal system is detailed in the In Comparative Perspective box, "China's Written Constitution Without Constitutionalism" in this Chapter.[29]

Israel's mixed legal system incorporates Talmudic, civil, common, and even Muslim law elements. Prior to Israel's independence in 1948, its territory was under Palestinian control as part of the Ottoman Empire. Because Ottoman law contained Muslim as well as European law components, until 1948 the territory had a combination of civil law, English common law, and Muslim law. Since independence, Israel's constitutional system has been constructed by codifying its basic laws and through the development of an Israeli common law. Moreover, the Israeli system has a separate body of religious courts that adjudicate disputes involving marriage and divorce. In other domestic relations cases, Talmudic law applies only if the parties consent. In recent years, Israel has witnessed the emergence of many new nonstate Jewish religious courts offering adjudication of private and commercial law disputes according to Jewish law (Halacha). Accordingly, in the words of Aharon Barak, the former president of the Supreme Court of Israel, Israel stands apart from most Western legal systems because it has a "duality of civil and religious law" along with common law tradition.[30]

In Comparative Perspective: China's Written Constitution Without Constitutionalism

After the 1949 revolution by the Chinese Communist Party (CCP), the new People's Republic of China (PRC) began a process of developing a new constitutional and legal structure. In doing so it at once abandoned the 2,000 year-old tradition of Confucianism's teaching of *li* ("rites" or "propriety"), which had formed the basis for a kind of social constitution, on the one hand, and, on the other, rejected "Western rule-of-law constitutionalism" as imperialistic. In the last sixty years, China has had one provisional and four formal constitutions.

Initially, a provisional Common Programme was enacted in 1949. It proclaimed the "people's democratic dictatorship" and laid out, in seven chapters and sixty articles, principles that became the basis for later constitutions. In 1954 the National People's Congress (NPC) adopted the first written constitution, containing 106 articles in four chapters. That constitution, however, was neither seriously implemented nor provided a barrier to the abuse of governmental power and denial of human rights. Subsequently, Mao Zedong initiated a series of political campaigns—from the "anti-rightists movement" (1957) to the "Great Leap Forward (1958) and the "great Proletarian Cultural Revolution" (1966–1976)—resulting in a Chinese Holocaust and eliminating virtually any basis for the constitutionalism.

A second constitution was adopted shortly before the end of the "Cultural Revolution." The 1975 Constitution was actually more of a political outline and basically removed most of the 1954 Constitution's provisions for individual rights and institutional powers, with only 30 articles remaining. After Mao's death in 1976, the NPC enacted a third constitution. The 1978 Constitution included 60 articles-deleting some of the previous constitution, adding some human rights and institutional provisions, and laying down "Four Modernisations" as primary objectives in the area of agriculture, defense, industry, and science and technology. Subsequently, that constitution was revised and amended in 1979 and 1980, and then replaced in 1982.

The 1982 Constitution is in some respects a return to the pre-"Cultural Revolution" period in establishing the People's Congress, a dualist judiciary, and tripartite national administrative structure: (1) the State President (largely symbolic); (2) the State Council, which wields substantial powers in operation as the Central People's Government (CPG); and, (3) a separate Central Military Commission (CMC), which actually overlaps with the CCP. This constitution was subsequently amended in 1988, 1993, 1999, and 2004. Most of the amendments in various ways primarily promoted a market economy-moving away from communal or collective ownership, particularly in rural areas—and, at least until the 2004 amendments, paid little attention to human rights.

In 2018, the 18th National People's Congress of the Communist Party approved further constitutional amendments that made it possible for President Xi Jinping to hold a third or more terms, in contrast to prior constitutional limitations on two terms; created a party-controlled National Supervision Commission, above the judiciary, to combat corruption; and provided for legal reforms, including greater professionalism and transparency within the judiciary.

The Chinese judiciary remains weak, when viewed in terms of Western standards. The Communist Party controls all judicial appointments, assignments, and reappointments. There is no power of judicial review, akin to that established in *Marbury v. Madison* (1803), the European Court of Justice, and elsewhere. China remains influenced by the civil law tradition, and neither do judges exercise "judicial independence," nor are thy bound by "precedents," as in common law countries. Over the last decade, the People's Supreme Court has developed a system of "guiding cases" but they are only *de facto* binding—that is, only in the sense that they must be considered by lower courts.

In sum, the socialist legal system and constitutionalism in China bears, as often is said, distinctive "Chinese characteristics."

Sources: See Qianfan Zhang, *The Constitution of China: A Contextual Analysis* (Oxford: Hart Publishing, 2012); Qianfan Zhang, "A Constitution without Constitutionalism? The Paths of Constitutional Development in China," 8 *I*Con* 950–976 (2010); Note, "Chinese Common Law? Guiding Cases and Judicial Reform," 129 *Harvard Law Review* 2213–2234 (2016); and Tu Yunxin, "Guiding Cases in Chinese Legal System." Other important insight, which David M. O'Brien has gained and is indebted to receiving, comes from Professor Tu and to Fundan University, where Professor O'Brien worked as a Visiting Senior Fellow, 2017–2018.

LEGAL SYSTEMS AND GLOBALIZATION

Scholars have long recognized the significance of the role that law plays in an increasingly complex global legal order. Yet, the precise meaning of international law, generally understood as "those rules of law applicable to relations among sovereign states,"[31] is less clear today than it was in the early twentieth century. The binding effect of rules of international law—mostly consisting of treaties, customary international law, generalized legal principles, and decisions of international organizations or tribunals—has become more complicated, especially for domestic national courts trying to apply them in a transnational legal environment.[32]

The trend toward globalization has brought significant evolutionary changes to the modern international legal system, including: (1) the increasing codification of international law, thereby pushing courts to rely less on custom as a basis for their decisions; (2) the rapid growth of new global and regional institutions; (3) the development of international human rights and criminal law; (4) the growing acceptance of executive agreements and instruments created apart from the formal treaty processes; and, (5) the growing presence of international administrative or regulatory bodies, such as the International Civil Aviation Organization (a specialized agency of the United Nations that sets safety standards for international air travel). The demands placed on the global legal order have also brought a proliferation of multinational corporations, specialized law firms, and courts dealing with specific areas of international law and foreign affairs, such as the European Court of Human Rights, the Inter-American Court of Human Rights, the International Criminal Court, and the European Court of Justice.

One consequence of these changes is the growing fragmentation or disaggregation of sovereignty among nation states and, thus, the increasing role of nontraditional actors, such as nongovernmental organizations (NGOs). Accordingly, global governance increasingly is defined by the existence and influence of transnational or transgovernmental networks, which directly interact with each other through a myriad of cross-border and supranational alliances. These linkages affect global politics and policy by enhancing the quality of information among international institutions, promoting the international enforcement of policy initiatives, and facilitating international consensus and problem solving using "soft law" techniques (e.g., memoranda of understanding) that respond to challenges without going through established hierarchical channels. Such transnational networks promote the cross-fertilization of constitutional ideas and an evolving "community of courts." Not surprisingly, such networks have been reinforced by the Internet and electronic legal databases, such as Lexis Nexis and Westlaw, which provide rich databases of information that judges increasingly draw upon. Consequently, "(l)egal systems and actors within these legal systems are increasingly interconnected" which, in turn, "have obliged highest courts to develop expertise concerning the application of legal sources elaborated outside of their national legal system."[33]

THE NATURE AND SOURCES OF LAW

The preceding discussion of global legal systems and their interrelationships underscores that the nature of the law is socially constructed and registers the prevailing values of the larger culture of communities and countries. Most Americans would consider a legal system that punishes a woman for driving a car with a whipping to be barbaric and one that violates basic human dignity. Yet, for many Saudi Arabians, under Shariah law, the ban is a religious edict that commands obedience because Shariah is synonymous with preserving law and order, respecting government legitimacy, and achieving prosperity. As a result, its effect on the most powerless in society, such as women, is arguably irrelevant in Saudi Arabia.[34]

The differences in legal systems may be explained by identifying the sources and nature of law within a country. The former dean of Harvard Law School Roscoe Pound once observed that "laws are general rules recognized or enforced in the administration of justice."[35] While there is no universally accepted definition of law, a common understanding of it is that "law" is a rule of conduct, or societal norm, enacted by government that details what is right or wrong, and which is enforced through the imposition of a penalty. Those subject to the law's command obey it because it is just to do so; and complying with the law is the basis for political obligation. The law's legitimacy is also intertwined with the law's social purpose. Hence, the law's purpose is critical to appreciating how law regulates human activity, while simultaneously maintaining social order and securing justice. In conventional terms, "justice" is understood in two ways: corrective and distributive. Corrective justice "fixes" a wrong that has harmed an innocent third party. If someone has stolen a car or vandalized public property, corrective justice is delivered by punishing the offender. Distributive justice, on the other hand, rectifies an inequality existing between parties because it is just to do so.[36]

In the United States, law originates from the U.S. Constitution and Bill of Rights, as well as state constitutions. In addition to federal and state constitutions, law is made by legislatures, administrative agencies, and, on occasion, the president, as well as the courts. These various sources of law (detailed in Table 1.2) are analyzed in terms of typologies of law that broadly describe the U.S. legal system of public and private law.

Table 1.2	Types of Law
Public Law	**Subject Matter**
Constitutional law	Interpretation of constitutional documents
Administrative law	Enforceability of agency action or regulation
Criminal law	Enforcement of public moral code through sanction
International law	Maintaining stability of various legal relationships between nation and states
Taxation law	Collection of public revenues
Bankruptcy law	Discharge or reorganization of corporate and individual debt due to financial hardship
Antitrust law	Facilitation of free market competition between business competitors
Private Law	**Subject Matter**
Contract law	Enforceability of private agreements
Tort law	Imposition of liability for unreasonable acts between private individuals that proximately cause harm
Corporation law	Maintaining stability of various legal relationships affecting private enterprise and business corporations
Probate law	Facilitation of transfer of property upon death or disability
Family law	Maintaining stability of various legal relationships affecting families, including marriage, dissolution, and child custody
Property law	Facilitation of the various legal relationships affecting the possession and transfer of real (land) or personal (tangible items) property

Sources: Lawrence M. Friedman, *American Law: An Introduction,* 2nd ed. (New York: Norton, 1998), 163–79; Kermit L. Hall, *The Magic Mirror: Law in American History* (New York: Oxford University Press, 1989), 7–8.

Public Law

Law affecting the government embodies **public law**—that is, the legal relationships among governments and between governments and individuals. Statutory law, or legislation enacted by legislatures, is the major source of public law. The Americans with Disabilities Act (1990),[37] a federal statute designed to protect disabled persons from employment discrimination, is an example of statutory law. Federal and state constitutions delegate authority to legislatures to enact statutes. Article I of the U.S. Constitution, for instance, vests the U.S. Congress with broad legislative powers. Yet, because statutes are drafted in general language, they are often ambiguous and require administrative and judicial interpretation. The interplay between the legislative, executive, and judicial branches in determining the meaning of statutes raises important questions of separation of powers and, sometimes, of constitutional law.

Public law includes distinct but interrelated subcategories, such as constitutional law, administrative law, and criminal law, among others, that merit further discussion.

Constitutional Law

In the United States, constitutional rights, duties, and obligations are given final effect by the Supreme Court. The Court's rulings are binding as the "supreme Law of the land" under Article VI of the U.S. Constitution. Notably, though Article III vests judicial power in "one Supreme Court," the Constitution is silent on whether the Court has the authority to determine the constitutionality of legislation or official executive action.

In addition, because of the system of **judicial federalism**—that is, separate federal and state constitutions and courts (as further discussed in Chapter Three)—the highest state courts apply the law and exercise judicial review under their respective state constitutions. For instance, in 1892, before his appointment to the U.S. Supreme Court and while serving as a state supreme court judge, Oliver Wendell Holmes, Jr., rejected a policeman's claim that a New Bedford, Massachusetts, mayor improperly fired him under a state law prohibiting policemen from soliciting money for "any political purpose whatever." Judge Holmes ruled that the policeman has "a constitutional right to talk politics, but he has no constitutional right to be a policeman."[38] In one respect, Judge Holmes's decision settled the dispute at hand—the aggrieved policeman lost the case as well as his job because his free speech rights under the state constitution did not trump the mayor's power to dismiss him. But, in another respect, the outcome reaffirmed the legislature's power to condition the employment of public servants because, Judge Holmes ruled, the state constitution and constitutional law recognized the legislature's authority to define individual rights, duties, and obligations.

The Supreme Court asserted that power in the landmark case of *Marbury v. Madison* (1803).[39] In declaring that it is the Court's duty "to say what the law is" under the Constitution, Chief Justice John Marshall elucidated the enduring principle of **judicial review**. Since judicial review enables courts to check majority will and laws from the political branches, it remains a controversial and formidable power of appellate court policymaking (for a full discussion on appellate courts, see Chapter Nine; and, judicial policymaking, see Chapter Ten).[40]

Administrative Law

Although the U.S. Constitution omits any reference to a government bureaucracy, the realities of governing necessitated the creation of administrative agencies. At the federal and state level, the legislature makes statutory law, but administering or implementing it requires the creation and existence of agencies. Executive agencies play a formidable role in Washington, D.C., as well as in most state capitals, because they possess delegated legislative authority to make law. In the federal government, there are numerous executive departments, such as Commerce, Defense, Energy, Labor, Education, Justice, and Transportation. In addition, there are several independent agencies and government corporations (which compete with private enterprise), as well as a host of other boards, commissions, and advisory committees that perform specialized bureaucratic tasks and a range of services. The Environmental Protection Agency, the Federal Communications Commission, the Nuclear Regulatory Commission, the Securities and Exchange Commission, and the U.S. Postal Service are familiar examples of independent agencies and government corporations that have been delegated specific powers to regulate environmental protection, public broadcasting, nuclear energy and safety, financial securities in the marketplace, and the nation's postal service. Similar bureaucratic entities are infused into state legal systems.

Under the federal Administrative Procedure Act,[41] and similar state laws, administrative agencies are key sources of law because they are empowered to make administrative regulations. Federal regulations, which are published in the *Federal Register* and are accessible in the *Code of Federal Regulations*, are based on broad legislative mandates that are expressed in statutory law. Because Congress lacks the institutional capability to review the application of all the statutes it enacts, it falls to administrative agencies to interpret and implement them. As a result, agencies also have quasi-judicial functions in resolving disputes with other agencies, interest groups, and the public, typically after agency hearings before promulgating regulations.

A recurring constitutional issue affecting agency regulations in the modern post-New Deal era since 1937 is the amount of judicial deference courts owe to agencies when agency powers are questioned in litigation. The growth of the institutional presidency and the expanding role of the federal government since World War II have placed increasing pressure on courts to act as guardians or overseers of the administrative state. The battleground for testing the constitutional limits of agency power generally revolves around statutory interpretation (a topic discussed further in Chapter Nine). Agencies must construe and apply legislation, and in doing so, they issue rules and regulations that have binding legal effect. but which also may be legally challenged in federal courts. When reviewing the legality of agency interpretations and regulations, courts are generally deferential, which means that agency action will be upheld by the courts if challenged in a lawsuit. In theory, courts afford deference to agency decision-making because agencies are implicitly given delegated powers by legislatures to solve complex regulatory problems that are best resolved by the expertise agencies bring to any given area of public policy. By affording deference, courts are signaling that they do not want to second-guess the judgments of experts in the political branches; but there is also a risk that they are rubber-stamping executive action and ceding too much power to agencies.

Notably, in *Chevron, U.S.A., Inc. v. Natural Resources Defense Council, Inc.* (1984),[42] the Supreme Court established guidelines that frame judicial review of agency statutory interpretation. If Congress's legislative intent is clear, then the courts should defer to an agency's construction of the statute; but if the statute is ambiguous, then courts should only overturn an agency's action if its interpretation of the statute is unreasonable. Even though the Supreme Court continues to interpret the precise scope and application of the *Chevron* rule in subsequent cases, the judiciary still retains significant control over agency regulations and lawmaking.

Still, the exercise of judicial power in relation to the *Chevron legal* standard is increasingly politically controversial. Scholars, along with several conservative businesses and Supreme Court justices—most notably, the recent appointment of Justice Neil Gorsuch in particular, as well as Justices Clarence Thomas and perhaps even the Court's newest member, Brett Kavanaugh—have questioned its wisdom, constitutionality, and scope, mostly because it gives too much legislative authority to the executive branch and raises other constitutional difficulties, including separation-of-powers' conflicts. Even so, and while its precedential force remains uncertain, some empirical studies find that agency interpretations prevail most of the time in federal circuit courts that decide cases under the *Chevron* principle; and, as evidenced by *Kisor v. Wilkie* (2019)—a case involving the Department of Veteran's Affairs denial of benefits to a veteran with Post-Traumatic Stress Disorder-the Supreme Court, at least in some legal contexts, seems committed to a deference principle. Although the case was remanded to the lower courts for further review, the Court, in *Kisor*, did not overrule a line of precedents that held that courts should defer to an agency's decision, even when it was interpreting its own admittedly ambiguously written rules.[43]

Criminal Law

Criminal law deals with the use of governmental power to enforce violations of federal and state penal codes. The legal guilt for committing a crime is defined under statutory law that covers different kinds of illegal behavior, ranging from traffic offenses to capital murder. Generally, crimes are categorized in accordance with the harm they cause. Felonies, such as arson, rape, aggravated assault, and grand larceny, are serious offenses, punishable by lengthy prison sentences. Misdemeanors involve less property or bodily harm and include minor offenses, such as disorderly conduct, possession of marijuana (in small amounts), loitering, and public intoxication. Accordingly, misdemeanors carry less severe punishments, typically with shorter incarceration (less than one year) or the payment of restitution.

"[If] the Government becomes a lawbreaker," Justice Louis Brandeis once said, "it breeds contempt for the law."[44] Perhaps more than any other aspect of American jurisprudence, courts must ensure that those accused of a crime are treated fairly and swiftly. As Justice Brandeis recognized, courts are obliged to strike a balance between individual freedom and public safety in criminal law. From the time of arrest until sentencing or acquittal, courts exercise their discretion in different phases of the trial process in deciding the scope and application of criminal defendants' substantive and procedural rights.

For example, in *Gideon v. Wainwright* (1963),[45] a landmark case guaranteeing the right to counsel for indigent defendants, the Court protected Clarence Gideon's right under the Sixth Amendment to have an attorney appointed for him at trial. The rulings in *Mapp v. Ohio* (1961),[46] which upheld the exclusionary rule (requiring the exclusion at trial of evidence obtained from an unreasonable search or seizure under the Fourth Amendment), and *Miranda v. Arizona* (1966),[47] which requires police to read defendants their "*Miranda* warnings" in order to prevent violations of the Fifth Amendment's privilege against self-incrimination, are other oft-cited examples of cases expanding defendants' rights. Because the accused is presumed innocent and the government has the burden of proving guilt beyond a reasonable doubt, courts pay careful attention to whether rules of legal procedure and evidence are fairly applied in accord with constitutional requirements. Under the Sixth Amendment, for instance, defendants are entitled to "a speedy and public trial, by an impartial jury." In enforcing the right to a "speedy" and "public" trial with an "impartial jury," courts create legal standards to guarantee that the government respects those rights. *Batson v. Kentucky* (1986),[48] to illustrate further, held that the prosecution cannot use peremptory challenges— procedural requests to exclude persons from jury service for any reason—to remove African Americans from juries because racial considerations violate the defendant's right to an impartial jury. The Court's rulings pertaining to the process of arraignment, bail, and the introduction of evidence at trials are further examples of legal procedures that have significant consequences in criminal law (criminal procedure is further considered in Chapter Seven).

Private Law

Private law regulates the affairs of citizens in a variety of legal areas. It is the primary mechanism by which individuals resolve personal disputes. It defines personal obligations to other citizens, groups, or business entities. At the same time, it also gives citizens vested interests in remaining safe from physical or material harm. The law regulating corporate behavior is private law, as is the law establishing the rules governing civil marriage, divorce, and child custody. The assets and liabilities of a person's estate are distributed in accordance with the law of probate, another subunit of private law. These typologies and others (listed in Table 1.2) are also considered civil law.

Notably, civil law, as used here, has a different connotation from that of the (code-based) European civil law tradition, and it is most easily understood in contrast to criminal law. In criminal law, the government has an interest in the prosecution of offenders who commit crimes. Conversely, in civil law, the government's interest usually only extends to providing citizens with the means of resolving a private dispute. To illustrate, a person failing to fulfill a contract or causing personal injuries by acting negligently (a tort action) is a civil action in private law. Upon a finding of civil liability, the aggrieved party may seek to recover the monies lost upon breach of contract; or, in a negligence lawsuit, try to recover an amount of money that "compensates" them for the harm they suffered by being kept out of work, or losing a limb, due to the defendant's irresponsible conduct (civil litigation is further discussed in Chapter Eight).

Contract Law

The modern law of **contracts** grew out of the common law tradition. In the United States, contract law underwent a major transformation in the late eighteenth century. Under prior doctrine, contracting parties could avoid performing their agreements if it could be shown that the terms were clearly unfair. The emerging doctrine, often referred to as the "will theory of contracts," instead recognized that the law should honor agreements based on the intent of the parties. The inherent fairness of the exchange thus became less important than whether the contracting parties in fact made an agreement. Accordingly, the "convergence of wills"[49] became a basis for modern contract law. Because the intent to make a contract determines its enforceability, agreements reached in principle but not yet performed—so-called executory contracts—became enforceable as well. In short, in making contracts, parties may now be certain that their agreements would be legally binding documents.

Will theory had enormous consequences. One effect was to transform the judicial function: Courts began to share the responsibility with legislatures in determining statutory law. Hence, "antebellum judges dethroned the English common law by Americanizing it,"[50] a process hastened by the judiciary's rising stature as agents of economic lawmaking in all aspects of capitalism, including contract, antitrust, labor, bankruptcy, and commercial law. By the outbreak of the Civil War, contract law had become the predominant source of private law. A corresponding legal change occurred in the law of torts as well, particularly in the states.

Between the mid-nineteenth and early twentieth centuries, state courts were at the forefront of preserving the sanctity of private agreements. Federal courts also helped lay the basis for the expansion of capitalism and the sustained protection of private property by affirming Congress's power to enforce public contracts and, later, by preventing states from passing laws that would deny individuals the "liberty of contract" in the beginning of the twentieth century. Two decisions, *Fletcher v. Peck* (1810) and *Trustees of Dartmouth College v. Woodward* (1819),[51] interpreted Article I, Section 10, of the U.S. Constitution, which bars states from impairing the obligations of contracts, to hold that states could not deny the validity of public as well as private contracts—specifically, the land grant given to investors by the Georgia legislature in *Fletcher* and the English royal charter that devolved into an agreement with the state of New Hampshire to set up a college in *Dartmouth College*. Moreover, in *Allgeyer v. Louisiana* (1897),[52] the Fourteenth Amendment's due process clause was broadly construed to create a "liberty of contract" that protected "all contracts which may be proper, necessary, and essential" to a citizen's right to "be free in the enjoyment of all his faculties." The principle was, then, used to nullify a New York labor law regulating the number of hours bakery workers could work in *Lochner v. New York* (1905).[53] These early decisions underscored the vital role that federal and state courts played in developing the law of contracts as well as the general economic liberty principles of constitutional law.

Tort Law

Tort law provides remedies for private civil injuries and can be traced back to 1850 when it was recognized as a separate category of law. Before then, most legal claims seeking relief for harm caused by acts that did not arise from contract law— such as injury to a person's reputation (slander or libel), a threat to do bodily harm (assault), or harmful physical contact (battery)—were typically adjudicated under the common law system of writs, such as "trespass" (directly violating a person's property interest) or "trespass on the case" (indirectly violating a person's property interest). Advances in technology and industrialization after the Civil War exposed the difficulties of litigating newly discovered tort claims—often caused by steamboats, railroads, and industrial accidents—with the arcane rules of common law pleading. The law of torts thus emerged and eventually expanded to include fault-based conceptions of legal liability, like **negligence**, and related issues of the foreseeability of harm, such as "proximate cause."[54]

Under common law, tort claims did not have to prove fault or intent because rules of strict liability applied. That is, all an injured plaintiff had to show was that the defendant committed the act in question, without regard to fault. In *Brown v. Kendall* (1850),[55] however, the Supreme Court of Massachusetts helped revolutionize the law of torts by holding, in the words of Chief Justice Lemuel Shaw, "the plaintiff must come prepared with evidence to show either that the [defendant's] intention was unlawful or that the defendant was in fault; for if the injury was unavoidable, and the conduct of the defendant was free from blame, he will not be liable." The controlling standard of legal liability for the tort of negligence, he wrote, was that the parties exercise "ordinary care," or "that kind and degree of care, which prudent and cautious men would use, such as is required by the exigency of the case, and such as is necessary to guard against probable danger." In other words, a plaintiff could only win if there was proof that the defendant did not use ordinary care. Moreover, Chief Justice Shaw added there would be no liability if the plaintiff helped cause the accident—that is, if there was no "contributory negligence."

The new standards for tort liability, however, generally permitted corporate and business defendants to escape liability, while promoting the development of capitalism in the mid nineteenth and the early twentieth centuries. By fashioning rules based on fault liability and intentional conduct, courts rewrote tort law by creating precedents that transferred the cost of having accidents from employers to insurance companies and, sometimes, to injured plaintiffs. Such early common law decisions laid the basis for distinguishing three general types of torts that structure today's modern tort law: *Intentional torts* are those causing harm by intentional conduct. Familiar examples include assault and battery, trespassing, and false imprisonment. *Negligent torts* involve the imposition of liability without regard to legal intent. *Strict liability torts* are like common law torts of trespass in the sense that liability is imposed without regard to legal intent or fault. Simply engaging in the activity is enough, typically because it is abnormally dangerous or hazardous. To illustrate, product liability cases—those lawsuits that hold manufacturers strictly liable for the injuries they cause by making defective products—arise, for example, when harm is caused by a car's defective braking system or through an explosion resulting from a faulty fuel tank on a jet.

Incurring tort liability remains a contentious public policy issue that often pits trial lawyers against the insurance industry and business interests. In establishing the rules of tort liability, judges and legislators alike determine the legal standards by which individuals and corporations are held financially liable. Over the past generation, extensive efforts have been made to reform tort law (the politics of "tort reform" is discussed in the context of the civil litigation in Chapter Eight).

THE ROLE OF COURTS IN CONTEMPORARY SOCIETY

The different typologies and sources of law, just discussed, are the touchstone for the way courts function in the United States and elsewhere. Moreover, all courts function and discharge their duties in accordance with established judicial roles, or a "set of expectations, values, and attitudes about the way judges behave and should behave."[56] While not an exhaustive list, courts perform several functions and roles, the most important of which are as mediators of conflict, creators of legal expectations, guardians of individual and minority rights, therapeutic (problem-solving) agents, and policymakers.

Mediators of Conflict

The most basic function of a court is to resolve disputes or conflicts. As arbiters of private and public disputes, they not only provide security by preventing vigilantism but also help set priorities in public policy and distribute societal resources among competing interests. In the U.S. and the common law tradition, the courts perform this function through an adversary process that allows judges to render impartial decisions after gathering the facts and applying the law in cases.

Not everyone who believes he or she may have suffered some harm through the misfeasance of others seeks the help of attorneys and courts in civil actions, however (see "Contemporary Controversies over Courts: The Dispute Pyramid" in Chapter Eight). For those who do seek legal relief, the main participants in adversarial litigation (parties, lawyers, and judges) participate in criminal and civil cases—though, the lawsuits in those types are different because in criminal cases the law is enforced to maintain the public peace; whereas, in civil cases a private claim is asserted seeking monetary damages for a legal injury. In both types of cases, parties reach settlements either informally (before a trial) or formally (after a trial). Some disputes having significant legal ramifications, such as contract enforcement in construction projects, or property division in divorce cases, are resolved without invoking the full expense of the formal trial process through *alternative dispute resolution* (ADR) mechanisms, sometimes connected to court forums, but many times not (in private settings). The similarities and differences between adversarial litigation in criminal and civil cases, and the ADR alternatives, are analyzed further in Chapters Seven and Eight.

Creators of Legal Expectations

Courts create and order legal and social expectations through dispute resolution. Citizens know that legislatures make law and are aware that courts apply the law or establish rights. In defining the scope of legal duties and rights, courts thereby create and reinforce public expectations about the law. In this regard, the published opinions of courts are valuable in not only justifying their decisions but also orienting social behavior and enabling citizens to know the probable consequences of their actions.

The Supreme Court's decision in *Planned Parenthood of Southeastern Pennsylvania v. Casey* (1992)[57] is illustrative. There, in an unusual plurality-joint opinion by Justices Sandra Day O'Connor, Anthony Kennedy, and David Souter, the Court employed the doctrine of **stare decisis** to uphold *Roe v. Wade*, a 1973 ruling recognizing a woman's fundamental right to choose an abortion. The decision to affirm *Roe*'s "central holding" registered the Court's reluctance to upset legal and social expectations by changing the legality of a controlling common law precedent in abortion cases. In the words of the plurality opinion in *Casey*:

> For two decades of economic and social developments, people have organized intimate relationships and made choices that define their views of themselves and their places in society, in reliance on the availability of abortion in the event that contraception should fail. The ability of women to participate equally in the economic and social life of

the Nation has been facilitated by their ability to control their reproductive lives. . . .The Constitution serves human values, and while the effect of reliance on *Roe* cannot be exactly measured, neither can the certain cost of overruling *Roe* for people who have ordered their thinking and living around that case be dismissed.

In addition to concluding that the social cost of overruling *Roe* was too great, the Court pragmatically recognized that reversing *Roe* would significantly damage the public's confidence in the Court as an institution. Although the dissenting justices thought otherwise, the plurality asserted that the Court's institutional legitimacy depends on fulfilling the expectations that courts create by demonstrating a commitment to existing precedent.

Guardians of Individual and Minority Rights

Constitutional framer Alexander Hamilton thought that the responsibility of courts was to act as "faithful guardians of the Constitution." In defending the judiciary's power to exercise judicial review, he observed that courts safeguard the values underlying the Constitution by exercising the authority to overrule laws originating from "occasional ill humors in the society." Since the Constitution provided for judicial independence from the other branches of government, Hamilton believed the judiciary was a bulwark against legislation threatening to compromise constitutional rights and the rule of law. In defending the role of courts in *Federalist* No. 78, he observed that "the judiciary, from the nature of its functions, will always be the least dangerous to the political rights of the Constitution; because it will be least in the capacity to annoy or injure them." In democracy with separation of powers, the courts are limited in what they can do. As Hamilton further explained:

> The judiciary. . . has no influence over either the sword or the purse; no direction either of the strength or of the wealth of the society; and can take no active resolution whatever. It may truly be said to have neither FORCE nor WILL, but merely judgment; and must ultimately depend upon the aid of the executive arm even for the efficacy of its judgments.[58]

Although Hamilton favored what is called **judicial self-restraint** (i.e. that courts should defer to the legislature and the laws it creates on behalf of the people it represents in the democratic process), there is little doubt that the court's exercise of judicial review enables the judiciary to assume the important role of safeguarding individual and minority rights against dominant political majorities in the legislative process. In *United States v. Carolene Products Co.* (1938) and its famous "Footnote Four" (of that decision), the U.S. Supreme Court signaled that the Court has a special obligation to safeguard the rights of "discrete and insular minorities" when they are diminished by legislative action in the political system— otherwise known as the "preferred freedoms" doctrine. Under Footnote Four's rationale, courts are obliged to invoke strict scrutiny (a rigorous standard of judicial review) to test the constitutionality of laws that may infringe upon fundamental rights. Accordingly, since World War II, the Court's agenda and decision-making has become more progressive in scope: Instead of mostly deciding constitutional cases testing the limits of economic regulation, increasingly the Court has reviewed civil rights and liberties appeals that implicate the scope of the Court's guardian role in affirmative action, free speech, and other cases.[59]

The guardian role of courts inherently requires the judiciary to seek justice within a constitutional and public policy framework that is dynamic, challenging, and complex. Judges are often called to decide cases that strike a difficult balance between majority rule and minority rights. In some instances, the judicial lines that are drawn in reconciling competing interests, such as the government's interest in protecting public safety while preserving a respect for individual rights, are influenced by the unique character of the court and its operation in the legal culture or political system. One such United States court, the Foreign Intelligence Surveillance Court (FISC), is tasked under law to review wiretap applications submitted by the federal government in order to gather intelligence that may lead to a criminal prosecution of foreign agents or spies that seek to harm the United States in terrorist plots or other illicit activity. Its importance has grown significantly in the post-9/11 era because it plays a key role in high profile criminal activity or preventing terrorist attacks to the homeland. Unlike other courts in the public domain, it operates in secrecy and it does not typically afford the targets of the surveillance the due process right to be notified (or be represented by counsel) when the government asks the court to review and grant or deny its wiretap application, which sometimes are directed against U.S. citizens. Also, while a record of kept of the judicial proceedings, the judicial opinions it writes do not ordinarily get published in the public domain since much of what it reviews involves classified information or other sensitive law enforcement matters. But, in some instances, the work that the secret court does is thrust into the public eye for political reasons. The legal and public policy implications of the FISC's role in safeguarding public safety while trying to protect basic rights is illustrated by the highly unusual decision to criticize the court through the release of the so-called "Nunes memo" in the second year of the Trump administration (see in the Contemporary Controversies over Courts box, The Secret Foreign Intelligence Court and its Politicization in the Trump Era).

Contemporary Controversies over Courts: The Politics of Secret Foreign Intelligence Surveillance Court During the Trump Administration

Shortly after Donald Trump's historic 2016 presidential victory, the U.S. House of Representative Permanent Select Committee on Intelligence and its chair, Devin Nunes (R-CA), released a memorandum to the public alleging that the Department of Justice (DOJ) and the Federal Bureau of Investigation (FBI) abused their law enforcement powers by conducting wiretap surveillance of Carter Page, a U.S. citizen and former Trump foreign policy advisor, during the presidential campaign process. The January 18, 2018 memorandum, which contained classified material of the FBI's surveillance of Page under the Foreign Intelligence Surveillance Act (FISA), questioned the "legitimacy and legality of certain DOJ and FBI interactions with the Foreign Intelligence Surveillance Court" (FISC) and concluded that there was "a troubling breakdown of legal processes established to protect the American people from abuses related to the FISA [probable cause] process." By taking the unusual step of publicly disclosing the Nunes memo, Republicans sought to discredit political critics alleging that the DOJ and FBI are biased and conspiring against Trump during Special Counsel Robert Mueller's investigation of Russian meddling in the presidential election campaign.

The allegations asserted that the initial FISA surveillance application (and three other successive renewals) was improperly granted by FISC because the DOJ and FBI omitted facts showing political animus against Trump. According to the Nunes memo, the Page FISA applications relied heavily upon the information gathered from a "dossier" compiled from Christopher Steele, an FBI informant that was paid $160,000 by the Democratic National Committee and the Hillary Clinton campaign (through the Perkins Cole law firm and Fusion GPS) to do opposition research against candidate Trump (that aimed to expose Trump's close political ties to Vladimir Putin and Russia). Also, the memo alleged that the Page FISA application did not disclose other facts revealing that Steele, and some FBI personnel that were part of or close the application process, exhibited clear anti-Trump bias which, in turn, show that Steele and the FBI were unreliable and ideologically driven. Because of these omissions, the Nunes memo asserted that the FISC, which is special tribunal of federal judges that are appointed by the Chief Justice of the U.S. Supreme Court and reviews in secret applications to surveil persons (including U.S. citizens) that are suspected of spying as foreign agents against the United

States, wrongfully approved of each application because it lacked the necessary legal probable cause to do so.

After President Trump decided to de-classify its contents, the Nunes memo was released to the public against the advice of federal law enforcement and national security officials or advisors. For critics, these actions were misleading because the memo did not outline what the facts were that led the FISC to grant the first Page FISA application or the successive ones that are legally required to demonstrate that the continuing investigation and surveillance are producing viable intelligence. As Stephanie Douglas, a former senior FBI official in charge of counterintelligence operations observed, the Nunes memo "nicely sits together to support a narrative that obviously is very consistent with what politics wants it to be consistent with, at least the Republican version."

Subsequently, House Democrats prepared a counter-memo in reply, but President Trump refused to de-classify and release the document to the public, citing national security concerns. Trump defended his decision by tweeting, "The Democrats sent a very political and long response memo which they knew, because of sources and methods (and more) would have to be heavily redacted, whereupon they would blame the White House for a lack of transparency. Told them to re-do and send back in proper form!" In a response tweet, House Minority Leader Nancy Pelosi (D-CA) countered, "The hypocrisy is on full display. What does the President have to hide?"

The political saga continued with the House Intelligence Committee's release of a heavily redacted version prepared by Democrats. In addition to contesting their rendition of the facts surrounding the FISA surveillance process, the Democratic memo, dated January 29, 2018 and styled "Correcting the Record—The Russia Investigation," chastised Republicans for releasing the Nunes memo, calling is "a transparent effort to undermine [the FBI and DOJ], the Special Counsel, and Congress' investigations." Predictably, Republicans countered that the Democratic version was just another attempt "to undercut the president politically." In a tweet, President Trump wrote that "The Democrat memo response on government surveillance abuses is a total political and legal BUST. . .Just confirms all of the terrible things that were done. SO ILLEGAL!" These events, thereafter, spurred on a Department of Justice Inspector report criticizing the FBI's handling of sensitive evidence in surveillance cases and, predictably, generated ongoing calls for Congress to reform the operation of the Foreign Intelligence Surveillance Court.

The politicization of the Nunes memo controversy raises important questions about the propriety of handling of foreign intelligence information at the highest level of government and the role that the FISC plays in authorizing surveillance warrants that are done in proceedings that are held in secret, purportedly in the interest of protecting national security. From one perspective, FISC court operations are defensible because their secret deliberations—which also in practice result in the majority of wiretaps sought by the U.S. government being approved without the target of surveillance (or their counsel) even knowing about the investigation or grounds for securing a wiretap—represent the best chance to uncover illicit foreign activities which, in turn, prevent foreign attacks from happening. Yet, the secret and *ex parte* nature of the proceedings (not allowing any defense or objection by the surveillance target or his or her counsel in the FISC) are criticized for expanding or abusing government powers while undermining due process and other constitutional rights. For some observers, as well, the extraordinary circumstances surrounding the Nunes memo controversy generates fundamental questions about the political legitimacy of this special tribunal and whether it has an institutional duty to launch its own investigation about its own procedures and perhaps order the government to take remedial action so that it can preserve the integrity of the judicial function in a nation governed by the rule of law.

Sources: Steve Vladeck, "Congress Has a Second Chance to Fix FISA," NBC News (May 14, 2020). Accessed June 17, 2020. https://www.nbcnews.com/think/opinion/congress-has-second-chance-fix-fisa-has-it-learned-anything-ncna1207001; Ryan Lucas, "Nunes Memo: What's In It And What's Not," *NPR 90.3 WCPN Ideastream* (February 2, 2018). Accessed February 20, 2019. https://www.npr.org/2018/02/02/582713363/memo-russian-overtures-to-trump-aide-triggered-fbi-investigation; Kyle Cheney, "Trump blocks release of Democratic Russian Memo," *Politico* (February 9, 2018). Accessed February 20, 2018. https://www.politico.com/story/2018/02/09/trump-blocks-release-of-democratic-memo-402083; Daniel S. Alter, "The Nunes Memo Attacks the Legitimacy of the Foreign Intelligence Surveillance Court. It Should Act to Repair the Damage." *Time* (February 6, 2018). Accessed February 20, 2018. http://time.com/5135266/nunes-memo-foreign-intelligence-surveillance-court/; Nicholas Fandos, "2 Weeks After Trump Blocked It, Democrats' Rebuttal of G.O.P. Memo is Released." *N.Y. Times* (February 24, 2018). Accessed February 28, 2018. https://www.nytimes.com/2018/02/24/us/politics/democratic-memo-released-fbi-surveillance-carter-page.html.

Therapeutic (Problem-Solving) Agents

In recent years, one of the most important trends in the U.S. courts has been the growing acceptance of therapeutic jurisprudence, or "the role of the law as a therapeutic agent."[60] Increasingly, problem-solving courts, which let judges use the law as a form of mental health therapy to enhance individual well-being, are becoming a significant part of the legal landscape. Most, but not all, problem-solving courts are specialized courts that assist underage offenders, defendants accused of domestic violence or drug crimes, and those with mental health problems. Several states use such courts to address problems of homelessness, prostitution, sexual predators, gambling, and (through so-called reentry courts) offenders who have been released from prison but cannot assimilate into the community. Since 1993, at least seventy nonspecialized problem-solving courts also have been created. Styled as "community courts," these judicial bodies tackle broad social problems relating to crime, public safety, and quality of life at the neighborhood level.[61]

While the origin of problem-solving courts can be traced back to the creation of juvenile courts in 1899, they have gained wider appeal since the opening of a drug court in Dade County, Florida, in 1989. In response to the problems of recidivism and prison overcrowding, the basic model of therapeutic courts aims to let problem-solving judges manage their **dockets** and impose sentences requiring long-term monitoring instead of incarceration. That court's success encouraged others to adopt similar programs.

In general, problem-solving courts have three characteristics: (1) intensive judicial monitoring, requiring offenders to report to the court regularly on the status of their efforts in drug treatment, securing employment, completing restitution, and the like; (2) aggressive professional outreach, involving judicial efforts to create a symbiotic relationship with off-site professionals, such as social workers or social scientists; and, (3) community engagement, involving judicial efforts to establish a relationship with community leaders and laypersons and encouraging them to participate actively in the justice system. These traits enable a better informed and trained staff to give immediate, hands-on intervention, an approach that provides individualized justice in a well-structured collaborative program that can take into account a participant's progress by constant evaluation and supervision.[62]

Most significantly, problem-solving courts are nonadversarial and aim at solving the underlying problems contributing to a crime, instead of focusing on assigning guilt or innocence. They also differ from traditional adversarial processes and courts, which are essentially backward looking in resolving legal disputes involving the claims of only a few participants. Therapeutic or problem-solving courts are forward looking in focusing on dispute avoidance and reaching results based on a collaborative process that serves the interests of individuals and the larger community.[63] In problem-solving courts, trial judges function more like social workers. Instead of simply handing down sentences or verdicts without getting to the root of a defendant's problems, problem-solving judges embrace a holistic approach in addressing an offender's problems by providing motivation, monitoring progress, and connecting the offender to social services. In contrast to the adversarial approach, which contemplates taking a dispassionate stance and impersonal attitude towards the offender, the problem-solving judge takes a direct interest in securing the well-being of the offender through empathy, and by keeping an open line of communication and dialogue with the litigant, counsel, and program participants. During the process, judges also educate the public about the best methods to prevent antisocial behavior. Notably, offenders in therapeutic programs are expected to fulfill the conditions of treatment while in the program; and, the failure to do so will mean that their original criminal sentences will be re-instituted, with no leniency. New York's innovative "Opioid Intervention Court," begun under the leadership of the Honorable Janet DiFiore, the Chief Judge of the N.Y. Court of Appeals, is a successful illustration the operation of a problem-solving approach in response to that state's Opioid and Addition Crisis in recent years.[64] Another is the growth of Veteran's Courts, discussed in the "Contemporary Controversies over Courts: Veteran Treatment Courts" box in this Chapter.

Advocates of problem-solving courts argue that they are a necessary response to the failures of traditional courts and the adversary process, which exact great costs and emotional toll from defendants, their families, and communities. In this respect, they are a more efficient and humane method of providing justice. Although the evidence is mixed, they also may help to reduce crime rates, prevent prison overcrowding, and address caseload problems typically found in adversarial courts. The promise of therapeutic courts is evident from the over 3,000 problem-solving courts currently in operation.[65]

Still, therapeutic courts remain controversial. Critics assert that the advantages of such courts are offset by judges having to assume the time-intensive role of a collaborator—a task for which they are untrained. Some victims and victims' rights groups also oppose them for moving away from the traditional function of courts, namely, serving justice by handing down penalties and other kinds of punishment. Other criticisms include that it is improper for the government to be paternal in delivering legal services; that the problem-solving approach wrongly diverts public funds and judicial resources away from other areas of criminal justice; and that defendants are basically coerced into sacrificing their due process rights by agreeing to participate in treatment programs that they may not fully understand.[66]

Contemporary Controversies over Courts: Veteran Treatment Courts

There are over 3,000 problem-solving, or treatment courts, throughout the United States. The most common are drug (44%) and mental health courts (11%); but family (9%), youth specialty (8%), hybrid DWI/drug (7%), DWI (6%), domestic violence (6%), veterans (4%), tribal wellness (1%), and other miscellaneous types of treatment (5%) courts are available as well. The success of drug courts, which treat substance addition as a disease that needs treatment instead of as a moral failing that deserves punishment, has been responsible for the growing trend to apply non-adversarial methods to resolve the problems that cause criminal misconduct. Generally, they follow a diversionary format: if eligibility is established and the court's guidelines for treatment are followed, participants may avoid criminal prosecution or incarceration after they complete a collaborative treatment plan by social service counselors, court personnel and former veterans that have experienced similar difficulties. Though not without their critics, supporters hail them as a justice reform movement by saving lives and tax dollars, along with enhancing public safety by reducing crime and recidivism.

Among treatment courts, the emergence of veteran treatment courts—which stand apart from U.S. military courts and remain independent from the Department of Veterans Affairs (but supported by the U.S. Department of Veterans Affairs program, an organization of direct outreach for veterans caught in the criminal justice system)—is a significant development in the American judicial process. The opioid crisis, which has reached epic proportions in the United States, underscores their importance for veterans, policymakers and the justice system. The first veteran treatment courts (VTC) opened in Anchorage, Alaska (in 2004) and Buffalo, N.Y. (in 2008). Since then, there has been a rapid growth of VTCs, with most opening after 2009. Thus, VTCs are found in nearly all the U.S. states and territories.

Today, there are over 461 VTCs, which include veterans drug courts, veterans mental health courts, and general veterans courts. While sometimes they work with active-duty personnel and violent offenders, a majority of VTCs try to aid veterans that are facing prosecution for less serious crimes stemming from substance abuse or mental health disorders. While the eligibility and court procedures vary by jurisdiction, typically VTCs treat veterans with post-traumatic stress and traumatic brain injuries, along with non-combat issues of substance abuse, financial difficulties, unemployment, homelessness, or suicide. After acceptance into the program, veterans may avoid incarceration or having their charges reduced if they successfully complete an individualized treatment program. In this respect, they operate differently than traditional criminal courts, which adjudicate questions of guilt or innocence in a punitive and adversarial framework. Instead, VTCs use principles of restorative justice that are designed to permit the offender to reintegrate into the community after treatment. VTCs adopt a collaborative approach, uniting the community, victim and offender in a common plan for treatment that lets the offender back into society. Who helps veterans while in treatment is also an important characteristic of VTCs. After a veteran is screened for their willingness and commitment to participate in the treatment plan, veteran mentors, sometimes called "Veterans Service Representatives," work as counselors or caseworkers along with other professionals to assist the mentees progress through the treatment plan and VTC judicial process.

While critics of VTCs claim they only reinforce negative stereotypes and strain judicial resources while affording special treatment to only a certain segment of the community, supporters laud that their non-confrontational approach to identifying and resolving the roots of criminal misfeasance, including the restoration of personal empowerment and hold out the promise that veterans, which comprise eight percent of all inmates in federal and state prisons, will not return to jail after receiving treatment. Yet the evidence is mixed as to whether VTCs accomplish their goals. While some research indicates that there is no significant difference in outcomes in VTCs as opposed to traditional criminal courts, other studies show that VTC treatment plans have a moderate but positive effect in improving veteran lives in their experiences in the criminal justice system or as they try to secure various housing, employment, and VA benefits. Still, VTC participants with histories of prior incarceration or a track record of violating probation or parole conditions, or those with chronic substance abuse or mental health problems, predictably tend to fare worse.

Sources: National Association of Drug Court Professionals, "Treatment Courts are Advancing Justice," *National Association of Drug Court Professionals* (YouTube Video, February 26, 2018). Accessed February 26, 2018. https://www.nadcp.org/; Douglas B. Marlowe, Carolyn D. Hardin, and Carson L. Fox, *Painting the Current Picture: A National Report on Drug Courts and Other Problem-Solving Courts in the United States (June 2016)*. Accessed February 26, 2018. https://www.ndci.org/wp-content/uploads/2016/05/Painting-the-Current-Picture-2016.pdf; Suzanne M. Strong, Ramoa R. Rantala, and Tracey Kyckelhahn, *Census of Problem-Solving Courts, 2012 (revised October 12, 2016)*. Bureau of Justice Statistics. Accessed February 26, 2018. https://www.bjs.gov/content/pub/pdf/cpsc12.pdf; Jack Tsai, Andrea Finlay, Bessie Flatley, and Wesley J. Kasprow, "A National Study of Veterans Treatment Court Participants: Who Benefits and Who Recidivates," *Administration and Policy in Mental Health and Mental Health Services Research* (2018) 45: 236–244; Julie Marie Baldwin, "Investigating the Programmatic Attack: A National Survey of Veterans Treatment Courts," *Journal of Criminal Law & Criminology* (2015)

105(3): 705–751; Michael L. Perlin, "John Brown Went Off to War: Considering Veterans Courts as Problem-Solving Courts," (2013) *Nova Law Review* 37: 445–477.

Policymakers

Courts not only decide what the law means in legal judgments or judicial rulings and opinions; they also create and enforce public policies by deciding disputes. Judicial policymaking occurs in all courts and at all levels of the state and federal judiciaries. Although courts decide only particular cases and controversies raised by the parties in a lawsuit seeking judicial relief, their decisions and outcomes often have wider public policy implications, especially in dealing with politically highly charged controversies, like abortion, affirmative action, and governmental surveillance. For example, in a study of U.S. district courts' decisions in cases challenging the USA PATRIOT Act (the key antiterrorism legislation enacted in the aftermath of September 11), political scientists Christopher Banks and Steven Tauber found that district court judges are highly deferential to law enforcement officials during times of emergency and "war," while nonetheless forging judicial policy in the fight against international terrorism.[67] The national opioid crisis, as well, has forced some trial court judges, such as U.S. District Court Judge Dan Aaron Polster of the Ohio Northern District to don the unconventional role of using judicial power to solve social problems. In 2018, Judge Polster was tasked in multi-district litigation to supervise over four hundred lawsuits brought against manufacturers and distributers of prescription opioids that grossly misrepresented the risks of using them. In doing so, he irked the parties' legal counsel by expediating the cases and putting them on a fast-track of limited discovery (the process by which information is gathered to resolve the case), soliciting the input from state attorneys general (even though they are not directly involved in the federal action), and immediately commencing settlement discussions. After reading the transcript of Polster's first settlement hearing, one law professor aptly captured the high stakes of the litigation and the daunting challenges the court faced in the opioid litigation by observing, "We say we want judges to be umpires, [b]ut when there's a large social problem at stake, judges can be umpires for only so long, before they decide that it has to be solved." A former law clerk of Polster, too, was not surprised by how the judge opted to solve an intractable social issue. As he recounted, "At the end of a long day where it looked like there wouldn't be a settlement, he'd walk out with one [a]nd he'd wink and say, 'Sometimes it takes a federal judge.' "[68]

Likewise, federal and state appeals courts, especially the U.S. Supreme Court and state supreme courts, have assumed important roles in public policymaking (as further analyzed in Chapters Nine and Ten). They have creatively established new legal rules in a variety of controversial areas of social policy, such as school desegregation, abortion, gun rights, and same-sex discrimination and same-sex marriage, among other hotly contested areas of public policy. However, judges, which are presumed to be impartial arbiters of the law that merely "declare" the law, run the risk of being labeled "judicial activists" whenever they decide cases that "makes" law by advancing rights or justice in these areas of contentious social policy. Also, among academics, the role courts play as policymakers and whether they actually "create" social change through their decision-making is a topic of intense debate (see Contemporary Controversies over Courts: Do Courts Forge Major Social Change? in Chapter Ten).

Chapter Summary

The nature and sources of law and relation to diverse legal systems are examined. The main legal systems are based on common law, civil law, customary law, or a mixture of either or any of those plus religious law. Two principal categories of law are public law (which involves disputes between the government and individuals or groups) and private law (which involves disputes between two private parties), including common law and civil law. Within each of those categories, there are different types of law: Public law includes constitutional law, statutory law, and criminal law, among others, while private law includes contract law and tort law, among others. Courts employ different methods and processes. The two most notable are the adversarial system, in which judges act as impartial arbitrators of disputes, and which is used in the United States and other common law countries, and the inquisitorial system, in which judges are proactive, as generally found in civil law countries. Courts and judges may play various roles in society. Besides being adjudicators of disputes, they may serve as mediators of private and public conflicts, creators of legal expectations, guardians of individual and minority rights, and agents of therapeutic justice as well as important makers of legal and public policy.

Key Questions for Review and Critical Analysis

1. What are some of the problems nations face in applying the law if they have a mixed legal system?

2. Why is it important to distinguish public law from private law?

3. Is the adversarial legal system in the United States better than the inquisitorial systems used in other parts of the world?

4. Relative to the roles courts play in society, do judges simply "declare" the law instead of "making" it, especially in high-stakes political or policy issues?

5. What are the strengths and weaknesses of having problem-solving courts in a common law adversarial system?

Web Links

1. Supreme Court of the United States home page (www.supremecourt.gov)

    *   A rich source to learn about the U.S. Supreme Court, its justices, how it performs its judicial role, and how it decides constitutional law cases. The site contains past and present judicial opinions from the Court and has links to other legal and judicial information.

2. World Legal Systems, by University of Ottawa Law Faculty (www.juriglobe.ca)

    *   A comprehensive explanation and listing of all world legal systems.

3. National Center of State Courts (www.ncsc.org)

    *   An exhaustive repository of information pertaining to the work and policymaking of all state courts in the United States. The site is home to the *Justice System Journal*, an important publication outlet for academic studies related to key issues confronting state judiciaries.

Selected Readings

Cardozo, Benjamin N. *The Nature of the Judicial Process.* New Haven, Conn.: Yale University Press, 1921.

Daly, Paul. Ed. *Apex Courts and the Common Law.* Toronto: University of Toronto Press, 2019.

David, Rene, and John E. C. Brierley. *Major Legal Systems in the World Today: An Introduction to the Comparative Study of Law.* Delran, N.J.: Legal Classics Library, 2000.

DeMatteo, David, Kirk Heilbrun, Alice Thornewill, and Shelby Arnold. *Problem-Solving Courts and the Criminal Justice System.* New York: Oxford University Press, 2019.

Flango, Victor E. and Thomas M. Clarke, *Reimagining Courts: A Design for the Twenty-First Century,* Philadelphia, PA.: Temple University Press, 2015.

Friedman, Lawrence M. *American Law in the 20th Century.* New Haven, Conn.: Yale University Press, 2002.

Glenn, Patrick H. *Legal Traditions of the World: Sustainable Diversity in Law*. 5th ed. New York: Oxford University Press, 2014.

Guarnieri, Carlo, and Patrizia Pederzoli. *The Power of Judges: A Comparative Study of Courts and Democracy*. Translated by C. A. Thomas. London: Oxford University Press, 2002.

Hall, Kermit L. *The Magic Mirror: Law in American History*. New York: Oxford University Press, 1989.

Jackson, Vicki C. *Constitutional Engagement in Transnational Era*. Oxford: Oxford University Press, 2010.

Kaye, Kerwin. *Enforcing Freedom: Drug Courts, Therapeutic Communities, and the Intimacies of the State*. New York: Columbia University Press, 2020.

Keck, Thomas M. *Judicial Politics in Polarized Times*. Chicago: University of Chicago Press, 2014.

Kritzer, Herbert M., ed. *Legal Systems of the World: A Political, Social and Cultural Encyclopedia*. Volume 1. Santa Barbara, Calif.: ABC-CLIO, 2002.

Mak, Elaine. *Judicial Decision-Making in a Globalised World: A Comparative Analysis of the Changing Practices of Western Highest Courts*. Oxford: Hart Publishing, 2013.

Merryman, John Henry. *The Civil Law Tradition: An Introduction to the Legal Systems of Western Europe and Latin America*. 4th ed. Stanford, Calif.: Stanford University Press, 2019.

Miller, Monica K., and Brian H. Bornstein, eds. *Stress, Trauma, and Wellbeing in the Legal System* [Electronic Resource]. New York: Oxford University Press, 2013.

O'Brien, David M., and Peter H. Russell, eds. *Judicial Independence in the Age of Democracy*. Charlottesville: University Press of Virginia, 2001.

Otto, Jan Michiel, ed. *Sharia Incorporated: A Comparative Overview of the Legal Systems of Twelve Muslim Countries in Past and Present*. Leiden, Netherlands: Leiden University Press, 2010.

Powell, Emilia Justyna. *Islamic Law and International Law: Peaceful Resolution of Disputes*. New York: Oxford University Press, 2019.

Rakove, Jack. *Original Meanings: Politics and Ideas in the Making of the Constitution*. New York: Knopf, 1996.

Siems, Mathias M. *Comparative Law*. New York: Cambridge University Press, 2018.

Susskind, Richard E. *Online Courts and the Future of Justice*. Oxford, U.K.: Oxford University Press, 2019.

Wheatley, Steven. *The Idea of International Human Rights Law*. Oxford: Oxford University Press, 2019.

Wilmot-Smith, Frederick. *Equal Justice: Fair Legal Systems in an Unfair World*. Cambridge, Harvard University Press, 2019.

Zenker, Olaf and Markus Virgil Hoehne, eds. *The State and the Paradox of Customary Law in Africa*. New York: Routledge, 2018.

Endnotes

1   Human Rights Watch, *Boxed In: Women and Saudi Arabia's Male Guardianship System* (July 2016), available at https://www.hrw.org/sites/default/files/report_pdf/saudiarabia0716web.pdf (last retrieved February 16, 2018), 21–22. See also Hugh Tomlinson, "Two Days After Getting Vote, a Mother Is Sentenced to 10 Lashes for Driving," *The Times* (London) (September 28, 2011), 23. See also Mohammed Jamjoon, "Women Drive for Change in Saudi Arabia," *CNN Video Report* (October 25, 2013), available at http://www.cnn.com/2013/10/25/world/meast/saudi-women-drivers-jamjoom/ (last retrieved November 4, 2013).

2   The quotation and example of discriminatory treatment is in Kelly LeBenger, *Behind the Veil: The State of Women in Saudi Arabia* (December 2013), available at http://www.gulfinstitute.org/wp-content/uploads/2013/12/Behind-the-Veil.pdf (last retrieved February 17, 2018), 4–5. See Human Rights Watch, *Boxed In: Women and Saudi Arabia's Male Guardian System* (July 2016), https://www.hrw.org/sites/default/files/report_pdf/saudiarabia0716web.pdf (last retrieved February 17, 2018).

3   RadioFreeEurope/RadioLiberty, "Russian Supreme Court Upholds Ruling Banning Jehovah's Witnesses (July 17, 2017), available at https://www.rferl.org/a/russia-jehovah-s-witness-ban-upheld/28621481.html (last retrieved February 17, 2018); Associated Press, "India hangs 4 men convicted for fatal New Delhi gang rape (March 20, 2020)," available at https://www.nbcnews.com/news/world/india-hangs-4-men-convicted-fatal-new-delhi-gang-rape-n1164586 (last retrieved March 23, 2020).

4   *Hawaii v. Trump*, 138 S. Ct. 2392 (2018).

5   Christopher P. Banks, "National Security and Anti-Terrorism Policies: The Federalism Implications of Trump's Travel Ban," in *Controversies in American Federalism and Public Policy*, ed. Christopher P. Banks (New York: Routledge, 2018), 35–54. See also Associated Press, "Veil Bans by Country: A Look at Restrictions on Muslim Headscarves Around the World," *Huffington Post* (September 18, 2013), available at www.huffington post.com (last retrieved October 14, 2013); Associated Press, "Quebec, Once Again Going Its Own Way, Defies Protest to Push Curbs on Showy Religious Symbols," *Washington Post* (October 9, 2013), available at www.washingtonpost.com (last retrieved October 14, 2013); Associated Press, "Spanish Court Overturns City's Ban on Burqas," *Fox News* (February 28, 2013), available at www.foxnews.com (last retrieved October 15, 2013); Stephan Castle, "Britain Is Pulled, Reluctantly, Into Debate Over Wearing Full-Face Veils in Public," *New York Times* (September 16, 2013), available at www.nytimes.com (last retrieved October 15, 2013); and Liam Stack, "Saudi Men Go to Polls; Women Wait," *New York Times* (September 30, 2011), A12.

6   Lawrence M. Friedman, Rogelio Perez-Perdomo, and Manuel A. Gomez, "Introduction," in *Law in Many Societies: A Reader*, edited by Lawrence M. Friedman, Rogelio Perez-Perdomo, and Manuel A. Gomez (Stanford, Calif.: Stanford Law Books, 2011), 2; Susan S. Silby, "J. Locke, op. cit.: Invocations of Law on Snowy Streets," in *Using Legal Culture*, edited by David Nelken (London: Wildy, Simmonds & Hill, 2012), 120–52.

7   See Lawrence M. Friedman, *The Legal System: A Social Science Perspective* (New York: Russell Sage Foundation, 1975), 11–16.

8   Esin Orucu, "General Introduction: Mixed Legal Systems at New Frontiers," in *Mixed Legal Systems at New Frontiers*, edited by Esin Orucu (London: Wildy, Simmonds & Hill, 2010), 1–18.

9   See, e.g., Konrad Zweigert, and Hein Kotz, *An Introduction to Comparative Law*, 3rd ed., translated by Tony Weir (New York: Oxford University Press, 1998); Rene David and John E. C. Brierley, *Major Legal Systems in the World Today*, 3rd ed. (London: Stevens & Sons, 1985).

10   John Henry Merryman, *The Civil Law Tradition: An Introduction to the Legal Systems of Western Europe and Latin America*, 2nd ed. (Stanford, Calif.: Stanford University Press, 1985), 13; Martin Shapiro, *Courts: A Comparative and Political Analysis* (Chicago: University of Chicago Press, 1981), 128–29; James T. McHugh, *Comparative Constitutional Traditions* (New York: Peter Lang, 2002), 18–19.

11   Philippe Bruno, "The Common Law From a Civil Law Perspective," in *Introduction to Foreign Legal Systems,* edited by Richard A. Danner and Marie-Louise H. Bernal (New York: Oceana Publications, 1994), 2, 8. See also Aharon Barak, "A Judge on Judging: The Role of a Supreme Court in a Democracy," *Harvard Law Review* 116 (2002), 16, 25.

12   Merryman, *The Civil Law Tradition*, 111–13.

13   David and Brierley, *Major Legal Systems in the World Today*, 316–17.

14   Benjamin N. Cardozo, *The Nature of the Judicial Process* (New Haven, Conn.: Yale University Press, 1921), 124.

15   Daniel J. Boorstin, *The Americans: The Colonial Experience* (New York: Vintage Books, 1958), 201. See also A. E. Dick Howard, *The Road for Runnymede: Magna Carta and Constitutionalism in America* (Charlottesville: University Press of Virginia, 1968), 117–25, 129–32.

16   *The Federalist Papers* (No. 78), edited by Clinton Rossiter (New York: Mentor, 1999), 433.

17   Zweigert and Kotz, *An Introduction to Comparative Law*, 242.

18   Jerome Frank, *Courts on Trial: Myth and Reality in American Justice* (Princeton, N.J.: Princeton University Press, 1973), 85.

19   David and Brierley, *Major Legal Systems in the World Today*, 169–80; James Feinerman, "Introduction to Asian Legal Systems," in *Introduction to Foreign Legal Systems*, edited by Richard A. Danner and Marie-Louise H. Bernal (New York: Oceana Publications, 1994), 98.

20   David and Brierley, *Major Legal Systems in the World Today*, 159–88, 191–224.

21   Joshua White, "Mohammed and Madison: A Comparison of the Qur'an and the U.S. Constitution," *Journal of Transnational Law and Policy* (Spring 2002), 310. See generally Kathleen M. Moore, "Islamic Law," in *Legal Systems of the World: A Political, Social and Cultural Encyclopedia, Volume 1*, edited by Herbert M. Kritzer (Santa Barbara, Calif.: ABC-CLIO, 2002), 755.

22   Sam Souryal, "The Religionization of a Society: The Continuing Application of Shariah Law in Saudi Arabia," *Journal for the Scientific Study of Religion* 26 (1987), 431.

23   Frank E. Vogel, *Islamic Law and Legal System: Studies of Saudi Arabia* (London: Brill, 2000), 154. See generally Walid Iqbal, "Courts, Lawyering and ADR: Glimpses Into the Islamic Tradition," *Fordham Urban Law Journal* 28 (2001), 1039–40.

24   Reuters, *HAARETZ*, "With Over $100 Billion Recovered, Saudi Arabia Ends High-profile Anti-corruption Crackdown (March 1, 2019)," available from https://www.haaretz.com/middle-east-news/with-over-100-billion-recovered-saudi-high-profile-anti-corruption-crackdown-ends-1.6895953; David Ignatius, "Are Saudi Arabia's reforms for real? A recent visit says yes." *Washington Post* (March 1, 2018), available at https://www.washingtonpost.com/opinions/global-opinions/are-saudi-arabias-reforms-for-real-a-recent-visit-says-yes/2018/03/01/a11a4ca8-1d9d-11e8-9de1-147dd2df3829_story.html?utm_term=.cf9e2c1b7f47 (last retrieved on March 4, 2018); Ziad A. Al-Sudairy, "The Constitutional Appeal of Shari'a in a Modernizing Saudi State," *Middle East Law and Governance* 2 (2010), 1–16; Abdullah Fakhry Ansary, "Saudi Judicial Reform and the Principle of Independence," *Sada* (May 5, 2009), available at http://carnegieendowment.org/2009/05/05/saudi-judicial-reform-and-principle-of-independence/fhpy (last retrieved November 13, 2013). See also Esther van Eijk, "Sharia and National Law in Saudi Arabia," in *Sharia Incorporated: A Comparative Overview of the Legal Systems of Twelve Muslim Countries in Past and Present*, edited by Jan Michiel Otto (Leiden: Leiden University Press, 2010), 139–80.

25   McHugh, *Comparative Constitutional Traditions*, 144. See also David and Brierley, *Major Legal Systems in the World Today*, 548–76; A. N. Allott, "African Law," in *An Introduction to Legal Systems*, edited by J. Duncan M. Derret (New York: Praeger, 1968), 145.

[26] H. Patrick Glenn, *Legal Traditions of the World: Sustainable Diversity in Law*, 4th ed. (New York: Oxford University Press, 2010), 319–60; James T. McHugh, *The Essential Concept of Law* (New York: Peter Lang, 2001), 24–27; David and Brierley, *Major Legal Systems in the World Today*, 518–21.

[27] Elizabeth M. Lynch, "China's Rule of Law Mirage: The Regression of the Legal Profession Since the Adoption of the 2007 Lawyers Law," *George Washington International Law Review* (2010), 535, 537.

[28] Lynch, "China's Rule of Law Mirage, 541–42. See also Sida Liu, "Lawyers, State Officials and Significant Others: Symbiotic Exchange in the Chinese Legal Services Market," *The China Quarterly* (2011), 276–93; "Legal Report," *Beijing Review* 56, no. 27 July 4, 2013), 5; Xin He and Kwai Hang Ng, "Inquisitorial Adjudication and Institutional Constraints in Chinese Civil Justice," *Law and Policy* 35, no. 4 (2013), 290–318; and Wang Hong, "Building a Guiding Precedents System With Chinese Characteristics," *Dui Hua Human Rights Journal* (December 7, 2012), available at http://duihuahrjournal.org/2012/12/can-chinas-legal-reform-survive-without.html?m=1 (last retrieved January 19, 2014).

[29] Tian Feilong, "Beyond term limits: China's new constitution is written for a nation on the rise," *South China Morning Post* (March 23, 2018), available at https://www.scmp.com/comment/insight-opinion/article/2138542/beyond-term-limits-chinas-new-constitution-written-nation (last retrieved March 1, 2019); Nectar Gan, "Xi Jinping cleared to stay on as China's president with just 2 dissenters among 2,964 votes," *South China Morning Post* (March 12, 2018), available at https://www.scmp.com/news/china/policies-politics/article/2136719/xi-jinping-cleared-stay-president-chinas-political (last retrieved March 1, 2019); Andrew Jacobs and Chris Buckley, "Chinese Activists Test New Leader and Are Crushed," *New York Times* (January 15, 2014), available at www.nytimes.com, (last retrieved January 20, 2014); Elizabeth M. Lynch, "China's Rule of Law Mirage: The Regression of the Legal Profession Since the Adoption of the 2007 Lawyers Law," *George Washington International Law Review* (2010), 535–85.

[30] Aharon Barak, "Some Reflections on the Israeli Legal System and Its Judiciary," *Electronic Journal of Comparative Law* (April 2002). See also Adam S. Hofri-Winogradow, "A Plurality of Discontent: Legal Pluralism, Religious Adjudication and the State," *Journal of Law and Religion* 26, no. 1 2010–2011), 57–89.

[31] David Haljan, *Separating Powers: International Law Before National Courts* [Electronic Resource] (The Hague: T.M.C. Asser Press, 2013), 2.

[32] Dinah Shelton, "Introduction," in *International Law and Domestic Legal Systems: Incorporation, Transformation, and Persuasion*, edited by Dinah Shelton (Oxford: Oxford University Press, 2011), 1. See also Philippa Webb, *International Judicial Integration and Fragmentation* (New York: Oxford University Press, 2013), 3–9.

[33] Elaine Mak, *Judicial Decision-Making in a Globalised World: A Comparative Analysis of the Changing Practices of Western Highest Courts* (Oxford: Hart Publishing, 2013), 1; Jenia Iontcheva Turner, "Transnational Networks and International Criminal Justice," *Michigan Law Review* 105 (March 2007): 985, 992–94. See also Anne-Marie Slaughter, *A New World Order* (Princeton, N.J.: Princeton University Press, 2004), 68–69, 72; Anne-Marie Slaughter, "A Global Community of Courts," *Harvard International Law Journal* 44 (Winter, 2003), 191–219; Robert O. Keohane and Joseph S. Nye, Jr., "Introduction," in *Governance in a Globalizing World*, edited by Joseph S. Nye, Jr., and John D. Donahue (Washington, D.C.: Brookings Institution Press, 2000), 12.

[34] Jill Crystal, "Saudi Arabia," in *Legal Systems of the World: A Political, Social and Cultural Encyclopedia, Volume 1*, edited by Herbert M. Kritzer (Santa Barbara, Calif.: ABC-CLIO, 2002), 1418. See also Ziad A. Al-Sudaitry, "The Constitutional Appeal of Shari'a in a Modernizing Saudi State," *Middle East Law and Governance* 2 (2010), 1–16; Abdullah Fakhry Ansary, "Saudi Judicial Reform and the Principle of Independence," *Sada* (May 5, 2009), available at http://carnegieendowment.org/2009/05/05/saudi-judicial-reform-and-principle-of-independence/fhpy (last retrieved November 13, 2013), 6.

[35] Roscoe Pound, "The Decadence of Equity," *Columbia Law Review* 5 (1905), 28.

[36] Richard A. Posner, *The Problems of Jurisprudence* (Cambridge, Mass.: Harvard University Press, 1990), 220–21, 313–15.

[37] 42 U.S.C. § 12101 et seq. (1990).

[38] *McAuliffe v. Mayor and Board of Aldermen of New Bedford*, 155 Mass. 216 (1892).

[39] *Marbury v. Madison*, 5 U.S. 137 (1803).

[40] See generally Paul W. Kahn, *The Reign of Law: Marbury v. Madison and the Construction of America* (New Haven, Conn.: Yale University Press, 2003).

[41] 5 U.S.C. Section 550, et seq. (2000).

[42] *Chevron, U.S.A., Inc. v. Natural Resources Defense Council, Inc.,* 467 U.S. 837 (1984).

[43] *Kisor v. Wilkie,* 139 S.Ct. 2400 (2019). See also, Amy Howe, "Opinion analysis: Justices leave agency deference doctrine in place—with limits (Updated)," *SCOTUSblog* (June 26, 2019), available at https://www.scotusblog.com/2019/06/opinion-analysis-justices-leave-agency-deference-doctrine-in-place/ (last retrieved April 3, 2020). For an analysis of criticism of the *Chevron* and related deference standards by Supreme Court Justices, see Eric Citron, "The roots and limits of Gorsuch's views on Chevron deference," *SCOTUSblog* (March 17, 2017), available https://www.scotusblog.com/2017/03/roots-limits-gorsuchs-views-chevron-deference/ (last retrieved April 3, 2020); and, Daniel Hemel, "Argument analysis: Hating on *Chevron,*" *SCOTUSblog* (November 7, 2018), available at https://www.scotusblog.com/2018/11/argument-analysis-hating-on-chevron/ (last retrieved April 3, 2020). For scholarly and judicial commentary on *Chevron's* legal standard, see Kent Barnett and Christopher J. Walker, "Chevron in the Circuit Courts," *Michigan Law Review* 116 (2018), 1–73; Stephen Breyer, "Judicial Review of Questions of Law and Policy," *Administrative Law Review* 38 (1986): 363–398; Antonin Scalia, "Judicial Deference to Administrative Interpretations of Law," *Duke Law Journal* 1989 (1989): 511–521.

[44] *Olmstead v. United States,* 277 U.S. 438, 485 (1928) (Brandeis, L., dissenting).

[45] *Gideon v. Wainwright,* 372 U.S. 335 (1963).

[46] *Mapp v. Ohio,* 367 U.S. 643 (1961).

[47] *Miranda v. Arizona,* 384 U.S. 436 (1966).

[48] *Batson v. Kentucky,* 476 U.S. 79 (1986).

[49] Howard Gillman, *The Constitution Besieged: The Rise and Demise of Lochner Era Police Powers Jurisprudence* (Durham, N.C.: Duke University Press, 1993), 49; Morton J. Horwitz, *The Transformation of American Law, 1780–1860* (Cambridge, Mass.: Harvard University Press, 1976), 160–61.

[50] Kermit L. Hall, *The Magic Mirror: Law in American History* (New York: Oxford University Press, 1989), 109.

[51] *Trustees of Dartmouth College v. Woodward,* 17 U.S. 518 (1819); *Fletcher v. Peck,* 10 U.S. 87 (1810).

[52] *Allgeyer v. Louisiana,* 165 U.S. 578 (1897).

[53] *Lochner v. New York,* 198 U.S. 45 (1905).

[54] Kermit L. Hall, William M. Wiecek, and Paul Finkelman, *American Legal History: Cases and Materials,* 2nd ed. (New York: Oxford University Press, 1996), 179.

[55] *Brown v. Kendall,* 60 Mass. 292 (1850).

[56] Carlo Guarnieri and Patrizia Pederzoli, *The Power of Judges: A Comparative Study of Courts and Democracy* (Oxford: Oxford University Press, 2002), 68.

[57] *Planned Parenthood of Southeastern Pennsylvania v. Casey,* 505 U.S. 833 (1992), 856.

[58] Alexander Hamilton, "The Federalist Papers: No. 78," *The Avalon Project: Documents in Law, History and Diplomacy,* available at http://avalon.law.yale.edu/18th_century/fed78.asp (last retrieved November 10, 2013).

[59] See, e.g., *Schuette v. Coalition to Defend Affirmative Action,* 572 U.S. 291 (2014) (affirmative action). See also Guarnieri and Pederzoli, *The Power of Judges,* 159, 161; Barry Cushman, "Carolene Products and Constitutional Structure," *The Supreme Court Review* (2012), 321–77; Richard L. Pacelle, *The Transformation of the Supreme Court's Agenda: From the New Deal to the Reagan Administration* (Boulder, Colo.: Westview Press, 1991); and *United States v. Carolene Products Co.,* 304 U.S. 144 (1938).

[60] Lorie L. Sicafuse and Brian H. Bornstein, "Using the Law to Enhance Wellbeing: Applying Therapeutic Jurisprudence in the Courtroom," in *Stress, Trauma, and Wellbeing in the Legal System* [Electronic Resource], edited by Monica K. Miller and Brian H. Bornstein (New York: Oxford University Press, 2013), 15.

[61] National Center for State Courts, *A Community Court Grows in Brooklyn: A Comprehensive Evaluation of the Red Hook Community Justice Center: Final Report* (Williamsburg, Va.: National Center for State Courts, 2013), available at https://www.courtinnovation.org/sites/default/files/documents/RH%20Evaluation%20Final%20Report.pdf (last retrieved June 18, 2020). See also Bruce J. Winick, "Problem Solving Courts: Therapeutic Jurisprudence in Practice," in *Problem-Solving Courts: Social Science and Legal Perspectives,* edited by Richard L. Wiener and Eve M. Brank [Electronic Resource] (New York: Springer, 2013); Sicafuse and Bornstein, "Using the Law to Enhance Wellbeing," 15.

[62] Victor E. Flango and Thomas M. Clarke, *Reimagining Courts: A Design for the Twenty-First Century* (Philadelphia: Temple University Press, 2015), 97–8; David Rottman and Pamela Casey, "Therapeutic Justice

and the Emergence of Problem-Solving Courts," *National Institute of Justice Journal* (July 1999), available at https://www.ncjrs.gov/App/publications/abstract.aspx?ID=178120 (last retrieved December 10, 2003); Bruce J. Winick, "Therapeutic Justice and Problem-Solving Courts," *Fordham Urban Law Journal* 30 (2003), 1055–90; Eve M. Brank and Joshua A. Haby, "The Intended and Unintended Consequences of Problem-Solving Courts," in *Problem-Solving Courts: Social Science and Legal Perspectives*, edited by Richard L. Wiener and Eve M. Brank [Electronic Resource] (New York: Springer, 2013), 241.

63   Victor E. Flango, "Problem-Solving Courts Under a Different Lens," in *Future Trends in State Courts 2007* (Williamsburg, Va.: National Center for State Courts, 2007), available at http://cdm16501.contentdm. oclc.org/cdm/ref/collection/spcts/id/177 (last retrieved November 14, 2013).

64   Janet DiFiore, "New York State's Opioid Intervention Court," available at https://ncsc.contentdm. oclc.org/digital/collection/spcts/id/316/ (last retrieved January 31, 2020). See also, Flango and Clarke, *Reimaging Courts*, 117 (Table 7.2); Bruce J. Winick, "Problem Solving Courts: Therapeutic Jurisprudence in Practice," in *Problem-Solving Courts: Social Science and Legal Perspectives*, edited by Richard L. Wiener and Eve M. Brank [Electronic Resource] (New York: Springer, 2013), 212, 217.

65   See National Center for State Courts, "Census of Problem-Solving Courts," available at http://www. ncsc.org/Services-and-Experts/Areas-of-expertise/Problem-solving-courts.aspx; Brank and Haby, "The Intended and Unintended Consequences of Problem-Solving Courts," 241; Sicafuse and Bornstein, "Using the Law to Enhance Wellbeing," 23, 25–26, 34–36, 241; and Eric L. Sevigny, Harold A. Pollack, and Peter Reuter, "Can Drug Courts Help to Reduce Prison and Jail Populations?" *ANNALS: The Annals of the American Academy* 67 (2013), 190–212.

66   Brank and Haby, "The Intended and Unintended Consequences of Problem-Solving Courts," 240–43. See also Sicafuse and Bornstein, "Using the Law to Enhance Wellbeing," 32–35.

67   Christopher P. Banks and Steven Tauber, "Federal District Court Decision-Making in USA PATRIOT ACT Cases," *Justice System Journal* 35, no. 2 (2014), 139–61. Tauber and Banks extended their research to consider whether district court judges took into account the immediate threat terrorism acts posed in their policy-making decisions in Steven Tauber and Christopher P. Banks, "The Impact of the Threat of Terrorism on U.S. District Court Decisions During Wartime," *Terrorism and Political Violence* 29 (2015): 7930829. See also Matthew E. K. Hall, *The Nature of Supreme Court Power* (New York: Cambridge University Press, 2011); Robert J. Hume, *Courthouse Democracy and Minority Rights* (New York: Oxford University Press, 2013).

68   Jan Hoffman, "Can This Judge Solve the Opioid Crisis?," *The N.Y. Times* (March 5, 2018), available at https://www.nytimes.com/2018/03/05/health/opioid-crisis-judge-lawsuits.html (last retrieved March 9, 2018).

CHAPTER 2

The Politics of Law and Jurisprudence

In defending Donald J. Trump's actions during his Senate impeachment trial in January 2020, lawyer Alan M. Dershowitz asserted that "If a president does something which he believes will help him get elected in the public interest, that cannot be the kind of quid pro quo that results in impeachment." Liberal critics, in denouncing Dershowitz's comments and Trump's foreign policy decision to condition, initially, military aid to Ukraine on the promise of investigating the alleged corruption of a political rival, countered that Trump's defense is based on an unsupportable legal theory that flouts the rule of law and eliminates any constitutional checks that prevents Trump from acting solely in his own personal, and not the public, interest. For conservative defenders, Trump's foreign policy decisions, which also include launching drone attacks at the Syrian government and in ordering another airstrike that killed a top Iranian general without Congress's approval, are constitutionally legitimate under broad Article II powers that sanctions the President's unilateral actions in an effort to protect national security.[1]

The intersection of law and politics, which often centers on competing policy justifications that defend or reject a President's foreign policy decision-making under the U.S. Constitution, is also well illustrated by President Trump's hardline immigration policy that, among other things, exerts political pressure on Congress to authorize money to build a border wall between the U.S. and Mexico; deploys border patrol agents to sanctuary cities to help Immigration and Customs Enforcement agents to remove undocumented aliens from the country; and uses executive orders, or "travel bans," that significantly restricts entry to or from the U.S. by foreign nationals—and all of these actions, significantly, are routinely defended because they are undertaken under the auspices of legal authority and in the interest of national security. Not surprisingly, when the President's actions are challenged, the U.S. Supreme Court remains the final arbiter in interpreting the scope of presidential powers under specific legal theories.[2] For example, in *Trump v. Hawaii* (2018), a 5:4 decision, the U.S. Supreme Court upheld President Trump's controversial executive order imposing travel ban restrictions on eight countries, six of which had predominately Muslim populations. Writing for the Court, Chief Justice John Roberts, Jr. accepted the President's contention that the travel conditions were not due to a racially motivated "Muslim ban," but instead were necessary to protect the national security against terrorist attacks. In examining the merits of the legal claims, the Court reviewed briefs directly from the parties as well as from *amicus curiae* ("friend of the court") litigants, or third parties that presented a variety of legal perspectives on whether the President had the constitutional and statutory authority to issue the proclamation.

Drawing on precedent and different legal theories, several friend-of-the-court briefs reached opposition conclusions about the scope of the President's authority to impose the travel ban. In its brief, counsel for The Foundation of Moral Law, a Christian organization, used natural law reasoning to claim that the Bible, the Declaration of Independence, and the writings from English jurists William Blackstone and John Locke support Trump's actions because the government is empowered to punish evildoers, safeguard the innocent, and exclude hostile foreign nationals from U.S. borders. Yet, other Christian organizations, the U.S. Conference for Catholic Bishops, Catholic Charities USA, and the Catholic Legal Organization, relied upon the Bible, Gospel requirements, and speeches by the Pope to argue that the Proclamation wrongly targeted Muslims for exclusion and thus violated the First Amendment's Free Exercise Clause. Similarly, the liberal NAACP Legal Defense Fund's *amicus curiae* brief cited to the writings of Angela Davis, a 1960s political black activist and feminist, to contend that the ban creates an odious discrimination that punishes a group of people according to their race and ethnicity, a principle that the courts have a democratic obligation to reject.[3]

The *Trump* case, along with the racial violence and civil unrest that erupted in the nation and across the globe following George Floyd's death at the hands of a white police officer in Minneapolis, as well as similar episodes in Ferguson and Charlottesville that has led to ongoing public policy controversies about whether Confederate symbols should be removed from public spaces across the nation, highlight the deep divisions over issues of law and morality, race, and justice that persist in society and which are often played out in the legal system. Trump's impeachment, as well as the Trump travel ban litigation that preceded it, is not the only example of how courts and judges shape their rulings based upon competing understandings of constitutional powers and distinct legal theories that, sometimes, exacerbate racial conflict and foment related tensions over the proper scope of personal freedoms in the context of race, sex, and equality principles.

An earlier illustration is in 2013, when a federal judge made headlines by criticizing New York City's police department's "stop and frisk policy" of racial profiling, an issue that has resurfaced in light of billionaire Mike Bloomberg's (and then-citizen Donald Trump's) defense of it while it was in effect during Bloomberg's N.Y. earlier mayoral term and which became part of the run up to the 2020 presidential election in the Democratic Party's nomination process. Notably, that anticrime strategy has been a longstanding part of police tactics; but it also has been consistently criticized for stirring up racial discord and violating individuals' constitutional rights.[4] Similarly, in *Shelby County v. Holder* (2013), the Supreme Court struck down a key part of the 1965 Voting Rights Act, which aimed to protect the voting rights of minorities in states that historically discriminated against African Americans during elections. As well, the Trump administration's hardline immigration policies, along with a growing recognition of anti-sexual discrimination principles as manifested by the allegations made by women celebrities against Harvey Weinstein, among others, and the rise of the #MeToo movement, show that ethnicity and feminist equality advocacy are deeply embedded into United States law and political culture.[5] Such legal episodes underscore the role courts play in society in managing the ongoing tensions between the rule by Presidents, legislative majorities, and individual claims of minority rights. They also register the ongoing controversy over race and women's rights in constitutional law, judicial policymaking, and, broadly speaking, jurisprudence.

Jurisprudence refers to legal theory and questions about the nature of law, the social impact of law and legal systems, and the relationship of law to justice and morality. *Schuette v. Coalition to Defend Affirmative Action* (2014), another Supreme Court ruling that upheld Michigan's ban on affirmative action, further demonstrates the importance jurisprudence has in linking legal theory to legal practice. Before *Schuette* was decided, several legal and political science scholars invoked references to critical race theory (discussed later in this chapter) in their *amicus curiae* briefs to persuade the Court to strike down the ban.[6] Although a majority of the Court approved of the ban in *Schuette*, courts and judges routinely consider arguments drawn from legal theory and political jurisprudence. In the judicial process, abstract questions of law frame the creation of legal principles that inform substantive court rulings and the operation of legal systems. Thus, understanding the law's relationship to jurisprudence is important for several reasons. Judges may use legal theory to ground their decisions, and lawyers may give advice to clients about what courts are likely to do considering legal theories. Furthermore, citizens become informed about the broader implications of laws that, in turn, may also inspire a change in their legal behavior or the enactment of reforms.[7]

In sum, as law evolves over time, classical and contemporary theories of jurisprudence address fundamental questions about the meaning of law and how it regulates public and private relationships. Although not an exhaustive list, these questions include: (1) What is the origin of law?; (2) What is and what should be law's substantive meaning?; (3) What is the relationship of morality to law?; (4) In what ways is law "just," and how does it (or does it not) promote social justice?; and, finally, (5) how does law change or evolve while preserving the stability of a political and legal system? At bottom, these are questions of legal philosophy. They elucidate the ideas and reasoning behind law's purpose, application, and normative content. Jurisprudence also addresses the legitimate exercise of judicial power and principles of democratic accountability, legitimacy, equality, and justice.

The discussion first turns to considering classical schools of jurisprudence because they are the touchstone for analyzing law in relation to individuals' rights and liberties, social justice, and the role of courts in society. They also provide a basis for later examining and contrasting contemporary jurisprudential theories.

CLASSICAL THEORIES OF JURISPRUDENCE

Natural Law

Natural law is thought of in divine terms as God's law. The earliest statement of natural law theory can be traced to Greek philosophy. A Greek orator, Demosthenes, described it as follows: "Every law is a discovery, a gift of God, a precept of wise men."[8] Both Plato (428–348 B.C.) and Aristotle (384–322 B.C.) spoke of universal truths that could be discovered, either as abstractions (Plato) or as empirical observations (Aristotle). Subsequently, Grotius (1583–1645 B.C.), a Roman statesman and philosopher, built on the Greek idea of rationality by describing law as "right reason in agreement with nature" that was universally applied beyond the borders of Rome.

In the Middle Ages, Christian theology adopted principles of natural law as well. Saint Thomas Aquinas (1224–1274 A.D.) was an important legal theorist because he made a distinction between divine law (God's universal law) and natural law (laws of nature capable of human discovery by reason). Put differently, faith in God alone was not enough to understand the nature of the world. Instead, reason could lead to the discovery of the laws of nature and, hence, the role of government in creating law. As a result, Aquinas's work legitimized the idea that it was possible for humans to create laws that reflected those revealed by God in Holy Scripture, and law could order human behavior in accordance with fixed principles consistent with God's will.[9]

More recently, natural law theory has been extended by Oxford's law and philosophy professor John Finnis in *Natural Law and Natural Rights* (1980). Unlike classical natural law theory, however, Finnis argues that universal and immutable principles of natural law are expressed through several "basic requirements of practical reasonableness" that, in turn, can be realized by institutions and instruments of human law that enhance human flourishing.[10] In his words, "law is a rational standard for conduct," and it is "of the nature of law to provide a set of standards that rational agents should take as a guide to their conduct."[11]

Still, at the time of the American founding, the classical view of natural law was predominant but increasingly under sharp attack from skeptics who questioned its validity. In his *Commentaries on the Laws of England*, William Blackstone (1723–1780), an influential English theorist, suggested that there was no legal authority to obey any law that was contrary to an immutable natural law. Accordingly, for Blackstone, the law of nature was

> co-equal with mankind and dictated by God himself, [and] is of course superior in obligation to any other. It is binding over all the globe, in all countries, and at all times: no human laws are of any validity, if contrary to this; and such of them as are valid derive all their force, and all their authority, mediately or immediately, from this original.[12]

Blackstone's theory was influential in America, and colonists would derive from natural law theory important **natural rights** arguments. But the concept of natural rights focuses on the relationship between individuals and the government, instead of explaining law's origin and whether there is a duty to respect law.

Besides Blackstone, two other influential English legal and political philosophers, Thomas Hobbes (1588–1679) and John Locke (1632–1704), had a profound and enduring effect. In *Leviathan* (1651), Hobbes argued that men in a pre-political state of existence ("a state of nature") seek security and freedom by forming a social contract establishing an absolute monarchy and give up most of their rights in exchange for security and legal stability. John Locke made a somewhat similar argument in his *Second Treatise of Government* (1690). Locke theorized that men agree to enter into a social contract establishing government, but their consent is predicated upon the condition that the sovereign serves the public good and protects individuals' fundamental natural rights, such as the right to property. The social contract thus became a model for limited government under majority rule, and the sovereignty of the divine rule by the Crown was replaced by the idea of popular sovereignty. Moreover, in Locke's theory, government plays a key role in acting as an "umpire" in resolving individual disputes arising from the distribution of property in society and balancing liberty against security.

In articulating a theory of limited government based on consent and individual natural rights, Locke greatly influenced the thinking of the Founders, particularly Thomas Jefferson (1743–1826), the principal draftsman of the Declaration of Independence in 1776. Relying on Locke's theory, Jefferson based the Declaration of Independence on principles of popular sovereignty, consent, and natural rights: that governments "derive their just powers from the consent of the governed"; that "all men are created equal [and] that they are endowed by their Creator with certain unalienable Rights [such as] Life, Liberty and the pursuit of Happiness"; and that "whenever any Form of Government becomes destructive of these ends, it is the Right of the People to alter or to abolish it." A decade later, the U.S. Constitution also registered these principles. Indeed, the Constitution not only represents the idea of limited government but also embraces natural rights theory by the addition in 1791 of a written Bill of Rights, or declaration of rights that includes the freedom of expression (in the First Amendment) and the freedom from "unreasonable searches and seizures" (in the Fourth Amendment), among other rights' guarantees.

Notably, the Supreme Court has also looked to natural law as a basis for some of its early rulings. In *Calder v. Bull* (1798),[13] the *ex post facto* clause of Article I, Section 10, forbidding the passage of laws that penalize acts after the fact, was held not to nullify a state law permitting a civil appeal in a contest over a will, because that clause applies only to criminal laws and cases. In the case, Justices Samuel Chase and James Iredell debated the Court's power of judicial review (discussed in Chapter One) and whether it could be used to overturn state laws. Whereas Justice Chase argued that the Court possessed such authority, Justice Iredell countered that the Court did not have the power to strike the law down even if it violated principles of natural law. In other cases, the Court appealed to natural law principles in asserting that blacks were not citizens entitled to constitutional rights in *Dred Scott v. Sandford* (1857).[14] In *Bradwell v. Illinois* (1873),[15] the Court ruled that women could not practice law because it was "in the nature of things" for them to remain relegated to the "domestic sphere as that which properly belongs to the domain and functions of womanhood." More recently, Justice Clarence Thomas cited natural law and the Declaration of Independence in criticizing the rationale in *Brown v. Board of Education* (1954),[16] the landmark case ending racial discrimination in public schools. Yet, Justice Thomas's reliance upon natural law is more of an exception, as opposed to being a general rule, in regard to the Court's contemporary approach to deciding cases.

The application of natural law to cases remains controversial, and the debate over the meaning of law is not settled. A natural law theorist, Lon Fuller, argues that all law contains an inner morality that judges must apply if they wish to remain faithful to the purposes of law. Fuller's position is illustrated by a West German prosecution of a Nazi officer's wife for alerting Nazi officials that her husband broke the law by making critical remarks about the Third Reich during World War II. Her husband was convicted and sentenced to death. After the war, she was put on trial and argued that Nazi law made her actions legal. Using natural law principles, Fuller rejected the wife's defense, arguing that the Nazi law was unjust and therefore not valid law. In contrast, H. L. A. Hart, an English philosopher associated with a legal theory of positivism, countered that the Nazi law was a valid enactment of positive law and must be respected, regardless of its moral purpose or application.[17] In short, Hart maintained a sharp division between morality and law. His position, and the scope and application of classical legal positivism, is considered next.

Legal Positivism

H. L. A. Hart's legal positivism—the separation of law and morality—built on the work of two earlier English legal philosophers, Jeremy Bentham (1748–1832) and John Austin (1790–1859). Their respective writings comprise the core of classical legal positivism: law is best conceived of in scientific and objective terms—that is, law is empirically discovered by reason and free from moral judgments about what the law should be.

Both Bentham and Locke disagreed with Blackstone's position that judges simply discover the law and recognize rights based on the morality of natural law. Their legal positivism and utilitarianism—that, simply put, the greatest good is for the greatest number—maintained that morality and law are distinct, and that law only creates an obligation to obey, and rights emerge, only when there is a breach of a recognized legal duty. Bentham's theory of law, thus, reduced law to a principle of utility. For Bentham, law is not simply a command or an order from a divine ruler, but rather aims at achieving the greatest happiness for the greatest number of people, and thereby benefits the community. As a result, people obey or disobey the law because they seek pleasure or fear pain, and not because of moral principles. Exercising the choice to follow the law brings pleasure because the law against murder benefits the majority, whereas the decision to flout the law, in committing the act of murder, results in severe punishment for the few who violate the criminal prohibition. A legal command preventing murder, therefore, reaps the greatest happiness for the greatest number of people who are obliged to follow the rule.[18]

Bentham's theory suggested that multiple sovereigns (as created by constitutions, legislatures, and courts) could command obedience because law is an imperative—something that has to be obeyed—as well as an empirical fact affecting behavior. Because the failure to perform a legal obligation risks punishment, compliance with law rests on a utilitarian calculation of experiencing pleasure or pain, and that determines the law's validity. People adhere to law as a command, regardless of whether it comes from one source. In this regard, both Bentham and Austin envisioned a strict separation between law and morality because law (as an "is") cannot be law at all if the decision to obey it rests on some moral principle or guide (i.e., one "ought" to obey only it if it is a "good" law). Accordingly, Bentham sharply criticized natural law and its corollary doctrine of natural rights, which he referred to as "nonsense upon stilts."[19] Indeed, he disagreed, for example, that the Declaration of Independence recognized or afforded citizens natural rights. In this sense, Bentham and Austin agreed; however, Austin contended that law is simply the command of a single sovereign (a person or institution with supreme lawmaking power) backed by sanctions, regardless of the morality of the law.

Although natural law theorists continue to struggle with the positivist criticism that morality is separate from law, positivists in turn confront the objection that people will not (and should not) obey a law if it is immoral. H. L. A. Hart, one of the most influential legal positivists in the twentieth century, addressed that controversy in *The Concept of Law* (1961). Hart did not believe that the law is simply a series of commands or habitual responses to coercive orders. Instead, law is a set of rules established by social convention: the union of what Hart called primary and secondary rules. Primary rules create legal duties that lay down legal guidelines for social conduct. They oblige citizens to conform to legal standards pertaining, for example, to making a valid contract or complying with criminal law. Secondary rules are procedural rules that confer power. They control how primary rules are identified (the rule of recognition), altered (the rule of change), and ultimately enforced (the rule of adjudication). Secondary rules, such as a law that vests an official with the power to perform a civil marriage, enable the law to be understood and carried out, both by citizens and by officials. Of the secondary rules, the most critical is what Hart termed the rule of recognition, which validates the criteria and social practices of what people understand to be law and ensures that officials who oversee applying the law are doing so under a set of legal standards commonly shared in society. In Hart's ideal paradigm, therefore, a legal system does not exist simply because there is a pressure to conform to a set of external commands from a sovereign. Rather, legal systems operate under an "internal aspect"—that is, a shared assumption that the law imposes certain duties and obligations that are accepted by society. The internal view facilitates compliance with the law because, in complex legal systems, those who apply the law and those who are subject to it share a common perspective about controlling legal standards.[20]

Although Hart's theory may provide a better explanation for why people obey a law than Austin's or Bentham's, it did not completely overcome the natural law criticism that positive law must have moral content. On that point, Hart acknowledged that a legal system of social rules was not a "suicide club." Morality is expressed in social norms that reflect a "minimum content of natural law"— the basic ideas shared by all about the minimal legal protections for human survival, such as rules against murder and stealing property. In other words, there is an inherent overlap between moral and legal behavior. Whereas Hart insisted that law is not derived from morality, and although he tried to maintain a separation between the two concepts, he ultimately conceded that morality plays a minimal role in constructing society's legal rules.[21]

"Constitutional Morality"

Positivists' separation between law and morality remains a significant issue in legal theory as well as in the politics of constitutional jurisprudence. Judge Robert Bork, a former appellate judge in the District of Columbia circuit and President Ronald Reagan's unsuccessful appointee to the U.S. Supreme Court in 1987, championed a positivist view. He sharply criticized, for example, the Supreme Court's recognition of an unenumerated (that which is not listed in writing) constitutional "right of privacy" and defenses of controversial rulings based on morality and theories of justice as fairness. In his view, judges only have discretion to consider a law's morality from the standpoint of a properly enacted law. In other words, the morality of the community is expressed in the positive law (i.e., statutes and rules). Hence, for Bork and others, judges act illegitimately when they impose their own views of morality because "in a constitutional democracy, the moral content of law must be given by the morality of the framer or the legislator, never by the morality of the judge."[22]

By contrast, Ronald Dworkin, a leading late-twentieth-century liberal legal philosopher, criticized legal positivism by attacking the presumption that judges ignore law's moral foundations. In books such as *Taking Rights Seriously* (1977), *Law's Empire* (1986), *Freedom's Law* (1996), and *Justice for Hedgehogs* (2011),[23] Dworkin embraces the importance of political morality in the application of legal principles. In Dworkin's view, a legal principle "is one which officials must take into account, if it is relevant, as a consideration inclining in one direction or another" during adjudication. As such, principles are more flexible than "all or nothing" rules, and, accordingly, moral considerations are a necessary part of legal interpretation because value judgments must be made by judges in deciding how legal principles apply in concrete cases. Although judges look to positive law, they must also weigh whether the outcome best fits the underlying purposes of the political system and its "constitutional morality." Accordingly, Dworkin maintained that determining the proper "fit" between positive law and the controlling legal principle also has the advantage of reducing the discretion exercised by judges because the application of legal principles always leads to one "right" answer in the process of interpretation. To illustrate, a judge should (and would properly) apply the principle that "no man shall profit from his own wrongdoing" in denying a murderer the inheritance from the victim even though the victim's will was legally valid. In this fashion, contrary to positivists like Bork, the "law is effectively integrated with morality: lawyers and judges are working political philosophers of the democratic state."[24]

Whereas Judge Bork and philosopher Hart deny a connection between law and morality, Dworkin embraces and celebrates their intimate connection. The implications of these contrasting views are illustrated by the Supreme Court's rulings on the criminalization of sexual behavior between same-sex couples. In *Bowers v. Hardwick* (1986),[25] a bare majority held that there was no constitutional right under the Fourteenth Amendment's due process clause to engage in consensual homosexual sodomy. In upholding Georgia's antisodomy law, Justice Byron White dismissively observed that "the law is constantly based on notions of morality, and if all laws representing essentially moral choices are to be invalidated under the Due Process Clause, the courts will be very busy indeed."[26] Chief Justice Warren Burger's concurring opinion likewise contended that Georgia's legislation reflected a moral choice made by the legislature, which the judiciary should not disturb, and that homosexual sodomy is inconsistent with traditional norms of Judeo-Christian morality.[27]

When the Court revisited *Bowers* in the controversy in *Lawrence v. Texas* (2003), the Court struck down Texas's criminal prohibition of "deviate sexual intercourse with another individual of the same sex." By a 6 to 3 vote, *Lawrence* overturned *Bowers*. Justice Anthony Kennedy's **Opinion for the Court** reasoned that homosexuals have a substantive right of privacy under the Fourteenth Amendment and are entitled to the same protections afforded heterosexuals. Whereas *Bowers* emphasized that "for centuries there have been powerful voices to condemn homosexual conduct as immoral," Justice Kennedy highlighted the "emerging awareness" over the past fifty years that "liberty gives substantial protection to adult persons in deciding how to conduct their private lives in matters pertaining to sex." In short, Texas's morals legislation was invalidated because the Fourteenth Amendment guarantees a right of personal autonomy that includes the personal and moral choice of individuals to engage in private, consensual relationships—regardless of whether they are heterosexual or homosexual.[28]

In *Lawrence*, dissenting Justice Antonin Scalia sharply countered that the Court's ruling "effectively decree[d] the end of all morals legislation." For Justice Scalia and the other dissenters, *Lawrence* wrongly overturned *Bowers* because *Bowers* respected the right of democratic majorities to define the boundaries of morally acceptable behavior. Justice Scalia complained that "countless judicial decisions and legislative enactments have relied on the ancient proposition that a governing majority's belief that certain sexual behavior is 'immoral and unacceptable' constitutes a rational basis for regulation." In his view, the Court overstepped its authority by replacing the moral judgment of the Texas legislature with its own moral conception. As he explained:

> One of the most revealing statements in today's opinion is the Court's grim warning that the criminalization of homosexual conduct is "an invitation to subject homosexual persons to discrimination both in the public and in the private spheres." It is clear from this that the Court has taken sides in the culture war, departing from its role of assuring, as neutral observer, that the democratic rules of engagement are observed. Many Americans do not want persons who openly engage in homosexual conduct as partners in their business, as scoutmasters for their children, as teachers in their children's schools, or as boarders in their home. They view this as protecting themselves and their families from a lifestyle that they believe to be immoral and destructive.

This passage underscores that for Justice Scalia (and Judge Bork and philosopher Hart), there is a clear separation between law and morality, and judges must respect the boundaries set by democratically elected majorities, instead of using the power of the judiciary to impose their own moral viewpoints of law. Not surprisingly, the legal morality of same-sex marriage has been debated in other countries as well (see "In Comparative Perspective: Law, Morality, and Same-Sex Marriages").

In Comparative Perspective: Law, Morality, and Same-Sex Marriages

In the last several decades, a movement has grown, both abroad and at home, toward legally recognizing same-sex marriages and the rights of LGBT (lesbian, gay, bisexual, and transgendered) individuals. Same-sex marriages have been recognized in the Netherlands (2000); Belgium (2003); Canada and Spain (2005); South Africa (2006); Norway (2008); Sweden (2009); Argentina, Portugal, and Iceland (2010); Denmark (2012); Brazil, France, New Zealand, and Uruguay (2013); the United Kingdom (England and Wales, 2013); and, more recently, the United States (2015) and Australia (2017) legally approved same-sex unions by court decree or legislative action. State jurisdictions in Mexico do so as well, and over a dozen other countries across Western Europe recognize civil unions.

The movement nonetheless has met with fierce opposition. Prior to 2015, in the United States thirty-two states had banned same-sex marriages through constitutional amendments or by statute. Russia and Uganda, among other counties in Africa, the Middle East, and Eastern Europe, also enacted laws criminalizing homosexual conduct. On the U.S. Supreme Court, the late Justice Antonin Scalia has been one of the sharpest critics. Dissenting in *Romer v. Evans*, 517 U.S. 620 (1996), which struck down a Colorado state constitutional amendment forbidding employers from discriminating against homosexuals, Justice Scalia expressed outrage over the invalidation of the state's legally enforced "moral disapproval of homosexual conduct, the same sort of moral disapproval that produced centuries-old criminal laws," like other "reprehensible [conduct]—murder, for example, or polygamy, or cruelty to animals—[that government deems] morally wrong and socially harmful." When the Court subsequently overturned Texas's law criminalizing homosexual sodomy in *Lawrence v. Texas*, 539 U.S. 558 (2003), he charged that the ruling "effectively decrees the end of all morals legislation. . . [including] criminal laws against fornication, bigamy, adultery, adult incest, bestiality, and obscenity."

But *United States v. Windsor*, 570 U.S. 744 (2013), invalidated a section of the Defense of Marriage Act of 1996 that had denied federal recognition of state-approved same-sex marriages, and Justice Scalia again warned against litigation that would lead to overturning state laws denying same-sex couples marital status and benefits. Indeed, after the Court's ruling in *Windsor*, several federal and state courts invalidated state prohibitions on same-sex marriages. By January 2015, some thirty-five states recognized same-sex marriages based on state legislation and judicial decisions; but some state bans on same-sex marriage, however, were upheld by federal appellate courts, thus suggesting that the Supreme Court would have to weigh in on the controversy, which it did in 2015.

In *Obergefell v. Hodges*, 576 U.S. 644 (2015), the Court narrowly affirmed the fundamental right of marriage, including the right of same-sex couples to marry. Relying upon the Fourteenth Amendment's due process and equality principles, in a 5–4 decision the Court held that states must license and recognize same-sex marriages performed in their own states as well as in others. Justice Anthony Kennedy cast the decisive vote in an opinion that was joined by liberal Justices Stephen Breyer, Ruth Bader Ginsburg, Sonia Sotomayor and Elena Kagan. In contrast, four conservative justices, Chief Justice Roberts and Justices Antonin Scalia, Clarence Thomas, and Samuel Alito, dissented by denouncing the Court's action as an activist decision that undermined the democratic and legislative processes of states to define marriage. For his part, in a separate dissent Justice Scalia wrote "to call attention to this Court's threat to American democracy" because the ruling stood as "a naked judicial claim to legislative—indeed, super-legislative—power." Notably, *Obergefell* may be reversed if the membership of the Court changes or public opinion forces the legislature to alter the ruling's effect through legislation or constitutional amendment (see Chapter Ten). For example, within nine months after the Bermuda Supreme Court legally recognized same-sex marriage, in February 2018 the Bermuda Parliament passed the Domestic Partnership Act, a law that recognized domestic partnerships but also banned same-sex marriage after most voters registered opposition to same-sex marriage unions.

Although opposition to same-sex marriages has been based on numerous grounds—religious reasons, the protection of children, and the preservation of "traditional marriages," among other political reasons—the controversy, as Justice Scalia's dissents suggest, has centered on the limits of the criminal sanction and the legal enforcement of "public morality." That controversy remains, perhaps, exemplified in the debate over England's decriminalization of homosexual sodomy and prostitution, sparked by the Report of the Committee on Homosexual Offenses and Prostitution—the so-called Wolfenden Report, named after Sir John Wolfenden.

The Wolfenden Report recommended decriminalization based on freedom of individual choice and the privacy of morality. As the report put it:

> The function of the criminal law is to preserve public order and decency, to protect the citizen from what is injurious, and to provide sufficient safeguards against exploitation and corruption of others, particularly those who are specifically vulnerable. . . .It is not. . .the function of the law to intervene in the private lives of our citizens.

Opposition to the report was led by Sir (later Law Lord) Patrick Devlin, who maintained that law without morality would destroy freedom and lead to "tyranny" by abandoning norms of public morality that keep social order from unraveling. In lectures, articles, and a book, *The Enforcement of Morals* (1959), Lord Devlin contended that "it is not possible to set theoretical limits to the power of the State to legislate against immorality. It is not possible to settle in advance exceptions to the general rule or to define inflexibly areas of morality into which the law is in no circumstances to be allowed to enter." For Lord Devlin, public morality was evident in asking "what is acceptable to the ordinary man, the man in the jury box, who might also be called the reasonable man or the right-minded man."

By contrast, Oxford University philosophy professor H. L. A. Hart countered that the "populism" of conventional morality denied individuals' liberty upon a contemporary majority's prejudices. He invoked the "harm principle" of British philosopher John Stuart Mill. In his classic works, *Utilitarianism* and *On Liberty*, Mill argued against legal paternalism and moralism, observing that

> the sole end for which mankind are warranted, individually or collectively, in interfering with the liberty of action of any of their number is self-protection. That is the only purpose for which power can rightfully be exercised over any member of a civilized community against his will is to prevent harm to others. His own good, whether physical or moral, is not a sufficient warrant.

Furthermore, Hart criticized Devlin for failing to show any empirical evidence that deviations from "public morality" threaten society, or that an identifiable "public morality" is based on reason, rather than simply moral feelings against (or animus toward) a practice deemed socially harmful. Oxford law professor and philosopher Ronald Dworkin went further, arguing that some conduct—like adult consensual sexual relations, abortion, and "the right to die"—involve fundamental liberties that may never be taken away or limited by the government.

Sources: Megan Specia, "Bermuda Outlaws Gay Marriage, Less Than a Year After It Become Legal," *N.Y. Times* (February 8, 2018), available at https://www.nytimes.com/2018/02/08/world/americas/bermuda-gay-marriage.html (last retrieved March 26, 2018); Damien Cave and Jacqueline Williams, "Australia Makes Same-Sex Marriage Legal," *N.Y. Times* (December 7, 2017), available at https://www.nytimes.com/2017/12/07/world/australia/gay-marriage-same-sex.html (last retrieved March 26, 2019); Pew Research Center (Religion & Public Life), "Gay Marriage Around the World," available at http://www.pewforum.org/2017/08/08/gay-marriage-around-the-world-2013/ (August 8, 2017) (last retrieved March 26, 2019); Michael Lipka," Where Europe stands on gay marriage and civil unions," *Pew Research* Center (Factank, News in the Numbers), available at http://www.pewresearch.org/fact-tank/2017/06/30/where-europe-stands-on-gay-marriage-and-civil-unions/ (June 30, 2017) (last retrieved March. 26, 2019); Patrick Devlin, *The Enforcement of Morals* (Oxford: Oxford University Press, 1965); H. L. A. Hart, *Law, Liberty, and Morality* (Oxford: Oxford University Press, 1963); John Stuart Mill, *Utilitarianism; On Liberty, and Considerations of Representative Government* (London: Dent Publishers, 1993); Ronald Dworkin, "Lord Devlin and the Enforcement of Morals," *The Yale Law Journal* 75 (1966): 986; and Ronald Dworkin, *A Matter of Principle* (Cambridge, Mass.: Harvard University Press, 1985).

Sociological Jurisprudence and Legal Realism

Natural law theories largely fell out of favor due to positivism and the emergence of sociological jurisprudence and legal realism in the late nineteenth and early twentieth centuries. A progressive response to late-nineteenth-century *laissez-faire* economic theory and legal formalism, sociological jurisprudence conceptualizes law as a social phenomenon and a method of social control (much like the positivists previously discussed). Pivotal sociological theorists include Émile Durkheim (1858–1917), Max Weber (1864–1920), and Roscoe Pound (1870–1964). In *The Division of Labor in Society* (1964), Durkheim postulates that law is a function of societal solidarity. Primitive societies resort to "mechanical" applications of laws that are penal and "repressive": punishing offenders reaffirms the collective consciousness and reinforces societal cohesion. In contrast, organic societies, which are more evolved and based on a division of labor and interdependence of social groups, place a premium on restitutive law (such as contract and administrative law) to resolve disputes, which promotes both more social integration and greater individualism.[29]

Weber's sociology of law proposes that law is infused with four elements—rationality, irrationality, formality, and substance—that help to explain the development of legal systems and political economies, especially capitalism. The formal rational administration of justice is based on codified rules and procedures that are predictable, confer legitimacy, and enable the growth of capitalism in the modern bureaucratic state.[30]

While Durkheim's and Weber's contributions to sociological jurisprudence loom large in law and society studies, former Harvard law school dean Roscoe Pound's scholarly impact has also been profound.[31] Through many writings that were consolidated into five volumes on *Jurisprudence* (1959), Pound focused on social justice and argued that it may be achieved through "law in action," instead of through a formalistic adherence to "law in books." Since law's evolution reflects social progress, Pound reasoned that law should be dynamically applied, and academics and judges should become "social engineers." Deductive reasoning, or a "mechanical jurisprudence," he maintained, was deficient because it does not recognize the different legal interests of individuals who seek social justice in the legal system. At the same time, he acknowledged that private interests, spanning from property rights to personal autonomy, must be balanced against the public interests of government in providing safety and security to citizens. Accordingly, the "task of the sociological jurist," he emphasized, was to harmonize competing interests efficiently in order "to attain a pragmatic [and] sociological legal science."[32]

Pound's early writings captured the attention of legal realists, a diverse group of scholars with an influential presence in leading law schools (Columbia, Yale, and Harvard) in the 1920s and 1930s. Legal realism embraced the skepticism that law is logically and predictably derived from formal rules and shared the sociological view that judges make law and should consider a law's practical consequences.[33]

Legal realism thus became associated with scientific inquiry in seeking to identify the sociological and psychological factors affecting judicial decision-making and, more broadly, the impact of laws. Its philosophical preoccupation is determining what is empirically and pragmatically "realistic" about judging. Since judges are not constrained by legal rules, they exercise considerable discretion in deciding cases. As a result, legal realism criticized the casebook method of legal instruction and formalistic legal reasoning that was the standard in law schools (see Chapter Five). Realist theory exposes the political reality of judicial lawmaking by questioning the position that law is a predictable creation of formal doctrinal rules deduced from logical reasoning. As a "fact" and a "rule" skeptic, legal realists question the certainty of legal doctrine and whether law could honestly be said to be "found" or "discovered" by judges.[34]

Supreme Court Justice Oliver Wendell Holmes, Jr., Karl Llewellyn, and Judge Jerome Frank were among the most visible in the early legal realist movement.[35] Holmes (1841–1935), a wounded Civil War soldier who served on the Massachusetts Supreme Court (for twenty years) and, then, the U.S. Supreme

Court (for thirty years), argued the law cannot be explained in terms of simple logic. "The life of the law has not been logic," he wrote in *The Common Law* (1880); "it has been experience." Holmes maintained that law is the embodiment of human history but is also the sum of social values of the prevailing, dominant majority. In his famous 1897 essay, "The Path of the Law," he advanced the perspective of a "bad man" to illustrate that law is a result of a prediction of what a court will do in deciding a case, and not discovered or logically derived from, as he put it, "some brooding omnipresence in the sky." For Holmes, the bad man "cares only for the material consequences [that enable] him to predict" what the law will do to him if he is caught breaking it, with little concern for "axioms or deductions." Yet the bad man wants to know "what. . .[the] courts are likely to do in fact." Hence, law is nothing more than "prophecies of what the courts will do in fact."[36] By casting aside logic, Holmes's "bad man" or prediction theory laid the foundation for the realist critique that the law is much more than logically deduced legal principles. He thus strongly implied that law is indeterminate, and open to rival interpretations and applications.

Karl N. Llewellyn (1893–1962), an influential legal scholar, linguist, and poet, also challenged the view that the language of statutes and judicial opinions—"paper rules"—adequately describes judicial behavior. Instead of formal legal doctrine, judges follow "real rules" and "working rules" when they decide cases. Llewellyn's books, *The Bramble Bush* (1930) and *The Common Law Tradition* (1960), advanced a functionalist approach to understanding law: legal institutions and judges perform certain functions, or "law-jobs," in society. For Llewellyn, "getting 'the' job done" acknowledges that courts resolve "trouble-cases," legal grievances and disputes. In addition, he argued, legal officials simply use law to prevent, set, and adjust individual conduct in accordance with societal norms and expectations. These and other "clusters" of law-jobs are central to law in society.[37]

Some of the implications of Holmes's and Llewellyn's ideas were further elaborated by Jerome N. Frank (1889–1957), an appellate judge and scholar. His major book, *Law and the Modern Mind* (1930), advocated rule skepticism—rejecting the idea that formal rules are discovered by judges using deductive legal reasoning. Frank challenged the view that judges reason syllogistically and that legal outcomes result from finding a legal principle and applying it to a set of facts. Instead, as he put it, "judicial judgments, like other judgments, doubtless, in most cases, are worked out backward from conclusions tentatively formulated." A backward-reasoning process thus proceeds from "a judge's hunches" and each particular judge's perception of what the facts and law are in any given case. Basically, the law is indeterminate because judicial decision-making is post-*ad hoc* rationalization of what a judge initially thinks the result should be. In Frank's words, "The law may vary with the personality of the judge who happens to pass upon any given case."[38]

Judge Frank's description of judicial decision-making led to other theories that jurisprudence would only become "realistic" if the legal community accepted psychological and sociological explanations for law's uncertainty. Once that first step is taken, then it follows that lawyers and judges should use methods of social science to predict legal behavior. Making predictions based on rigorous empirical inquiry would also improve the law by making it more responsive to social life. Likewise, Frank continuously pressed for legal reform and giving lawyers a clinical education to make them more relevant to the social purposes of law. Reform efforts to incorporate social science into the legal process, however, never fully came to fruition. World War II and the rise of Nazi Germany served to undermine Frank's and other legal realists' view that law is nothing more than a judge's personal hunch, because critics claimed realism was nihilistic, antidemocratic, and amoral.[39]

In sum, sociological and realist jurisprudence envisioned lawyers and judges as either innovative "social engineers" or pragmatic "hunch" lawmakers.[40] An important legacy of these theories is that they became the touchstone for developing the policy science and legal process schools of legal thought that emerged in the 1940s and 1950s. Policy science emphasized the integration of interdisciplinary studies (social sciences) into law and to the development of legal policy grounded in the political and moral values of Western liberal democracies—freedom, toleration, and equality—and that applied universally. Process jurisprudence assumed that the legal process was the elaboration of legal principles that were rationally discovered from the normative and political values at the core of the democratic process; and the legal process school also taught that the elaboration of judicial decisions gave legitimacy to the law. Policy science and legal process scholars, though, were perhaps too ambitious in their attempt to conceptualize law in these terms, and, hence, both were ultimately unsuccessful.[41] Nonetheless, contemporary jurisprudential theories developed from their insights and other classical legal theory concepts.

CONTEMPORARY THEORIES OF JURISPRUDENCE

Classical sociological, realist, policy science, and legal process theories of jurisprudence tried to develop a common framework for explaining judicial behavior within the context of law's social purpose. They in turn also invited new and divergent approaches after World War II. Law and economics, pragmatism, feminist legal thought, and critical legal studies collectively represent the contemporary challenge to classical theories. Advancing a rational economic perspective on law, the "Chicago school of law and economics" focused on maximizing individual self-interest along with law's instrumental role in securing social ends. Feminist jurisprudence, along with critical theories of law and race, likewise question whether traditional legal liberalism indeed reconciles competing notions of gender and race in an increasingly multicultural society. Ultimately, these theories maintain that law is manipulated by and reinforces oppressive political forces that institutionalize the unequal distribution of socioeconomic resources.

Economics in Law and Pragmatism

The law and economics school of thought holds that economic principles best explain legal arrangements affecting markets and noneconomic social behavior. Originating in the late 1930s, the theory presumes that individual freedom is best achieved in unregulated markets and that the legal process should be determined by the rational behavior of individuals seeking to maximize their material self-interests.[42]

Richard Posner, a leader of the law and economics school and a federal appeals court judge on the Seventh Circuit, maintains that "the science of human choice" treats individuals as "rational maximizer[s]." In his view, resources are allocated efficiently, and wealth is maximized only if free exchange is permitted. Because economic self-interest (not selfishness) drives behavior, human satisfaction is maximized only when highly valued resources are obtained through barter or exchanges. An "efficient" breach of contract, for example, occurs when one party agrees to perform the terms of a contract but fails to do so because a third party is willing to pay more for the same service. The breach is efficient if the nonperforming party is willing to compensate the victim of the breach for damages suffered by not having the contract fulfilled. In economic terms, none of the parties suffered because of the breach, and the happiness of the original parties to the contract is maximized by having the contract remain in force.[43]

In short, law is conceptualized in terms of a cost-benefit analysis and the related concepts of utility, value, and the marketplace. The value of a resource (or legally protected interest) is gauged by the maximum (or, conversely, the minimum) amount a consumer is willing to pay for it. In ordinary economic terms, such legal arrangements are either *Pareto optimal* (when one person's economic position is not improved at the expense of another) or *Pareto superior* (when at least one person's economic position is better but only when no one else's situation is made worse). Significantly, the Pareto efficiency principles are only meaningfully applied when it is possible to measure economic behavior objectively, which then allows for a comparison of the effects that changes make on the economic status quo. As such, it remains difficult to translate legal matters into a specification of the transaction costs for parties directly affected, or for those of third parties that are indirectly affected. With that in mind, Posner's innovation was to develop an economic analysis in law that overcomes that limitation through the so-called Kaldor-Hicks criteria, a standard that fully compensates those who lose in a situation in which another gains. By compensating the loser for any damage that is suffered at the expense of those who profit, Pareto principles remain intact because efficacy is promoted by the utility of maintaining a legal arrangement between those who stand to win or lose when the harmony of an economic relationship is threatened.[44]

Notably, Posner applies economic analysis to a full range of legal topics that go beyond the regulation of markets. In *Law, Pragmatism, and Democracy* (2003), he argues that economic analysis allows judges to make decisions that promote market efficiency. As such, law is an instrumental tool to achieve the best outcome in a political democracy and free-market economy. Accordingly, Posner defends the Supreme Court's decision in the disputed 2000 presidential election in *Bush v. Gore* (2000) as pragmatic.[45] Based on weighing the costs and the practical consequences of not deciding the election against those of judicial intervention, Posner concludes that the Court needed to act, and stop the ballot recount by Florida election officials, to avert a constitutional crisis.[46]

Similarly, *Mathias v. Accor Economy Lodging, Inc.* (2003) illustrates the connection between economic analysis or pragmatic theory of judicial decision-making. In *Mathias*, Motel 6, a hotel chain, challenged an award of $186,000 in punitive damages to a family that was bitten by bed bugs while staying in one of its motels. Attorneys for Motel 6 argued that the award was excessive because it was 37.2 times more than the $5,000 awarded the family as compensatory damages. In rejecting that claim, Judge Posner reasoned the amount was in fact justified because Motel 6 had to absorb the costs of trying to conceal illegally the infestation in an attempt to maximize its profits. As he put it, "If a tortfeasor is 'caught' only half the time he commits torts, then when he is caught he should be punished twice as heavily in order to make up for the times he gets away." Judge Posner reasoned that, in economic terms, punitive damages were required to "offset" the risk that tortfeasors would not be deterred from committing wrongful acts in the future, since there is always the possibility that they might escape liability and reap the rewards of their illicit conduct.[47]

Still, applying cost-benefit and policy analysis in deciding cases remains controversial. To illustrate, in a coauthored study, Posner argues that laws should permit adoption agencies to use the fees charged to parents as the means to subsidize the cost of having babies that pregnant women might otherwise abort. In economic terms, this scenario gives pregnant women an incentive not to abort the child and saves them the cost of having unwanted babies; and the increased supply in babies will give more parents a greater range of adoption choices, thus creating a market in babies that would benefit the parties and society. Other controversial studies using economic analyses contend that legalized abortions (authorized by *Roe v. Wade* in 1973) reduced crime rates in the 1990s, thus supporting the hypothesis that women in the high-risk category (teenagers, unmarried mothers, and the less fortunate) had more abortions, which in turn decreased criminality because fewer children grew up to become criminals.[48] Such studies have been criticized as morally bankrupt because they focus solely on cost-benefit analysis and market forces, and thereby dismissing or neglecting the importance of democratically determined moral principles as a check on free markets.[49]

Feminist Jurisprudence

Feminist jurisprudence, or the study of how law perpetuates gender inequality and cultural bias by distorting identity and sexual orientation, emerged from the struggle to achieve equality during the 1960s and 1970s. Since its inception, feminist jurisprudence has evolved into several distinct theoretical criticisms of liberal legalism.

Equality theory, growing out of the 1970s liberal feminist movement, posits that legal institutions discriminate against women and subjugates them based on gender difference. Consequently, equality theorists, such as Justice Ruth Bader Ginsburg and Wendy Williams, argue women must be treated in the same way as men when they are similarly situated. Such advocates of equal treatment tend to be liberal feminists who work within the legal system and push for legal reforms that give women equal rights and access to public institutions and benefits, such as "equal pay for equal work."[50]

Other feminists in the 1980s began to advance *difference theory*, which holds that women are too biologically, psychologically, and socially different to be simply and satisfactorily compared with males. Difference or dominance theorists argue that social norms and laws must be changed more radically than earlier liberal feminists maintained if equality between the sexes is to be achieved. Accordingly, dominance theory hypothesizes that the differences in power between men and women results from male domination in law, economics, and throughout society. The power difference is illustrated by rape and pornography laws that permit the subjugation of women through violence and exploitation of their bodies as objects of sexual pleasure. For dominance theorists, such as law school professor Catherine MacKinnon, radical legal reform is necessary to eliminate oppressive laws that simply perpetuate male supremacy.[51]

In contrast, *cultural theory* feminists challenge earlier liberal feminists in celebrating (rather than lamenting) the differences between men and women. Such feminists argue that women are different from men in the ways they construct their social identity, solve problems, and view the world. As a result, cultural feminists disagree with liberal feminists who contend that law must de-emphasize stereotypical or traditional portrayals of motherhood. Instead, they contend that maternal qualities, such as empathy, nurturing, and caring, should find expression in laws and be taught in law school courses on feminism and human sexuality.[52]

In the 1990s and 2000s, a third generation of feminism theory and criticism emerged in response to liberal, dominance, and cultural feminist jurisprudence. Three major strands of feminist thought arose, each registering the complexity of female identities with an underlying narrative or discourse. *Intersectional feminism* centers on "anti-essentialism," an argument denying that women can be identified as having a single voice or gender experience. Instead of defining women by a generic identity or "essence," multiple factors such as race, class, gender, and the like combine to create gender discrimination that takes many forms. By contrast, *autonomy feminism* focuses on "victimization" in arguing that while women are victims of discrimination, they retain the ability to resist as agents of their own destinies. Finally, *postmodernism feminism* is associated with the "normalization" of gender bias—that is, discrimination that reinforces conventional norms and practices, like heterosexuality and marriage, while marginalizing and stigmatizing lesbians, transgendered individuals, and other gender nonconformists.[53]

Feminist theories raise ongoing legal questions about deeply rooted male bias, cultural distortions of personal identity, and gender-based inequities. Whether feminist theories have had a positive effect on reform remains an open question and controversial. Although dominance theorist MacKinnon helped draft state legislation to protect women from erotic exploitation and sexual violence, for example, in *American Booksellers Association v. Hudnut* (1981), a federal appeals court ruled that the law violated the First Amendment guarantee for freedom of speech by improperly regulating the content of the ideas. Because the law defined pornography as the "graphic sexually explicit subordination of women" through media (pictures or words) that "dehumanizes" them as "sexual objects," the court struck it down. In this sense, *Hudnut* underscores the radical feminist's claim that law is an extension of male domination or confirms the values underlying individual freedom.[54] A similar setback for women's rights advocates resulted in *United States v. Morrison* (2000), a Supreme Court ruling that invalidated a part of the federal Violence Against Women Act, which had given victims of gender-motivated crimes standing to sue their attackers in federal courts.[55] Still, supporters claim that feminist theory has influenced the law and legal reforms by (1) creating a universal acceptance of the legal doctrine of gender neutrality in same-sex and family law cases; (2) facilitating the recognition of new claims of legal rights for victims of sexual harassment, domestic violence, and rape; and, (3) helping reform criminal and international human rights enforcement of rape, prostitution, and sex-trafficking laws.[56]

Notably postmodern feminist jurisprudence has spawned other movements, among them the LGBT (lesbian, gay, bisexual, and transgender) movement pushing for the expansion of same-sex marriage rights, along with "queer theory" (analyses of sexuality, sexual desire, and gender nonconformity). Whereas LGBT studies critique discriminatory practices related to sexual orientation and gender identity, queer theorists focus on understanding the law's effect on how LGBT individuals express their sexuality.[57] Not surprisingly, the debates over the proper scope of feminist theory are political in nature, though at times the interests and goals of partisan advocates merge in the political arena (see Contemporary Controversies over Courts: The Politics of Title IX, Sexual Assault on Campus, and Feminist Legal Reform).

Contemporary Controversies over Courts: The Politics of Title IX, Sexual Assault on Campus, and Feminist Legal Reform

The prevalence on universities and colleges of sexual harassment, including sexual assault, has been a growing public concern. Highly publicized incidents involving allegations of campus rape and violence against women at some of the most prestigious schools in the nation—including that of a Columbia University student, Emma Sulkowicz, who carried around a mattress for an entire year (and across the graduation stage) in 2015 in protest over how the administration allegedly mishandled her rape case against a fellow male student—has brought into sharp relief whether purported victims of sexual harassment, as well as their accusers, are equally and fairly having their respective voices heard in campus adjudicatory proceedings under federal law.

First signed into law in 1972 during the Nixon administration, Title IX of the Education Amendments, 20 U.S.C. Section 1681, et. seq., prohibits sex discrimination in education. The chief agency for its enforcement is the Department of Education's Office for Civil Rights (OCR). Since the 1990s, the agency and court decisions have established that Title IX sexual discrimination includes sexual harassment, which meant that colleges and universities are under a legal mandate to have sufficient policies and procedures in place to adjudicate claims of sexual harassment by employees or students. Significantly, the failure to meet that obligation risks the loss of federal financial aid and student loans.

In an abrupt shift in focus from past administrations, in 2011 the Obama administration's OCR issued a "Dear Colleague" letter (or guidance letter) to college and university administrators that specified that sexual violence harassment is a type of sex discrimination prohibited by Title IX. While not setting a uniform policy or procedure for how schools should review sexual discrimination cases, the letter stipulated that schools receiving financial aid were required to use a less rigorous "preponderance of the evidence" (i.e. it is more likely than not that sexual harassment or violence occurred) standard in their administrative proceedings to resolve sexual discrimination cases. The preponderance of evidence standard, which is typically adopted in civil lawsuits, is less stringent than the "clear and convincing evidence" employed in certain types of serious civil trial proceedings, and less strict than the "beyond a reasonable doubt" burden of proof that is mandated in criminal prosecutions. The letter also changed some of the rules that were in place about how sexual harassment cases were adjudicated in school administration hearings relating to notice, comment, and evidence gathering in the investigative and hearing stages.

Fearful of losing federal dollars, schools created their own Title IX offices, policies and procedures that varied widely from campus-to-campus. While some schools used only one Title IX administrator to investigate and decide such cases (the single-investigator model) after learning of an potential violation from a student, others vested Title IX officers with the power to use an external party or staff member trained in Title IX procedures to conduct panel hearings and issue a report once an investigation is held by notifying the parties, interviewing witnesses, and gathering evidence (the responsible employee model). The lack of firm guidance from the OCR led to criticisms from the political left and right about whether the Obama regulations are properly safeguarding not only the rights of victims of sexual assault, but also whether those accused of committing the violations are being given their procedural rights to be treated equally in accordance with due process norms of fair notice and an opportunity to be hear in administrative proceedings.

Shortly after Donald Trump's 2016 election, the President named Betsy DeVos to lead the Department of Education and, temporarily, the OCR. DeVos appointed Candice Jackson, a conservative who expressed skepticism that campus rape incident are legitimate, noting that ninety percent are likely a result of unenforceable allegations steeped in alcohol and relationship complications. DeVos also chimed in by stating that the Obama regulations reflect a "failed system" of "kangaroo courts" and "weaponized" civil rights, thus prompting her to repeal the 2011 OCR "Dear Colleague" letter, an action that aligned with the views of conservative-leaning donors and groups such as the Charles Koch Institute, the Foundation for Individual Rights in Education, and the American Legislative Exchange Council.

Notably, a coalition of Harvard law professors and other liberal feminists agreed that the Obama policies were well-intentioned but went too far in protecting sexual assault victims. Before DeVos rescinded the "Dear Colleague" letter, they complained that the Obama era Title IX regulations used definitions of sexual misconduct that were too broad, which blurred the distinction between consensual and non-consensual acts; lowered the threshold of proof, which made it easier to convict wrongfully accusers; encouraged the adoption of non-neutral administrative officials and proceedings, which undermined checks on the exercise of arbitrary decision-making and the use of administrative hearings that often turned out to be unfair in application to both victims and alleged perpetrators. Even the liberal organization American Association of University of Professors (AAUP) acknowledged that the Obama OCR actions were problematic, with a spokesperson noting that it has caused liberals and conservatives to unite and urge for reform. As the AAUP spokesmen quipped, "Funny what strange bedfellows politics makes sometimes."

The unity did not last, though. In November 2018, Secretary DeVos unveiled a new set of proposals that extensively rolled back the Obama rules and offered more formal protections to those accused of campus sexual assault instead of the victims. They, among other things, changed the standard of proof from a preponderance of evidence to a clear and convincing standard, a burden that makes it harder for school administrators to conclude that a sexual assault took place. Moreover, students would be guaranteed the right to cross-examination, something that is a major shift from the previous norm of doing investigations of allegations "behind-the-scenes" due to their sensitive nature. In general, victims would have to establish misconduct under stricter definitions and different standards that would trigger school investigations under what the Secretary argues are a clearer set of formal rules that protect the due process interests of both the accuser and victims more fairly.

Critics, which are likely to be found in supporters of the #MeToo movement and other liberal detractors, claim these changes, along with the others that favor a more adversarial and formal litigation setting to resolve sexual harassment allegations, will have the damaging effect of re-traumatizing victims instead of encouraging them to come forward and register a complaint with school officials. In particular, liberal critics denounced them as a return to the days when "rape, assault and harassment were swept under the rug" and, as well, a poor reflection of the Trump administration's "attitude about assault that we saw from Senate Republicans during the Kavanaugh hearing—disparage and diminish survivors and discourage them from reporting." The intensity of the public reaction is measured, in part, by the breadth of the public comments (124,000) to the proposed final rules that will not only impact college campuses, but also K–12 instruction. In addition, whether the final rules become legally binding is an open question since the DeVos plan is expected to generate multiple legal challenges. Indeed, Brett Sokolow, a Title IX advisor and attorney, foresees that it will result in a "systemic failure" in the college and K–12 school environment which, in turn, "potentially collapses under the weight of the litigation" that is likely to occur before final rule adoption.

Sources: Juan Perez Jr. and Bianca Quilantan, "How the New DeVos rules on Sexual Assault Will Shock Schools—And Students," *Politico* (March 6, 2020), available at https://www.politico.com/news/2020/03/06/betsy-devos-school-sexual-assault-rules-122401 (last retrieved April 7, 2020); Tovia Smith, "Education Dept. Proposes Enhanced Protection For Students Accused Of Sexual Assault," *NPR* (November 16, 2018), available at https://www.npr.org/2018/11/16/668556728/education-dept-proposes-enhanced-protection-for-students-accused-of-sexual-assau (last retrieved March 26, 2019); Kathryn Joyce, "The Takedown of Title IX," *NY Times Magazine* (December 5, 2017) (last retrieved March 26, 2019). https://mobile.nytimes.com/2017/12/05/magazine/the-takedown-of-title-ix.html; Elizabeth Bartholet, Nancy Gertner, Janet Halley & Jeannie Suk, "Fairness for All Students Under Title IX" (August 21, 2017) (last retrieved March 26, 2019). https://dash.harvard.edu/bitstream/handle/1/33789434/Fairness%20for%20All%20Students.pdf?sequence=1; Stephanie Ebbert. "Why are some feminists siding with Trump on sexual assault policy?" *Boston Globe* (September 15, 2017). (last retrieved March 26, 2019). https://www.bostonglobe.com/metro/2017/09/14/surprisingly-some-feminist-lawyers-side-with-trump-and-devos-campus-assault-policy/ArigBzO86tERWpDW17DbTI/story.html.

Critical Legal Studies and Critical Race Theory

Postmodern feminism is also closely linked with critical race theory (CRT) scholarship that emerged from the earlier **critical legal studies** (CLS) and civil rights movements in the 1970s and 1980s. Following the first Critical Legal Studies Conference in 1977, the leaders of the CLS—David Trubek, Mark Tushnet, Morton Horwitz, Roberto Unger, and Duncan Kennedy—advanced a critique of law and legal reasoning: Judges use deductive reasoning and formal rules, but the results are based on personal preferences. In other words, CLS theory maintains that there is no separation between law and politics. As Horwitz puts it, "The simple message that CLS delivered was. . .that law in American society was and is heavily influenced by politics."[58]

CLS theorists thus agree with the legal realist claim that law is indeterminate (the idea that not every legal case has one outcome),[59] but with one key difference. Unlike legal realism, CLS theory holds that the rule of law does not exist precisely because of law's uncertainty and political manipulation. As a result, resorting to legal doctrine never produces one single answer to a legal question, and doing so is inexorably arbitrary and incoherent. The CLS theory derives its skepticism from history, sociology, and political science in maintaining that all legal institutions are political and beset by contradictions that make the law inevitably unjust. CLS thus rejects law's neutrality under a principle of *antiformalism*, and its coherency under principles of *indeterminacy* and *contradiction*.[60] Legal regimes are value-laden but operate under the pretense of an objective (value-free) jurisprudence that simply empowers elites at the expense of the disadvantaged and the larger community. From the CLS theory point of view, law is a coercive instrument of power used to repress individuals' and minorities' freedoms.[61]

The thrust of CLS theory, therefore, has a socialist or neo-Marxist bent. In *Legal Education and the Reproduction of Hierarchy* (1983), Harvard law professor Duncan Kennedy argued that traditional legal education should be abolished and replaced by an ultra-egalitarian system of legal instruction, including reforms, such as law school admissions by lottery with racial or gender quotas, the termination of grading systems, and the equalization of all salaries in law schools.[62]

Similarly, Mark Tushnet, a former law clerk to Justice Thurgood Marshall and Harvard law school professor, argued that the contradictions of law prove that it is wholly political and in need of reform. In *The New Constitutional Order* (2003), Tushnet provided a "descriptive sociology" of the prevailing structure of political institutions, claiming America had entered into a new, more conservative constitutional order—rooted in the Reagan-Bush regime of the 1980s and early

1900s, which replaced the former political system defined by the New Deal and Great Society social programs of the 1930s to 1960s. The new conservative order is characterized by divided government, elevated polarization in Congress, and a limited government policy orientation. Its constitutional structure is basically a device for private market interests to use law to further its own objectives, and the judiciary does little to resist the interests of the new regime. Tushnet concluded that "democratic experimentalism" is "the most promising candidate" for creating a new constitutional order, mainly because it is a style of governing that works from the ground up: nonexperts at the local level experimenting with finding practical solutions to policy problems in coordination with national officials, who merely superintend the process rather than control it.[63]

Critics of CLS theory, however, charge that it is "largely defunct," and its adherents are "nihilistic" and locked into a "jurisprudence of despair." Tushnet and other proponents counter that CLS scholarship continues to exert great influence in the legal academy and that the critique merely reflects the growth of formalist legal philosophy and political conservatism. Still, for many others, CLS has become less relevant because of its inability to go beyond criticisms and develop more compelling and competing critical theories.[64]

Critical race theory (CRT), a movement that coalesced after its first conference at the University of Wisconsin Institute for Legal Studies in 1989, is another example of contemporary legal theory deeply skeptical of liberalism (and its emphasis on individual rights). However, CRT does not share CLS theory's premise that law does not exist. Instead, CRT contends that law and legal institutions are deeply ingrained with racism. Racial categories are socially constructed and manipulated by the dominant white legal, economic, and political power structure. CRT scholars view history as demonstrating a "differential racialization" pattern within society that stereotypes and stigmatizes minority groups to fit dominant economic interests. Thus, through *interest convergence* and *material determinism*, the dominant white elites and those in the working class perpetuate racism.[65] CRT goes so far as to argue that the civil rights movement was in fact a failure. Former Harvard law professor Derrick Bell, for one, asserts that the landmark desegregation ruling of *Brown v. Board of Education* (1954) only advanced Southern economic interests, and generally benefited an elite white culture more interested in preserving its image as a liberator of the free world and an enemy of Communism. In other words, *Brown* reflected an "interest convergence" at a brief moment in time, serving the mutual interests of whites in racial tolerance and economic self-interest, on the one hand, and blacks' interests in equality, on the other.[66]

In addition, critical race feminists, such as Angela Harris and Kimberlé Crenshaw, observe that most of the founders of the women's movement were white, relatively affluent, heterosexual, and college educated. As such, they were not representative of all women and cannot speak authoritatively about the experiences of black, Hispanic, and Latino women. Hence, the CRT principles of *intersectionality*—the idea that individuals and classes all share the same attitudes and interests—and *anti-essentialism*—which rejects the claim that all persons of a particular group uniformly fit into a discrete class—are used to show the limitations of battling racial bias by treating all members of a minority group in the same fashion. In other words, law only counters discrimination by first acknowledging that racism oppresses in different ways, depending upon a group's race or ethnicity. Accordingly, *structural determinism*—discriminatory biases built into the structure and vocabulary of society—must be overcome by legal reforms premised on a complete understanding of the unique history and perspectives of different groups suffering discrimination in a complex multicultural and racially diverse society.[67]

A distinguishing characteristic of CRT jurisprudence is also the use of narratives and discourse to unmask racial discrimination. Richard Delgado, a Latino law professor and a CRT leader, uses "legal storytelling" and "counter-storytelling" to highlight the discriminatory impact of racial bias. The dominant group, argues Delgado, uses its own narratives as "the prevailing mindset [to] justify the world as it is, that is, with whites on top and browns and blacks at the bottom." Oppressed minorities therefore must employ their own "[s]tories, parables, chronicles, and narratives," because they are "powerful means for destroying [the dominant group's] mindset—the bundle of presuppositions, received wisdoms, and shared understandings against a background of which legal and political discourse takes place." Engaging in narrative is but one method of CRT to break down the dominant hierarchies of wealth and power. In books such as *The Rodrigo Chronicles* (1995), *Justice at War* (2003), and *The Law Unbound!* (2007), Delgado lets his alter ego, "Rodrigo Crenshaw," tell stories about the difficult experiences minorities confront within the contexts of law school hiring practices, the regulation of hate speech and affirmative action, and the Bush administration's war against terrorism, among others.[68]

Like feminist jurisprudence, CRT has influenced the development of Asian American, Latino-critical (LatCrit), and gay (QueerCrit) scholarship that studies immigration, language rights, and national-origin racial discrimination.[69] CRT supporters also observe that racial perspectives have directly affected judicial outcomes in areas such as environmental justice, racial profiling, hate speech, and

English-only language discrimination cases. Federal Judge Shira Scheindlin's decision, which was overturned on appeal, to halt the New York police department's stop-and-frisk policy because it violated minority rights through racial profiling, may be further evidence of the impact of CLS theory and CRT.[70]

Contemporary Controversies over Courts: Is Cannibalism Ever Legally Justified?

The legal theories outlined in this chapter are "about" jurisprudence. The following hypothetical involves "doing" jurisprudence, as opposed to simply theorizing about important legal questions. Use the hypothetical situation and the questions posed afterward to answer the jurisprudential question of whether cannibalism is ever legally justified.

Imagine five cave explorers from the Speluncean Society in the year 4300 who are trapped in an underground cave after a landslide blocks the entrance. Considerable time and expense are put into a rescue effort, which spans more than two weeks and results in the deaths of ten rescuers. After twenty days in the cave and with diminishing supplies, the group members decide they must kill one of their own in order to survive. Roger Whetmore, one of the group, proposes that they cast dice to determine who should be killed and eaten. After much deliberation and hesitation, the group agrees. But shortly thereafter, Whetmore gets scared and withdraws from the agreement he had proposed. Nonetheless, the group goes ahead with the plan. Then Whetmore refuses to participate, so the dice is thrown for him, and the throw goes against him. Whetmore is then killed and eaten on the twenty-third day. The remaining survivors are rescued on the thirty-second day. Afterward, they are put on trial for murder. The statute under which they are tried states: "Whoever shall willfully take the life of another shall be punished by death."

Suppose the jury finds all of the survivors guilty and the trial judge promptly sentences the defendants to death by hanging. After the jury is released from duty, however, its members petition the Supreme Court to reconsider the verdict and commute the sentence to six months' imprisonment, although they are uncertain whether clemency would be granted under such circumstances.

Five justices on the Supreme Court review the petition, thus appealing the murder convictions and death sentences. The legal philosophy of each justice is well known:

- Chief Justice Truepenny is a textualist but favors executive clemency.

- Justice Foster is a natural law theorist.

- Justice Tatting is not associated with any legal philosophy and, before the justices vote, withdraws from the case.

- Justice Keen is a legal positivist who prefers using the "plain meaning" of the statute but disfavors executive clemency.

- Justice Handy is a legal realist.

Based on these facts:

(1) Will the Supreme Court affirm the murder convictions and death sentences, or will the defendants be acquitted?

(2) How would each justice (except for Tatting) vote based on his or her legal philosophy?

(3) The justices' race, ethnicity, or gender is not known in the hypothetical. But assign a race, ethnicity, and gender classification to each of the justices. Does that make a difference, and if so, how does race, ethnicity, or gender affect each justice's vote?

(4) What is the legislative purpose of the murder statute, and how would that affect each justice's vote?

(5) Are there any moral exceptions to the application of the statute, like "self-defense," "necessity," or "emergency"?

Sources: This hypothetical was created by Lon L. Fuller in a law review article, "The Case of the Speluncean Explorers," in *Harvard Law Review* 62 (1949): 616–45. The hypothetical was inspired by actual cases, *United States v. Holmes*, 26 F. Case 350 (E.D. Pa. 1842), and *Regina v. Dudley and Stephens*, 14 Q.B.D. 273 (1884). For further discussion, see William Twining, "Cannibalism and the Case of the Speluncean Explorers," in *The Speluncean Case: Making Jurisprudence Seriously Enjoyable*, edited by James Allen (Little London: Barry Rose Publishers, 1998); and Allan C. Hutchinson, *Is Eating People Wrong? Great Legal Cases and How They Shaped the World* (Cambridge, U.K.: Cambridge University Press, 2011).

Chapter Summary

The law's evolution is influenced by classical and contemporary theories of jurisprudence. Legal theories give meaning to the law and define the scope of the legal regulation of public and private affairs. Important questions of jurisprudence address the origins of law, law's substantive and normative meaning, and the relationship of morality to law and justice, as well as the role law plays in preserving and challenging the political and social order.

Classical legal theories include natural law, legal positivism, sociological jurisprudence, and legal realism. The writings of Saint Thomas Aquinas, Thomas Hobbes and John Locke, Sir William Blackstone, Jeremy Bentham, Lon Fuller and H. L. A. Hart, Max Weber, Roscoe Pound, Oliver Wendell Holmes, and Jerome Frank greatly influenced classical theories of jurisprudence. Contemporary legal theories include economics and law, feminist jurisprudence, critical legal studies, and critical race theory. Those schools of thought have been shaped by the contributions of philosophers Richard Posner, Catherine MacKinnon, Duncan Kennedy, Mark Tushnet, and Richard Delgado, among others. The application of legal theory to judicial practice and institutional reform is ongoing but often controversial and contingent upon prevailing social, economic, and political conditions.

Key Questions for Review and Critical Analysis

1. How would you characterize the origins of law? How do classical and contemporary legal theories differ?

2. Should judges decide cases only on the basis of the text of statutes and the Constitution, as legal positivists like H. L. A. Hart claim, or must judges take into account background principles and morality, as philosopher Ronald Dworkin argues?

3. What is the significance of Justice Oliver Wendell Holmes's observation that "the law is nothing more than 'prophecies of what the courts will do in fact' "? What is its relation to legal realism?

4. How defensible is the claim made by Judge Richard Posner, and others in the law and economics movement, that cost-benefit economic analysis results in greater efficiency and "maximizes" the public good?

5. Which strand of feminist theory (equality, difference and domination, or *postmodern* approaches) is most persuasive, and why?

6. What do you think of the critical race theorists' claim that the landmark school desegregation ruling in *Brown v. Board of Education* (1954) was a failure in law and society?

Web Links

1. Cornell Legal Information Institute ("Jurisprudence") (www.law.cornell.edu/wex/jurisprudence)

- Sponsored by Cornell University's Law School, this link provides an introduction to jurisprudence and a list of resources about specific schools of thought and cases.

2. Law and Society Association (www.lawandsociety.org)

- Website containing information and links to annual meetings, journals, research, publications, and networks relating to the Law and Society Association.

3. Jurist (www.jurist.org)

- Sponsored by the University of Pittsburgh School of Law, a comprehensive legal news and legal research website.

4. Justia's BlawgSearch (http://blawgsearch.justia.com/blogs/categories/legal-theory)

- A comprehensive listing of most popular legal theory blogs.

5. Social Science Research Network (www.ssrn.com/en)

- A widely used source of legal scholarship, spanning topics in law, political science, legal theory, and jurisprudence, and with links to SSRN blogs and relevant journals.

Selected Readings

Corwin, Edward S. *The "Higher Law" Background of American Constitutional Law.* Ithaca, N.Y.: Cornell University Press, 1968.

Chartier, Gary. *Flourishing Lives: Exploring Natural Law Liberalism.* New York: Cambridge University Press, 2019.

Cotterrell, Roger. *The Politics of Jurisprudence: A Critical Introduction to Legal Philosophy.* 2nd ed. New York: Oxford University Press, 2003.

Cotterrell, Roger. *Sociological Jurisprudence: Juristic Thought and Social Inquiry.* New York: Routledge, 2018.

Crenshaw, Kimberle, Neil Gotanda, Gary Peller, and Kendall Thomas, eds. *Critical Race Theory: The Key Writings That Formed the Movement.* New York: New Press, 1995.

Delgado, Richard. *Critical Race Theory: An Introduction.* 3rd ed. New York: New York University Press, 2017.

DeMatteo, David, Kirk Helbrun, Alice Thornewill and Shelby Arnold, eds. *Problem-Solving Courts and the Criminal Justice System*. New York: Oxford University Press, 2019.

Duxbury, Neil. *Patterns of American Jurisprudence*. New York: Oxford University Press, 1997.

Dworkin, Ronald. *Law's Empire*. London: Fontana Press, 1986.

Dworkin, Ronald. *Taking Rights Seriously*. Cambridge, Mass.: Harvard University Press, 1977.

Ehrenberg, Kenneth. *The Functions of Law*. New York: Oxford University Press, 2016.

Frank, Jerome. *Law and the Modern Mind*. New York: Brentano's Publishers, 1930.

Freeman, M.D.A. *Lloyd's Introduction to Jurisprudence*. 9th ed. London: Wiley & Sons, 2014.

Fuller, Lon L. *The Morality of Law*. New Haven, Conn.: Yale University Press, 1964.

George, Robert P., ed. *Natural Law, Liberalism, and Morality: Contemporary Essays*. Oxford: Oxford University Press, 2001.

Gibson, Katie L. *Ruth Bader Ginsburg's Legacy of Dissent: Feminist Rhetoric and the Law*. Tuscaloosa: University of Alabama Press, 2018.

Hart, H. L. A. *The Concept of Law*. New York: Oxford University Press, 1961.

Helmholz, R.H. *Natural Law in Court: A History of Legal Theory in Practice*. Cambridge, MA.: Harvard University Press, 2015.

Kelsen, Hans. *Pure Theory of Law*. Berkley, CA.: University of California Press, 1967.

Leiter, Brian. *Naturalizing Jurisprudence: Essays on American Legal Realism and Naturalism in Legal Philosophy*. New York: Oxford University Press, 2007.

MacKinnon, Catherine A. *Feminism Unmodified: Discourses on Life and Law*. Cambridge, Mass.: Harvard University Press, 1987.

Page, Anthony, and Wilfred Prest, eds. *Blackstone and His Critics*. Oxford: Hart Publishing, 2018.

Posner, Richard A. Law, *Pragmatism, and Democracy*. Cambridge, Mass.: Harvard University Press, 2003.

Rawls, John. *A Theory of Justice*. Cambridge, MA.: Belknap Press. 1971.

Rumble, Wilfrid E., Jr. *American Legal Realism.* Ithaca, N.Y.: Cornell University Press, 1968.

Sandel, Michael J. *Justice: What is the Right Thing to Do?* London: Penguin. 2010.

Stefancic, Jean, and Richard Delgado. *Critical Race Theory: The Cutting Edge.* 3rd ed. Philadelphia: Temple University Press, 2013.

Tamanaha, Brian Z. *A Realistic Theory of Law.* Cambridge: Cambridge University Press, 2017.

Twining, William. *Globalisation and Legal Theory.* Evanston, Ill.: Northwestern University Press, 2001.

Twining, William. *Karl Llewellyn and the Realist Movement.* 2nd ed. Cambridge, U. K.: Cambridge University Press, 2012.

Wacks, Raymond. *Understanding Jurisprudence: An Introduction to Legal Theory.* 5th ed. New York: Oxford University Press, 2017.

Endnotes

[1] Charlie Savage, "Trump Lawyer's Impeachment Argument Stokes Fears of Unfettered Power," *New York Times* (January 30, 2020), available at https://www.nytimes.com/2020/01/30/us/politics/dershowitz-trump-impeachment.html (last retrieved February 16, 2020).

[2] Brittny Mejia, Molly Hennessy-Fiske, and Leila Miller, "New ICE crackdown in sanctuary cities sparks backlash in L.A.," *Los Angeles Times* (February 15, 2020), available from https://www.latimes.com/california/story/2020-02-15/new-ice-crackdown-sanctuary-cities-sparks-backlash-la (last retrieved February 16, 2020).

[3] See Brief, *Amici Curiae* of the United States Conference of Catholic Bishops, et al, in Support of Respondents, available from https://www.supremecourt.gov/DocketPDF/17/17-965/41839/2018033017 0127467_No.%2017-965%20Amicus%20Brief%20ISO%20Respondents%20Final.pdf (last retrieved June 17, 2018); Brief of NAACP Legal Defense & Educational Fund, Inc., as *Amicus Curiae* in Support of Respondents State of Hawaii, et al., available from https://www.supremecourt.gov/DocketPDF/17/17-965/41700/ 20180330113458777_17965%20NAACP%20Legal%20Defense%20Educational%20Fund%20Inc.%20 AmicusBrief.pdf (last retrieved March 26, 2019); Brief, *Amicus Curiae* of the Foundation For Moral Law in Support of Petitioners," available from https://www.supremecourt.gov/DocketPDF/17/17-965/36554/ 20180226115307275_17-965%20FML%20Amicus%20Brief.pdf (last retrieved March 26, 2019); and, *Trump v. Hawaii*, 138 S.Ct. 2392 (2018).

[4] Tobias Hoonhout, "Bloomberg Defends Racial Profiling by Police in 2015 Recording: 'They Are Male Minorities' ", *National Review* (February 11, 2020), available at https://www.nationalreview.com/news/ bloomberg-defends-racial-profiling-by-police-in-2015-recording-they-are-male-minorities/ (last retrieved February 16, 2020). See also, New York Advisory Committee to the U.S. Commission on Civil Rights, "Civil Rights Implications of Post-September 11 Law Enforcement Practices in New York (March 2004)," available at https://www.usccr.gov/pubs/sac/ny0304/ny0304.pdf (last retrieved February 16, 2020); Joseph Goldstein, "Court Blocks Stop-and-Frisk Changes for New York Police," *New York Times* (October 31, 2013), available at www.nytimes.com/2013/11/01/nyregion/court-blocks-stop-and-frisk-changes-for-new-york-police.html? _r=0 (last retrieved November 22, 2013).

[5] See Eliana Dockterman, "Harvey Weinstein's Arrest Marks a Pivotal Turning Point for the #MeToo Movement," *Time* (May 25, 2018), available from http://time.com/5291663/harvey-weinstein-arrest-metoo-movement/ (last retrieved March 26, 2019); Jack Stripling, "Beyond a President's Worst Fears, a Mob with Torches Arrived," *The Chronicle of Higher Education* (August 13, 2017), https://www.chronicle.com/article/

Beyond-a-President-s-Worst/240914 (last retrieved March 26, 2019); *Shelby County v. Holder*, 570 U.S. 529 (2013).

6   See, e.g., "Brief, *Amicus Curiae* of Anti-Defamation League in Support of Respondents," available from www.supremecourtpreview.org (American Bar Association) (last retrieved November 22, 2013), 20; "Brief, *Amicus Curiae* of Political Scientists Gary Segura, Shaun Bowler, Todd Donovan, Zoltan Hajnal, Rodney Hero, Stephen Nicholson, and Caroline Tolbert in Support of Respondents," available from www.supremecourt preview.org (last retrieved November 22, 2013), 12–14; and, "Brief, *Amicus Curiae* of the Society of American Law Teachers in Support of Respondents," available from www.supremecourtpreview.org (last retrieved November 22, 2013), 24, 26, 29.

7   Ruggero J. Aldisert, *A Judge's Advice: 50 Years on the Bench* (Durham, N.C.: Carolina Academic Press, 2011), 172.

8   As quoted in Edward S. Corwin, *The "Higher Law" Background of American Constitutional Law* (Ithaca, N.Y.: Cornell University Press, 1988), 5.

9   Edgar Bodenheimer, *Jurisprudence: The Philosophy and Method of the Law*, rev. ed. (Cambridge, Mass.: Harvard University Press, 1974), 3–30; David Van Drunen, *Law and Custom: The Thought of Thomas Aquinas and the Future of the Common Law* (New York: Peter Lang, 2003), 30–37.

10   Such human flourishing is described by Finnis as "basic forms of good," including the drive for self-preservation (life), the acquisition of information (knowledge), engaging in enjoyment (play), having an appreciation of beauty, art, or nature (aesthetic experience), experiencing friendship (sociability), intelligently solving problems (practical reasonableness), and having faith (religion). The basic requirements of practical reasonableness are those (nine) principles that structure one's life, including remaining open-minded, detached, committed, impartial, and efficient in the pursuit of living a life that is respectful toward others and in pursuit of communal goals. Raymond Wacks, *Understanding Jurisprudence: An Introduction to Legal Theory*, 3rd ed. (Oxford: Oxford University Press, 2012), 24. Some label Finnis's work as representing the "new natural law." Steven D. Smith, "Which Come First: The Person or the Goods?" *Legal Theory* 13 (2007), 285–313, 286; and it is hailed as "groundbreaking in its application of the methodology of analytical jurisprudence to a body of doctrine [classical natural law] usually considered to be its polar opposite." Wacks, *Understanding Jurisprudence*, 23. See also N. E. Simmonds, *Central Issues in Jurisprudence: Justice, Law and Rights*, 4th ed. (London: Sweet & Maxwell, 2013), 142. Finnis's original book, published in 1980, has been revised slightly in John Finnis, *Natural Law and Natural Rights* (New York: Oxford University Press, 2011).

11   Mark C. Murphy, "Natural Law Jurisprudence," *Legal Theory* 9 (2003), 241–67, 244.

12   Blackstone's *Commentaries on the Laws of England in Four Volumes*, edited by Wayne Morrison (London: Cavendish, 2001), 41.

13   *Calder v. Bull*, 3 U.S. 386 (1798).

14   *Dred Scott v. Sandford*, 60 U.S. 393 (1857).

15   *Bradwell v. Illinois*, 83 U.S. 130 (1873).

16   *Brown v. Board of Education*, 347 U.S. 483 (1954). See Clarence Thomas, "Toward a 'Plain Reading' of the Constitution: The Declaration of Independence in Constitutional Interpretation," *Howard Law Journal* 30 (1987), 983, 991–997.

17   Lon L. Fuller, "Positivism and Fidelity to Law: A Reply to Professor Hart," *Harvard Law Review* 71 (1958), 630–72. See also Wacks, *Understanding Jurisprudence*, 33.

18   See generally M. D. A. Freeman, *Lloyd's Introduction to Jurisprudence*, 9th ed. (London: Sweet & Maxwell, 2015); H. L. A. Hart, *Essays on Bentham: Studies in Jurisprudence and Political Theory* (Oxford: Clarendon Press, 1982).

19   George P. Fletcher, *Basic Concepts of Legal Thought* (New York: Oxford University Press, 1996), 146. See generally Freeman, *Lloyd's Introduction to Jurisprudence*, 199–221; Hart, *Essays on Bentham*.

20   H. L. A. Hart, *The Concept of Law* (Oxford: Oxford University Press, 1961).

21   Ibid.

22   Robert H. Bork, "Tradition and Morality in Constitutional Law," in *Judges on Judging: Views from the Bench*, edited by David M. O'Brien, 5th ed. (Washington, D.C.: CQ Press, 2016), 203.

23   Ronald Dworkin, *Taking Rights Seriously* (Cambridge, Mass.: Harvard University Press, 1977); Ronald Dworkin, *Freedom's Law: The Moral Reading of the American Constitution* (Cambridge, Mass.: Harvard University

Press, 1996); Ronald Dworkin, *Law's Empire* (London: Fontana Press, 1986); Ronald Dworkin, *Justice for Hedgehogs* (Cambridge, Mass.: Belknap Press, 2011).

24 Dworkin, *Justice for Hedgehogs*, 414. The murder/inheritance illustration is from *Riggs v. Palmer*, a case Dworkin uses in his analysis of principles. Simmonds, *Central Issues in Jurisprudence*, 200. See also Dworkin, *Taking Rights Seriously*, 22, 26; Dworkin, *Freedom's Law*, 1–38; Dworkin, *Law's Empire*, 176–224.

25 *Bowers v. Hardwick*, 478 U.S. 186 (1986).

26 Ibid., 196.

27 Ibid. (CJ. Burger, concurring opinion).

28 *Lawrence v. Texas*, 539 U.S. 558 (2003), 563, 571–72, 576.

29 Kenneth Veitch, "Social Solidarity and the Power of Contract," *Journal of Law and Society* 38 (2011), 189–214.

30 Sally Ewing, "Formal Justice and the Spirit of Capitalism: Max Weber's Sociology of Law," *Law and Society Review* 21 (1987), 487–512; Anthony T. Kronman, *Max Weber* (Stanford, Calif.: Stanford University Press, 1983).

31 See Alan Hunt, *The Sociological Movement in Law* (Philadelphia: Temple University Press, 1978), 118–46.

32 Roscoe Pound, "The Need of a Sociological Jurisprudence," *Green Bag* 19 ("law in books" 1908), 611–12. See also Roscoe Pound, "Law in Books and Law in Action," *American Law Review* 44 (1910), 12–21; Roscoe Pound, "The Causes of Popular Dissatisfaction With the Administration of Justice," *The American Lawyer* 14 (1906), 445–52. See also Hunt, *The Sociological Movement in Law*, 22–29.

33 These scholars included John Chipman Gray (1839–1915), Herman Oliphant (1884–1939), William Underhill Moore (1879–1949), Walter Wheeler Cook (1873–1943), Arthur Linton Corbin (1874–1966), and Wesley Newcomb Hohfeld (1879–1918), all of which helped found American legal realism. American realism has a pragmatist orientation and differs from the skepticism of Scandinavian legal realism, which is described as "a philosophical assault on the metaphysical foundations of law" and directed at criticizing conventional understandings of the legal system instead of courts and judging. Wacks, *Understanding Jurisprudence*, 145. Scandinavian realism is best represented by the writings of Axel Hagerstrom (1868–1939), Alf Ross (1899–1979), Karl Olivecrona (1897–1980), and A. V. Lundstedt (1882–1955). Wacks, *Understanding Jurisprudence*, 145–47, 154.

34 Neil Duxbury, *Patterns of American Jurisprudence* (New York: Oxford University Press, 1995), 84–85, 122–25, 140–49.

35 Ibid.

36 Oliver Wendell Holmes, Jr., "The Path of the Law," *Harvard Law Review* 10 (1896), 42–43.

37 Karl N. Llewellyn, "The Normative, the Legal, and the Law-Jobs: The Problem of Juristic Method," *Yale Law Journal* 49 (1940), 1355–400. See also Wacks, *Understanding Jurisprudence*, 149–51; Hunt, *The Sociological Movement in Law*, 48–55.

38 Jerome Frank, *Law and the Modern Mind* (New York: Brentano's Publishers, 1930), 101–11.

39 Duxbury, *Patterns of American Jurisprudence*, 135–62. See also Wacks, *Understanding Jurisprudence*, 147.

40 See Duxbury, *Patterns of American Jurisprudence*, 123.

41 Duxbury, *Patterns of American Jurisprudence*, 161–299. See, e.g., Harold D. Laswell and Myres S. McDougal, "Legal Education and Public Policy: Professional Training in the Public Interest," *Yale Law Journal* 52 (1943), 203–95.

42 Duxbury, *Patterns of American Jurisprudence*, 316–64.

43 Richard A. Posner, *The Economics of Justice* (Cambridge, Mass.: Harvard University Press, 1981), 65–66, 75, 88–99.

44 Ibid.

45 *Bush v. Gore*, 531 U.S. 98 (2000).

46 Richard A. Posner, *Law, Pragmatism, and Democracy* (Cambridge, Mass.: Harvard University Press, 2003), 78–80, 188–203, 296–99, 322–56. See generally *Bush v. Gore: The Question of Legitimacy*, edited by Bruce Ackerman (New Haven, Conn.: Yale University Press, 2002).

47 A. Mitchell Polinsky and Steven Shavell, "Punitive Damages: An Economic Analysis," *Harvard Law Review* 111 (1998), 869–962; Robert J. Rhee, "A Financial Economic Theory of Punitive Damages," *Michigan*

Law Review 111 (2012), 33–87. See also *Matheis v. Accor Economy Lodging, Inc.*, 347 F.3d 672, 677 (7th Cir. 2003) (J. Posner).

48 John J. Donohue III and Steven D. Levitt, "The Impact of Legalized Abortion on Crime," *Quarterly Journal of Economics* 116 (2001), 379–420; and Elizabeth M. Landes and Richard A. Posner, "The Economics of the Baby Shortage," *Journal of Legal Studies* 7 (1978), 323–48. Other studies report that the Ku Klux Klan's illegal activities in the 1920s demonstrate the Klan was merely a successful marketing enterprise selling hate and profits instead of being a terrorist organization. Roland G. Fryer, Jr., and Steven D. Levitt, "Hatred and Profits: Under the Hood of the Ku Klux Klan," *Quarterly Journal of Economics* 127 (2012), 1883–925. See also Duxbury, *Patterns of American Jurisprudence*, 414–15.

49 See Eyal Zamir and Barak Medina, *Law, Economics, and Morality* (New York: Oxford University Press, 2010).

50 Martha Chamallas, *Introduction to Feminist Legal Theory* (New York: Wolters Kluwer Law and Business, 2013), 19–20; Wacks, *Understanding Jurisprudence*, 302.

51 Catherine MacKinnon, *Feminism Unmodified: Discourses on Life and Law* (Cambridge, Mass.: Harvard University Press, 1987); Catherine MacKinnon, *Feminist Theory of the State* (Cambridge, Mass.: Harvard University Press, 1989); Carol Gilligan, *In a Different Voice: Psychological Theory and Women's Development* (Cambridge, Mass.: Harvard University Press, 1982).

52 Chamallas, *Introduction to Feminist Legal Theory*, 20–23; Wacks, *Understanding Jurisprudence*, 303–304.

53 Chamallas, ibid. Wacks, *Understanding Jurisprudence*, 305–308.

54 *American Booksellers Association v. Hudnut*, 771 F.2d 323 (7th Cir., 1981). See also, Katharine T. Bartlett, "Feminist Legal Methods," *Harvard Law Review* 103 (1990), 829; Denise Schaeffer, "Feminism and Liberalism Reconsidered: The Case of Catharine MacKinnon," *American Political Science Review* 95 (2001), 699–708; Cass R. Sunstein, "Pornography and the First Amendment," *Duke Law Journal* 1986 (1986), 589.

55 *U.S. v. Morrison*, 529 U.S. 598 (2000). See also Catherine A. MacKinnon, "Disputing Male Sovereignty: On *United States v. Morrison*," *Harvard Law Review* 114 (2000), 135–77.

56 Chamallas, *Introduction to Feminist Legal Theory*, 405–8. Chamallas cites the entrenchment of gender neutrality legal doctrine (ibid., 406); the increased availability of sexual harassment lawsuits and routine use of protection orders (ibid., 406); the rapid growth and success of "family responsibility discriminatory" or caregiver lawsuits (ibid., 260); Pennsylvania's legislative reform of criminal penalties for nonconsensual sex in rape cases in response to *Commonwealth v. Berkowitz*, 641 A.2d 1161 (Pa. 1994) (ibid., 291); influencing federal court and international court decisions in mass rape cases as violations of federal law and human rights violations (ibid., 294–95); strengthening federal law and United Nations protocols that protect women's rights in prostitution cases and sex trafficking cases through lobbying efforts (ibid., 354–56).

57 Chamallas, *Introduction to Feminist Legal Theory*, 202, 216. See, e.g., Ernesto Javier Martinez, *Queer Race Narratives of Intelligibility* (Stanford, Calif.: Stanford University Press, 2013); Michael Sadowski, *In a Queer Voice: Journeys of Resilience From Adolescence to Adulthood* (Philadelphia: Temple University Press, 2013).

58 Morton Horowitz, "Legal History," in *Legal Intellectuals in Conversation*, edited by James R. Hackney, Jr. (New York: New York University Press, 2012), 80.

59 Richard Delgado and Jean Stefancic, *Critical Race Theory: An Introduction* (New York: New York University Press, 2012), 5.

60 Wacks, *Understanding Jurisprudence*, 284.

61 See, e.g., Duncan Kennedy, "Form and Substance in Private Law Adjudication," *Harvard Law Review* 89 (1976), 1689–778; Roberto Mangabeira Unger, "The Critical Legal Studies Movement," *Harvard Law Review* 96 (1983), 560–675; Mark V. Tushnet, "Following the Rules Laid Down: A Critique of Interpretivism and Neutral Principles," *Harvard Law Review* 96 (1983), 781–827.

62 Duncan Kennedy, *Legal Education and the Reproduction of Hierarchy: A Polemic Against the System* (Cambridge, U. K.: Afar, 1983). See also Michigan Law Review Association, "Legal Education and the Reproduction of Hierarchy: A Polemic Against the System" [Book Review], *Michigan Law Review* 82 (1984), 961–65; Pauline T. Kim, "The Colorblind Lottery," *Fordham Law Review* 72 (2003), 20 n. 62.

63 Mark Tushnet, *The New Constitutional Order* (Princeton, N.J.: Princeton University Press, 2003), ix–x, 1–7, 111–12, 167–72. Tushnet reiterates these themes in Mark Tushnet, *Why the Constitution Matters* (New Haven, Conn.: Yale University Press, 2010).

64 Mark Tushnet, "Critical Legal Theory (Without Modifiers) in the United States," *Journal of Political Philosophy* 13 (2005), 99–112. But see Duxbury, *Patterns of American Jurisprudence*, 509; David Jabbari, "From Criticism to Construction in Modern Critical Legal Theory," *Oxford Journal of Legal Studies* 12 (1992), 507–42. See also Richard A. Epstein, "Tushnet's Lawless World," *The University of Chicago Law Review Dialogue* 80 (2013), 1–23. Epstein attacks Mark Tushnet by describing him as "a grizzled hanger-on" of the defunct CLS movement that has an "unwholesome negativism." Ibid., 1, 22.

65 Richard Delgado and Jean Stefancic, *Critical Race Theory: An Introduction*, 2nd ed. (New York: New York University Press, 2012), 20–30.

66 Derrick A. Bell, Jr., "*Brown v. Board of Education* and the Interest-Convergence Dilemma," *Harvard Law Review* 93 (1980), 518. See generally Kimberle Crenshaw, Neil Gotanda, Gary Peller, and Kendall Thomas, eds., *Critical Race Theory: The Key Writings That Formed the Movement* (New York: New Press, 1995).

67 Delgado and Stefancic, *Critical Race Theory: An Introduction*, 2nd ed. (New York: New York University Press, 2012), 30–34. See also Kathryn Abrams, "The Constitution of Women," *Alabama Law Review* 48 (1997), 867–74; Patricia A. Cain, "Feminism and the Limits of Equality," *Georgia Law Review* 24 (1990), 804–5, 829–40.

68 Richard Delgado, "Storytelling for Oppositionists and Others: A Plea for Narrative," *Michigan Law Review* 87 (1989), 2411, and *Critical Race Theory: The Cutting Edge* (Philadelphia: Temple University Press, 2013). See also Richard Delgado, *The Rodrigo Chronicles: Conversations About America and Race* (New York: New York University Press, 1995); Richard Delgado, *Justice at War: Civil Liberties and Civil Rights During Time of War* (New York: New York University Press, 2003); and Richard Delgado, *The Law Unbound! A Richard Delgado Reader*, edited by Richard Delgado and Jean Stefancic (Boulder, Colo.: Paradigm, 2007).

69 Delgado and Jean Stefancic, *Critical Race Theory*, 3.

70 Delgado and Jean Stefancic, *Critical Race Theory*, 143–51. See ibid., 122–23—citing *Jersey Heights Neighborhood Association v. Glendening*, 174 F.3d 180 (4th Cir., 1999) (environmental justice); 129–30—citing *United States v. Leviner*, 31 F. Supp.2d 23 (D. Mass., 1998) (mandatory sentencing); 133—citing *Taylor v. Metzger*, 706 A.2d 685, 691 (N.J., 1998) (hate speech); 134—citing *Ruiz v. Hull*, 957 P.2d 984 (Ariz., 1998) (English-only language law). See also Goldstein, "Court Blocks Stop-and-Frisk Changes for New York Police."

PART II

Judicial Organization and Administrative Processes

Judicial Organization and Administration

Some court watchers claim that "state courts have become a new battleground" for politicians and special interest groups who disagree with their rulings—ranging from capital punishment and public school financing, to abortion rights. At the federal level, hyper-partisan attacks are fueled by the high profile use of social media and public statements on both sides of the aisle. Liberal judges, such as Supreme Court Justices Ruth Bader Ginsburg and Sonia Sotomayor, have been the target of President Donald Trump's "tweetstorms" accusing them of being biased against him or his administration's policies; and, among other denunciations of different federal judges, he lambasted U.S. District Court of the District of Columbia Judge Amy Berman Jackson for unfairly presiding over the criminal prosecution and sentencing of his close political ally, Roger Stone, which, in turn, may have influenced the Department of Justice to reverse itself and recommend a lighter sentence. Similarly, Senate Minority Leader Chuck Schumer (D-N.Y.) stood in front of the Supreme Court and publicly declared during an abortion rally on the day of oral arguments that conservative Justices Neil Gorsuch and Brett Kavanaugh will "pay the price" for their "awful decisions." Increasingly, public attacks on courts are not simply rhetorical, as the Berman-Stone incident suggests. Justices and judges, for example, face actionable threats of impeachment and millions of special interest dollars are spent on attack ads aimed at limiting their life-tenure or unseating them in retention elections. Other schemes include introducing legislation that would sharply cut court funding, reduce judicial salaries, or impose term limits and retirement age requirements.[1]

A widely-used tactic is using judicial reform as a pretext for acting in retaliation for politically controversial rulings, which sometimes jeopardizes the basic operation of political governance. To illustrate, in seeking to stimulate the state's economy through deep tax cuts and other business-friendly legislation, in 2015 Kansas Governor Sam Brownback (R-KS) and the Republican legislature retaliated against the Kansas Supreme Court when it ordered the legislature to increase funding for public schools after it ruled that state's system of educational financing was unconstitutional. In response, the legislature passed two laws that stripped the Supreme Court of its administrative authority over the lower courts and defunded the entire judicial branch if the Supreme Court later ruled that first law was unconstitutional. Shortly thereafter, the Supreme Court nullified the first retaliatory law on constitutional grounds. A constitutional crisis was only averted when the Kansas legislature reversed the second defunding law. Perhaps more ominously, the political battle for control of the court and Kansas' public educational financing system did not stop there. In 2016, the Republican Party and conservative interest groups who were unhappy with the Court's decision-making in educational funding, abortion, and capital punishment cases raised nearly a million dollars in an unsuccessful attempt to unseat four Kansas Supreme Court justices that were up for election; and, in 2018, in its sixth ruling on the educational financing issue, the Kansas Supreme Court held that the remedial funding laws passed by legislature met the equity, but not the adequacy, constitutional requirements to fund public schools properly. Among other things, the episode registers the depth, and institutional effects, that partisanship has on the courts and political governance in times of hyper-polarization at the state and national level (see Chapter Ten for additional discussion of state judicial policymaking in the area of public school financing).[2]

Critics of these trends, including retired Supreme Court Justice Sandra Day O'Connor, argue that there is a growing "national war on state courts" that threatens judicial independence and public confidence in the courts. As O'Connor declared shortly after leaving the bench: "In too many states, judicial elections are becoming political prizefights where partisans and special interests seek to install judges who will answer to them instead of the law and the Constitution."[3] Moreover, partisan efforts to reconstitute the courts are not confined to the states or defined by a particular political ideology or a political era. Historically, federal courts also have often been easy targets. Liberals and conservatives alike have tried to curb the courts by reshuffling them and changing how they administer justice— the alleged activism of the District of Columbia and Ninth Circuit courts has been the basis of reform legislation and proposals to change their jurisdiction and structure to make them more efficient, but also to curb their liberal decision-making in controversial areas of social and legal policy. Political meddling also occurs in other countries. In 2018, for instance, Poland's right-wing Law and Justice Party, which controls the country's Parliament and claims that the judiciary has still not purged itself of corrupt Communist-era judges that thwart popular will, ushered through legislation that forced Polish Supreme Court Justices to retire at the age of 65, a move that affected Chief Justice and 26 others in the 72-person Court.[4] The political struggles to limit judicial authority by enacting reform to change the judiciary's structure or composition illustrate the ongoing conflicts over judicial architecture.

As these examples and many others imply, politics is infused into the basic structure and operation of courts, a concept sometimes referred to as "judicial architecture." *Judicial architecture* is defined as the organization and administration of court operations, including judicial administration, budgeting, rulemaking, staffing, education, and discipline.[5] Partisan debates over architectural issues influence a judiciary's institutional identity and internal operations, such as whether there is sufficient funding and resources to manage caseloads efficiently. In addition, they may impact the quality and substance of judicial decision-making. As Justice O'Connor suggests, the underlying politics of judicial architecture greatly affect whether the judiciary retains independence from the political branches, an essential **separation of powers** principle and one consistent with the rule of law.

This chapter focuses on the basic issues of the politics of judicial architecture: the structure, organization, and administration of courts. First, a brief history of the origin of U.S. courts is discussed to situate the growth of state and federal courts in a constitutional framework. Next, the basic organization, and respective dockets, of state and federal courts is analyzed and illustrates the principles and politics of judicial federalism (the independence and interrelationship of state and federal courts). The chapter concludes by addressing the politics of judicial administration and how courts internally operate or respond to external forces within the political system.

THE ORIGINS OF U.S. COURTS

U.S. courts arose with the struggle for independence. Before the Constitutional Convention in Philadelphia in 1787, the states were in the forefront of experiments to limit governmental power by separating institutions and imposing checks and balances. Consequently, a diverse network of independent state courts emerged that resemble, but remain distinct from, the federal judiciary. The federal judiciary was created only after the U.S. Constitution's ratification in June 1788. Yet, the structure and organization of state and federal judiciaries remain largely the same as that which took shape during the founding period.

Before the American Revolution, town, county, and representative assemblies were sources of colonial law. Colonial governments typically consisted of a governor (appointed by the Crown), an appointed council, and an elected assembly. Of the three institutions, the assembly had most of the people's allegiance because the governor and courts were viewed as symbols of the Crown. The divisions of authority, however, were blurred because the governor shared legislative powers and the councils often served as high courts. Accordingly, colonial legal institutions consisted of a confusing and sometimes overlapping layer of courts that included superior courts and county or local courts, each with varying **jurisdiction** over specific criminal and civil matters.[6]

Colonists grew increasingly hostile over England's attempt to assert more formal control through magisterial rule. The lack of separated governmental institutions was perceived as a source of political corruption and destructive of personal freedoms. In 1775, the colonies responded by calling special conventions for the purpose of drafting constitutions, based on the principles of popular consent and the separation of powers between legislative and judicial branches. Several 1776 constitutions added bills of rights, established rotating terms of office, and required annual elections. Some made explicit reference to the principle of separation of powers, and most removed the power to appoint judges from governors and placed it with the legislature. Following the lead of Virginia, six states identified the judiciary as a distinct branch of government. Most states as well granted judges tenure on the basis of "good behavior." Although the extent of the judiciaries' power remained largely untested in practice, the highest courts in some states (Virginia, Pennsylvania, and Massachusetts) asserted the power of judicial review—the power to declare legislation and other official acts unconstitutional.[7]

The Articles of Confederation, drafted in 1777 and approved by the Continental Congress in 1781 did not establish a separate national judiciary. Congress was the "last resort of appeal," but, with few exceptions, congressional power was only effective if nine of the thirteen states approved of legislative action.[8] Because each state had sovereign rights in a loose confederation of voluntary cooperation, state legislatures were dominant in a system of weak central government. There was no power to coerce the states into cooperating on issues affecting the national interest. With a unicameral assembly and a diluted executive and nonexistent judiciary, the Articles made difficult or prevented united national action to repel domestic or foreign threats.[9]

The lack of a federal coercive sanction against state laws was a structural defect that James Madison thought was "mortal to the ancient Confederacies, and [a] disease of the modern."[10] Madison's experience in the Continental Congress and the Virginia General Assembly in the 1780s convinced him of the need for centralization and a national veto over state laws because dominant majorities often put their interests above those of minorities and the nation. Although Madison's proposal for a "council of revision," with the power to strike down state laws, was ultimately rejected at the Constitutional Convention, he realized the political system required a strong central government in order to curb factionalism, conduct foreign relations, regulate commerce, and protect natural rights. State legislatures also acted unpredictably, passing laws favoring debtor relief at the expense of the creditors in an uncertain economy struggling with the problem of paying Revolutionary War debts. State courts, on the other hand, tended to protect creditors and the mercantile class, forcing many farmers and debt-ridden citizens into foreclosures.[11]

Under the Articles of Confederation, the nation was fatally beset by problems. Those favoring an invigorated centralized government, including Madison, Alexander Hamilton, and John Dickinson, met in Annapolis, Maryland, at a convention in September 1786. Although only five states and twelve delegates attended, the occasion was used to call for a second convention to convene in Philadelphia in May 1787 for the purpose of considering remedies to meet the "exigencies of the Union."[12]

Most of the fifty-five delegates to the Constitutional Convention were lawyers, Revolutionary War heroes, and political statesmen. James Madison, a nationalist from Virginia, advanced the "Virginia Plan" to set the Convention's agenda and to replace the Articles. In addition to establishing a legislature and giving it the power to veto state laws, the Virginia Plan proposed creating an executive, a national judiciary, and a council of revision that could veto laws passed by Congress and the states. By contrast, William Paterson's "New Jersey Plan" countered that all states must be represented equally, and the Articles should just be revised, not replaced. By June, the differences over the key issue of representation forced the Convention into deadlock. The stalemate was then effectively broken by the Great Compromise, an agreement among the large and small state delegates. That compromise divided Congress into a bicameral institution elected by the states and the people. The states were represented in the Senate by allowing state legislatures to select its senators, whereas the House of Representatives' membership was determined through popular elections held in each of the states. The federal judiciary consisted of a Supreme Court staffed by justices appointed by the president after Senate confirmation.[13] Notably, the establishment and organization of the lower federal courts was left to the First Congress to determine.

Likewise, the nature and scope of the Court's jurisdiction and power was also debated. The Convention rejected Madison's proposal for a veto over state laws, but the ensuing deliberation produced Article VI—the Supremacy Clause, requiring both federal and state courts to adhere to the Constitution. Accordingly, the Framers appeared to anticipate that federal courts would exercise judicial review over acts of the federal and state governments, although it was less clear whether state courts had the same power to nullify national law.[14]

The 1789 Judiciary Act

Following the Constitution's ratification, the First Congress swiftly enacted the Judiciary Act of 1789, which laid the foundation for the federal judiciary—its organizational structure and jurisdiction. State judiciaries were left untouched and retained jurisdiction over cases not otherwise raising issues under federal law. Just as significantly, with the exception of diversity cases (in which citizens of one state sue another for monetary damages exceeding a certain amount), the act ensured that state courts would have **concurrent jurisdiction** with federal courts over many federal questions—questions involving the interpretation of the Constitution and federal law. That decision reflected a political and economic compromise. Anti-Federalists (those opposing the U.S. Constitution's ratification), who were mostly rural landowners, feared the creation of a federal judiciary and favored state courts that they thought would protect local economic interests. In addition, the act generally limited federal courts' jurisdiction to admiralty, forfeitures, penalties, federal criminal law, and cases in which the national government is a plaintiff. The restrictions on federal judicial power meant that the state courts, which were more numerous, would play a central role as the principal trial courts.[15]

Congress's decision to create lower federal courts was nonetheless a key political victory for Federalists (those who favored commercial nationalism and supported the Constitution's ratification). Federalists worried that all trials would occur in state courts and mercantile interests might be threatened as the nation grew. As a result, Congress created thirteen district (trial) courts, one in each state, along with three appellate or circuit courts in three geographical regions (eastern, southern, and middle). District courts heard mostly admiralty cases and were presided over by a single judge in quarterly sessions during the year. Circuit courts were specially convened to hear cases twice a year in each circuit's district. Their main function was to adjudicate diversity and criminal cases, but also appeals in certain cases from district courts. Notably, Congress did not authorize judgeships for the circuit courts. Instead, they were staffed by two Supreme Court justices who traveled to the location where the circuit court was held with a district judge and sat as a three-judge court. The practice became known as "riding circuit."

Although it was physically demanding and unpleasant for most justices, the measure was practical because justices had very few cases in the first decades of the new republic. It also contributed to the process of nation building at a time when many citizens were unfamiliar with, or even deeply distrustful of, the national government. Still, the justices resented the practice because they thought of themselves as "traveling postboys," who were placed in the uncomfortable position of having to hear the appeals of cases they originally heard while serving on circuit courts.[16]

The Judiciary Act of 1789 established the Supreme Court's membership at six (one chief justice and five associate justices). In addition to authorizing federal courts to make procedural rules and appoint clerks, the act set the Court's **appellate jurisdiction**—jurisdiction over appeals from the lower federal courts. However, Article III of the Constitution created the Court's **original jurisdiction**—specifically, what kinds of cases the Court would hear as a trial court or court of first instance. Subsequently, Section 13 of the Judiciary Act of 1789 appeared to expand the Court's original jurisdiction beyond "all Cases affecting Ambassadors, other public Ministers and Consuls, and those in which a State shall be Party" by giving it the power to issue writs of *mandamus*—writs ordering government officials to perform or stop some action. That provision proved contentious, and Chief Justice John Marshall (a Federalist), in the landmark ruling in *Marbury v. Madison* (1803),[17] declared Section 13 unconstitutional because it was deemed to expand the Court's original jurisdiction, as established in Article III, by mere legislation and thus violated the Supremacy Clause of Article VI of the Constitution. In addition, Section 25 of the Judiciary Act empowered the Court to hear appeals from the highest state court rulings that either invalidated federal law or upheld state law in opposition to federal law. By bringing state court judgments under federal appellate review, Section 25 was essentially an important restatement of the principle found in the Supremacy Clause.[18]

The Federal Judiciary's Evolution

After the American Revolution, more new states and territories emerged as the country rapidly expanded westward. The growth increased the federal courts' responsibilities and caseloads. Congress periodically enacted legislation that added more circuits and judges in response to rising litigation.[19] The difficulties were compounded by the acquisition of the Louisiana Purchase and the emergence of the modern business corporation, which both produced more commercial and maritime activity that expanded the role of federal courts. As a result, by 1863 the size of the federal judiciary had grown to ten circuits, and the total number of justices on the Supreme Court rose to ten, its highest level.[20]

President Abraham Lincoln in 1861 warned in his first inaugural address that "the country has outgrown our present judicial system." Of particular concern were the limitations of circuit courts and a backlog of Supreme Court cases. At least eight newly admitted states could not convene circuit courts with Supreme Court justices in attendance. Between 1860 and 1880, the Court's docket rose from 310 to 1,212 cases, and the Court had to decide all appeals. Moreover, lower federal courts faced similar caseload pressures. From 1873 to 1890, the caseloads of lower federal courts grew from 29,013 to 54,194 cases. As former Justice Felix Frankfurter observed, the prevalence of federal litigation indicated that the "fear of rivalry with state courts and respect for state sentiment were swept aside by the great impulse of national feeling born of the Civil War."[21]

In short, the Framers' understanding that federal courts would be largely "subsidiary courts" was gradually replaced by an acceptance of the need for a federal judiciary with "national administration."[22] Relief finally came with the Circuit Court of Appeals Act of 1891, or the so-called Evarts Act, named after Senator William M. Evarts (R-N.Y.). Besides eliminating the justices' circuit riding, the Evarts Act restructured the federal courts. It retained the circuit courts but abolished their appellate jurisdiction and created a new set of intermediate courts, the circuit courts of appeals. Organized in nine geographical circuits, each new circuit court of appeals was originally staffed with a circuit court judge, a district court judge, or a Supreme Court justice assigned to the circuit. These courts convened, though, with a quorum of two judges. In practice, the Evarts Act allowed the circuit courts of appeals to absorb the Court's caseload. In certain cases, the circuit courts of appeals could certify appeals to the Court for review, or, conversely, the Court had the option to grant review by **writ of *certiorari***— an order transferring the appellate record from the lower court, which the Court could simply deny and thus give it **discretionary jurisdiction**. Subsequent legislation, the Judicial Code of 1911, provided for appointing circuit judges to each new circuit court of appeals.

Although the reconfiguration of circuit courts helped ease the Supreme Court's workload, its caseload continued to rise in the early twentieth century. That increase led President William H. Taft to assert, in his second annual address in 1910, that "no man ought to have, as a matter of right, a review of his case by the Supreme Court." Rather, "he ought to be satisfied by one hearing before a court of first instance and one review by a court of appeals."[23] As president and later chief justice, Taft maintained that the state courts of last resort and the federal circuit courts both played a vital role in deflecting the bulk of federal appellate litigation away from the nation's highest court. In his view, the Supreme Court was overburdened by frivolous appeals and should decide only those cases with national social and legal significance.

Accordingly, Chief Justice Taft lobbied Congress to pass the Judiciary Act of 1925, which expanded the Court's discretionary jurisdiction. That act, known as the "Judges' Bill," was drafted by a committee of justices before it was sent to Capitol Hill. A milestone in judicial administration, it replaced many mandatory appeals (which the Court had to decide) with petitions for *certiorari* (which could simply be denied review)—hence the Court's greater power to manage its docket and to set its substantive agenda. By letting the Court "decide what to decide," Congress shifted a substantial portion of the Court's docket to the circuit courts of appeals, because the Court's expanded discretionary jurisdiction gave it the power to deny appeals of lower court decisions. The Judges' Bill, though, did not completely eliminate **mandatory jurisdiction** in certain instances. But it became the model for subsequent legislation that incrementally expanded the Court's discretionary jurisdiction. The Judicial Improvements and Access to Justice Act of 1988 finally eliminated virtually all remaining non-discretionary jurisdiction.

Congress also added lower court judges and administrative apparatuses in response to expanding caseloads. Federal caseloads in the district and circuit courts of appeals experienced especially sharp increases after 1960. Thus, Congress established federal magistrates at the district court level in order to reduce caseloads and created two new appellate courts (the Eleventh Circuit and the U.S. Court of Appeals for the Federal Circuit, in 1980 and in 1982, respectively). In addition, Congress took a number of steps to improve judicial administration—most notably with the creation of the Administrative Office of the U.S. Courts (1939) and the Federal Judicial Center (1969).[24] These agencies, discussed in this chapter's last section, are the basis for the contemporary federal judiciary's administrative support over matters of caseload management, human relations, judicial education, and budget, among other things.

The manner in which federal courts interact with state courts in reviewing cases and administering justice is analyzed next.

CONTEMPORARY JUDICIAL FEDERALISM: STATE AND FEDERAL COURTS

The United States dual judicial systems of state and federal courts that stands in contrast with unitary systems elsewhere around the world. U.S. courts are geographically based and predominantly hierarchical in structure (trial courts are first level, and appellate courts sit above them in successive or ascending tiers). In general, both state and federal courts organizationally have three levels, or tiers, and each court system has general and specialized courts.

With the exception of the Supreme Court and other specialized courts, federal appellate courts generally consist of large circuits covering several states within a region, and within each state are one or more district courts (depending on population and litigation). In contrast, state judiciaries have different types of trial, appellate, and special courts in each state. The federal system is also smaller in size and handles fewer cases than state judiciaries. As a result, state courts handle the bulk of the nation's judicial business because they are larger and more diverse, compared to the federal judiciary (see Figure 3.1). Although each state court system hears similar types of cases, there are notable differences. For example, while federal and state courts each interpret constitutions, only federal courts handle bankruptcy cases, and state courts exclusively review a majority of criminal and civil law matters, along with probate, family law, and traffic cases (see Table 3.1).

There are other key differences in how state and federal courts relate to each other. Although judicial power is divided between the two systems of courts, Article III and the Supremacy Clause in Article VI of the Constitution give the Supreme Court appellate jurisdiction over appeals of state supreme court rulings that conflict with federal law. Yet, in many areas, state and federal courts share concurrent jurisdiction (both have power to decide the same type of case); however, jurisdiction not expressly given to federal courts remains the province of the state courts. In addition, in those areas of constitutional law in which the Court declines review or in which a state court has based its decision solely on its own state constitution, the Court will not review or overturn a state court decision, even if it is inconsistent with prevailing federal law. Since the Court's ruling in *Michigan v. Long* (1983),[25] state court decisions must expressly make a "plain statement" that their decisions have "adequate and independent state grounds" for resting their decisions on their state constitution, not the Supreme Court's rulings or the Constitution. Otherwise, the Supreme Court presumes that state courts are interpreting federal law and therefore reverse state court decisions with which it disagrees.

| Figure 3.1 | **Dual System of Courts** |

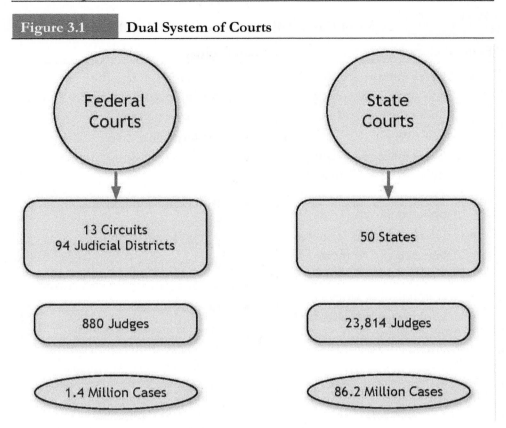

Federal Courts

State Courts

13 Circuits
94 Judicial Districts

50 States

880 Judges

23,814 Judges

1.4 Million Cases

86.2 Million Cases

Sources: U.S. Supreme Court petition data is excluded. Administrative Office of U.S. Courts, "Authorized Judgeships-From 1789 to Present," available from http://www.uscourts.gov/judges-judgeships/authorized-judgeships (last retrieved April 10, 2020); Administrative Office U.S. Courts, "Federal Judicial Caseload Statistics 2019 Tables (U.S. Federal Courts)," available from https://www.uscourts.gov/federal-judicial-caseload-statistics-2019-tables (last retrieved April 10, 2020); National Center for State Courts, "National Overview," available from http://www.courtstatistics.org/NCSC-Analysis/National-Overview.aspx (last retrieved April 10, 2020); National Center for State Courts, "State Court Organization," available from http://stage.ncsc.org/microsites/sco/home (last retrieved June 24, 2020).

Table 3.1	Types of Cases Adjudicated in Federal and State Courts
Federal Courts	**State Courts**
<ul><li>Cases interpreting the constitutionality of laws under the U.S. Constitution</li><li>Cases interpreting laws and treaties of the United States, ambassadors, and public ministers</li><li>Diversity claims (disputes between two or more states)</li><li>Admiralty law cases</li><li>Bankruptcy law cases</li></ul>	<ul><li>Cases interpreting the constitutionality of laws under state constitutions</li><li>Most criminal cases</li><li>Tort cases (personal injury)</li><li>Contract cases</li><li>Real estate and personal property cases</li><li>Family law (marriages, dissolutions, adoptions)</li><li>Probate, trusts, and wills cases</li><li>Juvenile law cases</li><li>Small claims or minor civil cases (e.g., landlord/tenant, creditor/debtor, municipal cases)</li><li>Traffic cases</li><li>Therapeutic or problem-solving cases (mental health, substance abuse, domestic violence, veterans' issues)</li></ul>

Sources: Administrative Office of the U.S. Courts, "Comparing Federal & State Courts," available at http://www.uscourts.gov/about-federal-courts/court-role-and-structure/comparing-federal-state-courts (last retrieved March 26, 2019); Integrated Justice Information Systems, Courts Advisory Committee," *Courts 101: An Understanding of the Court System* (October 2, 2012), available at https://www.fjc.gov/sites/default/files/2015/Courts%20101%20An%20Understanding%20of%20the%20Court%20System.pdf (last retrieved April 10, 2020), 2.

Moreover, state courts play a vital role in the administration of justice in construing their own state constitutional provisions and bills of rights. Although some state supreme courts review issues of state constitutional law in "lockstep" with the Supreme Court's rulings, studies show that state supreme courts are active in expanding individual rights in areas not recognized by the Supreme Court. State supreme courts have extended broader protection to the free exercise of religion, searches and seizures, capital punishment, the right to privacy, and equal protection. These examples of state judicial policymaking generate support and political opposition: In some states, ballot initiatives and constitutional amendments have been used to reverse them, and not all states have joined progressive inroads. Nonetheless, a "new judicial federalism" has emerged since the late 1970s, during which time the Supreme Court became more conservative, while some state supreme courts became more liberal in certain areas of civil rights and liberties. Even so, the reality is that judicial decision-making often cuts across conservative and liberal lines. For example, while conservatives may lament extending same-sex or transgender-friendly rulings in the states, the same conservatives also celebrate state rulings that retrench abortion rights, expand police authority in searches and seizures, or support increase corporate powers in avoiding environmental protection regulation. A similar political dynamic happens if the ideological impact of state judicial opinions is reversed.[26]

State Trial and Tribal Courts

The evolution of state judiciaries is closely tied to the diverse legal cultures and traditions of each state. Early state court organization drew from the multitier English and colonial judicial systems. Multiple trial and appellate courts existed in villages, towns, and cities: all had jurisdiction over specific areas of law, and trial and appellate judges interchanged their responsibilities frequently. As the nation grew, the demands on courts increased and became less efficient and lacked administrative cohesion. Especially at the trial court level, state judges generally lacked professionalism and were susceptible to the influences of local politics and bar associations.

Between the Civil War and the early twentieth century, reformers strove to make courts more autonomous and to simplify their operations. At the turn of the twentieth century, Harvard Law School dean Roscoe Pound raised these concerns by arguing that the nation's courts were "archaic," too numerous, and inefficient.[27] A reform movement, led by the American Judicature Society and the American Bar Association (ABA), aimed to improve judicial selection and retention methods (discussed in Chapter Four) and promote professional judicial administration through "unification." The early goals of unification focused on enhancing court performance through *consolidation* (structurally reorganizing courts), *centralization* (giving state chief justices or supreme courts authority over administrative processes and personnel), and *empowerment* (granting to state supreme courts or judicial councils, made up of state judges throughout the state, rulemaking authority). Many of these reforms became institutionalized in the late 1930s with the *Standards of Judicial Administration*, created by ABA president Arthur Vanderbilt and Judge John Parker.[28]

In the second half of the twentieth century, state courts continued to advance case management by increasing their staff and research support, adopting new technologies, and centralizing administrative control over their dockets. In light of that progress, the unification movement began to encompass budgeting goals that gave courts greater control over their financial operations.

In sum, since the 1950s, the **court unification movement** has fostered five interrelated trends in state judicial administration: (1) trial court consolidation, (2) centralized management, (3) centralized rulemaking, (4) centralized budgeting, and (5) state, rather than local, financing. Together, these reforms have enabled courts to reduce the impact of local politics on their operation and brought them under the administrative control of a statewide court of last resort or chief justice.[29] Organizations such as the Conference of State Court Administrators, the National Association for Court Management, and the National Center for State Courts also emerged. They assist state judiciaries in adopting bureaucratic practices and improving state court administration.

Still, the precise nature of court unification and whether it has resulted in better court performance remains subject to debate. Although many states claim they have unified court systems, not all state judiciaries have uniformly worked toward or achieved the same reform objectives. Consequently, state courts continue to be highly diverse in terms of their organizational structures and administrative operations, and each state court system remains to some extent subject to legislative or executive control.[30]

Single-Tier vs. Two-Tier Trial Courts

Today, the complexity of state courts is reflected in the diversity of their organizational structure, function, and funding. Eleven states and territories—California, Idaho, Illinois, Iowa, Maine, Minnesota, Montana, Vermont, the District of Columbia, Puerto Rico, and Guam—have **single-tier trial courts** that operate with general jurisdiction over a wide array of civil and criminal cases.[31] However, neither the single-tier trial court structure nor the source of funding is uniform. An illustration of a single-tier court structure that has a three-level hierarchy of trial and appellate courts is found in Illinois (see Figure 3.2).

The remaining forty-two states retain **two-tier trial courts** that are split into one or more sets of courts of general and limited jurisdiction (discussed more in the next section). Depending on the state, these trial courts handle a wide range of legal disputes, including general criminal and civil matters, as well as more specialized cases such as probate, juvenile, family, small claims, and traffic violation. Typically, both tiers in two-tier trial court system have jurisdiction over a similar category of cases and the tier in which the case is adjudicated depends upon the case's complexity, case type, the case's monetary value, and geographical region.[32] As with single-tier trial court forums, there is little organizational or administrative consistency across two-tier court systems. Many states, such as Ohio, using two-tier systems have a hierarchical framework of trial courts that are split between different general jurisdiction and limited jurisdiction courts and two types of appellate courts (intermediate appellate courts and courts of last resort) (see Figure 3.3).[33]

Figure 3.2	**Illinois Single-Tier Trial Court System**

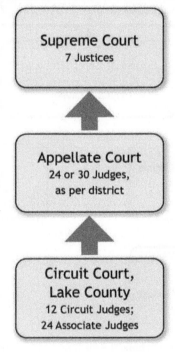

Source: Nineteenth Judicial Circuit Court of Lake County, "Organizational Chart of the Illinois Courts," available from http://www.19thcircuitcourt.state.il.us/DocumentCenter/View/69/Illinois-Courts-Organizational-Chart-PDF?bidId= (retrieved April 10, 2020).

Figure 3.3	Ohio's Two-Tier Trial Court System

Supreme Court
(Chief Justice and 6 Justices)

Court of Appeals
(12 Districts with 3 Judge Panels)

Courts of Common Pleas
(Civil, Criminal, Juvenile, Family, Probate Cases)

Municipal and County Courts
(Misdemeanor, Traffic, Minor Civil Cases)

Court of Claims
(Suits Against State)

Mayor's Courts
(Local Traffic, Ordinances Cases)

Source: The Supreme Court of Ohio, "Judicial System Structure," available from http://www.supreme court.ohio.gov/judsystem/ (retrieved April 10, 2020).

Limited Jurisdiction Courts

Most people only encounter the judicial process in a court of **limited jurisdiction**—that is, trial courts that deal with a narrow set of legal issues, such as traffic, minor civil, and less serious (non-felony) criminal cases. Often litigants choose to represent themselves (*pro se*) in these courts. Most are simply called *municipal or district courts*; at one time, they were typically known as *police courts, or justice of the peace* courts, usually staffed by non-lawyers and handling disputes between landlords and tenants, for instance, or domestic violence cases.[34]

There are approximately fourteen to sixteen thousand limited jurisdiction courts in forty-six states. Only four states (California, Illinois, Iowa, and Minnesota), plus the District of Columbia, do not have them. Caseload statistics show that 64 percent of the 86.2 million filings in two-tier state courts were processed in these courts, and of those, 61 percent were traffic cases. Many states also use limited jurisdiction courts to adjudicate other civil matters, including probate (Alabama, Michigan, Rhode Island), family (Delaware, New York, South Carolina), and juvenile (Georgia, Nebraska, Tennessee) cases. In a few states, they deal with other kinds of disputes, such as workers' compensation (Nebraska), tax (New Jersey), land (Massachusetts), and claims made against state government (New York and Ohio). Two states (Louisiana and Ohio) still retain mayor's courts that adjudicate traffic, drunken driving, and other misdemeanor cases. With high caseloads and because they have frequent contact with the public, limited jurisdiction courts are vitally important in generating revenue for localities and funding court operations.[35]

General Jurisdiction Courts

Other trial courts have **general jurisdiction**. Although they are most commonly referred to as *superior, district, or circuit courts*, states use a wide variety of other classifications. There are approximately 3,747 general jurisdiction state courts. Their dockets primarily consist of serious criminal and civil cases. Caseload data indicates that 17 percent of all case filings in two tier courts were processed in these courts. The right to a jury trial may be offered, but it generally depends on the kind of dispute and whether it involves a serious civil or criminal action. These courts share some similarities with limited jurisdiction courts. For example, some states give them authority over specific areas, such as probate (Indiana and Tennessee), family disputes (Kentucky), workers' compensation (Montana), tax (Arizona and Oregon), and even water (Colorado and Montana) claims.[36] Still, there are important differences as well. In general jurisdiction courts, litigants are afforded more procedural rights because the risk of liberty and out-of-pocket loss is greater. Furthermore, litigants generally may appeal, which is often not possible in courts of limited jurisdiction.

The subject matter on state trial courts' dockets is shown in Table 3.2. Notably, in handling nearly 55 million cases, or 65 percent, of all state court filings, limited jurisdiction courts in two tier systems are the "workhorses" of the state judicial system. In those courts, and in single tier court systems, most judges hear traffic cases; whereas, two tier general jurisdiction courts process roughly the same amount of criminal cases but a greater number of civil, domestic relations and juvenile matters. Even though general jurisdiction and single tier courts handle far fewer cases than courts of limited jurisdiction, the fines and fees they collect make them key sources of revenue. Also, they are no less important in adjudicating serious civil and criminal matters that may be appealed to a higher court.

Table 3.2	State Trial Court Docket		
	Single Tier (of 15.4 Million Cases)	**General Jurisdiction** (of 14.9 Million Cases)	**Limited Jurisdiction** (of 55.8 Million Cases)
Traffic	63%	16%	62%
Criminal	17%	21%	22%
Civil	14%	34%	15%
Domestic Relations	5%	23%	1%
Juvenile	1%	6%	Less than 1%

Note: N = 86.2 million cases filed in 2015. Totals may not sum due to rounding error.

Source: "Caseload Composition, Total by Tier, 2015" in Robert C. LaFountain, Shauna M. Strickland, and Kathryn A. Holt, and Kathryn J. Genthon, *Examining the Work of State Courts: An Overview of 2015 State Court Caseloads* (Williamsburg, Va.: National Center for State Courts, 2016), 3.

Tribal Courts

It bears noting that roughly a third of the states have tribal courts. Native American and Alaska Native tribes operate their own courts due to a unique combination of federal and state law. Federal treaties, congressional legislation, administrative regulations, and court rulings have determined the scope of their jurisdiction. In addition, some states, and in over five hundred American Indian and Alaskan Native federally-recognized tribes, enter into compacts and other agreements governing concurrent areas of legal policy, such as law enforcement, health care, taxation, gaming, and environmental conservation. Thus, while the scope of tribal sovereignty remains based on federal law, state governments also regulate Indian affairs and shape the contours of tribal justice.[37]

Tribal courts, nevertheless, exist independently of the state and federal judiciaries. Early Supreme Court rulings, *Cherokee Nation v. Georgia* (1831) and *Worcester v. Georgia* (1832), established that tribes are "domestic dependent nations" and that state law does not apply to Indian reservations. Likewise, *Ex Parte Crow Dog* (1883) held that federal courts do not have jurisdiction over criminal cases involving acts committed on Indian land. In 1883, however, the federal Bureau of Indian Affairs (BIA) created the "Court of Indian Offenses" or "Courts of Federal

Regulations" (CFR Courts) to handle minor criminal actions and to adjudicate civil disputes between tribal members in accordance with federal law. Subsequently, the Indian Reorganization Act of 1934 recognized Indian tribes' authority to adopt their own constitutions and establish their own laws and justice systems.[38] While some tribes continue to use CFR Courts, most adopted tribal constitutions that created diverse tribal justice systems—some of which incorporate the adversarial and restorative justice models of federal and state courts. In this sense, adversarial conflicts are resolved with cooperative solutions that help restore balance to the individuals and the community. Consequently, the boundaries of tribal court jurisdiction remain in flux and controversial. In 1953, Congress gave to the states (and withdrew federal) authority over criminal and civil law disputes occurring on tribal lands. Furthermore, a series of Supreme Court rulings since the 1970s have limited tribal sovereignty and judicial powers. More recently, at the urging of the Obama administration, Congress enacted the Tribal Law and Order Act of 2010. That law responded to a growing problem of violent crime on Indian lands. It has increased federal court prosecutions of serious crimes, promoted coordination of federal criminal investigations with tribal prosecutors, and expanded tribal court powers to impose enhanced felony sentences.[39]

Intermediate State Appellate Courts

Appellate courts are different than trial courts because they usually decide issues of law—what the law is or should be—instead of adjudicating the factual circumstances underlying a dispute. They also are distinct with respect to how they review cases. While all of the justices of a state court of last resort typically sit as a full *en banc* court, usually an intermediate appellate court decides cases by a **panel** of three randomly selected judges from that court.[40] In short, appellate courts are collegial entities that work in small groups, unlike trial courts that typically have only one judge.

Like state courts of last resort, intermediate appellate courts primarily serve to correct legal errors in lower courts, such as when a trial judge gives improper jury instructions or wrongly excludes evidence. Moreover, 90 percent of their decisions are not appealed to the state's court of last resort. Therefore, they are the *de facto* courts of last resort for most litigants, which give them a significant policymaking role in state judicial systems.[41]

Thirty-seven states and Puerto Rico have intermediate appellate courts. The remaining states and the District of Columbia do not, due to lower caseloads. In states that have intermediate appellate courts, they function as screening tribunals that help reduce the caseloads of state courts of last resort.[42] Furthermore, the structure of these courts, and how jurisdiction is divided among the courts, varies extensively. Although most states with a middle-tier court have a single intermediate appellate court, there are some that retain two, such as Alabama, Tennessee, Indiana, and Pennsylvania. Of those states, Alabama and Tennessee have two separate criminal and civil intermediate appellate courts, whereas Indiana has a court of appeals and a separate tax court; Pennsylvania has bifurcated midlevel appellate courts but under different court designations.[43]

Roughly 263,000 appeals are filed in state courts. Of those, intermediate appellate courts handled 71 percent because they were **appeal by right** cases—mandatory appeals—that may not be denied review. Notably, almost three-quarters of the intermediate appellate docket are appeals by right cases. These courts cannot control their docket, like courts of last resort, which generally have the discretion to pick which cases to hear, because most of their cases are discretionary **appeals by permission**. Also, middle-tier appellate court jurisdiction varies from state to state, though mandatory appeals primarily involve criminal, civil, and administrative agency cases. With little or no power to shape their dockets, intermediate appellate courts are truly the engines of state appellate courts that confront extremely heavy caseloads.[44]

Despite large caseloads, appellate courts are remarkably efficient. They typically affirm lower court rulings, and a large percentage of their rulings are a result of a combination of pre-argument dismissals, summary memoranda or orders, and signed judicial opinions. Indeed, one study found that nearly half of the twenty-two intermediate appellate courts had a 100 percent clearance rate of mandatory appellate caseloads.[45] In other words, although they guarantee litigants the right to appeal, intermediate appellate courts have a filtering function that enables a state's highest court to adjudicate only cases raising the most important questions of legal and public policy.

State Courts of Last Resort

Although there are only fifty states, there are fifty-four courts of last resort. Two states (Oklahoma and Texas) have two separate courts for civil and criminal cases. While most states identify them as "supreme courts," some, like New York, refer to them as "Courts of Appeals" or other designations like "Supreme Judicial Court" or "Supreme Court of Appeals". Courts of last resort provide a second level of review and a final opportunity for appeal. In terms of workload, state supreme courts have substantial dockets and can issue up to an average of 112 full written opinions per year. Moreover, besides deciding appeals, courts of last resort perform other administrative and supervisory roles within the legal system. How the Vermont Supreme Court is structured and operates is good illustration: it creates rules that govern court procedures, and it superintends the entire state judiciary (through a state court administrator) as well as overseeing the processes by which lawyers gain admission to the bar and how they are disciplined for ethical violations.[46]

State courts of last resort, like intermediate appellate courts, are collegial courts that perform their judicial functions in small groups. Most sit *en banc*, though some states use panels of rotating judges, as intermediate courts do in many states.[47] Yet, there are significant differences. Courts of last resort handle fewer appeals and have greater discretion over the cases they hear. They may review a large proportion of criminal appeals and resolve conflicts arising from lower state courts; and, they interpret the meaning and application of state constitutions.[48] Moreover, although intermediate appellate courts and courts of last resort both hear mandatory appeals, courts of last resort do so much more infrequently. Furthermore, a large percentage of special appeals bypass the middle-tier courts altogether because they are directly reviewable by the state's highest court, such as death penalty appeals. Also, courts of last resort handle slightly more "original proceedings" and miscellaneous appeals, such as election disputes, specialized writs (**habeas corpus**, **mandamus**, and **quo warranto** proceedings), or bar and judiciary proceedings, although some of those cases are directly filed with the highest court in some states.[49]

In addition, state courts of last resort are significant policymakers. Of the approximately seven thousand cases they annually decide, a vast majority of their rulings remain undisturbed; only one-half of one percent of their decisions are reviewed by the U.S. Supreme Court.[50]

Federal Courts

Congress has reorganized the federal judiciary's structure, jurisdiction, and operation through periodic legislation. Still, the federal judiciary's original three-tier organization has remained intact. At the apex is the Supreme Court of the United States, sitting above federal courts of appeals and district (trial) courts. There are thirteen appellate circuits: eleven numbered circuits spanning twelve geographic areas covering all fifty states, one circuit for the District of Columbia Circuit, and one—the Court of Appeals for the Federal Circuit in Washington, D.C.—with nationwide jurisdiction over certain specialized areas of litigation (see Figure 3.4). The smallest is the First Circuit in the Northeast, and the largest is the

Ninth Circuit, covering multiple western states the size of Western Europe. The typical federal appellate court has between twelve and fifteen judges.

U.S. District Courts

Federal district courts are the federal judiciary's trial courts. There are ninety-four federal district courts, with at least one in each state, staffed by 677 judges (along with some who have taken senior status and continue to hear cases on a part-time basis). District court judges are appointed by the president and confirmed by the Senate. Although they generally decide cases alone or with a jury, in certain cases—involving voting rights and election cases—they may sit in three-judge panels. In addition to authority over bankruptcy cases, they have general jurisdiction over federal questions arising from the interpretation of federal statutes and regulations, treaties, and the Constitution, as well as diversity cases (between citizens of different states or between U.S. citizens and those of another country, if the lawsuit claims $75,000 or more). Caseload date indicates that 50 percent of all private civil cases in district courts raised federal questions, and only 35 percent were diversity cases.[51]

| Figure 3.4 | Geographical Boundaries of the U.S. Courts of Appeals |

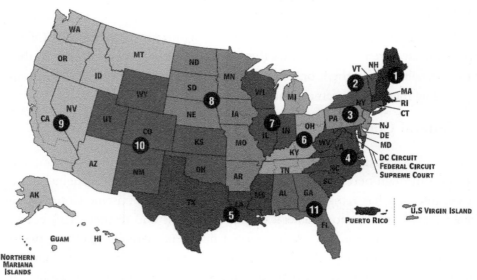

Geographic Boundaries
of United States Courts of Appeals and United States District Courts

Source: Administrative Office of U.S. Courts, available at http://www.uscourts.gov/sites/default/files/u.s._federal_courts_circuit_map_1.pdf (last retrieved August 24, 2020).

District courts have original and **general jurisdiction**. District judges may sit with a jury or alone in a bench trial. As trial courts, they adjudicate far more cases than federal appellate courts. They annually review about 390,896 civil and criminal case filings, whereas federal circuit appellate courts only handle about 49,421 per year.[52] Also, since 1960, district court dockets have steadily grown, and in turn so has the number of authorized judgeships. Over the past forty years, roughly 80 percent of their dockets have been civil cases (see Table 3.3). Notably, cases involving the interpretation of federal statutes represent over 60 percent of all civil actions. As well, a significant part of district court judges' time is spent hearing prisoner petitions and civil rights claims. The latter tend to drain judicial resources because most are frivolous writs alleging constitutional deprivations; nonetheless, some prove especially important and deserve to be heard (like *habeas corpus* actions asserting illegal confinement). The remaining types of civil cases involve ordinary contract, tort, and real property claims.[53]

A substantial portion of the district courts' criminal law docket consists of handling drug, immigration, and property offenses. Miscellaneous criminal actions, including general offenses like bribery, extortion, and gambling; sex crimes; and other offenses relating to firearms, explosives, and perjury or contempt, also consume a good deal of district judges' time. Less frequently, they preside over prosecutions of violent crimes, such as homicide, armed robbery, and assault.[54]

As in state trial courts, most cases in district courts are disposed of before trial. In cases involving court action, eighty-six percent of civil filings are settled at the pretrial stage. Another 13 percent end during or after pretrial proceedings, and only 1 percent terminate at trial or afterward. A similar pattern appears with criminal cases, but with the important difference that a defendant's guilty plea, instead of a negotiated settlement, is the basis for ending the proceedings. Only eight percent of criminal defendants are acquitted or have their prosecutions dismissed at the trial level; and, of those who are found guilty, ninety-seven percent of criminal convictions result from guilty pleas. Less than 2 percent of criminal convictions come after a jury or bench (or, acting only with a judge only) trial. Thus, it is a common misconception that citizens usually get their day in court by having a trial.[55]

Table 3.3			**U.S. District Court Caseload and Docket Composition, 1970–2018**			
			Civil Cases		Criminal Cases	
Year	Total Cases	Authorized Judgeships	Filings	Percentage of Docket	Filings	Percentage of Docket
1970	127,280	401	87,321	68.6	39,959	31.3
1980	200,461	516	171,074	85.3	29,387	14.6
1990	265,048	575	217,013	81.8	48,035	18.1
2000	322,262	655	259,517	80.5	62,745	19.5
2010	361,323	678	282,895	78.3	78,428	21.7
2012	349,745	677	278,442	79.6	71,303	20.4
2019	390,896	677	296,691	75.9	94,205	24.0

Note: U.S. bankruptcy, post-conviction supervision, and pretrial services cases are excluded. All percentages are subject to rounding error.

Sources: Administrative Office of the U.S. Courts, *Judicial Facts and Figures* (Tables 1.1, 4.1, and 5.1), available at www.uscourts.gov (last retrieved March 26, 2019) (for years 1970 to 2012); and, Administrative Office of the U.S. Courts, "Table JCI-U.S. Federal Courts, Work of the Federal Judiciary (12-Month Period Ending December 31, 2010, 2015, 2018 and 2019)," available at www.uscourts.gov (last retrieved April 11, 2020) (for 2019).

In processing their caseloads, district court judges work with other judicial divisions and personnel. These include territorial courts, U.S. magistrates, and bankruptcy courts. District courts in U.S. territories are Article IV courts, whereas U.S. district courts are created under Article III of the U.S. Constitution. District court judges serving in the territories (Northern Mariana Islands and Guam in the Ninth Circuit, and Virgin Islands in the Third Circuit) are placed on the bench by presidential appointment and Senate approval for renewable ten-year terms. The U.S. District Court for Puerto Rico was a territorial court between 1900 and 1966. After 1966, Congress established that its judges would get Article III protections, including life tenure. The American Samoa, a U.S. territory, has a High Court of American Samoa and a local district court.[56]

U.S. Magistrate Judges

Historically, U.S. magistrates filled a need of federal courts in unique ways. In 1793, Congress gave circuit courts the power to appoint individuals to take bail in criminal cases; they worked only part-time and were paid from fees. Then, in 1896, Congress institutionalized the position by giving district court judges the power to appoint "U.S. commissioners" and established a uniform fee schedule for their services. Over the next century, their responsibilities grew to the point that further reform was necessary. In 1968, Congress enacted the Federal Magistrates Act, replacing the fee system with salaries and requiring "magistrates" to have been admitted to the bar.[57]

Magistrate judges serve in either a full-time or a part-time capacity for an eight- or four-year term, respectively. There are 531 authorized full-time magistrates, along with some forty or so part-time judges. They are appointed by district judges, but their appointments are processed by a citizen's merit nomination screening commission. Since Congress has not limited the number of times a magistrate judge can be reappointed, it is not unusual for them to stay on for long periods of time.[58]

Although they do not enjoy the prestige or reputation of Article III judges, magistrate judges play a key role in helping district courts manage their caseloads. Collectively, they dispose of more than a million cases. Since the vast majority of cases do not go to trial, often times the only interactions counsel and clients have in the federal litigation process is with magistrate judges, who handle much of the criminal misdemeanor and civil trial docket. With consent of the parties, they assign cases for trial, issue warrants, conduct pretrial hearings, and set bail in criminal cases. They also have the power to try minor criminal offenses; however, their decisions may be appealed to a district court judge.[59]

U.S. Bankruptcy Courts

Besides magistrates, bankruptcy judges also play a crucial part in handling lower court cases. Bankruptcy courts are linked to federal district courts, and handle debtor-creditor claims emerging from personal and corporate bankruptcies. Although they are considered subunits of federal district courts, they are anomalous because bankruptcy judges do not have Article III status. In 1978, Congress enacted a new bankruptcy code that created new U.S. bankruptcy courts as Article I legislative courts. They were vested with broad jurisdiction over all civil actions arising under the bankruptcy code. Yet, these judges were not given Article III life tenure or salary protections, even though they are Presidential appointees, and they are confirmed by the Senate for fourteen-year terms. In *Northern Pipeline Construction Company v. Marathon Pipeline Company* (1982),[60] the Supreme Court held that it was unconstitutional for bankruptcy courts to exercise jurisdiction over state law claims because the principle of separation of powers was violated by Congress vesting Article III jurisdiction in Article I judges who lacked the status of Article III judges.

In response to that decision, Congress enacted the Bankruptcy Amendments and Federal Judgeship Act of 1984. It fixed the constitutional problems in two ways. First, while ensuring that the district courts retained jurisdiction, the law let the district courts delegate judicial power to the bankruptcy court for the purpose of handling bankruptcy litigation. Second, the act transferred the power to appoint bankruptcy judges from the president to federal appellate courts. The changes remain important because they eliminated the Article III basis for exercising bankruptcy jurisdiction by Article I judges over "core" proceedings in bankruptcy, thereby conforming to *Northern Pipeline*. "Non-core" bankruptcy matters are referred to U.S. district courts. As a result, bankruptcy judges are now considered "units" of the district courts and have the status of judicial officers instead of Article III judges, because they have limited tenure and no salary protection.[61]

Bankruptcy judges play a huge role in an overloaded bankruptcy system. In 2005, Congress enacted the Bankruptcy Abuse Prevention and Consumer Protection Act (BAPCPA), a major reform designed to increase debtor accountability and restrict opportunistic or abusive filings. Credit card companies, banks, and various creditor organizations lobbied extensively for the change. Unlike past law, the act requires debtors filing consumer bankruptcies to repay some of their obligations if they have the financial ability to do so. For certain bankruptcies, the law requires a financial "means test" to see if a debtor is eligible to file. BAPCPA also increased the cost of filing bankruptcies by imposing new fees and requiring more paperwork, as well as expanded the list of nondischargeable debts and imposed penalties on filers providing inaccurate financial information.[62] Although the 2005 act created twenty-eight new judgeships to help administer the new requirements, some feared that the law would result in a sharp increase in bankruptcy filings. But, BAPCPA's operation and effect has probably reduced bankruptcy filings. Still, whether BAPCPA has done more harm than good in creating more obstacles for consumers filing for bankruptcies remains an open question, subject to ongoing debate.[63]

Other Specialized Lower Federal Courts and Tribunals

There are a number of other courts and tribunals performing federal trial functions. They have specialized jurisdiction over cases relating to international trade disagreements, public contracts, veteran benefits appeals, taxpayer disputes, and national security wiretaps. The U.S. Court of International Trade, an Article III court, sits in New York and is staffed by nine judges who review civil cases over import transactions and international trade. The U.S. Court of Federal Claims, an Article I court in Washington, D.C., has sixteen judges who serve fifteen-year terms and adjudicate monetary claims over government contracts, tax refunds, Fifth Amendment "takings" cases, civilian and military pay claims, intellectual property, and Indian tribe cases. The U.S. Tax Court, also an Article I court, is also located in the nation's capital. It has nineteen judges and hears taxpayer disputes.[64]

One other specialized forum that sits in Washington, D.C. is the Judicial Panel on Multidistrict Litigation, which consolidates multiple civil actions that are pending in one or more federal judicial districts by transferring them to the appropriate district court for resolution. Created by Congress and staffed by seven judges appointed by the Supreme Court's chief justice, the panel deals with complex civil actions ranging from airplane crashes to patent infringements and securities fraud.[65]

Finally, two other courts, the Alien Terrorist Removal Court (ATRC) and the Foreign Intelligence Surveillance Court (FISC), were created in response to terrorism. Enacted by Congress in 1996, a year after the Oklahoma City federal court bombing, the ATRC is a "court of deportation" with five district court judges authorized to order the deportation of a resident alien suspected of being a terrorist. Yet, the ATRC has never been used.[66]

Of more significance in the post-9/11 era is the FISC, an Article III court created by the Foreign Intelligence Surveillance Act of 1978 (FISA). Because of Supreme Court rulings and the disclosure of executive abuse in gathering domestic intelligence in the 1960s civil rights era, Congress enacted the FISA in order to control the surveillance operations of agencies charged with protecting national security. Under the act, the FISC initially had authority to review government applications for electronic surveillance. However, over time, its jurisdiction was expanded to include reviewing government applications for conducting physical searches, using pen registers, and orders requiring the production of business records deemed relevant to criminal prosecutions. Notably, due to its secretive nature and the political salience of its operations in the post-9/11 era, there has been growing interest in reforming FISC in recent years. Notably, legislation enacted in 2008, the FISA Amendments Act, created some additional safeguards to protect U.S. citizens and other persons living abroad who are targeted for surveillance in national security investigations.[67] Furthermore, even though Congress extended two controversial USA Patriot Act provisions that authorized roving wiretaps and so-called "lone wolf" surveillance, the USA Freedom Act (2015) outlawed the bulk collection of data of American's telephone records and Internet-generated metadata as well as providing more oversight of FISC activities, including the imposition of new reporting requirements and permitting the designation of a panel of "amicus curiae" advocates to represent the public's interest in cases of legal significance.[68] Finally, as discussed in Chapter One (Contemporary Controversies over Courts: The Politics of Secret Foreign Intelligence Surveillance Court During the Trump Administration), the operation and legitimacy of the FBI and FISC was thrust into the public spotlight and political realm when Republicans and Democrats sparred over the issue of whether the secret court abused its authority in sanctioning surveillance of Carter Page, a former Trump campaign adviser who was at the center of allegations that Trump colluded with the Russians in the 2016 presidential race.[69]

The FISC performs an appellate function with eleven district court judges, who are assigned by the chief justice of the Supreme Court and come from seven different circuits. Ordinarily, a FISC judge acts alone in making decisions, but the court may sit as a whole as well. The FISC is also different because it operates with little transparency: one of the FISC judges review cases for a one-week period, on a rotating basis, in a secure courtroom in a federal courthouse in Washington, D.C. Not only are court sessions held behind closed doors, but they are held *ex parte*—that is, only the government presents its case, and after the hearing, the FISC's written opinions are generally not available to the public. The role and implications of the FISC in the war against terrorism assumed greater significance after 9/11 when President George W. Bush authorized, without full disclosure to Congress, the National Security Agency (NSA) to conduct domestic wiretaps on anyone suspected of communicating with terrorists abroad without utilizing the FISC's approval for such wiretaps. Subsequently, in light of disclosures—made by WikiLeaks founder Julian Assange and former NSA whistle-blower Edward Snowden—of classified documents detailing surveillance activities on U.S. citizens domestically and across the globe, critics (on the left and the right) persuaded Congress to explore possible reforms that would make the FISC more transparent and accountable.[70]

U.S. Courts of Appeals

The U.S. circuit courts of appeals, with 179 authorized judges, are located in eleven regional circuit courts, plus the D.C. Circuit and the Court of Appeals for the Federal Circuit. All have general jurisdiction spanning civil, criminal, and administrative law appeals. But the D.C. Circuit has a high concentration of agency cases because of its location in the nation's capital. The Court of Appeals for the Federal Circuit, also in Washington, D.C., review appeals in international trade, government contracts, and cases involving claims against the government for monetary damages. Another special area of the Court of Appeals for the

Federal Circuit is patent and intellectual property appeals from district courts and the U.S. Patent and Trademark Office.[71]

As with other federal judgeships, the president, with the Senate's confirmation, appoints circuit court judges. They ordinarily hear appeals in panels of three randomly selected judges. Like state appellate courts, they correct the errors of federal trial courts, establish a uniform body of national law, and function to screen out cases for the Supreme Court. They also do not determine the facts of a case and show great deference to lower courts. As a collegial court, circuit judges engage in a dynamic process of small-group decision making. They function thus as "courts of last resort for the great mass of federal litigants" because only a very few of their decisions are reviewed by the Supreme Court.[72]

Federal circuit courts may convene ***en banc*** (the entire court) to reconsider a three-judge panel's ruling. The Federal Rules of Appellate Procedure permit *en banc* review if a majority of a circuit's judges agree that it "is necessary to secure or maintain uniformity of the court's decisions," or if "the proceeding involves a question of exceptional importance." Ordinarily, the party losing the appeal must petition for an *en banc* rehearing; however, the vast majority of such petitions are denied. Despite their infrequency, *en banc* judicial opinions represent an appellate court's collective judgment and resolve intra-circuit court conflicts among three-judge panels.[73]

Judicial workload statistics illustrate the vital role federal appellate courts play in nationalizing federal law uniformity over a wide range of matters. Annually, circuit courts review about a total of 49,977 appeals. Roughly three-fourths of their docket consists of civil and criminal appeals from the district courts, with the remaining appeals coming from federal agencies (12 percent), original proceedings (10 percent), and bankruptcy courts (1 percent), More than half of the appeals from district courts are civil actions, and the remainder are criminal appeals. Because a substantial portion of the district courts' caseloads involve civil prisoner petitions and criminal drug cases, a majority of the federal appeals courts' dockets are prisoner and drug-related appeals.[74]

Caseload pressures affect circuit court decisional practices and the time it takes for appeals to reach final disposition after filing. During the last fifty years, circuit court dockets grew by 1,436 percent—from about four thousand appeals in 1960 to the present level of close to fifty to sixty thousand appeals per year. According to some estimates, during that time filings rose from 57 to 357 filings per judgeship—almost a 600 percent increase. Burgeoning caseloads also created delay in case processing. In 1980, the average time of case termination was between six and nine months, but today it is closer to a year. Notably, swelling dockets have not been accompanied by an increase in the number of authorized judgeships. Consequently, circuit courts now rely upon a large contingent of central staff attorneys to process appeals; roughly 75 percent of appeals are denied oral argument, and only 15 percent of appeals result in published opinions. Significantly, a majority of appeals are decided by central staff in unpublished rulings that cannot be used by lawyers seeking to apply precedents in future litigation. Thus, the practical solutions devised to meet high caseloads have arguably hurt the legal system because only a small percentage of litigants get published decisions from full appellate review.[75]

U.S. Courts of Appeals with Limited Jurisdiction

Other specialized appellate courts deal with military justice and national security. The most notable are three Article I courts: the U.S. Court of Appeals for Veterans Claims, the Court of Appeals for the Armed Forces, and the Foreign Intelligence Surveillance Court of Review (FISCR). The Veterans Claims court has seven judges that are appointed by the president for fifteen-year terms and handles veteran disability, survivor, and education benefits appeals. Staffed by five civilian judges through presidential appointments for fifteen-year terms, the Armed Forces court reviews court-martial convictions and referrals from the Judge Advocate General. The third court, the FISCR, is composed of three district or appeals court judges that are appointed for seven year terms by the Chief Justice of the Supreme Court of the United States, and it reviews appeals from the denial of applications from FISC. Still, it is rarely used as roughly 90 percent of FISC (trial court) surveillance applications are granted annually.[76]

U.S. Supreme Court

At the top of the federal judiciary is the Supreme Court of the United States. It resolves legal disputes arising from both federal and state courts. Approximately 65 percent of the Court's docket comes from federal courts, and about 30 percent comes from state courts. In managing its docket, the court's role has changed over time in response to its expanding caseload. Before 1925, the Court's primary function was to decide cases in order to correct legal errors below, but Congress gave it discretionary jurisdiction and now decides what to decide. The Court now only grants review in cases involving "substantial questions of federal law" and inter-circuit conflicts among federal appellate courts. Because it has the discretion to set its agenda, the Supreme Court "assume[s] the role of super legislature."[77]

The Court sits with one chief justice and eight associate justices. The chief justice, presently John Roberts, Jr., is also the titular head of the entire federal judiciary. In addition to performing their regular judicial duties, each associate justice serves as circuit justice for one or more of the regional circuits. Each justice hires up to four law clerks, who screen *writ of certiorari* petitions, perform legal research, prepare "bench memos" (used in preparation for oral argument), and draft opinions. The justices have their own conference and robing rooms, and lawyers practicing before the Court have a separate lounge. The solicitor general, a frequent litigator representing the federal government, has its own office. The Court has a library, a barber shop, a museum, dining, and its own basketball court. The Marshal's Office is in charge of building security and public safety. Like other government institutions, it has a website (www.supremecourt.gov), along with a public information office for access to filings, briefs, and opinions.[78]

The Court has original and appellate jurisdiction. It adjudicates cases as specified in Article III—its original jurisdiction—between certain parties (e.g., ambassadors, public ministers, and consuls, and between two states) and cases arising from its appellate jurisdiction over appeals from state and lower federal courts. Filings are inspected by the Clerk of the Court for procedural correctness in accordance with the Court's rules and placed in one of three categories of the docket: paid cases, unpaid cases, and original proceedings. About one-quarter of the filings are put on what is somewhat ambiguously termed the "appellate docket" because they are paid cases (which require a $300 fee and another $100 for oral argument if granted). Most of the remaining three-quarters go on the miscellaneous docket, which includes unpaid cases or **in forma pauperis** petitions from indigents for which the filing fee is waived. A handful of cases come on original jurisdiction and are decided after a special master has made a recommendation on how it should be decided. The Supreme Court's docket between 2014 and 2018 is shown in Figure 3.5. Notably, only a fraction of all petitions are given **plenary consideration**. Of the nearly 5,800 cases on the docket, in the 2017–2018 Term only 85 cases were granted plenary review, 56 were decided without oral argument, and 69 cases were decided by full written opinions.[79]

Cases come to the Court in basically three ways: as a writ for certification, as a mandatory appeal, or as a petition for a *writ of certiorari*. A *writ of certification* is reserved for the unusual situation where a lower federal court asks the Court to clarify a legal issue. Once but no longer, most cases came as mandatory appeals, which the Court had to decide. But as discussed earlier, the Court's burgeoning caseload led Congress in a series of legislation to replace mandatory appeals with petitions for *certiorari*, which the Court may simply deny unless four of nine justices vote to grant *cert.*—in an informal practice known as "the rule of four." Congress's expansion of the Court's discretionary jurisdiction gave it the power to manage its docket in deciding what to decide, in terms of both how many cases to grant and what substantive issues are addressed.[80] As an institutional norm, the Court's discretionary jurisdiction enables it to decide only those cases that have broad national legal and political importance. Notably, since the 1990s, the Court has reduced the number of cases given full consideration (with briefs and oral argument).[81] About thirty years ago, the Court routinely had about 5,000 cases on its docket and decided between 150 and 180, about 3 percent of those filings. Today, the docket is considerably larger, but the Roberts Court gives full consideration to only about 80 cases per year, less than 1 percent of its docket.

| Figure 3.5 | U.S. Supreme Court Membership and Docket Composition |

The Roberts Court

G.H.W. Bush	Clinton	G.W. Bush	Obama	Trump
Clarence Thomas (1991)	Ruth Bader Ginsburg (1993)	Chief Justice John Roberts, Jr. (2005)	Sonia Sotomayor (2009)	Neil Gorsuch (2017)
	Stephen Breyer (1994)	Samuel Alito (2006)	Elena Kagan (2010)	Brett Kavanaugh (2018)

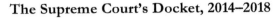

The Supreme Court's Docket, 2014–2018

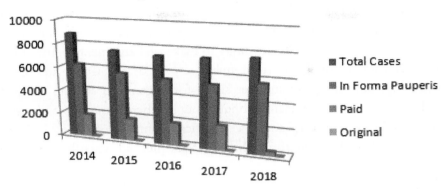

Sources: Administrative Office of U.S. Courts, "Supreme Court of the United States-Cases on Docket, Disposed of, and Remaining on Docket at Conclusion of October Terms, 2014 Through 2018" (Table A-1), available at www.uscourts.gov (last retrieved April 11, 2020). The official portrait of the justices is from U.S. Supreme Court, "About the Court, Justices," available at https://www.supremecourt.gov/about/justices.aspx (last retrieved August 20, 2020).

The Court is a collegial institution, and much of what it does is conducted behind closed doors. Its term begins on the first Monday of October and usually ends in late June. From October to April, the Court hears oral arguments on the cases granted review, but in May and June, none are scheduled. During the months that oral arguments are held, the Court meets in conferences on Wednesdays and Fridays to discuss new filings and to decide cases that were orally argued. In May and June, conferences are held on Thursdays. Throughout the term, on "opinion days" (which by tradition are not known in advance), the justices assemble in the courtroom to publicly announce their decisions.[82]

In the summer preceding the beginning of a new term, the justices' law clerks begin the process of screening *certiorari* petitions that flood the Court throughout the year. Since 1972, a majority of the Court (except now for Justices Alito and Gorsuch) have their clerks join in a **cert. pool** that screens and recommends which cases should be granted review. Before each new term, the justices also meet in a one- to two-day preterm conference to clear about two thousand cases that have come in since the last term. The preterm conference is significant because about one-fourth of the docket is eliminated before the new term even begins and for the most part is screened out by law clerks and never evaluated by the justices.[83]

Once the justices grant cases, they hear oral arguments from the litigants, who are referred to as the **petitioner** (the party bringing the appeal) and the **respondent** (the party defending against the appeal). Upon request, interested nonparties may present their views in ***amicus curiae*** ("friend of the court") briefs. In highly visible cases, such as abortion, school prayer, or affirmative action appeals, *amicus* briefs are routinely used as a strategic device to advocate a special interest group's policy position. After *cert.* is granted, litigants in some cases and even *amicus* parties have the opportunity to make oral arguments before the high bench. Oral argument is the most public aspect of the Court and the only chance—typically thirty minutes per side—for litigants to address the justices directly. As Chief Justice William Rehnquist put it, "there is more to oral argument than meets the eye—or ear," and in a "significant minority of cases," he had "left the bench feeling different about the case than [he] did when he came on the bench."[84]

After oral argument, the justices meet in conference to screen *cert.* petitions and to consider the merits of the small number of cases given oral argument. Two lists were traditionally used to structure deliberations—the Discuss List (includes jurisdictional statements, *cert.* petitions, and motions that the Chief Justice determines are worthy of discussion; and a second list, once called the Dead List, has cases on it that are not deemed worthy of conference time, though it is no longer circulated by Chief Justice Roberts. Justices may also ask that cases be put on the Discuss List. The size of the Court's contemporary docket has made conferences into largely symbolic and non-deliberative meetings at which most of the time is spent on denying petitions review and briefly voting on orally argued cases. As former Justice Antonin Scalia described it, "to call our discussion of a case a conference is really something of a misnomer. It's much more a statement of the views of each of the nine justices."[85] All votes at conference are tentative, and it is not uncommon for justices to change their minds after voting in conference.

Traditionally, after conference, if in the majority, the chief justice assigns a justice to write the opinion for the court. If the chief justice is not in the majority, then the task falls to the most senior associate justice. Once an assignment is made, law clerks help prepare an initial draft that is then circulated among the justices for revision. The process of circulating opinions is dynamic and interactive. Beginning in the last century, justices have increasingly issued concurring opinions (agreeing with the result but not the majority's rationale) and dissenting opinions (disagreeing with the result and the majority's rationale). As a result, more individual opinions are issued than institutional opinions for the Court's decisions.[86]

Notably, apart from the U.S. Supreme Court, which is the final arbiter of constitutional law interpretations, other types of "constitutional courts" have gained prominence in Europe (for further discussion, see "In Comparative Perspective: Constitutional Courts in Europe").

In Comparative Perspective: Constitutional Courts in Europe

Historically, European nations have not adopted the type of approach to judicial review that is linked to legal practice in the United States. European judges may still not invalidate or refuse to enforce national laws as unconstitutional. European courts remain subordinate to the legislature. The French law of August 16, 1790, which remains in force, for instance, stipulates that "Courts cannot interfere with the exercising of legislative powers or suspend the application of the laws." The recently established supreme court in the United Kingdom, which began hearing cases in 2009, may not exercise judicial review *per se* but only issue rulings finding "incompatibility" between national laws and those of the European Union (EU); the case is then sent to Parliament to reconcile national and EU law.

Separate constitutional courts, which sit outside and are set apart from the ordinary judicial branches linked to national or domestic dispute resolution and have the power to annul unconstitutional statutes, have emerged in most countries in Western and Eastern Europe. They are modeled after the constitutional court of the Austrian Second Republic (1920–1934), which was established in 1920 by Hans Kelsen, drafter of the constitution and an influential legal philosopher. No other country established a constitutional court, though, until after World War II. Then, constitutional courts were established as a result of the bitter experiences of fascism having taken hold in Germany and Italy, as an institutional precaution against that happening again. Austria's constitution of 1945 preserved its constitutional court, and others were created in Italy (1948), the Federal Republic of Germany (1949), France (1958), Portugal (1976), Spain (1978), and Belgium (1985).

After the collapse of the former Soviet Union in 1989, constitutional courts were likewise established in the former communist countries of central and eastern Europe, including the Czech Republic, Hungary, Poland, Romania, Russia, Slovakia, the Baltics, and the countries of the former Yugoslavia.

A new European model of constitution judicial review thus emerged. In contrast to the U.S. Supreme Court and federal judiciary, which have general jurisdiction over issues of constitutional and statutory law (and which all judges and courts are vested with the power to decide a law's constitutionality), regular courts in Europe still have no jurisdiction over constitutional matters. Only constitutional courts may decide constitutional issues. That was a new development, but it is not all that separates the European model of judicial review from the American one. European constitutional courts (1) are formally detached from the national judiciary, (2) have exclusive jurisdiction over constitutional disputes, and (3) are authorized to exercise review over and issue opinions on the constitutionality of legislation.

Moreover, unlike the U.S. federal judiciary's jurisdiction over only "actual cases and controversies," European constitutional courts may exercise both *abstract* and *concrete* review of legislation. Some also have jurisdiction based on individuals' constitutional complaint procedures.

Abstract constitutional review of legislation is initiated by elected officials or national and regional governmental bodies with respect to legislation that has been recently adopted but that either (a) has not yet been put into force, as in France; or (b) has not yet been enforced, or has been suspended, pending review by the constitutional court, as in Germany, Italy, and Spain. The executive and legislative branches in Germany, France, and Spain; the federal states or regional governments in Germany, Italy, and Spain; and an ombudsman in Spain may file suits challenging the constitutionality of legislation before constitutional courts. In short, before controversial legislation goes into effect, the constitutional court must pass on its constitutionality, and thereafter the legislation may be revised.

By contrast, *concrete* constitutional review arises from challenges to legislation in the courts when regular judges are uncertain about the constitutionality of a national statute or ordinance, and its compatibility with EU law. In such cases, regular judges refer the constitutional question or complaint to the constitutional court for resolution. Once the constitutional court renders its ruling, the case is remanded back to the referring judge, who then must decide the case in light of the constitutional court's decision.

In addition, in Germany and Spain individuals (and in Spain the ombudsman) may file constitutional complaints after they have exhausted all other remedies. Notably, once the process of constitutional review has been initiated, constitutional courts must consider the matter and render a decision. Unlike the U.S. Supreme Court, they have no discretionary jurisdiction or power to deny cases review.

The jurisdiction and operation of the constitutional courts in France, Germany, Italy, and Spain are summarized in the following table.

	France	Germany	Italy	Spain
Court/Date of creation	Constitutional Council (1958)	Federal Constitutional Court (1949)	Italian Constitutional Court (1956)	Spanish Constitutional Court (1978)
Jurisdiction				
Abstract review	Yes	Yes	Yes	Yes
Authority to initiate review	President, Presidential Assembly, or Senate	Federal and lander (state) governments or one-third of the Bundestag	National government (against regional laws); and regional governments (against national laws)	Prime minister, president of Parliament, fifty deputies or senators, executives of autonomous regions, and ombudsmen
Laws referred	National	Federal and lander legislation	National and regional legislation	National and regional legislation
Laws must be referred	Within fifteen days of adoption	Within thirty days of adoption	Within thirty days of adoption	Within ninety days of adoption
Concrete review	Yes (as of 2008)	Yes	Yes	Yes
Authority to initiate concrete review	Judiciary	Judiciary and individuals	Judiciary	Judiciary, ombudsmen, and individuals
Composition, Selection & Tenure				
Number of judges	Nine	Sixteen	Fifteen	Twelve
Appointing bodies	Named by President (3), Presidential Assembly (6)	Elected by Bundestag (8), Bundesrat (8)	Named by national government (5), elected by Parliament (5)	Named by national government (2), judiciary (5), elected by Congress (4), Senate (4)

Length of tenure	Nine years	Twelve years	Nine years	Nine years
Age limit	None	Forty-year minimum; sixty-eight-year maximum	None	None
Requisite qualifications	None	Six in sixteen must be federal judges; all must be qualified to be judges	All must be judges with twenty years' experience	May be judges, professors, lawyers, or civil servants with at least fifteen years' experience

Western European constitutional courts also differ with respect to their composition, judges' qualifications for appointment, and term limits on judicial service. In general, constitutional judges are either appointed by political bodies, as in France, or subject to some combination of nomination and election, as in Italy and Spain. Moreover, unlike appointments to the U.S. Supreme Court, constitutional courts have precise quotas for the appointment of professional/career judges, professors, and so on. In the Federal Republic of Germany, for example, the sixteen-member constitutional court must always have at least six former federal judges. In Italy, five of the fifteen judges on its constitutional court must be representatives of the federal judiciary, but in Spain only two of its twelve judges must be. Some of the differences in the composition and requirements for appointment to the constitutional courts in France, Germany, Italy, and Spain are highlighted above.

Sources: Carlo Guarnieri and Patrizia Pederzoli, *The Power of Judges: A Comparative Study of Courts and Democracy* (London: Oxford University Press, 2002); and Allan R. Brewer-Carias, *Constitutional Courts as Positive Legislators* (New York: Cambridge University Press, 2011). Portions of the box have been reprinted with permission from David M. O'Brien and Gordon Silverstein, *Constitutional Law and Politics: Struggles for Power and Governmental Accountability (Vol. 1)*, 11th ed. (New York: W.W. Norton, 2020); and David M. O'Brien and Gordon Silverstein, *Constitutional Law and Politics: Civil Rights and Civil Liberties (Vol. 2)*, 11th ed. (New York: W.W. Norton, 2020), as well as earlier editions solely authored by the late David M. O'Brien.

THE POLITICS OF JUDICIAL ADMINISTRATION

Solving legal problems is complex and bureaucratic. All of a court's resources—its building, courtroom, computers, library, staff offices, judges' chambers, and security system—are a part of what some say has become "bureaucratic justice."[87] Since the 1960s, burgeoning caseloads have transformed the ideal model of justice—in which litigants receive their "day" in court—into a delay-ridden process that forces courts to rely upon administrative solutions to cope with rising dockets. Bureaucratic justice has important consequences because the quality of the justice may be diminished as judges delegate their responsibilities to subordinate staff attorneys, law clerks, and administrative personnel, and accordingly spend less time on cases. After exploring the main elements of state and federal judicial administration, the chapter concludes by considering how courts respond to the political attacks and challenges they face in delivering justice in the twenty-first century.

State Court Administration

Historically, court administration has evolved from a series of intermittent reforms that sought to integrate court operations and to assert judicial independence from other political branches. In the past, state courts were decentralized, and most judges lacked professional training and were often beholden to the local bar associations because they were elected. As a result, a growing backlog of cases and other problems led to judicial reforms to make courts more democratically accountable and improve their operations and professionalism.[88] In the twentieth century, state courts worked on centralizing and streamlining operations through *court unification* (discussed earlier in this chapter). In 1949, the Conference of Chief Justices was founded to develop, and advance policies directed at professionalizing court management and enhancing court funding and resources.[89]

Still, court administration varies from state to state. State courts typically use **clerks of court** or **trial administrators** to keep records, establish court calendars, schedule cases, and manage the flow of litigation between judges, attorneys, and the public. Many states have **administrative offices of the courts** (AOCs) to perform similar tasks. In states having AOCs, a **state court administrator** (SCA) usually provides administrative support for the chief justice and other personnel within the judicial branch. The SCA's responsibilities are diverse, significant, and wide-ranging. They include managing unified budgets, centralizing judicial records and workload data, and supervising all organizational activities pertaining to human resources, information technology, facilities administration, community outreach, and external relationships with the state executive and legislative branches.[90]

State courts interact with other judicial organizations on caseload management, coordinating lobbying efforts, and providing educational training for judicial personnel and staff. Established in 1964, the National Judicial College in Reno, Nevada, offers continuing education for judges. In the early 1970s, the Institute for Court Management (ICM) and the National Center for State Courts (NCSC) were created. As a result, many states now use non-legal administrators to manage the non-adjudicative matters, such as personnel management, accounting, and the incorporation of new technologies. Although each state assigns to the highest court the responsibility for rulemaking, supervising attorney admissions, imposing discipline, and maintaining external relations with other branches and the public, the Conference of Chief Justices assists in setting the policy agenda for all the states.[91]

Federal Court Administration

Like state courts, federal courts struggled with establishing a professionalized bureaucracy that met the goals of increasing judicial autonomy and achieving the fair administration of justice. Congress originally required federal courts to adopt the same type of procedural rules that were used in the states. That decentralization, however, thwarted the development of consistent legal practices across the federal circuits.[92] But, in the early part of the twentieth century, Congress and the federal courts undertook steps to improve court administration. In 1922, Congress created the Judicial Conference of the United States, which serves as the national policy-making body for federal courts. In 1938, Congress gave the Supreme Court the power to promulgate the Federal Rules of Civil Procedure, which now govern the basic litigation practices in the federal judiciary. The following year, the Judicial Conference's significance grew when Congress created the Administrative Office of the U.S. Courts and transferred budgetary control and judicial statistics preparation from the Department of Justice to it. That legislation also instituted circuit judicial councils in order to supervise the docket management of district courts. In 1969, Congress created the Federal Judicial Center (FJC), an influential source of research and training for federal court judges and judicial personnel.[93]

Judicial Administration Reform

Judicial reform proposals are often driven by political motives, or attacks, and counter-responses that may compromise judicial independence. In the 2012 presidential election, state and federal judicial decision-making amplified political controversies because the electorate was polarized over public policy issues involving health care, same-sex marriage, affirmative action, and immigration. Before that, *Bush v. Gore* (2000), the landmark Supreme Court ruling that stopped the Florida vote recount in the 2000 presidential race, registered the public debate over the role federal courts should play in actively supervising the electoral process. But state courts have also been at the center of heated electoral conflicts: before the Supreme Court's ruling in *Obergefell v. Hodges* (2015), state courts in California and elsewhere legalized same-sex marriage, a trend that generated intense public and electoral resistance across the country. Identical political conflicts have emerged in the highly polarized electorate across the nation in not only the Obama era, but also in the Trump administration, especially regarding global, foreign affairs and domestic issues of immigration, climate change, health care, tax and spending policies, education reform, abortion politics, and the governmental responses to the coronavirus pandemic.[94] Courts, in turn, respond to such political challenges in different ways.

The success of courts in beating back or repelling political attacks is often determined by their behind-the-scenes management of bureaucratic administration and public statements that are strategically designed to cultivate positive external political and legal stakeholder relationships. Courts, that is, are extremely mindful of recurring funding issues because, for example, roughly only two-tenths of 1 percent of the federal budget is allocated to federal courts. Court appropriations thus are a constant political concern because judiciaries must rely to some degree on the legislative and executive budgetary processes for resources. The lobbying skills of judges and chief justices are important because legislatures are not afraid to use their fiscal authority to influence or protest court rulings—a common problem in the states. As a result, it is not unusual for federal and state courts, at year's end, to give speeches to political elites and publish "state of the judiciary" reports that advocate for changes, and sometimes they have a decidedly political bent.[95]

In short, courts and their leaders must be adept at understanding their administrative processes to respond and lobby for reform that benefits their organizations and their respective states or the country as a whole. In this light, long-range plans, which result from task forces or committees within the judicial branch, are used to help set judicial priorities in dealing with the political branches.

Courts routinely publicize strategic long-range plans and current assessments of judicial trends reports to alert the public about the challenges facing courts. For example, in several of his Year-End Reports on the Federal Judiciary, Chief Justice Roberts has regularly highlighted the role courts and judges play in (1) responding to emergencies, natural disasters, and the problem of sexual harassment in the workplace, (2) performing key legal and administrative functions at the federal trial court level, including public outreach and advancing civic responsibility and education, (3) creating fair and efficient rules of procedure that govern court operations, (4) adapting to changes in information technology, and (5) working with law clerks and the vital role they play in assisting Justices handle their workload. State chief judges write similar annual reports and also engage in extensive lobbying efforts. Before his retirement, Jonathan Lippman, the Chief Justice of New York's highest court, aggressively pushed for judicial reforms that would permit law students to pass the bar early if they agreed to devote their last semester to providing *pro bono* work to indigents; and he pursued other measures that tried to stop judicial patronage abuses and make it easier for defendants to get bail in criminal cases.[96]

In sum, the political reality is that state and federal courts are complex bureaucracies that require flexibility, and a certain political savviness, to help them manage their operations and long-term institutional health. At least in part because of caseload demands and constant political pressures, today's judges cannot play the role of a passive or neutral and detached adjudicator. Rather, a judge must be an efficient manager of court resources and, at times, an engaged mediator, problem solver and policy advocate. Appellate court judges, which are often the most visible judicial representatives in the public eye, must be prepared to adopt a leadership role that is inherently political when lobbying for additional resources in the areas of judicial compensation, retirement benefits, administrative personnel, or new technologies. In this regard, the next chapter explores some additional challenges confronting courts within the context of the politics of judicial recruitment, retention, and removal.

Chapter Summary

The structure, organization, and administration of courts are detailed and examined. The U.S. judicial system has evolved. Seminal legislation, such as the 1789 Judiciary Act, allowed for federal courts to emerge alongside state courts in a dual system of courts that is held together under principles of judicial federalism. Subsequently, state courts developed through "unification," a reform movement consolidating trial courts and centralizing court operations and increasing judicial autonomy from the political branches. State courts handle the bulk of the nation's litigation. Federal courts review less case, but their focus is on deciding federal questions of law. While state and federal courts remain distinct, their basic structure and organization are identical in terms of operating in a hierarchical format, with trial courts—tasked with the duty to decide the facts of cases and apply the law, at the bottom tier—and appellate courts—obliged to decide only issues of law, at the middle or uppermost tier, as intermediate adjudicators or courts of last resort.

Courts operate as bureaucratic organizations, so how they administer justice is highly significant. State courts' administrative offices perform essentially the same administrative and agenda-setting function as clerks of the federal courts. State and federal judicial organizations play key roles as research and training centers, as well as in helping courts manage budgets, human resources, courtroom facilities, and informational technology. Lastly, because they are not completely autonomous from the political branches, state and federal court administrators must engage in external lobbying, internal self-examination, and strategic long-range planning in order to compete for scarce resources in the political system while administering justice fairly.

Key Questions for Review and Critical Analysis

1. What are the key similarities and differences between state and federal courts with respect to their structural organization, dockets, and the role they play in deciding trial and appellate cases?

2. Why is it politically difficult for states to unify or centralize their court structures, funding, and internal operations?

3. In practice, which level of the state or federal judiciary is the "court of last resort" for most litigants, and why?

4. What principles of the fair administration of justice are threatened when courts are attacked politically for making unpopular judicial decisions?

5. What are the different administrative strategies that federal and state courts use to manage high caseloads when they have limited financial or staffing resources?

Web Links

1. State Justice Institute (www.sji.gov)
   - A non-profit corporation's site that provides grant information and news about current issues facing state and federal courts.

2. Conference of Chief Justices (https://ccj.ncsc.org/)

    • Established for chief justices of state courts of last resort that supply insight into the issues and problems facing state courts.

3. Conference of State Court Administrators (http://cosca.ncsc.org)

    • A rich source for news and research about state courts. It also provides additional information about case management strategies, relevant websites, and the policy issues state courts face in administering justice.

4. Administrative Office of the U.S. Courts (http://www.uscourts.gov/)

    • A comprehensive site that supplies current news, federal court workload statistics, annual reports, and long-range planning initiatives.

5. Federal Judicial Center (https://www.fjc.gov/)

    • The site provides access to publications and videos, information about international judicial relations, and significant research about federal judicial history, including a rich source of federal judge biographies.

Selected Readings

ABA Conference Judicial Division. *The Improvement of the Administration of Justice*, 8th ed. Peter Koelling, ed. Chicago: American Bar Association, 2016.

Banks, Christopher P. *Judicial Politics in the D.C. Circuit Court*. Baltimore: Johns Hopkins University Press, 1999.

Banks, Christopher P., and John C. Blakeman. *The U.S. Supreme Court and New Federalism: From the Rehnquist to the Roberts Court*. Lanham, Md.: Rowman & Littlefield, 2012.

Baum, Lawrence. *Specializing the Courts*. Chicago: University of Chicago Press, 2011.

Clark, Tom C. *The Supreme Court: An Analytic History of Constitutional Decision Making*. New York: Cambridge University Press, 2019.

Cross, Frank B. *Decision Making in the U.S. Courts of Appeals*. Stanford, Calif.: Stanford University Press, 2007.

Crowe, Justin. *Building the Judiciary: Law, Courts and the Politics of Institutional Development*. Princeton, N.J.: Princeton University Press, 2012.

Devins, Neal and Lawrence Baum. *The Company They Keep: How Partisan Divisions Came to the Supreme Court.* New York: Oxford University Press, 2019.

Fish, Peter Graham. *The Politics of Federal Judicial Administration.* Princeton, N.J.: Princeton University Press, 1973.

Howard, J. Woodford, Jr. *Courts of Appeals in the Federal Judicial System: A Study of the Second, Fifth, and District of Columbia Circuits.* Princeton, N.J.: Princeton University Press, 1981.

Landfried, Christine, ed. *Judicial Power: How Constitutional Courts Affect Political Transformations.* New York: Cambridge University Press, 2019.

O'Brien, David M. Storm Center: *The Supreme Court in American Politics,* 12th ed. New York: Norton, 2020.

Ostrom, Brian J., Charles W. Ostrom, Jr., Roger A. Hanson, and Matthew Kleiman. *Trial Courts as Organizations.* Philadelphia: Temple University Press, 2007.

Redish, Martin H. *Judicial Independence and the American Constitution: A Democratic Paradox.* Stanford: Stanford University Press, 2017.

Richman, William M., and William L. Reynolds. *Injustice on Appeal: The United States Courts of Appeals in Crisis.* New York: Oxford University Press, 2013.

Sutton, Jeffrey S. *51 Imperfect Solutions: States and the Making of American Constitutional Law.* (New York: Oxford University Press, 2018).

Wheeler, Russell R., and Cynthia Harrison. *Creating the Federal Judicial System,* 3rd ed. Washington, D.C.: Federal Judicial Center, 2005.

Zackin, Emily. *Looking for Rights in All the Wrong Places.* Princeton: Princeton University Press, 2013.

Endnotes

[1] Ronn Blitzer, "Schumer Unloads on Gorsuch, Kavanaugh at Abortion Rights Rally: 'You Will Pay the Price!'", *Fox News* (March 4, 2020), available at https://www.foxnews.com/politics/schumer-unloads-on-gorsuch-kavanaugh-at-abortion-rights-rally-warns-they-will-pay-the-price-for-awful-decisions (last retrieved April 8, 2020); Brennan Center for Justice, "In His Own Words: The President's Attacks on the Courts (February 14, 2020), available at https://www.brennancenter.org/our-work/research-reports/his-own-words-presidents-attacks-courts (last retrieved April 8, 2020). See also, Jay L. Jackson, "The Siege on State Courts," *ABA Journal* 99 (2013), 54–61.

[2] Special to the Gazette, "Supreme Court Rules School Finance Adequacy Not Quite Met: One Year to Make Adjustments." *The Emporia Gazette* (June 25, 2018), available at http://www.emporiagazette.com/area_news/article_fff9d44e-788f-11e8-ac8f-6f3e7f614f0c.html (last retrieved on March 26, 2019); Sam Zeff, "All Kansas Supreme Court Justices Retained," *WKUR* (November 9, 2016), available at http://www.kcur.org/post/all-kansas-supreme-court-justices-retained#stream/0 (last retrieved March 26, 2019); Lincoln Caplan, "The Political War Against the Kansas Supreme Court," *The New Yorker* (February 5, 2016), available

at https://www.newyorker.com/news/news-desk/the-political-war-against-the-kansas-supreme-court (last retrieved March 26, 2–19). See also *Gannon v. State*, 420 P.3d 477 (2018).

3   Justice O'Connor is quoted in Ryan J. Reilly, "Sandra Day O'Connor's New Judgment: Judicial Campaign Reform Is Necessary," *TPM* (August 17, 2010), available at https://talkingpointsmemo.com/muckraker/sandra-day-o-connor-s-new-judgment-judicial-campaign-reform-is-necessary (last retrieved on March 26, 2019); and, Jackson, "The Siege on State Courts."

4   Marc Santora, "Poland Purges Supreme Court, and Protesters Take to the Streets," *N.Y. Times* (July 3, 2018), available at https://www.nytimes.com/2018/07/03/world/europe/poland-supreme-court-protest.html (last retrieved March 26, 2019). In the U.S., in response to liberal activism, federal legislation in the 1970s restructured District of Columbia courts by weakening the D.C. Circuit's criminal law precedent and ultimately replacing the circuit's criminal jurisdiction with administrative law jurisdiction. Christopher P. Banks, *Judicial Politics of the D.C. Circuit Court* (Baltimore: John Hopkins University Press, 1999), 26–32. In the 1990s, the Ninth Circuit's liberal activism prompted legislative proposals to reorganize the court into smaller divisions to curb its ideological decision making. Christopher P. Banks, "The Politics of Court Reform in the U.S. Courts of Appeals," *Judicature* 84 (2000), 34–43. More recently, special interests reportedly lobbied extensively to reduce the size of the Michigan Supreme Court in order to oust two conservative Republican justices. Jackson, "The Siege on State Courts," 54–61. In his 2011 bid for the presidency, Republican Newt Gingrich vowed to abolish activist courts and arrest judges with U.S. Capitol Police in order to make them testify before Congress to explain their controversial rulings. Amy Gardner and Matt Delong, "Newt Gingrich's Assault on 'Activist Judges' Draws Criticism, Even From the Right," *Washington Post* (December 17, 2011), available at www.washingtonpost.com (last retrieved March 1, 2014); Ariane de Vogue, "Gingrich's Judiciary Hunt Riles Conservatives, Reformists," *ABC News* (December 20, 2011), available at www.abcnews.go.com (last retrieved March 1, 2014).

5   See generally, *The Improvement of the Administration of Justice*, 7th ed., edited by Gordon M. Griller and E. Keith Stott, Jr. (Chicago: Lawyers Conference, Judicial Division, American Bar Association, 2002); Robert W. Tobin, *Creating the Judicial Branch: The Unfinished Reform* (Williamsburg, Va.: National Center for State Courts, 1999); Deborah J. Barrow, Gary Zuk, and Gerard S. Gryski, *The Federal Judiciary and Institutional Change* (Ann Arbor: University of Michigan Press, 1996).

6   Melvin I. Urofsky and Paul Finkelman, *A March of Liberty: A Constitutional History of the United States, Volume I: From the Founding to 1890*, 2nd ed. (Oxford: Oxford University Press, 2002), 41–58; Kermit L. Hall, *The Magic Mirror: Law in American History* (Oxford: Oxford University Press, 1989), 17–22.

7   G. Alan Tarr, *Understanding State Constitutions* (Princeton, N.J.: Princeton University Press, 1998), 60–93.

8   Sue Davis, *American Political Thought: Four Hundred Years of Ideas and Ideologies* (Englewood Cliffs, N.J.: Prentice Hall, 1996), 91–93.

9   Jack N. Rakove, *Original Meanings: Politics and Ideas in the Making of the Constitution* (New York: Vintage Books, 1996), 25–26, 44; Edward A. Purcell, Jr., *Originalism, Federalism, and the American Constitutional Enterprise: A Historical Inquiry* (New Haven, Conn.: Yale University Press, 2007), 22. See also Michael Hail and Stephen Lange, "Federalism and Representation in the Theory of the Founding Fathers: A Comparative Study of U.S. and Canadian Constitutional Thought," *Publius: The Journal of Federalism* 40, no. 3 (2010), 360, 370; Raoul Berger, *Federalism: The Founder's Design* (Norman: University of Oklahoma Press, 1987), 46.

10   Letter from James Madison to Thomas Jefferson (October 24, 1787), *The Writings of James Madison*, edited by Gaillard Hunt (New York: G.P. Putnam's Sons, 1904), 17, 23.

11   Rakove, *Original Meanings*, 25–26, 44. See also Alison L. LaCroix, *The Ideological Origins of American Federalism* (Cambridge, Mass.: Harvard University Press, 2010), 148–49.

12   Rakove, *Original Meanings*, 32.

13   Max Farrand, *The Framing of the Constitution of the United States* (New Haven, Conn.: Yale University Press, 1967), 119.

14   Farrand, *The Framing of the Constitution of the United States*, 119–21, 156–57; Rakove, *Original Meanings*, 173–77.

15   Justin Crowe, *Building the Judiciary: Law, Courts, and Politics of Institutional Development* (Princeton, N.J.: Princeton University Press, 2012), 31–32. See also Maeva Marcus and Natalie Wexler, "The Judiciary Act of 1789: Political Compromise or Constitutional Interpretation," in *Origins of the Federal Judiciary: Essays on the Judiciary Act of 1789*, edited by Maeva Marcus (New York: Oxford University Press, 1992), 13–39.

[16] David M. O'Brien, *Storm Center: The Supreme Court in American Politics*, 12th ed. (New York: Norton, 2020), 113–14. See also Crowe, *Building the Judiciary*, 38–39.

[17] *Marbury v. Madison*, 5 U.S. 137 (1803).

[18] Akhil Reed Amar, *"Marbury,* Section 13, and the Original Jurisdiction of the Supreme Court," *University of Chicago Law Review* (Spring, 1989), 443–98.

[19] Kathryn Turner, "Federalist Policy and the Judiciary Act of 1801," *William and Mary Quarterly* 22 (1965), 3–32.

[20] Felix Frankfurter and James M. Landis, *The Business of the Supreme Court: A Study in the Federal Judicial System* (New York: Macmillan, 1928), 56–64. See also Eleanore Bushnell, *Crimes, Follies, and Misfortunes: The Federal Impeachment Trials* (Urbana: University of Illinois Press, 1992).

[21] Frankfurter and Landis, *The Business of the Supreme Court*, 60, 64. President Lincoln's quote is found in Russell R. Wheeler and Cynthia Harrison, *Creating the Federal Judicial System*, 3rd ed. (Washington, D.C.: Federal Judicial Center, 2005), 12.

[22] Frankfurter and Landis, *The Business of the Supreme Court*, 60, 64.

[23] As quoted in Frankfurter and Landis, *The Business of the Supreme Court*, 259, n. 13.

[24] Richard A. Posner, *The Federal Courts: Challenge and Reform* (Cambridge, Mass.: Harvard University Press, 1996), 87–123. For a detailed historical survey of the evolution of the structure of federal courts, see Federal Judicial Center, "Timelines of the Federal Judiciary," available at https://www.fjc.gov/history/timeline (last retrieved March 26, 2019).

[25] *Michigan v. Long*, 463 U.S. 1032 (1983).

[26] See Jeffrey S. Sutton, *51 Imperfect Solutions: States and the Making of American Constitutional Law.* (New York: Oxford University Press, 2018), 10–12. For an analysis of new judicial federalism trends, see Christopher P. Banks and John C. Blakeman, *The U.S. Supreme Court and New Federalism: From the Rehnquist to the Roberts Court* (Lanham, Md.: Rowman & Littlefield, 2012). See also Kenneth P. Miller, "Defining Rights in the States: Judicial Activism and Popular Response," *Albany Law Review* 76 (2012), 2061–103; William J. Brennan, Jr., "State Constitutions and the Protection of Individual Rights," *Harvard Law Review* 90 (1977), 489.

[27] Roscoe Pound, "The Causes of Popular Dissatisfaction with the Administration of Justice," *American Bar Association Report* 29 (1906), 395–417; Robert W. Tobin, *Creating the Judicial Branch: The Unfinished Reform* (Williamsburg, Va.: National Center for State Courts, 1999), 3, 21–22.

[28] William Rafferty, "Unification and 'Urgency': A Century of Court Organization and Reorganization," *Judicature* 96 (2013), 337–46. See also Tobin, *Creating the Judicial Branch: The Unfinished Reform*, 119–21.

[29] Tobin, *Creating the Judicial Branch: The Unfinished Reform*, 23. See also Larry C. Berkson, "The Emerging Ideal of Court Unification," *Judicature* 60 (1977), 372, 373.

[30] Rafferty, "Unification and 'Bragency,'" 337–46. See also Tobin, *Creating the Judicial Branch*, 155–57.

[31] Whereas single-tier systems report their caseloads as one number for every case category, two-tier systems divvy up their caseloads between a general jurisdiction and limited jurisdiction tier. Robert C. LaFountain, Shauna M. Strickland, and Kathryn A. Holt, and Kathryn J. Genthon, *Examining the Work of State Courts: An Overview of 2015 State Court Caseloads* (Williamsburg, Va.: National Center for State Courts, 2016), 3.

[32] LaFountain, Schauffler, Strickland, Holt and Genthon, *Examining the Work of State Courts: An Overview of 2015 State Court Caseloads*, 2.

[33] Shauna M. Strickland, Richard Y. Schauffler, Robert C. LaFountain, and Kathryn A. Holt, "State Court Organization," *National Center for State Courts* (last updated on June 30, 2017), available at https://www.ncsc.org/sco (last retrieved April 10, 2020).

[34] James G. Cornell, "Limited-Jurisdiction Courts: Challenges, Opportunities, and Strategies for Action," in *Future Trends in State Courts (2012): Special Focus and Courts and Community*, edited by Carol R. Flango, Amy M. McDowell, Deborah W. Saunders, Nora E. Sydow, Charles F. Campbell, and Neal B. Kauder (Williamsburg, Va.: National Center for State Courts, 2012), 67–70.

[35] Cornell, "Limited-Jurisdiction Courts," 67–70. See also LaFountain, Schauffler, Strickland, Holt and Genthon, *Examining the Work of State Courts: An Overview of 2015 State Court Caseloads*, 3. See also Strickland, Schauffler, LaFountain, and Holt, "State Court Organization" (for data indicating number of limited jurisdiction courts and how they are named).

36   LaFountain, Schauffler, Strickland, Holt and Genthon, *Examining the Work of State Courts: An Overview of 2015 State Court Caseloads,* 3 (listing types of subject matter handled by general jurisdiction courts). See also Strickland, Schauffler, LaFountain, and Holt, "State Court Organization" (for data indicating number of general jurisdiction courts and how they are named).

37   Tribal Law and Policy Institute's Tribal Court Clearinghouse, "Tribal Courts," available at http://www.tribal-institute.org/lists/justice.htm (last retrieved April 10, 2020); Susan Johnson, Jeanne Kaufman, John Dossett, and Sarah Hicks (updated by Sue Davis), *Government to Government: Models of Cooperation Between States and Tribes* (Denver, Colo.: National Conference of State Legislators, 2009); Susan Johnson, Jeanne Kaufman, John Dossett, and Sarah Hicks, *Government to Government: Understanding State and Tribal Government* (Denver, Colo.: National Conference of State Legislators, 2000); Bureau of Indian Affairs, "Frequently Asked Questions: What is a Federally-Recognized Tribe?," available at https://www.bia.gov/frequently-asked-questions (last retrieved April 10, 2020).

38   Tribal Law and Policy Institute's Tribal Court Clearinghouse, "Tribal Courts." See also *Cherokee Nation v. Georgia*, 30 U.S. 1 (1831), *Worcester v. Georgia*, 31 U.S. 515 (1832), and *Ex Parte Crow Dog*, 109 U.S. 556 (1883).

39   Office of Inspector General, U.S. Department of Justice, "Review of Department's Tribal Law Enforcement Efforts Pursuant to Tribal Law and Order Act of 2010 (December 2017)," available at https://www.oversight.gov/sites/default/files/oig-reports/e1801.pdf (last retrieved April 10, 2020); Tribal Law and Policy Institute's Tribal Court Clearinghouse, "Public Law 280," http://www.tribal-institute.org/lists/pl280.htm (last accessed April 10, 2020); Philip P. Frickey, "(Native) American Exceptionalism in Federal Public Law," *Harvard Law Review* 119 (2005), 433–90. See also *Montana v. United States*, 450 U.S. 544 (1981) (tribal court jurisdiction restricted over nonmember activities taking place on the reservation); *Nevada v. Hicks*, 533 U.S. 353 (2001)(tribal court lacks jurisdiction over civil claims against state officials who entered tribal land to execute a search warrant against a tribe member suspected of having violated state law outside the reservation); *Plains Commerce Banks v. Long Family Land and Cattle Co., Inc.,* 554 U.S. 316 (2008)(tribal court lacks jurisdiction to adjudicate a discrimination claim concerning the non-Indian bank's sale of land it owned on an Indian reservation); but see *United States v. Lara*, 541 U.S. 193 (2004) (federal government and tribal courts have authority to prosecute an Indian from another nonmember tribe for offenses in separate, successive prosecutions without violating the Double Jeopardy Clause).

40   Intermediate appellate courts in thirty-six states, plus Puerto Rico, sit in panels, but, Connecticut, Massachusetts and Oregon use permanent, or the same, panels. Most jurisdictions rotate judges in panels. Some states, such as Alaska, do not sit in panels. Also, there is considerable variation in the number of panels used (how many the court uses relative to a certain size, which sometimes is more than three judges) and the frequency of their rotation (either by case, by the court's discretion or through the chief judge, or by certain time intervals, either by week, month, year, and so forth). Courts of last resort sit *en banc* in most states, with only eight states, plus the District of Columbia and Guam, deciding cases through panels, mostly on a rotating basis with three justices (only Guam, Virginia and Utah use permanent panels; and, Florida and Montana use panels of five instead of three judges); but there is a wide variation in the number of panels and their frequency of rotation. See also Strickland, Schauffler, LaFountain, and Holt, "State Court Organization" (for data indicating structure of appellate panels).

41   John P. Doerner and Christine A. Markman, *The Role of State Intermediate Courts: Principles for Adopting to Change* (a white paper produced by the Council of Chief Judges of the State Courts of Appeal [November 2012]), available at https://www.sji.gov/wp/wp-content/uploads/Report_5_CCJSCA_Report.pdf (last retrieved June 24, 2020), 27–28. See also Victor E. Flango, "A Taxonomy of Appellate Court Organization," *Caseload Highlights: Examining the Work of State Courts* 3, no. 1 (July 1997), available at http://ncsc.contentdm.oclc.org/cdm/singleitem/collection/appellate/id/88/rec/16 (last retrieved April 10, 2020).

42   Harry P. Stumpf and John H. Culver, *The Politics of State Courts* (New York: Longman, 1991), 149. See also Robert C. LaFountain, Richard Y. Schauffler, Shauna M. Strickland, and Kathryn A. Holt, *Examining the Work of State Courts: An Analysis of 2010 State Court Caseloads* (Williamsburg, Va.: National Center for State Courts, 2012), 40.

43   Strickland, Schauffler, LaFountain, and Holt, "State Court Organization" (for data indicating structure of intermediate appellate courts).

44   LaFountain, Schauffler, Strickland, Holt and Genthon, *Examining the Work of State Courts: An Overview of 2015 State Court Caseloads*, 18–20.

45   LaFountain, Schauffler, Strickland, and Holt, *Examining the Work of State Courts: An Analysis of 2010 State Court Caseloads*, 44. See also Richard Y. Schauffler, Robert C. LaFountain, Neal B. Kauder, and Shauna M. Strickland, *Examining the Work of State Courts, 2004: A National Perspective From the Court Statistics Project* (Williamsburg, Va.: National Center for State Courts, 2004), 68.

46   See, e.g., Vermont Supreme Court, "Supreme Court," available at https://www.vermontjudiciary.org/ supreme-court (last retrieved April 10, 2020)(identifying five distinct roles in the state judicial system); and, Matthew E. K. Hall and Jason Harold Windett, "New Data on State Supreme Court Cases," State Politics and Policy Quarterly 13 (2013), 427, 436. See also Strickland, LaFountain, and Holt, "State Court Organization."

47   At least eight states, plus the District of Columbia and Guam, have courts of last resort that decide cases in panels. Strickland, Schauffler, LaFountain, and Holt, "State Court Organization" (for data indicating structure of appellate court panels).

48   LaFountain, Schauffler, Strickland, Holt and Genthon, *Examining the Work of State Courts: An Overview of 2015 State Court Caseloads*, 19–20. See also LaFountain, Schauffler, Strickland, and Holt, *Examining the Work of State Courts: An Analysis of 2010 State Court Caseloads*, 45–46.

49   LaFountain, Schauffler, Strickland, Holt and Genthon, *Examining the Work of State Courts: An Overview of 2015 State Court Caseloads*, 19. See also LaFountain, Schauffler, Strickland, and Holt, *Examining the Work of State Courts: An Analysis of 2010 State Court Caseloads*, 41, 43. See also Doerner and Markman, *The Role of State Intermediate Courts*, 4.

50   Benjamin Kassow, Donald R. Songer, and Michael P. Fix, "The Influence of Precedent on State Supreme Courts," Political Research Quarterly 65 (2012), 372, 375.

51   Administrative Office of the U.S. Courts, Table C-2: U.S. District Courts—Civil Cases Commenced, by Basis of Jurisdiction and Nature of Suit, During 12-Month Period Ending December 31, 2018 and 2019, available at https://www.uscourts.gov/statistics/table/c-2/statistical-tables-federal-judiciary/2019/12/31 (last retrieved April 11, 2020). The number of authorized judgeships is detailed in Administrative Office of the U.S. Courts, "Authorized Judgeships—1789 to Present," available at http://www.uscourts.gov/judges-judgeships/authorized-judgeships (last retrieved April 11, 2020).

52   Judicial workload statistics for the federal courts are detailed in Administrative Office of the U.S. Courts, "Table JCI-U.S. Federal Courts, Work of the Federal Judiciary (12-Month Period Ending December 31, 2010, 2015, 2018 and 2019)," available at www.uscourts.gov (last retrieved April 11, 2020).

53   Administrative Office of U.S. Courts, U.S. District Courts-Civil Cases Commenced, by Nature of Suit, During the 12-Month Periods Ending September 30, 2015 through 2019 (Table C-2A), available at www.uscourts.gov (last retrieved April 11, 2020).

54   Administrative Office of U.S. Courts, U.S. District Courts-Civil Cases Commenced, by Nature of Suit, During the 12-Month Periods Ending September 30, 2015 through 2019 (Table D-2), available at www.uscourts.gov (last retrieved April 11, 2020).

55   Case termination and method of disposition statistics in civil and criminal cases are derived from 2019 filings. Administrative Office of U.S. Courts, U.S. District Courts—Civil Cases Terminated, by Nature of Suit and Action Taken, During the 12-Month Period Ending September 30, 2019 (Table C-4) and U.S. District Courts—Criminal Defendants Disposed of, by Type of Disposition and Offense, During the 12-Month Period Ending September 30, 2019 (Table D-4), both available at www.uscourts.gov (last retrieved April 11, 2020).

56   Federal Judicial Center, "Territorial Courts," available at https://www.fjc.gov/history/courts/ territorial-courts (last retrieved April 11, 2020); American Samoa, "Judicial Branch of American Samoa," available at https://www.americansamoa.gov/judicial-branch (last retrieved April 11, 2020).

57   Federal Judicial Center, "Landmark Legislation: Federal Judicial Center," available at https://www.fjc. gov/history/legislation/landmark-legislation-federal-judicial-center-0 (last retrieved April 11, 2020).

58   McCabe, Peter G., *A Guide to the Federal Magistrate Judges System* (A White Paper Prepared at the Request of the Federal Bar Association (August 2014, Updated October 2016), available at https://www. fedbar.org/wp-content/uploads/2019/10/FBA-White-Paper-2016-pdf-2.pdf (last retrieved April 11, 2020).

59   McCabe, *A Guide to the Federal Magistrate Judges System*. They dispose of nearly 5,716 Class A misdemeanors (e.g., traffic, theft, food/drug, weapons, trespass, fraud, assault) and 70,629 petty offenses (e.g., DUI/DWI, immigration, food/drug, littering, drunk/disorderly, hunting, trespassing, theft). They participate in over 380,269 felony preliminary hearings (e.g., search and arrest warrants, initial appearances, arraignments, bail review) and perform 57,707 miscellaneous duties (e.g., seizure/inspection warrants, calendar calls, grand juries). They conduct almost 514.464 matters relating to pretrial in criminal and civil cases, and process over 50,000 reports pursuant to statute, with over half of those coming from prisoner petitions. Administrative Office of the U.S. Courts, "Judicial Business of the U.S. Courts" (Tables S-17, M-1, M-2, M-3 M-3A, M-4, M-4A, M-4B), available at www.uscourts.gov (last retrieved March 26, 2019).

[60]   *Northern Pipeline Construction Company v. Marathon Pipeline Company*, 458 U.S. 50 (1982).

[61]   David S. Kennedy and R. Spencer Clift III, "An Historical Analysis of Insolvency Laws and Their Impact on the Role, Power, and Jurisdiction of Today's United States Bankruptcy Court and Its Judicial Officers," *Journal of Bankruptcy Law and Practice* 9 (January/February 2000), 165–200.

[62]   Stephen J. Spurr and Kevin M. Ball, "The Effects of a Statute (BAPCPA) Designed to Make It More Difficult for People to File for Bankruptcy," *American Bankruptcy Law Journal* 87 (2013), 27–47. CCH, "CCH Bankruptcy Reform Act Briefing: Bankruptcy Abuse Prevention and Consumer Protection Act of 2005" (updated April 21, 2005), available at www.cch.com/bankruptcy/Bankruptcy_04-21.pdf (last retrieved December 2, 2005).

[63]   Angela Littwin, "Adapting to BAPCPA," *American Bankruptcy Law Journal* 90 (2016), 183–234. See also Spurr and Ball, "The Effects of a Statute (BAPCPA) Designed to Make It More Difficult for People to File for Bankruptcy," 29–33; Christian E. Weller, Bernard J. Morzuch, and Amanda Logan, "Estimating the Effect of the Bankruptcy Abuse Prevention and Consumer Protection Act of 2005 on the Bankruptcy Rate," *American Bankruptcy Law Journal* 84 (2010), 327–60; and Christine Duga, "Reform Has Made Filing Bankruptcy More Costly," *USA Today* (December 23, 2011). See also Administrative Office of the U.S. Courts, "New Law Creates Rush to File in Federal Court," *The Third Branch* 11 (November 2005), 1.

[64]   For more detailed information about these courts, see United States Court of International Trade, "About the Court," available at https://www.cit.uscourts.gov/ (last retrieved April 11, 2020); United States Court of Federal Claims, "About the Court," https://www.uscfc.uscourts.gov/about-court (last retrieved April 11, 2020); and, United States Tax Court, "About the Court," https://www.ustaxcourt.gov/ (last retrieved April 11, 2020).

[65]   See Judicial Panel on Multidistrict Litigation, available at http://www.jpml.uscourts.gov/ (last retrieved April 11, 2020).

[66]   John Dorsett Niles, "Assessing the Constitutionality of the Alien Terrorist Removal Court," *Duke Law Journal* (2008), 1833–64.

[67]   Section 207 of the FISA Amendments Act gave the federal government the power to conduct targeted surveillance of foreign persons outside of the U.S., but it could not be used to target Americans abroad, or anyone located in the U.S. Still, Section 207 encouraged the FBI to collect information on not only the surveillance target, but also incidental or inadvertent communications between the target and Americans without a warrant. Geoffrey Stone and Michael Morell, "The One Change We Need to Surveillance Law," *Washington Post*, available at https://www.washingtonpost.com/opinions/the-one-change-we-need-to-surveillance-law/2017/10/09/53a40df0-a9ea-11e7-850e-2bdd1236be5d_story.html?utm_term=.361b0c0ba 221 (last retrieved March 26, 2019). See also, President Barack Obama, "Obama's Speech on N.S.A. Phone Surveillance (Transcript)," *New York Times* (January 17, 2014), available at www.nytimes.com (last retrieved March 4, 2014); Lauren Fox, "Democrats Seek to Reform FISA Court in Light of NSA Revelations," *USA Today* (August 2, 2013); James Risen and Eric Lichtblau, "Court Affirms Wiretapping Without Warrants," *New York Times* (January 15, 2009), available at www.nytimes.com (last retrieved March 4, 2014); Nolan and Thompson, "Reform of the Foreign Intelligence Surveillance Courts: Procedural and Operational Changes"; *In re Directives Pursuant to Section 10b of the Foreign Intelligence Surveillance Act*, 551 F.3d 1004 (FISA Ct. Rev. 2008); and *In re Sealed Case*, 310 F.3d 717 (FISA Ct. Rev. 2002).

[68]   The Washington Post, "USA Freedom Act: What's In, What's Out," available at https://www.washingtonpost.com/graphics/politics/usa-freedom-act/ (last retrieved April 11, 2020).

[69]   Charlie Savage, "Carter Page FISA Documents Are Released by the Justice Department," NY Times (July 21, 2018), available at https://www.nytimes.com/2018/07/21/us/politics/carter-page-fisa.html (last retrieved April 11, 2020). See also, Andrew Nolan and Richard M. Thompson II, "Reform of the Foreign Intelligence Surveillance Courts: Procedural and Operational Changes," *Congressional Research Service* (August 26, 2014), available at http://www.fas.org/sgp/crs/intel/R43362.pdf (last retrieved October 27, 2014), 1–2. See also Edward C. Liu, "Reauthorization of the FISA Amendments Act," *Congressional Research Service* (April 8, 2013), available at http://fas.org/sgp/crs/intel/R42725.pdf (last retrieved October 27, 2014), 1–2.

70   Such reforms include requiring FISC to review amicus curiae (or third-party) briefs to make FISC judges aware of privacy and civil rights and liberties interests in government wiretap applications; requiring FISC judges to sit en banc, or with a full court of eleven judges in making wiretap decisions; altering FISC or its appellate body, the Foreign Intelligence Surveillance Court of Review; raising the bar of permitting government surveillance; and requiring a "public advocate" be present during the FISC review process. Andrew Nolan and Richard M. Thompson II, "Reform of the Foreign Intelligence Surveillance Courts: Procedural and Operational Changes," *Congressional Research Service* (January 16, 2014), available at www.fas.org/sgp/crs/intel/R43362.pdf (last retrieved March 2, 2014). See also James Risen and Eric Lichtblau, "Bush Said to Have Secretly Lifted Some Spying Limits After 9/11," *Chicago Tribune* (December 16, 2005), C30.

71   U.S. Court of Appeals for the Federal Circuit, "Court Jurisdiction," available at http://www.cafc.uscourts.gov/the-court/court-jurisdiction (last retrieved April 11, 2020). See also Judicial Conference of the United States, Long Range Plan for the Federal Courts (December 1995), 43, n. 6; R. Polk Wagner and Lee Petherbridge, "Is the Federal Circuit Succeeding? An Empirical Assessment of Judicial Performance," *University of Pennsylvania Law Review* 152 (2004), 1105–80.

72   J. Woodford Howard, Jr., *Courts of Appeals in the Federal Judicial System: A Study of the Second, Fifth, and District of Columbia Circuits* (Princeton, N.J.: Princeton University Press, 1981), 8. See generally Jonathan Matthew Cohen, *Inside Appellate Courts: The Impact of Court Organization on Judicial Decision-Making in the United States Courts of Appeals* (Ann Arbor: University of Michigan Press, 2002); David E. Klein, *Making Law in the United States Courts of Appeals* (Cambridge, U.K.: Cambridge University Press, 2002); Donald R. Songer, Reginald S. Sheehan, and Susan B. Haire, *Continuity and Change on the United States Courts of Appeals* (Ann Arbor: University of Michigan Press, 2000).

73   Christopher P. Banks, "The Politics of En Banc Review in the 'Mini-Supreme Court,' " *Journal of Law and Politics* (Spring 1997), 377–414.

74   Administrative Office of U.S. Courts, U.S. Courts of Appeals-Civil Cases Commenced, Terminated, and Pending, By Circuit and Nature of Proceeding, During the 12-Month Periods Ending March 31,2019 (Table B-1) available at www.uscourts.gov (last retrieved April 11, 2020).

75   The caseload statistics cited and the argument that appellate justice is compromised are detailed in William M. Richman and William L. Reynolds, *Injustice on Appeal: The United States Courts of Appeals in Crisis* (New York: Oxford University Press, 2013), xi–9. Caseload data for 2019 and the process by which cases are terminated on procedural grounds or by the merits is located in Administrative Office of U.S. Courts, U.S. Courts of Appeals Federal Judicial Caseload Statistics.

76   Zack Whittaker, "In Trump's first year, FISA court denied record number of surveillance orders," *ZDNet* (April 25, 2018), available at https://www.zdnet.com/article/fisa-court-denied-record-surveillance-orders-trump-first-year/ (last retrieved on April 11, 2020)(citing an eleven percent FISC rejection rate of FISA applications during the Trump Administration's first year in office, a historical high). For information on the other courts mentioned, see U.S. Court of Appeals for Veteran Claims, "About the Court," available at http://m.uscourts.cavc.gov/About.php (last retrieved April 11, 2020); U.S. Court of Appeals for the Armed Forces, "About the Court," available at http://www.armfor.uscourts.gov/newcaaf/about.htm (last retrieved April 11, 2020); and United States Foreign Intelligence Surveillance Court, "United States Foreign Intelligence Court of Review," available at http://www.fisc.uscourts.gov/FISCR (last retrieved on April 11, 2020).

77   O'Brien, *Storm Center*, 235.

78   See David Lat, "Supreme Court Clerk Hiring Watch: The Complete Clerk Roster for October Term 2018," available at https://abovethelaw.com/2018/08/supreme-court-clerk-hiring-watch-the-complete-clerk-roster-for-october-term-2018/ (last retrieved April 11, 2020); and, Barbara A. Perry, *The Priestly Tribe: The Supreme Court's Image in the American Mind* (Westport, Conn.: Praeger, 1999), 25–45.

79   Administrative Office of U.S. Courts, "Supreme Court of the United States—Cases on Docket, Disposed of, and Remaining on Docket at Conclusion of October Terms, 2014 Through 2018" (Table A-1), available at www.uscourts.gov (last retrieved April 11, 2020).

80   H. W. Perry, Jr., *Deciding to Decide: Agenda Setting in the United States Supreme Court* (Cambridge, Mass.: Harvard University Press, 1991).

81   David M. O'Brien, "A Diminished Plenary Docket: A Legacy of the Rehnquist Court," *Judicature* (November/December 2005), 134–37, 183.

82   William H. Rehnquist, *The Supreme Court: How It Was, How It Is* (New York: William Morrow, Inc., 1987), 253.

83   O'Brien, *Storm Center*, 147, 209.

84   Rehnquist, *The Supreme Court*, 276.

85   As quoted in O'Brien, *Storm Center*, 216.

86   O'Brien, *Storm Center*, 288–89, 297–308.

87   Owen M. Fiss, "The Bureaucratization of the Judiciary," *Yale Law Journal* 92 (1983), 1442; Wade H. McCree, Jr., "Bureaucratic Justice: An Early Warning," *University of Pennsylvania Law Review* 129 (1981), 777.

88   Conference of Chief Justices and National Center for State Courts, *The History of the Conference of Chief Justices (1949–2009)* (Williamsburg, Va.: National Center for State Courts, 2009); Robert W. Tobin, *Creating the Judicial Branch: The Unfinished Reform* (Williamsburg, Va.: National Center for State Courts, 1999), 51–115.

89   Larry C. Berkson, "A Brief History of Court Reform," in *Managing the State Courts: Text and Readings*, edited by Larry C. Berkson, Steven, W. Hays, and Susan J. Carbon (St. Paul, Minn.: West, 1977), 7–8.

90   Gregory J. Linhares, "Vision, Function, and the Kitchen Sink: The Evolving Role of the State Court Administrator," in *Future Trends in State Courts* (2012), edited by Carol R. Flango, Amy M. McDowell, Deborah W. Saunders, Nora E. Sydow, Charles F. Campbell, and Neal B. Kauder (Williamsburg, Va.: National Center for State Courts, 2012), 20–25. Although many states let the chief justice of the court of last resort act as chief executive officer for the judiciary, some states use judicial councils, where other members of the judiciary sit on committees that establish policy, practices, and rules. A common format for governance is what Robert Tobin calls a "modified executive model," an arrangement that allows the chief justice to remain in charge of administration but also permits the state court administrator to use delegated authority to run court operations and to implement, to the extent possible, established judicial priorities. Tobin, Creating the Judicial Branch, 105–6.

91   Tobin, *Creating the Judicial Branch*, 105–6.

92   Fish, *The Politics of Federal Judicial Administration*, 32–33, 61–62, 125–45, 387. See Felix Frankfurter and James M. Landis, *The Business of the Supreme Court: A Study in the Federal Judicial System* (New York: Macmillan, 1928).

93   Russell Wheeler, "The Administration of the Federal Courts: Understanding the Entities and Interrelationships That Make Federal Courts Work," in *The Improvement of the Administration of Justice*, 7th ed. (Chicago: Judicial Division, American Bar Association, 2001), 54–57. See Federal Judicial Center, "Federal Judicial Center," available at www.fjc.gov (last retrieved March 7, 2014); and, Administrative Office of U.S. Courts, "Governance & the Judicial Conference," available at https://www.uscourts.gov/about-federal-courts/governance-judicial-conference (last retrieved on June 30, 2020).

94   See Edward-Isaac Dovere, "The Coronavirus Killed the Policy Primary," *The Atlantic* (April 4, 2020), available   at   https://www.theatlantic.com/politics/archive/2020/04/coronavirus-climate-change-policy-primary/609280/ (last retrieved April 11, 2020); Pew Research Center for the People and the Press, "Partisan Polarization Surges in Bush, Obama Years" (June 4, 2013) (Washington, D.C.: Pew Research Center for the People and the Press, 2012), available at www.people-press.org (last retrieved March 7, 2014). See *Bush v. Gore*, 531 U.S. 98 (2000). See also, *Obergefell v. Hodges*, 135 S.Ct. 2071 (2015).

95   See Richard L. Vining, Jr. and Teena Wilhelm, "The Chief Justice as Advocate-in-Chief: Examining the Year-End Report on the Federal Judiciary," *Judicature* 95 (2012): 267–274.

96   See, e.g., Supreme Court of the United States, "Chief Justice's Year-End Reports on the Federal Judiciary (2014 to 2019), available at https://www.supremecourt.gov/publicinfo/year-end/year-endreports. aspx (last retrieved on April 11, 2020); Editorial, "Lippman's legacy: The chief judge of New York's highest court retires with plenty to be proud of," Daily News (Jan. 1, 2016), available from http://www.nydailynews. com/opinion/lippman-legacy-article-1.2482144# (last retrieved April 11, 2020); James C. McKinley Jr., "New York State's Top Judge Permits Early Bar Exam in Exchange for Pro Bono Work," *N.Y. Times* (February 11, 2014), available from https://www.nytimes.com/2014/02/12/nyregion/top-judge-allows-for-early-bar-exam-in-return-for-pro-bono-work.html (last retrieved April 11, 2020); Judicial Conference of the United States, "Strategic Plan for the Federal Judiciary" (September 2010), available from www.uscourts.gov (last retrieved March 8, 2014); and Judicial Conference of the United States, "Long Range Plan for Information Technology in the Federal Judiciary," available from www.uscourts.gov (last retrieved March 8, 2014).

CHAPTER 4

Judicial Selection and Removal

At the start of his presidency Donald J. Trump was poised to reshape the federal courts for decades to come. By exercising his constitutional power to appoint judges with the advice and consent of the Senate, his White House victory gave him the chance to fill over a hundred judicial vacancies with life-time appointments, including one at the Supreme Court due to Justice Antonin Scalia's sudden death in February 2016. In contrast, at the start of his administration Barack Obama only had roughly half that number; and, even though Obama successfully placed more nominees on the bench in eight years than his predecessor, George W. Bush, Obama's prospects of putting an enduring stamp on the federal judiciary dimmed after the Republicans seized control of the U.S. Senate during the 2014 midterm elections. Indeed, buoyed by a change in Senate rules that let a simple majority (51) of senators to confirm presidential and judicial appointees, Majority Leader Mitch McConnell (R-KY) and the Senate Judiciary Committee led by Charles Grassley (R-IA) refused to grant an up-or-down vote to dozens of Obama's picks after 2015. Also, whereas Obama chose to fill the federal courts with a more diversified bench—elevating a greater number of females, minorities, and even openly gay nominees at historically unprecedented levels—Trump correctly sensed that his base (social conservatives, Rust Belt workers, evangelicals, and the alt-right) and his electoral fortunes would turn on his decision to appoint judges that shared the textualist and originalist judicial philosophy of the late Justice Scalia. As he explained at his Republic National Convention acceptance speech, "The replacement of our beloved Justice Scalia will be a person of similar views, principles and judicial philosophies. Very important. This will be one of the most important issues decided by this election."[1]

Once in office, President Trump told his closest advisers that his judicial nominees must be young (under 50, but sometimes under 40 years of age), conservative, and a strict constructionist. With the close supervision of his White House counsel, Donald McGahn, and the extensive cooperation of key conservative interest groups, such as the Federalist Society and the Heritage Foundation, Trump raced to turn his campaign promise into a reality before the 2018 midterm elections and the end of his first term (the Federalist Society's role in federal judicial selection is discussed in this chapter in the "The Federalist Society's Role in Federal Judicial Selection" box). Although much of his first term was dogged by special counsel Robert Mueller's investigation of Trump's involvement in Russian meddling in the 2016 presidential election, and impeachment proceedings, with few exceptions the President has been immensely successful in packing the federal courts. By the end of June 2020, the Senate confirmed two hundred lifetime appointments to the federal courts, with fifty-three on the influential court of appeals (circuit courts) and over twice that number on the district (trial) courts. Along with Senate rule changes that put few barriers in front of getting speedy confirmations, the Republicans' ability to hold on to the Senate in the 2018 elections allowed Trump to accelerate rapidly the pace and quantity of judicial confirmations to unprecedented levels. Trump's imprint at the circuit court level is particularly impressive, as the number of judges he put on the appeals court in three years are almost as many as President Barack Obama did over his entire eight years in office. Trump's success in reshaping federal circuit courts is highly significant because they are often, in practice, the court of last resort for many litigants. Put differently, in the words of Justice Sonia Sotomayor, "the court of appeals is where policy is made," a fact that is especially salient because the nation's highest court, the Supreme Court, is increasingly inclined to review fewer cases on their legal merits.[2]

Apart from the federal lower courts, Trump has also deeply influenced the Supreme Court's political composition. In light of the Senate changing hands after the 2014 election, Justice Scalia's death paved the way for the Senate to confirm the Tenth Circuit's Judge, Neil M. Gorsuch, shortly before the Court's 2017–2018 Term. Even though Gorsuch was eminently qualified to serve, his confirmation was politically controversial: Gorsuch was given the chance to replace Scalia only after the Senate's Republican leadership took the unprecedented step of denying Obama's choice, Merrick Garland (the Chief Judge of the D.C. Circuit), a Senate confirmation hearing for over a year. Notably, the refusal to give Garland a hearing—and ultimately, the impending reality of Gorsuch's Senate confirmation—arose when the Republicans invoked the so-called "nuclear option" of changing the Senate rules to permit Gorsuch to be confirmed by a simple majority vote, rather than the tradition of requiring 60 votes to cut off a filibuster. The political gambit worked and fully vindicated the GOP's strategy of not giving Obama a third Supreme Court appointment (Justices Sonia Sotomayor and Elena Kagan were the first two) when there was a possibility that Trump would win the White House in the 2016 presidential campaign (for further analysis, see "The (Constitutional) Hardball Politics of Federal Judicial Selection" box in this chapter).[3]

The political controversies involving President Trump's Supreme Court appointments continued into the next year with the announcement of Anthony Kennedy's retirement at the end of the Court's Term. The President's pick, Brett Kavanaugh of the D.C. Circuit, surprised many court watchers who thought his hardline conservative views were too extreme.[4] In addition, as the Republican-held Senate quickly moved to have a confirmation vote before the midterm elections, the nominee's hearings were first marred by loud protests and persistent complaints by Democratic senators that the hearings were fundamentally unfair because the Republicans did not make reasonably available all of the nominee's record pertaining to his involvement in the G.W. Bush White House and the Starr impeachment investigation of President Bill Clinton for review. The partisan rancor intensified when Professor Christine Blasey Ford subsequently accused Kavanaugh of sexual assault in high school, which Republicans called a political sham designed to delay the Senate's vote, but one defended by Democrats and sexual assault victims as necessary to prevent a nominee with questionable character and judicial temperament from serving on the nation's highest court. A special hearing of the Senate Judiciary Committee heard testimony from Ford and Kavanaugh, but not others who alleged sexual misconduct, though, and Kavanaugh was confirmed by one of the closest confirmation votes in the Senate's history (50:48) shortly after the beginning of the Court's 2018–19 Term.[5]

To be sure, Trump and the Republican Party understood the political significance of securing two appointments to the Supreme Court. Both Kavanaugh and Gorsuch have impeccable conservative credentials, and each adheres to a textual and originalist judicial philosophy to deciding cases. But unlike Gorsuch's appointment, which filled the vacancy of a like-minded Scalia, Kavanaugh replaced Justice Kennedy, who often served as a pivotal fifth vote in controversial areas of social policy, such as abortion and same-sex marriage cases. In short, Trump anticipated that Kavanaugh would join the Court's most reliable conservative bloc (Chief Justice John Roberts and Justices Gorsuch, Samuel Alito, and Clarence Thomas) and enable it to push the Court further to the right as it would most likely revisit, and possibly reverse, some of the Court's most progressive precedents that even Kennedy helped to maintain when he was on the bench. With Kennedy off the Court, some researchers and court watchers speculate that not only will Chief Justice Roberts will become the new "swing" or median vote, but also that the conservative bloc will increasingly undercut rulings on abortion, affirmative action, and same-sex anti-discrimination rights while strengthening business interests and rejecting claims of judicial deference to agency power as well as challenges to capital punishment or solitary confinement.[6]

The Trump administration's impact in reconfiguring the federal courts registers how the federal judicial selection process has become highly politicized in recent decades. That trend, perhaps, is even more apparent in state judicial selection processes that have increasingly become political battlegrounds, which in turn may diminish judicial impartiality and independence. This chapter explores the politics of judicial selection by examining (1) the different methods of judicial selection in the states, (2) the appointment politics of filling vacancies on the federal bench, and, (3) whether there should be reforms affecting judicial retirement, discipline, and removal.

STAFFING STATE COURTS

The debate over how to select judges originated during the American Revolution. In the colonies, royalist judges were appointed by the Crown and perceived to be corrupt and tyrannical. The Declaration of Independence thus identified royalist judges as one of several grievances against the King of England, stating that he "made Judges dependent on his Will alone, for the tenure of their offices, and the amount and payment of their salaries." That objection highlighted the need to separate the judiciary from the executive and legislative branches. Still, **judicial independence**—the principle requiring the insulation of courts from the ordinary political processes—had to be balanced with **judicial accountability**—that courts and judges are democratically accountable to the people. Historically, both directly condition the role of courts and judges in the legal and political system.[7]

In historical perspective, after the Constitution's 1789 ratification, judges were appointed either by the legislature or by the governor in all thirteen states. Judges were given some measure of independence through the imposition of tenure for "good behavior" and fixed or "adequate" salary provisions. But judges were also subject to impeachment and removal for misconduct or abuse of power.[8]

Some states, however, began to change their judicial selection processes during the era of Jacksonian democracy. Economic crises in the states led to political reform proposals to strengthen and democratize courts across the country in the 1840s and 1850s. Many populist reformers thought that having judicial elections would secure judicial independence from the political branches and empower the courts to protect the people from corrupt elected officials and state legislatures—who were thought to be responsible for the economic crises that damaged the country.[9]

By the Civil War, twenty-three of the then thirty-one states elected all or some of their judges. Most states held partisan elections. However, the problem of cronyism and the growing impact of political parties soon overwhelmed the states' judicial selection systems. A major criticism of appointive and electoral systems was that they made judges too dependent upon politicians. That dependency was made worse because the electorate generally lacked knowledge about judicial candidates. The problems of voter ignorance, political bias, and corruption were magnified because judges campaigned to get elected, which created a sometimes obvious appearance of impropriety.[10]

Consequently, in the early twentieth century, there was a movement to take the politics out of judicial selection through the adoption of nonpartisan ballots—ballots omitting the partisan affiliation of judicial candidates.[11] A related reform focused on judicial candidates' qualifications and the adoption of some form of **judicial "merit" plan**. Those plans, as a first step, allowed the governor to make an appointment from a list of nominees that was generated by a nonpartisan nomination commission (a panel composed of public officials, lawyers or judges, and citizens). After the appointment and a term of service by the judge, subsequently voters would have the choice to let the judge continue to serve after an uncontested retention election.[12]

Merit Judicial Selection Systems

The prospect of corruption led to efforts to depoliticize judicial selection in the states. In 1913, at the suggestion of one of its founders, Albert Kales, a Northwestern University law professor, the American Judicature Society (AJS) developed the prototype of state "merit judicial selection" systems. It featured the appointment of lower court judges by elected state court chief judges who made their selections from a preapproved list of candidates compiled by a non-partisan judicial council or commission. States then could hold periodic retention elections with judges retaining their seats only if they received a majority vote in an unopposed, nonpartisan election. Retention elections were thought to be different from ordinary elections because voters could evaluate the judge's record instead of comparing the judge to another challenger, a common pathway in ordinary elections to decide who to vote for. Indeed, the AJS reform was styled as a "nonpartisan court plan," built on the assumption that it would attract highly qualified lawyers—instead of rote politicians—to the bench while encouraging public participation through voting behavior. In 1926, political scientist Harold

Laski modified the plan's design in an effort to depoliticize it further. Under Laski's version, a multimember advisory board, picked by judges, prepared a slate of candidates for selection by the governor, and appointments were made subject to Senate confirmation.[13]

In 1934, California became the first state to adopt a version of the merit plan, but it differed from the AJS version in one important respect. As originally proposed, the plan called for the governor to pick a judge from a list of candidates proposed by a nominating panel composed of judges and prosecutors, with a retention election held at the next general election. Under the so-called California plan, however, the governor's office (not a commission) first compiled the list of candidates. Thereafter, the nominating panel, consisting of the chief justice, the presiding judge of a district court of appeal, and the attorney general, reviewed and approved (or rejected) the governor's appointment. Also, at the next general election, a noncompetitive retention election was held. With only the judge's name on the ballot, voters were given a "yes" or "no" option for retention. Judges who were retained subsequently served a twelve-year term (instead of for life, as the AJS originally proposed). By giving the governor more control over judicial selection at the initial stages, California's merit plan, ironically, had the effect of increasing the governor's powers to pick nominees sharing his or her political ideology; still, it also limited judicial service to a fixed term.[14]

Shortly thereafter, the American Bar Association (ABA) endorsed the AJS type of merit plan—but one that allowed the nominating panel, and not the governor's office, to compile the initial list of judicial candidates for gubernatorial appointment. While several other states considered the reform, only Missouri, in 1940, adopted the ABA-endorsed appointment-elective plan. Under the so-called **Missouri merit plan**, a multimember nomination commission (consisting of citizens and attorneys) proposes a list of three candidates whose choice is then ratified or rejected in an unopposed, nonpartisan retention election held in the next general election. For appellate judges, a favorable vote guarantees a twelve-year term, whereas other judges are elected for six-year terms. If a judge is voted out of office, the commission compiles another list from which the governor fills the vacancy. After Missouri ratified its merit plan, twenty-three other states adopted some version of merit selection for some or all of their judges. With the exception of Hawaii, every one of those states added a retention election to let voters decide if judges should remain on the bench.[15]

The realistic prospect of achieving a depoliticized system of state judicial selection through the adoption of merit plans has, nonetheless, diminished over time. Even the Missouri merit plan, which for years was the "model system for merit selection in states across the country," has been under sharp political attack.[16] While "judicial merit plan" supporters contend that they limit gubernatorial control over appointments and ensure that the public has a role in removing judges through retention elections,[17] critics counter that merit systems are flawed because they grant a "functional equivalent of life tenure" due to the legal profession's dominance on judicial commissions, and judges facing retention elections rarely face any opposition. As a result, for some scholars there is not enough evidence that merit systems truly depoliticize the state judicial selection process. Accordingly, judicial merit selection systems are facing growing legislative scrutiny and possible reform.[18] Although many states incorporate input from a nomination commission into their judicial selection process, only five states— Alaska, Colorado, Iowa, Nebraska, and Wyoming—continue to use an apolitical classic merit plan format across all levels of their court system. In these systems, before having to face a retention election, state judges serve a term of years between one to three years, depending upon the state.

Judicial Election and Appointment Systems

States use a variety of formats to select their judges that typically serve for a term of years. In addition to using classic merit plans, the selection process is generally by popular election, appointment, or some combination that incorporates gubernatorial appointment and merit with election designs (Table 4.1). Whereas twenty-two states use judicial election systems, twelve others let the governor or legislature appoint judges. Ten more states use a combination of gubernatorial appointments (as informed by nominating commissions) or judicial elections at different levels (trial or appellate) of the judiciary. One state, Tennessee, permits the governor to select appellate judges after House and Senate confirmation; but partisan elections determine who sits on trial courts (Table 4.1).

Either partisan or non-partisan elections decide who sits on the bench in states using judicial elections. In partisan elections, the judge's political affiliation appears on the ballot after the political party's choice to serve is ratified by a primary election or party convention. For nonpartisan elections, it is absent. Notably, a few states have mixed election systems. In Michigan, nonpartisan elections are held to pick trial and intermediate court of appeals judges; but partisan nomination and nonpartisan elections determine who will sit on Michigan's court of last resort. In North Carolina, trial court judges are chosen through non-partisan ballots and appellate judges are subject to popular elections. In contrast, after a partisan primary, Ohio voters choose their judges after a non-partisan general election. Of the states with judicial elections as their primary means to pick judges, twelve hold nonpartisan elections—the dominant method (Table 4.1).

The remaining states are typically modeled after a gubernatorial appointment system that is structured to give governors or legislatures more control over judicial selection; or they generally combine merit with an election method at different levels of the judiciary. In states using gubernatorial appointments, a judge may be selected by a gubernatorial appointment and a nomination commission (i.e., merit), but the appointment is subject to additional executive or legislative approval. Accordingly, governors may add or remove judicial nomination commissioners, or governors or legislatures may reappoint judges instead of letting them face a retention election. Another common variation is to allow governors to appoint judges with senatorial consent.[19] Moreover, two states, South Carolina and Virginia, empower the legislature to staff the state courts; but that process is more the exception that the rule in appointment jurisdictions because most states opt for gubernatorial appointment. Finally, several states use hybrid gubernatorial merit appointment and election systems to select judges at different levels of the judiciary. For example, after a nominating commission weighs in, the governor in Indiana picks appellate judges; but lower court judges are chosen through popular elections.[20] Even though there is wide diversity in state judicial selection, state governors play an influential role in staffing the courts because they are at the forefront in determining who sits on the bench in classic merit, gubernatorial appointment, and combined appointment-merit and election systems in over half the states.

Table 4.1	Judicial Selection Methods in the States			
Classic Merit	**Election**	**Gubernatorial Appointment**	**Legislative Appointment**	**Combined Merit and Other Methods**
Alaska	Alabama*	Connecticut^	South Carolina	Arizona
Colorado	Arkansas**	Delaware^	Virginia	California
Iowa	Georgia**	Hawaii^		Florida
Nebraska	Idaho**	Maine^^		Indiana
Wyoming	Illinois*	Massachusetts^^		Kansas
	Kentucky**	New Hampshire^^^		Maryland
	Louisiana*	New Jersey^^		Missouri
	Michigan***	Rhode Island^		New York
	Minnesota**	Utah^		Oklahoma
	Mississippi**	Vermont^		South Dakota
	Montana**			Tennessee
	Nevada**			
	New Mexico*			
	North Carolina****			
	North Dakota%			
	Ohio*****			
	Oregon**			
	Pennsylvania*			
	Texas*			
	Washington**			
	West Virginia**			
	Wisconsin**			

Notes: * Partisan Election; ** Non-Partisan Election; *** Partisan Nomination and Non-Partisan Election for Supreme Court and Non-Partisan Election for Court of Appeals and Circuit Court; ****Non-partisan election for Superior Court and Partisan Election for Court of Appeals and Supreme

Court; *****Partisan Primary and Non-Partisan General Election; % Non-partisan election for Superior and Supreme Court but Court of Appeals chosen by judges and lawyers; ^ with nominating committee and house and/or senate confirmation; ^^ with house and/or senate and/or governor council confirmation (Massachusetts uses nominating commission as well in Appeals and Superior Courts); ^^^Gubernatorial recommendation from selection commission and executive council appointment.

All columns except for last generally use the method identified across all levels (trial and appellate) of the state judicial system. Except for Tennessee (which does not use a nominating commission), States in the last column use gubernatorial appointment (sometimes subject to legislative or executive consent) with a merit component (a nomination commission) along with another method (election) for selecting judges at different levels of the state judicial system.

Source: National Center for State Courts, "Methods of Judicial Selection," available from http://www.judicialselection.us/judicial_selection/methods/selection_of_judges.cfm?state=f (last retrieved April 14, 2020).

Staying on the Bench

Unlike their federal counterparts (which enjoy life-tenure), a majority of state judges serve for a term of years after their initial selection to the bench. The process for staying in judicial service is just as diverse as the way state judges are put onto their respective courts. Across the states, and depending upon which specific court is at issue, the length of service generally ranges from as little as one year to as much as fourteen years; but many fall in the six to eight-year time frame. After the initial term of years expires, the process by which they continue to serve is also quite varied. In Florida, Kansas and Wyoming, for example, Supreme Court justices serve at least one year before having to face a retention election that asks the voters to decide if they (as incumbents) should stay in office; but, in Delaware, justices at the highest court enjoy twelve-year terms that are renewable for another dozen-years if they receive gubernatorial reappointment from a nomination commission and senate consent. In states using partisan or non-partisan elections, judges in many states, such as Georgia and Texas, must be reelected once their term expires. In still other states, such as Massachusetts and New Hampshire, after gubernatorial appointment judges can stay on the bench until they reach the age of 70; and many other states impose mandatory retirement requirements as well. Only one state, Rhode Island, vests its judges with lifetime tenure, a benefit that is given to federal courts that are constituted under Article III of the U.S. Constitution.[21]

In sum, all but two states use either merit or elective systems to staff their courts initially; and, as with initial selection designs, the process by which state judges remain on the bench varies from state-to-state. Of the two general selection methods, gubernatorial-based merit plans (or some hybrid combination thereof) are responsible for staffing some or all of the courts in more states, although judicial elections are still widely used and have many defenders. Furthermore, although the merit plan format is the preferred reform method to take the politics out of judicial selection,[22] several states are actively trying to pass new laws in order to reduce their effectiveness in depoliticizing judicial selection. In response, some judicial reform efforts have abandoned serious efforts to expand merit selection plans. Instead, they have begun to concentrate on finding ways to improve the underlying mechanisms linked to conducting judicial elections, such as creating public financing laws to limit special interest group influence or exploring initiatives to enhance voter information by the use of voter guides and judicial evaluation programs.[23] The recent movement toward diminishing merit selection and retention processes underscores the difficulties of striking an appropriate balance between judicial independence and judicial accountability. At bottom, the diversity and debate surrounding the issue of how to best put judges on the bench is a potent reminder that political factors cannot be entirely removed from the state judicial selection process. Moreover, as the next section details, courts are always vulnerable to political attacks when they make politically unpopular decisions by special interest groups or organizations trying to change the composition of courts to favor their ideological viewpoints in judicial elections.[24]

The Politics of Judicial Campaigns

Despite merit selection systems, most state judges face some type of election in the initial selection or retention process. As a result, since the 1980s judicial races are getting "nastier, nosier, and costlier" and the underlying mechanisms that serve to staff state courts has become increasingly politicized.[25] Special interest groups have become an established part of judicial campaigns and elections, typically pitting trial lawyers and labor unions against the insurance industry and the business community. Dysfunctional national politics, and heightened partisanship across the states, has allowed groups to become especially influential in what have become judicial election wars.[26]

In 2011–2012, the first full election cycle after the Court's ruling in *Citizens United v. Federal Election Commission* (2010)—a decision that permitted unlimited corporate and labor union spending in federal elections but also led to removing restrictions on campaign spending in about half the states—judicial candidates raised a total of over $56 million in state supreme court elections. The most money was spent in battleground states, like Alabama, Michigan, Florida, North Carolina, Ohio, and Wisconsin. In these states and a growing number of others, contested (partisan and nonpartisan) supreme court elections have had an influx of negative television advertisements. Unlike past election cycles, much of the mudslinging was the result of independent spending by super PACs—so-called 501(c)(4)s, or social welfare organizations (which do not have to disclose their donor under the tax code) and political parties that use social media venues (e.g., Facebook, Twitter, and YouTube) and television to get their message to voters. Of the $56 million spent in 2011–2012, 57 percent was by candidates, but special interest groups accounted for 27 percent, and political parties spent 15 percent on judicial races.[27]

According to the Brennan Center for Justice, the trend of high outside spending in state supreme court races has continued to grow in the aftermath of *Citizens United.* In a study of the 2015–16 supreme court election cycle, PACs, social welfare organizations, and non-party groups spent $27.8 million dollars on those races and special interest groups were responsible for 40 percent of total expenditures (up from the 29 percent in the year before). The Center documented other trends that register a lack of transparency and implicit influence on the supreme court election process, such as the increasing presence of "dark money" (spending by groups whose funding sources are not disclosed) and "gray money" (super PAC spending that disclose other PACS as donors, which makes the donation sources difficult or impossible to trace). Together, a total of 82 percent of dark (54 percent) and gray (28 percent) money was spent in the 2015–16 state supreme court campaigns. In a subsequent study, the Center underscored that as of January 2017 over twenty states had at least one justice on their supreme court that were the object of a one-million-dollar election, fueled by special interest group money.[28]

Furthermore, the judicial media campaigns are consistently negative. In 2011–2012, for instance, a Michigan Democratic Party ad accused a judicial candidate of having "worked to deny benefits to a cancer patient," while an ad from the Judicial Crisis Network (a conservative Washington, D.C., group) claimed another candidate had "volunteered to free a terrorist" because she sought to provide legal representation to a Guantánamo Bay detainee. In the same campaign cycle, justices who unanimously legalized same-sex marriage in Iowa in 2009 were labeled "open enemies of God" by a conservative radio host. The Justice for All Political Action Committee, composed of trial lawyers and labor groups, broadcast an ad accusing a Republican judicial candidate of being too lenient on criminals because he gave probation to kidnappers who "tortured and nearly beat a ninety-two-year-old grandmother to death."[29] Such ads are increasingly common in state court of last resort races: whereas in 2000 only four states had T.V. ads broadcast in state supreme court elections, by 2016 they were prevalent in at least 16 states. In addition to more money being spent on such ads, their tone and character are quite nasty. In a 2016 Washington State judicial election, a supreme court justice's re-election bid was characterized as the candidate favoring "child predators" following his support of a decision that ruled against the police in conducting a warrantless search of a private home. In another race, an ad by the group Kansans for Justice attacked the Kansas Supreme Court as "repeatedly pervert(ing) the law to side with murderers and rapists" for its decision to overturn the death sentences of convicted murders. While these ads often portray courts or justices as being "tough" or "too soft" on criminal defendants in their decision-making, other ad themes across the states range from highlighting more "traditional" content (involving a person's experience and professional or personal accomplishments) to other types of sordid depictions suggesting that specific judges are "for sale" or "in the pocket" of moneyed interests that pressure them to decide cases in accordance with the donor's political preferences.[30]

A disturbing aspect of state judicial elections, which are supposed to ensure judicial accountability, instead foster political attacks that may actually mislead voters about the merits of a judge and, therefore, undercut judicial independence and democratic participation. The problem is compounded by two other interrelated factors: low voter information and the high retention rates of judges. One study of retention elections in ten states between 1964 and 1994 found that most judges are retained in office, except in the rare instance when a portion of the electorate targets a judge for defeat. Indeed, only fifty judges, or 1.3 percent, were defeated in that period. Furthermore, the average rate of "voter rolloff"— the portion of voters who vote for the lead partisan office on the ballot but omit voting for the judicial retention candidates—was 34.5 percent. These findings show that a significant portion of voters do not bother to cast a vote for judges, even though they do so for other non-judicial candidates. Accordingly, in the "typical retention election there is little voter differentiation among judges, and they are all routinely returned to the bench for another term."[31] Although it is unclear what prompts voters to target and remove a particular judge, studies indicate that the electorate is constrained due to a lack of information or confused about judges' performance, or even the nature of the election process itself.[32]

The politicization of judicial campaigns also presents special ethical problems. Although judges are bound by ethical rules to remain impartial and independent from the political influence, they are nonetheless forced to engage in campaigns increasingly infused with negative advertising. Until the decision in *Republican Party of Minnesota v. White* (2002),[33] judges on the campaign trail could not announce their views on disputed political or legal issues on the grounds that it would compromise their impartiality. But *White* held that judicial candidates who wish to express their political viewpoints in judicial elections deserve First Amendment protection. Notably, Justice Antonin Scalia's Opinion for the Court tested the constitutionality of the state bar's "announce clause" against the strict scrutiny test, a rigorous legal standard that requires that the justification for burdening speech must be rooted in a compelling interest that is narrowly tailored to achieve that interest. Although Scalia acknowledged that the announce clause may serve a compelling interest in ensuring that a judge remains impartial and open-minded to hearing the different legal views surrounding a case, he reasoned that it was not a narrowly tailored interest that could be achieved well because it was "under-inclusive" in its application to judicial campaigns; therefore, the announce clause was an unconstitutional content-based restriction on electoral speech that could not achieve its intended purpose (i.e. that judges must remain impartial) (See the "In Comparative Perspective: Are Judges "Politicians in Robes" or Not?" box in this Chapter for further discussion.) Furthermore, Scalia's opinion rejected dissenting Justice Ruth Bader Ginsburg's argument that a litigant's due process are violated by striking down an ethical canon that is designed to ensure that a campaigning judge will not be tempted to commit to a position that was taken on the campaign trail once they are elected into office.[34] In response, the federal and state judiciaries, along with the American Bar Association and many state bar associations, have wrestled with *White*'s implications and whether it is permissible for judges to engage in aggressive political campaigning.

In Comparative Perspective: Are Judges "Politicians in Robes" or Not?

In recent decades, justices, judges, and court watchers have debated "the globalization of judicial power" and the role of courts in democracies. That trend has been described as "the judicialization of politics" not only in European democracies but also elsewhere around the world. In the 1990s, for example, the growth of judicial power in Italy was illustrated by the "clean hands" investigations by prosecutors and judges, which resulted in displacing a political class that had governed the country for over fifty years. The German Constitutional Court imposed restrictions on abortion and banned religious symbols in public school classrooms, which ignited fierce political controversies. And Egyptian courts were at the center of democratic protests that ousted President Hosni Mubarak, and they remain pivotal actors in the ongoing struggle to democratize the political process.

The expansion of judicial power, domestically and internationally, has been both praised and condemned. Some argue that courts reinforce the basic principles of constitutional democracy. Others contend that judges are usurping the democratic process. Ultimately, though, both sides disagree about the role of courts and whether judges are political actors.

The question of whether judges are political actors was put into bold relief in the United States in an exchange between the majority and dissenting opinions in *Republican Party of Minnesota v. White* (2002). At issue was the constitutionality of prohibiting state judicial candidates, during their election campaigns, from announcing their positions on legal and political controversies. Writing for the majority, Justice Antonin Scalia—joined by Chief Justice William H. Rehnquist and Justices Anthony Kennedy, Sandra Day O'Connor, and Clarence Thomas—maintained that such a restriction (the "announce" clause) violates the First Amendment because "it prohibits speech on the basis of its content and burdens a category of speech that is at the core of First Amendment freedoms—speech about candidates for public office." By contrast, Justice Ruth Bader Ginsburg—joined in her dissent by Justices John Paul Stevens, David Souter, and Stephen Breyer—defended the power of states to regulate judicial campaigns and elections. Notably, as the excerpts from the judicial opinion below indicate, the majority and the dissenters advance competing conceptions of whether judges are political actors.

Judges Are Political Actors—Justice Scalia's View:

We think it plain that the announce clause is not narrowly tailored to serve impartiality (or the appearance of impartiality) . . . .Indeed, the clause is barely tailored to serve that interest at all, inasmuch as it does not restrict speech for or against particular parties, but rather speech for or against particular issues. To be sure, when a case arises that turns on a legal issue on which the judge (as a candidate) had taken a particular stand, the party taking the opposite stand is likely to lose. But not because of any bias against that party, or favoritism toward the other party. Any party taking that position is just as likely to lose. The judge is applying the law (as he sees it) evenhandedly.

It is perhaps possible to use the term "impartiality" in the judicial context (though this is certainly not a common usage) to mean lack of preconception in favor of or against a particular legal view. This sort of impartiality would be concerned, not with guaranteeing litigants' equal application of the law, but rather with guaranteeing them an equal chance to persuade the court on the legal points in their case. Impartiality in this sense may well be an interest served by the announce clause, but it is not a **compelling (state) interest**, as strict scrutiny requires. A judge's lack of predisposition regarding the relevant legal issues in a case has never been thought a necessary component of equal justice, and with good reason. For one thing, it is virtually impossible to find a judge who does not have preconceptions about the law. . . .

A third possible meaning of "impartiality" (again not a common one) might be described as open-mindedness. This quality in a judge demands, not that he have no preconceptions on legal issues, but that he be willing to consider views that oppose his preconceptions, and remain open to persuasion, when the issues arise in a pending case. This sort of impartiality seeks to guarantee each litigant, not an equal chance to win the legal points in the case, but at least some chance of doing so. It may well be that impartiality in this sense, and the appearance of it, are desirable in the judiciary, but we need not pursue that inquiry, since we do not believe the Minnesota Supreme Court adopted the announce clause for that purpose.

The short of the matter is. . .a candidate for judicial office may not say "I think it is constitutional for the legislature to prohibit same-sex marriages." He may say the very same thing, however, up until the very day before he declares himself a candidate and may say it repeatedly (until litigation is pending) after he is elected. As a means of pursuing the objective of open-mindedness that respondents now articulate, the announce clause is so woefully under-inclusive as to render belief in that purpose a challenge to the credulous. . . .

There is an obvious tension between the article of Minnesota's popularly approved Constitution which provides that judges shall be elected, and the Minnesota Supreme Court's announce clause which places most subjects of interest to the voters off limits. The disparity is perhaps unsurprising, since the ABA, which originated the announce clause, has long been an opponent of judicial elections. That opposition may be well taken (it certainly had the support of the Founders of the Federal Government), but the First Amendment does not permit it to achieve its goal by leaving the principle of elections in place while preventing candidates from discussing what the elections are about.

Judges Are Not Political Actors—Justice Ginsburg's View:

Unlike their counterparts in the political branches, judges are expected to refrain from catering to particular constituencies or committing themselves on controversial issues in advance of adversarial presentation. Their mission is deciding "individual cases and controversies" on individual records, neutrally applying legal principles, and, when necessary, "stand[ing] up to what is generally supreme in a democracy: the popular will.". . .

The speech restriction must fail, in the Court's view, because an electoral process is at stake; if Minnesota opts to elect its judges, the Court asserts, the State may not rein in what candidates may say. . . .I do not agree with this unilocular, "an election is an election," approach. Instead, I would differentiate elections for political offices, in which the First Amendment holds full sway, from elections designed to select those whose office it is to administer justice without respect to persons. . . .

Legislative and executive officials serve in representative capacities. . . . Judges, however, are not political actors. They do not sit as representatives of particular persons, communities, or parties; they serve no faction or constituency. They must strive to do what is legally right, all the more so when the result is not the one "the home crowd" wants. Even when they develop common law or give concrete meaning to constitutional text, judges act only in the context of individual cases, the outcome of which cannot depend on the will of the public. . . .

Thus, the rationale underlying unconstrained speech in elections for political office—that representative government depends on the public's ability to choose agents who will act at its behest—does not carry over to campaigns for the bench. . . .In view of the magisterial role judges must fill in a system of justice, a role that removes them from the partisan fray, States may limit judicial campaign speech by measures impermissible in elections for political office. . . .

Sources: *Republican Party of Minnesota v. White*, 536 U.S. 765 (2002). For further reading, see Ursula Lindsey, "Egypt's Judges Strike Back," *The New Yorker* (March 26, 2014), available at https://www.newyorker.com/news/news-desk/egypts-judges-strike-back (last retrieved April 14, 2020); Donald W. Jackson, Michael C. Tolley, and Mary L. Volcansek, eds., *Globalizing Justice: Critical Perspectives on Transnational Law and the Cross-Border Migration of Legal Norms* (Albany: State University of New York Press, 2010); Aharon Barak, *The Judge in a Democracy* (Princeton, N.J.: Princeton University Press, 2006); Carlo Guarnieri and Patrizia Pederzoli, *The Power of Judges: A Comparative Study of Courts and Democracy* (New York: Oxford University Press, 2002); C. Neal Tate and Torbjorn Vallinder, eds., *The Global Expansion of Judicial Power* (New York: New York University Press, 1995); Robert H. Bork, *Coercing Virtue: The Worldwide Rule of Judges* (Washington, D.C.: American Enterprise Institute, 2003).

At the time *White* was decided, critics warned that the ruling "threatens to turn judges into a set of politicians in black robes."[35] In this respect, *White* intuitively promotes the image that justice is "for sale." Perhaps this is why the Supreme Court decided to revisit the legal question in a subsequent decision that flatly declared that judges *are* different than ordinary politicians, at least in some judicial campaigning contexts. At issue in *Williams-Yulee v. Florida Bar Association* (2015) was whether a judicial candidate for a seat on a Florida county court was protected by the First Amendment after she made direct personal solicitations for campaign money to fund her election bid, a violation of Florida bar regulations. In a 5:4 ruling, the Court sided with the Florida bar, reasoning that it had the legal authority to discipline the campaigning judge because making a direct appeal to voters for campaign cash undermines the public's confidence in having an impartial and independent bench. As in *White*, in his Opinion for the Court Chief Justice John Roberts, Jr. used the strict scrutiny test to hold that Florida had a compelling interest in safeguarding the public's confidence in its courts by enacting a ban on the personal solicitations of funds; and that the Canon 7C(1)— the rule in the state judicial code to do so—was narrowly tailored to serve that interest, especially since there were numerous other ways that candidates can raise money in their judicial campaigns. In reasoning that Canon 7C(1) met the demanding test of strict scrutiny, Chief Justice Roberts declared that "Judges are not politicians. . .[a]nd a State's decision to elect its judiciary does not compel its people that judges will apply the law without fear or favor—and without having personally asked anyone for money." In this respect, the Court agreed with concurring justice Ruth Bader Ginsburg, who first expressed a similar (but losing) viewpoint in *Republican Party of Minnesota;* and she added, like Roberts did, that courts do not serve the same political constituencies as ordinary politicians. Finally, she cited to extralegal sources and research reports to make the point that the rise in "disproportionate spending" by special interest groups in the aftermath of *Citizens United* "threatens both the appearance and actuality of judicial independence."

In addition, unethical judicial behavior during campaigns and elections is subject to other constitutional limitations and state judicial codes of conduct provisions. In *Caperton v. Massey Coal Company* (2009), the Supreme Court held that judges who receive large campaign donations and have a personal stake in the outcome must recuse, or disqualify, themselves from the proceedings if there is a "serious risk of actual bias."[36] Moreover, research on *White*'s impact has found that it has not generated more contested elections. Also, for some scholars, judicial elections actually enhance, rather than diminish, institutional legitimacy.[37]

For some scholars, as well, both *Caperton* and *Williams-Yulee* establish clearer "bright-line" legal principles on where to draw the judicial lines in separating permissible and impermissible conduct in judicial campaigns that raise recusal and direct solicitation issues.[38] But *White's* long-term impact remains uncertain because state legislatures, courts, and bar associations have struggled with determining the proper legal and ethical boundaries in judicial elections. In the aftermath *of White*, a few states, including Arkansas, actually changed their selection systems from having partisan to nonpartisan elections;[39] other states, such as North Carolina, amended their judicial conduct rules and made it easier for judicial candidates to engage in overt political activity while Georgia amended its canons by eliminating its "pledge or promise" clause. However, in still other states, such as Missouri and Texas, the prohibitions on judicial candidates making campaign pledges, promises, or commitments were strengthened.[40] Although *White* invalidated Minnesota's "announce clause," the ruling has prompted ongoing litigation over whether judges may directly raise money, negatively attack opponents, "mislead" or "misrepresent" qualifications, or make "pledges or promises" or "commitments."[41]

While state and federal courts applying *White* have not been uniform in their responses, most seem inclined to allow for greater political activity so long as judicial candidates do not make pledges, promises, or commitments to vote a particular way once on the bench.[42] Notably, some federal courts have interpreted *White* to permit judicial candidates to make direct appeals to voters and actively engage in fund-raising during campaigns.[43] In addition, several states and local communities have formed campaign conduct committees to oversee judicial election practices—they operate in official or informal capacities to provide information and advice to candidates about what constitutes ethical campaign behavior in the judicial context.[44]

Beyond these measures, reformers interested in changing the rules of judicial campaigns and elections have made other proposals that have not yet been tested or had a mixed record of success in depoliticizing them. The Brennan Center for Justice, for example, maintains that judicial elections must be abolished, and states should, instead, adopt a "merit selection" system; thus, after initial gubernatorial appointment by a non-partisan nomination commission, judges wishing to stay in office must run in retention elections that keep them on the bench through an "up or down" vote by the electorate. Moreover, it argues that state supreme court justices must only serve a single, lengthy term on the bench in order to diminish the influence of political pressures that may affect their decision-making; or, alternatively, let them serve indefinite terms, subject to the constitutional and ethical rules placed upon federal judges to remain on the bench if they exhibit "good behavior."[45] In addition, the ABA recommends the adoption of nonpartisan judicial elections and public financing of judicial campaigns or, alternatively, the imposition of campaign contribution limits, as well as the distribution of voter guides, based on judicial performance evaluations. While many states and jurisdictions have instituted an official system of judicial performance evaluation, the methods and procedures for doing so vary widely.[46]

Yet, only a few states—New Mexico, North Carolina, West Virginia, and Wisconsin—have tried to sustain public financing programs for some or all judicial elections. Up through the 2015–16 election cycle, the National Conference of State Legislatures reports that of those states only New Mexico and West Virginia allow for public financing in respect to candidates seeking a position on their respective Supreme Courts.[47] Indeed, in light of *Arizona Free Enterprise Club's Freedom Club PAC v. Bennett* (2011), a Court ruling casting doubt about the constitutionality of some public financing programs by nullifying Arizona's publicly funded matching program, it seems that there is little momentum to enact laws that are designed to help underfunded candidates compete with over-resourced competitors by giving them the same amount of public money that a self-financed candidate can raise and spend.[48]

STAFFING FEDERAL COURTS

While the diversity of state judicial selection methods is largely absent at the federal level, the process for picking Article III (lifetime appointments) judges is more uniform, but nonetheless extremely political. Under Article II of the U.S. Constitution, the President has the power to select and the Senate the power to confirm or reject the appointment of federal judges. The specific steps of the nomination and confirmation process, and the roles that are played by the main political actors in the process, are considered next.

The Framers and Judicial Selection

Article II declares that the President has the power "by and with the Advice and Consent of the Senate" to appoint "Judges of the supreme Court, and all other officers of the United States." Significantly, the President also has authority "to fill up all Vacancies that may happen during the Recess of the Senate, by granting Commissions which shall expire at the End of their Next Session."

In *The Federalist Papers*, Alexander Hamilton argued that the President's "sole duty" was to nominate judges. The Senate, on the other hand, rendered "advice and consent" and only "ratify or reject the choice" of the President. In Hamilton's view, the Senate was "an excellent check upon a spirit of favoritism in the President, and. . .to prevent the appointment of unfit characters from State prejudice, from family connection, from personal attachment, or from a view to popularity."[49] The Framers' decision to give the President authority to fill vacancies when the Senate is adjourned in recess—and, thus, to make temporary judicial appointments that lapse at the end of the next congressional session unless they receive Senate confirmation—is further evidence that judicial appointments were envisioned to be the result of negotiated compromises. Moreover, because Article III judges basically enjoy life tenure, presidents have increasingly turned federal judgeships into a way to extend their political legacy well beyond their time in the White House. At the same time, the Senate also realized how valuable judgeships are as patronage tools.

Ideology or Merit?

Although all Presidents seek qualified and meritorious judicial candidates who will withstand Senate scrutiny, a host of interrelated political factors drive the selection and confirmation processes. Before announcing their nominations, Presidents generally base their selection decisions on ideological considerations and political expediency. Still, as the late political scientist Henry J. Abraham emphasized, nominees should also demonstrate "objective merit": a proven judicial temperament; professional expertise and competence; personal and professional integrity; an able, agile, and lucid mind; appropriate professional educational background or training; and the ability to communicate well, both orally and in writing. But Abraham also notes that Supreme Court appointments are often affected by the president's personal relationship to the candidate, the nominee's political compatibility with the president, and whether the president believes the selection brings a geographic, racial, gender-based, or religious balance to the Court.[50] In his study of circuit court appointments, political scientist J. Woodford Howard likewise found similar criteria. Personal competence, extensive political participation, personal ambition, and a "pinch of luck" all contribute to securing a federal judgeship. A variation of these ideas is presented by still other theories that assert presidents take a "characteristics approach" to making Supreme Court appointments; that is, presidents do not evaluate individual nominees *per se*, but rather base their choices on an evaluation of a nominee's "bundle of characteristics", such as their ideology, their reliability in making policy choices, and their diversity (race, gender and ethnicity), which are thought to reap the greatest political gains at the least political cost to the president.[51]

Although "objective merit" or "professional competence" is a part of a President's criteria, the terms are not entirely useful (and may be misleading) in describing the process of federal judicial selection. For one thing, defining merit is notoriously difficult because "a credible case can be made for the competence of almost any nominee."[52] Further, emphasizing merit-based explanations obscures the reality that all appointments are inescapably political, and Presidents generally try to "pack" the courts with their preferred nominees. Indeed, political scientists George L. Watson and John A. Stookey argue that finding the most qualified candidate is "the motivation least likely to drive presidential considerations" in selecting judges.[53] Exceptionally qualified nominees, such as President Ronald Reagan's nomination of Robert Bork to the Supreme Court in 1987, are meritorious selections, but the Senate nonetheless rejected Bork as ideologically "out of the mainstream." Or, similarly, the Senate leadership decides to make a political calculation that denies a fully qualified nominee, such President Barack Obama's selection of Merrick Garland, a hearing or an up-or-down Senate vote in an effort to prevent that nominee from assuming a lifetime position on the Court (as this Chapter's introduction explains).

In short, federal judicial recruitment is more complex and usually based on a combination of four broad considerations: (1) a candidate's professional competence; (2) whether the selection is a patronage-based reward for those loyal to the party; (3) "representative" factors, such as religion, race, ethnicity, and gender, or in the past geographical balance on a court; and (4) whether a nominee's ideological orientation is likely to promote the president's legal policy goals over the long run. Moreover, presidents assign different priorities to these factors in their judicial selections, depending upon the level of the court, and the amount of political opposition they are likely to encounter in the Senate.[54] As a result, federal judicial selection is best described in terms of three general types of presidential selection models: the **classic Democratic**, **Bipartisan**, and **Republican ideological** judicial selection models.

The classic Democratic model—embraced by Presidents Franklin D. Roosevelt, Harry Truman, John F. Kennedy, and Lyndon B. Johnson—de-emphasizes the pursuit of specific policy agendas and, instead, stresses rewarding the party faithful and distributing political patronage in making judicial appointments. Moreover, patronage and a candidate's professional qualifications are sometimes symbolic representation. President Johnson's selection of the Court's first African American justice, Thurgood Marshall, is illustrative, as is his appointment to the Court a close friend, Jewish Justice Abe Fortas, to replace another Jewish Justice, Arthur J. Goldberg.[55]

The Bipartisan approach, on the other hand, puts a premium on the nominee's professional competence while emphasizing, to some degree, patronage or symbolic representation characteristics like race or gender. Republican presidents Dwight D. Eisenhower and Gerald R. Ford, along with Democratic presidents Jimmy Carter, Bill Clinton, and Barack Obama, took this approach to judicial selection. With the exception of President Clinton, these presidents delegated to their attorney generals the job of judicial selection based on merit and not stringent ideological considerations. In addition, these presidents placed a premium on confirmability in the Senate, because they either were unelected (Ford) or faced strong opposition in the Senate to more ideological appointees.[56]

Finally, Republican Presidents Richard M. Nixon, Ronald Reagan, George H. W. Bush, George W. Bush and Donald J. Trump have tended to give highest priority to ideological considerations because they viewed judgeships as symbols and instruments of presidential power. For these Presidents, their policy agenda was the touchstone for judicial selection. As a result, rewarding party faithful and even professional qualifications was less critical. Nixon made judgeships symbols of presidential power and vowed to appoint only judges who would exercise "judicial restraint" (in contrast to the "judicial activism" of the Warren Court) and advance his "law and order" policy agenda, a centerpiece of his 1968 presidential campaign. He was not entirely successful, and for that reason Reagan's administration adopted a more rigorous judicial selection process for the appointment of conservative lower court judges and justices—hence the elevation of Justice William Rehnquist to the chief justiceship and the appointment of Justice Antonin Scalia.[57] Likewise, President George W. Bush gave high priority to appointing judges based on their conservative ideology, as with the naming of Judge John G. Roberts to fill the seat of Chief Justice Rehnquist and in appointing Judge Samuel Alito to fill Justice Sandra Day O'Connor's seat, despite countervailing pressures to appoint another woman or Hispanic.

Regardless of which approach is taken, the federal judicial selection process begins with the president's staff initiating a search for an acceptable nominee and conducting a preliminary screening process. Vetting a candidate helps in ensuring that the nominee will withstand Senate review, though it does not guarantee confirmation success. The subsequent Senate confirmation process is no less fluid and dynamic. Any number of political factors—including presidential style and power; the Senate's political composition, and especially whether the president and the Senate majority are from opposite political parties; and organized interest activity; as well as the media, public opinion, and the electorate's polarization—may trigger strong opposition and defeat confirmation. The nomination and confirmation process is outlined in Figure 4.1, and we give a more detailed examination in the following sections.

Figure 4.1   The Nomination and Confirmation Process for Federal Judges

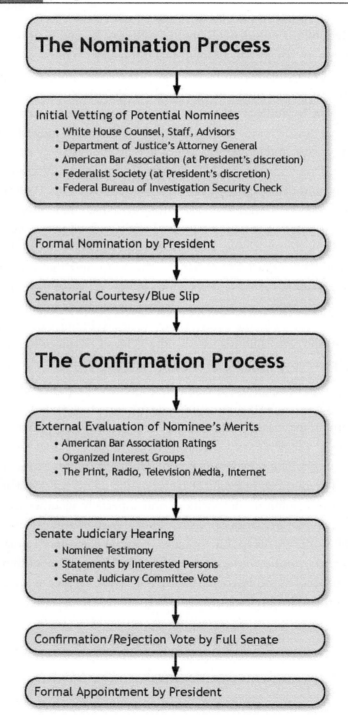

The Nomination Process

Initial Vetting of Potential Nominees
- White House Counsel, Staff, Advisors
- Department of Justice's Attorney General
- American Bar Association (at President's discretion)
- Federalist Society (at President's discretion)
- Federal Bureau of Investigation Security Check

Formal Nomination by President

Senatorial Courtesy/Blue Slip

The Confirmation Process

External Evaluation of Nominee's Merits
- American Bar Association Ratings
- Organized Interest Groups
- The Print, Radio, Television Media, Internet

Senate Judiciary Hearing
- Nominee Testimony
- Statements by Interested Persons
- Senate Judiciary Committee Vote

Confirmation/Rejection Vote by Full Senate

Formal Appointment by President

The Nomination Process

Since the New Deal and FDR's presidency, the President's closest advisors in the White House and the Department of Justice (DOJ) have largely controlled the selection process. Although most Presidents have taken a keen interest in personally making Supreme Court appointments, to varying degrees all routinely rely on DOJ attorneys for generating a list of names of acceptable candidates. Much of this behind-the-scenes activity usually occurs either before or immediately after a vacancy arises on the bench.[58]

Though the procedure for compiling a list of nominees varies from president to president, all modern presidencies from Jimmy Carter to Donald J. Trump have delegated the initial selection process, though with different legal policy goals in mind. Each president, of course, sets priorities for the selection process. The Carter and Reagan presidencies are especially significant in highlighting sharply different presidential priorities and how those priorities changed the process.

President Carter's chief objective was the appointment of qualified nominees who would diversify the federal bench. After striking a deal with the powerful chair of the Senate Judiciary Committee (SJC), James Eastland (D-MS), Carter issued an executive order establishing that federal appellate court judgeships were to be initially recommended by nominating or "merit" commissions, composed of a diverse mix of genders, minorities, lawyers, and nonlawyers. Subsequently, Congress enacted the Omnibus Judgeship Act of 1978, creating 152 new judgeships. And that inspired a second executive order encouraging senators to set up their own nominating commissions for district court vacancies. But, because of protracted resistance by some senators to Carter's initial circuit court plan, Carter could only ask them to cooperate on a voluntary basis, and in the end only about thirty senators did so.[59]

Carter's initiatives were historic and achieved diversity on the bench; but, they had mixed success. Although he appointed an unprecedented number of women, African Americans, and other minorities, Carter alienated powerful senators who strongly opposed relinquishing the traditional patronage practice of deferring to their recommendations on the selection of lower court judgeships. Moreover, the merit commissions did little to depoliticize the selection process. Not only did Carter personally select who sat on the commissions, but also many of the judicial candidates were asked questions about their views on divisive social issues, such as affirmative action, women's rights, abortion, capital punishment, and desegregation.[60] Those inquiries were part of an unparalleled attempt to vet judicial candidates on the basis of how they would decide controversial cases.

Ironically, that contributed to the Reagan administration's adoption of an even more rigorous screening process. Even though Carter and his Attorney General Griffin Bell did not make a candidate's ideology the primary criteria for selection, the reality was that most judgeships went to party faithful: 94.1 percent of Carter's district court judges and 89.3 percent of circuit court judges were Democrats.[61] Likewise, though, Republican presidents rarely cross party lines.

Initial Vetting of Nominees

"Most presidents name justices who, they think, will vote the way they would vote. That is what I would do were I president." Those words of liberal justice William O. Douglas capture the thrust of Reagan's approach to judicial recruitment. Like Carter, the Reagan administration's staffing methodology broke with convention, but in a different way. The selection process became centralized in the White House with the creation of the Federal Judicial Selection Committee, chaired by the White House counsel and composed of administration attorneys with oversight responsibility for personnel and legislative affairs, as well as legal policy. The committee worked in conjunction with the DOJ's newly created Office of Legal Policy, which initially screened all potential nominees. Critics charged that the Reagan administration imposed an "ideological litmus test," requiring not just loyalty to the Republican Party, but also a commitment to the conservative "Reagan revolution." To an unprecedented degree, the Reagan White House and Justice Department sifted through the political and professional qualifications of candidates by inspecting their written record (past judicial opinions, academic writings, and written commentary) and conducting personal interviews to discover their ideological compatibility. In the process, the American Bar Association's (ABA) pre-nomination advisory role, which began with the Eisenhower presidency, was greatly reduced.[62]

Reagan's more rigorous and ideological judicial selection process had an enormous, long-lasting impact. Reagan appointed 290 district and 78 circuit court judges, for a total of 368 lower federal court judges. Reagan also elevated Justice William H. Rehnquist (the Court's most conservative justice) to chief justice and named Justices Sandra Day O'Connor, Antonin Scalia, and Anthony Kennedy. Not a single nominee from the Democratic Party was put on a circuit court during his two administrations; no prior president (Republican or Democrat) had done that since Warren G. Harding's administration. Overall, the voting behavior of Reagan's judges extended a conservative revolution started by Nixon and reinvigorated by George W. Bush's judicial appointees.[63]

The changes made during the Carter and Reagan years established the basic framework and process for subsequent administrations. Presidents George H. W. Bush, Bill Clinton, and George W. Bush anchored their selection processes in the White House and DOJ, and used vetting processes spearheaded by a judicial selection committee. Although George H. W. Bush dismantled the DOJ's Office of Legal Policy, Presidents Clinton and George W. Bush revived its role in screening judicial nominees. All three administrations relied upon recommendations made from a judicial selection committee. Moreover, unlike the H. W. Bush and Clinton presidencies, George W. Bush's administration also drew on the conservative Federalist Society and gave it a voice in judicial selection-a practice taken to new heights during the Trump presidency (see the Contemporary Controversies over Courts: The Federalist Society's Role in Federal Judicial Selection box, later in this Chapter). In contrast, the Obama administration relied less on interest group input (other than the ABA) and avoided using a judicial selection committee. Instead, prospective nominees were vetted in a collaborative process involving the White House Office of General Counsel, the DOJ's Office of Legal Policy, and the White House Office of Legislative Affairs.[64]

To varying degrees, every president since Reagan has relied on White House and DOJ counsel to oversee the vetting process, although other political actors have been a part as well. For example, the Obama administration used the White House Counsel's Office (and the Office of Legislative Affairs to work directly with Senators) as a means to shepherd the nominees through the political landscape to confirmation; but the responsibility of professionally vetting them was lodged in the Justice Department's Office of Legal Policy. In contrast, in Trump's first two years in office, the Trump administration has de-emphasized the DOJ's role and instead squarely relied upon White House counsel, including Donald McGahn and others, along with input from the Senate's leadership (Senate Majority Leader Mitch McConnell [R-KY.]) and the Federalist Society (through Executive Vice President Leonard Leo, who took a leave of absence to work in the Trump administration), to generate a list of prospective nominees.[65] The vetting process includes examining a potential nominee's professional qualifications, financial status, physical condition, and judicial philosophy, along with past work experience and written record (academic writings, judicial opinions, or political commentary). Accordingly, potential nominees are asked to complete lengthy questionnaires from not only the DOJ, but also the American Bar Association, the Federal Bureau of Investigation, and the Internal Revenue Service. Also, Supreme Court nominees are interviewed by administration staff and taken to senators' offices in "courtesy calls" on influential senators; and recently, lower court nominees have also been interviewed. Typically, DOJ attorneys also seek out the views of members of Congress, state governors, and state or local bar associations, as well as interest groups that have a keen interest in judicial selection.[66]

Contemporary Controversies over Courts: The Federalist Society's Role in Federal Judicial Selection

Once merely a debating society in law schools at Harvard, the University of Chicago, and the University of Virginia, after a spring 1982 symposium at Yale Law School on Federalism, The Federalist Society for Law and Public Policy Studies was created. Over time, it has grown into a multifaceted conservative organization with considerable influence over federal judicial selection from a conservative and libertarian perspective. It now boasts over 70,000 members committed to "reform[ing] the current legal order," ostensibly by cultivating a "greater appreciation for the role of separation of powers, federalism, limited constitutional government, and the rule of law in protecting individual freedom and traditional values." Fueled by in-kind contributions (volunteer work of its members) and donations from conservative foundations and elites in and out of the Washington, D.C. establishment, the Federalist Society has more than 200 law school chapters, 80 city lawyer chapters, and 15 national lawyer practice groups, along with a multi-million-dollar budget.

Since its inception, it has evolved into a "central nervous system for a network of conservative lawyers," which, in turn, strongly influences the selection of law clerks and federal judges, particularly during the administrations of Ronald Reagan, George H.W. Bush, George W. Bush, and Donald J. Trump. Its founders include the late Antonin Scalia (as a University of Chicago law professor, before he was a judge), federal circuit court Judge Richard Posner; former Attorney General Edwin Meese; former D.C. Circuit Judge Robert Bork; former Energy Secretary Spencer Abraham; former Interior Secretary Gale A. Norton; former Attorney General John Ashcroft; former Solicitor General Theodore Olsen; and several lawyers in the White House counsel's office, among others.

As political scientist Amanda Hollis-Brusky observes, the Federalist Society is a conservative and libertarian group that proves that "ideas have consequences." In the context of the 1980s "Reagan Revolution" and President Reagan's promise to "get government off the backs of the American people," the organization emerged as an aggressive challenge to liberal orthodoxy. Its ideological advocacy is premised on the need to achieve individual freedom by limiting government powers, an operational principle that is grounded on three inter-related ideas: (1) that the government exists to safeguard individual freedom; (2) that a separation of powers framework is at the structural core of the U.S. Constitution; and, (3) that the courts have a duty to say what the law is, and not what is ought to be. Together, these ideas and principles animate the Federalist Society's support for filling the federal courts with judges that subscribe to the constitutional philosophy of "originalism." Placing originalist judges on the bench is important because those jurists are committed to finding the "original" meaning of constitutional provisions through an analysis of the text and what the founders thought the words meant at the time they were written. For its advocates, originalist judges are faithful to the idea of judicial self-restraint: they declare what the law is, instead of simply making it up when they decide cases. For critics, though, originalist judges are activists that use that methodology as a pretext for undermining or destroying rights as they are currently understood or what they might become to be.

The Federalist Society aims to "act as the network, forum, and information clearinghouse for its members," often espousing the values underlying a conservative agenda that includes filling the courts with those who rhetorically decry judicial activism and advocate judicial restraint. The law clerkship has become a valuable tool in the Federalist Society's organizational strategy. As one prominent appeals judge mused, "a clerkship is a useful credential, and if I want to advance my philosophy I'd rather give it to someone who thinks like me"; and, so, clerks affiliated with the Federalist Society are selected for service. In this light, the Federalist Society advances its cause through indirect strategies that focus on engaging its membership and exerting its influence through training, education, and networking—so, unlike many interest groups, it does not directly lobby for policies or represent clients in litigation. In addition to holding national conferences twice a year, it has a large array of student chapters in law schools, lawyer chapters located in cities, and practice groups that centered around functional interests.

Spearheaded initially by White House Counsel Donald McGahn, the Trump administration has worked closely with the Federalist Society's Executive Vice President Leonard Leo and Senate Majority Leader Mitch McConnell (R-KY) to fill the federal bench with originalists and textualists that are ideologically committed to limiting government powers in cases addressing agency regulation, abortion, LGBTQ protections, gun rights, environmental protection, campaign finance, affirmative action, and health care, among others. Indeed, President Trump has relied heavily on a list of nominees to the

Supreme Court complied by the Federalist Society. Apart from the successful confirmations of Neil Gorsuch and Brett Kavanaugh—both originalists and adherents of the jurisprudence of the late Justice Antonin Scalia—the rest of the controlling majority on the Roberts Court—namely, Chief Justice John Roberts, Samuel Alito, and Clarence Thomas, all consist of all Reaganites that once worked in the Reagan administration in the Department of Justice or the Equal Employment Opportunity Commission.

Besides the influence the Supreme Court will have in moving the nation's jurisprudence further to the right, the Trump administration and Republican-controlled Senate has confirmed dozens of lower court federal judges in Trump's first term. With the help of the Federalist Society, the Trump administration's streamlined federal judicial selection process has "flipped" (or is poised to flip) the ideological composition of several circuit courts in the nation after only a short time in office. Because the Court decides far less cases, circuit courts are especially significant "courts of last resort" that will enable Trump to extend his presidential legacy far beyond the number of years he remains in office. As conservative Newt Gingrich, remarked: "[President Trump] could, by the end of his time in office, be the most important president since Franklin Delano Roosevelt in shaping the judiciary." Indeed, there is little doubt that the Federalist Society has greatly contributed to establishing Trump's presidential legacy of reconstituting the federal courts, especially if he continues to stay in office.

Finally, in response to the success of the Federalist Society, liberal activists, under the leadership of Georgetown law professor Peter Rubin, created the Madison Society for Law and Policy at Georgetown University Law School in 1999, later renamed to the American Constitution Society (ACS). The impetus for the ACS's creation was the 2000 Supreme Court ruling in *Bush v. Gore*. Although the influence of the American Constitution Society is not as pervasive as the Federalist Society, it underscores the growing and significant role organized interests play in the federal judicial confirmation process on both sides of the political aisle.

Sources: Amanda Hollis-Brusky, *Ideas with Consequences: The Federalist Society and the Conservative Counterrevolution* (New York: Oxford University Press 2015); Steven M. Teles, *The Rise of the Conservative Legal Movement: The Battle for Control of the Law* (Princeton: Princeton University Press 2008); The Federalist Society, "Frequently Asked Questions," *Federalist Society*, available at https://fedsoc.org/frequently-asked-questions (last retrieved March 29, 2019); American Constitution Society, available at https://www.acslaw.org/ (last retrieved April 14, 2020); Michael Kruse, "The Weekend at Yale that Changed American Politics," *Politico Magazine* (September/October 2018), available at https://www.politico.com/magazine/story/2018/08/27/federalist-society-yale-history-conservative-law-court-219608 (last retrieved April 14, 2020); Jason Zengerle, "How the Trump Administration is Remaking the Courts," *New York Times Magazine* (August 22, 2018), available from https://www.nytimes.com/2018/08/22/magazine/trump-remaking-courts-judiciary.html (last retrieved April 14,

2020); Elliot Slotnick, Sara Schiavoni and Sheldon Goldman, "Obama's Judicial Legacy: The Final Chapter," *Journal of Law and Courts* 5 (No. 2, Fall 2017), 364–422; Terry Carter, "Conservatives Who Sought Refuge in the Federalist Society Gain Clout," *American Bar Association Journal* (September, 2001), 46; Thomas B. Edsall, "Federalist Society Becomes a Force in Washington," *Washington Post* (April 18, 2001), A04.

The American Bar Association and Its Ratings

With the notable exception of the presidencies of George W. Bush and Donald J. Trump, since 1956 all presidents have solicited an informal evaluation of potential nominees from the American Bar Association, which has rated every judicial candidate since the Eisenhower administration. In 2001, Bush stopped sending nominees' names to the ABA, arguing that the organization should not be given a special advising role and that it was too liberal, though that policy was reversed by Obama and reinstated by President Trump. Trump's action, for some, might signal a "durable GOP policy change," as some influential GOP representatives, such as Senator Mike Lee (R-Utah) and former Senator Orrin Hatch (R-Utah), have gone on record declaring because, in their view, the ABA must be treated as any other special interest group and not be given a privileged role in judicial selection. In any event, the ABA remains an active player in confirmation politics, because its evaluations are still used by Democrats on the Senate Judiciary Committee and, for them, may very well be a prerequisite to beginning the confirmation process.[67]

The ABA's Standing Committee on the Federal Judiciary has fifteen members appointed by the president of the ABA for staggered three-year terms. It rates candidates as *well qualified*, *qualified*, or *not qualified*, after examining their professional qualifications. In addition, members of the committee disclose whether a rating carries a *substantial majority*, *majority*, or *minority* designation.[68] At a minimum, the ABA's assessment of judicial nominees ensures scrutiny of a candidate's alleged objective merits to evaluate the law, and perform the judicial function, impartially and with a high level of professional competence. Even so, critics, especially conservatives, have charged that the ABA's rating is politically biased and should not be part of the judicial selection process. Some empirical data suggests otherwise. For example, as of April 1, 2020, roughly seventy percent of Trump's nominees have been rated "well-qualified," twenty-seven percent were assessed as "qualified," and only four percent have been declared "not qualified."[69]

Senatorial Courtesy and the "Blue Slip"

Another significant player in federal judicial selection is the U.S. Senate Judiciary Committee (SJC), which initially screens nominees but later also evaluates them in the confirmation process. The SJC's investigation of candidates may greatly affect the fate of nominees. The views of senators from a nominee's home state are guaranteed by two closely guarded Senate traditions: **senatorial courtesy** and the **blue slip** procedure.

Traditionally, senatorial courtesy necessitated that presidents consult with senators from a nominee's home state prior to the nomination as part of the Article II requirement of seeking "advice and consent" from the Senate. The practice dates back to George Washington's administration, where one of the President's choices for port collectors (of an import tax), Benjamin Fishbourn, a navy officer stationed at a Savannah Georgia port, was not approved by a Georgia senator, James Gunn. Senator Gunn's rejection of Washington's nominee registers that home state senators must have a say in the selection of officials that could have an impact on policies.[70] In more recent times, Senator Orrin Hatch (R-UT), who chaired the SJC when Clinton was in office, referred to it when he said that "there was no way to confirm . . . nominations without completely ignoring the senatorial courtesy we afford to home state Senators in the nomination process."[71]

The senatorial courtesy tradition is the foundation for the "blue slip" process, a custom that was first introduced for a judicial nomination in 1917 when Georgia Senator Thomas Hardwick returned a negative blue slip to the SJC for President Woodrow Wilson's nomination of U.V. Whipple for a district court seat in southern Georgia. On a blue piece of paper, Hardwick wrote that he found the appointment "personally offensive and objectionable" and, after the SJC reported it to the full Senate, Whipple's nominated was rejected. Since that time, all judicial nominees have blue slips in their files.[72]

The blue slip process begins when the president formally sends a nomination to the Senate. Thereafter, the chair of the SJC sends out a form requesting the home-state senator's opinion on whether a nominee should be approved or opposed. The home-state Senator has two options: endorse or reject the nominee by returning the blue slip, or block confirmation hearings by not returning it (amounting to a "pocket veto"). Depending upon how the SJC chair interprets and applies the blue slip tradition, the blue slip practice may be used defensively or offensively, and advance or hinder a president's attempt to pack the courts.

It matters a great deal whether the chair of the SJC honors the blue slip tradition because the procedures governing it are not in the U.S. Constitution or codified in the SJC rules; thus, the chair sets the blue slip policy and how it is implemented in practice. Although there are many variations in practice, the SJC chair confronts the basic choice of whether to treat the blue slip as an advisory tool or whether it will be an absolute veto. For example, until the mid-1950s, SJC chairs only used it to solicit the opinion of home state senators about whether judicial nominations were suitable; so, negative blue slips did not automatically sink a nomination. In contrast, from the mid-1950s to 1978, when Senator James O. Eastland (D-Miss.) was the SJC chair, the blue slip was treated as a unilateral veto, purportedly in an effort to stop racial integration and the appointment of federal judges that opposed ending Jim Crow laws in the aftermath of the *Brown v. Board of Education* (1954) desegregation ruling. During the Trump administration, SJC chair Lindsey Graham (R-SC) initially declared that he would follow the one-time practice of his predecessor, Senator Chuck Grassley (R-Iowa), who allowed blue slips for federal district court nominees but not for circuit court nominees so long as the White House consulted the senators. That commitment was short-lived, as Trump appointments are increasingly not derailed by the blue slip process at the district or circuit court level. For example, a Third Circuit nominee, Paul Matey, was confirmed in March 2019 over the objections of Senators Cory Booker and Bob Menendez, Democrats who both complained the White House did not talk to them before Matey's confirmation. The Matey episode was not an aberration, as Senate Republicans confirmed a Ninth Circuit nominee, Eric Miller, even though neither home-state Senators (Patty Murray [D-WA] and Maria Cantwell [D-WA] returned a blue slip in support of Miller. Not surprisingly, as Republicans once said when they were in the Senate minority, Democratic senators are issuing warnings that Republicans will not have a chance to weigh in on the acceptability of judicial nominees through the blue slip process should they retake the Senate in upcoming election cycles, thus exacerbating partisanship tensions even further.[73]

Such threats of political retaliation are increasingly becoming a function of the political dynamics of the time and, of course, which party controls the White House, Senate and the SJC chair position. Those in power and who are uncompromising, or more lax, in exercising it may adopt rule changes or, instead, opt to stick to old-time Senate traditions to accomplish their political goals or preserve Senate norms. In 2013, after the Democrats, who controlled the Senate, invoked the so-called "nuclear option" that changed Senate rules to allow a filibuster debate to be ended by a simple majority vote (except for Supreme Court nominees), a procedural move that prevented minority Republicans from filibustering Obama nominees, Democratic chairman Patrick Leahy (D-VT) chose to return to a more "institutional" or traditional blue slip approach: confirmation hearings were not scheduled unless positive blue slips from both home-state senators were returned. Leahy defended the tradition of honoring blue slips by saying, "I assume no one will abuse the blue-slip process like some have abused the use of the filibuster to block judicial nominees on the floor of the Senate. As long as the blue slip process is not being abused by home-state senators, then I will see no reason to change that tradition." Yet, in practice, for the first six years of the Obama presidency (when the Democrats controlled the Senate), Leahy's blue slip procedure ironically gave senators in states with two Republican senators virtually unlimited power to block Obama's judicial appointments.[74]

In subsequent years, Leahy's institutional approach has yielded to more hardball political maneuvering. In the last two years of the Obama presidency, the blue-slip procedure was altered again after the Republicans captured the Senate in the 2014 mid-term elections. At first, with Republicans in the Senate minority while Obama was still in office, the SJC Chair, Chuck Grassley (R-IA), honored the blue slip tradition, thus giving Democrats or Republicans more opportunities to stop Obama's judicial picks from getting a hearing and an up-or-down vote in the Senate. If both home-state senators did not return the blue slips, a nominee would not get a hearing. But, as noted above, after Trump was elected President, Grassley changed the blue slip process to give Republicans every opportunity to pack the courts with conservative, life-time appointments at the trial and appellate level. Notably, Lindsey Graham (R-SC), who took over as SJC chair from Grassley, defended the change in blue slip practice by observing that the Democrats used the nuclear option to end filibusters in 2013 for certain judicial nominees; and he, along with Grassley, argue that the blue slip was never intended to operate as a unilateral veto to block the President's judicial appointments, especially at the circuit court level. As Grassley put it, "Circuit courts cover multiple states. . .There's less reason to defer to the views of a single state's senator for such nominee." As a result, President Trump has placed a record number of judges on the federal appellate courts, in part because Democrats cannot use the blue slip to stop them from being confirmed.[75]

The Confirmation Process

After the President announces a nomination and the blue slip is not returned by a home-state senator, the Senate Judiciary Committee (SJC) holds hearings and makes a recommendation to the full Senate as part of an up-or-down vote. Historically, the Senate has confirmed 99 percent of all nominees, typically consisting of tens of thousands of military and civilian appointments. That high rate of confirmations is because the appointments are considered a presidential prerogative and most are for non-policymaking positions.[76] Similarly, in spite of recent Senate practice, historically most appointments for federal court vacancies are routinely confirmed if a home-state senator does not object. A subcommittee of the SJC typically spends little time on hearings—some last for five minutes or less. Barring unexpected objections, the nomination is reported out of the committee and then moves to the full Senate for a confirmation vote.

Still, the increasingly strident partisanship and growing dysfunctional governance in Washington, D.C., has affected the historical norms and the prospect of "easy" confirmations.[77] The Senate's confirmation vote has also been progressively influenced by the media, special interest groups, and public opinion. As a result, presidential "court packing" has become more contingent on the politics of convincing the SJC to consider nominees without unnecessary delay or obstruction, and then reporting them to the Senate for up-or-down votes.

The Confirmation Politics of Evaluating the Nominee's Merits

For the Supreme Court, and increasingly for circuit courts, the scrutiny given a nominee's merits during the confirmation process has become much more rigorous. Senate scrutiny has intensified when opposition senators work to delay a nomination in the Senate Judiciary Committee, or to deny an up-or-down vote by using **filibusters**—a procedure preventing legislative action by continuously debating an issue on the Senate floor. In the aftermath of *Bush v. Gore* (2000),[78] Senate Democrats filibustered ten Bush circuit court nominees, and in response, Republicans threatened to invoke the so-called nuclear option—that is, preventing filibusters by rewriting the Senate rules for closing the debate, and thus permitting a confirmation vote. In May 2005, the White House and the so-called Gang of 14 senators (a bipartisan coalition) reached an agreement on voting on nominees: a list of filibuster targets would be confirmed by a simple majority vote in the Senate, so long as the President Bush agreed not to make any more recess appointments.[79]

After Bush left office, the political calculus changed again, and the "Gang of 14 Agreement" dissolved. When Obama entered the White House in 2008 and Democrats became the Senate majority, the political tables turned, and Senate Republicans now in the minority began to filibuster disfavored Obama judicial nominees, thereby preventing up-or-down votes. This time, however, after Republicans blocked three Obama appointments to the powerful U.S. Court of

Appeals for the District of Columbia Circuit and several administrative appointees, in late November 2013 Democratic Senate majority leader Harry Reid (D-NV) and fifty-one other senators invoked the "nuclear option" of revising the Senate cloture rules to allow a simple majority vote (instead of the sixty-vote supermajority that had been in force for forty years) to stop a filibuster and permit a vote on most presidential nominees, including those for the lower federal courts.[80] Thereafter, Obama was able to fill over a hundred judgeships in a year's time; but Republicans were incensed. In referring to Reid's decision to trigger the nuclear option, then-Senate Minority Leader Mitch McConnell (R-KY) warned that "You'll regret this, and you may regret this a lot sooner than you think." After the 2014 midterm elections, McConnell, now Senate majority leader, and Senate Judiciary Chair Chuck Grassley (R-IA), turned their threats into action by using their influence to obstruct and delay most of Obama's judicial appointments in the remaining two years of his administration; and, they refused to give Obama's pick, D.C. Circuit Judge Merrick Garland, a hearing to fill Justice Scalia's seat on the Supreme Court after Scalia died unexpectedly in early 2016. So, when President Trump nominated Neil Gorsuch to fill Justice Scalia's seat, it was not surprising that the Republicans invoked the nuclear option to change the Senate rules to prevent the Democrats from filibustering Trump's first Supreme Court selection. Before the second invocation of the nuclear option by McConnell, the 60-vote filibuster rule that would have ended a filibuster remained intact for Supreme Court nominations (but not lower court nominations). Thus, McConnell's action eliminated that exception, thereby paving the way for Gorsuch's (and ultimately Brett Kavanaugh's) successful confirmation with a simple majority fifty-one Senator vote.[81]

Those historic decisions to rewrite the Senate rules, though, are not likely to end the political controversy over confirming highly coveted judicial nominees. The growing polarization in national politics registers that each party that has control over the Senate is willing to rewrite the rules and change the traditional practices that have governed federal judicial selection for many decades; thus neither the filibuster nor, increasingly, the blue slip are effective procedural tools that can stop the confirmation of judicial appointments, especially when the Senate and Presidency remain in the control of the same party. Another tactic that presidents can use to counter senatorial obstruction, though, is by making recess appointments, a topic discussed in the "Contemporary Controversies over Courts: The (Constitutional) Hardball Politics of Federal Judicial Selection" box.

Contemporary Controversies over Courts: The (Constitutional) Hardball Politics of Federal Judicial Selection

The appointment of federal judges has become increasingly contentious over the last forty years. The principal reason is divided government—when one party controls the presidency and the opposition party has a majority, or even a hard-line minority unwilling to compromise, in the Senate. Another is the high stakes of securing lifetime judicial appointments and the value they have to presidential administrations pushing an ideological agenda. Since President Ronald Reagan's administration in the 1980s, federal judgeships have become both symbols and instruments of presidential power. Because judgeships are basically lifetime appointments, they offer presidents the opportunity to appoint judges who are likely to carry on their ideological positions long after they have left the Oval Office. As a result, the selection process became more rigorous. And, in turn, the Senate confirmation process became more prolonged and contested, with the opposition party aiming to thwart presidential attempts to pack the federal bench. Whether Democratic or Republican, the party in opposition has increasingly sought to delay or deny confirmation votes. One indicator of delay and obstruction is the increasing length of time from nomination to confirmation of district court judges: on average 60 days for Reagan's nominees, 135 days for Bill Clinton's, 166 for George H. W. Bush's, 178 for George W. Bush's, and 223 for Barack Obama's (in his first term and to 2014). Also, in the final two years the Obama presidency (during the 114th Congress, when Republicans controlled the Senate), there were 42 unconfirmed district court nominations; and, of the 18 that were confirmed, 9 were holdovers from 2014, 9 were from 2015, and none were confirmed in 2016. Except for two district court nominees coming from the home state of the Senate Judiciary Committee, Chuck Grassley (R-(Iowa)(from July and September nominations to February confirmations), the median time from nomination to confirmation was eleven months (in contrast, the median time for confirmation of President Trump's 17 district court nominations was six months in his first year in office with the Republicans controlling the Senate). Additional data shows that, in the Trump Administration's first three years, the delay is substantially less in red states with two Republican senators (217 median days); whereas, for nominees in states with two Democratic senators it was much more (412 median days).

More recently, another indicator is the length to which the party in opposition, or the one in control in a time of unified government (when the same party is dominates the White House, the House of Representatives, and the Senate) will go to push or go beyond the boundaries of old political conventions or notions of what was considered to be the unspoken rules of fair play in politics in order to gain political advantages. Some scholars, such as Mark Tushnet, have termed this phenomenon "constitutional hardball," a tactic that does not technically break the law but one that creates new political norms of behavior that encourages an almost never-ending pattern of outrage, dysfunction, and political reprisals. Examples include the decision by Democrats and Republicans to revise and replace longstanding Senate traditions to invoke the "nuclear option" to end filibuster debates in order to push judicial nominations to the full Senate to get an up-or-down vote in spite of vigorous minority party opposition; or the unprecedented decision by the Republican party Senate leadership to shut down the lower federal lower court confirmation process in President Obama's final two years in office; and, significantly, the failure of Republicans to grant a hearing to President Obama's nomination of the Chief Judge of the District of Columbia Circuit, Merrick Garland, to join the Supreme Court after Justice Antonin Scalia's death in February 2016, even though there was over ten months left in Obama's final year in office. Mitch McConnell, the Republican Senate Majority (R-KY) leader, defended the action by declaring that the American people, in choosing the next President in the 2016 election between Donald Trump and Hillary Clinton, must have a voice in choosing who should sit on the Supreme Court. The GOP's hardball political strategy worked when Trump unexpectedly won, which allowed Republicans to fill Scalia's seat with Neil Gorsuch, a staunch conservative and originalist, in the first year of his presidency. Still, it is unlikely that Democrats will easily forget these episodes and they are likely to retaliate in kind when they return to power in the Senate and the political conditions call for an equally hardball response.

Notably, the politics of constitutional hardball is registered with other procedural tactics underlying Senate obstruction and delay. Other than specifying that the president shall make judicial appointments with the "advice and consent" of the Senate, the Constitution is silent on the process of appointing judges—unlike the requirement of a two-thirds majority vote for ratifying treaties, expelling members of either house, or approving proposed constitutional amendments. In *United States v. Ballin*, 144 U.S. 1 (1892), the Supreme Court affirmed that each house of Congress may make or change procedural rules by simple majority vote. Over time, the exercise of that legislative prerogative began to affect how smoothly the President was able to get his judicial nominations confirmed by the Senate.

For example, in 1789, the Senate permitted lengthy debate over nominees, subject to a simple majority vote to cut off debate. But in 1837, senators in the opposition party began giving lengthy speeches in order to prevent votes on legislation (and later also on judicial nominees). That practice became known as *filibustering*. The increasing use of filibusters led to a series of changes in the Senate's rules for voting on cloture—voting to cut off a filibuster. In 1917, the rule for cloture votes was changed to require a supermajority of two-thirds (67) of the entire Senate (if all 100 senators are present). Subsequently, that rule was changed in 1975 to require a three-fifths vote (60 votes) to cut off filibusters. Still, as with other Senate rules, the rule on cloture votes remained subject to change by a simple-majority vote.

This background is important because the use of filibusters to obstruct confirming judicial nominees grew, which in turn and heightened tensions between both parties over what either deemed "extremist" or "out of the mainstream" judicial nominees. An indication of the escalating conflict is that of the 168 cloture votes ever filed (or reconsidered) with respect to judicial and other nominations, almost half occurred during Obama's administration; that is, by November 2013 Obama's nominees had faced 79 cloture votes, whereas during the preceding eight years George W. Bush's nominees confronted only 38 such votes. In addition, the attempted filibusters of nonjudicial executive appointments, including the unprecedented one directed at preventing Chuck Hagel from entering the Pentagon as defense secretary as well as a bevy of selections to assume leadership positions in the National Labor Relations Board and the Consumer Financial Protection Bureau, only intensified partisan divisions and made any hope for reaching a compromise on bipartisan grounds all but nearly impossible.

Consequently, in November 2013, Senate majority leader Harry Reid (D-NV) invoked the so-called nuclear option—namely, changing the rule requiring a supermajority vote for cloture to requiring a simple-majority vote for ending debate and proceeding to a vote on confirming judicial and other nominees, except for those to the Supreme Court (or to ordinary legislation). That rule change was approved by a vote of 52 to 48, with all Republican and three Democratic senators voting in opposition.

Republicans decried the change in the cloture rule on filibusters from requiring 60 to 50 votes. However, in 2005, Republican senators had threatened the "nuclear option" in order to have votes on George W. Bush's appellate court nominees who were blocked by Democrats, then in the minority. And in 2013, Republicans warned that the rule change would come back to haunt Democrats when they lost control of the Senate. As Senator Richard C. Shelby (R-AL) observed, "Democrats won't be in power in perpetuity," and the political fallout is likely to be felt for years to come. Shelby's prediction came true in April 2017, when the Republicans controlling the Senate invoked their own nuclear option by changing the Senate's cloture rule to end filibusters with a simple majority Senate vote for Supreme Court nominees, a move that allowed President Trump's first two picks to the high court, Neil Gorsuch and Brett Kavanaugh, to be confirmed without Senate Minority Democratic interference.

Even with the rule change, senators in the minority party may still give marathon speeches on the Senate floor in opposition to judicial nominees. In addition, at least until recent times, senators in the minority party could block or delay confirmation of judicial nominees by means of the "blue slip" practice of having home-state senators endorse a judicial nominee before holding confirmation hearings and a Senate vote. However, like the rules on filibusters and cloture, the blue slip practice remains subject to the political winds and, increasingly today during the Trump presidency, more of an abandoned practice, especially at the circuit court level. Before Trump, though, and at the end of the Carter presidency, and during a period of unified party control, Senator Edward Kennedy (D-MA) altered the blue slip process to make sure that Carter's selections got a hearing in an attempt to increase the federal bench's gender and racial diversity. In the 1980s, the committee's chair at the time, Republican senator Orrin Hatch, ignored the blue slip tradition in order to get around Democratic opposition to some of Reagan's judicial nominees. And, in 2017, Republican Senate Chair Chuck Grassley altered the blue slip process to prevent Democrats from using blue slips to object to President Trump's circuit court nominations. Grassley's change of blue slip practice has been followed by his successor, Lindsey Graham (R-South Carolina) in 2019; and should Democrats recapture the Senate while a Republican remains in the White House in 2020, Democrats have vowed to use the blue slip procedure in a similar fashion, which means they will not defer automatically to the preferences of Republican home-state senators on judicial nominees.

Finally, another hardball political response to Senate obstructionism over judicial nominations is "recess appointments" that presidents can make under Article II of the U.S. Constitution. If the Senate is not in session, presidents have the constitutional authority to bypass senatorial approval over nominees and may temporarily appoint judges to the bench while the Senate is in recess. In practice, recess appointments are often made permanent when a new congressional session begins, and since the Eisenhower administration, presidents only use them for federal lower court appointments. As such, it remains a formidable weapon: a president may award a judgeship regardless of political opposition. Still, the scope of the recess power is subject to ongoing constitutional review, as illustrated by *National Labor Relations Board v. Canning*, 573 U.S. 513 (2014), a case in which the Supreme Court limited the president's authority to make recess appointments during *pro-forma* sessions—the time when the Senate declares to be in session but does not do any governmental business. Hence, the change in the rules governing filibusters and the blue slip practice, as well as the constitutional threat by presidents to bypass the Senate through recess appointments, is likely to only further deepen conflicts and discourage compromise over the Senate's confirmation of judicial nominees in the emerging era of constitutional hardball politics.

Sources: Russell Wheeler, "Judicial Appointments in Trump's First Three Years: Myths and Realities," *Brookings* January 28, 2020), available at https://www.brookings.edu/blog/fixgov/2020/01/28/judicial-appointments-in-trumps-first-three-years-myths-and-realities/ (last retrieved April 14, 2020); Seung Min Kim, "Senate GOP Confirms Kavanaugh's Replacement, Trump's 36th Pick for Powerful Appeals Court, *Washington Post* (March 13, 2019), available at https://www.courthousenews.com/dozens-of-judicial-nominees-advance-to-full-senate/ (last retrieved April 14, 2020); Jason Zengerle, "How the Trump Administration is Remaking the Courts," *New York Magazine* (August 22, 2018), available at https://www.nytimes.com/2018/08/22/magazine/trump-remaking-courts-judiciary.html (last retrieved April 14, 2020); Barry J. McMillion, "The Blue Slip Process for U.S. Circuit and District Court Nominations: Frequently Asked Questions," *Congressional Research Service (R44975, October 7, 2017)* (Washington, D.C.: Government Printing Office, 2017); Russell Wheeler, "Senate obstructionism handed a raft of judicial vacancies to Trump—what has he done with them?," *FIXGOV (Brookings Institution, June 4, 2018)*, available at https://www.brookings.edu/blog/fixgov/2018/06/04/senate-obstructionism-handed-judicial-vacancies-to-trump/ (last retrieved April 14, 2020); Russell Wheeler, "Judicial Nominations and Confirmations: Fact and Fiction," *FIXGOV's Review of 2013* (Washington, D.C.: Brookings Institution, December 30, 2013); Congressional Research Service, Report RL 32013, *The History of the Blue Slip in the Senate Committee on the Judiciary, 1917–Present* (Washington, D.C.: U.S. Government Printing Office, 2003); and Congressional Research Service, Report RS21308, *Recess Appointments: Frequently Asked Questions (June 7, 2003, 7-5700)* (Washington, D.C.: U.S. Government Printing Office, 2013); Mark Tushnet, "Constitutional Hardball," *John Marshall Law Review* 37 (2004): 523, 523.

The Politics of Organized Interests, the Media, and Public Hearings

The confirmation process has become much more political during its evolution during the nation's history. Early on, those nominated to serve on federal courts were largely invisible to the public eye, but that changed because of technological advancements and the growing role that organized interests and the media played in affecting judicial appointments. Before 1925, Supreme Court nominees were relatively uninvolved in the confirmation process and were not asked to testify before the Senate Judiciary Committee. Before then, only one confirmation hearing, for Harlan F. Stone, in 1916, was held in open session and not behind closed doors. After 1925 and up until the late 1930s, the Senate did not even bother to hold confirmation hearings for three of five Supreme Court nominees. Senate practices, however, began to change in the mid-twentieth century and thereafter. After 1938, the Senate has held hearings for all but four Supreme Court nominees. And since John M. Harlan's nomination in 1955, every Supreme Court nominee has testified before the Senate Judiciary Committee. A key event that signaled what was to come was the confirmation hearings in 1981, with Sandra Day O'Connor's historic nomination (as the first woman on the Supreme Court). She was given unprecedented, for the time, "gavel-to-gavel" television coverage, something that has since become the norm for important judicial candidates in the twenty-first century with the advent of cable and social media news coverage.[82]

The increased transparency of the Senate confirmation process, along with the growing influence of interest groups, has come at a cost because it has resulted in the confirmation process becoming more contentious and politicized over time. In the words of one legal reporter, "Groups want certain policies kept in place or struck down by the courts."[83] Furthermore, as shown by Robert Bork's bitter confirmation battle (discussed below), the confirmation process has become more susceptible to demands of 24/7 cable news and, later on, social media coverage and, as a result, increasingly contentious, if not unstable, in regards to high-profile appointments due to hyper-partisanship and divided government. Consequently, Presidents can expect their selections to receive more intense Senate scrutiny if their choices are portrayed as ideologically extreme or if have any number of skeletons in their closet that can be exposed for political gain, even if they are fully qualified to hold the judgeship.[84]

The Battle over Robert Bork's 1987 Nomination

A seminal event in the politicization of the federal judicial confirmation process occurred in the summer of 1987, when President Reagan announced that Robert Bork, then a Judge on the influential D.C. Circuit, was his pick to replace Justice Lewis F. Powell, a critical swing vote of the Supreme Court, who was retiring. Shortly thereafter, Massachusetts's Democratic Senator Edward Kennedy denounced the nominee in his famous "Robert Bork's America" on the floor of the Senate speech:

> Robert Bork's America is a land in which women would be forced into back-alley abortions, blacks would sit at segregated lunch counters, rogue police could break down citizens' doors in midnight raids, and

schoolchildren could not be taught about evolution, writers and artists would be censored at the whim of government, and the doors of the federal courts would be shut on the fingers of millions of citizens for whom the judiciary is, and is often, the only protector of the individual rights that are at the heart of our democracy. America is a better, and freer nation, than Robert Bork thinks.[85]

Kennedy predicted and lamented that "the damage that President Reagan will do with this nomination, if it is not rejected by the Senate, could live on far beyond his presidential term. . .No justice would be better than this injustice."[86]

Despite Senator Kennedy's partisan hyperbole, Bork had strong legal credentials: He earned a law degree at the University of Chicago Law School; he had been a Yale University law professor; he served as U.S. Solicitor General and as acting U.S. Attorney General during the Nixon administration; and, for a short time, he served on the Court of Appeals for the D.C. Circuit. Some of those activities led to Kennedy's assessment, as then-Solicitor General Bork was an instrumental part of the so-called "Saturday Night Massacre" on October 20, 1972, when Bork agreed to fire the special prosecutor, Archibald Cox, who was investigating President Nixon's misfeasance in the 1970s Watergate scandal when Attorney General Elliot Richardson and Deputy Attorney General William Ruckelshaus refused to do so (both resigned thereafter).[87] In addition, Bork was also a well-known conservative, so liberals took aim at his outspoken advocacy of a jurisprudence of "original understanding" and opposition to unenumerated constitutional rights, like the right to privacy. In this light, Bork's conservative judicial philosophy, and not his professional merits or competence, defined the events that would ultimately determine the fate of his success as a judge on the nation's highest court.

In contrast to most prior Supreme Court nominees, Bork's constitutional views galvanized interest groups and gave Democratic senators many political incentives to question him intently about the public policy implications of his judicial views.[88] As an opponent of abortion rights and an advocate of a judicial philosophy of "original understanding," Bork had drawn the ire of a multitude of liberal interest groups. Liberals were especially concerned about the prospect of replacing Justice Powell, who had been a swing vote on abortion and civil rights issues. Over 150 interest groups mobilized for battle, with at least eighty-three liberal organizations opposed to the nomination.[89] Although historically it is not unusual for organized interests to fight or support a Supreme Court nominee, the Bork controversy was unprecedented at the time for its extensive media coverage and intense mobilization of (liberal and conservative) interest groups.

In order to win the votes of about twenty-five undecided senators, organized interests from both sides of the aisle mounted extensive letter-writing campaigns, and an estimated 250 op-ed articles (expressing support or opposition) appeared in newspapers. The People for the American Way, a liberal interest group founded by Norman Lear of television fame, launched a $2 million media campaign against Bork's confirmation. Conservative groups, such as the National Conservative Political Action Committee, did the same, spending over $1 million in support. Other conservative groups chartered an airplane to fly over the Iowa state fair with a banner castigating "Bork Bashers" and "liberal lap-dogs," whereas the liberal Concerned Women for America initiated a sophisticated phone bank and letter-writing campaign in order to influence the votes of senators.[90]

The mobilization of organized interests resembled the kind of political activity usually confined to general political campaigns. Interest groups used a variety of tactics, including: (1) testifying at congressional hearings; (2) engaging in direct lobbying of legislators and their staff; (3) generating large amounts of fund-raising and campaign contributions; (4) organizing grassroots support; (5) launching direct mail or letter-writing campaigns; (6) facilitating the dissemination of salient information (e.g., written opinions, law review articles, voting records) to educate the public about the nominee; (7) airing media advertisements; and (8) organizing demonstrations, marches, and protests. To be sure, the tactics sometimes distorted Bork's position on key issues, but they were effective in affecting Senator's views and perhaps public opinion on the acceptability of Bork's appointment.[91]

For some critics, the Bork controversy overwhelmed the traditional sanctity of the Senate confirmation process. For others, the vitriolic emergence of interest group advocacy was an ominous sign that some high-profile confirmations were destined to become mired in political considerations.[92] That signal became a self-fulfilling prophesy because in the last few decades interest groups have increasingly initiated the practice of targeting certain judicial nominees for political gain which, in turn, has encouraged the strident mobilization of voters at the grassroots level to support or oppose certain judicial appointments. In this respect, pro-choice interest groups played a key role in Bork's defeat by threatening to divert money away from senators supporting Bork; and, just a few years later, the same forces were at work when civil rights and women's interest groups rallied in their opposition to Clarence Thomas's confirmation by threatening to unseat senators who had publicly discredited Anita Hill's allegations of sexual harassment.[93] Although the Bork and Thomas confirmation battles were politically divisive for different reasons, it is worth noting that Bork's judicial philosophy, as opposed to his alleged personal foibles, was probably the most important factor in the Senate's decision to reject his nomination by a 58:42 vote.[94]

An enduring consequence of Bork's failed nomination is the dramatic proliferation of interest groups (across the political spectrum) who monitor and mobilize support or opposition to critical judicial appointments and nominees.[95] Scholars, in particular, have observed that there has been a significant increase in conservative groups' attempts to counter the influence of liberal groups and defeat nominees at all levels of the federal judiciary.[96] Such advocacy has been facilitated by the omnipotence of the Internet and social media in recent years. By taking positions and asking questions at confirmation hearings that are instantly transmitted throughout the world, senators speak not only to the nominees but also to their constituencies. Notably, since Bork's failed confirmation, more nominees have faced more frequent, and more rigorous, questions in the Senate hearings. In 1962, senators asked then-Supreme Court nominee Byron White only six questions at his confirmation hearings. By contrast, in 2005, Chief Justice John Roberts and Justice Samuel Alito were each asked over seven hundred questions. Another by-product of Bork's defeat has been for nominees to invoke the so-called Ginsburg rule—named after Justice Ruth Bader Ginsburg's decision to refuse to discuss legal issues that she was likely to consider on the bench. Accordingly, post-Bork nominees are more apt to "duck difficult questions in a way that their predecessors did not," a trend that Justice Elena Kagan has lamented has made confirmation hearings less meaningful because they present "to the public a vapid and hollow charade, in which repetition of platitudes has replaced discussion of viewpoints and personal anecdotes have supplanted legal analysis."[97]

Senate Confirmation Hearings and Reporting the Nomination

A pivotal phase of the federal confirmation process is the Senate Judiciary Committee's (SJC) assessment of the President's nomination. The SJC's recommendation to support or reject the appointment is based on a variety of factors, including the written record of the nominee's background and professional qualifications, as compiled by the committee's staff, the ABA, interest groups, academics, and interested persons. At the hearing, the committee also considers the nominee's answers to questions about his or her views of the law. The increasing importance of the SJC's hearings and report on recommending confirmation or not is underscored by the amount of time devoted to controversial nominees and the increasing length of the hearing transcript.

Between 1930 and 1949, the length of a transcript for Supreme Court justices' hearings averaged only 42 pages. But, since 1970, the average has grown to 1,117 pages or more. Moreover, since 1992, the SJC has held closed-door sessions with each nominee after his or her hearing in order to let the nominee further respond to issues that arose.[98] As suggested above, confirmation proceedings have become lengthier because they are now increasingly the principal forum for attacking the ideological views, or the personal character, of a controversial nominee—a tactic that is not uncommon in non-judicial, or ordinary, political milieus.

Senatorial Obstruction and Delay

The role the U.S. Senate plays in the process of evaluating federal judicial nominations is a key factor in the confirmation process, but increasingly it is defined by political, instead of objectively meritorious, considerations. In the past, lower court nominations were reported out of committee in short order and delivered to the Senate floor for a vote. Delaying the vote, however, has become more the rule than the exception that largely (as noted above) is due to divided government and increased hyper-partisanship. Other factors—such as presidential election year politics, or whether the appointment will shift the ideological balance of a court—also contribute to delaying final Senate action.[99] In addition to filibusters to delay or deny confirmations, senators may manipulate a variety of other Senate floor rules—such as putting "holds" on nominees and not giving unanimous consent to their being taken up on the Senate floor—which underscores the reality that judges are key change agents of legal and social policy.[100]

The trend toward delaying Senate action is especially apparent for court of appeals judgeships and, in recent times, even district court nominees. On average, between 1979 and 1994, it took 71 days to confirm a judicial nominee. During the first term of Obama's presidency, the average length of the confirmation process was 220 days for circuit court nominees and 190 days for district court positions. In targeting Obama's district court nominees, Republicans appeared committed to blocking all of his judicial appointments, in a sharp break from the past.[101] To illustrate further, in the last two years of the Obama administration—in the 114th Congress, a time when the Republicans controlled a Senate majority—Obama was only able to appoint successfully 18 of 62 (29%) district court nominations and only one of eight (13%) of his circuit court nominations. Those figures are the lowest percentages of successful appointments going back to the Carter administration. In comparison, in the 109th Congress, President G.W. Bush had fifty-five percent of his district court nominees confirmed; and, in the 106th

Congress, President Bill Clinton had forty-one percent of his circuit court choices ratified, even though he was in the midst of a Senate impeachment trial due to his extra-marital affair with Monica Lewinsky.[102] These patterns indicate that the politics of "obstruction and delay" has been the norm in recent presidencies (see Figure 4.2). In what some scholars call a "dysfunctional game of tit-for-tat" politics,[103] however, major obstruction and delay is not likely to be a factor or continue in the post-Obama presidency years, so long as a Republican President remains in office at a time when the Senate is also in Republican hands, or vice versa.

Figure 4.2	Senate Obstruction and Delay of Lower Federal Court Nominations

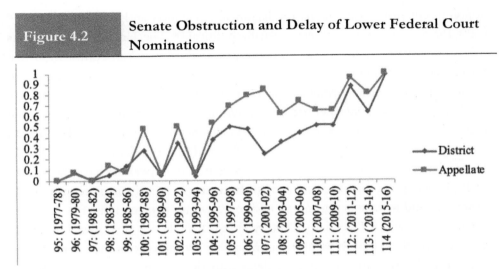

Source: Figure 4.2 is constructed using Goldman's "obstruction and delay" index. The index computes the number of nominees who remain unconfirmed at the end of Congress, which are added to the number for whom the confirmation took longer than 180 days, which is then divided by the number of total nominees for that Congress. A calculation that is "0.0000" indicates an absence of obstruction and delay, whereas "1.0000" shows maximum obstruction and delay. An index calculation that moves closer to 1 indicates a greater level of obstruction and delay. Elliot Slotnick, Sara Schiavoni and Sheldon Goldman, "Obama's Judicial Legacy: The Final Chapter," *Journal of Law and Courts* 5 (No. 2, Fall 2017), 363–422 (Tables 2 and 3).

Is the Confirmation Process "Broken"?

"This confirmation process has become a national disgrace," said Brett Kavanaugh, President Trump's second nominee to the Court in defending himself before the Senate Judiciary Committee in September 2018 against allegations of sexual harassment of Christine Blasey Ford while in high school. As he continued: "The Constitution gives the Senate an important role in the confirmation process, but you have replaced advice and consent with search and destroy." Although he was ultimately confirmed by narrow Senate vote, he characterized the confirmation as a "circus" and "a calculated and orchestrated political hit fueled with apparent pent-up anger about President Trump and the 2016 election" that was the result of a left-wing conspiracy led by political operatives aligned with the Clintons. In attacking the confirmation process as politically-motivated, Kavanaugh's response was immediately compared to Clarence Thomas' Senate hearings in 1991 in which the nominee accused the Senate Judiciary as conducting a "high tech lynching" after he was forced to defend himself against similar allegation of sexual harassment by Anita Hill, who worked for Thomas at the Equal Employment Opportunity Commission before he was nominated.[104]

For some court watchers, the politicization of the federal judicial appointment process threatens the legitimacy of courts and access to justice.[105] Calls for reform are nevertheless usually political.[106] The University of Virginia Miller Center of Public Affairs, however, created a bipartisan commission that concluded that a number of steps could be taken to shorten the time it takes to fill judicial vacancies, including: (1) encouraging senators to identify and vet candidates before a vacancy occurs or within thirty days thereafter and then recommending at least two or more candidates no later than ninety days after a vacancy occurs; (2) suggesting that the White House and the Department of Justice complete their investigations of potential nominees within ninety days; and, (3) asking the Senate to forego confirmation hearings for noncontroversial nominees and to take action on all nominees within two months after receiving them.[107] An earlier Twentieth Century Fund Task Force on Judicial Selection recommended using bipartisan nominating commissions to screen and recommend candidates for lower federal court judgeships. Specifically, the task force argued that candidates must be selected for their professional qualifications, based on their written records. For Supreme Court nominations, the task force went further in recommending that the Senate Judiciary Committee depoliticize confirmation hearings by abolishing the practice of having nominees appear before the committee.[108]

In addition to these proposals, other suggested reforms have included having the Senate Judiciary Committee hold confirmation hearings within thirty (for district courts) or sixty (for circuit courts) days. If the committee or full Senate does not act on the nomination in a timely fashion, then a referral is made to a confirmation commission (staffed by the Senate majority leader and Senate Judiciary Committee's chair), which would hold its own hearing and make a recommendation to the full Senate within two months. If the Senate fails to act on that recommendation, the Senate will be deemed to consent to it, and a certification of confirmation will be forwarded to the president.[109] By contrast, another proposal would increase participation by the electorate in confirming nominees through federal judicial elections (along the lines used in many states).[110]

Still, the claim that the confirmation process is in need of repair must be weighed against data showing that over eight years President Obama had put 263 district court judges on the bench (of 479 opportunities, or 56%), representing about forty percent of authorized district court positions; and, even though he was less successful due to senatorial obstruction and delay, he managed to confirm forty-eight circuit court judges (of 98 opportunities, or 49%); plus, he placed two Supreme Court Justice, Sonia Sotomayor and Elena Kagan, on the nation's highest court. Moreover, in comparison to his predecessor, G.W. Bush, Obama transformed the federal judiciary by greatly enhancing its gender/racial/ethnic diversity and reconstituting the courts with non-traditional judges that were moderate to liberal instead of staunchly conservative.[111] In terms of his first-term numbers, among which are successfully confirming nearly two hundred new federal judges and two Supreme Court Justices (Gorsuch and Kavanaugh) in that time span, President Trump is having a similar impact on the federal courts; but the effects of his selections will be more like G.W. Bush and Ronald Reagan in securing judicial appointments that are less diverse and lean heavily in the conservative direction (though Trump has also been adept at securing a greater number, and younger (below age fifty) judges at the influential circuit court level than past Presidents).[112] In historical context, the post-Reagan confirmation trends largely mirror what has gone on before in the area of federal judicial appointments, suggesting that politics is an inevitability that defines a President's legacy in shaping the federal bench—and that the confirmation process is not necessarily "broken." As political scientist Sheldon Goldman explains after surveying federal judicial appointments over a fifty-six-year period from Roosevelt to Reagan:

> [D]espite occasional dissatisfaction with how a particular nomination is handled, or charges that excessive partisanship or ideological litmus tests are being applied, our current judicial selection process, with the checks and balances envisioned by the framers (and even with some that were not, such as the role of the ABA), appears under most circumstances (with the possible exception of presidential election years) to be working reasonably well. There will always be tension between patronage, merit, and ideological considerations, and how that tension is resolved will differ from administration to administration. It will depend upon the point in political time in which an administration is functioning. It will depend upon the personalities and the nature of the interactions within and between the executive branch and the Senate.[113]

In sum, the judicial confirmation process is inherently political and will remain so, whether reformed or not.[114]

TOWARD A REPRESENTATIVE BENCH AND A CAREER JUDICIARY?

For most citizens, the prestige of serving as a state or federal judgeship is enviable. As federal appellate Judge James Buckley reminds us, "The federal judiciary is recruited from a professional elite, it enjoys life tenure, and, at the appellate level at least, it is sheltered from the rough and tumble of everyday life."[115] Yet, the judges across state and federal courts routinely confront political challenges that test their mettle. The balance of this Chapter considers, on the one hand, whether the American judiciary is moving toward greater diversity or a **career judiciary**— a relatively homogeneous cadre of professional judges—and, on the other hand, the disincentives for serving on the bench and why some judges opt to leave or are removed from the bench.

A Representative Bench?

A crucial characteristic of the judiciary is how representative it is of the general population. The personal and professional background of judges influence how they perform their judicial function and decide cases; and they affect the public's perception of the court's fairness, impartiality and legitimacy.[116] With this in mind, the demographic statistics—the racial, ethnic, religious, and socioeconomic characteristics of the state and federal judiciaries—reveal that the makeup of state and federal courts is identical despite different selection methods. Though the composition of U.S. courts has become more diversified over the past half-century, both state and federal courts remain relatively homogeneous and elitist. In general, judges are white, male, and Protestant. One study found that in 2005 African Americans represented only 8 percent of the nation's state supreme court justices, and only twenty-seven percent were women. As of 2009, thirty-one states failed to have an African American on their courts of last resort, nineteen states had yet to have an African American in the entire history of their state supreme court, and two states have never had a female justice. Subsequent research by the Brennan Center of Justice (2019) reports identical percentages of gender and minority under-representation across state high courts and the federal judiciary, noting especially that: (1) twenty-four states have an all-white supreme court bench (of which eight states have people of color at least in a quarter of their population); (2) fifteen percent of state supreme court seats in the national are staffed by Black, Asian, Latino, or Native Americans, even though nearly forty percent of the nation consists of people of color; and, (3) since 1960, thirteen states have never had a person of color service as a justice, and only six states have had one such person—and, over a third of the states have never seated a Black justice.[117]

The Brennan Center's findings are consistent with other studies by legal scholars Tracy George and Albert Yoon showing that state benches are not only "overwhelmingly white," but that there is an important gender gap as well. George and Yoon thus found that although more women have entered law school and the legal profession in the past forty years, less than one-third of state judges are women, and none of the states have women on the bench that are representative of their general populations. In addition, they report that fifty-seven percent of trial judges and fifty-eight percent of state appellate judges are white men even though they comprise only thirty percent of the population; and, only eight percent women of color are in state courts even though they represent twenty percent of the population.[118]

Empirical studies of the composition of the federal courts find similar general trends. The backgrounds of appointees from the Reagan to the Trump administrations underscore the lack of diversity in federal courts. Tables 4.2 and 4.3 show that since the 1980s lower federal court judges are typically fifty years old at the time of appointment and roughly eight out of ten judges are white. People of color represent less than eighteen percent, even though African Americans and Latinos increasingly represent larger segments of the general population. Also, beginning with the Reagan administration and extending through the first Bush, Clinton, second Bush, and Obama presidencies, appointments of women have become more numerous—almost three of every ten judges have been women in the post-Reagan years. In contrast to the pre-Reagan administrations, the Clinton and especially the Obama presidencies have had more success in putting women on the federal bench. Still, since the Reagan administration over 50 percent of the lower federal courts are white males. Likewise, President Trump's judicial appointments also largely consist of white men, a trend that some liberal critics allege shows no signs of abating.[119]

| Table 4.2 | | | | Diversity of Federal District Court Judges | | | | | |

		Gender		Race/Ethnicity					White/Male
President	Age	Male	Female	White	African American	Hispanic	Asian	Native American	
Reagan	48.6	91.7	8.3	92.4	2.1	4.8	.7	___	84.8
G. H. W. Bush	48.2	80.4	19.6	89.2	6.8	4.0	___	___	73.0
Clinton	49.5	71.5	28.5	75.1	17.4	5.9	1.3	.3	52.4
G. W. Bush	50.1	79.3	20.7	81.2	6.9	10.3	1.5	___	67.4
Obama	50.5	59.0	41.0	63.4	19.0	11.2	6.0	.4	38.1
Trump	51.0	76.0	24.0	92.0	2.0	2.0	4.0	___	___
Total Avg.	49.6	76.3	23.6	82.2	9.0	6.3	2.2	.11	52.6

Note: Some percentages within a category do not equal 100 percent because of exclusions. All data except for Trump relate to confirmed nominees; the Trump data relates to nominees in Trump's first year in office. Except age, all figures are percentages.

Sources: Elliot Slotnick, Sara Schiavoni and Sheldon Goldman, "Obama's Judicial Legacy: The Final Chapter," *Journal of Law and Courts* 5 (No. 2, Fall 2017))(Table 6), 364–422; Barry J. McMillion, "U.S. Circuit and District Court Nominations During President Trump's First Year in Office: Comparative Analysis with Recent Presidents," *Congressional Research Service (R45189, May 2, 2018)* (Washington, D.C.: Government Printing Office, 2018), 1, 11–12 (Figures 3–4).

| Table 4.3 | | | | Diversity of Federal Court of Appeals' Judges | | | | | |

		Gender		Race/Ethnicity					White/Male
President	Age	Male	Female	White	African American	Hispanic	Asian	Native American	
Reagan	50.0	94.9	5.1	97.4	1.3	1.3	___	___	92.3
G. H. W. Bush	48.7	81.1	18.9	89.2	5.4	5.4	___	___	70.3
Clinton	51.2	67.2	32.8	73.8	13.1	11.5	1.6	___	49.2
G. W. Bush	49.6	74.6	25.4	84.7	10.2	5.1	___	___	64.4
Obama	51.8	54.2	45.8	66.7	18.8	8.3	6.3	___	29.2
Trump	49	79.0	21.0	89.0	11.0	___	___	___	___
Total Avg.	50.0	75.1	24.8	83.4	9.9	5.2	1.3	___	50.9

Note: Some percentages within a category do not equal 100 percent because of exclusions. All data except for Trump relate to confirmed nominees; the Trump data relates to nominees in Trump's first year in office. Except age, all figures are percentages.

Sources: Elliot Slotnick, Sara Schiavoni and Sheldon Goldman, "Obama's Judicial Legacy: The Final Chapter," *Journal of Law and Courts* 5 (No. 2, Fall 2017), 364–422 (Table 7); Barry J. McMillion, "U.S.

Circuit and District Court Nominations During President Trump's First Year in Office: Comparative Analysis with Recent Presidents," *Congressional Research Service (R45189, May 2, 2018)* (Washington, D.C.: Government Printing Office, 2018), 1, 9–10 (Figures 1–2).

Moreover, like state judges, federal judges are basically recruited from three religious groups and, on balance, represent the upper class. Sixty percent of judges are Protestants, whereas roughly 26 percent are Catholic and about 10 percent are Jewish. Notably, judicial appointments by Democratic presidents Carter, Clinton, and especially Obama broke with the trend by making significant inroads in diversifying the federal bench.[120]

In addition, both state and federal judges are well-compensated, although they probably would earn more money in the private sector (see Table 4.4). Federal appellate judges, as well, do not have to draw from their salaries to contribute to retirement funds while in active service and, upon retirement, retire with full pay under certain conditions. An important trend registering these factors is that since the 1980s the proportion of millionaires on the federal bench has progressively increased. 22 percent of district court judges and 17 percent of circuit court judges in the Reagan administration reported their net worth as over a million dollars. By the end of the Obama administration, that figure has risen to 67 percent and 77 percent, respectively; and, at the start of the Trump presidency, the median net worth of Supreme Court justices was close to 5 million dollars.[121] Still, Chief Justice Roberts and other Supreme Court justices have aggressively lobbied Congress for pay increases on the grounds that it is becoming difficult to recruit the best from the private legal sector, and some federal judges are resigning before they are eligible for retirement in search of better-paying employment.[122]

Table 4.4	Judicial Salaries of State and Federal Judges			
State Courts				**Federal Courts**
Position	**Mean Salary**	**Salary Range**	**Position**	**Salary**
Chief, Highest Court	$ 186,098	$125,000–$273,712	Chief Justice, U.S. Supreme Court	$270,700
Associate Judge, Court of Last Resort	$ 179,785	$120,000–$261,013	Associate Justice, U.S. Supreme Court	$258,900
Judge, Intermediate Appellate Court	$ 173,132	$105,000–$244,700	Judge, U.S. Court of Appeals	$223,700
Judge, Trial Court	$ 161,750	$89,600–$216,400	Judge, U.S. District Court	$210,900
State Court Administrator	$ 161,221	$70,000–$299,004	Administrative Director, U.S. Courts	$199,100

Sources: National Center for State Courts, "Survey of Judicial Salaries (Vo. 45, No. 1; Data and Rankings as of January 1, 2020)" available from https://www.ncsc.org/__data/assets/pdf_file/0023/25358/2020-jss.pdf (last retrieved June 25, 2020); Administrative Office of the U.S. Courts, "Judicial Compensation," available from http://www.uscourts.gov/judges-judgeships/judicial-compensation (last retrieved April 15, 2020). Federal judicial compensation is based on 2019 wage levels. The salary for the Administrative Director, U.S. Courts was reported by the National Center for State Courts, as of 2015.

Nonetheless, the professionalization of the judiciary is apparent.[123] State and federal courts are distinct and stand in sharp contrast to the kind of professionalized judiciaries found in Europe and elsewhere (see "In Comparative Perspective: The Career Judiciary in Japan"). Notwithstanding the comparative differences between the U.S. courts and other career judiciaries across the globe, the fact remains that state and federal judges are professionally homogeneous and financially affluent.

In Comparative Perspective: The Career Judiciary in Japan

In the aftermath of World War II, Japan's Constitution (1947) vested the judicial system's highest Court, the Supreme Court of Japan, with the authority to nullify laws that were contrary to the constitution—similar to what is done in the United States under its own judicial review practice. Also, the Supreme Court has assumed considerable sway in controlling the recruitment and training of Japan's lower court judges, mostly through its management and supervision of the country's Legal Training and Research Institute (LTRI). Becoming a Justice on the Supreme Court is a function of elite legal bureaucratic practices and norms which also explain how lower court judges are recruited to become, ultimately, "career judges" that result only after completing several decades of professional training in the Japanese judicial system.

The Japanese judiciary is a unitary system of justice that has no separate national or state courts, like in the U.S. But, similar to the U.S., Japan features essentially a three-tier hierarchy, or levels, of different courts that handle each of their respective caseloads. The highest court, *the Supreme Court of Japan*, has fifteen justices that decides minor cases in groups of five justices each, and more significant cases are heard *en banc*, or by the full court membership. Sitting beneath the Supreme Court are eight *high courts* that are dispersed throughout Japan's major cities, but there six other branches in less-populated cities. High courts are staffed by nearly three hundred judges that are appointed by the prime minister and the Cabinet, with the recommendation of the Supreme Court. Notably, these judges are prone to have reassignments at different time periods, and there is a mandatory retirement age of sixty-five years old.

The trial courts at the bottom tier consist of *district and family courts*. Approximately fifty district courts operate in major urban areas, and a much larger contingent (about 200 courts) serve justice in much smaller regions, towns and localities. Like U.S. federal middle-tier appellate courts in the U.S., district courts in Japan hold trials with three-judge panels, except in minor cases. Apart from district courts, roughly fifty family courts and just over two hundred branches operate as limited jurisdiction, or specialized courts that decide cases through lay conciliators. Underneath family courts sit several hundred *summary courts* that adjudicate minor criminal and civil cases with the help of nearly eight hundred judicial officers. Notably, summary court judgeships are distinctive because they consist of former judicial or court-related personnel, like clerks, prosecutors, and judges, who extend their service in the Japanese court system by working past the retirement ages in their previous positions because they are allowed to work in summary courts until the age of seventy years old.

As with many court systems across the world, the Japanese court system operates as a complex bureaucracy that employ thousands of judges, clerks of court, and administrative personnel. A key element that distinguishes its operation and function is an elaborate recruitment, training and appointment process that takes years to negotiate through if one is interested in achieving a high degree of professional success. It is not an over-simplification to describe that process has having the effect of creating, and fostering, an elite cadre of career judges that possess a highly professional skill-set to dispense justice in Japan. In particular, but apart from Supreme Court justices, aspirants vying for lower court judgeships must begin their training at a university by earning a Bachelor's degree in law (in the U.S., undergraduate pre-law training is different, see Chapter Five). Thereafter, they must study for, and pass, a National Law Examination (NLE)-a requirement that less than one percent of applicant-test takers succeed in passing (although it can be taken multiple times). There are other requirements as well: if the NLE is passed, students must write a thesis and be successful in a personal interview in order to matriculate into the LTRI. After LRTRI admission, students then must finish four separate internships that last four months each in an attorney's office and a prosecutor's office, plus one each in a criminal and civil court, respectively. Once all of these steps have been completed, graduates may apply for assistant judgeship positions that last for ten years-though such appointments are very limited in number, and many aspirants do not have much success in landing them in practice. If a student receives an appointment as an assistant judge, the ten year period in which they serve operates more like on-the-job training, or an apprenticeship; but, in practice, after five years they begin to act more in the capacity of full judges, and they may also become associate judges that work on a three-judge court or as a single judge presiding in one court. Indeed, it is common for judges to move to different courts and positions throughout their professional careers, though only a few become chief judges on the most reputable courts. At the end of ten years, most become full judges subject to reappointment in each subsequent decade.

In contrast to lower court appointments, the process by which Supreme Court justices achieve their positions evolved differently. In the early post-war years, the constitution and statutory law drew from the Missouri "merit plan" model that began to take hold in the United States in the 1940s (see that discussion earlier in this chapter). Over time, the Japan abandoned the use of judicial nomination commissions (but retained a system of using retention elections after ten years of service-though few justices face elections because there is a mandatory retirement age of seventy, and most are appointed in their sixties), and a new practice emerged that empowered the chief justice, in essence, to appoint Supreme Court justices in consultation with Cabinet officials and the General Secretariat, as well as other legal stakeholders from the Japanese bar and other legal administrators. In terms of qualifications, statutory law (the Court Organization Law) requires that justices who are appointed to the Supreme Court "shall be among persons of broad vision and extensive knowledge of law, who are not less than 40 years of age"-in practice, appointments generally come from three types of groups in Japan's legal establishment: (1) lower court judges; (2) lawyers; and (3) public prosecutors, law professors, or others with extensive knowledge and professional experience. As a result, a convention developed that encourages the Supreme Court to consist of six career judges, four lawyers, two former bureaucrats, two prosecutors, and one law professor on the Supreme Court.

In sum, the appointment of judges in Japan is largely determined by the recruitment, training, and promotion of career judges admitted into the LTRI and overseen by the chief justice. Most judges begin their careers in their mid-twenties and serve until sixty-five, though some may extend their careers until age seventy by serving on the Supreme Court or a summary court. Throughout their careers, they are periodically reassigned to various courts, and their careers are overseen by senior judges and the bureaucracy of the LTRI. These two features—spiraling career paths within a judicial hierarchy closely controlled by a judicial bureaucracy—set the Japanese judiciary apart from not only other judicial selection systems within Asia, but also those in Western Europe and North America. From beginning to end, judicial careers are determined by senior judges, not political branches or agencies outside the courts. As a result, the Japanese judiciary maintains institutional independence at the price of conformity and the sacrifice of individual judges' independence on the bench.

Source: David M. O'Brien (with Yasuo Ohkoshi), *To Dream of Dreams: Religious Freedom and Constitutional Politics in Postwar Japan* (Honolulu: University of Hawaii Press, 1996)(chapter three).

LEAVING THE BENCH

"Fortunately most of the judiciary is honest," Judge Jerome Frank once remarked, but "a very few scamps manage to get on the bench, and the best way to avoid unfairness to the vast majority of judges is to oust the few rascals."[124] Judges, of course, voluntarily leave the bench because of ill health, due to advancing age and retirement, or for personal reasons. But, as Judge Frank suggested, on occasion there is a need to force a judge off the bench because of misconduct, incompetence, intemperance, neglect, or disability. Judges may also be targeted for making unpopular rulings and impeached.

Forcing qualified judges to step down raises separation of powers and broader constitutional concerns: How much power should legislatures have in policing the internal affairs of the judiciary? Should court administrators, judges, and lawyers have the flexibility to discipline judges without external political interference? In short, the problem of judicial removal and discipline arises from the inherent tension between judicial independence and accountability and has been an ongoing political struggle. The rest of this chapter explores the methods used to persuade or force judges to leave the bench.

Historically, state constitutions or statutes have authorized the disciplining of state judges by the legislature through a variety of means, including impeachment (removal by trial by the upper house after the lower house votes to impeach), *legislative resolution* (removal by concurrent vote of each legislative chamber), *legislative address* (by majority vote the legislature directs the governor to remove a judge), and, since the first decades of the twentieth century, *legislative recall* (after petition for a special election to vote on removal).[125]

Each method, however, has proven subject to political abuse or has been rarely used.[126] As a result, beginning in the 1940s, the task of disciplining judges incrementally shifted to state courts themselves. In 1960, California established the prototype for judicial discipline and removal that became a model for sanctioning judges in virtually all other states. California's Commission on Judicial Performance, a multimember commission of judges, lawyers, and citizens, was empowered to investigate complaints about judicial performance and then, with or without a hearing, to make recommendations to the state's highest court about final disposition. Today, every state and the District of Columbia has some type of judicial conduct organization that is charged with investigating allegations of judicial misfeasance or disability.[127]

State supreme courts, the state bar, or the governor usually determine a judicial commission's membership, and the size and jurisdiction vary. Typically, once a written complaint is filed, the commission first investigates the allegations—in confidence—and then, after concluding its inquiry, resolves the case through dismissal, informal private sanction, or formal referral to the state's highest court after conducting a public hearing on the charges. The kind of informal or formal sanction levied—including removal, involuntary retirement, suspension without pay, the payment of a fine, public or private censure, public or private reprimand, professional counseling and education, admonishment, or advisory letters—typically depends on the offense and whether there is a pattern of misconduct.[128]

Although the imposition of penalties is relatively infrequent, state judicial commissions have nonetheless disciplined judges, sometimes severely. One study reports that in 1980, only 22 state judges were disciplined; but, by 2012, the number had risen to 137.[129] Still, while the frequency of disciplining state judges has grown, the numbers likely reflect that there are also many more judgeships because of the nation's growth. In general, most of the complaints about judges are dismissed. For example, in 2014 the New Mexico Judicial Standards Commission dismissed seventy-six percent of the 188 complaints it received, mostly because the claims were not substantiated or on procedural grounds (such as raising an appellate issue or that the judge was not within the commission's jurisdiction). Likewise, in 2014 the Washington State Commission on Judicial Conduct dismissed eighty-seven percent of the 319 complaints it processed for similar reasons. In addition, in a national investigation of thousands of judicial misconduct cases it reviewed over the past dozen years or so, Reuters, a news agency, discovered that ninety percent of sanctioned judges were able to return to the bench, even in egregious instances—such as when, in California, a judge was disciplined for having sex in his chambers; or, in Utah a judge texted a video of a man's scrotum to court clerks; or, in Indiana, a trio of judges got in a drunkard fight outside a White Castle hamburger joint at 3 a.m., with two even being shot.[130]

Apart from disciplining state judges, federal judges may be removed only by impeachment for criminal activities, treason, or committing "other high Crimes and Misdemeanors." Under Article I, Section 2, of the Constitution, the House of Representatives passes articles of impeachment, and then the Senate tries impeachment cases. Historically, impeaching federal judges has been problematic for the same reasons that the procedure proved unwieldy in the states. Impeachment may be politically abused and awkward. Moreover, not all instances of judicial misfeasance rise to the level of impeachable offenses, and the Constitution is silent about the removal of inept, intemperate, or disabled judges. Only fifteen federal judges have been impeached, and of those only eight were convicted; the rest either resigned, had their charges dismissed, or were acquitted.[131]

Consequently, Congress and the federal courts have moved toward adopting the same type of commission format for disciplining judges that became prevalent in the states. However, the federal procedure is distinct because public citizens and attorneys do not play a role in sitting on the committee that is empowered to discipline judges. Under the Administrative Office Act of 1939, and then through the Judicial Code in 1948, circuit court councils (staffed by appellate judges from all circuits) were given responsibility to set ethical standards and discipline judges by certifying cases of physical or mental disability. The constitutionality of the authority of circuit courts to sanction federal judges, however, remained unclear. Hence, Congress enacted the Judicial Councils Reform and Judicial Conduct and Disability Act of 1980. In conjunction with the Rules for Judicial Conduct and Judicial Disability Proceedings, that legislation, as amended by the Judicial Improvements Act of 2002, remains the principal means for disciplining federal judges, except Supreme Court justices in non-impeachment cases.[132]

Under the Judicial Conduct and Disability Act, a complaint must be filed with a federal court of appeals asserting that a judge has become disabled or "prejudicial to the effective and expeditious administration of the business of the courts." After reviewing the charges, the chief judge of the circuit may dismiss the complaint on procedural grounds or upon finding that corrective action has already been undertaken; or, alternatively, a special committee of district and circuit court judges may be created to investigate further and make a written recommendation to the circuit council about what action should be taken. After conducting its own review, the circuit council may disregard or adopt the recommendation and, if necessary, may levy sanctions against the judge. Penalties include certifying that there is a disability, requesting voluntary retirement, or otherwise reprimanding the judge, either publicly or privately. Notably, the council does not have the power to compel removal but instead refers such cases to the House of Representatives for impeachment proceedings.

As in the state courts, the process of disciplining federal judges has had little impact in removing judges. Between October 2018 to September 2019, for example, 1,412 complaints were filed against federal judges. Of those complaints, ninety-two percent were filed by litigants or prison inmates, and most allegations centered on issues relating to making an "erroneous decision" or exhibiting "personal bias against litigant or attorney" or "hostility toward litigant or attorney." Seventy-two percent of complaints were dismissed with no further review, and the balance were rejected or withdrawn as either frivolous, lacking sufficient evidence or merit, or not germane. The large number of complaints that were filed did not lead to disciplinary sanctions since only two judges were ultimately censured or reprimanded.[133]

In sum, federal and state court judges are likely to stay on the bench, and they are infrequently disciplined or removed.

Chapter Summary

The politics of state and federal judicial selection, as well as whether the American judiciary is moving toward a professionalized "career judiciary" that limits opportunities to remove judges from public service, is analyzed. The circumstances under which federal or state judges leave the bench are discussed.

While a handful of states use legislative and gubernatorial appointment systems, a majority uses a combined mix of elective-appointment methods in order to keep judges accountable to the people. Electing judges creates the risk of political corruption and inherently diminishes judicial independence from the political branches. Thus, many states use merit judicial selection commissions to depoliticize judicial campaigns and elections, but they have met with little success. Moreover, Supreme Court decisions have expanded the free speech rights of judges when campaigning for office and have put few limits on how judges use political money in judicial elections. As a result, state judicial selection has become highly politicized, and critics argue that state judges are merely politicians in black robes.

In contrast, federal judicial selection involves presidential nomination and Senate confirmation through "advice and consent." Presidents tend to take different approaches to judicial selection. Typically, the White House General Counsel's Office and the Department of Justice's Office of Legal Policy engage in a "vetting process" that screens candidates. Other entities, such as the American Bar Association, the Federalist Society, the media, and interest groups, also evaluate the candidate's merits. In recent years, the Federalist Society in particular has had great influence on federal judicial selection process, especially during the vetting stage. The Senate Judiciary Committee holds public hearings and decides whether to send the name to the full Senate for an up-or-down vote. As Brett Kavanaugh's appointment to the Supreme Court illustrates, federal judicial selection has become increasingly politicized; thus, some critics claim that the confirmation process is "broken" and in need of reform. In 1987, the Senate's rejection of Judge Robert Bork's nomination to the Supreme Court registers the significant role organized interests play in defeating an otherwise meritorious nomination; and special interest groups continue to affect contemporary confirmation politics. In addition, senatorial obstruction and delay of federal lower court appointments is a growing issue in periods of sustained divided government. As a result, the Senate has changed its rules or abandoned traditions such as the blue slip process.

Apart from judicial selection, the chapter analyzes whether the American judiciary is moving toward a "career judiciary." While U.S. courts have increasingly become more diversified in recent years, the racial, ethnic, religious, and socioeconomic characteristics of the state and federal judiciaries still remain relatively homogeneous and elitist. In general, judges are white, male, Protestant, and affluent. Moreover, although subject to removal for illicit conduct, in practice they are infrequently removed. As a result, most federal and state court judges stay on the bench unless they voluntarily retire, become disabled, or die in office.

Key Questions for Review and Critical Analysis

1. How do state judicial selection methods strengthen or undermine the values of judicial accountability or judicial independence from the political branches?

2. Is the criticism that state judges are "politicians in black robes" when campaigning for office justified or accurate? Why or why not?

3. Some recent presidents, like Barack Obama and Bill Clinton, have been more interested in diversifying the federal bench; others, like Ronald Reagan, George W. Bush and Donald J. Trump, have tried to pack the courts with judges who share the president's political ideology. Does that mean that Presidents Obama and Clinton are not interested in packing the courts? Do you think presidents Reagan, Bush and Trump were not interested in filling the bench with meritorious candidates? What role does ideology or merit play in federal judicial selection? Should presidents try to "pack" the federal bench?

4. In a growing era of constitutional hardball politics, do you think it is appropriate for the Senate to use obstructive and delaying tactics, such as invoking the "nuclear option" to stop filibusters, or to using the blue slip process aggressively to prevent or delay votes, on nominees to the federal courts? Is it appropriate for the party in power during unified government to invoke nuclear options or to manipulate the blue slip process as well?

5. How important is it to have a diversified or "representative" bench in the state and federal judiciaries?

Web Links

1. National Center for State Courts (Judicial Selection and Retention Resource Guide) (https://www.ncsc.org/)

- The NCSC has taken over the data from the American Judicature Society, an organization that was interested in judicial selection. The AJS was founded in 1913 (but in 2014 the AJS operations shifted from the Dwight D. Opperman Center at Drake University to the AJS Hawaii Chapter. At the same time, AJS's assets and programs were transferred to several institutions which include the National Center for State Courts, the Duke Law Center for Judicial Studies, the Hunter Center of the Communities Foundation of Texas, and the South Texas College of Law. It remains an organization focused on maintaining the integrity of the American justice system.

2. The Department of Justice's Office of Legal Policy (https://www.justice.gov/olp)

- The Department of Justice's Office of Legal Policy undertakes policy initiatives and gives advice to the president, including on the selection process of federal judges. The site provides current data on the nomination and confirmation activity of federal judges in relation to the U.S. Congress.

3. Alliance for Justice (https://www.afj.org/)

- A national organization representing progressive political values. It monitors federal judicial selection and provides an array of information, reports, publications, and advocacy resources on the topic.

4. The Federalist Society for Law and Public Policy Studies (https://fedsoc.org/)

- A national group of conservatives and libertarians interested in the current state of the legal order.

Selected Readings

Abraham, Henry J. *Justices, Presidents, and Senators: A History of the U.S. Supreme Court Appointments from Washington to Bush* II. 5th ed. Lanham, Md.: Rowman & Littlefield Publishers, 2007.

Binder, Sarah A., and Forrest Maltzman. Advice and Dissent: *The Struggle to Shape the Federal Judiciary.* Washington, D.C.: Brookings Institution, 2010.

Bonneau, Chris W. and Melinda Gann Hall, eds. *Judicial Elections in the 21st Century.* New York: Routledge, 2017.

Collins, Paul M., Jr., and Matthew Eshbaugh-Soha. *The President and the Supreme Court: Going Public on Judicial Decisions from Washington to Trump.* New York: Cambridge University Press, 2019.

Epstein, Lee, and Jeffrey Segal. *Advice and Consent: The Politics of Judicial Appointments.* New York: Oxford University Press, 2005.

Geyh, Charles Gardner. *Who is to Judge?: The Perennial Debate Over Whether to Elect or Appoint America's Judges.* New York: Oxford University Press, 2019.

Gibson, James L. *Electing Judges: The Surprising Effects of Campaigning on Judicial Legitimacy.* Chicago: Chicago University Press, 2012.

Goelzhauser, Greg. *Judicial Merit Selection: Institutional Design and Performance for State Courts.* Philadelphia, PA.: Temple University Press, 2019.

Goldman, Sheldon. *Picking Federal Judges: Lower Court Selection From Roosevelt Through Reagan.* New Haven, Conn.: Yale University Press, 1997.

Haire, Susan B. and Laura P. Moyer. *Diversity Matters: Judicial Policy Making in the U.S. Courts of Appeals.* Charlottesville, Va.: University of Virginia Press, 2015.

Hall, Melinda Gann. *Attacking Judges: How Campaign Advertising Influences State Supreme Court Elections.* Stanford, CA.: Stanford University Press, 2015.

Hasen, Richard L. *Plutocrats United: Campaign Money, The Supreme Court, and the Distortion of American Elections.* New Haven: Yale University Press, 2016.

O'Brien, David M. *Judicial Roulette: Report of the Twentieth-Century Fund Task Force on Judicial Selection.* New York: Priority Press, 1988.

Peters, C. Scott. *Regulating Judicial Elections: Assessing State Codes of Judicial Conduct.* New York: Routledge, 2018.

Scherer, Nancy. *Scoring Points: Politicians, Activists, and the Lower Federal Court Appointment Process.* Stanford, Calif.: Stanford University Press, 2005.

Shugerman, Jed Handelsman. *The People's Courts: Pursuing Independence in America.* Cambridge, Mass.: Harvard University Press, 2012.

Steigerwalt, Amy. *Battle Over the Bench: Senators, Interest Groups, and Lower Court Confirmations.* Charlottesville: University of Virginia Press, 2010.

Tarr, G. Alan. *Without Fear or Favor: Judicial Independence and Judicial Accountability in the States.* Stanford, Calif.: Stanford University Press, 2012.

Volcansek, Mary L. *Judicial Impeachment: None Called for Justice.* Urbana: University of Illinois Press, 1992.

Yalof, David Alistair. *Pursuit of Justices: Presidential Politics and the Selection of Supreme Court Nominees.* Chicago: University of Chicago Press, 1999.

Endnotes

1   Philip Rucker and Robert Barnes, "Trump to Inherit More than 100 Court Vacancies, Plans to Reshape Judiciary," *Washington Post* (December 25, 2016), available at https://www.washingtonpost.com/politics/trump-to-inherit-more-than-100-court-vacancies-plans-to-reshape-judiciary/2016/12/25/d190dd18-c928-11e6-85b5-76616a33048d_story.html?utm_term=.92d1fe0c493c (last retrieved April 11, 2020). See also Elliot Slotnick, Sara Schiavoni and Sheldon Goldman, "Obama's Judicial Legacy: The Final Chapter," *Journal of Law and Courts* 5 (No. 2, Fall 2017), 363–64.

2   Devan Cole and Ted Barrett, "Senate Confirms Trump's 200th Judicial Nominee," *CNN* (June 24, 2020), available at https://www.cnn.com/2020/06/24/politics/trump-200-judicial-appointments-cory-wilson/index.html (last retrieved June 24, 2020); Ian Millhiser, "What Trump Has Done to the Courts, Explained," *Vox* (December 19, 2019), available at https://www.vox.com/policy-and-politics/2019/12/9/20962980/trump-supreme-court-federal-judges (last retrieved April 11, 2020)(quoting Justice Sotomayor); Mark Joseph Stern, "While the House Impeaches, the Senate Will Confirm 13 More Trump Judges," *Slate* (December 18, 2019), available at https://slate.com/news-and-politics/2019/12/senate-impeachment-trump-judicial-nominees.html (last retrieved April 11, 2020); Kevin Schaul and Kevin Uhrmacher, "How Trump is Shifting the Most Important Courts in the Country," *Washington Post* (September 4, 2018), available at https://www.washingtonpost.com/graphics/2018/politics/trump-federal-judges/?utm_term=.7595095f4866 (last retrieved April 11, 2020). See also, American Constitution Society, "On the Bench: Federal Judiciary," available at https://www.acslaw.org/judicial-nominations/on-the-bench/ (last retrieved December 20, 2019).

3   Adam Liptak and Matt Flegenheimer, "Neil Gorsuch Confirmed by Senate as Supreme Court Justice," *New York Times* (April 7, 2017), available at https://www.nytimes.com/2017/04/07/us/politics/neil-gorsuch-supreme-court.html (last retrieved April 11, 2020).

4   Dylan Matthews, "Brett Kavanaugh, Donald Trump's Supreme Court nominee, explained," *Vox* (July 9, 2018), available at https://www.vox.com/explainers/2018/7/9/17540334/brett-kavanaugh-trump-supreme-court-anthony-kennedy (last retrieved April 11, 2020); Ron Elving, "Kavanaugh Pick Shows Trump Bowing Again To The GOP Legal Establishment (July 10, 2018)," available at https://www.npr.org/2018/07/10/627561071/kavanaugh-pick-shows-trump-bowing-again-to-the-gop-legal-establishment (last retrieved April 11, 2020).

5   Sheryl Gay Stolberg, "Kavanaugh Is Sworn In After Close Confirmation Vote in Senate," *N.Y. Times* (October 6, 2018), available https://www.nytimes.com/2018/10/06/us/politics/brett-kavanaugh-supreme-court.html (last retrieved April 11, 2020); Russell Berman, "Democratic Frustration Over the Supreme Court Finally Boils Over," *The Atlantic* (September 6, 2018), available at https://www.theatlantic.com/politics/archive/2018/09/democrats-cory-booker-brett-kavanaugh-supreme-courts-emails/569488/ (last retrieved April 11, 2020); Jason Breslow, "The Resistance At The Kavanaugh Hearings: More Than 200 Arrests," *NPR* (September 8, 2018), available at https://www.npr.org/2018/09/08/645497667/the-resistance-at-the-kavanaugh-hearings-more-than-200-arrests (last retrieved April 11, 2020).

6   See Andrew Nolan and Caitlain Devereaux Lewis, "Judge Brett M. Kavanaugh: His Jurisprudence and Potential Impact on the Supreme Court," *Congressional Research Service*, Order Code R45293 (August 21, 2018) (Washington, D.C.: Congressional Research Service, 2018); Dylan Matthews, "America under Brett Kavanaugh," *Vox* (September 4, 2018), available at https://www.vox.com/2018/7/11/17555974/brett-kavanaugh-anthony-kennedy-supreme-court-transform (last retrieved April 11, 2020).

7   G. Alan Tarr, *Without Fear or Favor: Judicial Independence and Judicial Accountability in the States* (Stanford, Calif.: Stanford University Press, 2012), 8–9.

8   Geyh, "The American Judicature Society and Judicial Independence: Reflections at the Century Mark," "The American Judicature Society and Judicial Independence: Reflections at the Century Mark," *Judicature* 96 (2013), 257–63; Lauren C. Bell, "Federal Judicial Selection: In History and Scholarship," *Judicature* 96 (2013), 296, 297; Charles H. Sheldon and Linda S. Maule, *Choosing Justice: The Recruitment of State and Federal Judges* (Pullman: Washington State University Press, 1997), 2–3.

[9]   Jed Handelsman Shugerman, *The People's Courts: Pursuing Independence in America* (Cambridge, Mass.: Harvard University Press, 2012), 84–102.

[10]   Shugerman, *The People's Courts*, 105, 148–49. See also Geyh, "The American Judicature Society and Judicial Independence," 260.

[11]   Larry C. Berkson, "Judicial Selection in the United States: A Special Report," in *Judicial Politics: Readings From Judicature*, edited by Elliot E. Slotnick (Chicago: American Judicature Society 1999), 45.

[12]   Geyh, "The American Judicature Society and Judicial Independence," 260. For the American Judicature Society, for "merit selection" states, retention can be accomplished *either* through a retention election or by a judicial commission making a retention evaluation. American Judicature Society, "Merit Selection: The Best Way to Choose the Best Judges," available at http://www.judicialselection.us/uploads/documents/ms_descrip_1185462202120.pdf (last retrieved March 29, 2019).

[13]   Evan Haynes, *The Selection and Tenure of Judges* (Newark, N.J.: National Conference of Judicial Councils, 1944), 235–36; Shugerman, *The People's Courts*, 174. See also Geyh, "The American Judicature Society and Judicial Independence," 260; and Rachel Paine Caufield, "How the Pickers Pick: Finding a Set of Best Practices for Judicial Nominating Commissions," *Fordham Urban Law Journal* 34 (2007): 163, 169–170.

[14]   After the twelve-year term, the judge would then serve for life. Malcolm Smith, "The California Method of Selecting Judges," *Stanford Law Review* 3 (1951), 571–72, 583. See also Shugerman, *The People's Courts*, 185–86. Notably, California's merit plan was contested by organized labor, which supported partisan elections, but favored by lawyers and business interests that were concerned with the close connection between judicial corruption, machine party politics, and organized crime. It was thus part of a crime control package that was spearheaded by Earl Warren, a state prosecutor who would later become California's governor as well as Chief Justice of the U.S. Supreme Court. Shugerman, *The People's Courts*, 177–207; Smith, "The California Method of Selecting Judges," 579–80.

[15]   Geyh, "The American Judicature Society and Judicial Independence," 260. See also Shugerman, *The People's Courts*, 197–203.

[16]   Alicia Bannon, Eric Velasco, Linda Casey, and Lianna Reagan, *The New Politics of Judicial Elections, 2011–12: How New Waves of Special Interest Spending Raised the Stakes for Fair Courts* (Report written by Justice at Stake, the Brennan Center for Justice at NYU School of Law, and the National Institute on Money in State Politics), available at https://www.brennancenter.org/sites/default/files/publications/New%20Politics%20of%20Judicial%20Elections%202012.pdf (last retrieved March 29, 2019), 35.

[17]   Rachel Paine Caufield, *Inside Merit Selection: A National Survey of Judicial Nominating Commissioners (2012)*, available at http://www.judicialselection.us/uploads/documents/JNC_Survey_ReportFINAL3_92E04A2F04E65.pdf (last retrieved April 11, 2020).

[18]   G. Alan Tarr and Brian T. Fitzpatrick, "Judicial Selection Should Return to Its Roots," *USA Today* (March 29, 2013), available at https://www.usatoday.com/story/opinion/2013/03/29/judges-states-missouri/2028705/ (last retrieved April 11, 2020).

[19]   For example, in Connecticut, the governor appoints trial and appellate judges from a nomination commission, but the gubernatorial choice must be ratified by the legislature. Also, incumbent Connecticut judges are kept on *only if* the governor decides to renominate *and* the legislative opts to reappoint. See also Bannon, Velasco, Casey, and Reagan, *The New Politics of Judicial Elections, 2011–12*.

[20]   National Center for State Courts, "Methods of Judicial Selection," available from http://www.judicialselection.us/judicial_selection/methods/selection_of_judges.cfm?state=f (last retrieved April 14, 2020).

[21]   Ibid.

[22]   Bannon, Velasco, Casey, and Reagan, *The New Politics of Judicial Elections, 2011–12*. See also Joel F. Knutson, "Judicial Selection in the States: Historical Context and Ongoing Debates," in *The Improvement of the Administration of Justice,* 7th ed. (Chicago: Judicial Division, American Bar Association, 2002), 205; G. Alan Tarr, "Selection of State Appellate Judges: Reform Proposals, Rethinking the Selection of State Supreme Court Justices," *Williamette Law Review* (Fall, 2003), 1445–46.

[23]   John F. Kowal, *Judicial Selection for the 21st Century (A Report Written for the Brennan Center for Justice)*, available at https://www.brennancenter.org/sites/default/files/publications/Judicial_Selection_21st_Century.pdf (last retrieved April 14, 2020), 3–4. See also Bannon, Velasco, Casey, and Reagan, *The New Politics of Judicial Elections, 2011–12*, 27–37.

24 Richard A. Watson and Rondal G. Downing, *The Politics of Bench and Bar: Judicial Selection Under the Missouri Non-Partisan Court Plan* (New York: Wiley, 1969); Beth M. Henschen, Robert Moog, and Steven Davis, "Judicial Nominating Commissioners: A National Profile," *Judicature* (April/May 1990), 328–34; Charles H. Sheldon, "The Role of State Bar Associations in Judicial Selection," *Judicature* (May/June 1994), 300–305.

25 James L. Gibson, " 'New-Style' Judicial Campaigns and the Legitimacy of State High Courts," *Journal of Politics* 71 (2009), 1285–304; Roy Schotland, "Comment," *Law and Contemporary Problems* (Summer, 1998), 150. See also Rachel P. Caufield, "The Changing Tone of Judicial Election Campaigns as a Result of White," in *Running for Judge: The Rising Political, Financial, and Legal Stakes of Judicial Elections*, edited by Matthew J. Streb (New York: New York University Press, 2007), 34–58.

26 Shugerman, *The People's Courts*, 4.

27 Bannon, Velasco, Casey, and Reagan, *The New Politics of Judicial Elections, 2011–12*, 4, 23. See also Linda Casey (for National Institute on Money in State Politics), "Courting Donors: Money in Judicial Elections, 2011 and 2012," available at https://www.followthemoney.org/research/institute-reports/courting-donors-money-in-judicial-elections-2011-and-2012 (last retrieved April 25, 2014); Politico, "2012 Swing States," available at www.politico.com/2012-election/swing-state/ (last accessed April 14, 2020); and *Citizens United v. FEC*, 558 U.S. 310 (2010).

28 Alicia Bannon, *Choosing State Judges: A Plan for Reform*, available at https://www.brennancenter.org/sites/default/files/publications/2018_09_JudicialSelection.pdf (last retrieved April 14, 2020); Alicia Bannon, Cathleen Lisk, and Peter Hardin, *Who Pays for Judicial Races? The Politics of Judicial Elections, 2015–16*, available at https://www.brennancenter.org/publication/politics-judicial-elections (last retrieved April 14, 2020), 2; Chisun Lee and Douglas Keith, "How Semi-Secret Spending Took Over Politics," *The Atlantic* (June 28, 2016), available at https://www.theatlantic.com/politics/archive/2016/06/the-rise-of-gray-money-in-politics/489002/ (last retrieved April 14, 2020).

29 Bannon, Velasco, Casey, and Reagan, *The New Politics of Judicial Elections, 2011–12*, 22–24, 30–31; Adam Skaggs, Marla da Silva, Linda Casey, and Charles Hall, *The New Politics of Judicial Elections, 2009–10* (Report written by Justice at Stake, the Brennan Center for Justice at NYU School of Law, and the National Institute on Money in State Politics), available at https://www.brennancenter.org/our-work/research-reports/new-politics-judicial-elections-2009-10 (last accessed April 14, 2020), 20; Deborah Goldberg, Sarah Samis, Edwin Bender, and Rachel Weiss, *The New Politics of Judicial Elections 2004* (New York: Brennan Center for Justice, New York University Law School, 2005).

30 Alicia Bannon, et al., *Who Pays for Judicial Races?*, 32–39.

31 Larry Aspin, William K. Hall, Jean Bax, and Celeste Montoya, "Thirty Years of Judicial Retention Elections: An Update," *The Social Science Journal* 37 (2000), 12.

32 See, e.g., Jordan M. Singer, "The Mind of the Judicial Voter," *Michigan State Law Review* 2011 (2011), 1443–96; Lawrence Baum and Marie Hojnacki, "Choosing Judicial Candidates: How Voters Explain Their Decisions," *Judicature* (April/May 1992), 300–309.

33 *Republican Party of Minnesota v. White*, 536 U.S. 765 (2002).

34 Richard Briffault, "The Supreme Court, Judicial Elections, and Dark Money," *DePaul Law Review* 67 (2018), 287–288, 290.

35 Stephen Lubet, "Black Robe Politics," *The American Lawyer* (July 2003). See also Charles Gardner Geyh, "Why Judicial Elections Stink," *Ohio State Law Journal* 64 (2003), 43–79. The Supreme Court's rulings that significantly undercut campaigning financing regulations include *McCutcheon v. FEC*, 572 U.S. 185 (2014); and *Citizens United v. FEC*, 558 U.S. 310 (2010).

36 Still, *Caperton* also cautioned that not "every campaign contribution by a litigant or attorney creates a probability of bias that requires a judge's recusal." Randy N. Smith, "A Jurist and a Lawyer Consider Judicial Recusal After Caperton," *Judges' Journal* 52 (2013), 26–30. In light of *Caperton*, some states, such as Michigan and Wisconsin, strengthened their recusal standards while others, such as California, Georgia, Massachusetts, Montana, New York, and Texas, have considered recusal reform, such as allowing judicial peremptory challenges (adopted by one-third of the states, to allow counsel to remove judges peremptorily with disqualification "strikes") or requiring disqualification motions to be heard by a neutral judicial panel instead of the challenged judge. Tarr, *Without Fear or Favor*, 152–54; Elizabeth K. Lamphier, "Justice Run Amok: Big Money, Partisanship, and State Judiciaries," *Michigan State Law Review* 2011 (2011), 1327, 1351–52. See also *Caperton v. Massey Coal Company*, 556 U.S. 868 (2009).

37 James L. Gibson. *Electing Judges: The Surprising Effects of Campaigning on Judicial Legitimacy* (Chicago: Chicago University Press, 2012); "White Noise: The Unrealized Effects of *Republican Party of Minnesota v. White* on Judicial Elections," *Justice System Journal* 32 (2011), 247–68; Chris W. Bonneau and Melinda Gann Hall, *In Defense of Judicial Elections* (New York: Routledge, 2011).

38 Briffault observes, for example, that "the post-*Caperton* appeals court cases. . .involve restrictions on political activity in support of political parties or other candidates and not the judicial candidate's own campaign"; and, unlike *White*, because "bans on personal solicitation of campaign funds are widespread" many federal courts have turned back constitutional challenges to those types of bans, especially in the aftermath of *Williams-Yulee*. Briffault, "The Supreme Court, Judicial Elections, and Dark Money," 298, 302–305.

39 Matthew J. Streb, "Judicial Elections and Public Perception of the Courts," in *The Politics of Judicial Independence: Courts, Politics, and the Public*, edited by Bruce Peabody (Baltimore, Md.: John Hopkins University Press, 2011), 162.

40 David K. Stott, "Zero-Sum Judicial Elections: Balancing Free Speech and Impartiality Through Recusal Reform," *Brigham Young University Law Review* 2009 (2009), 481, 497. See also Julie Schuering Schuetz, "Judicial Campaign Speech Restrictions in Light of *Republican Party of Minnesota v. White*," *Northern Illinois University Law Review* (Spring, 2004), 340–41.

41 Federal lower courts are split on the constitutionality of candidates personally soliciting campaign contributions, and they remain divided or are still determining the constitutionality of "commit," "pledge or promise," and "misrepresent" clauses. Cynthia Gray, "Top Judicial Ethics Stories of 2010," *Judicature* 94 (2011), 94, 191; Walter M. Weber, "Judicial Campaign Speech Restrictions: Some Litigation Nuts and Bolts," *Albany Law Review* 68 (2005), 635–50.

42 See, e.g., *In re Matter Concerning a Judge (Kinsey)*, 842 So.2d 77 (Fla. 2003) (disciplining judge for making improper campaign statements). Also, many jurisdictions have consistently invalidated post-*White* judicial speech restrictions. Stott, "Zero-Sum Judicial Elections," 495–96.

43 See, e.g., *Weaver v. Bonner*, 309 F.3d 1312 (11th Cir. 2002) (striking down Georgia judicial canons that prohibited candidates from making misrepresentations or personally soliciting campaign funds where Weaver, a challenger running for a seat on the Georgia Supreme Court, distributed brochures and aired television ads portraying his opponent as endorsing gay marriage, disagreeing with criminal laws punishing pedophiles, and opposed to applying the death penalty); and *Spargo v. N.Y. State Commission on Judicial Conduct*, 244 F. Supp. 2d 72 (N.D.N.Y. 2003) (striking down New York's ethical prohibitions against judicial candidates engaging in political activities where Spargo, in running for a seat on the New York Appellate Court, offered free cider, donuts, alcohol, and gasoline while campaigning).

44 David B. Rottman, "Conduct and Its Oversight in Judicial Elections: Can Friendly Persuasion Outperform the Power to Regulate?" *Georgetown Journal of Legal Ethics* 21 (2008), 1295–321; Roy A. Schotland and Barbara Reed, "Judicial Campaign Conduct Committees," *Indiana Law Review* 35 (2002), 781–805.

45 Bannon, *Choosing State Judges: A Plan for Reform*, 1. Similarly, an earlier ABA report, *Justice in Jeopardy*, argues states should adopt merit-based appointive systems. American Bar Association, *Justice in Jeopardy: Report of the American Bar Association Commission on the 21st Century* (Chicago: American Bar Association, 2003), available from https://www.opensocietyfoundations.org/publications/justice-jeopardy-report-american-bar-assocation-commission-21st-century-judiciary#:~:text=The%20commission's%20final%20report%2C%20Justice, judiciary%20in%20the%20United%20States (last retrieved August 20, 2020).

46 Jurisdictions with evaluation programs are listed in National Center for State Courts, "State Court Organization, List of Tables, Judicial Performance Evaluation (Table 1.6)," available at http://stage.ncsc.org/microsites/sco/home/List-Of-Tables.aspx (last retrieved June 24, 2020). On the status of judicial performance evaluations and their effectiveness, see Jennifer K. Elek, David B. Rottman, and Brian L. Cutler, "Judicial Performance Evaluation: Steps to Improve Survey Process and Measurement," *Judicature* 96 (2012), 66–75. See also American Bar Association, *Justice in Jeopardy: Report of the American Bar Association Commission on the 21st Century*, iv-vi.

47 National Conference of State Legislatures, "Overview of State Laws on Public Financing," available at http://www.ncsl.org/research/elections-and-campaigns/public-financing-of-campaigns-overview.aspx (last retrieved April 14, 2020). Notably, Wisconsin had a program for publicly financed Supreme Court races, but it only lasted two years (2009–2011). Bill Raferty, "Wisconsin Democrats Try to Force Public Financing of Judicial Campaigns Out of Committee," available at http://gaveltogavel.us/2014/02/13/wisconsin-democrats-try-to-force-public-financing-of-judicial-campaigns-bill-out-of-committee/ (last retrieved April 14,

2020). As of 2014, North Carolina repealed its public financing program for certain judicial elections. North Carolina State Board of Elections, "Fact Sheet: Running for Judicial Offices, 2014 Election," available at www.ncsbe.gov/ncsbe/Portals/0/FilesP/FilingFactsJudge2014.pdf (last retrieved April 24, 2014). New Mexico's governor Susana Martinez vetoed legislation that would have updated a voluntary system of public financing for elections of appellate court judges. Peter Hardin, "Governor Vetoes Update to NM Public Financing Law," *Gavel Grab* (April 8, 2013), available at www.gavelgrab.org/?p=55216 (last retrieved April 24, 2014). See also Tarr, *Without Fear or Favor*, 155–60.

[48]   In *Arizona Free Enterprise Club's Freedom Club PAC v. Bennett*, 564 U.S. 721 (2011), candidates in the public financing program were eligible to get additional funds if privately financed challengers or independent organizations spent over a certain amount. See Stephen Ansolabere, "*Arizona Free Enterprise v. Bennett* and the Problem of Campaign Finance," *Supreme Court Review* 2011 (2011), 39–79.

[49]   Alexander Hamilton, "Federalist No. 76," in *The Federalist Papers*, edited by Clinton Rossiter (New York: Mentor, 1961), 457.

[50]   Henry J. Abraham. "A Bench Happily Filled: Some Historical Reflections on the Supreme Court Selection Process," *Judicature* (February 1983), 282–95.

[51]   Charles M. Cameron, Jonathan P. Kastellec and Lauren A. Mattioli, "Presidential Selection of Supreme Court Nominees: The Characteristics Approach," *Quarterly Journal of Political Science* 14 (2019): 439–474. See also, J. Woodford Howard, Jr., *Courts of Appeals in the Federal Judicial System: A Study of the Second, Fifth, and D.C. Circuit Courts of Appeals* (Princeton, N.J.: Princeton University Press, 1981), 90.

[52]   Michael J. Gerhardt, *The Federal Appointments Process: A Constitutional and Historical Analysis* (Durham, N.C.: Duke University Press, 2003), 190.

[53]   George L. Watson and John A. Stookey, *Shaping America: The Politics of Supreme Court Appointments* (New York: Longman, 1995), 64.

[54]   David M. O'Brien, "Federal Judgeships in Retrospect," in *The Reagan Presidency: Pragmatic Conservatism and Its Legacies*, edited by W. Elliot Brownlee and Hugh Davis Graham (Lawrence: University Press of Kansas, 2003), 329.

[55]   Ibid.

[56]   Ibid., 329–30.

[57]   Ibid., 330.

[58]   David Alistair Yalof, *Pursuit of Justices: Presidential Politics and the Selection of Supreme Court Nominees* (Chicago: University of Chicago Press, 1999), 12–18.

[59]   David M. O'Brien, *Judicial Roulette: Report of the Twentieth Century Fund Task Force on Judicial Selection* (New York: Priority Press, 1988), 58–60.

[60]   Ibid., 59 n. 38.

[61]   Sheldon Goldman, "Carter's Judicial Appointments: A Lasting Legacy," *Judicature* 64 (March 1981), 344–55 (Tables 2 and 3).

[62]   Sheldon Goldman, "Reagan's Judicial Legacy: Completing the Puzzle and Summing Up," *Judicature* (April/May 1989), 319–20. Justice Douglas is quoted in Graeme Browning, "Reagan Molds the Federal Court in His Own Image," *American Bar Association Journal* (August 1985), 60.

[63]   Jon Gottschall, "Reagan's Appointments to the U.S. Courts of Appeals: The Continuation of a Judicial Revolution," *Judicature* (June/July 1986), 48–54.

[64]   Sheldon Goldman, Elliot Slotnick, and Sara Schiavoni, "Obama's First Term Judiciary: Picking Judges in the Minefield of Obstructionism," *Judicature* 97 (2013), 7, 14–16; Sheldon Goldman, Elliot Slotnick, and Sara Schiavoni, "Obama's Judiciary at Midterm: The Confirmation Drama Continues," *Judicature* 94 (2011), 262, 264–65, 279.

[65]   Jason Zengerle, "How the Trump Administration is Remaking the Courts," *New York Magazine* (August 22, 2018), available at https://www.nytimes.com/2018/08/22/magazine/trump-remaking-courts-judiciary.html (last retrieved April 14, 2020); Slotnick, Schiavoni and Goldman, "Obama's Judicial Legacy: The Final Chapter," *Journal of Law and Courts*, 365.

[66]   Sheldon Goldman, Elliot Slotnick, Gerard Gryski, Gary Zuk, and Sara Schiavoni, "W. Bush Remaking the Judiciary: Like Father Like Son?" *Judicature* (May/June 2003), 285.

[67] Sheldon Goldman, Elliot Slotnick, Gerard Gryski, and Sara Schiavoni, "W. Bush's Judiciary: The First Term Record," *Judicature* (May/June 2005), 244, 254–55. See also, Slotnick, Schiavoni and Goldman, "Obama's Judicial Legacy: The Final Chapter," *Journal of Law and Courts*, 418; Ballotpedia, "ABA Ratings during the Trump administration," available at https://ballotpedia.org/ABA_ratings_during_the_Trump_administration (last retrieved April 14, 2020).

[68] American Bar Association, "ABA Standing Committee on Federal Judiciary" available at https://www.americanbar.org/groups/committees/federal_judiciary/ (last retrieved August 20, 2020).

[69] Ballotpedia, "ABA Ratings during the Trump administration." See also, Paul D. Kamenar, "The Role of the American Bar Association in the Judicial Selection Process," in *Judicial Selection: Merit, Ideology, and Politics* (Washington: D.C., National Center of the Public Interest, 1990), 93–101.

[70] Christine Blackerby, "The Origins of Senatorial Courtesy," *National Archives/Pieces of History* (August 3, 2014), available at https://prologue.blogs.archives.gov/2014/08/03/the-origins-of-senatorial-courtesy/ (last retrieved April 14, 2020). See also Mitchel A. Sollenberger, "The Blue-Slip Process in the Senate Committee on the Judiciary: Background, Issues, and Opinions," *CRS Report for Congress*, Order Code RS21674 (November 21, 2003) (Washington, D.C.: Congressional Research Service, 2003), 2–3. The history of senatorial courtesy is discussed in Gerhardt, *The Federal Appointments Process*, 143–44; see also John Anthony Maltese, *The Selling of Supreme Court Nominees* (Baltimore, Md.: John Hopkins University Press, 1995), 121.

[71] Senator Hatch is quoted in Betsy Palmer, "Evolution of the Senate's Role in the Nomination and Confirmation Process: A Brief History," *Report for Congress,* Order Code RL31948 (Updated March 29, 2005) (Washington, D.C.: Congressional Research Service, 2003), 8.

[72] Barry J. McMillion, "The Blue Slip Process for U.S. Circuit and District Court Nominations: Frequently Asked Questions," *Congressional Research Service (R44975, October 7, 2017)* (Washington, D.C.: Government Printing Office, 2017), 3.

[73] Seung Min Kim, "Senate GOP Confirms Kavanaugh's Replacement, Trump's 36th Pick for Powerful Appeals Court, *Washington Post* (March 13, 2019), available at https://www.courthousenews.com/dozens-of-judicial-nominees-advance-to-full-senate/ (last retrieved April 14, 2020); Jordain Carney, "Senate Confirms Trump court pick despite missing two 'blue slips,' " *The Hill* February 26, 2019), available at https://thehill.com/homenews/senate/431717-senate-confirms-trump-court-nominee-despite-missing-two-blue-slips (last retrieved April 14, 2020); Tim Ryan, "Dozens of Judicial Nominees Advance to Full Senate, *Courthouse News Service* (February 7, 2019), available at https://www.courthousenews.com/dozens-of-judicial-nominees-advance-to-full-senate/ (last retrieved April 14, 2020); Chuck Grassley, "100 Years of Blue Slip Courtesy," *The Hill* (November 15, 2017), available from https://thehill.com/blogs/congress-blog/judicial/360510-100-years-of-the-blue-slip-courtesy (last retrieved April 14, 2020). See also, McMillion, "The Blue Slip Process for U.S. Circuit and District Court Nominations: Frequently Asked Questions," 3; and, Blackerby, "The Origins of Senatorial Courtesy," *National Archives/Pieces of History* (August 3, 2014).

[74] Jeffrey Toobin, "Blue-Slip Battle: The Senate Obstructionists' Secret Weapon," *The New Yorker* (November 26, 2013), available at https://www.newyorker.com/news/daily-comment/blue-slip-battle-the-senate-obstructionists-secret-weapon (last retrieved October 21, 2018). See also Goldman, Slotnick, and Schiavoni, "Obama's First Term Judiciary: Picking Judges in the Minefield of Obstructionism," 7, 17; McElroy and Cannan, "Obama's Second Term and the Federal Courts," 100; Denning, "The Judicial Confirmation Process and the Blue Slip," 218, 221; Joseph A. Pike and John Anthony Maltese, *The Politics of the Presidency*, 6th ed. (Washington, D.C.: CQ Press, 2004), 264–65.

[75] Ryan, "Dozens of Judicial Nominees Advance to the Senate"; Kevin Schaul and Kevin Uhrmacher, "How Trump is shifting the most important courts in the country," *Washington Post (September 4, 2018)*, available at https://www.washingtonpost.com/graphics/2018/politics/trump-federal-judges/?noredirect=on&utm_term=.bf9f341179d5 (last retrieved April 14, 2020). Grassley's quote is found in Zengerle, "How the Trump Administration is Remaking the Courts." See also McMillion, "The Blue Slip Process for U.S. Circuit and District Court Nominations: Frequently Asked Questions," 12.

[76] Elizabeth Rybicki, *CRS Report for Congress: Senate Consideration of Presidential Nominations: Committee and Floor Procedure*, Order Code RL 31980 (Updated November 25, 2013), 1–2.

[77] See Barry J. McMillion, "U.S. Circuit and District Court Nominations During President Obama's First Five Years: Comparative Analysis With Recent Presidents," *Congressional Research Service (R43369, January 24, 2014)* (Washington, D.C.: Government Printing Office, 2014).

[78] 531 U.S. 98 (2000).

[79] Goldman, Slotnick, Gryski, and Schiavoni, "W. Bush's Judiciary: The First Term Record," 244–75.

[80] William Douglas and Anita Kumar, "Democrats Strip GOP of Power to Block Many Obama Appointees," *McClatchyDC* (November 21, 2013), available at https://www.mcclatchydc.com/news/politics-government/congress/article24759370.html (last retrieved June 25, 2020); Aaron Blake, "How Historic Is the GOP's Filibuster of Mell Watt?" *The Washington Post* (November 1, 2013), available at www.washingtonpost.com (last retrieved April 27, 2014).

[81] Jane C. Timm, "Senate rules have changed in recent years, allowing presidential picks to be confirmed with a simple majority," *NBC News (June 28, 2018),* available at https://www.nbcnews.com/politics/donald-trump/mcconnell-went-nuclear-confirm-gorsuch-democrats-changed-senate-filibuster-rules-n887271 (last retrieved April 14, 2020); Aaron Blake, "Democrats' nuclear-option gambles are coming up snake-eyes," (June 29, 2018), available at https://www.washingtonpost.com/news/the-fix/wp/2018/06/29/democrats-overplayed-their-hand-on-the-nuclear-option-and-here-we-are/?utm_term=.f1bb8de3c7f8 (last retrieved April 14, 2020).

[82] Denis Steven Rutkus, *Congressional Research Service: Supreme Court Appointment Process: Roles of the President, Judiciary Committee, and Senate,* Order Code RL 31989 (February 19, 2010), 20–21. See also James A. Thorpe, "The Appearance of Supreme Court Nominees Before the Senate Judiciary Committee," *Journal of Public Law* 18 (1969), 371–402.

[83] Jonathan Ringel (senior reporter for Legal Times), "Special Interest Groups and Judicial Nominations" (T.V. interview for C-SPAN, September 8, 2001), available at www.c-span.org (last retrieved April 29, 2014). See also Caldeira and Wright, "Lobbying for Justice: Organized Interests, Supreme Court Nominations, and the United States Senate," *American Journal of Political Science* 42 (1998), 499–523; Jeffrey A. Segal, Charles M. Cameron, and Albert D. Cover, "A Spatial Model of Roll Call Voting: Senators, Constituents, Presidents, and Interest Groups in Supreme Court Confirmations," *American Journal of Political Science* 36 (1992), 96–121 (finding that organized interest groups influence the confirmation process). Before Bork's nomination, President Nixon's 1969 nomination of Clement F. Haynsworth, Jr., and President Herbert Hoover's 1930 nomination of John J. Parker mobilized intense interest group opposition. Peter G. Fish, "Spite Nominations to the United States Supreme Court: Herbert C. Hoover, Owen J. Roberts, and the Politics of Presidential Vengeance in Retrospect," *Kentucky Law Journal* 77 (1989), 545–76.

[84] Lee Epstein, René Lindstädt, Jeffrey A. Segal, and Chad Westerland, "The Changing Dynamics of Senate Voting on Supreme Court Nominees," *Journal of Politics* 68 (2006), 296–307. See also Robert A. Kagan, *Adversarial Legalism: The American Way of Law* (Cambridge, Mass.: Harvard University Press, 2001), 50.

[85] As quoted in John Massaro, *Supremely Political: The Role of Ideology and Presidential Management in Unsuccessful Supreme Court Nominations* (Albany: State University of New York Press, 1989), 165. A video clip of the speech is in "Robert Bork's America," *C-Span,* available at https://www.c-span.org/video/?45973-1/robert-borks-america (last retrieved April 14, 2020).

[86] "Robert Bork's America," *C-Span,* available at https://www.c-span.org/video/?45973-1/robert-borks-america (last retrieved April 14, 2020).

[87] Eva Andrews, "What Was the Saturday Night Massacre?," *History* (December 4, 2013, updated: October 18, 2019), available at https://www.history.com/news/what-was-the-saturday-night-massacre (last retrieved April 15, 2020).

[88] See Ayo Ogundele and Linda Camp Keith, "Reexamining the Impact of the Bork Nomination to the Supreme Court," *Political Research Quarterly* 52 (1999), 403, 405–6. For a description of Bork's judicial philosophy, see, generally, Robert H. Bork, *The Tempting of America: The Political Seduction of the Law* (New York: Free Press, 1987), 143–60.

[89] Joyce A. Baugh, *Supreme Court Justices in the Post-Bork Era: Confirmation Politics and Judicial Performance* (New York: Peter Lang, 2002), 10; O'Brien, *Judicial Roulette,* 100.

[90] William G. Myers, III, "The Role of Special Interest Groups in the Supreme Court Nomination of Robert Bork," *Hastings Law Quarterly* 17 (1990), 411, 414; Bork, *The Tempting of America,* 288.

[91] Bork, *The Tempting of America,* 289. An analysis of interest group pressure tactics is found in Gregory A. Calderia, Marie Hojnacki, and John R. Wright, "The Lobbying Activities of Organized Interests in Federal Judicial Nominations," *Journal of Politics* (February 2000), 51–69. See also *Moore v. City of East Cleveland,* 431 U.S. 494 (1977).

[92] See Nancy Scherer, *Scoring Points: Politicians, Activists, and the Lower Federal Court Appointment Process* (Stanford, Calif.: Stanford University Press, 2005); Nancy Scherer, "The Judicial Confirmation Process:

Mobilizing Elites, Mobilizing Masses," *Judicature* (March/April 2003), 240–50; Lauren Cohen Bell, *Warring Factions: Interest Groups, Money, and the New Politics of Senate Confirmation* (Columbus: Ohio State University Press, 2002).

93 Gerhardt, *The Federal Appointments Process*, 222–23. For a critical view of interest group advocacy, see Gregory A. Caldeira, "Commentary on Senate Confirmation of Supreme Court Justices: The Roles of Organized and Unorganized Interests," *Kentucky Law Journal* 77 (1988), 531.

94 See Ayo Ogundele and Linda Camp Keith, "Reexamining the Impact of the Bork Nomination to the Supreme Court," *Political Research Quarterly* 52 (1999), 403–20; David Danelski, "Ideology as a Ground for the Rejection of the Bork Nomination," *Northwestern University Law Review* (1990), 900–920; and George Watson and John Stookey, "The Bork Hearings: Rocks and Roles," *Judicature* 71 (1988), 194–96.

95 In contrast to Bork's nomination, for Justice William Brennan's 1957 confirmation hearing, there was no interest group representation; but eighty-six witnesses aligned with organized interests participated in Bork's hearings. In the post-Bork era, ninety-six witnesses appeared in Justice Clarence Thomas's hearings; thirty-nine appeared in Justice David Souter's confirmation hearings; and twenty were a part of Justice Ruth Bader Ginsburg's hearings. In comparison, for the Bork hearings, 145 active groups participated, and another 81 (Thomas), 53 (Souter), 41 (Rehnquist), and 39 (Kennedy) were involved in other Supreme Court confirmation hearings. Calderia, Hojnacki, and Wright, "The Lobbying Activities of Organized Interests in Federal Judicial Nominations," 58 (Table 2); see also Gerhardt, *The Federal Appointments Process*, 219, 230.

96 Michael Avery, *The Federalist Society: How Conservatives Took the Law Back From Liberals* (Nashville, Tenn.: Vanderbilt University Press, 2013); Ann Southworth, *Lawyers of the Right: Professionalizing the Conservative Coalition* (Chicago: University of Chicago Press, 2008); Stephen M. Teles, *The Rise of the Conservative Legal Movement: The Battle for Control of the Law* (Princeton, N.J.: Princeton University Press, 2008).

97 Elena Kagan, "Confirmation Messes, Old and New" (Book Review of Stephen L. Carter's The Confirmation Mess), 62, *University of Chicago Law Review* (1992), 919, 941. See also Dion Farganis and Justin Wedeking, " 'No Hints, No Forecasts, No Previews': An Empirical Analysis of Supreme Court Nominee Candor From Harlan to Kagan," *Law and Society Review* 45 (2011), 525, 526 (but finding that invoking the Ginsburg rule is more of a perception rather than a reality, based on empirical evidence); ibid., 528 (noting past nominees were typically asked fewer than one hundred questions by the Senate Judiciary Committee). But see Dan Froomkin, "Kagan Under Obligation to Open Up," *Huffington Post* (May 12, 2010), available at www.huffingtonpost.com/2010/05/12/kagan-under-obligation-to_n_571733.html (last retrieved April 30, 2014); and Jonathan Turley, "Retire the Ginsburg Rule," *USA Today* (July 16, 2009), available at http://usatoday30.usatoday.com/printedition/news/20090716/column16_st.art.htm (last retrieved April 30, 2014).

98 Rutkus, *Supreme Court Appointment Process*, 31. See also Michael Comiskey, *Seeking Justice: The Judging of Supreme Court Nominees* (Lawrence: University Press of Kansas, 2004), 12–13.

99 See, e.g., Sarah Binder and Forrest Maltzman, "New Wars of Advice and Consent," *Judicature* 97 (2013), 48–56; Charles R. Shipan and Megan L. Shannon, "Delaying Justice(s): A Duration Analysis of Supreme Court Nominations," *American Journal of Political Science* (October 2003), 654–68; Sarah A. Binder and Forrest Maltzman, "Senatorial Delay in Confirming Federal Judges, 1947–1998," *American Journal of Political Science* 46 (January, 2001), 190–99; Wendy L. Martinek, Mark Kemper, and Steven R. Van Winkle, "To Advise and Consent: The Senate and Lower Federal Court Nominations, 1977–1998," *Journal of Politics* (May 2002), 337–61.

100 Binder and Maltzman, "New Wars of Advice and Consent," 48–56. See also Amy Steigerwalt, *Battle Over the Bench: Senators, Interest Groups, and Lower Court Confirmations* (Charlottesville: University of Virginia Press, 2010); Michael Teter, "Rethinking Consent: Proposals for Reforming the Judicial Confirmation Process," *Ohio State Law Journal* 73 (2014), 287–342.

101 Binder and Maltzman, "Senatorial Delay in Confirming Federal Judges, 1947–1998," 52. See also Robert A. Carp and Kenneth A. Manning, "The Obama Judges: A Midterm Assessment" (Unpublished Paper at the 2014 Annual Meeting for the Southwestern Social Science Association Meeting, San Antonio, Texas, April 16–19, 2004) (on file with the author); Shipan and Shannon, "Delaying Justice(s)," 665; and, Miller Center Commission on the Selection of Federal Judges, *Improving the Process of Appointing Federal Judges: A Report of the Miller Center Commission on the Selection of Federal Judges* (Appendix B) (Charlottesville: Miller Center of Public Affairs, University of Virginia, 1996).

102 Slotnick, Schiavoni and Goldman, "Obama's Judicial Legacy: The Final Chapter," *Journal of Law and Courts*, 376.

[103] Slotnick, Schiavoni and Goldman, "Obama's Judicial Legacy: The Final Chapter," *Journal of Law and Courts*, 380.

[104] Aaron Blake, "Brett Kavanaugh just got remarkably angry—and political—for a Supreme Court nominee," *Washington Post* (September 27, 2018), available at https://www.washingtonpost.com/politics/2018/09/27/brett-kavanaugh-just-got-remarkably-angry-political-supreme-court-nominee/?utm_term=.9a76 f85d0899 (last retrieved April 15, 2020); and, March A. Thiessen, "His reputation in tatters, Kavanaugh fights back," *Plain Dealer* (September 30, 2018), E6.

[105] Teter, "Rethinking Consent: Proposals for Reforming the Judicial Confirmation Process," 287, 297–99 (observing high vacancy rate in federal courts during Obama administration negatively affects case disposition time, erodes the administration of justice, diminishes public's confidence in courts, and deters recruitment of qualified persons willing to serve on the federal bench).

[106] See, e.g., "5/6/03 Letter From Counsel to the President Alberto R. Gonzales to Senator Schumer Regarding the Judicial Confirmation Process," reprinted in Subcommittee on the Constitution, Civil Rights, and Property Rights, "Judicial Nominations, Filibusters, and the Constitution: When the Majority Is Denied Its Right to Consent," *S. Hrg.* 108–227 (108th Congress, 1st Session, May 6, 2003) (Serial No. J-108-9); Charles E. Schumer, "Judging by Ideology," *New York Times* (June 26, 2001), A19; John Cornyn, "Our Broken Judicial Confirmation Process and the Need for Filibuster Reform," *Harvard Journal of Law and Public Policy* 27 (2003), 182–230; White House, "Infographic: President Obama's Judicial Nominees (September 24, 2013)," available at www.whitehouse.gov (last retrieved May 5, 2014).

[107] Miller Center Commission on the Selection of Federal Judges, *Improving the Process of Appointing Federal Judges*, 6–10.

[108] O'Brien, in "Report of the Task Force," 5, 10–11.

[109] Teter, "Rethinking Consent: Proposals for Reforming the Judicial Confirmation Process," 287, 301–4.

[110] Richard Davis, *Electing Justice: Fixing the Supreme Court Nomination Process* (New York: Oxford University Press, 2005), 170–72.

[111] Slotnick, Schiavoni and Goldman, "Obama's Judicial Legacy: The Final Chapter," *Journal of Law and Courts*, 413, 416.

[112] For precise numbers and trends in Trump's judicial appointment record during his first term, and/or in comparison to other presidential administrations, see Ballotpedia, "Federal Judges Nominated by Donald Trump," available at https://ballotpedia.org/Federal_judges_nominated_by_Donald_Trump (last retrieved April 15, 2020); Department of Justice, Office of Legal Policy, "Judicial Nominations," available at https://www.justice.gov/olp/judicial-nominations (last retrieved April 15, 2020); and, Russell Wheeler, "Judicial Appointments in Trump's First Three Years: Myths and Realities," Brookings January 28, 2020), available at https://www.brookings.edu/blog/fixgov/2020/01/28/judicial-appointments-in-trumps-first-three-years-myths-and-realities/ (last retrieved April 15, 2020).

[113] Sheldon Goldman, *Picking Federal Judges: Lower Court Selection From Roosevelt Through Reagan* (New Haven, Conn.: Yale University Press, 1997), 362–63; O'Brien, "Report of the Task Force."

[114] Comiskey, *Seeking Justice*, 81, 134; Gerhardt, *The Federal Appointments Process*, 287; O'Brien, "Report of the Task Force."

[115] As quoted in Michael J. Frank, "Judge Not, Lest Yee Be Judged Not Worthy of a Pay Raise," *Marquette Law Review* (Fall, 2003), 81.

[116] See Tracy E. George and Albert H. Yoon, "Measuring Justice in State Courts: The Demographics of the State Judiciary," *Vanderbilt Law Review* 70 (2017): 1887–1910, 1887.

[117] Laila Robbins and Alicia Bannon (with Malia Redick), "State Supreme Court Diversity (July 23, 2019)," *Brennan Center For Justice*, available at https://www.brennancenter.org/ (last retrieved April 15, 2020), 2. See also, Greg Goelzhauser, "Diversifying State Supreme Courts," *Law and Society Review* 45 (2011), 761–81; Mark S. Hurwitz and Drew Noble Lanier, "Diversity in State and Federal Appellate Courts: Change and Continuity Across 20 Years," *Justice System Journal* 29 (2008), 47–70. See also Chris W. Bonneau, "The Composition of State Supreme Courts 2000," *Judicature* (July/August 2001), 26–31 (Table 1); John B. Wefing, "State Supreme Court Justices: Who Are They?" *New England Law Review* (Fall 1997), 47–100.

[118] George and Yoon, "Measuring Justice in State Courts," 1903–1908. See also, Tracy E. George and Albert H. Yoon, "Gavel Gap: The differences between the race & gender composition of the courts & the

communities they serve," available at https://www.acslaw.org/analysis/reports/gavel-gap/ (last retrieved April 15, 2020) (Data reflects findings relative to judges serving on courts up to December 2014).

[119] Richard Wolf, "Trump's Conservative Judges Begin Takeover of Federal Appeals Courts," *USA Today* (March 12, 2019), available at https://www.yahoo.com/news/trump-apos-conservative-judges-begin-190131 514.html (last retrieved April 15, 2020); Carrie Johnson, "Trump Is Reshaping the Judiciary: A Breakdown by Race, Gender and Qualification," *NPR* (November 18, 2018), available at https://www.npr.org/2018/11/15/667483587/trump-is-reshaping-the-judiciary-a-breakdown-by-race-gender-and-qualification (last retrieved April 15, 2020). See also, American Bar Association Commission on Women in the Profession, "Current Glance of Women in the Law (April 2019)," available at https://www.americanbar.org/content/dam/aba/administrative/women/a-current-glance-at-women-in-the-law-jan-2018.authcheckdam.pdf (last retrieved April 15, 2020) (noting as of April 2019 women comprise 38 percent of all lawyers and 49 percent of law students are women).

[120] See Christopher P. Banks and David M. O'Brien, *The Judicial Process: Law, Courts, and Judicial Politics* (Thousand Oaks, CA.: Sage/CQ Press, 2015), 122–123 (Tables 4.2 and 4.3) (reporting percentages of religious affiliation from the Eisenhower to Obama [first term] presidencies).

[121] Jordan Muller, "Trump's top SCOTUS Picks Less Wealthy Than Current Court," OpenSecrets.org (July 6, 2018), available at https://www.opensecrets.org/news/2018/07/trumps-top-scotus-picks-less-wealthy/ (last retrieved April 15, 2020). See also, Albert Yoon, "Love's Labor's Lost? Judicial Tenure Among Federal Court Judges: 1945–2000," *California Law Review* (2003), 1055, 1056 n. 86. See also Slotnick, Schiavoni and Goldman, "Obama's Judicial Legacy: The Final Chapter," *Journal of Law and Courts*, 413, 394–395 and 400– (Tables 6 and 7) (reporting net worth of judges).

[122] Denis Stephen Rutkus, "Judicial Salary: Current Issues and Options for Congress" (updated September 16, 2008), *CRS Report for Congress*, Order Code R34281 (Washington, D.C.: Congressional Research Service, 2008) (noting that it is unclear if lower salaries are causing early retirements); Linda Greenhouse, "Chief Justice Advocates Higher Pay for the Judiciary," *New York Times* (January 7, 2007), available at www.nytimes.com (last retrieved May 5, 2014). See, e.g., *Atkins v. United States*, 556 F.2d 1028 (Ct. Cl. 1977); *Williams v. United States*, 48 F. Supp. 2d 53 (D.D.C. 1999), aff'd and rev'd, 240 F.3d 1019 (D.C. Cir. 2001), petition for cert. denied, 535 U.S. 911 (2002).

[123] Lee Epstein, Jack Knight, and Andrew D. Martin, "The Norm of Prior Judicial Experience and Its Consequences for Career Diversity on the U.S. Supreme Court," *California Law Review* (July, 2003), 912; Bonneau, "The Composition of State Supreme Courts 2000" (Table 1); Yoon, "Love's Labor's Lost?" 1029–60; Goldman, Slotnick, and Schiavoni, "Obama's First Term Judiciary: Picking Judges in the Minefield of Obstructionism," 41, 43 (Table 6, 8).

[124] Jerome Frank, *Courts on Trial: Myth and Reality in American Justice* (Princeton, N.J.: Princeton University Press, 1949), 241.

[125] Larry C. Berkson, "Judicial Selection, Compensation, Discipline and Mandatory Retirement," In *Improvement of the Administration of Justice*, Fannie J. Klein ed. (Chicago, Ill.: American Bar Association), 61–83.

[126] Ibid., 72–73.

[127] Cynthia Gray, *A Study of State Judicial Discipline Sanctions* (Chicago: American Judicature Society, 2002), 3, 5. See also Cynthia Gray, "The Center for Judicial Ethics: An Evolving Clearinghouse," *Judicature* 96 (2013), 305–13.

[128] Cynthia Gray, "How Judicial Conduct Commissions Work," *Justice System Journal* 28 (2007), 405–18. See also Cynthia Gray, A Study of State Judicial Disciplinary Sanctions (Des Moines, Iowa: American Judicature Society, 2002).

[129] Gray, "How Judicial Conduct Commissions Work," 405, 415–16.

[130] Michael Berens and John Schiffman, "Thousands of Judges Who Broke U.S. Laws or Oaths Remain on the Bench (June 30, 2020)," available at https://www.reuters.com/investigates/special-report/usa-judges-misconduct/ (last retrieved August 20, 2020). See also, Cynthia Gray, "Judicial Conduct Commissions: Rules and Variations." In *The Improvement of the Administration of Justice*, 8th ed. Peter Koelling ed. (Chicago, Ill.: American Bar Association 2016), 131, 140.

[131] Federal Judicial Center, "Impeachments of Federal Judges," available at https://www.fjc.gov/history/judges/impeachments-federal-judges (last retrieved April 15, 2020). See also Eleanore Bushnell, *Crimes, Follies, and Misfortunes: The Federal Impeachment Trials* (Urbana: University of Illinois Press, 1992); Mary L. Volcansek, *Judicial Impeachment: None Called for Justice* (Urbana: University of Illinois Press, 1992).

132 28 U.S.C. §§ 351–64, as amended by the Judicial Improvements Act of 2002, 28 U.S.C. §§ 11041, et seq. A significant challenge to circuit court council disciplinary authority is found in *Chandler v. Judicial Council of Tenth Circuit*, 398 U.S. 74 (1970). See also, Administrative Office of U.S. Courts, "FAQ: Filing a Judicial Conduct or Disability Complaint Against a Federal Judge," available at https://www.uscourts.gov/judges-judgeships/judicial-conduct-disability/faqs-filing-judicial-conduct-or-disability-complaint (last retrieved April 15, 2020).

133 Administrative Office of U.S. Courts, "Report of Complaints Commenced and Action Taken Under Authority of 28 U.S.C. 351–364" (Table S-22) (During the period from October 1, 2018 to September 30, 2019), available at www.uscourts.gov (last retrieved April 15, 2020).

PART III

Access to Courts and Judicial Decision-Making

The Practice of Law

In the 1830s, the French observer Alexis de Tocqueville noted that in the United States lawyers possess a "specialized knowledge of the law," enabling them to "fill most public functions" in society.[1] Twenty-five of fifty-six signers of the Declaration of Independence were lawyers. A majority of American presidents came from the legal profession and, more recently, a majority of state legislatures and almost half of the U.S. Congress consists of lawyers. In the private sector, lawyers occupy influential positions on corporate boards, in nonprofit organizations, and on community task forces or committees. Their specialized knowledge of the law allows lawyers to be at the forefront of securing personal freedoms; and they are vital agents of legal and political change. As law professor Kathleen Sullivan aptly put it, "It is a lawyer's job, taking the profession as a whole, to create, find, interpret, adapt, apply and enforce rules and principles that structure human relationships," a role that allows for human conflicts to be resolved by bring people together through "normative ordering."[2] In short, lawyers perform a variety of critical public and private functions, making them central figures in American culture. Most important, they are the "primary gatekeepers to the administration of justice" and have an instrumental role in providing access to courts.[3] This chapter examines the growth and changing nature of the legal profession, the business of legal practice, and the opportunities and limits of the profession in providing access to justice.

THE RISE OF THE AMERICAN LEGAL PROFESSION

In historical perspective, the public image of lawyers has almost always been dim because they are viewed as mercenaries who needlessly stir up litigation. In colonial times, a North Carolina vigilante group, "The Regulators," characterized lawyers as "cursed Hungry Caterpillars [who charged] fees that eat out the very bowels of [the] Commonwealth."[4] Colonial laws aimed at curbing the number and influence of lawyers by limiting their ability to make money and preventing them from assuming public leadership positions. In 1641, it was illegal for Massachusetts lawyers to charge a fee for their services, and they were barred from holding a seat in the legislature. Not only were such restrictions disincentives to practice law, but they also created a prejudice against lawyers that has endured.[5]

At that time, law schools as we know them did not yet exist, so the primary methods of colonial legal training were self-study or apprenticeships. Transplanted into the American colonies from the English legal system, students learned how to practice law under the tutelage of an experienced lawyer in a law office after paying a fee. The fee gave the student access to the lawyer's library and the prestige of the practitioner often determined how much the student had to pay. Apprenticeships were supposed to give students theoretical and practical experience by reading books in the law library, watching other attorneys in court, and performing menial tasks, such as drawing up contracts. Still, the value of an apprenticeship was questionable because most of the work was drudgery and there was often little time to read law books or to get meaningful instruction from the lawyer supervising the apprentice. In this regard, colonial lawyers "mastered the law not because of their legal apprenticeship, but in spite of it."[6]

Despite their shortcomings, apprenticeships were an important part of early attempts to institutionalize legal education. Another was the movement toward university instruction, first at the College of William and Mary in 1779 and then elsewhere. The first private law school opened under the direction of Judge Tapping Reeve in 1784 in Litchfield, Connecticut. Unlike William and Mary's approach, which taught principles of law through a formal interdisciplinary curriculum, Litchfield's pedagogy provided students with legal training from the practitioners' perspective. The issue of whether lawyers are best trained through formal academic study or by practical experience was partially resolved with Harvard University's decision to open a law school in 1826. Harvard reduced the practitioner's perspective to virtual insignificance and began the process of transforming law schools into the institutional basis for a legal education.[7]

The growth of the modern legal education, however, was slowed by Jacksonian democracy in the 1830s, a populist social reform movement that resulted in the legal profession becoming more accountable to the people. First, many state legislatures changed their methods of judicial selection by replacing the appointment of judges with popular elections. Second, the common law was assailed by attempts to replace it with the adoption of written codes. Third, the spirit of equality underlying the Jacksonian era mandated that legal practice remain open to all, and bar admission standards were relaxed or abolished.[8]

Diversifying the practice of law also created more opportunities to enter the profession. Anyone possessing minimum age and "good moral" requirements could be licensed. Lax standards also encouraged students to go to law schools because several states allowed direct bar admission (without taking an exam) upon graduation. Using the so-called diploma privilege, about 2,400 persons entered the legal profession between 1860 and 1875 in fifteen states. Some states even had "twenty dollar" lawyers, who simply paid that amount to be licensed to practice law. Moreover, apprenticeships could not compete with law schools in raising the professional standards. Although Jacksonian democracy encouraged greater access to the legal profession, it also created a corresponding movement for professional self-regulation by the bar.[9]

The post-Civil War and Reconstruction period expanded the scope of the national economy and in turn sharply increased the demand for law education.[10] Local bar associations, first established in New York City, Cleveland, Chicago, St. Louis, and Boston, worked with the American Bar Association (ABA), founded in 1878, to restrict entry into the profession. The bar argued that stricter standards were necessary to ensure the quality of the legal profession. Critics, though, observed that minorities, immigrants, and women were becoming excluded from being a part of the legal profession. Nonetheless, a new private accreditation organization, the Association of American Law Schools (AALS), founded in 1900, joined bar associations to lobby state legislatures in an ongoing effort to narrow the opportunities of law school entry and bar admissions. Ultimately, tightening these standards enabled ABA-approved law schools to become the exclusive path to the practice of law.[11]

The accreditation standards initiatives of the ABA, the AALS, and local bar associations eventually led to the creation of national standards for bar examinations. The corresponding push toward professional self-regulation allowed new requirements to be instituted, including ending the diploma privilege, imposing the requirement of college study as a precondition for law school admission, requiring compulsory attendance in law schools for three years, and making graduation a prerequisite for taking compulsory bar examinations. While lawyers defend their regulatory independence on the grounds that it is needed to protect clients and the public against outside interference that might undermine the profession's core values and legal practices, critics countered that self-regulation insulates and harms the legal profession because it can never look past its own occupational interests.[12]

The growth of the legal profession was also greatly affected by two other closely related developments: the institutionalization of the academic **casebook**

method and the establishment of the so-called **Wall Street law firm**. The casebook method was introduced in 1870 by Christopher Columbus Langdell, the dean of Harvard University's law school. In contrast to a lecture style of instruction, students learned law by studying appellate judicial opinions, reprinted in casebooks. For Langdell, "law, considered as a science, consists of certain principles or doctrines, [and] a mastery of these. . .is what constitutes a true lawyer. . .and [the]. . .best, if not the only way of mastering the doctrine effectually is by studying the cases in which it is embodied." Scientifically studying case law facilitated logical reasoning or, in popular terms, "thinking like a lawyer." Casebooks isolated key legal principles, and professors asked students to determine whether judges properly adhered to precedent (past decisions). In time, Langdell's "case method" of teaching common law doctrine became associated with the "Socratic method," or "case-dialogue" method of modern classroom instruction that was popularized in best-selling books (Scott Turow's *One L*) and movies (*The Paper Chase*) that depicted Harvard Law School's grueling first-year law school experience. In that type of classroom setting, law professors aggressively engage students in a systematic one-on-one questioning and answering dialogue about what the cases they study legally mean, thus forcing students to develop a unique analytical skill that helps them to discover legal principles and how the law applies to different factual circumstances.[13]

The casebook method became widely adopted as an effective tool to increase class size and to keep law schools profitable with higher enrollments. Its popularity made apprenticeships virtually irrelevant, and it facilitated the rise of the Wall Street law firm by encouraging law firms to hire young associates directly from law school, without prior legal experience. The Wall Street law firm emerged in the 1890s as an innovation of a Columbia Law School graduate and New York City attorney, Paul D. Cravath (a co-founder of Cravath, Swaine & Moore). Cravath structured the law office as a bureaucratically efficient and profitable entity—sometimes called a "factory system of law"—with a filing system, typewriters, stenographers, and typists. He also recruited new, aggressive associates who were in the top of their class from elite law schools. In this respect, the Cravath law firm produced meritorious but "anonymous organization men, steadfastly loyal to the firm that had hired them fresh out of law school, [and] moving only if the firm informed them it could not advance them to partnership." If the associate attorney made the grade by putting in long hours in a law firm environment that resembled a "sweat shop," a successful lawyer could expect to become a partner within five to nine years.[14]

The Cravath system and its recruiting practices caught on quickly, and several large firms appeared in major metropolitan areas—New York, Chicago, Boston, and Cleveland, among others. The institutionalization of the large corporate law firm brought with it legal specialization and commercialization, and both remain today. The advancement of office technologies pushed legal environments toward a business model predicated on generating a reliable source of revenue that was readily found in corporate, as opposed to sporadic, individual client representation. Though rhetorical skill in a courtroom was valued, it was no longer perceived to be the ticket to professional success. Instead, professional advancement was conditioned on generating a profitable client base (a precursor to the modern professional norm of "billable hours," which is one of the prominent methods by which lawyers earn fees on the basis of the time spent performing legal work). If an associate met the firm's expectations, promotion to partner was likely, and a promoted attorney would then receive a share of the firm's profits.[15]

The socialization of the contemporary lawyer remains a by-product of the historical changes made to law schools, accreditation standards, the structure of legal education, and law firm organization after 1870. Once admission standards were nationally applied, apprenticeship gave way to learning the skills of a professional lawyer in a classroom with a casebook. The academic rather than practice-based focus of legal training coincided with transforming the law degree into a graduate education that enabled the growth of university-affiliated law schools. And with the rise of the large corporate law firm, the traditional conception of the generalist lawyer gradually yielded to the reality that attorneys are specialists, cultivating the business of legal practice for its financial rewards. Under the traditional Cravath corporate law firm model, which exerted its biggest influence on the legal profession until the 1960s until it yielded to the advent of Big Law (an explosion of elite large law firms and megafirms, discussed later in this chapter), a "tournament" of legal norms and internal management practices was created that centered on taking advantage of promotion-to-partner incentives in a clearly defined hierarchical organization. Significantly, as well, a new emphasis on corporate practice brought with it an increasing stratification within the legal profession, separating the elite performers from the "also-rans."[16]

CONTEMPORARY LEGAL EDUCATION AND BAR ADMISSION

Since the 1960s, the number of attorneys has quadrupled due to a proliferation of new law schools and graduates between 1960 and 2000. Recent survey data from the American Bar Association indicate that there are over 1.3 million licensed lawyer that are in active practice, a total representing a 15 percent increase since 2008. In the U.S., most lawyers practice law in five states: New York (177,035), California (170,044), Texas (90,485), Florida (78,244) and Illinois (63,422). The fewest are found in North Dakota (1,694), Virgin Islands (776), Guam (270), North Mariana Islands (128) and American Samoa (59). Notably, the United States is not alone in experiencing a dramatic increase in the number of lawyers: other common law countries (such as England and Wales, and Canada) as well as many civil law countries (like Germany and Italy) saw a rapid increase at roughly the same time.[17]

There are over two hundred law schools in the United States: 203 with ABA accreditation and 31 nonaccredited institutions.[18] Moreover, the growth of the Internet has spawned distance learning and so-called MOOCs ("massive open online courses" that are free to take). Though several online law schools have emerged because of their low cost and flexibility, none are ABA approved, which greatly restricts their utility for passing a bar exam and practicing law. As a result, MOOCs are plagued by low graduation rates and other problems, so their impact on legal education in the future remains uncertain.[19] Still, because the structure, quality, and practicality of legal instruction is a longstanding debate in the legal academy, the growth of digital and informational technologies has prompted the ABA to give its approval to a growing number of so-called "hybrid" on campus/online J.D. (Juris Doctor) programs in several states.[20]

Today, the legal profession is now a $288 billion industry, with over 186,216 legal establishments; 175,653 law offices; and over 1.3 million lawyers, judges, and legal support staff. Indeed, in 1978, the rapid growth of lawyers in the U.S. prompted former Chief Justice Warren Burger to quip: "We may well be on our way to a society overrun by hordes of lawyers, hungry as locusts, and brigades of judges in numbers never before contemplated."[21] Other statistics confirm that there is at least some truth of that statement. Between 1947 and 2002, the ratio of population to lawyers shrunk from 790:1 to about 283:1. And, according to one recent estimate, there were 392 lawyers for every hundred thousand people, which at the time was reported to be the second highest ratio in the world next to Israel.[22]

| Figure 5.1 | Law School Enrollment & Bar Admissions, 1965–2019 |

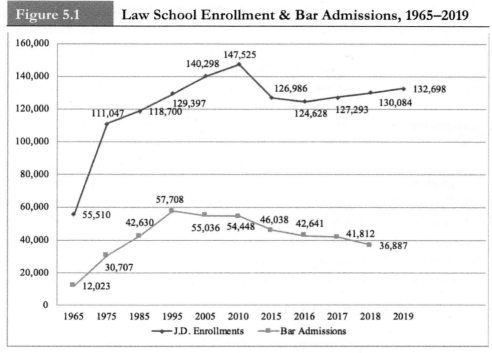

Sources: American Bar Association, Section of Legal Education and Admissions to the Bar, Standard 509 Information Report Data Overview for years 2016 to 2019, available from https://www. americanbar.org/groups/legal_education/resources/statistics/ (retrieved April 16, 2020)(reporting data from ABA approved law schools, comprising J.D. enrollment, non-J.D. enrollment programs, such as LL.M, masters and certificate Programs); National Conference of Bar Examiners, "Statistics and Research," available from http://www.ncbex.org/statistics-and-research/statistics/ (retrieved April 16, 2020)(2019 bar passage results not reported); American Bar Association, Section of Legal Education and Admissions to the Bar, "Enrollment and Degrees Awarded, 1963–2012 Academic Years," available at https://www.americanbar.org/content/dam/aba/administrative/legal_education_and_admissions_ to_the_bar/statistics/enrollment_degrees_awarded.pdf (last retrieved April 16, 2020).

Recently, however, legal practice in the United States has been growing at an anemic rate, and in turn, fewer students are pursuing legal education. Prior to the 2008 recession, there was a four to six percent annual growth in the demand for law firm services; thereafter, the demand growth sharply declined and remained essentially flat, with growth rates stagnant at one percent or less.[23] After 2008, law firms began to lay off attorneys and institute cost saving measures, and many of the tasks that ordinarily went to new associate attorneys, such as conducting time-intensive "document reviews" in preparation for litigation, were either automated or outsourced to contract attorneys and paralegals.[24] The constriction of the legal marketplace also caused law school applications to sharply decline: whereas nearly 88,000 applicants sought entry in the 2009–10 admission cycle, applications dipped and has remained below the 60,000 level from 2012 to 2016.[25] In addition, total enrollments in the Juris Doctor (J.D.) and non-J.D. programs (LL.M, masters and certificate programs) decreased from almost one hundred forty-eight to roughly one hundred thirty-three thousand between 2010 and 2019. Moreover, since the mid 1990s, the rate of new bar admissions has not appreciably grown: in 1995, almost 58,000 new lawyers were admitted but by 2018 that number had steadily declined to a little under 37,000. (see Figure 5.1). While there are some recent signs that the interest in law school may be increasing, many legal commentators observe that law schools, and the legal profession itself, is facing a crisis—in part brought on by high tuition rates, rising student loan debt, declines in law school enrollments, and the unpredictable success in landing employment after graduation. New Internet-based businesses, among them LawPivot, RocketLawyer, and LegalZoom, have reduced the need for lawyers, and law-licensed legal research is now readily available to anyone looking to cut back on high legal costs. Consequently, some legal experts fear that the demand for lawyers will continue to decline and a permanent restructuring of the profession will force law school closures, massive layoffs, and fewer new attorneys.[26]

U.S. Law School Education

Unlike many other legal systems throughout the world, in the United States, eligibility to practice law usually begins with admission into law school after graduating from an undergraduate university or college. By contrast, in most civil law countries, legal training is provided at the undergraduate level. Earning a law degree in some common law countries—notably, the United Kingdom and Canada—also differs from that in the United States (see "In Comparative Perspective: Legal Education and Lawyers in Western Democracies" in this chapter and "In Comparative Perspective: The Career Judiciary in Japan" in Chapter Four).

In Comparative Perspective: Legal Education and Lawyers in Western Democracies

Justice Felix Frankfurter once observed: "In the last analysis, the law is what lawyers are. And the law and the lawyers are what law school makes them." Whereas prospective lawyers in the United States complete a four-year undergraduate degree before they apply to a law school, it is possible in Canada to be professionally licensed with only two or three years of undergraduate education. That was once true in the United States until the early part of the twentieth century, and it was not until 1957 that all justices on the Supreme Court had formal law degrees. A few states, like Virginia, still allow people to take the bar exam without having earned a law degree. Now, though, most U.S.

students earn their undergraduate degree and then apply to one of the nation's 203 ABA-accredited law schools in fifty states to earn a JD (Juris Doctor) degree. By contrast, Canada has roughly over twenty law schools. Most Canadian law schools offer degree programs in the English or French common law. Canadian law students may earn an LLB (Bachelor of Laws), a BCL (Bachelor of Civil Law), or a JD degree, typically in three years. As in the United States, many Canadian law schools use the LSAT (along with grade point averages to evaluate applicants' merits, but some bilingual learning institutions, such as the McGill University Faculty of Law, do not require it because the LSAT is an English-only test). Unlike the U.S. schools, Canadian law schools also offer an alternative system of admissions that may admit "special" applicants—those lacking an undergraduate degree; those with special needs, disabilities, or financial hardship; or those historically disadvantaged because of race or ethnicity.

In contrast, U.K. law schools admit students into undergraduate law programs. Students may choose among roughly one hundred universities that offer law programs, including the most prestigious—Oxford and Cambridge. As in the United States and Canada, admission decisions are based on grades— though, high school grades—and other meritorious factors; some law schools also require the National Admissions Test for Law (LNAT), a standardized test analogous to the LSAT.

Moreover, unlike in the United States or in Canada, it is possible to become a U.K. lawyer without having an undergraduate law degree, although a degree in another discipline is required. For example, students who have an undergraduate degree in history or economics may take a one-year Postgraduate Diploma in Law (PGDL) course that assesses proficiency in seven core subjects (criminal law, constitutional law, tort law, contract law, land law, equity/trust law, and European Union law). Likewise, U.K. students with an undergraduate law degree must also take a one-year vocational course—the Legal Practice Course (LPC)—if they want to become "solicitors" in a law firm, or the Bar Vocational Course (BVC) if they want to become "barristers" who argue cases in court. Once the appropriate vocational course and the corresponding exams are passed, U.K. students begin an apprenticeship, or a period of practical training under the supervision of an experienced lawyer, before becoming a lawyer. Notably, the UK requires apprenticeships as a prerequisite for law licensing (in the UK, apprenticeships for solicitors are called "training contracts," and barristers complete a "pupilage"; the apprenticeship in Canada is called "articling").

Furthermore, in Canada, law graduates must successfully pass a bar admission course in order to qualify for bar admission. The Canadian bar admission program is regulated by rules established by the provincial or territorial "law society" in which the bar applicant intends to practice law. These law societies are akin to state bar associations in the United States that regulate professional licensing. In contrast, U.K. lawyers are regulated by "law societies" (for solicitors) or the Bar Council and its independent Bar Standards Board (for barristers). While the mandatory one-year vocational course in the United Kingdom that is taken before an apprenticeship is arguably functionally equivalent to the Canadian compulsory bar admission course, U.S. law schools generally do not provide similar courses; instead, U.S. bar applicants typically take expensive, bar preparation courses after law school that help them pass state bar examinations.

Finally, U.S. and Canadian lawyers are considered "generalists," whereas, in the United Kingdom, lawyers are distinguished by their respective solicitor or barrister expertise. Even so, most U.S. and Canadian lawyers informally develop specialties in law (criminal defense attorneys, real estate attorneys, family law attorneys, and the like) during the course of their careers.

The table below summarizes the prelaw, law, and bar admission requirements for the United States, Canada, and the United Kingdom.

	United States	Canada	United Kingdom
		Prelaw Admission	
Standardized Prelaw Test Used in Admission Decisions	LSAT	LSAT	LNAT
		Bar Admission	
Bar Regulatory Bodies	American Bar Association	Federation of Law Societies of Canada	Law Societies (Solicitors)
	State Bar Associations	Provincial/ Territorial Law Societies	Bar Council (Barristers)

Is "Law" a Graduate or Undergraduate Degree?	Graduate	Graduate	Undergraduate
Undergraduate Degree Required?	Yes	No	No
Apprenticeship Required?	No	Yes	Yes
Vocational Course Required Before Apprenticeship Begins?	No	No	Yes
Bar Admission Course Required?	No	Yes	No
Bar or Licensing Examination Format	Bar Exam Administered by State Bar Association	Licensing Exam Administered by Law Society	Completion of Vocational Course/Exams and Apprenticeship Under Supervision of Law Society or Bar Council

Sources: Federation of Law Societies of Canada, available at https://flsc.ca/ (last retrieved April 16, 2020); F. C. DeCoste, *On Coming to Law: An Introduction to Law in Liberal Societies*, 3rd ed. (Markham, Ontario: LexisNexis Canada, 2011) (J. Frankfurter's quote is on p. xxiii); Nicholas J. McBride, *Letters to a Law Student: A Guide to Studying Law at University*, rev. 3rd ed. (Edinburgh Gate, U.K.: Pearson Education Limited, 2013); *Comparative Law and Society*, edited by David S. Clark (Northampton, Mass.: Edward Elgar, 2012).

In the U.S., there is common belief that there is a special type of prelaw undergraduate study that "best" prepares students for law school. But neither the American Bar Association (ABA) nor the Law School Admission Council (LSAC) recommend that students choose any undergraduate majors or group of courses to prepare for a legal education.[27] Instead, those interested in going to law school can take a variety of undergraduate courses in the social sciences or other disciplines: there is no standard "prelaw" degree or program of study, though many college and university departments may house a specialized prelaw minor or similar programs that cater to students exploring a desire to attend law school. A department or college may have a prelaw advisor to help students structure their coursework or to help them prepare their law school applications. While there is no set prelaw degree or program in many instances, a popular major is Political Science, but others include Criminal Justice, Psychology, English, History, Economics and Philosophy, among others. While many students gravitate to the liberal arts for prelaw study, studies have shown that taking STEM (science, technology, engineering, math) or EAR (economics, accounting, finance) majors are useful predictors of law school success. Regardless, students aiming to apply to law school are typically advised to take courses that hone analytical reasoning, problem-solving, research, oral communications, and writing—all of which are part in building attorney competence once in law school and legal practice.[28]

ABA-accredited law schools require that students is take Law School Admissions Test (LSAT). Contrary to popular belief, the LSAT does not test a person's substantive knowledge about the law. Instead, the LSAT is an important admission metric because it registers the likelihood of an applicant's success in law school by testing the student's ability to perform the type of skills that lawyers use in legal practice. Students typically begin to prepare for it in the last two years of their undergraduate education. The LSAT score, which is computed on a scale of 120–180, is determined from the number of correct answers, and there is no deduction for wrong answers. The LSAT's test format consists of multiple choice questions in five thirty-five minute sections (four of which are scored). There is also a thirty-five-minute unscored writing sample that is taken at the end of the exam (that is not scored but forwarded to law schools where applications are sent). The multiple choice design has three question types: reading comprehension, analytical reasoning, and logical reasoning. Whereas the reading comprehension section has three long and two short comparative reading passages, the analytical reasoning part has four logic games and the logical reasoning section is based on short arguments.[29]

Along with earning a strong undergraduate grade point average (UGPA), performing well on the LSAT is vital: but, law schools routinely advise applicants that while UGPA and LSAT scores are significant, "they are only one of several pieces of the law school application puzzle." Admissions committees usually weigh a variety of factors in making admission decisions, such as the strength of the college attended and its undergraduate curriculum; graduate study; grade improvement; extracurricular activities; ethnic or racial background; individual character and personality traits; letters of recommendation; writing skills, especially as gleaned from the personal statement (the reasons why the applicant believes they are a good candidate for law study); relevant work experience and community activities or volunteer work; and, if there have been noteworthy past accomplishments and leadership activities, and so forth.[30]

Notably, applying to law school requires extensive preparation and money. Besides the standard preparatory steps of earning an undergraduate degree, studying for the LSAT and completing the law school application, prospective students and the law schools themselves often consult a popular, but controversial, ranking of law schools that is compiled annually by U.S. News & World Report (USNWR) (Table 5.1). Students look to them as an indicator of quality and law schools see them as a proxy for how well they are positioned against other competitor law schools that try to recruit students and their tuition dollars. While there are other venues and online sources that rank law schools, such as Princeton Review, Above the Law or Vault, empirical studies demonstrate that the USNWR rankings have an effect on the decision-making of both applicants and law schools.[31] Still, USNWR rankings have been heavily criticized because some law schools have used the ranking system as a recruitment tool to boost rankings their artificially. For example, law schools that were trying to remain competitive in a tight legal marketplace resorted to dubious recruitment tactics, such as fudging their post-JD employment data; offering "bait and switch" conditional scholarships (that lure students by the promise of guarantying three years of funding but then rescinding them when they did not meet conditions of the scholarship, such as keeping a high GPA); changing their admissions formula; or, using expensive promotional campaigns or adopting institutional strategies to inflate the school's (and faculty) reputation. Such tactics have led to additional criticisms that the USNWR rankings' methodology is deeply flawed and has caused other collateral damage, such as the firing of law school deans or the commencement of litigation by unhappy students claiming that law schools owe them damages for misrepresenting their employment data.[32] Significantly, the ABA has responded to the criticisms, in part, by requiring law schools to file and post on their websites so-called Standard 509 disclosure reports in an effort to improve consumer knowledge and law school transparency. These reports, among other things, mandate that law schools disclose a wide range of information that helps prospective law students understand admission standards, costs, student and faculty demographics, and the availability of scholarship money.[33]

Table 5.1	Law School Rankings, 2021			
Rank	**School**	**UGPA/ LSAT**	**Tuition and Fees**	**Acceptance Rate**
1	Yale University	3.93/173	$66,128	8.22%
2	Stanford University	3.91/171	$64,554	9.72%
3	Harvard University	3.89/173	$67,081	12.49%
4 (tie)	Columbia University	3.80/172	$72,465	15.86%
4 (tie)	University of Chicago	3.90/170	$66,651	18.61%
6	New York University	3.80/170	$68,934	21.60%
7	University of Pennsylvania	3.89/170	$67,998	14.51%
8#	University of Virginia	3.90/170	$63,200* $66,200**	14.69%
9 (tie)	Northwestern University	3.85/169	$66,806	18.01%
9 (tie)#	University of California, Berkeley	3.81/168	$52,017* $55,346**	19.68%
9 (tie)#	University of Michigan, Ann Arbor	3.81/169	$61,944* $64,944**	16.63%
12	Duke University	3.78/169	$67,358	18.91%

Source: *U.S. News and World Report* Rankings (law schools ranked as of 2020) and 2019 ABA-required Standard 509 disclosure reports. 50th percentile GPA/ LSAT reported. *=Resident; **=Non-resident. # = Public school, all others are private. U.S. News numerically ranks the top three-quarters of the law schools. The bottom quartile of law schools are listed alphabetically.

Furthermore, students spend several hundred, and sometimes thousands, of dollars in application fees for applying to several schools, taking the LSAT, and having the Law School Credential Assembly Service send their transcripts and letters of recommendation and any other required documentation to targeted schools. In addition, given the significance of scoring well on the LSAT, many applicants also take expensive LSAT-preparation classes (costing up to $1,400 or more); but, notably, the LSAC has begun to offer free prep course material (through the Khan Academy) and applicants can take at least one free test and receive a listing of multiple commercial providers and courses that incorporate licensed LSAT content in their programs directly on its website.[34]

Another important factor in legal education is rising tuition rates and determining how to pay for law school. Research shows that the prospect of paying back educational law school debt is increasingly a burden for those who are admitted and graduate, especially if there is also undergraduate loans to repay. Especially since the 2008 recession, the problem has become worst because many law students cannot find suitable employment to service their debt after graduation. Studies from the American Bar Association (ABA), non-profit advocacy groups and scholars document the scope of the problem. According to the ABA, in 1985 the median tuition rate for public law schools was $1,792 (resident; for non-residents, $4,786); for private schools, it was $7,385. But by 2013, it skyrocketed to $22,209 for residents going to public schools and $33,752 for non-residents, for private schools, it grew to $42,241. Apart from the tuition rate, for single students living on campus the average amount of living and book expenses has similarly risen from roughly $5,000 per year in 1990 to $15,000 by 2012–2013. Data from the non-profit advocacy group Law School Transparency registers analogous trends, reporting that increases in law school tuition rates have outpaced the inflation rate for the past thirty-five years. After adjusting for inflation, the average tuition cost for attending a private ($47,754) and public school ($41,628 for non-residents and $28,186 for residents) is 2.76 and 5.92 times as expensive as it was in 1985, respectively.[35]

Rising tuition has caused a corresponding increase in student loan debt. In the mid 1980s, the total amount of loan debt for undergraduate and law school was roughly $16,000. According to Law School Transparency, law students borrow an average $145,419 (for-profit school), $134,497 (private school) and $96,054 (public school). In addition, nearly 90 percent of law students borrow money to attend law school and, as one illustration, it is plausible that a law graduate making about $67,000 in their first full-time job will have to pay $1,400 per month on a $125,000 loan under a standard ten-year repayment plan.[36] Even though there are ways to mitigate educational debt—such as taking advantage of government loan forgiveness programs (under certain conditions), income-based repayment plans, or the possibility that highly qualified law school applicants might get an offer of receiving a tuition discount (which may be subject to conditions, like maintaining a certain GPA)—for many students the high debt is likely to linger long after graduation. One study found that less than half of lawyers paid off their loans after twelve years of legal practice; and the median debt for lawyers, which was roughly $50,000, was much harder to pay off for non-elites, such as African-Americans, Hispanics, and Asians (but not whites).[37] Accordingly, some scholars question whether law school offers a good return on investment, with mixed results. Regardless, as law professor Mary Ann Glendon quipped, at least for some law students the specter of paying off student loans certainly means that "the gilded cage has a trapdoor."[38]

Students that ultimately go to law school will quickly discover that there is some truth to the old adage that "the first year of law school scares you to death, the second works you to death, and the third bores you to death."[39] Once in law school, law students are trained through a combination of the Socratic casebook method, lectures, legal clinics, moot courts, legal research, and writing exercises. Although there are opportunities to gain practical law office or trial court experience, the thrust of legal training remains learning legal doctrine through casebook analysis—a reasoning process that allows students to discover general principles of law from specific cases decided by appeals courts. In this respect, legal questions are resolved deductively by first inductively using specific past precedents to identify general principles of law that are applied to the unique facts of the case. In conjunction with casebook analysis, a Socratic case-dialogue method of instruction—in which law professors systematically engage students in a one-on-one questioning and answering dialogue about what legal principles are in a judicial opinion and what they mean—is often used to sharpen a student's critical thinking and problem-solving skills.[40]

Teaching in a legal doctrinal-heavy format also means that there is little emphasis in law school on learning the practice of law. The lack of practical legal training underscores the divergent paths of law study: there is an academic focus by law professors to teach legal doctrine while ironically there is little instruction on how to practice law from a private practitioner's perspective. While law schools are increasingly being more responsive to the criticism that they must be more flexible and teach their students more "practice-ready" legal skills, in general law schools have been reluctant to change their standard curriculum, especially in the first year of study (see Table 5.2). After the first year, students have more choices to take elective courses that allow them to cultivate a more specific interest in certain areas of the law, such as Administrative Law, Corporations (or Business Organizations), Criminal Procedure, Evidence, Employment (or Labor) Law, Family Law (or Domestic Relations), Federal Taxation, and Wills and Estates, among others. Typically, the third year combines elective courses with other practice-ready experiences or clinical programs, such as externships, working in a local law firm or clerking for a judge, or participating in mock trial, moot court, and trial advocacy programs.[41] Over the usual three-year program, though, only a few practice skills are developed and, for those at the top of the class, there remains the possibility of learning how to do legal research and publishing journal articles in student-led and faculty-advised law reviews. The lack of practical training has led some observers, including the ABA, to criticize that the teaching of legal doctrine and theory is overemphasized and in need of reform. As legal scholar Deborah Rhode put it, reform is imperative because under the traditional model of legal instruction students "may have learned to 'think like a lawyer' but not how to make a living at it."[42] Moreover, a related concern is that many law professors have limited credentials to teach because they only have a law degree— only a few possess an additional master's degree in law (Master of Laws, or LLM) or, less often, a Doctor of the Science of Law (SJD) or a PhD in a related field. Most simply hold a JD and have little or no teaching experience.[43]

Table 5.2	Standard First Year Courses in Law School	
Course	Type of Law	Content
Contract law	Private law	Enforceability of private agreements
Tort law	Private law	Imposition of liability for unreasonable acts between private individuals that proximately cause harm
Property law	Private law	Facilitation of the various legal relationships affecting the possession and transfer of real (land) or personal (tangible items) property
Criminal law	Public law	Enforcement of public moral code through sanction
Constitutional law	Public law	Interpretation of constitutional documents
Civil Procedure	Procedural law (mostly dealing in private law subject matter)	Rules of legal procedure developed by courts relative to federal civil cases and litigation
Legal Research and Writing	Practice-ready skills in public and private law contexts	Legal research and writing strategies and skills

Sources: Christopher P. Banks, *The American Legal Profession: The Myths and Realities of Practicing Law* (Thousand Oaks, CA.: Sage/CQ Press 2017), 54; Sheldon Krantz, *The Legal Profession: What is Wrong and How to Fix It* (New Providence, N.J.: LexisNexis, 2014): 20–21.

The traditional preoccupation with legal doctrine underscores that it is "still almost entirely about law and. . .only incidentally and superficially about lawyering."[44] What is being taught in law schools and by whom has significant implications for the legal profession and, not surprisingly, is linked to modern law school hiring trends. For example, increasingly law schools are hiring faculty who have both a JD and a PhD in a nonlaw discipline, but who have little or no experience in practicing law. For Seventh Circuit Judge Richard A. Posner, hiring law professors with advanced non-legal degrees is problematic because the legal scholarship produced by law faculty has little relevance to legal practitioners or judges. In addition, a study of 872 professorships (about 15 percent of the profession) found that only about a handful of elite schools—Harvard, Yale, Columbia, Chicago, Michigan, and New York University—are responsible for producing almost one-third of the nation's law professors. And 60 percent of the professorate came from top-twenty schools. Another study shows graduates of the nation's top fifty law schools—especially Yale, Harvard, and Stanford—are more likely to be hired by other top-fifty law schools, and all law schools usually select faculty from schools that are ranked above them. More often than not, a different but related concern is that many law faculties are dominated by white males, and thus merely homogeneous "gatekeepers and molders" of the profession.[45]

Professional Ethics

An integral component of law school education involves teaching students the significance of professional responsibility and legal ethics. In most jurisdictions, passing the Multistate Professional Responsibility Examination (MPRE) is a condition for bar admission. Since the 1970s, and administered three times per year, the MPRE is important because it assesses whether lawyers understand the Model Rules of Professional Conduct (MRPC), the ethical rules that are promulgated by the American Bar Association. All states have adopted some version of the model rules.[46]

Under the MRPC, law students are taught that they are "officers of the court" and hold a special place in the community in representing clients. In general, the rules mandate that attorneys act with competence and due diligence in the cases they handle, and that they be free from conflicts of interest that undermine the position of trust that they hold in relation to their clients. These rules detail specific procedures for managing client monies and preventing a comingling of business and client funds. Moreover, they proscribe standards that govern client representation and managing or selling a law practice, including acting as advocates for client interests, maintaining client confidentiality, knowing the rules of advertising legal services, and other ethical issues.[47]

Furthermore, ethical training is reinforced by the threat of professional sanction. If attorneys transgress ethical codes, the MRPC makes them subject to penalties ranging from reprimand and suspension to disbarment. The responsibility for evaluating alleged acts of attorney misconduct ordinarily rests with the state's court of last resort and the state's authorized bar disciplinary commissions. Still, even though state courts are vested with the power to enforce professional code of ethics, disciplinary systems vary widely and, regardless, they tend to show great deference to the organized bar and its membership. Clients that are harmed by an attorney's ethical misfeasance thus often face difficulties in trying to sanction lawyer misconduct, simply because the process is bureaucratically complex and, for some observers, appear to prioritize protecting the attorney's due process and reputational rights instead of safeguarding client interests. As a result, critics complain that they are ineffectual because they are too idiosyncratic and fraught with bias because lawyers are mostly in charge of policing themselves.[48]

Bar Admissions

Bar admissions for the practice of law are inherently restrictive and operate to limit the number of practicing lawyers. In order to practice before most federal courts, lawyers must generally be a member of the bar within the jurisdiction of a federal court in which they will practice. With the exception of a few states, such as California, Vermont, Virginia, Washington and Wisconsin, that allow admission by apprenticeship (through law office study) or diploma privilege (bar admission after graduation from a state-run law school), most aspiring lawyers must prepare and sit for state-specific bar examinations once they graduate from an ABA-accredited law school.[49]

Most bar examinations are administered through a state board that is an agent of the highest court in the state or, less typically, the state bar association. In addition to passing the MPRE, most jurisdictions use a two-day bar examination format. On the first day, applicants must pass the standardized Multistate Bar Examination (MBE), offered semiannually by the National Conference of Bar Examiners (NCBE) (established in 1931). The MBE consists of two hundred multiple-choice questions typically covering most first-year law school subjects (Civil Procedure, Constitutional Law, Contracts, Criminal Law and Procedure, Evidence, Real Property, and Torts). Its purpose is to evaluate proficiency in legal reasoning and in understanding the application of legal principles to different situations. On the second day, jurisdictions test a wide range of legal substantive and procedural subject matter through written essays that are created by the state bar licensing authority; but a growing number of states are opting to test lawyer competence through two national NCBE-based tests, the Multistate Essay Examination (MEE) and the Multistate Performance Test (MPT).[50]

Whereas the MEE, which has six thirty-minute essay questions designed to test professional writing skills and competencies across twelve areas of substantive law, the MPT is structured by the completion of two ninety minute exams that evaluate the ability to use basic lawyering skills in real-life situations. Significantly, in response to the criticism that state bar licensing procedures are too geo-centric and interfere with establishing cross-jurisdictional legal practice across state lines, several states have adopted another type of bar examination, the Uniform Bar Examination (UBE). With the UBE, applicants take the MBE, the MEE and the MPT and the score is portable, or transferrable, to other UBE jurisdictions.[51]

Apart from testing applicants' substantive knowledge of the law through written examinations, bar licensing authorities also mandate that prospective lawyers satisfy state-specific character and fitness requirements. Accordingly, bar applicants must submit to a thorough investigation of their personal background in order to determine if they are qualified to be professionally licensed and be in a position to earn the public's trust. Character and fitness tests, however, are controversial: although the legal profession defends them as a means to prevent unqualified or unfit persons from getting a law license, historically they have been used to discriminate and exclude disfavored applicants from entering the legal profession, such as immigrants or indigents. Moreover, these questionnaires have been criticized on the grounds that they are too invasive, arbitrary, and expensive to administer fairly.[52]

Nonetheless, tens of thousands of lawyers are admitted into practice each year. Although law school applications and bar passage rates have declined in recent years, since 2015 the total number of enrolled J.D. candidates and bar admissions have remained relatively constant at roughly 127,000 enrollees and 41,000 admissions, respectively (see Figure 5.1). Indeed, between 2008 and 2017, the overall national passage rate ranged from a high of 71 percent (in 2008) to a low of 54 percent (2016) and the ten-year average is nearly 60 percent.[53] As measured by historical law school enrollment trends, more women, and to a lesser degree minorities, have been admitted. Before 1972, women represented less than 10 percent of the profession. By 1980, the number rose to 36 percent, and by 2019, it increased to 54 percent. Minority enrollments have not increased as quickly: whereas, in 1970 minorities constituted only 7 percent of law school matriculants, by 2019 they represented 31 percent.[54]

After Bar Passage: Trends in Diversity and Employment Inequality

Despite the incremental gains made by women and (to a lesser degree) minorities, social norms substantially prevent employment equality. While men and women retain an identical percentage of judicial or magistrate positions, men outpace women by a significant margin in working as lawyers and in judicial clerkships, while the reverse is true for in subordinate legal support workers, such as paralegal or legal assistants (see Table 5.3). According to the Bureau of Labor Statistics, the legal profession is not as diverse as the medicine, accounting, or academic professions and the disparities register a disproportionate advantage for men in terms of professional success. Women, for example, comprise only 18 percent of law firm equity partners and 24 percent of general counsel of Fortune 500 companies even though they represent over one-third of the legal profession. Moreover, various studies show that women generally earn less than men, and fewer succeed in getting promoted to high-status positions, such as becoming a partner in a law firm. Similar trends are found in minority or person of color representation: whereas roughly half of white lawyers have achieved partnership status in large law firms, far less African-American, Hispanic or Asian attorneys have done so; and, even fewer lawyers of color are equity partners.[55] As law professor Deborah Rhode observes:

> One irony of this nation's continuing struggle for diversity and gender equity in employment is that the profession leading the struggle has failed to set an example in its own workplaces. In principle, the bar is deeply committed to equal opportunity and social justice. In practice, it lags behind other occupations.[56]

Table 5.3	Legal Profession Occupations by Gender and Position		
Legal Occupation	**Male**	**Female**	**Total**
Lawyers/Judicial Law Clerks	38.4%	23.0%	61.4%
Judges/Magistrates/Other Judicial Workers	2.2%	2.0%	4.2%
Legal Support Workers	6.2%	28.3%	34.5%
Total	46.7%	53.3%	100.0%

Source: U.S. Census Bureau, "B24010. SEX BY OCCUPATION FOR THE CIVILIAN EMPLOYED POPULATION 16 YEARS AND OVER (Universe: Civilian employed population 16 years and over more information, 2017 American Community Survey 1-Year Estimates)," available at https://www.bls.gov/cps/tables.htm (last retrieved April 12, 2019).

Two studies, one from a 2019 report by the ABA's Commission on Women in the Profession and another from a 2019 Report on Diversity in Law Firms from the National Association for Law Placement (NALP), show how pervasive the disparities are across the full spectrum of the legal profession. Relative to women: (1) women only represent 30 and 24 percent of Fortune 500, and Fortune 501–1000 general counsel positions, respectively; (2) only 35 percent of law school deans are women; (3) women occupy 34 to 37 percent of federal district and appellate court judgeships; and, (4) between 2006 and 2018, women lawyers made only 80 percent of what men earned in salary.[57] The NALP report made analogous findings, but added that while 25 percent of associate attorneys in law firms were minorities, only 10 percent were partners and, of those, 3 percent were women. Among different ethnicities, there were less Asian (4 percent), African-American (2 percent) and Hispanic (3 percent) partners as well, and one percent or less were women. Finally, the NALP found that lawyers with disabilities in law firms represented less than one percent of the profession; whereas openly LGBT lawyers constituted 3 percent, and, of those, 2 percent were partners, 4 percent were associates, and 2 percent were staff or "of counsel" lawyers.[58]

THE BUSINESS OF LEGAL PRACTICE

Since the 1960s, the legal profession is facing several challenges relative to its structure and the integrity of the legal system of the in the twenty-first century. The oversupply of lawyers in a tight and increasingly competitive global legal marketplace has meant that the traditional career choice of a solo practitioner has yielded to the pressure of cost-effective employment in a law firm. Attorneys, once trained as trained as "generalists," now usually develop specialties, often during their first job after law school. Such specialization in discrete areas of law after many years of practice includes corporate, labor, tax, family, real estate, tort, and criminal law, among others. Moreover, the prestige of the law school from which a graduate is hired usually affects a lawyer's career path. Within private practice, graduates from more prestigious law schools are likely to wind up in large law firms, whereas students from less renowned schools tend to be employed in midsize to small law firms. Thus, some court watchers claim that aspiring lawyers are often too preoccupied with the business of legal practice, in part because of the perception that graduates must attend the best-ranked law schools in order to secure a job in a large corporate firm, thereby increasing chances of having a prosperous legal career. At the root of this criticism is the argument that law is a profession, not a business, and the economic stratification of lawyers into the "haves" and "have-nots" is doubly harmful. Not only do the most privileged get coveted employment, but their clients also have the most meaningful access to the lawyers and courts, which registers a broad inequality in the delivery of legal services. These trends and realities, critics say, are reinforced by the self-regulatory insularity of the legal profession and the resistance of law schools to change their traditional pedagogies to a more practical "practice-ready" law instruction.[59]

The way lawyers traditionally conducted business also began to change after the 1960s. Increasing global and domestic government regulation meant that the demand for legal services expanded into new areas of civil rights, employment, product liability, intellectual property, antitrust, securities, and contract law. But the rising costs of meeting the demand for services led corporate businesses to cut expenses and rely less upon expensive outside counsel in large law firms, a break from the past. In turn, the number and competition between large law firms grew; the relatively reliable time frame for many associates to reach partnership status became uncertain or considerably lengthened; and the lateral movement within the profession of partners and associates, once rare, began to become a common occurrence in the 1970s. Now, once employed, lawyers often make lateral career changes, taking the skills learned in one job to another. Government lawyers, for instance, may become criminal defense attorneys; likewise, a law firm associate's experience might be later channeled into corporate work or even a judgeship. By contrast, attorneys in civil law countries do not have nearly as much lateral mobility because their training as civil bureaucrats locks them into certain positions. Hence, at the beginning of his or her career, a civil law attorney has to decide to go into private practice or, alternatively, become a judge, prosecutor, or government attorney.[60] Some of the byproducts of the transformation of the legal profession are discussed next.

Lawyers as Counselors and Advocates

What lawyers do in practice is fundamentally affected by the basic roles they play as advocates or advisors. Lawyers are principally problem solvers, but they also routinely engage in negotiations, perform research, and conduct factual investigations. As counselors, or **transactional lawyers**, they meet clients in their offices and explain the strengths and weaknesses of different legal courses of action, such as buying a house or selling a business. More often than not, they do not spend any time in a courtroom litigating cases. In contrast, **advocates** are more likely to represent clients in court as litigators or trial attorneys. In this role, attorneys are under an ethical obligation to advocate zealously for their clients in legal cases. Contrary to popular opinion, relatively few lawyers regularly appear in court, and most attorneys are behind-the-scenes technicians serving a range of clientele spanning private practice, government, and corporate industry. Only a relatively small percentage of lawyers take public interest jobs or become judges or law teachers, and some increasingly pursue nonlegal careers, especially in the aftermath of the 2008 recession that had a pronounced negative effect on the American legal profession.[61] Another myth is the popular belief that most law graduates easily find employment that pay substantial salaries right after law school and that affluence defines one's professional reputation and legal career. As one legal expert explains, this mystique is a powerful incentive to become an attorney:

> Tens of thousands of people apply to law school each year because it is an avenue to a desirable career. There is prestige attached to the status of a lawyer. Lawyers are smart professionals who wear suits. Most lawyers earn a comfortable living, and very successful ones become wealthy. Many lawyers play leading roles in advising or managing corporations. Many public figures are lawyers. One can do good things as a lawyer-support a cause, work in public service, prosecute criminals, become a politician, serve as a judge, become a high-level government official, advocate for the poor, defend the unjustly accused. Lawyers are pillars of the community.[62]

While it is undoubtedly true that many law graduates have successful and lucrative careers, readily finding employment immediately after graduation is not a reality for others in today's competitive legal landscape.

Legal Employment Trends and Salaries

The growth and diversity of the legal profession has not changed the reality that private legal practice is still the bedrock of the profession. Although estimates vary, 55 percent of almost 30,000 law graduates work in private practice. 72 percent of those jobs required bar passage and 49 percent were in law firms of different sizes; but most were in small firms (1 to 10 attorneys, 34 percent) or extremely large firms (501 or more lawyers, 29 percent), and the vast majority (88 percent) were hired as entry-level associates instead of staff attorneys, law clerks, paralegals, among others.[63] Still, the growing competition among practitioners has caused the number of jobs in the private sector to dissipate, forcing many graduates to start legal careers either in government service or in entrepreneurial enterprise. In the mid 1990s, for example, less than 8 percent of graduates sought business and industry careers, but now roughly 13 percent find their first jobs in business/industry or government. The remainder law graduates secured employment in judicial clerkships (11 percent), public interest (7 percent) and academia (2 percent) (Figure 5.2).

| Figure 5.2 | Law School Graduate Employment |

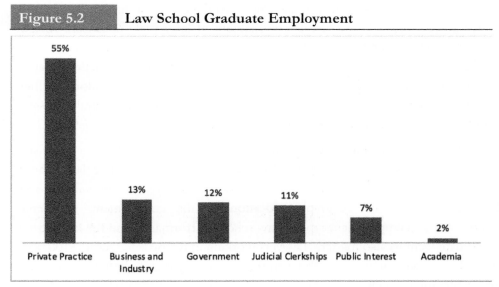

Source: National Association for Law Placement, "Class of 2018 National Summary Report," available at https://www.nalp.org/uploads/NationalSummaryReport_Classof2018_FINAL.pdf (last retrieved on April 16, 2020). Percentages do not include "Unknown Type" of employment (.17 percent) in graph.

Because every year there are only about 25,000 entry-level jobs are available for the roughly 35,000 to 40,000 law graduates entering the market, another trend is for law graduates to use their legal training in non-legal fields across the public and private sectors, such as in claims adjusting, risk or human resources management, financial advising, or as city or town managers. Many of these jobs are what the NALP and ABA styles "JD Advantage" jobs, or employment that does not require bar passage but allows the person to use the skills they acquired by earning a law degree as a "distinct" advantage. The number of these jobs has doubled in the ten years, and by 2018 they represent 14 percent of legal employment for new graduates. Notably, nearly half of these jobs are entry-level positions in business and government. Yet, for all types of positions, they tend to pay less in salary, though there is considerable variability depending upon the type of position secured. According to the NALP, the median salary for JD Advantage jobs is $65,000.[64]

Additionally, law students increasingly compete against not only their U.S. peers, but also foreign lawyers. The growth of transnational lawyering and the need for technology-driven efficiency has created a market for low-cost foreign lawyers to perform e-discovery, document review, legal research, contract management, and due diligence tasks related to mergers and acquisitions, a phenomenon called "legal process outsourcing (LPO)." LPO's "unbundle" mundane legal tasks from large corporate Big Law firms and delegate them to automation or low-cost professionals which sell their wares at half the legal costs of using fledging U.S. lawyers. The availability of large-scale document review through vendors such as Novus Law, Axiom Law, Cobra Legal Services or Bodhi Global Services, among others, is greatly affecting U.S. corporate practice because in-house counsel in corporations are increasingly using low-cost vendors in other countries, such as India, the Philippines, or South Africa, and Australia to save hundreds of thousands of dollars on outside counsel fees on each case.[65]

The global and domestic legal marketplace trends can also be juxtaposed against the amount of money lawyers can expect to earn after law school graduation. In general, the starting salaries of attorneys tend to be variable and contingent upon the geographic location of the employment, economic conditions, and employment type.[66] Law school performance and the law school a graduate went to also matters. Lawyers working in the private sector ($100,000) earn almost twice as much as those in the public sector ($56,000). Certain types of employment, such as working in private practice ($120,000) and business ($77,000) have a higher median starting salary; but attorneys that secure jobs in government ($60,000), education ($51,500), judicial clerkships ($57,000) and public interest ($50,500) earn less. Moreover, the distribution of salaries of lawyers in law firms is correlated to the size of the firm and the position taken: attorneys make more money in larger law firms simply because they tend to be the top recruits from the nation's most prestigious law schools. The median starting salaries for lawyers in 1 to 10 attorney firms is $60,000; $70,000 (11 to 25 attorneys); $80,000 (26 to 50 attorneys); $86,000 (51 to 100 attorneys); $120,000 (101 to 250 attorneys); $180,000 (251 to 500 attorneys); and, $190,000 (501 or more attorneys). First-year associate lawyers in law firms ($130,000) are compensated more than full-time staff attorneys ($63,000), law clerks ($50,000) and paralegals ($50,000).[67]

Legal Practice Areas

Private Practice

Attorneys in private practice work solo or in law firms of different sizes. Most solo practitioners and small firms, especially in rural areas, represent individual clients, often in criminal court or in civil cases involving domestic relations or personal injury claims, real estate transactions, drafting wills, or setting up estate plans. In contrast, attorneys working in large law firms (often referred to as "Big Law") tend to serve business clientele in tax, securities, acquisitions, franchise, antitrust, and commercial transactions. A majority of attorneys in large law firms specialize in areas linked to corporate business practice. The organizational structure of law firms and their underlying operational norms within the context of law school training or recruitment and the business of legal practice has evolved over time, and how law firm practice—especially in large organizations—has changed shapes recruitment and professional advancement incentives in a competitive domestic and globalized legal marketplace.[68]

In this light, the legal profession is highly stratified in what some scholars call the two "hemispheres." On the one hand, lawyer elites produced from the best law schools practice law for the affluent or political elites (large organizations, corporations, labor unions, and government). On the other hand, graduates from lesser-known law schools take care of small businesses and individuals. In 2005, a majority of top-ten law schools placed over half of their graduates into the biggest 250 law firms, whereas law schools ranking after the top quartile placed a mere 20 percent. According to some estimates, almost 55 percent of 2017 graduates from the top twenty law schools were given jobs in large law firms. Regardless, the type of employment secured by law graduates has been affected by the globalization and its corresponding competitive pressures that, some say, continuously transforms corporate legal practice.[69]

In this respect, the growth of Big Law has altered the scope and operation of traditional law firm practice. Under the Cravath model, law firms are structured as a partnership of senior lawyers. Associate attorneys are salaried employees who do not take part in ownership decisions and do not share in a firm's profits; however, under a so-called "lockstep" model of compensation, with good performance, associates graduating from the same class often receive the same compensation, with annual pay raises and bonuses, based on earned seniority.

While some law firms use the lockstep method to compensate partners, increased economic pressures has led to a growing trend to reward performance based on "merit." The distinction between using the lockstep method or merit-based calculations to compensating attorneys is significant: whereas the lockstep method signals that the firm is committed to maintaining norms of professional collegiality and high-quality work without an undue focus on the financial bottom-line, individual merit-based compensation schemes puts more intense pressure on associates and partners to generate revenue and firm profitability in a hyper-competitive legal market.[70]

The structural organization of law firms and their operations thus increasingly dictate the terms of law firm economics and culture and, ultimately, the pathways for professional advancement. In the mid-twentieth century, large firms (consisting of fifty or more lawyers) and many medium- to large-sized law firms were relatively similar in operation. Associates that performed well advanced to partner, while less successful ones left the firm and were replaced by new elite recruits. Associate attorneys thus had a stake in firm's overall financial well-being and professional reputation because both directly affected if they would be promoted to partner and begin to share in the firm's profits, typically within a five to nine year period. For this reason, there was little lateral movement in the legal profession because most partners and many associates stayed with the same firm for years. As Joseph Hinsey, a former partner for twenty years at New York City's White & Case, remarked, "Moving from Firm A to Firm B, and taking a client group, was basically unheard of, at least in New York."[71]

Due to increasing economic demands which were exacerbated by the 2008 recession, the traditional way of doing things began to yield to the workplace reality that associate attorneys had to work longer hours, and fewer became partners as the competition for legal services grew among law firms. Another development is that some of the top law firms began to not hire the best students from the most prestigious law schools for cost reasons, thus making it difficult to recruit or retain them—once a hallmark of the "historic 'Cravath model.' "[72] Moreover, the changes and incentives linked to professional advancement are closely tied to how clients are billed for legal services—which, in turn, facilitate or diminish the economic health of a law firm and regardless intensifies the need to become more entrepreneurial and fiscally responsible in generating law firm profits.

Notably, the introduction of the "billable hour" in the late 1950s was an early sign that legal practice was destined to become more entrepreneurial. As law became more voluminous, complex and globalized, lawyers found creative ways to market their increasingly specialized skills, especially after the Supreme Court struck down restrictions on legal advertising in the 1970s.[73] Corporate clients also have increasingly turned to cheaper, in-house counsel, and that has led to an aggressive, "eat what you kill" revenue-producing system of legal practice.[74] Loyalty to the firm gave way to longer partnership tracks and more lateral moves within the profession. These trends were reinforced by the introduction of "up-or-out" promotion policies for associates—that is, associates advance to partnerships only if they develop a productive client base—and even partners who do not meet revenue-producing expectations now may be "de-equitized," creating a two-tier senior management.[75]

The emergence of such two-tier structured law firms reduces the role that seniority plays as a traditional metric in determining who will become a profit-sharing partner in a firm. Instead, equity partnership status can only be achieved by remaining productive and bringing in clients; and, law firms could not afford to lose productive partners in equity status because they might leave the firm and take their list of clients (or, "book of business") with them. Moreover, unlike the traditional Cravath model, the two-tier law firm model altered the rules for individual professional success. Only associate attorneys that are good at generating firm revenue ("rainmakers") are put into a partnership-track, whereas other associates are relegated into a non-partnership track. Consequently, the two-tier model that is increasingly prevalent among Big Law firms is very different than the traditional Cravath organizational structure, which basically separates partners from associates that can only become partners if they are loyal to the firm, worked there a long time, and clearly demonstrated a commitment to hard work by stock-piling large volumes of billable hours. In contrast, under the two-tier partnership-track model of law firm practice, promotion to equity status is possible, but highly uncertain because associates must constantly prove their worth by bringing money into the firm. Those that cannot meet these standards become long-term non-equity partners or non-partnership track associates; and, below them in pay and status, are "of counsel" (typically, retired) attorneys, staff attorneys, and contract attorneys, among others.[76]

Some legal scholars characterize the organizational transformation of Big Law's practice through a "tournament" metaphor. Whereas the traditional law firm "tournament" model motivates associates to achieve partnership status after a successful probationary period within the firm, Big Law practice has morphed into an "elastic" tournament that consists of "a firm in which a core of owner-partners is surrounded by a much larger mantle of employed lawyers that includes not only ambitious associates, but also non-equity partners, permanent associates, of-counsel and de-equitized former partners." In the elastic tournament format, the rewards that used to be linked to promotional advancement and sharing in firm profits are contingent and may never be realized (or taken away) over the span of an attorney's career because there is an ever-present risk of being de-equitized, or being forced to retirement status, if the governing metrics underlying law firm revenue and profits are not met. Within this model, there is also a lower tier of subordinate attorneys, permanent associates, career or staff lawyers that may enjoy the benefits of having long-term job security (and receive promotions or other perks); and, contract attorneys, which are typically hired on a short-term basis and paid by the hour, thus leading some critics to classify them as "second-class" attorneys.[77]

Accordingly, unlike the lifetime security that once defined large law firm practice, a "new disloyalty" has become an enduring trait of contemporary law practice, especially in elite, large corporate Big Law firms. As political scientist Herbert Kritzer observed, "corporate legal practice has become a world of change and turmoil," with firms regularly losing partners, dissolving, or merging.[78] According to recent estimates, only about one-third of associates in their sixth year at a law firm worked at firms that they were hired from after graduating from law school. The expectations surrounding professional advancement often prove to be too much, as associates are told to generate anywhere between 1,800 and 2,300 billable hours per year. As a result, for many young attorneys achieving partnership is more of a pipe dream simply because working sixty-five to seventy hours a week in an effort to record in excess of two thousand hours of billable time annually is like "drinking water from a fire hose" and professionally unsatisfying and not simply worth it.[79]

Economic competitive pressures has led to two other interrelated developments in private law practice: (1) the growing tendency of corporate law firms to downsize their operations by laying off personnel, cutting back or freezing salaries, and moving to "flat-fee" billing methods (instead of relying on billable hours) or using contract lawyers or nonlawyer staff, like paralegals and interns[80]; and, (2) an explosion in the number of large law firms that are as complex as the corporate giants they service. By the 1990s, there were close to 300 large firms with 50 lawyers, plus nearly 250 other firms with over 100 or more attorneys. By 2001, the average size of the *American Lawyer* top hundred law firms was 621 lawyers.[81] One study found that 28 percent of lawyers who graduated in 2000 were working in large corporate firms with 100 or more lawyers, and 20 percent in firms with 251 or more lawyers.[82] The competition to secure the best legal talent has meant that the demographics and organizational culture of large corporate law firms is in constant flux. Some large, elite corporate law firms are no longer relying on hiring exclusively from top-tier schools, and the lack of job security or chance for professional advancement has led to more lateral movement of associates seeking better employment opportunities in light of a shifting client base that is no longer loyal to one firm.[83]

Today, one-stop, full-service global mega-firms with thousands of lawyers in numerous branch offices domestically and abroad are prevalent in the legal landscape. In 2010, the top seventeen law firms had over $1 billion in revenue. In 2017, the profits per equity partner (PEP) averaged 1.7 million dollars among Global100 law firms; and, in the top fifteen, an average of 3 to 5 million or more was allocated as PEP.[84] Chicago's Baker & McKenzie, for example, is one of the nation's largest global mega-firms. It generates nearly 3 billion in global revenues from seventy-seven offices in over forty-six countries. The firm maintains a press office and separate marketing and recruitment departments, as well as sixteen different legal practice areas staffed by hundreds of attorneys. Baker & McKenzie, along with other megafirms, typically handle a variety of corporate practice areas, such as "M & A" (mergers and acquisitions) work, corporate finance, tax, securities, environmental, employment, or antitrust law matters.[85]

A sample of some of the top mega-firms in the United States are summarized in Table 5.4.

| Table 5.4 | Mega-Firms in the United States & Abroad | | | | |
Offices & Revenue	Practice Areas	Attorneys	Equity and Non-Equity Partners	Profits Per Equity Partner	Associates/ Starting Salaries
DLA Piper • 94 Offices • 2.8 Trillion	• Corporate • Finance • Global Regulatory	3,702	401/845	$1,874,000	• 2,258 • $190,000
Hogan Lovells • 50 Offices • 2.1 Trillion	• Corporate • Finance • Global Regulatory	2,636	523/280	$1,381,000	• 1,833 • $190,000
Jones Day • 41 Offices • 2.0 Trillion	• Litigation • Labor & Employment	2,518	919/0	$1,093,000	• 1,301 • $180,000
Norton Rose Fulbright • 54 Offices • 1.9 Trillion	• Global Regulatory • Corporate • Finance	3,376	681/485	$907,000	• 2,145 • $190,000
Baker Botts • 14 Offices • 6.7 Million	• Corporate • Finance • Litigation	708	190/90	$1,662,000	• 367 • $190,000

Sources: Ben Seal, "The 2019 Am Law 100: Gross Revenue," Law.com/The American Lawyer (April 23, 2019), available at https://www.law.com/americanlawyer/2019/04/23/the-2019-am-law-100-gross-revenue/ (last retrieved April 17, 2020); Vault, "2020 Vault Law 100," available at https://www.vault.com/best-companies-to-work-for/law/top-100-law-firms-rankings (last accessed April 17, 2020).

Government Attorneys

In contrast to private practice, government attorneys work for and represent local, state, or federal government. Their function varies: they could be prosecutors, public defenders, legislative staff, or agency employees. At bottom, they are civil servants who, as Justice Stephen Breyer once observed, perform public service as "citizen-statesmen." Even so, Justice Breyer has lamented that a decreasing percentage of law graduates were interested in public service, in part because government jobs do not pay as well as the private sector. Yet, in his view, working as a government attorney provides valuable professional experience that may ultimately be used to obtain higher-paying jobs in private law practice. The path for his own success, he recounted, was first paved as a staff member of the Senate Subcommittee on Administrative Practice and Procedure. As Justice Breyer pointed out, many law graduates of his generation also began their career in government service. Most significantly, he concluded, the professional satisfaction derived as a public servant may substantially outweigh the benefits of earning higher salaries.[86]

Approximately thirty-six thousand attorneys work in federal agencies. Roughly 27 percent are employed in the Department of Justice; 15 percent are in Treasury, Homeland Security, and Army; and the balance is spread across as many as fourteen other agencies.[87] Regardless of their role in the agency they work for, governmental service is usually a stepping-stone for other legal career paths that might be more prestigious or profitable. As law professor Thomas O. McGarity explains,

> Government attorneys must live with the reality of very limited resources and maximize the attendant benefits. On the one hand, the offices will not be as large, the secretaries will not be as adept, the computers will not work as well, and the pay will not be as high as in private law firms. On the other hand, the fact of limited resources means that young government lawyers are given far more responsibility than their counterparts in private law firms, and they have a correspondingly greater opportunity to gain valuable professional experience at an early stage of their careers.[88]

Not surprisingly, then, one study found that between 2000 and 2007 almost 5 percent of lawyers left the state or federal government and joined other organizations, a trend that is becoming increasingly prevalent as attorneys decide to make lateral moves to private law firms. Moreover, working as a law clerk in public service, which is typically a short-term position, may offer the chance to make a lateral move to a Big Law corporate firm or getting an academic job as a law professor.[89]

Business and Industry Law Practice: The Role of In-House Counsel

A significant proportion of lawyers work in corporate law. Moreover, large Fortune 500 corporations—including Walmart, Exxon Mobil, Chevron, Apple, General Motors, General Electric, AT&T, Verizon Communications, JPMorgan Chase & Company, and others—have their own legal departments with "in-house" counsel. Corporate practice in highly diversified corporations, however, increasingly relies upon in-house counsel to cut costs.[90]

Smaller businesses, but even some corporations with their own legal departments, are likely to farm out specialized matters or other cases that involve major litigation. According to one survey, about 40 percent of a corporation's average legal budget (of $1.2 million, in 2001) was spent on outside fees.[91] The economic pressures and the uncertainty brought on by the 2008 financial crisis, however, reinforced the use of in-house counsel in an effort to cut legal costs. Accordingly, budgets for in-house counsel have increased by 18 percent with corporations sharply reducing the use of outside counsel in tax, merger, and acquisitions cases.[92] Still, there are an estimated sixty-five thousand in-house counsel working in more than twenty-one thousand for-profit and not-for-profit U.S. business organizations, and many of them are highly compensated. Estimates vary on in-house counsel salaries, but Robert Half Legal, an annual source of lawyer compensation data, reports that they range from $87,000 to $269,000, depending upon the lawyer's length of professional experience. Another survey reports that the base pay for general counsel can be over $600,000 and that total compensation packages, which include bonuses, stock options, and other perks, equal a million dollars or more.[93]

Public Interest Lawyers and Legal Academia

A small percentage of attorneys are policy advocates for a variety of private concerns and public-interest law firms. In general, public interest law organizations (PILOs) provide legal services to those who cannot afford private counsel. PILO lawyers might provide legal aid to the community, or sometimes their work is directed at producing public policy reform. Some devote their professional lives to the pursuit of discrete social political or moral objectives, such as legalizing same-sex marriage, protecting consumers, or restricting abortion rights.[94]

Those contemplating a career in public interest law, however, are often discouraged from doing so because of low salaries and high student loan debt. A study commissioned by the Illinois State Bar Association reported that annual salaries at several public interest organizations ranged from $39,000 to $46,000 per year, causing most graduates to avoid entering into public service or leaving it only after a few years. While the empirical research is not conclusive, some studies find that about 65 percent of law graduates avoid public service.[95] In response, a growing number of law schools offer loan forgiveness or debt reduction programs to entice their graduates to enter public service careers.[96]

Likewise, only a small percentage of law graduates become law professors or take administrative positions as career advisors, admissions personnel, or university counsel. Roughly 1,000 applicants seek for tenure-track law professor positions in the U.S. every year through a formal recruitment process managed by the American Association of Law Schools or by direct application to law schools. Many law professors increasingly have an advanced degree (a masters or a doctorate) in another discipline, or a higher level degree in law, such as an L.L.M. (a one year graduate degree that is earned after the three-year law degree). As in many facets of the legal profession, the competition to be hired as a law professor is especially keen, and some empirical studies report that only one in seven applicants are offered tenure-track positions among ABA-accredited law schools in the U.S.[97]

Today, there are approximately eleven thousand law faculty in ABA-approved law schools. As legal scholar Richard Abel points out, many law professors describe themselves as teachers instead of scholars and devote much of their time to classroom activities instead of publishing articles and books. Whether more time is spent in the classroom or publishing research remains debatable, however. Still, many professors enjoy their autonomy and job security, and those benefits tend to outweigh the prospect that practicing law in the private sector might yield greater incomes. In other words, law professors are endowed with professional independence and are well-compensated. Some surveys, in fact, indicate that law faculty earned $100,000 or more per year at the pre-tenure assistant or associate rank level, excluding three to twenty-five thousand dollars in compensation as a summer research stipends for research and other scholarly activities. Tenured associate or full professors earn even more, with a large proportion paid in the $150,000 to $195,000 range.[98]

Alternative Legal Careers

The realities of law practice in the twenty-first century are greatly influenced by a volatile legal marketplace that is affected by increasing competition and evolving Internet or digital technologies. For some legal scholars, the legal profession and law schools must recognize the emergence of a new "post-professional" era that encourages specialized non-lawyers to do the work traditionally assigned to licensed legal professionals. The post-professional era features a growing number of "law workers," or "all individuals who deliver services of a legal nature," such as tax preparation, tax law consulting, workers' compensation, or legal document preparation; or, in the advocacy realm, legal assistants, paralegals, and alternative dispute resolution mediators that are independent in performing their jobs but most likely to require licensed attorney supervision. Similarly, other positions may be in information technology employment where lawyers may become legal information engineers, legal consultants, or legal processors.[99]

In this light, critics argue that legal education must be reformed to teach lawyers "practice-ready" skills, especially in the third year of law school. Also, by their acknowledgment and promotion of "JD Advantaged" jobs, or employment that allows law graduates to get positions that do not require bar passage and can make good use of what a law degree has to offer (discussed earlier in this chapter), the American Bar Association and other legal institutional stakeholders have begun to realize that job-seekers (whether they pass the bar or not) need more flexibility to apply their legal talents and law skills in an alternative, or non-legal setting. Such opportunities permit graduates or licensed lawyers to work in the nonprofit and education sectors, the federal or state government, or in the real estate or financial markets as realtors or investment bankers. Accordingly, there is growing evidence that the number of recent law graduates opt to go into business or industry careers, especially after the 1990s. A discernible trend is that J.D. holders are taking positions as corporate contracts administrators, alternative dispute resolution specialists, government regulatory analysts, FBI agents, accountants, human resource or personnel employees, legal consultants, legal compliance specialists, educational admissions or career services officers, and employees working in law firm professional development, among others.[100]

ACCESS TO LAWYERS AND EQUAL JUSTICE

"Our system of justice is adversarial," Justice Harry Blackmun once said, "and depends for its legitimacy on the fair and adequate representation of all parties at all levels of the judicial process."[101] Justice Blackmun's vision of equal justice, however, has never been fully realized. Historically, common law rules allowed lawyers to represent misdemeanor offenders, but barred them from defending clients charged with felonies. Although most states and the federal government broke from that practice, it was also widely understood that the right to counsel extended only to those who could afford it. Though the Supreme Court now requires counsel for indigents in most criminal cases, some critics today still maintain that it remains a "shameful irony that the country with the world's most lawyers has one of the least adequate systems for legal assistance."[102]

The Right to Counsel in Criminal Cases

The Sixth Amendment to the Constitution provides that "in all criminal prosecutions, the accused shall. . .have the assistance of counsel for his defense." It was not until 1932 that the Supreme Court took the initial step of requiring the appointment of counsel for indigent defendants in death penalty cases. In *Powell v. Alabama* (1932), an all-white jury in Scottsboro, Alabama, convicted several young black men without the assistance of counsel of raping a white woman, an offense carrying the death penalty. In reversing their convictions, Justice George Sutherland held that the Fourteenth Amendment's due process clause required the appointment of counsel in such circumstances in order to preserve the defendants' right to a fair trial. Yet, the Court's holding was narrowly tailored to the facts of the case, as Justice Sutherland explained:

> All that it is necessary now to decide, as we do decide, is that in a capital case, where the defendant is unable to employ counsel, and is incapable adequately of making his own defense because of ignorance, feeble mindedness, illiteracy, or the like, it is the duty of the court, whether requested or not, to assign counsel for him as a necessary requisite of due process of law.[103]

Powell, thus, did not require state courts to appoint counsel for indigent defendants in all cases. Then, in *Johnson v. Zerbst* (1938), the Court extended the right to appointed counsel for indigent defendants in federal criminal cases. However, in *Betts v. Brady* (1942), the Court retreated and ruled that in state courts counsel was required in capital cases or cases presenting "special circumstances." *Betts* prompted a sharp attack from dissenting Justice Hugo Black, who argued that depriving counsel for the poor "defeat[s] the promise of our democratic society [of] providing equal justice under the law" and threatened "innocent men [with] increased dangers of conviction merely because of their poverty."[104]

The fuzzy line the Court drew in these cases remained until the landmark decision in *Gideon v. Wainwright* (1963).[105] In *Gideon*, the Warren Court reversed Clarence Gideon's state felony conviction for breaking into a pool hall because he had requested but was denied the appointment of an attorney to represent him. Writing for a unanimous court, Justice Black overruled *Betts v. Brady* and its so-called "special circumstances" rule, observing that "any person haled into court, who is too poor to hire a lawyer, cannot be assured a fair trial unless counsel is provided for him." He concluded that "government hires lawyers to prosecute, and defendants who have the money to hire lawyers to defend are the strongest indications of the widespread belief that lawyers in criminal courts are necessities, not luxuries." *Gideon* forced the states to recognize that the Fourteenth Amendment's due process clause establishes a constitutional obligation to provide indigents with appointed counsel in felony cases.

Subsequent cases expanded *Gideon*'s ruling to indigent defendants' right to appointed counsel to all types of offenses (petty, misdemeanor, and felony) that risk incarceration. Moreover, the right has been judicially extended to most stages of the adversarial criminal process, ranging from arrest, to preindictment preliminary hearings, arraignments, and post-sentencing proceedings, among others.[106] Although the conservative Burger and Rehnquist Courts substantially cut back on the scope of the right to appointed counsel in a number of post-*Gideon* cases,[107] the basic holding and mandate for legal counsel in *Gideon* has not been overturned.

In light of the *Gideon* mandate, the federal and state governments have a variety of programs and funding systems to provide indigents with legal services. In roughly thirty states, the state entirely funds and operates indigent defense systems. In all but one of the remaining states, the state and county share the cost for systems administered by the state in different proportions. In Pennsylvania, each county funds and locally administers indigent defense services. Among the state-administered systems, public defender programs, assigned counsel appointments, or competitive private contracts are the most common. Using these systems, almost 2.7 million cases are handled by public defenders in primarily non-felony and misdemeanor cases. In **public defender programs**, legal aid is given to criminal defendants by full- or part-time salaried government employees; or, they work through public or private nonprofit organizations. Typically, the program provides counsel in a centralized office that has some additional support staff, such as investigators or paralegals. In **assigned counsel systems**, judges appoint individual attorneys or law firms to deliver legal aid on an *ad hoc*, case-by-case basis. These attorneys are either paid by the case or by the hour. In jurisdictions with **competitive private contract systems**, individual attorneys, bar associations, law firms, and nonprofit organizations contract with the government to provide legal services. Oftentimes, the contract is on a year-to-year basis, and it can be awarded after a bidding process. Regardless of the system used, many state-administered indigent defender services are beset by chronic problems of large caseloads and a lack of adequate funding which, in turn, lead to issues of poor representation, access of justice and even rising incarceration rates. Whereas one study from the Bureau of Justice Statistics found that an estimated 66 percent of federal felony defendants and 82 percent of felony defendants in large state courts were represented by public defenders or assigned counsel, a report from the Justice Policy Institute determined that far more taxpayer money is spent on providing police protection and corrections rather than indigent defense; and, such "under-resourcing"—which is characterized by little access to money, time, investigators, training, independence and oversight—undermines even the best intentions to provide a meaningful and quality legal defense for most indigents.[108]

The Criminal Justice Act of 1964 controls legal services for indigents in federal courts. Counsel are assigned from panels of attorneys chosen from a list of lawyers on an *ad hoc* basis, federal defender organizations (staffed with salaried government employees and led by a public defender selected by the court of appeals), or community defender organizations (state-incorporated, nonprofit legal services). In contrast state public defense systems, several studies report that the quality of the defense bar is superior because its attorneys are well-qualified and better-trained at the federal level, in large part because of better funding. One leading federal appeals court judge, in fact, described the federal public defender system as "obviously" constitut[ing] the gold standard" vis a vis state indigent representation systems.[109]

Although federal and state governments spend an estimated $3.3 billion annually on legal services for the poor, critics lament how justice, especially at the state level, is administered—it is degraded by crushing caseloads, insufficient staffing, inadequate budgetary funding, mismanagement, and attorney incompetence or indifference (caused by low compensation)—so they argue that the criminal justice system is essentially broken and in need of significant reform.[110] In response, progressive interest groups, such the American Civil Liberties Union and its Criminal Law Reform Project, have resorted to litigation in several jurisdiction to compel states to fund the *Gideon* mandate and indigent defense. Also, some courts have taken the lead in amending their procedures to improve indigent defense. In *Wilbur v. City of Mount Vernon* (2013), a district court in Washington ruled that excessive caseloads systemically deprived defendants of their constitutional rights at critical stages of the prosecution. The judge ordered that attorneys in future cases must certify that they are competent to handle their cases and, most importantly, limit their annual caseload. *Wilbur* is also noteworthy because it led to the Department of Justice's launching its own reform initiative—the so-called Access to Justice Initiative (AJI) program—that encouraged states to undertake similar remedial action with federal grant dollars. Although the AJI has since been ended by the Trump Administration,[111] it cast a wide net in creating initiatives that encompassed "the Department of Justice, . . . federal agencies, and . . . state, local, and tribal justice system stakeholders" in an effort "to increase access to counsel and legal assistance and to improve the justice delivery systems that serve people who are unable to afford lawyers."[112]

Other inequities favoring the rich and discriminate against indigents further inhibit access to courts. Representation of indigents is qualitatively different than for those who can afford to hire counsel. These institutional conditions result in more plea bargains, less attorney contact, and more guilty pleas (see Table 5.5 and "Contemporary Controversies over Courts: Plea Bargaining, the Right to Counsel, and Global Trends" in Chapter Seven). The lack of financial resources for criminal defendants is problematic as well because in increasingly tight budgetary times states often resort to imposing a wide range of court fees, costs, and fines against those caught up in the criminal justice system. Such cost recovery, or "pay as you go" systems, can even require indigent defendants to pay for the cost of applying for a public defender (See in this chapter "Contemporary Controversies over Courts: The Right to Counsel and 'Pay-as-You-Go' Justice"). Moreover, as the next section discusses, the same kind of problems also affect the delivery of legal aid to indigents in civil cases.

Table 5.5	Salient Differences in Legal Representation in Indigent Criminal Cases			
	State Defendants		**Federal Defendants**	
Institutional and Legal Representation Characteristics	**Public Defender**	**Private Counsel**	**Public Defender**	**Private Counsel**
Total Number of Inmates	10,254	3,469	2,426	1,118
Contact with counsel				
Within twenty-four hours of arrest	7.0%	23.6%	18.2%	39.1%
Within week of arrest	25.1%	33.1%	31.4%	30.9%
More than week before trial	30.6%	28.5%	31.1%	21.2%
Within week of trial	15.2%	7.5%	9.9%	3.8%
At trial	15.3%	4.1%	5.0%	2.0%
Did not talk with counsel	4.6%	1.5%	1.4%	1.3%
Number of times talked with counsel				
0–1	28.6%	10.8%	11.5%	7.3%
2–5	55.4%	47.5%	60.4%	45.0%
6 or more times	12.1%	33.7%	21.2%	40.0%
Case disposition				
Not guilty plea	20.9%	24.8%	18.8%	21.7%
Bench trial	6.0%	7.6%	3.3%	4.0%
Jury trial	14.8%	17.1%	15.4%	17.2%
Guilty or no contest plea with plea bargain	49.2%	47.5%	46.9%	48.0%
Guilty or no contest plea without plea bargain	21.9%	19.3%	29.6%	25.9%

Source: U.S. Department of Justice: Bureau of Justice Statistics, "Survey of Inmates in State and Federal Correctional Facilities, 2004," ICPSR04572-v1 (Ann Arbor, MI: Inter-university Consortium for Political and Social Research [distributor]), available at https://www.icpsr.umich.edu/icpsrweb/NACJD/studies/4572 (last retrieved April 17, 2020).

Legal Representation in Civil Litigation

Roughly less than 1 percent of spending on legal services is devoted to civil legal aid. Consequently, a majority of legal needs of civil indigents remains unmet. In a speech delivered to the National Legal Center for the Public Interest, Justice Stephen Breyer estimated that 80 percent of low-income clients actually receive civil legal assistance, and that the United States government only spends about $2 per person in providing it, a figure that is far less than in comparable Western democracies. Another study reported that although the legal profession generates approximately $100 billion annually, less than $1 billion goes to low-income citizens. Other studies report that four of five indigents go unrepresented in the civil justice system.[113]

Unlike criminal prosecutions, receiving legal aid or counsel in a civil case is not a constitutional right. Although *Boddie v. Connecticut* (1971) held that welfare recipients had a due process right to maintain divorce proceedings in state court if they could not pay the filing fee, the ruling was limited to its facts. Thus, a broad right of access for all civil cases was not established. Subsequent cases, such as *United States v. Kras* (1973), held that there is no constitutional right to obtain a discharge of one's debts in bankruptcy even if the debtors could not afford to pay filing fees. In addition, an indigent parent was denied appointed counsel in a termination of parental rights lawsuit in *Lassiter v. Department of Social Services* (1981). But, in *M. L. B. v. S. L. J.* (1996), an indigent whose parental rights were terminated was permitted to obtain a free transcript for the purpose of filing an appeal. In addition, though reaffirming that there is no constitutional right to counsel in civil cases, in *Turner v. Rogers* (2011) the Court ruled that an indigent father's procedural rights of due process were violated after he was denied appointed counsel and was incarcerated for failing to pay thousands of dollars in past child support.[114]

Consequently, in most civil cases, clients must pay lawyers a fee plus expenses. In personal injury lawsuits, however, clients may hire lawyers on the basis of a **contingency fee**—agreements stipulating that legal fees are only paid as a percentage of the total amount of monetary damages recovered. Although clients remain responsible for litigation expenses, contingency fees facilitate access to attorneys because clients do not have to pay legal fees unless there is a successful conclusion. Alternatively, prepaid legal services may be available as part of an employee's insurance benefits by paying premiums to a group insurance plan, but such plans are not widespread, largely because of resistance from the organized bar.[115]

Contemporary Controversies over Courts: The Right to Counsel and "Pay-as-You-Go" Justice

In *Argersinger v. Hamlin*, 407 U.S. 25 (1972), in extending the right to court-appointed counsel to misdemeanor offenses carrying a six-month sentence of imprisonment, Justice Lewis Powell warned: "No one can foresee the consequences of such a drastic enlargement of the constitutional right to free counsel" by expanding the right too far. As Justice Powell predicted, Court decisions applying the right to appointed counsel to juveniles, as well as for cases involving misdemeanor offenses and suspended sentences, have severely strained the ability of state governments to supply court-appointed counsel for criminal defendants. The problem is aggravated by the reluctance of law schools to train students to become attorneys for indigents, budgetary constraints, and state legislation that incarcerates convicted defendants for longer time periods using mandatory sentencing.

All but a few states have enacted cost recovery systems that require state governments to be reimbursed for the cost of providing legal representation in criminal cases. There are two basic cost-saving strategies, recoupment and contribution. Each has the effect of shifting the financial burden of indigent defense to the accused. *Recoupment systems* require indigents to pay the actual cost of attorney's fees, and sometimes other investigative and expert service expenses. Recoupment orders are issued at the end of a case and levy a fee for representation, which requires state or county governments to collect it after legal services have been delivered. Some jurisdictions require recoupment only from those convicted, but others require it even from defendants who are acquitted. In contrast, contribution systems are fixed sums charged against indigents at the time counsel is appointed, an attribute that makes them akin to a precondition to getting legal aid. Contribution fees are routinely levied at the front end of a case, which usually (but not always) eliminates the need for a judicial hearing to assess the ability to pay, or to collect it after legal services are delivered. Approximately thirty jurisdictions use them.

Cost recovery systems have been criticized as unjust because they promote a "pay-as-you-go" criminal justice system that turns convictions into moneymaking enterprises for courts. Their impact is wide-ranging, especially on low-level offenders convicted of misdemeanor offenses, like most drug cases. The effect is intensified when combined with so-called "user fees" on defendants that require prisoners to repay the costs of incarceration. The table below illustrates some of Ohio's cost, fee, and surcharge structure under statutory law. As a result, high debts accrued in the criminal justice system often impede successful "reentry" into the community once sentences are served.

Predictably, these laws have been challenged as equal protection and due process violations that discriminate against indigents. A study from the National Juvenile Defender Center argues, for example, that while 40 percent of all states charge a probation "supervision fee" to children in the juvenile court system, only one jurisdiction holds an ability-to-pay hearing (which occurs without a right to counsel). For juvenile defender advocates, the lack of meaningful protections afforded to juveniles has the effect of punishing a child for simply being poor and therefore violates basic constitutional principles of due process and fair play. Another set of objections claims that recoupment practices are not cost-effective—that they remain punitive and lead to the creation of "debtor's prisons." Still, for the most part, the challenges have been turned back by the Supreme Court, in cases such as *Fuller v. Oregon*, 417 U.S. 40, 53–54 (1974), which held that recovering costs from indigent defendants is constitutional so long as it does not result in a "manifest hardship."

Ohio's Fees, Fines, and Surcharges

Statute	Description	Financial Obligation	Amount
Ohio Rev. Code § 120.36(A)(1)	Application fee for public defender	Fee	$25
Ohio Rev. Code § 1907.24(B)(1)	Fee for special projects if related to efficient operation of court	Fee	Actual costs
Ohio Rev. Code § 2303.20(E)	Clerk fee for calling jury	Fee	$25
Ohio Rev. Code § 2947.23(A)(1)(a)	Costs of prosecution to be included at sentencing in criminal cases	Fee	Actual costs
Ohio Rev. Code § 311.172(A)	Registration fee for sex offenders	Fee	$100

Ohio Rev. Code § 2929.28(D)	Stalking and domestic violence misdemeanors	Fine	$70–$500
Ohio Rev. Code § 2929.18(B)(10)	Financial sanctions for death of police horse of dog	Fine	$0–$10,000
Ohio Rev. Code § 2949.091(A)(1)(a)(ii)	Misdemeanor fee for violations other than moving violations	Fine	$20
Ohio Rev. Code § 4510.111	Misdemeanor driving under suspension	Fine	$0–$1,000
Ohio Rev. Code § 2152.20(A)(1)(k)	Fines, costs, restitution, forfeiture for delinquent or juvenile traffic offenders	Surcharge	$0–$2,000

Sources: Criminal Justice Policy Program at Harvard Law School, "50-State Criminal Justice Debt Reform Builder," available at https://cjdebtreform.org/ (last retrieved April 17, 2020); Mary Ann Scali and Hellela Simpson, "The Problem of Making Children Pay for Probation Supervision." In *2017 Trends in State Courts: Fees, Fines and Bail Practices,* edited by Deborah W. Smith (Williamsburg, VA.: National Center for State Courts, 2017), 55–58; National Association for Criminal Defense Lawyers, "Minor Crimes, Massive Waste: The Terrible Toll of America's Broken Misdemeanor Courts," (2009), available at https://www.nacdl.org/Document/MinorCrimesMassiveWasteTollof MisdemeanorCourts (last retrieved April 17, 2020); Travis Stearns, "Legal Financial Obligations: Fulfilling the Promise of Gideon by Reducing the Burden," *Seattle Journal for Social Justice* 11 (2013), 963–85; Ronald F. Wright and Wayne A. Logan, "The Political Economy of Application Fees for Indigent Criminal Defense," *William and Mary Law Review* 47 (2006), 2045–87.

Government-Subsidized Legal Aid

Legal assistance for low-income civil litigants remains available through federal and state government subsidies. As an outgrowth of President Lyndon B. Johnson's Great Society program and War on Poverty, in 1964 Congress created the federally funded Office of Economic Opportunity Legal Services Program (LSP). Designed to fight poverty by asserting federal control over local legal aid efforts, LSP attorneys made significant inroads in protecting the due process rights of welfare recipients from the denial of benefits. Still, the LSP encountered strident political opposition, especially from established business interests, and, consequently, in 1974, the LSP was removed from the executive branch and replaced by the Legal Services Corporation (LSC), an independent nonprofit corporation. The LSC continued the mission of providing legal services to the poor through federally funded grants.[116]

In the 1980s, the Reagan administration tried unsuccessfully to end the LSC program, but severely cut the LSC's funding and enacted a number of restrictions on the types of cases handled. By 1996, LSC's funding was cut by one-third, and LSC-funded organizations in the states were barred from participating in school desegregation cases, labor boycotts, class actions, and, among other controversial areas, cases involving abortion. In *Legal Services Corporation v. Velazquez* (2001), however, the Court ruled that the First Amendment prevented Congress from cutting funds to legal aid organizations representing indigent clients challenging welfare laws because it had a chilling effect on the free speech rights of their clients. In addition, *Brown v. Legal Foundation of Washington* (2002) upheld the constitutionality of state Interest on Lawyers Trust Accounts (IOLTA), which generates funds for legal aid based on interest accrued in lawyers' trust accounts, thereby preserving a significant source of public interest organization funding.[117]

Ironically, the conservative opposition to such liberal public interest initiatives led in the 1990s and early 2000s to litigation that expanded religious freedom and free speech rights in public institutions, on the one hand, and on the other limited federal powers in discrimination and affirmative action cases.[118] In addition, a recent legal services report found that the demand for legal aid is still great: on average, only 86 percent of civil legal problems get inadequate or no legal assistance across the nation and many of these legal problems relate to basic issues of family, housing and income maintenance. In spite of these political challenges and growing fluctuations in the economy, government-subsidized legal aid programs continue to supply civil legal services through local grants provided by the federal Legal Services Corporation and IOLTA in all states plus the District of Columbia and the Virgin Islands.[119]

Pro Se Representation

An old adage is that a person who represents himself has a fool for a client. Nonetheless, one of the most important trends in civil justice is the increasing number of citizens representing themselves in court. Since the 1990s, all courts and bar associations have chronicled a sharp upturn in self-representation filings.

In state courts, they appear most often in divorce and child support cases, landlord-tenant disputes, probate, foreclosures, and small claims or other miscellaneous actions. In federal courts, statistics show that 26 percent of all district court civil cases are from **pro se** filers, with many involving bankruptcies. Moreover, *pro se* filings are not confined to the poor because they are distributed across a wide range of incomes and educational levels.[120]

A number of interrelated factors have led to more *pro se* litigants, including the lack of affordable legal counsel, the increased demand for legal aid by moderate- to low-income litigants, the lack of *pro bono* help from the legal profession (discussed in the next section), and the proliferation of "do it yourself" legal aids, as facilitated by the Internet and evolving court website technologies. Even though *Faretta v. California* (1972) held that the Sixth Amendment incorporates a right of self-representation, the organized bar has traditionally resisted assisting *pro se* litigants. Unlike many other nations, the legal profession outlaws legal aid from nonlawyers. That has allowed the bar to claim it is trying to protect the consumer from fraud and non-licensed incompetent practitioners. But cynics counter that the legal profession is simply trying to preserve its monopoly over the practice of law. Courts have also been slow in upgrading facilities and training staff to assist *pro se* litigants.[121]

Nevertheless, several entities, among them the American Bar Association, the State Justice Institute, the National Center for State Courts and other non-profit organizations or independent research centers such as the Self-Represented Litigation Network and the Institute for the Advancement of the American Legal System at the University of Denver, have all launched extensive public relations campaigns and websites to help *pro se* litigants.[122] The response by the states, though, remains uneven: whereas several states have comprehensive *pro se* programs, others have partially integrated programs, and still others are in the process of developing them. A relatively few states offer little or no *pro se* assistance. Still, depending upon the state, *pro se* litigants have been given access to self-help centers, court-sponsored legal information assistance, Internet technologies, workshops, mobile service centers, videoconferencing, law school clinics, library improvements, and Web-based technologies that are increasingly "user-friendly" and allow litigants to prepare or file legal documents, often in multiple languages. Moreover, some states have revised their rules for civil or ethical practice to permit "unbundling"—a form of quasi-legal representation that lets lawyers contract with clients to perform specific legal tasks for a reduced fee. Such services might include appearing in court on a limited basis, rendering advice on the telephone or the Internet, or assisting in document preparation.[123]

Pro Bono Legal Services

An alternative type of legal representation includes the volunteer efforts of the organized bar and individual attorneys. The need is great, and millions of people are without legal aid in tenant evictions, child support and mortgage foreclosure cases, among others. Accordingly, a "civil Gideon" reform movement emerged in recent years, claiming that representation in civil cases involving basic human rights—such as in domestic violence, foreclosure, mental health, loss of government benefits, and immigration asylum or detention litigation—require attorney representation for indigents on due process, equality and access to justice grounds.[124] Whereas performing legal work ***pro bono publico*** ("in the public good") or delivering "low bono" (reduced fee) service has long been considered a public responsibility of the legal profession, relying upon the cooperation of private lawyers to give away free legal services is impractical.[125] Moreover, under most rules of professional ethics, attorneys need only set an aspirational goal of completing fifty hours of *pro bono* work annually, but the states do not penalize lawyers or law firms for not doing so. Indeed, very few states require *pro bono* activity at all. A recent initiative, started under the leadership of then-Chief Judge Jonathan Lippman the New York bar, created a Pro Bono Scholars Program that allows third-year law students to sit for the bar exam early in return for providing fifty hours of *pro bono* service. Similar reform proposals call for the volume of pro bono service must be exchanged as a substitution or credit for attending required continuing legal education courses as an effort to incentivize lawyers to give legal help to those who need it for free.[126] In addition, some inroads have been made in institutionalizing *pro bono* practice into private practice. But such efforts remain uneven. While large firms may have the capacity to tailor *pro bono* activities around the professional needs of the firm, in small firms *pro bono* work is only minimal and often accidental.[127] As one law professor concluded, "The central dilemma of *pro bono* remains: [it is a] system that depends on private lawyers [that] is ultimately beholden to their interests."[128]

Chapter Summary

The role lawyers play in delivering legal services and providing access to courts for litigants is significant. While lawyers have never been popular, they are generally recognized as society's leaders. The growth of the legal profession has been a function of the way in which lawyers are trained and socialized into legal practice. At first, historically, lawyers learned law through apprenticeships, but modern legal education was transformed by law schools and the casebook method of instruction, first introduced by Christopher Columbus Langdell, dean of

Harvard Law School in the 1870s. The legal profession, then, evolved into a business, starting with large Wall Street firms that outpaced solo practitioners, and was introduced in major urban areas by attorney Paul Cravath in the early twentieth century.

Today, the legal profession is a multibillion-dollar industry. Admission into law school is highly selective, and the cost of attending is prohibitive for some. Rising tuition rates, burgeoning student loan debt, and the uncertainty of securing employment after graduation have recently made it difficult to enter the legal profession. Law schools are now oriented around learning legal doctrine and knowing how to "think like a lawyer." There is less emphasis on learning practical skills. After bar admission, law students enter into an increasingly diverse workforce. Still, substantial differences remain in terms of gender, race, and ethnicity, and the most prestigious, high-paying positions generally go to white males.

Most lawyers find employment in law firms, business and industry, government, and less frequently solo practices or academic careers. Trained as generalists, most attorneys now develop specialties throughout their career. The legal profession remains highly stratified, split between those who represent corporate interests and those for smaller businesses and private individuals. While the Wall Street law firm model persists, due to competitive pressures, associates are expected to churn out a high rate of billable hours, and lawyers may no longer expect lifetime security by gaining partnership status. Other trends include rewarding attorney performance based on merit and the institutionalization of the Big Law mega-firm, a phenomenon that has led to a reorganization of the traditional Cravath corporate law firm format into a two-tier partnership "elastic" model of Big Law organizational structure that increasingly strives for achieving more entrepreneurial and cost-cutting management solutions that deemphasize partnership seniority and loyalty to the collegial values of the law firm.

The constitutional right to an attorney only applies to a narrow class of criminal defendants and not in civil cases. Although federal and state governments spend billions of dollars on providing legal services to the poor, high caseloads, inadequate funding, attorney incompetence, and other factors negatively affect legal aid to indigents. While there is no constitutional right to an attorney in civil cases, some governments and the legal profession try to deliver legal services to needy or unrepresented clients through subsidized legal aid programs, and with *pro se* and *pro bono* initiatives.

Key Questions for Review and Critical Analysis

1. Do you think legal training is best accomplished by learning legal doctrine and how to "think like a lawyer" through a Socratic, case-dialogue method of instruction, or by an apprenticeship?

2. Given high tuition rates, increasing student loan debt, and the uncertainty of securing stable employment after graduation, is earning a law degree a sound "investment" in choosing a professional career?

3. For years, modern legal practice has been highly stratified in delivering legal services to big corporate interests as opposed to representing smaller businesses and private individuals. Is there any way for law schools or the legal profession to lessen the impact of stratification and to close the gap between who has legal representation and who does not?

4. How can budget-strapped state governments best fulfill the mandate of *Gideon v. Wainwright* (1963) to provide appointed counsel to indigent criminal defendants?

5. Should clients in civil litigation have the constitutional right to appointed counsel if they cannot afford to hire an attorney, especially in cases involving an alleged violation of basic human rights, such as a loss of housing in a landlord-tenant eviction case?

Web Links

1. Law School Admission Council (www.lsac.org)

    *   A comprehensive source of information on all facets of law school admission, including LSAT registration and administration, information about law schools, and resources for prelaw advisors.

2. American Bar Association (https://www.americanbar.org/about_the_aba/)

    *   A national organization of lawyers that provides a variety of informational resources that address all aspects of the legal profession, including legal education, judicial selection, and areas of legal practice.

3. Jurist (www.jurist.org)

    *   Managed by law professor Bernard Hibbitts at the University of Pittsburgh School of Law, the site provides legal news, legal commentary, and legal research.

4.   Above the Law (http://abovethelaw.com)

- The site fashions itself as a "behind-the-scenes" look at the legal world, offering news and perspectives about law firms, law schools, legal technology, and legal careers.

5.   Law Professor Blogs Network (www.lawprofessorblogs.com)

- A national network of over forty legal blogs edited by law professors that provides legal news, information, commentary, and legal analysis.

6.   Law School Transparency (https://www.lawschooltransparency.com/)

- A 501(c)(3) non-profit organization that engages in consumer advocacy and public education about the legal profession.

Selected Readings

Abel, Richard L. *American Lawyers*. New York: Oxford University Press, 1991.

Auerbach, Jerold S. *Unequal Justice: Lawyers and Social Change in Modern America*. New York: Oxford University Press, 1976.

Banks, Christopher P., *The American Legal Profession: The Myths and Realities of Practicing Law*. Thousand Oaks, CA.: Sage/CQ Press, 2017.

Barton, Benjamin H., *Glass Half Full: The Decline and Rebirth of the Legal Profession*. New York: Oxford University Press, 2015.

Galanter, Marc, and Thomas Palay. *Tournament of Lawyers: The Transformation of the Big Law Firm*. Chicago: University of Chicago Press, 1991.

Harper, Steven J. *The Lawyer Bubble: A Profession in Crisis*. New York: Basic Books, 2013.

Heinz, John P., Robert L. Nelson, Rebecca L. Sandefur, and Edward O. Laumann. *Urban Lawyers: The New Social Structure of the Bar*. Chicago: University of Chicago Press, 2005.

Johnson, Earl. *To Establish Justice for All: The Past and Future of Civil Legal Aid in the United States*. Santa Barbara, CA.: Praeger, 2014.

Kiser, Randall. *American Law Firms in Transition: Trends, Threats, and Strategies*. Chicago: American Bar Association, 2019.

Kritzer, Herbert M. *When Lawyers Screw Up: Improving Access to Justice for Legal Malpractice Victims*. Lawrence: University Press of Kansas, 2018.

Lawrence, Susan E. *The Poor in Court: The Legal Services Program and Supreme Court Decision-Making.* Princeton, N.J.: Princeton University Press, 1990.

Mather, Lynn, Craig A. McEwen, and Richard J. Maiman. *Divorce Lawyers at Work: Varieties of Professionalism in Practice.* New York: Oxford University Press, 2001.

Mertz, Elizabeth. *The Language of Law School: Learning to "Think Like a Lawyer."* New York: Oxford University Press, 2007.

Moliterno, James E. *The American Legal Profession in Crisis: Resistance and Responses to Change.* New York: Oxford University Press, 2013.

Posner, Richard A. *Divergent Paths: The Academy and the Judiciary.* Cambridge: Harvard University Press, 2016.

Rhode, Deborah L. *Access to Justice.* New York: Oxford University Press, 2004.

Rhode, Deborah L. *The Trouble with Lawyers.* New York: Oxford University Press, 2015.

Rhode, Deborah L. and Amanda K. Packel. *Leadership for Lawyers.* New York: Wolters Kluwer, 2018.

Stevens, Robert. *Law School: Legal Education in America From the 1850s to the 1980s.* Chapel Hill: University of North Carolina Press, 1987.

Susskind, Richard. *Online Courts and the Future of Justice.* New York: Oxford University Press, 2019.

Tamanaha, Brian Z. *Failing Law Schools.* Chicago: University of Chicago Press, 2012.

West, Robin L. *Teaching Law: Justice, Politics, and the Demands of Professionalism.* New York, N.Y.: Cambridge University Press, 2015.

Wilmont-Smith, Frederic. *Equal Justice: Fair Legal Systems in an Unfair World.* Cambridge, MA.: Harvard University Press, 2019.

Endnotes

[1]   Alexis de Tocqueville, *Democracy in America*, translated by George Lawrence, edited by J. P. Mayer (New York: Harper & Row, 1988), 264, 268–69. Government lawyers, for example, in the Department of Justice's Office of Legal Counsel (OLC) are significant advisors to the president on post-9/11 national security and foreign policy issues. Case Note, "Presidential Power and the Office of Legal Counsel," *Harvard Law Review* 125 (2012), 2090–113; Arthur H. Garrison, "The Opinions by the Attorney General and the Office of Legal Counsel: How and Why They Are Significant," *Albany Law Review* 76 (2012–2013), 217–47; Frank M. Wozencraft, "OLC: The Unfamiliar Acronym," *American Bar Association Journal* 57 (1971), 33–37.

[2]   The reference to "normative ordering," and its attribution to Harvard Law School's Dean Robert Clark, is found in Kathleen M. Sullivan, "The Good That Lawyers Do," *Washington University Journal of Law & Policy* 4 (2000), 7, 10.

3   Christopher P. Banks, *The American Legal Profession: The Myths and Realities of Practicing Law* (Thousand Oaks, CA.: Sage/CQ Press 2017), 1; Stephen M. Sheppard, "The American Legal Profession in the Twenty First Century," *American Journal of Comparative Law* 62 (2014), 241, 243 (arguing lawyers perform key functions and roles that are essential to American society); Frances Kahn Zemans and Victor G. Rosenblum, *The Making of a Public Profession* (Chicago: American Bar Foundation, 1981), 2. A description of the leadership roles lawyers play in society is found in Deborah L. Rhode, *Lawyers as Leaders* (New York: Oxford University Press, 2013), 1.

4   Lawrence M. Friedman, *A History of American Law*, 2nd ed. (New York: Simon & Schuster, 1985), 96.

5   For a description of some of the colonial restrictions placed on lawyers, see Charles Warren, *A History of the American Bar* (New York: Howard Fertig, 1966), 8.

6   Charles R. McKirdy, "The Lawyer as Apprentice: Legal Education in Eighteenth Century Massachusetts," *Journal of Legal Education* 28 (1976), 134–35. See also, Banks, *The American Legal Profession*, 50.

7   Zemans and Rosenblum, *The Making of a Public Profession,* 5–6; Robert Stevens, "Two Cheers for 1870: The American Law School," in *Law in American History*, edited by Donald Fleming and Bernard Bailyn (Boston: Little, Brown, and Company, 1971), 413–16.

8   Kermit L. Hall, *The Magic Mirror: Law in American History* (New York: Oxford University Press, 1989), 126–27; Robert Stevens, *Law School: Legal Education in America From the 1850s to the 1980s* (Chapel Hill: University of North Carolina Press, 1983), 5–9.

9   Stevens, "Two Cheers for 1870," 417.

10   Stevens, *Law School,* 22.

11   Richard L. Abel, *American Lawyers* (New York: Oxford University Press, 1989), 41–73. See also Jerold S. Auerbach, *Unequal Justice: Lawyers and Social Change in Modern America* (New York: Oxford University Press, 1976), 106–8 (noting that ABA elites were interested in slowing the growth of new lawyers that were from specific types of ethnic or religious minority groups).

12   Banks, *The American Legal Profession*, 96; Stevens, *Law School,* 94–95, 105 n. 23. See also Olufunmilayo B. Arewa, Andrew P. Morriss, and William D. Henderson, "Enduring Hierarchies in American Legal Education," *Indiana Law Journal* 89 (2014), 941, 947–48.

13   Brian Z. Tamanaha, *Failing Law Schools* (Chicago: University of Chicago Press, 2012), 22 Elizabeth Garrett, "The Role of the Socratic Method in Modern Law Schools" *Green Bag* 2nd 1 (1998): 199–208. John Jay Osborn, Jr., wrote *The Paper Chase*, which was made into a 1973 movie. Law school's instructional method was additionally fictionalized in Reese Witherspoon's popular movie, *Legally Blonde* (MGM 2001). Joe Patrice, "*The Paper Chase*—The Law School Movie Without Reese Witherspoon—Turns 40," *Above the Law* (July 30, 2013), available at http://abovethelaw.com/2013/07/the-paper-chase-the-law-school-movie-without-reese-witherspoon-turns-40/#more-260798 (last retrieved May 11, 2014). See also Scott Turow, *One L: The Turbulent True Story of a First Year at Harvard Law School* (New York: Putnam, 1977).

14   Deborah L. Rhode, *Lawyers as Leaders*, 156. See also Wayne K. Hobson, "Symbol of the New Profession: Emergence of the Large Law Firm, 1870–1915," in *The New High Priests: Lawyers in Post-Civil War America*, edited by Gerard W. Gawalt (Westport, Conn.: Greenwood Press, 1984), 19–20; and Robert T. Swaine, *The Cravath Firm and Its Predecessors: 1819–1947* (New York: Ad Press, 1948).

15   See Marc Galanter and Thomas Palay, *Tournament of Lawyers: The Transformation of the Big Law Firm* (Chicago: University of Chicago Press, 1991); David Wilkins, Ronit Dinovitzer, and Rishi Batra, "Urban Law School Graduates in Large Law Firms," *Southwestern University Law Review* 36 (2007), 433, 439.

16   Elizabeth Chambliss, "Two Questions for Law Schools About the Future Boundaries of the Legal Profession," *The Journal of the Legal Profession* 36 (2013), 329–52. The seminal study of the legal profession's "two hemispheres" is John P. Heinz, Robert L. Nelson, Rebecca L. Sandefur, and Edward O. Laumann, *Urban Lawyers: The New Social Structure of the Bar* (Chicago: University of Chicago Press, 2005). The history and transformation of legal education is detailed in Olufunmilayo B. Arewa, Andrew P. Morriss, and William D. Henderson, "Enduring Hierarchies in American Legal Education," *Indiana Law Journal* 89 (2014), 941–1068. For a description of the "tournament" in corporate legal practice, see Galanter and Palay, *Tournament of Lawyers*.

17   David S. Clark, "Legal Professions and Law Firms," in *Comparative Law and Society*, edited by David S. Clark (Northampton, Mass.: Edward Elgar, 2012), 379–82. The ABA survey represents data to December 31, 2017. See American Bar Association, "New ABA data reveals rise in number of U.S. lawyers, 15 percent

increase since 2008," available at https://www.americanbar.org/news/abanews/aba-news-archives/2018/05/new_aba_data_reveals/ (last retrieved April 16, 2020).

18   American Bar Association, "ABA-Approved Law Schools," available at https://www.americanbar.org/groups/legal_education/resources/aba_approved_law_schools/ (last retrieved April 16, 2020); American Bar Association, "Non-ABA-Approved Law Schools," available at https://www.lsac.org/choosing-law-school/find-law-school/non-aba-approved-law-schools (last retrieved April 16, 2020).

19   Philip G. Schrag, "MOOCS and Legal Education: Valuable Innovation or Looming Disaster?" *Villanova Law Review* 59 (2014), 83–134. See also Mansfield J. Park, "The Best Online Law Schools: JD and LLM Programs," *Above the Law* (May 3, 2013), available at https://abovethelaw.com/2013/05/from-the-career-files-the-best-online-law-schools-j-d-and-ll-m-programs/ (last retrieved April 16, 2020); Brian Bursed, "Online Law Schools Have Yet to Pass the Bar," *U.S. News & World Report* (Education: Online Education, Updated June 20, 2012), available at https://www.usnews.com/education/online-education/articles/2011/03/23/online-law-schools-have-yet-to-pass-the-bar) last retrieved April 16, 2020).

20   Online programs at ABA-accredited U.S. law schools have emerged in Mitchell Hamline, Syracuse, Southwestern and Dayton law schools. Henry Kronk, "The Ice is Melting for Hybrid J.D. Programs, (February 22, 2018)," available at https://news.elearninginside.com/the-ice-is-melting-for-hybrid-j-d-programs/ (last retrieved April 16, 2020); Mike Stetz, "University of Dayton to Offer New Hybrid J.D. Program (June 21, 2018), available at http://www.nationaljurist.com/national-jurist-magazine/university-dayton-offer-new-hybrid-jd-program (last retrieved April 16, 2020). See also, National Jurist, "Prelaw: William Mitchell gets ABA approval to offer first hybrid online/on-campus JD" (January 8, 2014)," available at http://www.nationaljurist.com/prelaw/william-mitchell-gets-aba-approval-offer-first-hybrid-onlineon-campus-jd (last retrieved April 16, 2020); and Banks, *The American Legal Profession*, 103–106.

21   As quoted by Jeff Jacoby, "US legal bubble can't pop soon enough," *Boston Globe* (May 9, 2014), available at https://www.bostonglobe.com/opinion/2014/05/09/the-lawyer-bubble-pops-not-moment-too-soon/qAYzQ823qpfi4GQl2OiPZM/story.html (last retrieved April 16, 2020). See also Charles Saxon, "Those ✻✻@⚡✻✻!! Lawyers!," *Time* (Vol. 11, Issue No. 16, April 10, 1978). For a statistical overview of the legal profession, see American Bar Association, "ABA National Lawyer Population Survey: Historical Trend in Total National Lawyer Population 1878–2019," available at https://www.americanbar.org/about_the_aba/profession_statistics/ (last retrieved April 16, 2020); U.S. Census Bureau, "Number of Firms, Number of Establishments, Employment, and Annual Payroll by Enterprise Employment Size for the United States, All Industries: 2015 [Sector 54, Professional, Scientific, Technical Services, NAICS Code 5411]," available at www.census.gov (last retrieved April 16, 2020); Statista, "Legal services industry in the U.S.—Statistics & Facts," available at https://www.statista.com/topics/2137/legal-services-industry-in-the-us/ (last retrieved April 16, 2020).

22   Clark, "Legal Professions and Law Firms," 380. See also American Bar Association, Section of Legal Education and Admissions to the Bar, *Legal Education and Professional Development—An Educational Continuum. Report of the Task Force on Law Schools and the Profession: Narrowing the Gap* (Chicago: American Bar Association, July 1992), 13, 15 (The "MacCrate Report").

23   Georgetown Law Center on Ethics and the Legal Profession, *2019 Report on the State of the Legal Market*, available at https://images.ask.legalsolutions.thomsonreuters.com/Web/TRlegalUS/%7B7f73da9c-0789-4f63-b012-379d45d54cdf%7D_2019_Report_on_the_State_of_the_Legal_Market_NEW.pdf (last retrieved June 27, 2020), 3 (Figure 1). See also, Marketline, "Legal Services in the United States" (October 2012, Reference Code: 0072-0423), available at www.marketline.com (last retrieved May 12, 2014).

24   Derek Hawkins, "Did law school applications get a 'Trump bump'? Maybe.", *Washington Post* (February 23, 2018), available at https://www.washingtonpost.com/news/morning-mix/wp/2018/02/23/did-law-school-applications-get-a-trump-bump-maybe/?utm_term=.f59dae66244e (last retrieved April 16, 2020); Asma Khalid, "From Post-it Notes To Algorithms: How Automation Is Changing Legal Work" (November 7, 2017), available at https://www.npr.org/sections/alltechconsidered/2017/11/07/561631927/from-post-it-notes-to-algorithms-how-automation-is-changing-legal-work (last retrieved April 16, 2020). See also, Law School Transparency, "Law School Enrollment," available at https://data.lawschooltransparency.com/enrollment/demand-for-law-school/ (last retrieved April 16, 2020) (Prospective Student Data Chart).

25   Law School Transparency, "Law School Enrollment."

26   Banks, *The American Legal Profession*, 95; see ibid, 019 (note 1); Mike Stetz, "People are flocking to law school again. Will there be jobs?," *National Jurist* (October 9, 2018), available at http://www.nationaljurist.com/

national-jurist-magazine/people-are-flocking-law-school-again-will-there-be-jobs (last retrieved April 16, 2020). See also Richard Susskind, *Tomorrow's Lawyers: An Introduction to Your Future* (Oxford, U.K.: Oxford University Press, 2013); Steven J. Harper, *The Lawyer Bubble: A Profession in Crisis* (New York: Basic Books, 2013); Chambliss, "Two Questions for Law Schools About the Future Boundaries of the Legal Profession," 342.

27 American Bar Association: Section of Legal Education and Admissions to the Bar, "Pre Law," available at http://www.americanbar.org/groups/legal_education/resources/pre_law.html (last retrieved April 16, 2020); Law School Admissions Council, "How to Prepare for your Legal Education," http://www. lsac.org/jd/thinking-about-law-school/preparing-for-law-school (last retrieved April 16, 2020).

28 Banks, *The American Legal Profession*, 23–27.

29 Law School Admission Council, "LSAT," available at http://lsac.org/jd/lsat/about-the-lsat (last retrieved April 16, 2020). See also, Dave Killoran, "A Brief Overview of the LSAT." *In Getting into Law School: A Guide for Pre-Law Students (An AdmissionsDean.org Publication)*, available from https://luc.edu/media/lucedu/prehealth/pdfs/Getting%20into%20Law%20School%20Guide.pdf (last retrieved April 16, 2020), 3.

30 Law School Admission Council and the American Bar Association Section of Legal Education and Admissions to the Bar, *ABA-LSAC Official Guide to ABA-Approved Law Schools (2013 Edition)*, 9. The quote is from Ann Perry, a University of Chicago law school Dean. See Ann Perry, "Interpreting the Numbers: The Importance of LSAT and UGPA in an Admission Decision." *In Getting into Law School: A Guide for Pre-Law Students (An AdmissionsDean.org Publication)*, available from https://www.uc.edu/content/dam/uc/preproadvising/docs/GettingIntoLawSchoolGuide.pdf (last retrieved April 16, 2020).

31 Michael Sauder, *Fear of Falling: The Effects of U.S. News & World Report Rankings on U.S. Law Schools* (LSAC RESEARCH REPORT SERIES, available at lsac.org (last retrieved November 1, 2018)(available by request and on file with author); Jeffrey Evans Stake and Michael Alexeev, "Who Responds to U.S. News & World Report's Law School Rankings?," *Journal of Empirical Legal Studies* 12 (2015): 421–480. See also, Banks, *The American Legal Profession*, 31–34.

32 Banks, *The American Legal Profession*, 31–34. See also Brian Z. Tamanaha, *Failing Law Schools* (Chicago: University of Chicago Press, 2012).

33 The ABA imposed the requirement to disclose by revising Standard 509 in 2013. American Bar Association, Section on Legal Education and Admission to the Bar, "Memorandum (August 2013)," available at http://www.americanbar.org/content/dam/aba/administrative/legal_education_and_admissions_to_the_bar/governancedocuments/2013_standard_509_memo.authcheckdam.pdf (last accessed April 16, 2020).

34 Law School Admissions Council, "Prepare for LSAT Success," available at https://www.lsac.org/lsat/lsat-prep (last retrieved April 16, 2020). KAPLAN LSAT is not listed on the lsac.com website and, in 2018, their preparation costs are $799 (self-paced), $1299 (live online), in person ($1,299), all access ($1,699) and between $2,399–4,999 (online personal tutor). Kaplan, "LSAT Prep Your Way," https://www.kaptest.com/lsat (last retrieved April 16, 2020). The various fees and costs of filing a law school application through the Law School Admission Council is found at https://www.lsac.org/ (last accessed April 16, 2020).

35 Law School Transparency, "Law School Costs," available at https://data.lawschooltransparency.com/costs/tuition/ (last retrieved April 16, 2020)(reporting 2019 tuition rates as compared to 1985), See also American Bar Association, "Data from the 2013 Annual Questionnaire: ABA Approved Law School Tuition History Data," available from http://www.americanbar.org/groups/legal_education/resources/statistics.html (last retrieved April 16, 2020); American Bar Association, "Average Living and Book Expenses For Single Students Living on Campus, 1990–2012," available at http://www.americanbar.org/content/dam/aba/administrative/legal_education_and_admissions_to_the_bar/statistics/average_living_book_expenses.authcheckdam.pdf. (last retrieved April 16, 2020).

36 Kyle McEntee, *A Way Forward: Transparency in 2018 (A Report on behalf of Law School Transparency and the Iowa State Bar Association, Young Lawyers Division)*, available at https://data.lawschooltransparency.com/documents/2018_Report.pdf (last retrieved April 16, 2020), 4. On the high price of law school tuition and the problem of growing law school student debt, see Brian Z. Tamanaha, *Failing Law Schools* (Chicago: University of Chicago Press, 2012), 109–10; Debra Cassens Weiss, "Average Debt of Private Law School Grads is $125K; It's Highest at These Five Schools," *ABA Journal* (March 28, 2012), available at www.abajournal.com (last retrieved May 12, 2014).

37 Rebecca Sandefur, Bryant G. Garth, and Joyce Sterling, "Financing Legal Education: The View Twelve Years Out of Law School. In *After the JD III: Third Results from a National Study of Legal Careers* Ed.

Gabriele Plickert (Chicago, Ill.: American Bar Foundation; Dallas, TX.: NALP Foundation for Law Career Research and Education, 2014), 80–84.

38   Mary Ann Glendon, *A Nation Under Lawyers: How the Crisis in the Legal Profession Is Transforming American Society* (Cambridge, Mass.: Harvard University Press, 1996), 90. Herwig Schlunk, "Mamas 2011: Is a Law Degree a Good Investment Today?" *Journal of the Legal Profession* 36 (2011), 301–27; David Segal, "Is Law School a Losing Game?" *New York Times* (January 8, 2011).

39   R. Michael Cassidy, "Reforming the Law School Curriculum from the Top Down," *Journal of Legal Education* 64 (2015): 428, 437.

40   Jamie R. Abrams. "Reframing the Socratic Method." *Journal of Legal Education* 64 (2015): 562, 564. American Bar Association Section of Legal Education and Admissions to the Bar, "Legal Education and Professional Development—An Educational Continuum (Report of the Task Force on Law Schools and the Profession: Narrowing the Gap)," 236–237; William M. Sullivan, Anne Colby, Judith Welch Wegner, Lloyd Bond, Lee S. Shulman, *Educating Lawyers: Preparation for the Profession of Law (A Publication of the Carnegie Foundation for the Advancement of Teaching)* (San Francisco: Jossey-Bass, 2007): 49–50. See also, Melissa J. Marlow, "Does Kingsfield Live?" Teaching with Authenticity in Today's Law Schools." *Journal of Legal Education* 65 (2015): 229, 233; Robin L. West. *Teaching Law: Justice, Politics, and the Demands of Professionalism* (New York, N.Y.: Cambridge University Press, 2015): 30.

41   Banks, *The American Legal Profession*, 53–56.

42   Deborah L. Rhode, *In the Interests of Justice: Reforming the Legal Profession* (New York, N.Y.: Oxford University Press, 2000), 186. Commentary about the need to reform legal instruction can be found in American Bar Association, Task Force on the Future of Legal Education. *Report and Recommendations (January 2014),* available at http://www.americanbar.org/content/dam/aba/administrative/professional_responsibility/ report_and_recommendations_of_aba_task_force.authcheckdam.pdf (last retrieved April 16, 2020); William M. Sullivan, Anne Colby, Judith Welch Wegner, Lloyd Bond, and Lee S. Shulman, *Educating Lawyers: Preparation for the Profession of Law (A Publication of the Carnegie Foundation for the Advancement of Teaching)* (San Francisco: Jossey-Bass, 2007); Harry T. Edwards, "The Growing Disjunction between Legal Education and the Legal Profession." *Michigan Law Review* 91 (1992): 34, 38–39, 59–63; American Bar Association, Section of Legal Education and Admissions to the Bar, *Legal Education and Professional Development: An Educational Continuum (Report of the Task Force on Law Schools and the Profession: Narrowing the Gap)* (Chicago, Ill.: American Bar Association, 1992).

43   Yet law schools ranked in the top ten are increasingly hiring faculty holding PhDs. Brent E. Nelson, "Preaching What They Don't Practice: Why Law Faculties' Preoccupation With Impractical Scholarship and Devaluation of Practical Competencies Obstruct Reform in the Legal Academy," *South Carolina Law Review* 62 (2010), 105, 131.

44   As quoted by UCLA law professor Gerald Lopez, in Deborah L. Rhode, *In the Interests of Justice: Reforming the Legal Profession* (New York: Oxford University Press, 2000), 198.

45   Richard E. Redding, "Where Did You Go to Law School? Gatekeeping for the Professoriate and Its Implications for Legal Education," *Journal of Legal Education* 53 (2003), 594, 595. The "divergent paths" of legal scholars and judges or legal practitioners, as manifested by law school hiring trends, is discussed in Richard A. Posner, *Divergent Paths: The Academy and the Judiciary* (Cambridge, Harvard University Press 2016), 40–42. See also Tracey E. George and Albert H. Yoon, "The Labor Market for New Law Professors," *Journal of Empirical Legal Studies* 11 (2014), 1–38; Robert J. Borthwick and Jordan R. Schau, "Gatekeepers of the Profession: An Empirical Analysis of the Nation's Law Professors," *University of Michigan Journal of Law Reform* 25 (Fall, 2001), 191–92.

46   The Model Rules of Professional Responsibility are found in American Bar Association, "Model Rules of Professional Conduct: Table of Contents," available at http://www.americanbar.org/groups/professional_ responsibility/publications/model_rules_of_professional_conduct/model_rules_of_professional_conduct_ table_of_contents.html (last accessed April 16, 2020). A listing of states and the date of adoption of the model rules is found in American Bar Association, "State Adoption of the ABA Model Rules of Professional Conduct," http://www.americanbar.org/groups/professional_responsibility/publications/model_rules_of_ professional_conduct/alpha_list_state_adopting_model_rules.html (last accessed April 16, 2020). See also, National Conference of Bar Examiners, "Jurisdictions Requiring the MPRE," *The National Conference of Bar Examiners,* available at http://www.ncbex.org/exams/mpre/ (last accessed April 16, 2020).

47   See American Bar Association, "Model Rules of Professional Conduct: Table of Contents."

48 Banks, *The American Legal Profession*, 101–103. A state-by-state analysis of lawyer disciplinary systems is found in Debra Moss Curtis, "Attorney Discipline Nationwide: A Comparative Analysis of Process and Statistics," *Journal of the Legal Profession* 35 (2011), 209–337.

49 Banks, *The American Legal Profession*, 56–58.

50 American Bar Association, "Bar Admissions Basic Overview," https://www.americanbar.org/groups/legal_education/resources/bar_admissions/basic_overview/ (last retrieved April 16, 2020). See also National Conference of Bar Examiners, *2018 Year in Review*, 10–12 (providing a summary of bar testing procedures for 2018 for participating jurisdictions), available at http://www.ncbex.org/pdfviewer/?file=%2Fdmsdocument%2F231 (last retrieved April 16, 2020). See also National Conference of Bar Examiners and American Bar Association Section of Legal Education and Admissions to the Bar, *Comprehensive Guide to Bar Admission Requirements: 2019*, available at http://www.ncbex.org/assets/BarAdmissionGuide/NCBE-CompGuide-2019.pdf (last retrieved April 16, 2020).

51 National Conference of Bar Examiners, *Understanding the Uniform Bar Examination (Jurisdictions that have adopted the UBE, as of August 26, 2019)*, available at http://www.ncbex.org/pdfviewer/?file=%2Fdmsdocument%2F209 (last retrieved April 16, 2020).

52 Leslie C. Levin, Christine Zozula, and Peter Siegelman, "The Questionable Character of the Bar's Character and Fitness Inquiry," *Law & Social Inquiry* 40 (2015): 51, 52. See also, Banks, *The American Legal Profession*, 60–61.

53 National Conference of Bar Examiners, "2017 Statistics," available at http://www.ncbex.org/pdfviewer/?file=%2Fdmsdocument%2F218 (last retrieved April 16, 2020), 27. See also, National Conference of Bar Examiners, "Persons Taking and Passing the 2018 Bar Examination," available at https://thebarexaminer.org/wp-content/uploads/2019/880119/Persons-Taking-and-Passing-the-2018-Bar-Examination.pdf (April 16, 2020).

54 American Bar Association, "2019 IL Enrollment by Gender, Race/Ethnicity," available https://www.americanbar.org/groups/legal_education/resources/statistics/ (last retrieved April 16, 2020). See also, American Bar Association, "First Year J.D. and Total J.D. Minority Enrollment: 1971–2012," available at https://www.americanbar.org/content/dam/aba/administrative/legal_education_and_admissions_to_the_bar/statistics/jd_enrollment_1yr_total_minority.authcheckdam.pdf (last retrieved April 16, 2020); American Bar Association, "First Year and Total J.D. Enrollment by Gender: 1947–2011," available at https://www.americanbar.org/content/dam/aba/administrative/legal_education_and_admissions_to_the_bar/statistics/jd_enrollment_1yr_total_gender.authcheckdam.pdf (last retrieved April 16, 2020).

55 Deborah L. Rhode, "Leadership in Law," *Stanford Law Review* 69 (June 2017): 1603–1645–1646.

56 Deborah L. Rhode, *Women in Leadership* (New York: Oxford University Press 2017), 76. See also, Deborah L. Rhode, *In the Interests of Justice: Reforming the Legal Profession* (New York: Oxford University Press, 2000), 192; Clark, "Legal Professions and Law Firms," 382; Helia Garrido Hull, "Diversity in the Legal Profession: Moving From Rhetoric to Reality," *Columbia Journal of Race and Law* 4 (2013), 1–23; Wynn R. Huang, "Gender Differences in the Earnings of Lawyers," *Columbia Journal of Law and Society Problems* 30 (1997), 267.

57 American Bar Association, Commission on Women in the Profession, "A Current Glance at Women in the Law (April 2019)," available at https://www.americanbar.org/content/dam/aba/administrative/women/current_glance_2019.pdf (last retrieved April 16, 2020).

58 National Association for Law Placement, *2019 Report on Diversity in U.S. Law Firms*, available at https://www.nalp.org/uploads/2019_DiversityReport.pdf (last retrieved April 16, 2020)(Tables 1 to 8).

59 Banks, *The American Legal Profession*, 68, 85–86. The ill-effects of lawyer elitism is discussed in Marc Galanter, "Why the 'Haves' Come Out Ahead: Speculations on the Limits of Legal Change," *Law and Society Review* 9 (1974): 95–160; and, John P. Heinz, Robert L. Nelson, Rebecca L. Sandefur, and Edward O. Laumann, *Urban Lawyers: The New Social Structure of the Bar*. (Chicago, Ill.: University of Chicago Press 2005). Criticisms (and reform proposals) the legal profession are found in Deborah L. Rhode, *The Trouble with Lawyers* (New York, N.Y.: Oxford University Press 2015); Benjamin H. Barton, *Glass Half Full: The Decline and Rebirth of the Legal Profession* (New York, N.Y.: Oxford University Press, 2015); William Domnarski, *Swimming in Deep Water: Lawyers, Judges, and Our Troubled Legal Profession* (Chicago, Ill.: American Bar Association 2014); Creola Johnson, *Is a Law Degree Still Worth the Price?: It Depends on What the Law School Has To Offer* (Durham, N.C.: Carolina Academic Press, 2014); Steven J. Harper, *The Lawyer Bubble* (New York, N.Y.: Basic Books 2013); James E. Moliterno, *The American Legal Profession in Crisis: Resistance and Responses to Change* (New York, N.Y.: Oxford University Press, 2010); Thomas D. Morgan, *The Vanishing Lawyer* (New York: Oxford University Press 2010);

Douglas Litowitz, *The Destruction of Young Lawyers: Beyond One L.* (Akron, OH.: University of Akron Press 2006); Anthony Kronman, *The Lost Lawyer: Failing Ideals of the Legal Profession* (Cambridge, MA.: Belknap Press of Harvard University Press 1993).

[60] Clark, "Legal Professions and Law Firms," 362. See also Banks, *The American Legal Profession*, 72; Abel, *American Lawyers*, 175–76; *MacCrate Report*, 226.

[61] Banks, *The American Legal Profession*, 2–5; F. C. DeCoste, *On Coming to Law: An Introduction to Law in Liberal Societies*, 3rd ed. (Markham, Ontario: LexisNexis Canada, 2011), 24.

[62] Tamanaha, *Failing Law Schools*, 135. See also, Banks, *The American Legal Profession*, 5–6.

[63] National Association of Law Placement, "Class of 2018 National Summary Report," available at https://www.nalp.org/uploads/NationalSummaryReport_Classof2018_FINAL.pdf (last retrieved April 16, 2020). See also, Emily A. Spieler, "The Paradox of Access to Civil Justice: The 'Glut' of New Lawyers and the Persistence of Unmet Need," *University of Toledo Law Review* 44 (2013), 365, 377–79 (evaluating lawyer demographic statistics from various sources, as of 2005).

[64] National Association for Law Placement, "JD Advantage Career Guide (Spring 2020)," available at https://www.nalp.org/uploads/JDAdvantage/JDAdvantageGuide.pdf (last retrieved April 16, 2020). See also, Thomas W. Lyons, "Legal Education: Learning What Lawyers Need." In *The Relevant Lawyer: Reimaging the Future of the Legal Profession.* Edited by Paul A. Haskins (Chicago, Ill.: American Bar Association, 2015), 226; Debra Cassens Weiss, " 'After the JD' Study Shows Many Leave Law Practice," *ABA Journal* 100 (2014), 1; Hollee Schwartz Temple, "Law Students Prepare for Jobs Outside Firms," *ABA Journal* 99 (December 2013), 1.

[65] Rachel Zahorsky and William D. Henderson, "Who's Eating Law Firms' Lunch?" *ABA Journal* 99 (2013), 1; John Okray, "Legal Process Outsourcing—Coming to a Practice Area Near You?" *Federal Lawyer* 60 (September 2013), 4; Ron Friedmann, "The Impact of Legal Process Outsourcing (LPO) You Might Not Have Noticed," *Law Practice Today* (January 2012), 1–4; David A. Steiger, The rise of global legal sourcing: how vendors and clients are changing legal business models," *ABA Business Law Section* 19 (No. 2, November/December 2009), 1.

[66] Stephen M. Sheppard, "The American Legal Profession in the Twenty First Century," *American Journal of Comparative Law* (2014): 62: 241, 270.

[67] National Association of Law Placement, "Class of 2018 National Summary Report." See also, Kathryn Rubino, "Biglaw Jobs Are Not Spread Out Equally Among Law Schools: Where you go to law school impacts where you'll work after graduation (November 8, 2018)," available at https://abovethelaw.com/2018/11/biglaw-jobs-are-not-spread-out-equally-among-law-schools/ (last retrieved April 16, 2020). See also Banks, *The American Legal Profession*, 21.

[68] Herbert M. Kritzer, "The Professions Are Dead, Long Live the Professions: Legal Practice in a Postprofessional World," *Law and Society Review* 33 (1998), 735. See also National Association for Legal Career Professionals, "Prelaw—What Do Lawyers Do?," available at https://www.nalp.org/what_do_lawyers_do (last retrieved November 9, 2018).

[69] Kathryn Rubino, "Biglaw Jobs Are Not Spread Out Equally Among Law Schools: Where you go to law school impacts where you'll work after graduation (November 8, 2018)." See also Chambliss, "Two Questions for Law Schools About the Future Boundaries of the Legal Profession," 336, 339; John P. Heinz and Edward O. Laumann, *Chicago Lawyers: The Social Structure of the Bar*, rev. ed. (Evanston, Ill.: Northwestern University Press, 1994), 127–28.

[70] Milton C. Reagan, Jr. and Lisa H. Rohrer, *A Fragile Balance: Business, Profession and Culture in the Large Law Firm* (Law School Admission Council Grants Report 15-02, October 2015), 17–18 (on file with author). See also Martha Neil, "Some Law Firms End Lockstep Pay for Associates, as Economy Plummets," *ABA Journal* (March 16, 2009), available at www.abajournal.com (last retrieved May 18, 2014); National Association for Law Placement, "Industry Leaders Discuss the Future of Lawyer Hiring, Development, and Advancement," available at www.nalp.org/future_pressrelease?s=lockstep (June 30, 2009) (last retrieved May 18, 2014). See also Clark, "Legal Professions and Law Firms," 385, 387.

[71] Martha Neil, "Brave, New World of Partnership," *American Bar Association Journal* (January 2004), 56; Erwin Orson Smigel, *The Wall Street Lawyer: Professional Organization Man?* (Bloomington: Indiana University Press, 1969). See also Banks, *The American Legal Profession*, 70–71.

[72] Deborah L. Cohen, "End of the Road for the 'Cravath Model'?" *ABA Journal* 94 (2008), 36–38.

73 *Bates v. State Bar of Arizona*, 433 U.S. 350 (1977) (striking down legal advertising restrictions).

74 Glendon, *A Nation Under Lawyers*, 24 ("eat what you kill" business orientation). See also *Goldfarb v. Virginia State Bar Association*, 421 U.S. 773 (1975) (striking down minimum fee schedules).

75 Joyce S. Sterling and Nancy Reichman, "So You Want to Be a Lawyer? The Quest for Professional Status in a Changing Legal World," *Fordham Law Review* 78 (2010), 2289, 2295–96. See also Marc Galanter and Thomas Palay, *Tournament of Lawyers: The Transformation of the Big Law Firm* (Chicago: University of Chicago Press, 1991), 28 ("up-or-out" policy); Neil, "Brave, New World of Partnership," 30 (two-tier partnerships).

76 Banks, *The American Legal Profession* 74–76. The different titles, roles, and performance obligations of equity versus non-equity partners are discussed in William D. Henderson, "An Empirical Study of Single-Tier Versus Two-Tier Partnerships in the Am Law 200," *North Carolina Law Review* 84 (2006): 1691, 1707–1711.

77 Creola Johnson, *Is a Law Degree Still Worth the Price?: It Depends on What the Law School Has To Offer* (Durham, N.C.: Carolina Academic Press, 2014), 175–179. The quote describing the elastic tournament is from Marc Galanter and William Henderson, "The Elastic Tournament: A Second Transformation of the Big Law Firm." *Stanford Law Review* 60 (2008): 1867, 1877. See also, Marc Galanter and Thomas Palay, *Tournament of Lawyers: The Transformation of the Big Law Firm* (Chicago: University of Chicago Press (1991); and, Banks, *The American Legal Profession,* 73–75.

78 Kritzer, "The Professions Are Dead, Long Live the Professions," 731–32.

79 As quoted by a lawyer referred to in Stephen Breyer, "The Legal Profession and Public Service" (lecture given in New York, September 12, 2000), available at https://www.supremecourt.gov/publicinfo/speeches/sp_10-10-00.pdf (last retrieved April 17, 2020), 2. In 2014, in law firms of all sizes was the average hours worked was 2,081 and the average billable hours was 1,806; both represent an increase from the prior year. Almost 17 percent of law firms had attorneys working 2,000 billable hours; and, of those, 26 percent documented those hours in law firms with over 701 attorneys. National Association for Law Placement, "Update on Associate Hours Worked," available at https://www.nalp.org/0516research (last retrieved April 17, 2020). These trends are consistent with earlier years. In 2010, the average billable hours across law firms of all sizes were 2,044. Smaller law firms (50 lawyers or fewer, averaged 1,912), whereas the largest firms (over 701 lawyers) averaged 2,202. National Association for Law Placement, "Number of Associate Hours Worked Increases at Largest Firms (February 2012)," available at www.nalp.org/billable_hours_feb2012 (last retrieved April 17, 2020). See also Sterling and Reichman, "So You Want to Be a Lawyer?" 2296, 2300–301; Stephanie B. Goldberg, "Then and Now: 75 Years of Change," *American Bar Association Journal* (January 1990), 56–61; Marie Beaudette, "Associates Leave Firms in Droves," *National Law Journal* (October 26, 2003), 8.

80 Sterling and Reichman, "So You Want to Be a Lawyer?" 2297–98, 2309–2311. There are calls for reform due to increasing criticism of using the traditional billable hour compensation format. See, e.g., Evan R. Chesler, "Kill the Billable Hour," *Forbes* (January 12, 2009), available at www.forbes.com/forbes/2009/0112/026.html (last retrieved April 17, 2020); Jonathan D. Glater, "Billable Hours Giving Ground at Law Firms," *New York Times* (January 29, 2009), available at https://www.nytimes.com/2009/01/30/business/worldbusiness/30iht-30hours.19799084.html (last retrieved April 17, 2020); Scott Turow, "The Billable Hour Must Die," *ABA Journal* (August 1, 2007), available at www.abajournal.com/magazine/the_billable_hour_must_die (last retrieved May 21, 2014). Some lawyers argue though that billable hours will not disappear, especially in high-stakes litigation, unless there is structural reform in law schools. Lucy Muzy, "Maximizing the Value of Outside Counsel," *Federal Lawyer* (September 2013), 56–61.

81 Scott L. Cummings, "The Politics of Pro Bono," *University of California Law Review* (October 2004), 1, 36–37 (discussing growth of large corporate law firms).

82 Wilkins, Dinovitzer, and Batra, "Urban Law School Graduates in Large Law Firms," 445–46.

83 Bryant G. Garth and Joyce Sterling, "Exploring Inequality in the Corporate Law Firm Apprenticeship: Doing the Time, Finding the Love," *Georgetown Journal of Legal Ethics* 22 (2009), 1361–94. See also Wilkins, Dinovitzer, and Batra, "Urban Law School Graduates in Large Law Firms," 443–44; Association for Legal Career Professionals, "Lateral Hiring Continues to Outpace Entry-Level Hiring," available at www.nalp.org/2008maylateralhiring?s=number%20law%20firms (last retrieved April 17, 2020).

84 The American Lawyer, "Most Profits Per Equity Partner," *The American Lawyer* 40 (Issue 10, October 2018): 48. See also Clark, "Legal Professions and Law Firms," 385–86; Goldberg, "Then and Now: 75 Years of Change," 56 (analyzing the emergence of the mega-firm). See also Wilkins, Dinovitzer, and Batra, "Urban Law School Graduates in Large Law Firms," 434.

85   Banks, *The American Legal Profession,* 72. The firm's "facts" and different areas of legal practice is found on Baker & McKenzie's website, https://www.bakermckenzie.com/-/media/files/about-us/bm_firm_facts-aug19.pdf?la=en (last retrieved April 17, 2020).

86   Breyer, "The Legal Profession and Public Service," 9. See also Hope Viner Samborn, "Government Agents: Some Find Perks of Public Sector Work Beat the Potential of Private Practice," *American Bar Association Journal* (December 2002), 64. See also Joe D. Whitley, "In the Service of Justice: A U.S. Attorney Defines His Role," *ABA Journal* 79 (1993), 120.

87   U.S. Office of Personnel Management, "The Twenty Largest White-Collar Occupations as of September 2012 and Compared to September 2011" and "Number of General Attorneys in Cabinet Level Agencies, Non-Seasonal Full-Time Permanent, as of February 2014" (prepared by agency's Data Analysis Group, on file with author). For some of the roles government attorneys play and their unique ethical responsibilities, see Neil M. Peretz, "The Limits of Outsourcing: Ethical Responsibilities of Federal Government Attorneys Advising Executive Branch Officials," *Connecticut Public Interest Law Journal* 6 (2006), 23–63; Anonymous, "Rethinking the Professional Responsibilities of Federal Agency Lawyers," *Harvard Law Review* 115 (2002), 1170–92; John C. Yoo, "Lawyers in Congress," *Law and Contemporary Problems* (Spring 1988), 1–19.

88   Thomas O. McGarity, "The Role of Government Attorneys in Regulatory Agency Rulemaking," *Law and Contemporary Problems* 61 (Winter 1988), 19, 32. Critics of legal education assert that law school does not adequately train lawyers for government policymaking careers in executive agencies. Peter H. Schuck, "Lawyers and Policymakers in Government," *Law and Contemporary Problems* (Winter, 1998), 7, 10.

89   Banks, *The American Legal Profession,* 83. See also William D. Henderson and Leonard Bierman, "An Empirical Analysis of Lateral Lawyer Trends From 2000 to 2007: The Emerging Equilibrium for Corporate Law Firms," *Georgetown Journal of Legal Ethics* 22 (2009), 1395, 1400–401.

90   Banks, *The American Legal Profession,* 81–82.

91   Susan Hackett, "Inside Out: An Examination of Demographic Trends in the In-House Profession," *Arizona Law Review* (Fall/Winter 2002), 613. See also Abel, *American Lawyers,* 168–72.

92   Association of Corporate Counsel, "Association of Corporate Counsel Census Reveals Power Shift From Law Firms to Corporate Legal Departments," available at www.acc.com/aboutacc/newsroom/pressreleases/acc_census_press.cfm (last retrieved May 14, 2014).

93   William Vogeler, "Startup Counsel Salaries Going Up in Silicon Valley, *FindLaw* (May 11, 2017), available at https://blogs.findlaw.com/in_house/2017/05/startup-counsel-salaries-going-up-in-silicon-valley.html (last retrieved April 17, 2020). See also, Staci Zaretsky, "Who are America's Best-Paid General Counsel? (2016)," *Above the Law* (July 18, 2016), available at http://abovethelaw.com/2016/07/who-are-americas-best-paid-general-counsel-2016/ (last retrieved April 17, 2020); David Lat, "Who Are America's Best-Paid General Counsel? (2012 Rankings)," *Above the Law* (July 18, 2012), available at http://abovethelaw.com/2012/07/who-are-americas-best-paid-general-counsel-2012-rankings/ (last retrieved April 17, 2020).

94   *Cause Lawyers and Social Movements,* edited by Austin Sarat and Stuart A. Scheingold (Stanford, Calif.: Stanford Law and Politics, 2006); Stuart A. Scheingold and Austin Sarat, *Something to Believe In: Politics, Professionalism, and Cause Lawyering* (Stanford, Calif.: Stanford University Press, 2004), 3–4; and Catherine R. Albiston and Laura Beth Nielsen, "Funding the Cause: How Public Interest Law Organizations Fund Their Activities and Why It Matters for Social Change," *Law and Social Inquiry* 39 (2014), 62–95.

95   Gita Z. Wilder, *Law School Debt Among New Lawyers* (Washington, D.C.: National Association for Legal Career Professionals, 2007), 19; Equal Justice Works, National Association for Legal Career Professionals, and Partnership for Public Service, *From the Paper Chase to Money Chase: Law School Debt Diverts Road to Public Service* (Washington, D.C.: Equal Justice Works, National Association for Legal Career Professionals, and Partnership for Public Service, 2002), 6; see also ABA Commission on Loan Repayment and Forgiveness, *Lifting the Burden: Law Student Debt as a Barrier to Public Service* (Chicago: American Bar Association, 2003), 10. Empirical research contests the finding that debt is diverting students away from public interest work. Christa McGill, "Educational Debt and Law Student Failure to Enter Public Service Careers: Bringing Empirical Data to Bear," *Law and Social Inquiry* 31 (2006) 677, 679. The Illinois study and its findings on the impact of debt on public interest work is found at Illinois State Bar Association, "Final Report, Findings, and Recommendations on the Impact of Law School Debt on the Delivery of Legal Services" (Adopted by the Assembly of the Illinois State Bar Association, June 22, 2013), available at www.isba.org/sites/default/files/committees/Law%20School%20Debt%20Report%20-%203-8-13.pdf (last retrieved April 17, 2020), 15–16.

96   A listing of the types of loan forgiveness or debt reduction programs, and the entities that offer them, is found in American Bar Association, "Loan Repayment Assistance Programs (LRAP)," available at https://www.americanbar.org/groups/center-pro-bono/resources/directory_of_law_school_public_interest_pro_bono_programs/definitions/pi_lrap/ (last retrieved April 17, 2020). See also Doug Rendleman and Scott Weingart, "Collection of Student Loans," *Washington and Lee Journal of Civil Rights and Social Justice* 20 (2014), 215, 231–34; Tresa Baldas, "Paying the Way: Loan Programs Booming for Grads in Public Service Jobs," *National Law Journal* (July 5, 2004), 1.

97   Tracey E. George and Albert H. Yoon, "The Labor Market for New Law Professors," *Journal of Empirical Legal Studies* 11 (2014): 1–38. An increasing trend is for law schools to hire J.D.-Ph.D's. Lynn M. LoPucki, "Dawn of the Discipline-Based Law Faculty," *Journal of Legal Education* 65 (2016): 506–542.

98   Society of American Law Teachers, "2017–18 SALT Salary Survey," *SALT Equalizer 2019* (November 2019), available https://www.saltlaw.org/wp-content/uploads/2015/03/SALT-salary-survey-2019-final-draft.pdf (last retrieved April 17, 2020). See also Abel, *American Lawyers*, 174.

99   Herbert M. Kritzer, *Lawyers at Work* (New Orleans, LA.: Quid Pro Books, 2015), 319 (acknowledging the rise of the post-professional era); and, ibid, 321, 323 (observing that "legal information engineer" design and manage rote legal service delivery systems, whereas a "legal consultant" uses specialized knowledge to create protocols for the delivery of legal services that are administered by either legal information engineers or legal processors; and "legal processor" develop or apply specialized services in basic tasks across a wide variety of legal practice areas, such, estate planning, or routine civil or criminal matters). See also, Richard Susskind, *Tomorrow's Lawyers: An Introduction to Your Future* (New York, N.Y.: Oxford University Press, 2013).

100   Banks, *The American Legal Profession,* 84–85. See also, Young Lawyer Editorial Board, "Law School Reimaged," *American Lawyer* 40 (No. 4, April 2018), 1–4.

101   *McFarland v. Scott*, 512 U.S. 1256 (1994) (Blackmun, J., dissenting).

102   Deborah L. Rhode, *Access to Justice* (New York: Oxford University Press, 2004), 3. See also David Cole, *No Equal Justice: Race and Class in the American Criminal Justice System* (New York: New Press, 1999), 65–66.

103   *Powell v. Alabama*, 287 U.S. 45, 71 (1932).

104   *Betts v. Brady*, 316 U.S. 455 (1942). See also *Johnson v. Zerbst*, 304 U.S. 458 (1938).

105   *Gideon v. Wainwright*, 372 U.S. 335 (1963).

106   See, e.g., *Argersinger v. Hamlin*, 407 U.S. 25 (1972) (misdemeanors); *Alabama v. Shelton*, 535 U.S. 654 (2002) (suspended sentences); *In re Gault*, 387 U.S. 1 (1967) (juveniles); and *Douglas v. California*, 372 U.S. 353 (1963) (first, mandatory appeals). David M. O'Brien, *Constitutional Law and Politics: Civil Rights and Liberties*, 11th ed., Vol. 2 (New York: Norton, 2020), 1098.

107   See, e.g., *Scott v. Illinois*, 440 U.S. 367 (1979); *Ross v. Moffitt*, 417 U.S. 600 (1974); *Pennsylvania v. Finley*, 481 U.S. 551 (1987). David M. O'Brien, *Constitutional Law and Politics: Civil Rights and Liberties*, 1100.

108   Justice Policy Institute. *System Overload: The Costs of Under-Resourcing Public Defense (July 2011)* (Washington, D.C.: Justice Policy Institute), available at http://www.justicepolicy.org/uploads/justicepolicy/documents/system_overload_final.pdf (last retrieved April 17, 2020); Suzanne M. Strong, *State-Administered Indigent Defense Systems, 2013 (Revised May 3, 2017)*(Bureau of Justice Statistics Special Report, November 2016, NCJ 250249), available at https://www.bjs.gov/content/pub/pdf/saids13.pdf (last retrieved April 17, 2020 and, Caroline Wolf Harlow, *Defense Counsel in Criminal Cases* (Bureau of Justice Statistics Special Report, November 2000, NCJ 179023), available at https://www.bjs.gov/content/pub/pdf/dccc.pdf (last retrieved April 17, 2020).

109   The quote is from the Honorable Fourth Circuit Judge, J. Harvie Wilkinson, "In Defense of American Criminal Justice," *Vanderbilt Law Review* 67 (May 2014): 1099, 1127. See also, Richard A. Posner and Albert H. Yoon, "What Judges Think of the Quality of Legal Representation," *Stanford Law Review* 63 (January, 2011): 317: 319–320 (reporting survey responses from federal judges rating "prosecutors as comparable in quality to public defenders and significantly better than court-appointed counsel or retained counsel); and, Margareth Etienne, "The Declining Utility of the Right to Counsel in Federal Criminal Courts: An Empirical Study on the Diminished Role of Defense Attorney Advocacy Under the Sentencing Guidelines," *California Law Review* 92 (March, 2004): 425, 478 (citing Inga L. Parsons, "Making it a Federal Case": A Model for Indigent Representation, 1997 *Annual Survey of American Law* 837, 839 n.7).

110   See American Bar Association, Standing Committee on Legal Aid and Indigent Defense," *Gideon's Broken Promise: America's Continuing Quest for Equal Justice (December 2004)*, available at https://www.americanbar.

org/content/dam/aba/administrative/legal_aid_indigent_defendants/ls_sclaid_def_bp_right_to_counsel_in_criminal_proceedings.authcheckdam.pdf (last retrieved April 17, 2020); National Association for Criminal Defense Lawyers, *Minor Crimes, Massive Waste: The Terrible Toll of America's Broken Misdemeanor Courts* (April, 2009), available at https://www.nacdl.org/Document/MinorCrimesMassiveWasteTollofMisdemeanorCourts (last retrieved June 27, 2020).

[111] Jonathan Lippman, et al., "A 'quiet' closing with resounding impacts on equal justice," *The Hill* (March 2, 2018), available at https://thehill.com/opinion/criminal-justice/376254-a-quiet-closing-with-resounding-impacts-on-equal-justice (last retrieved April 17, 2020).

[112] The ACLU's strategy to use litigation to force indigent defense funding is cited in Aditi Juneja and Nidhi Vij Mali, "Value of Improving Funding for Indigent Defense and Recommendations for Implementation," *Gonzaga Law Review* 54 (2018–2019): 23, 25. See also, Alan W. Houseman, "Civil Legal Aid in the United States (An Update for 2017)," available at https://palegalaid.net/sites/default/files/attachments/2018-07/CIVIL-LEGAL-AID-IN-THE-UNITED-STATES-2017.pdf (last retrieved April 17, 2020); Department of Justice, "About the Initiative," available at http://www.justice.gov/atj/about-initiative (last retrieved August 13, 2015). See also Department of Justice, "ATJ's Four-Year Anniversary Major Accomplishments," available at www.justice.gov/atj/access-to-justice-accomplishments.html (last retrieved May 17, 2014); *Wilbur v. City of Mount Vernon*, No. C11–1100RSL, 2013 WL 6275319, at *2 (W.D. Wash. Dec. 4, 2013); Andrea Woods, "The Undersigned Attorney Hereby Certifies: Ensuring Reasonable Caseloads for Washington Defenders and Clients," *Washington Law Review* 89 (2014), 217–51.

[113] Deborah L. Rhode, "Access to Justice: An Agenda for Legal Education and Research," *Journal of Legal Education* 62 (2013), 531; David Luban, "Taking Out the Adversary: The Assault on Progressive Public Interest Lawyers," *California Law Review* (January 2003), 209, 211; Tom Lininger, "Deregulating Public Interest Law," *Tulane Law Review* 88 (2014), 727–71. See also Stephen Breyer, "The Legal Profession and Public Service" (Speech Sponsored by the National Legal Center for the Public Interest, The Pierre Hotel, New York, N.Y., September 12, 2000), available at www.supremecourt.gov (last retrieved May 22, 2014), 4.

[114] *Turner v. Rogers*, 564 U.S. 431 (2011). See also *M. L. B. v. S. L. J.*, 519 U.S. 102 (1996); *Lassiter v. Department of Social Services*, 452 U.S. 18 (1981); *United States v. Kras*, 409 U.S. 434 (1973); and *Boddie v. Connecticut*, 401 U.S. 371 (1971).

[115] See Jerold S. Auerbach, *Unequal Justice: Lawyers and Social Change in Modern America* (New York: Oxford University Press, 1976), 285–88.

[116] Albiston and Nielsen, "Funding the Cause: How Public Interest Law Organizations Fund Their Activities and Why It Matters for Social Change," 64–66; Susan E. Lawrence, *The Poor in Court: The Legal Services Program and Supreme Court Decision Making* (Princeton, N.J.: Princeton University Press, 1990), 25–36.

[117] Albiston and Nielsen, "Funding the Cause: How Public Interest Law Organizations Fund Their Activities and Why It Matters for Social Change," 66–67. See also *Brown v. Legal Foundation of Washington*, 538 U.S. 216 (2002); *Legal Services Corporation v. Velazquez*, 531 U.S. 533 (2001).

[118] See Steven M. Teles, *The Rise of the Conservative Legal Movement: The Battle for Control of the Law* (Princeton, N.J.: Princeton University Press, 2008).

[119] Terry Carter, "IOLTA Programs Find New Funding to Support Legal Services," *ABA Journal* 99 (2013), 61; Ed Finkel, *ABA Journal* 97 (2011), 24–25. The American Bar Association's Directory of IOLTA programs is found in American Bar Association, "Directory of IOLTA Programs," available at https://www.americanbar.org/groups/interest_lawyers_trust_accounts/resources/directory_of_iolta_programs/ (last retrieved April 17, 2020). Information about the Legal Services Corporation and an evaluation about the problems of meeting the challenge of meeting the legal aid needs of indigents is found at Legal Services Corporation, "The Justice Gap: Measuring the Unmet Civil Legal Needs of Low-income Americans," available at https://www.lsc.gov/sites/default/files/images/TheJusticeGap-FullReport.pdf (last retrieved April 17, 2020). See also Legal Services Corporation, "Fact Sheet on the Legal Services Corporation," available at https://www.lsc.gov/about-lsc/who-we-are (last retrieved April 17, 2020).

[120] National Center for State Courts, "Access to Justice: The Self-Represented Litigant (2006, Ten Trends Impacting State Courts)," available at https://ncsc.contentdm.oclc.org/digital/collection/accessfair/id/135 (last retrieved April 17, 2020); Rhode, *Access to Justice*, 82. Federal district court *pro se* civil filings are in Administrative Office of the U.S. Courts, "Table C-13. U.S. District Courts-Civil *Pro Se* and Non-*Pro Se* Filings, by District, During the 12-Month Period Ending September 30, 2017," available at https://www.uscourts.gov/sites/default/files/data_tables/jb_c13_0930.2019.pdf (last retrieved April 17, 2020); and, for federal

bankruptcy courts, in Administrative Office of the U.S. Courts, "By the Numbers—*Pro Se* Filers in the Bankruptcy Courts, *Third Branch News*, October 2011," available at www.uscourts.gov (last retrieved May 22, 2014) (reporting *pro se* bankruptcy petitions grew 187 percent from 2006 to 2011).

121 Paula L. Hannaford-Agor, "Helping the *Pro Se* Litigant: A Changing Landscape," *Court Review* 39 (Winter, 2003), 8–16; Rhode, *Access to Justice*, 82–83; Deborah L. Rhode, "Reforming American Legal Education and Legal Practice: Rethinking Licensing Structures and the Role of Nonlawyers in Delivering and Financing Legal Services," *Legal Ethics* 16 (2013), 243, 247. See also *Faretta v. California*, 422 U.S. 806 (1972).

122 See, e.g., the Self-Represented Litigation Network, available at https://www.srln.org/ (last retrieved April 17, 2020) (sponsored by the New Venture Fund, a 501(c)(3) public charity that provides full fiscal sponsorship including grant and contract management along with several law-related organizations).

123 National Center for State Courts, "Access to Justice: The Self-Represented Litigant (2006, Ten Trends Impacting State Courts)," available at http://ncsc.contentdm.oclc.org/cdm/ref/collection/accessfair/id/135 (last retrieved April 17, 2020); Richard Zorza, "Access to Justice: Economic Crisis Challenges, Impacts, and Responses (2009, Court Innovations to Consider in a Tight Economy)," available at http://ncsc.contentdm. oclc.org/cdm/ref/collection/accessfair/id/185 (last retrieved April 17, 2020).

124 Mitchell Levi, "Empirical Patterns in Pro Se Litigation in Federal District Courts," *University of Chicago Law Review* 85 (November 2018): 1819, 1828; Tom Lininger, "Exploring Strategies to Promote Access to Justice," *Georgetown Journal of Legal Ethics* 31 (2018): 357, 359. See also James G. Leipold, "Being Mindful About the Connection Between Pro Bono and PD," NALP Bulletin (May 2013), available at www.nalp.org/uploads/ 0513ConnectionBetweenProBonoandPD.pdf (last retrieved April 17, 2020).

125 See, e.g., Ruth Bader Ginsburg, "In Pursuit of the Public Good: Lawyers Who Care" (speech delivered on April 9, 2001, University of District of Columbia), available at https://www.supremecourt.gov/publicinfo/ speeches/viewspeech/sp_04-09-01a (last retrieved April 17, 2020); Margaret Graham Tebo, "Lag in Legal Services: Conference Speakers Make the Case for More Pro Bono Efforts by Lawyers," *American Bar Association Journal* (July 2002), 67; Rhode, *Access to Justice*, 145–84.

126 James C. McKinley, Jr., "New York State's Top Judge Permits Early Bar Exam in Exchange for Pro Bono Work," *New York Times* (February 11, 2014), available at www.nytimes.com (last retrieved April 17, 2020).

127 Lininger, "Exploring Strategies to Promote Access to Justice," 367–368. See also Scott L. Cummings, "The Pursuit of Legal Rights and Beyond," *U.C.L.A. Law Review* 59 (2012), 506, 535–36; Scott L. Cummings and Deborah L. Rhode, "Managing the Pro Bono: Doing Well by Doing Better," *Fordham Law Review* 78 (2010), 2357, 2364–65, 2373–74; Leslie C. Levin, "Pro Bono Publico in a Parallel Universe: The Meaning of Pro Bono in Solo and Small Law Firms," *Hofstra Law Review* 37 (2009), 699, 701.

128 Cummings, "The Politics of Pro Bono," 147. See also David J. Dreyer, "Culture, Structure, and Pro Bono Practice," *Journal of the Legal Profession* 33 (2009), 185, 198–99.

Access to Courts and Justice

For the first time in over forty years, in 2011 the Republican-controlled Wisconsin legislature enacted Wisconsin Act 43, a redistricting plan that allowed the Republican Party to capture 49 percent of the two-party statewide vote and 60 of 90 seats in the state legislature. In 2012, Republicans increased their stronghold in the state assembly by winning 63 seats and receiving 52 percent of the state-wide vote. In response, several Wisconsin voters challenged the redistricting plan because it allegedly diluted the votes of Democrats that were either put into a few districts by a process of "packing," or thinly spreading them across other districts through a process of "cracking." For the plaintiffs, the redistricting plan violated their rights under the Fourteenth Amendment's Equal Protection Clause; that is, they were discriminated against because they could only cast "wasted" votes for candidates who could only lose (under cracking), or who could only win by overwhelming margins (under packing).[1]

After a lower federal court sided with the plaintiffs and struck down the redistricting plan as the product of an unconstitutional partisan gerrymandering, in *Gill v. Whitford* (2018)[2] the Supreme Court held that the challengers did not have standing to sue because they claimed only a state-wide injury and not a personal injury based on their individual voting districts. Writing for a unanimous Court and quoting the landmark reapportionment decision *Baker v. Carr* (1962),[3] Chief Justice John Roberts reasoned that they did not have a legal basis to challenge the statewide map. In other words, they failed to demonstrate a "personal stake in the outcome," which is distinct from asserting a "generally available grievance about government." Rather than hear the case on whether the redistricting plan violated their voting rights under Fourteenth Amendment, the Court remanded the case to the lower court to determine the threshold issue of whether the affected voters could establish they suffered an individualized injury or harm, allowing them to bring an action in federal court.

Notably, after *Whitford* the Court decided to review two additional partisan redistricting cases—one arising in Maryland (*Lamone v. Benisek*) involving a map drawn by Democrats, and another from a map crafted by Republicans in North Carolina (*Rucho v. Common Cause*). After consolidating both cases, the Court split, 5:4, to hold that partisan gerrymandering lawsuits are non-justiciable (unreviewable by the courts) because they present political questions that are best resolved by the political branches. In his Opinion for the Court in *Rucho v. Common Cause*, which was joined by the conservative bloc of Justices Clarence Thomas, Samuel Alito, Neil Gorsuch and Brett Kavanaugh, Chief Justice John Roberts explained that there are no constitutional standards that courts can use to determine if gerrymandered districts are too political, or unfair, to one political party or not. Moreover, allowing courts to weigh in on such claims represents "an unprecedented expansion of judicial power" that, in turn, spawns an almost endless cycle of litigation that "would recur over and over again around the country with each new round of districting" after every ten-year census. The liberal bloc, Justices Ruth Bader Ginsburg, Stephen Breyer, Elena Kagan and Sonia Sotomayor, dissented. Reading her dissent from the bench, Justice Kagan argued that the Court's decision in and of itself was "unprecedented" because it, "for the first time ever," declined to "remedy a constitutional violation because it thinks the task beyond judicial capabilities." In her view, partisan gerrymanders not only take away the fundamental rights of citizens, they operate to "debase" and "dishonor" democratic governance in a way that "may irreparably damage of system of government."[4]

By requiring litigants to overcome threshold barriers, the law of standing and other jurisdictional doctrines allow courts to avoid, delay, or reach out to resolve contentious issues of public policy. *Whitford* and the Court's most recent redistricting decisions illustrate that judicial policymaking is often formulated in the preliminary stages of lawsuits when determining whether a litigant may bring a lawsuit in the first place. The political implications of judicial doctrines governing **justiciability** (whether a court has jurisdiction to hear a case and to provide a remedy) are thus important in defining litigants' access to courts but also for the elucidating policy making role of courts. Federal and state courts routinely use so-called threshold doctrines as a filter for reaching the legal merits of cases and controversial disputes over, for example, same-sex marriage, religious freedom, environmental protection, governmental surveillance, educational financing, redistricting, and many others.[5]

Notably, the public policy significance of high-profile litigation routinely also draws the attention of third-party advocacy and special interest groups who also want to be heard in courts so as to assert their ideological agendas.[6] In *Rucho*, several liberal and conservative nonprofit organizations—among them the American Civil Rights Union and Judicial Watch, Inc.—filed *amicus curiae* (third-party "friend of the court") briefs in support of their legal positions supporting or rejecting judicial interference in deciding partisan gerrymandering cases. Moreover, congressional and state committees and/or representatives, along with States, academics and private individuals, did the same in trying to influence the Court's decision. In total, the fact that nearly forty *amicus curiae* briefs were filed by a range of political and legal stakeholders—among them historians, political scientists, elected officials, and legal experts offering different theories of constitutional law and social science methodologies—registers the case's legal significance on the vital question of whether the federal courts ought to enter into the "political thicket" and resolve redistricting questions of law that are inherently political in nature.[7]

Whether litigants and outside groups gain judicial access is thus a crucial threshold question that defines the scope and limits of a court's power to hear a case and, ultimately, affect public policy. In general, the Constitution and state constitutions, federal or state statutes, and rules of courts are the principal sources establishing the jurisdiction of courts. After reviewing some of these formal barriers to judicial access, this Chapter considers the informal constraints, along with the different methods organized interests and public advocacy groups use to win access to the courts and shape policy.

FORMAL BARRIERS

The legal doctrines defining the scope of courts' jurisdiction originate in state or federal constitutions and judicial practices. While state and federal courts share similar constitutional frameworks, there are important differences distinguishing their operation, function, and decisional processes. Judicial selection for federal and state courts differs (as discussed in Chapter Four), and state constitutions may be more easily amended than the federal Constitution. As a result, state constitutional development is more closely tied to the democratic values and preferences that orient how the courts determine jurisdiction and exercise their judicial authority. Given these differences, some legal scholars argue that the formal constraints that delineate judicial powers—among them separation of powers or federalism principles—do not uniformly apply in state and federal courts.[8] In other words, the same formal barriers that determine whether a federal court has jurisdiction to adjudicate a case may not control state court jurisdictional powers. Even so, many state courts nonetheless tend to draw on the provisions of the Constitution when interpreting their jurisdiction.[9]

The Constitution's Article III "Cases" or "Controversies" Requirement

Under Article III of the Constitution, federal courts may decide only "cases or controversies." As explained by Chief Justice Charles Evans Hughes, jurisdiction extends to controversies that are "definite and concrete, touching the legal relations of parties having adverse legal interests," and that may be resolved by courts giving "specific relief through a decree of a conclusive character, as distinguished from an opinion advising what the law would be upon a hypothetical state of facts."[10]

Article III bars federal courts from entertaining friendly lawsuits—those that do not raise adverse interests. Nor do courts give **advisory opinions** about hypothetical cases. In 1793, for example, the Supreme Court rejected President George Washington's request to interpret an international law. Most state courts adhere to the tradition of not rendering advisory opinions, though there are exceptions: at least eight state constitutions permit their courts to advise the governor or legislature on questions of policy, and several state courts have assumed jurisdiction over legal and political disputes that ordinarily are nonreviewable ("nonjusticiable") in the federal courts.[11]

The Procedural Rules of Courts

Both federal and state courts rely on procedural rules to manage their dockets and determine whether litigants have standing to bring legal claims. Under the 1789 Judiciary Act, federal courts followed the rules of state judiciaries. But as the federal system grew, Congress authorized federal courts to develop their own procedural rules. With the passage of the Rules Enabling Act in 1934, Congress gave the Supreme Court the power to create its own rules on the basis of recommendations made by the Judicial Conference of the United States (the policymaking body that administers the operation of federal courts, as discussed in Chapter Three). As a result, the Court enacted the 1938 Federal Rules of Civil Procedure (FRCP), which now govern federal judicial procedure.[12]

The FRCP quickly became the model for most states as well. The model rules require pretrial meetings between judges and lawyers, a practice that helps settle cases without trials. In 1946, the Court created the Federal Rules of Criminal Procedure, and in the 1970s, the Federal Rules format was adopted for administrative actions as well as for evidentiary hearings and other proceedings.

Today, the Federal Rules of Appellate Procedure, the Federal Rules of Bankruptcy Procedure, and the Federal Rules of Evidence all govern specialized trial practices and case procedures.[13]

The proliferation of judicial rulemaking has been both a boon and a bane, however. Though the goal of greater uniformity has been arguably achieved to some degree, the simplicity of procedure is undermined when each judicial district promulgates its own set of rules. Some studies have shown that the federal model of procedural rules has had a diminishing impact on state courts over time, thus allowing nonfederal practices to govern the legal processes of most of the heavily populated states.[14] In the federal courts, Congress has also complicated the development of uniform rules by amending the federal rules, often without consulting the U.S. Judicial Conference or the Supreme Court.[15]

The struggles over the development of rules of judicial procedure—complicated by the growth of Internet technologies and the movement toward digital "e-formats" that regulate the flow of court paperwork—has also had some contradictory effects.[16] On the one hand, the open and deliberative nature of the rulemaking process contributes to transparency and public accountability. On the other hand, its openness resulted in some state and federal courts promulgating their own sets of procedural rules. As a result, litigants seeking access to justice often confront parochial rules that make the judicial process complicated, costly, and time-consuming.[17]

Lastly, the use of procedural rules by courts and litigants has the potential to be manipulated politically and doing so can either facilitate or restrict access to courts. Some scholars argue, for example, that the Roberts Court has been adept at accomplishing a "procedural retrenchment" in deciding cases interpreting how the rules of federal civil procedure must operate in certain controversial areas of legal and public policy, such as class action, criminal justice, or consumer protection lawsuits, to name a few (see Chapter Eight for a discussion of how the rules of notice and pleading affect civil litigation). The effect of those decisions have a conservative bent as, in the words of one scholar, they "systematically [are] closing the courthouse doors to those suing corporations, to those suing the government, to criminal defendants, and to plaintiffs in general. . .[As such], the Roberts Court often has been able to achieve substantive results favored by conservatives through these procedural devices."[18] Yet, as suggested above, state courts are not obliged to follow federal rules, and it is within their authority to ignore or reject outright Supreme Court precedents interpreting procedural rules at the federal level, and several high and lower state courts have expressly rejected Supreme Court precedents governing restrictive pleading and class action requirements.[19] Moreover, some research argues that a variety of institutional actors and interests, among them Congress, businesses, organized groups, and bureaucrats laid a bi-partisan foundation for changing the rules of the game in an effort to promote access to courts, such as in the area of alternative dispute resolution, to relieve plaintiffs from the high cost of litigation; but, ultimately, the same rules were co-opted and applied by conservative courts and judges in later political time periods to restrict it. Consequently, the causes of retrenchment can only be explained by a pattern of institutional occurrences within in American political development over time and, therefore, cannot solely be associated with the outcomes of rulings by recent Supreme Courts and the exercise of its ideological preferences.[20]

DISCRETIONARY BARRIERS

The case and controversy limitations on judicial power are also the basis for discretionary doctrines that determine whether a case is *justiciable*—that is, reviewable. Doctrines of justiciability allow courts to exercise restraint and deny access to cases not deemed "fit" for resolution. Scholars and courts, however, have never reached a consensus on the wisdom of invoking such jurisdictional doctrines in order to grant or deny litigants access to the courts (see "Contemporary Controversies over Courts: Tactics for Constitutional Avoidance: 'Passive Virtues' or 'Subtle Vices'?"). Political scientists refer to these doctrines as "access policy making" principles because, in determining whether litigants have the legal merits of their cases heard, courts express ideological preferences in the choices they make about access whenever they consider whether litigants have standing, or whether lawsuits are **moot** or **ripe** or improperly raise a **political question**.[21]

Contemporary Controversies over Courts: Tactics for Constitutional Avoidance: "Passive Virtues" or "Subtle Vices"?

Justice Louis Brandeis (1916–1939) famously outlined rules for avoiding deciding constitutional questions. They remain important—though controversial and not always followed—for understanding the ways the Court may forestall addressing constitutional questions that might bring it into conflicts with Congress or the president. Justice Brandeis and other liberal progressives advocated "judicial self-restraint" and deference to the political process because, in the 1930s, a conservative majority on the Court was striking down early New Deal and other progressive state legislation. In an opinion in

Ashwander v. Tennessee Valley Authority (1936), he objected to granting standing—that is, recognizing a personal injury entitling the petitioner to bring a lawsuit challenging the constitutionality of federal legislation—and maintained that, if standing was granted in a case, the Court should still avoid striking down legislation or a law unless it was "beyond all reasonable doubt" that there was a constitutional violation. In setting forth seven rules for constitutional avoidance, Justice Brandeis explained:

The Court developed, for its own governance in the cases confessedly within its jurisdiction, a series of rules under which it has avoided passing upon a large part of all the constitutional questions pressed upon it for decision. They are:

1. The Court will not pass upon the constitutionality of legislation in a friendly, non-adversary, proceeding, declining because to decide such questions "is legitimate only in the last resort, and as a necessity in the determination of real, earnest and vital controversy between individuals. It never was the thought that, by means of a friendly suit, a party beaten in the legislature could transfer to the courts an inquiry as to the constitutionality of the legislative act."

2. The Court will not "anticipate a question of constitutional law in advance of the necessity of deciding it. . . .It is not the habit of the Court to decide questions of a constitutional nature unless absolutely necessary to a decision of the case."

3. The Court will not "formulate a rule of constitutional law broader than is required by the precise facts to which it is to be applied."

4. The Court will not pass upon a constitutional question although properly presented by the record, if there is also present some other ground upon which the case may be disposed of. This rule has found most varied application. Thus, if a case can be decided on either of two grounds, one involving a constitutional question, the other a question of statutory construction or general law, the Court will decide only the latter. . . .Appeals from the highest court of a state challenging its decision of a question under the Federal Constitution are frequently dismissed because the judgment can be sustained on an independent state ground.

5. The Court will not pass upon the validity of a statute upon complaint of one who fails to show that he is injured by its operation. . . .Among the many applications of this rule, none is more striking than the denial of the right of challenge to one who lacks a personal or property right. Thus, the challenge by a public official interested only in the performance of his official duty will not be entertained.

6. The Court will not pass upon the constitutionality of a statute at the instance of one who has availed himself of its benefits.

7. When the validity of an act of the Congress is drawn in question, and even if a serious doubt of constitutionality is raised, it is a cardinal principle that this Court will first ascertain whether a construction of the statute is fairly possible by which the question may be avoided.

Justice Brandeis's disciple, former liberal Harvard Law School professor Justice Felix Frankfurter, subsequently championed avoiding deciding many cases by invoking standing requirements—whether there is a true adversarial dispute over a personal injury that is ripe, not moot, and does not present a "political question." As a result, the Court delayed deciding many cases involving claims of constitutional rights, and Justice Frankfurter became more conservative during his time on the bench (1939–1962).

The rules for constitutional avoidance and threshold questions of standing to sue, thus, became and remain controversial. One of Justice Frankfurter's former law clerks, Yale Law School professor Alexander Bickel, defended them as the "passive virtues" of judicial review. Since the Court is an antidemocratic, countermajoritarian institution, he argued, it therefore should generally defer to the outcomes of the democratic process. By contrast, another of Justice Frankfurter's former law clerks, Stanford Law School professor Gerald Gunther, along with other liberals, countered that such rules and standing requirements were "subtle vices." Important questions of constitutional rights are thereby avoided, but the Court in fact has "a duty to decide" them, given its obligation to enforce the Constitution and the Bill of Rights.

After Justice Frankfurter retired, less attention was paid to such rules and standing requirements by the Court—from the latter years of the tenure of Chief Justice Earl Warren (1953–1969) through the chief justiceships of Warren E. Burger (1969–1986) and William H. Rehnquist (1986–2005). More recently, however, a majority of the Court under Chief Justice John G. Roberts,

Jr., has renewed interest in avoiding constitutional questions and, if reaching them, deciding them on the narrowest possible grounds.

Sources: *Ashwander v. Tennessee Valley Authority*, 297 U.S. 288 (1936); Alexander Bickel, *The Least Dangerous Branch: The Supreme Court at the Bar of Politics* (New York: Bobbs-Merrill, 1962); Gerald Gunther, "The Subtle Vices of 'Passive Virtues,'" *Columbia Law Review* 64, no. 1 (1964); and Lisa Kloppenberg, *Playing It Safe: How the Supreme Court Sidesteps Hard Cases and Stunts the Development of Law* (New York: New York University Press, 2001).

The Standing Doctrine

Although the law of standing has been called one of "the most amorphous concepts in the entire domain of public law,"[22] it simply means that a party must have a personal stake in the outcome of a case. In making that determination, a court decides whether the party has suffered a "concrete and particularized" injury that is "fairly traceable" to the challenged conduct and is likely to be resolved (or "redressed") by a judicial decision.[23] In applying these principles of "injury," "causation," and "redressability," courts often focus on the party's injury. For example, in California, two same-sex couples sued state officials because they claimed that California's Proposition 8, a ballot initiative banning same-sex marriage, violated their due process and equality rights. Yet the state officials, who included the governor, the attorney general, and others who were responsible for enforcing California's marriage laws, refused to defend Proposition 8—so the official proponents of Proposition 8 sought to intervene and defend it in court on behalf of the state. In *Hollingsworth v. Perry* (2013), however, the Supreme Court denied the official proponents of the ballot measure standing because they merely had a "generalized grievance" that did not give them a "direct stake" in Proposition 8's enforcement. As Chief Justice John Roberts put it, "Without a judicially cognizable interest of their own, [the official proponents of Proposition 8] attempt to invoke that of someone else," namely state officials. Therefore, they did not have a "sufficiently concrete interest" in the dispute and did not suffer an "injury in fact."[24]

It bears emphasizing that the doctrine of standing resolves only questions of a litigant's status and not whether the underlying claim is meritorious. The common sense, or intuitive legitimacy of the lawsuits' substantive claims may not be enough to convince a court that it has the jurisdiction, or fitness, to resolve them. To illustrate, in *Juliana v. United States* (2019),[25] in a 2:1 ruling the Ninth Circuit reversed a district court judgment that sanctioned a lawsuit brought by citizens and pro-environmental interest groups claiming that they were harmed by governmental policies promoting the use of fossil fuels by the federal government on the grounds that the federal courts were not empowered to enact legislation that would diminish the effects of climate change. Under the standing doctrine, the circuit court concluded that it was not within its judicial competency to fix, or "redress" the harm; thus, it could not order a decree that would force the federal government to come up with a legislative plan that would curb fossil fuel emissions and reduce harmful carbon dioxide emissions, even though the court determined that the government's fossil fuel policies caused the type of significant harm and damage that the plaintiffs sought relief from. As circuit Judge Andrew Hurwitz explained, "it was beyond the power of an Article III court to order, design, supervise, or implement the plaintiffs' requested remedial plan where any effective plan would necessarily require a host of complex policy decisions entrusted to the wisdom and discretion of the executive and legislative branches." In dissent, district court Judge Josephine Staton (sitting by designation on the circuit court) countered the plaintiffs must be granted standing to vindicate the principle that "the Constitution does not condone the Nation's willful destruction" by climate change.[26]

Apart from climate change lawsuits, federal courts likewise have been reluctant to accept to the advocacy arguments raised by animal rights' groups claiming that non-humans animals must be given the right to sue in cases where they are harmed by their owner's or caretakers neglect or abuse. Simply put, courts have not let animals, such as injured horses or the "cetacean community" (e.g. whales, dolphins, or porpoises) bring their actions into court because, from the courts' perspective, the law does not give them any legal status to do so; and, they are fearful that courts would be inundated with lawsuits if they entertained the merits of lawsuits that animals sought to litigate (see Contemporary Controversies over Courts: Animal Rights, Standing & Justice box). As in the climate change context, generally the courts are unwilling to unlock the keys to the courthouse door to give litigants the chance under the standing doctrine to effectuate legal and policy change based on the case's lawful merits.

Contemporary Controversies over Courts: Animal Rights, Standing & Justice

In a civil action filed in Washington County Circuit Court in Hillsboro, Oregon, the Animal Legal Defense Fund sued on behalf of an 8-year-old horse named Justice. The suit claimed that the horse's owner broke Oregon law by abusing it with severe neglect. The horse's owner left him outside for extended periods of time in the cold and failed to give him food and water, which lead to starvation and frostbite. When discovered, the horse had multiple injuries, some of which were permanent: he was 300 pounds underweight; his coat was lice-ridden; his skin was scabbed due to "rain rot" and; and the frostbite caused a prolapsed penis, an injury that might require partial amputation in the future. While the horse was relocated to a farm with other rescued equines, and even though the defendant, Vercher, pleaded guilty to criminal neglect and agreed to pay restitution for past medical costs, the civil suit sought $100,000 for ongoing veterinary care, plus damages for "pain and suffering." In September 2018, the state trial court granted the defendant's motion to dismiss, ruling that Justice lacked standing to bring the suit because he was a non-human animal that "lacks the legal status or qualifications necessary for the assertion of legal rights and duties in a court of law." In so ruling, the court reasoned that allowing the case to go forward "would likely lead to a flood of lawsuits whereby non-human animals could assert claims we now reserve just for humans and human creations such as business and other entities. Furthermore, non-human animals are incapable of accepting legal responsibilities."

While Justice's case might seem unusual, it is part of a growing social movement in the last 30 years to achieve legal and rights' protections for non-human animals. While a few ancient philosophers thought that animals' welfare must be taken into consideration in human society, the notion of extending legal protections to animals has not been an integral part of Western political philosophy until the 1970s. Thereafter, the animal rights' movement started to take hold with the publication of Peter Singer's *Animal Liberation* (1990), a book arguing that the United States engaged in "speciesism," or "a prejudice or attitude of bias in favor of the interests of members of one's own species and against those of members of another species." For Singer, who was a utilitarian, the interests of non-human animals and humans must be equally considered and, in weighing them, the benefits of human domination over non-human animals do not outweigh the costs imposed on those species. As opposed to other political philosophers arguing against giving legal protections to non-human animals because they do not have the capacity to speak, think or reason, Singer and other utilitarians countered it is morally ethical and just to safeguard the legal interests of non-human animals because they do have the capacity to endure suffering at the hands of humans. While Singer does not emphasize that non-human animals deserve rights' recognition, his view that speciesism results in unethical behavior, such as using animals for medical experimentation or product-testing, resonates with contemporary animal protection group advocacy which asserts that animals must not be used for human entertainment, food, clothing and scientific research.

Today, the modern animal law scholarship mostly consists of normative arguments taking one of three positions: (1) supporting the prevailing view of lawyers and courts that animals are property, so existing laws protecting non-human animals, e.g. animal cruelty laws, are sufficient; (2) supporting the view that animals are property but argue for laws that strengthen animal welfare; and, (3) supporting an absolutist view that animals must be given full legal status and rights' protections. The leading animal advocacy groups and the approach they take to advancing animal welfare is generally aligned with one of these positions. Whereas the Humane Society of the United States and the American Society for the Prevention of Cruelty to Animals take a moderate, welfarist approach that stresses rescuing and caring for abused or neglected animals, more radical and confrontational groups such as People for the Ethical Treatment of Animals and the Animal Liberation Front undertake action that highlights animal suffering in order to draw attention to the problem of animal cruelty and abuse. The latter group has even resorted to engaging in sabotage, arson, and vandalism against facilities that exploit animals, such as circuses, research laboratories and slaughterhouses, to make its point, leading the federal government to classify it as a terrorist organization.

Some of these groups are involved with other well-resourced specialist litigation organizations, such as the Animal Legal Defense Fund (ALDF) and state and federal governmental actors, in litigation to advance non-human animal rights and interests in the courts. As the ALDF's case that tried to convince a state court that Justice, an abused horse, could sue in his own right illustrates, courts generally follow the longstanding principle that non-human animals are property and do not have legal "personhood" status to sue or have rights. This is true even though the law recognizes artificial entities, such as corporations, as legal persons that have the legal right to sue. Still, with few exceptions, the Supreme Court's three-prong test established in *Lujan v. Defenders of Wildlife*, 504 U.S. 555 (1992), makes it very difficult for pro-animal rights advocates to argue successfully that non-human animals deserve standing to sue. In order to satisfy *Lujan*'s standing doctrine principles, litigants must show that there is proof of a "concrete and particularized" "injury-in-fact" that is "traceable" to an action causing the harm, and which is capable of being "redressed" by a favorable decision on the merits. Most cases applying this standard limit standing to human actors and not their "property," such as a pig, goat or horse.

Critics counter that easing standing restrictions would do more harm than good: permitting animal litigants and their human representatives to sue would invite difficult, if not irreconcilable, questions about what kinds of legal actions may be brought by animals or humans (on their behalf). Thus far, courts have recognized these implications by refusing to grant standing or relief in cases that test the limits of animal law, such as: whether captive Chimpanzees can be issued a *habeas corpus* to gain release; if animal protection groups can bring a federal action on behalf of the cetacean community that is allegedly harmed by sonar waves used by the military; or whether a beloved pet that died because of a veterinarian's medical mistake entitles the owner to non-economic damages (e.g. pain and suffering) because the pet is considered to be "family" instead of property, like a toaster or a chair.

Sources: Opinion Letter by Judge John S. Knowles in *Justice v. Gwendolyn Vercher (18 CV17601, Washington County Circuit Court)*(September 17, 2018), available at https://www.portlandmercury.com/images/blogimages/2018/09/17/1537229464-documentfragment_66832151.pdf (last retrieved April 17, 2020); Karin Brulliard, "Seeking Justice for Justice the Horse," *Washington Post* (August 13, 2018), available at https://www.washingtonpost.com/news/national/wp/2018/08/13/feature/a-horse-was-neglected-by-its-owner-now-the-horse-is-suing/?utm_term=.fe9e5379d3d9&wpisrc=nl_az_most&wpmk=1 (last retrieved April 17, 2020); Animal Legal Defense Fund, "Justice the Horse Sues Abuser," available at https://aldf.org/case/justice-the-horse-sues-abuser/ (last retrieved April 17, 2020); Nicole Pallotta, "Advocating for Justice in Oregon: Neglected Horse Sues Former Owner," available at https://aldf.org/article/advocating-for-justice-in-oregon-neglected-horse-sues-former-owner/ (last retrieved April 17, 2020); Joseph Lubinski, "Introduction to Animal Rights (2nd Ed.)," *Animal Legal and Historical Center*, available at https://www.animallaw.info/article/introduction-animal-rights-2nd-ed (last retrieved April 17, 2020); Kim Masters Evans, *Animal Rights* (Farmington Hills, MI.: Gale Cengage Learning, 2018); Steven C. Tauber, *Navigating the Jungle: Law, Politics, and the Animal Advocacy Movement* (New York: Routledge, 2016).

State and federal courts, however, are not uniform in deciding standing issues. Taxpayer lawsuits—suits by citizens alleging that the government unlawfully is spending taxpayer monies in support of disfavored legislative programs—is a good example.[27] Whereas Article III constrains federal court jurisdiction in taxpayer lawsuits, it does not affect state courts. Consequently, many state courts permit taxpayer standing, but federal courts generally prohibit it.[28]

Moreover, in the 1960s, the Warren Court (1953–1969) relaxed the barriers to taxpayer standing, but subsequently a more conservative Court has limited taxpayer standing. In *Flast v. Cohen* (1968),[29] the Court granted taxpayer standing to challenge the federal government's giving religious schools a subsidy for instructional materials and textbooks under the Elementary and Secondary Education Act. *Flast* is important because it liberalized taxpayers' standing to challenge the constitutionality of legislation if they could satisfy a two-prong test: first, whether there is a nexus between their status as taxpayers and the challenged legislation; and, second, whether there is a nexus between their status and the "precise nature of the constitutional infringement alleged." These principles made it easier for taxpayers in Establishment Clause cases to bring lawsuits in federal courts and expanded the role of courts in determining public policy.

However, as the Court became more conservative, the law on taxpayer standing has been increasingly limited. In *Valley Forge Christian College v. Americans United for Separation of Church and State, Inc.* (1982), the Burger Court (1969–1986) denied standing to a citizen challenging a land grant to a religious college, because it was a challenge to an administrative decision—and not, as in *Flast*, a challenge to the constitutionality of congressional legislation.[30] Subsequently, in *Hein v. Freedom From Religion Foundation, Inc.* (2007) and *Arizona Christian School Tuition Organization v. Winn* (2011), the Roberts Court (2005–present) rejected taxpayer standing in cases raising other Establishment Clause issues. In *Hein*, taxpayers were not permitted to challenge President George W. Bush's "faith-based initiatives" program because the funds used to support religious organizations were dispersed at the discretion of the executive branch and not as authorized by Congress. In *Winn*, Arizona taxpayers were denied standing to challenge a state law permitting taxpayers to receive tax credits for making contributions to so-called school tuition organizations, including some that were religious, because the credits were not deemed a legislative appropriation.[31] Justices Antonin Scalia and Clarence Thomas would have gone further and entirely overturned *Flast*.[32]

In addition to taxpayer suits, the courts apply the standing doctrine to so-called citizen suits, or the lawsuits by citizens who by statute may bring suits in order to vindicate certain public interests against federal agencies' regulations. Citizen-suit provisions are often located in federal environmental laws, such as the Clean Water Act, the Clean Air Act, the Resource Conservation and Recovery Act, and the Endangered Species Act (ESA), among others—though, to use them successfully, plaintiffs cannot assert a generalized grievance against government. In *Lujan v. Defenders of Wildlife* (1992) the Supreme Court dismissed a citizen-suit lawsuit by a group of environmental activists because its claim—that a change in the ESA that limited its protection to the United States and the high seas (and not foreign nations)—did not cause an "injury in fact" to one or more of its members since none of them harbored any concrete plans or particularized intentions to visit the habitats of the species in the foreign countries at issue.[33] The *Lujan* principle that alleged injuries must be specifically concrete *and* particular before standing is granted was tightened further in *Spokeo, Inc. v. Robins* (2016). There, the Supreme Court denied standing to a citizen alleging that a company operating a "people search engine" violated the Federal Credit Reporting Act (1970) by reporting false and inaccurate information about him because it was a harm that is "particularized" (Spokeo's handling of Robins' credit information personally affected him), but not "concrete" (*de facto*, which is real and actually existed). As Justice Samuel Alito emphasized, Congress cannot authorize a citizen to sue through a statute if the plaintiff only alleges a "bare procedural violation, divorced from any concrete harm, and satisfy the injury-in-fact requirement of Article III."[34]

Similarly, in "legislative standing" cases, the judiciary sometimes hear (but increasingly reject) the claims of elected representatives who challenge the constitutionality of recently enacted legislation on which they were outvoted. Public advocacy groups, governmental entities, and other third parties also routinely seek judicial access, and do so in not always ideologically predictable alliances.[35] For example, in *Massachusetts v. Environmental Protection Agency* (2007),[36] a bare majority of the Roberts Court granted Massachusetts and other environmental groups standing to challenge the federal government's decision not to regulate harmful greenhouse gas emissions under the Clean Air Act. However, in *Clapper v. Amnesty International USA* (2013),[37] another 5:4 decision, the Court denied standing to attorneys, human rights activists, labor organizations, and journalists that did not want their private telephone conversations to suspected terrorists in foreign countries to be monitored under the federal government's wiretap surveillance program. In sum, while the law of standing continues to evolve, critics lament the inability to draw clearly fixed lines and what appears to be *ad hoc* judicial decision-making—even "lawless, illogical, and dishonest" judicial behavior.[38]

The Timing Doctrines: Mootness and Ripeness

Mootness and ripeness are two sides of the same coin for denying a litigant the chance to argue a lawsuit's merits: a case may be dismissed as *moot* if the factual basis for the dispute has changed; alternatively, a review may be denied if it is not *ripe* because appeals in lower courts or other agencies have not been exhausted. In both instances, the timing of the lawsuit in relation to its facts and the law are at issue and a significant factor in allowing or preventing full access to the courts.

In *DeFunis v. Odegaard* (1974),[39] for example, the Court dismissed a lawsuit challenging the University of Washington School of Law's affirmative action program because the student bringing the suit had been admitted, was in his third year of law school, and would graduate before the justices could decide the case. *DeFunis* illustrates that a live controversy can lose its adverseness upon a change in facts or law after a lawsuit is filed. Similarly, during its 2019–20 Term, in a case involving the scope of gun rights under the Second Amendment the Roberts Court sent it back to the lower courts on the grounds of mootness after New York

City repealed a rule banning them from transporting their licensed guns to areas beyond the City. Still, the sharply critical dissents from three of the Court's conservatives—Justices Samuel Alito, Neil Gorsuch and, in part, Justice Clarence Thomas—signaled that the controversy over gun rights will not stay dormant for long, and the full Court might review the merits of a similar challenge sometime in the near future—something that it has not done in the decade since its landmark rulings declaring there is a personal right to self-defense in the home in *District of Columbia v. Heller* (2008), and its follow-up decision, *McDonald v. City of Chicago* (2010), confirming that the *Heller's* Second Amendment principle applied uniformly across the nation, and not just in the District of Columbia, under the Fourteenth Amendment's incorporation doctrine.[40]

In contrast to federal courts, though, state judiciaries are, arguably, more inclined to hear, and not avoid, disputes involving important public policy questions, sometimes under the rhetoric of advancing the "public interest."[41] But, as with federal justiciability questions, determining the public interest is a matter of judicial discretion. To illustrate, in Illinois, after a lower court ruled that a state law was unconstitutional because it denied a convicted sex offender visitation rights to his children, county and state officials filed an appeal to reverse the court's ruling. But, while the appeal was pending, the father filed another petition claiming that he was entitled to visit his children under the same law that was held to be unconstitutional because he successfully completed a treatment program, a precondition that established his legal right to visitation. In *In re Marriage of Donald B. and Roberta B.* (2014),[42] the Illinois Supreme Court agreed, holding that the issue of the state law's constitutionality no longer needed to be decided on appeal because it was moot in light of the father's compliance with the controlling statute.

The *ripeness* doctrine, as explained in *Abbott Laboratories v. Gardner* (1967),[43] is invoked "to prevent courts, through the avoidance of premature adjudication, from entangling themselves in abstract disagreements" with other government institutions over legal interpretations. Thus, for many federal courts, issues of ripeness are determined by the "fitness of the issues" for judicial resolution and the type of "hardship" the parties will face if the court does not review the case. The first factor ensures that the court is hearing a legal question and the second evaluates how the litigants are affected if the court declines to act.[44] In *Renne v. Geary* (1991),[45] on First Amendment free speech grounds, several registered voters and political party representatives sued county election officials to stop them from deleting political endorsements that are printed in voting pamphlets in nonpartisan elections, in accordance with a state constitutional provision. But, absent an allegation that county officials had actually removed the endorsements, the Supreme Court held that the case did not present a live controversy to decide.

Notably, the doctrines of mootness and ripeness may be manipulated, either to avoid deciding contentious social issues of public policy or, conversely, to confront them. Although *DeFunis* declined to review the merits of reverse affirmative-action claims, four years later, in *Regents of the University of California v. Bakke* (1978),[46] the Court did so and upheld such programs so long as they do not impose a quota system. Likewise, in *Roe v. Wade* (1973),[47] the landmark abortion decision, the Court decided the case even though Jane Roe had delivered a baby by the time the Court handed down its decision. Instead of mooting the case, the Court held because a woman may become pregnant again and the litigation process would have taken longer than nine months, the issues raised had to be judicially resolved because they were "capable of repetition, yet evading review."

The Political Question Doctrine

As this chapter's introduction shows the implications of denying on a merits' review of partisan gerrymandering cases, the political question doctrine is a powerful tool of judicial discretion that raises fundamental questions about a court's fitness to adjudicate highly controversial matters of public policy affecting the U.S. political system. Notably, the political question doctrine has a longstanding constitutional history because it originated from a landmark Supreme Court case, *Marbury v. Madison* (1803), that is best known for re-enforcing the principle of judicial review, or a court's power to strike down laws or executive action that violates constitutional principles.[48] In an important aside, Chief Justice Marshall said, "The province of the court is, solely, to decide on the rights of individuals, not to inquire how the executive, or executive officers, perform duties in which they have discretion. Questions in their nature political, or which are, by the constitution and the laws, submitted to the executive, can never be made in this court." The doctrine limits a court's jurisdiction by removing political disputes from judicial consideration. Similar to the standing doctrine's application in the *Juliana* climate change case, it rules that disputes are better resolved by the political branches because there is no clear judicial remedy.

Although state courts may decline to hear political questions, Article III requires federal courts to apply the doctrine with more rigor.[49] Yet, even the federal judiciary has assumed jurisdiction over matters that were once thought to be best resolved by other political branches. Before 1962, for instance, the Court generally refused to hear "political questions" involving challenges to legislative redistricting.[50] In *Colegrove v. Green* (1946),[51] Justice Felix Frankfurter famously stated that political disputes over redistricting would require the judiciary to do "what is beyond its competence to grant," and therefore "courts ought not to enter this political thicket." Yet in *Baker v. Carr* (1962)[52] the Supreme Court signaled that it was ready to take that step in a subsequent redistricting case challenging the malapportionment of a state legislature as violation of equal voting rights. The Court delineated six factors that were intended to guide courts in deciding if a legal issue should be heard or avoided as a political question, and among them was whether there is a "lack of judicially discoverable and manageable standards for resolving the issue."[53] These factors, when applied, give the justices more discretion to decide the types of cases that previously were thought to be unreviewable. Since *Baker*, the Court has increasingly supervised the electoral process in a wide range of areas, including the regulation of political parties, campaign finance regulation, political patronage, voting, and redistricting.

The political question doctrine's scope and application remains controversial in the area of political elections and campaigns, especially when the Court is criticized as taking ideological sides. In *Bush v. Gore* (2000), an election saga and legal contest that Justice Ruth Bader Ginsburg later referred to as a "December storm over the U.S. Supreme Court,"[54] the Court bypassed the political question doctrine and decided that the manual recount conducted in certain Florida voting districts violated the Equal Protection Clause by not providing precise standards for determining a voter's intent in casting a ballot. Four justices—John Paul Stevens, David Souter, Ruth Bader Ginsburg, and Stephen Breyer—disagreed. Justice Breyer made the most forceful case for nonintervention, arguing that the Twelfth Amendment and the federal Electoral Count Act vested in Congress, not the Court, the power to decide the outcome of presidential elections. For Justice Breyer, the Court should have invoked the political question and followed the advice of Justice Louis Brandeis who once said that "the most important thing we do is not doing."

Bush v. Gore is perhaps the most dramatic illustration of the political question doctrine's significant public policy and electoral consequences. By not using the political question doctrine, one could argue that the Court was complicit in *Bush* in helping G.W. Bush enter the White House in a sharply contented presidential contest. Also, the doctrine can be the focus of lesser known cases that routinely go under the radar in terms of general public awareness. For example, it is often the focal point of land-use disputes and state educational finance suits challenging public school funding formulas devised by legislatures and whether they meet constitutional standards,[55] and its application can define the role unregulated political money plays in campaigns and elections in protecting the free speech rights or ideological interests of individuals and special interest groups.[56]

In sum, all of the justiciability doctrines are critical gateways for litigants to gain access to courts and possibly help change legal and social policy. In the next section, the central role lawyers and organized interests play in strategically positioning themselves to gain access to the courts and influence legal policy is analyzed.

ORGANIZED INTERESTS AND STRATEGIC LITIGATION

"We can now look forward to at least another term," complained Justice Antonin Scalia, "with carts full of mail from the public, and streets full of demonstrators, urging us—their unelected and life-tenured judges who have been awarded those extraordinary, undemocratic characteristics precisely in order that we might follow the law despite the popular will—to follow the popular will." Justice Scalia's disappointment, expressed in a concurring opinion in *Webster v. Reproductive Health Services* (1989), was over the Court's failure to overturn *Roe v. Wade* (1973), its landmark ruling on abortion. For its time, *Webster*—which tested the limits of Missouri law that enacted a variety of restrictions on abortion, such as banning most public facilities and employees from performing the procedure, and requiring fetus viability tests on women in their twentieth week of pregnancy— generated an unprecedented amount of attention from organized interests and public advocacy groups from both sides of the political spectrum—seventy-eight *amicus curiae* briefs were filed, and over four hundred different interest groups cosponsored the litigation; and, significantly, all participated with the anticipation that their policy desires would be recognized by the Court, including, perhaps, that the Justices would take the bold step of using *Webster* to reverse *Roe*. Although the Court upheld the restrictions, and it declined to revisit's *Roe's* precedential effect, Justice Scalia's comments affirms that courts and judges are very mindful of the strong influence that interest groups have on the legal system, both in the United States and in foreign jurisdictions.[57]

Also, as Justice Scalia predicted, the abortion controversy did not go away after *Webster*. In fact, it resurfaced nearly thirty-five years later under remarkably identical circumstances in the conservative Roberts Court's review of *June Medical Services LLC v. Russo* (2020), a case that struck down Louisiana's law mandating that abortions be performed only by doctors with admitting privileges at nearby hospitals. As with *Webster*, court watchers, at the time, speculated that Justice Anthony's recent arrival on Supreme Court—who replaced retiring Justice Lewis

Powell's "swing vote" on a bench equally split on the abortion issue—would be enough to tip the ideological balance and lead to *Roe's* demise, the same scenario generally was in play in the Court's review of *June Medical Services LLC*—though, this time, the key vote was thought to be from President Donald Trump's newest appointee and Kennedy's replacement, Brett Kavanaugh, who many observers conjectured might be the difference in leading to a ruling that would severely diminish abortion rights to the point where *Roe* becomes constitutionally meaningless. Although former Justice Kennedy did not attend *June Medical Services LLC's* oral argument, a full panoply of political, legal and academic stakeholders, was well as multiple organized interest groups representing liberal and conservative views, packed the courtroom as part of the public debate on the abortion controversy.[58]

Academic studies show a growing increase in the use of **amicus curiae** briefs in United States appellate courts—sometimes called "intervener" briefs that affect apex, or high Court, venues in other countries. In the latter context, such briefs are increasingly prevalent and exert a considerable influence across several foreign courts, particularly in civil rights and liberties cases, between 1970 and 2002.[59] Likewise, researchers exploring the decision-making of the Roberts Courts in its first ten Terms report that 97 percent of "full-opinion decisions" featured the input of third-party briefs, with an average of eleven being filed in each case—a ten-fold increase from pre-1960s levels.[60] In many of these cases—which resolved disputes in the most divisive issues of our time, including not only abortion, but also same-sex marriage, affirmative action and health care, interest group activity was increasingly conspicuous, a phenomenon that expands the range of public policy influence that such interests can wield at a time when the Supreme Court is taking less cases for plenary review.[61] That organized groups have become a pervasive part of appellate litigation in controversial cases is a rough measure of their significance in law and courts. Accordingly, the rest of this Chapter examines the different methods by which organized interest groups attempt to influence judicial policymaking.

Interest Group Politics and Litigation Strategies

The significance of interest group politics is widely acknowledged in political science, and scholars have demonstrated that all levels of government are susceptible to group pressure. Interest groups broadly consist of institutional or membership-based entities, such as nonprofit corporations, private foundations, think tanks, public advocacy groups, trade associations, or public interest law firms. One study reports there are over 1,600 organizations in Washington, D.C., that advocate public policy positions along a wide spectrum of ideological, vocational, religious, ethnic, race, and gender-specific interests. "Organized interests," therefore, are groups that seek objectives through political action.[62] They exert pressure by lobbying legislators with letter-writing campaigns; organizing public demonstrations at executive agencies, courts, or assembly buildings; donating money for political campaigns; mobilizing grassroots support; arranging public appearances; and testifying at public hearings. The Internet has become a powerful tool for organized interests as well.[63]

Interest groups may influence judicial appointments and elections, and they may organize protests that send political messages to the judiciary.[64] Interest groups seeking economic, social, or political change adopt several litigation strategies to achieve their goals. They may file a lawsuit and become direct parties to litigation. Alternatively, they may set up "test cases," either on their own initiative or after being solicited to file a lawsuit by an outside individual or group. For example, in *District of Columbia v. Heller* (2008), libertarian lawyers linked to the Institute for Justice and the Cato Institute actively sought out and filed a lawsuit on behalf of Dick Anthony Heller, a federal security guard who was already involved in challenging the District of Columbia's restrictive gun laws. As a test case, *Heller* was successful because the Supreme Court's landmark ruling struck down D.C.'s restrictive gun regulations for violating an individual's right to self-defense in the home under the Second Amendment. While such a test case strategy has the advantage of framing the legal issues, ordinarily only organizations with enough time, money, and legal resources may pursue that course of litigation.[65]

A closely related interest group litigation tactic is to "sponsor" cases filed by other parties. Sponsoring litigation is time-intensive and costly because groups supply the legal talent and pay for litigation expenses. The classic example is *Brown v. Board of Education* (1954), the landmark ruling on racial discrimination in public schools. In *Brown*, the National Association for the Advancement of Colored People (NAACP) Legal Defense and Educational Fund sponsored five cases in the South, Midwest, and District of Columbia against segregated schools. Still, judicial support for a group's policy goals is not guaranteed. As Susan Lawrence's study of the Legal Services Program's sponsorship of litigation demonstrated, the victories in the high court that expanded the rights of indigents were often offset by the defeats in cases that restricted the rights of the poor for decades afterward.[66]

A third litigation strategy is to submit an *amicus curiae* brief. Filing *amicus* briefs is less costly, but organizations cannot control the litigation or make tactical decisions. Submitting *amicus* briefs alerts the bench to information that is not provided by the parties and, in this sense, they help "democratize an undemocratic component of the American policy-making process" and may even supply courts with "an informal tally of public opinion."[67] On a pragmatic level, organizations use them to assert their ideological view of the law in an effort to persuade judges to side with them. In addition, groups may simultaneously file them in multiple locations, giving them higher exposure and publicity in certain instances.[68]

In general, federal and state court rules permit organized groups to file *amicus* briefs if they have the parties' consent or the leave of court. Some courts, such as the Ohio Supreme Court, do not even require the court's leave, and *amici* briefs can be filed without limitation.[69] The U.S. Solicitor General, or a state attorney general, may be exempted from having to ask permission to file a brief. Though organizations may be permitted to file briefs, they are rarely allowed to participate in oral arguments. Court procedures may impose other requirements for *amicus* filers. Under the Supreme Court's rules, for instance, *amicus* briefs must disclose who provided financial support for writing the brief and whether an attorney representing a party to the case assisted in the brief's submission.[70]

In spite of the procedural hurdles *amici* briefs must overcome, courts have increasingly allowed greater *amici* participation, and their filings in state supreme courts and in the Supreme Court have sharply increased in the past sixty years.[71] Moreover, *amici* filings provide more information about legal doctrine and extralegal sources (such as social science studies, public opinion polls, or foreign law precedent) that might otherwise be omitted. For example, extralegal sources were an important reference point for the Court in *Hall v. Florida* (2014) and its holding that Florida could not use an IQ test score of 70 or less to determine if a convicted but intellectually disabled murderer was eligible for death penalty. In writing the Court's 5:4 decision, Justice Anthony Kennedy drew on the opinion of psychologists and psychiatrists—information provided in an *amicus* brief filed by several professional medical associations.[72]

Whether *amici* filings actually explain judicial outcomes is, nevertheless, subject to considerable debate. One study found that the number of *amicus* briefs filed by organizations influences the ideological direction of the Court's decision making, but only because of the quality of the legal argument, and not the justices' ideology. Yet, an analysis of the decision-making of the first ten terms of the Roberts Court found that *amicus* briefs exerted an impact on the justices' voting behavior across the ideological spectrum, and that influence is greater upon the Court's moderate justices. Moreover, another study of federal appellate court behavior found that the number of *amicus* briefs filed supporting the appellant (the party appealing the case) increases the chances for litigation success, but the same was not true for briefs filed on behalf of the appellee (the party who won in the earlier proceeding). In contrast, other research suggests that organized interests use their *amici* arguments to target strategically state supreme courts that are thought to be ideologically disposed (and publicly accountable if they are staffed through judicial elections) to making decisions that align with the groups' ideological goals; but still other studies show that they did not affect state supreme court decision making. In short, *amici* filings remain important sources of legal information, but there is no consensus on whether they actually make a difference in determining judicial behavior.[73]

What does seem clear is that certain *amici* participants, such as the U.S. Solicitor General, enjoy more access and have more success because they are "repeat players." Established in the Department of Justice in 1870, the *Solicitor General* (S.G.) is the sole legal representative of the federal government in Supreme Court litigation. Consequently, the S.G. has many advantages over individual litigants who litigate infrequently, and often with scant resources or expertise. It is therefore not surprising that the justices rely on the S.G.'s office's institutional expertise and, accordingly, are predisposed to grant *certiorari* in cases in which the S.G. participates. For the same reasons, studies have shown that the S.G. is more successful on the merits than are other organized litigants in cases argued before the Court, simply because the S.G. enjoys the reputation among the justices as being an especially credible litigator.[74]

In sum, litigant status is a key factor in determining the Court's agenda as well as the outcome of its decisions.[75] Yet it remains an open question whether comparable organized litigants with equal experience and resources win as often as the S.G. does. Political scientists Paul Brace and Melinda Hall found that state supreme courts' agenda setting and decision making turned on multifaceted institutional factors—including the supply of lawyers in states, whether state judiciaries had the professional resources (financial and administrative staff) to manage their courts, and the type of judicial selection system process used—and significantly affected whether the "have-nots" in civil litigation involving *amicus* participation had more access to courts and whether they won or not. As such, a variety of institutional and other factors in the legal environment are probably a better explanation of who won access to courts, and whether they won or lost.[76] Another study likewise reported that the underlying institutional resources of the legal system—number of lawyers, organized interests, money, and standing doctrines that encourage litigation—are related to mobilizing litigants and producing legal policy change.[77] And still another illustration of the impact of *amici* activity is that well-established organizations like the American Civil Liberties

Union (ACLU) and other international human rights groups have greatly influenced the development of comparative constitutional law standards with respect to capital punishment and other legal areas (for further discussion, see "In Comparative Perspective: Comparative Constitutional Law, Interest Group Litigation, and Capital Punishment"; and Chapter Ten for an analysis of capital punishment jurisprudence).

In Comparative Perspective: Comparative Constitutional Law, Interest Group Litigation, and Capital Punishment

Comparative constitutional law commands greater attention as a result of supranational courts, like the European Court of Justice (discussed in Chapter Ten), and other transnational courts, such as the European Court of Human Rights, as well as national high courts, citing the decisions of other courts in their rulings. There are a number of reasons for that development. Following the collapse of the Soviet Union, constitutional courts in Central and Eastern Europe turned to comparative constitutional law analysis when construing their new constitutions. High courts in Canada, Germany, and Japan also have frequently looked to the decisions of the U.S. Supreme Court when interpreting similar provisions in their post-World War II constitutions. The South African Constitution and Bill of Rights specifically requires its judiciary to consider foreign and international law.

Moreover, interest groups like the National Association for the Advancement of Colored People Legal Defense and Educational Fund (LDF) and the American Civil Liberties Union (ACLU), bar associations, and business and human rights organizations, both domestic and international, have promoted the development of international standards, and comparative constitutional analysis became easier with Internet access to high court decisions from around the world. An illustrative development is the reliance on comparative constitutional law in striking down capital punishment laws. To be sure, U.S. Supreme Court justices disagree about the use of comparative constitutional law, and some foreign jurists have been critical of the Court for not paying more attention to comparative law, particularly with respect to human rights. Still, increasingly, attorneys, interest groups, and organizations—like the Council of Europe—file *amici curiae* ("friend of the court") briefs and cite foreign judicial decisions in support of their arguments.

When holding that the execution of mentally retarded criminals violates the Eighth Amendment in *Atkins v. Virginia* (2002), for example, Justice John

Paul Stevens noted that "within the world community, the imposition of the death penalty for crimes committed by mentally retarded offenders is overwhelmingly disapproved." Yet, that reference invited a sharp rebuke from Chief Justice William H. Rehnquist and Justice Antonin Scalia, who maintained that "the viewpoints of other countries simply are not relevant to interpreting constitutional standards." Nonetheless, the Court has throughout its history taken judicial notice or in *dicta* taken note of comparative legal developments.

In fact, the decades-old debate over the abolition of the death penalty in the United States was sparked by Justice Arthur J. Goldberg's 1963 opinion dissenting from the denial of *certiorari* in *Rudolph v. Alabama*. There, Justice Goldberg cited international developments and documents in urging lawyers and interest groups, like the LDF and ACLU, to challenge the constitutionality of imposing capital punishment for rape as disproportionate and cruel and unusual punishment. As a result of challenges to capital punishment, there was a ten-year-old moratorium on executions and a broader assault on the death penalty.

One widely cited example of comparative constitutional analysis is the South African Constitutional Court's ruling striking down capital punishment as a violation of "human dignity" based on its constitutional guarantee of "the right to life." Chief Justice Arthur Chaskalson emphasized the importance of taking into account international and comparative legal developments—such as the efforts of interest groups in Europe and the United States to abolish capital punishment. He then focused on Justice William J. Brennan's concurrence in *Furman v. Georgia* (1972) and dissent in *Gregg v. Georgia* (1976), along with rulings going back to *Trop v. Dulles* (1958), recognizing the "evolving standards of decency" and "the concept of human dignity." (For further discussion of the U.S. Supreme Court's capital punishment jurisprudence, see Chapter Ten).

From that, Chief Justice Chaskalson buttressed his analysis that capital punishment violates human dignity by turning to Canadian and German high court rulings on the death penalty, as well as rulings of the European Court of Human Rights. On the basis of these sources, Chief Justice Chaskalson concluded that the South African Constitution embraced the concept of "human dignity" and invalidated South Africa's laws for imposing capital punishment.

Subsequently, constitutional courts in Albania, Lithuania, and the Ukraine invalidated capital punishment, as did the Hungarian Constitutional Court. They based their decisions on, among other legal developments, a 1983 protocol abolishing capital punishment in Western European countries. The Eastern Caribbean Court of Appeal likewise struck down mandatory death penalty laws for certain crimes in St. Vincent and the Grenadines. And in 2002 the Organization of American States Inter-American Court of Human Rights invalidated mandatory death sentences in Trinidad and Tobago.

Sources: Sujit Choudrhry, "Globalization in Search of Justification: Towards a Theory of Comparative Constitutional Interpretation," *Indiana Law Review* 74 (1999), 819; Paolo G. Carozza, " 'My Friend Is a Stranger': The Death Penalty and Global Ius Commune of Human Rights," *Texas Law Review* 81 (2003), 1031; David Fontana, "Refined Comparativism in Constitutional Law," *UCLA Law Review* 49 (2001), 539; David Fontana, "The Rise and Fall of Comparative Constitutional Law in the Postwar Era," *Yale Journal of International Law* 36, no. 1 (2011); Roger Hood, *The Death Penalty: A Worldwide Perspective*, 4th ed. (New York: Oxford University Press, 2008); and Carstein Anckar, *Determinants of the Death Penalty: A Comparative Study of the World* (New York: Routledge, 2013).

Chapter Summary

Litigant access to the courts is examined. Whether direct parties or outside groups gain judicial access is a threshold legal question that defines the scope and limits of jurisdiction to hear a case. Gaining threshold access through the use of jurisdictional and procedural doctrines allows, or denies, litigants to argue the substantive merits, or legal grounds, of their lawsuits before judges and courts. U.S. and state constitutional provisions, federal or state statutes, and the rules of courts provide the formal basis for the judiciary's "gate-keeping" and agenda-setting jurisdiction. Informal constraints include judge-made legal doctrines that give courts the discretion to permit or deny litigant access to courts. Of central importance is the legal concept of "justiciability" and the law of standing, the doctrines of mootness and ripeness, and political questions.

In addition, organized interest groups that are not direct parties may gain access through strategic litigation. Apart from filing lawsuits, organized interests may bring "test cases"; sponsor litigation from other litigants that have already filed suit; and file third-party "friend of the court," or *amicus curiae*, briefs that provide additional information for courts to consider. Organized interest groups' decisions to litigate, and their impact, are often dependent upon the organizations' goals and whether they have enough resources to sustain protracted litigation. Filing *amicus curiae* briefs is the most cost-efficient method, but it remains unclear whether they influence judicial behavior. Often litigation success is determined by a host of legal, political, and institutional factors, including whether organizations are "repeat players" like the solicitor general.

Key Questions for Review and Critical Analysis

1. Why do courts "decide not to decide" cases? Should all litigants have a right to have their cases heard "on the merits"?

2. Many legal scholars claim that the standing doctrine—the threshold requirement foe litigants bringing a lawsuit have a personal stake in the outcome—is incoherent and fragmented. Similarly, do you think that the justices' ideology, or personal preferences, is an important factor in determining which litigants can sue?

3. Do you agree with some scholars that the "political question doctrine" merely masks a court's political preferences? Conversely, what are the main reasons for relying on the political question doctrine?

4. Why do organized interest groups engage in strategic litigation, and what strategies may they pursue in trying to change the law and legal policy?

Web Links

1. American Conservative Union (https://conservative.org/)

   - A website of a broad-based conservative organization that adheres to a political philosophy that sovereignty resides in the person.

2. Public Citizen (https://www.citizen.org/)

   - An online resource of non-profit liberal consumer advocacy group that advances the public interest in a variety of legal areas, including access to justice, climate change, consumer safety and financial reform, among others.

3. NAACP Legal Defense and Educational Fund, Inc. (www.naacpldf.org)

   - A source of information, analysis, and the legal activities of a national legal organization committed to fighting for racial injustice.

4. Judicial Crisis Network (https://judicialnetwork.com/)

   - The home page for conservatives and libertarians that expresses support for the Founder's vision of limited government, the rule of law and an impartial judiciary.

Selected Readings

Bickel, Alexander M. "Foreword: The Passive Virtues." *Harvard Law Review* 75 (1961), 40–79.

Brown, Steven. Trumping Religion: *The New Christian Right, The Free Speech Clause, and the Courts*. Tuscaloosa: University of Alabama Press, 2003.

Caldeira, Gregory A., Marie Hojnacki, and John R. Wright. "The Lobbying Activities of Organized Interests in Federal Judicial Nominations." *Journal of Politics* 62 (2000), 51–69.

Chemerinsky, Erwin. *Closing the Courthouse Door: How Your Constitutional Rights Became Unenforceable*. New Haven: Yale University Press, 2017.

Collins, Paul M., Jr. *Friends of the Supreme Court: Interest Groups and Judicial Decision Makers*. New York: Oxford University Press, 2008.

Coomans, Fons, ed. *Justiciability of Economic and Social Rights: Experiences From Domestic Systems*. Cambridge, U.K.: Intersentia, 2006.

Decker, Jefferson. *The Other Rights Revolution: Conservative Lawyers and the Remaking of Government*. New York: Oxford University Press, 2016.

Diver, Alice and Jacinta Miller, eds. *The Justiciability of Human Rights Law in Domestic Jurisdictions*. Cham: Springer, 2016.

Doyle, Kelly R. ed. *Constitutional Inquiries: The Doctrine of Constitutional Avoidance and the Political Question Doctrine*. New York: Novinka, 2015.

Epp, Charles R. *Making Rights Real: Activists, Bureaucrats, and the Creation of the Legalistic State*. Chicago: University of Chicago Press, 2010.

Epp, Charles R. *The Rights Revolution: Lawyers, Activists, and Supreme Courts in Comparative Perspective*. Chicago: University of Chicago Press, 1998.

Epstein, Lee. *Conservatives in Court*. Knoxville: University of Tennessee Press, 1985.

Galanter, Marc. "Why the 'Haves' Come Out Ahead: Speculations on the Limits of Legal Change." *Law and Society Review* 9 (1974), 96–160.

Gunther, Gerald. "The Subtle Vices of the 'Passive Virtues'—A Comment on Principle and Expediency in Judicial Review." *Columbia Law Review 64* (January 1964), 1–25.

Hershkoff, Helen. "State Courts and the 'Passive Virtues': Rethinking the Judicial Function." *Harvard Law Review* 114 (May 2001), 1833–1941.

Hollis-Brusky, Amanda. *Ideas with Consequences: The Federalist Society and the Conservative Counter-Revolution*. New York: Oxford University Press, 2015.

Rhode, Deborah L. *Access to Justice*. New York: Oxford University Press, 2004.

Sossin, Lorne M. *Boundaries of Judicial Review: The Law of Justiciability in Canada*. 2nd ed. Scarborough, Ontario: Carswell, 2012.

Staszak, Sarah. *No Day in Court: Access to Justice and the Politics of Judicial Retrenchment.* New York: Oxford University Press, 2017.

Teles, Steven M. *The Rise of the Conservative Legal Movement: The Battle for Control of the Law.* Princeton, N.J.: Princeton University Press, 2008.

Endnotes

1   *Whitford v. Gill*, 218 F.Supp.3d 837 (W.D. Wisconsin, 2016).

2   *Gill v. Whitford*, 138 S.Ct. 1916 (2018). While Justices Clarence Thomas and Neil Gorsuch joined most of Chief Justice Roberts' opinion, Gorsuch joined Thomas' separate opinion that would have dismissed the plaintiffs' claims. See ibid., at 1941 (Thomas, J., concurring in part and concurring in the judgment). See also, Amy Howe, "Opinion analysis: Court stays out of merits on partisan gerrymandering, at least for now," *SCOTUSblog* (June 18, 2018), available at http://www.scotusblog.com/2018/06/opinion-analysis-court-stays-out-of-merits-on-partisan-gerrymandering-at-least-for-now/ (last retrieved April 17, 2020).

3   369 U.S. 186 (1962).

4   Amy Howe, "Opinion Analysis: No Role for Courts in Partisan Gerrymandering (Updated)," *SCOTUSblog* (June 27, 2019), https://www.scotusblog.com/2019/06/opinion-analysis-no-role-for-courts-in-partisan-gerrymandering/ (last retrieved April 17, 2020). See also, *Rucho v. Common Cause*, 139 S.Ct. 2484 (2019).

5   Helen Hershkoff, "State Courts and the 'Passive Virtues': Rethinking the Judicial Function," *Harvard Law Review* 114 (May 2001), 1833–941. See also Richard M. Re, "Relative Standing," *Georgetown Law Journal* 102 (2014), 1191–250; Jonathan H. Adler, "Standing Still in the Roberts Court," *Case Western Reserve Law Review* 59 (2009), 1061–87.

6   Heather Elliott, "Standing Lessons: What We Can Learn When Conservative Plaintiffs Lose Under Article III Standing Doctrine," *Indiana Law Journal* (2012), 551–98.

7   Rucho v. Common Cause, *SCOTUSblog*, available at https://www.scotusblog.com/case-files/cases/rucho-v-common-cause-2/ (last retrieved April 17, 2020). See also *Colegrove v. Green*, 328 U.S. 549 (1946) (ruling that courts should not enter into the "political thicket" of legislative apportionment cases).

8   Hershkoff, "State Courts and the 'Passive Virtues,' " 1838–39.

9   John C. Reitz, "Standing to Raise Constitutional Issues," *American Journal of Comparative Law* 50 (2002), 437, 439.

10   *Aetna Life Insurance Company v. Haworth*, 300 U.S. 227 (1937), 240–41.

11   Hershkoff, "State Courts and the 'Passive Virtues,' " 1836 n. 17 and 1845–46. See also Mel A. Topf, *A Doubtful and Perilous Experiment: Advisory Opinions, State Constitutions, and Judicial Supremacy* (New York: Oxford University Press, 2011).

12   Judith Resnik, *Processes of the Law: Understanding Courts and Their Alternatives* (New York: Foundation Press, 2004), 131–40.

13   Saul Zipkin, "A Common Law Court in a Regulatory World," *Ohio State Law Journal* 74 (2013), 285–337.

14   Carl Tobias, "The Past and Future of the Federal Rules in State Courts," *Nevada Law Journal* 3 (2002–2003), 400, 400–401 (citing and updating John B. Oakley and Arthur F. Coon, "The Federal Rules in State Courts: A Survey of State Court Systems of Civil Procedure," *Washington Law Review* 61 [1986], 1367–426).

15   Richard D. Freer, "The Continuing Gloom About Federal Judicial Rulemaking," *Northwestern University Law Review* 107 (2013), 447, 458–59. See also Resnick, *Processes of the Law*, 132–37; Judicial Conference of the United States, *Long Range Plan for the Federal Courts* (December 1995), available at http://www.uscourts.gov/sites/default/files/federalcourtslongrangeplan_0.pdf (last retrieved April 18, 2019), 58–59.

16   Jennifer M. Smith, "Electronic Discovery and the Constitution: Inaccessible Justice," *Journal of Legal Technology and Risk Management* 6 (2012), 122–72.

17   Freer, "The Continuing Gloom About Federal Judicial Rulemaking," 447–74. See also Jack B. Weinstein, "Rule-making by the Courts," in *The Improvement in the Administration of Justice*, 6th ed., edited by Fannie J. Klein (Chicago: American Bar Association, 1981), 127–35.

[18]   Zachary D. Clopton, "Procedural Retrenchment and the States," *California Law Review* 106 (2018), 411, 413 (quoting Dean Erwin Chemerinsky).

[19]   Ibid., 423–434.

[20]   Sarah Staszak, *No Day in Court: Access to Justice and the Politics of Judicial Retrenchment* (New York: Oxford University Press, 2017).

[21]   Harold J. Spaeth and Stuart H. Teger, "Activism and Restraint: A Cloak for the Justices' Policy Preferences," in *U.S. Supreme Court Behavior Studies*, edited by Harold J. Spaeth and Saul Brenner (New York: Garland, 1990), 240. See also C. K. Rowland and Bridget Jeffery Todd, "Where You Stand Depends on Who Sits: Platform Promises and Judicial Gatekeeping in the Federal District Courts," *Journal of Politics* 53 (1991), 175–85. Burton Atkins and William Taggart, "Substantive Access Doctrines and Conflict Management in the U.S. Supreme Court: Reflections on Activism and Restraint," in *Supreme Court Activism and Restraint*, edited by Stephen Halpern and Charles Lamb (Lexington, Mass.: Lexington Books, 1982).

[22]   *Flast v. Cohen*, 392 U.S. 83 (1962), 99 (quoting Professor Paul A. Freund).

[23]   See *Lujan v. Defenders of Wildlife*, 504 U.S. 555 (1992).

[24]   *Hollingsworth v. Perry*, 570 U.S. 693 (2013), 2663–64. See also Adam Rosenzweig, "The Article III Fiscal Power," *Constitutional Commentary* 29 (2014), 127, 141–42; Scott L. Kafker and David A. Russcol, "Standing at a Constitutional Divide: Redefining State and Federal Requirements for Initiatives after *Hollingsworth v. Perry*," *Washington and Lee Law Review* 71 (2014), 229–303.

[25]   *Juliana v. United States*, 947 F.3d 1159 (January 17, 2020, 9th Cir. 2020).

[26]   Ibid., 33 (J. Staton, dissenting). Judge Hurwitz's quotation on behalf of the majority opinion is (the quoted material in the paragraph is at ibid, 25.

[27]   Nancy C. Staudt, "Taxpayers in Court: A Systematic Study of a (Misunderstood) Standing Doctrine," *Emory Law Journal* 52 (2003), 771–847.

[28]   See, e.g., *Frothingham v. Mellon*, 262 U.S. 447 (1923) (establishing the general rule that taxpayers could not challenge the constitutionality of federal laws unless they suffered a "direct injury"). See also Joshua G. Urquhart, "Disfavored Constitution, Passive Virtues? Linking State Constitutional Fiscal Limitations and Permissive Taxpayer Standing Issues," *Fordham Law Review* 81 (2012), 1263, 1267. An early influential survey of the differences in state and federal taxpayer standing jurisprudence is found in Comment, "Taxpayers' Suits: A Survey and Summary," *Yale Law Journal* 69 (1960), 895–924.

[29]   *Flast v. Cohen*, 392 U.S. 83 (1968).

[30]   *Valley Forge Christian Coll. v. Americans United for Separation of Church and State, Inc.*, 454 U.S. 464 (1982), 485.

[31]   *Arizona Christian School Tuition Organization v. Winn*, 563 U.S. 125 (2011); *Hein v. Freedom of Religious Foundation, Inc.*, 551 U.S. 587 (2007).

[32]   *Arizona Christian School Tuition Organization v. Winn*, 563 U.S. 125 (2011) (J. Scalia, with J. Thomas, concurring in the judgment); and ibid., (J. Kagan, with JJ. Ginsburg, Breyer, and Sotomayor, dissenting). See also Bryan Dearinger, "The Future of Taxpayer Standing in Establishment Clause Tax Cases," *Oregon Law Review* 92 (2013), 263–335.

[33]   *Lujan v. Defenders of Wildlife*, 504 U.S. 555, 564 (1992).

[34]   *Spokeo, Inc. v. Robins*, 136 S.Ct. 1540, 1548 (2016).

[35]   Comparisons of state and federal standing doctrine cases involving citizen's suits, claims of elected representatives, and other advocacy groups are found in Re, "Relative Standing," 1191–250; Hershkoff, "State Courts and the 'Passive Virtues,' " 1852–59; Avis K. Poai, "Hawaii's Justiciability Doctrine," *University of Hawaii Law Review* 26 (2004), 537, 557–64; Sylvia Ewald, "State Court Adjudication of Environmental Rights: Lessons From the Adjudication of the Right to Education and the Right to Welfare," *Columbia Journal of Environmental Law* 36 (2011), 413–59.

[36]   *Massachusetts v. EPA*, 549 U.S. 497 (2007).

[37]   *Clapper v. Amnesty International USA*, 568 U.S. 398 (2013).

[38]   Heather Elliot, "The Functions of Standing," *Stanford Law Review* 61 (2008), 459, 501. See also Re, "Relative Standing," 1201–4; Richard H. Fallon, Jr., "The Linkage Between Justiciability and Remedies: And Their Connections to Substantive Rights," *Virginia Law Journal* 92 (2006), 633–705.

39 *DeFunis v. Odegaard*, 416 U.S. 312 (1974), quoting *Aetna Life Ins. Co. v. Haworth*, 300 U.S. 227, 240–41 (1937).

40 Amy Howe, "Opinion Analysis: Court Sends New York Second Amendment Case Back to the Lower Courts Without Ruling on the Merits" *SCOTUSblog* (April 27, 2020), available at https://www.scotusblog.com/2020/04/opinion-analysis-court-sends-new-york-second-amendment-case-back-to-lower-courts-without-ruling-on-the-merits/ (last retrieved April 27, 2020). See also, *District of Columbia v. Heller*, 554 U.S. 570 (2008); and, *McDonald v. City of Chicago*, 561 U.S. 742 (2010). The case to be decided in the 2019–20 Term is being appealed from *New York State Rifle & Pistol Association Inc. v. City of New York, New York*, 883 F.3d 45 (2nd Cir. 2018).

41 Hershkoff, "State Courts and the 'Passive Virtues,' " 1859–60.

42 *In re Marriage of Donald B. and Roberta B.*, 2014 *Illinois* 115463 (Illinois Supreme Court, 2014).

43 *Abbott Laboratories v. Gardner*, 387 U.S. 136 (1967), 148–49.

44 William Grayson Lambert, "Toward a Better Understanding of Ripeness and Free Speech Claims," *South Carolina Law Review* 65 (2013), 411–62; Gene R. Nichol, Jr., "Ripeness and the Constitution," *University of Chicago Law Review* 54 (1987), 153–83.

45 *Renne v. Geary,* 501 U.S. 312 (1991).

46 *Regents of the University of California v. Bakke*, 438 U.S. 265 (1978).

47 *Roe v. Wade,* 410 U.S. 113 (1973).

48 *Marbury v. Madison*, 5 U.S. (1 Cranch) 137 (1803), 170.

49 Hershkoff, "State Courts and the 'Passive Virtues,' " 1861–67; Poai, "Hawaii's Justiciability Doctrine," 565–72.

50 The seminal case is *Luther v. Borden*, 48 U.S. 1 (1849) (ruling that the judiciary lacked the power to address whether Rhode Island's charter government or the government set up by insurgents in the Dorr rebellion was a lawful state government).

51 *Colegrove v. Green*, 328 U.S. 549 (1946).

52 *Baker v. Carr*, 369 U.S. 186 (1962).

53 Richard H. Fallon, Jr., "Judicially Manageable Standards and Constitutional Meaning," *Harvard Law Review* 119 (2006), 1274–332.

54 Christopher P. Banks, "A December Storm over the U.S. Supreme Court," in *Superintending Democracy: The Courts and the Political Process*, edited by Christopher P. Banks and John C. Green (Akron, Ohio: University of Akron Press, 2001), 238. See also *Bush v. Gore*, 531 U.S. 98 (2000).

55 Comment, "Colorado Supreme Court Upholds State's School Finance System as Rationally Related to the 'Thorough and Uniform' Mandate of the Colorado Constitution's Education Clause," *Harvard Law Review* 127 (2013), 803–10 (analyzing *Lobato v. State*, 304 P.3d 1132 [Colorado, 2013] in light of how the political question doctrine affected a challenge to the state's educational financing system). See also Hershkoff, "State Courts and the 'Passive Virtues,' " 1861–67; and Poai, "Hawaii's Justiciability Doctrine," 568–72.

56 Samuel Issacharoff and Jeremy Peterman, "Special Interests After *Citizens United*: Access, Replacement, and Interest Group Response to Legal Change," *Annual Review Social Science* 9 (2013), 185–205; Deborah Hellman, "Defining Corruption and Constitutionalizing Democracy," *Michigan Law Review* 111 (2013), 1385, 1402. Notably, the political question doctrine has allowed courts to assume or to avoid taking jurisdiction to decide basic separation of powers issues that implicate the procedures used to impeach federal judges, the enforcement of international treaties, the recovery of damages in post-9/11 "counter-terrorism" civil lawsuits, and the scope of human rights in foreign policy cases. See, e.g., Gwynne Skinner, "Misunderstood, Misconstrued, and Now Clearly Dead: The 'Political Question Doctrine' as a Justiciability Doctrine," *Journal of Law and Politics* 29 (2014), 427–80 (documenting federal courts using the political question doctrine to deny individual rights in foreign policy cases); Stephen I. Vladeck, "The New National Security Canon," *American University Law Review* 61 (2012), 1295–329 (arguing the political question defense has prevented civil litigants from recovering civil damages against government officials for misconduct in fighting terrorism and protecting national security). See also Rachel E. Barkow, "More Supreme Than Court? The Fall of the Political Question Doctrine and the Rise of Judicial Supremacy," *Columbia Law Review* 102 (2002), 237–336.

57 *Webster v. Reproductive Health Services*, 492 U.S. 490 (1989). See also *Roe v. Wade*, 410 U.S. 113 (1973). The extensive role public interest groups played in *Webster* is analyzed in Susan Behuniak-Long, "Friendly Fire: *Amici Curiae* and *Webster v. Reproductive Health Services*," *Judicature* (February/March 1991), 261–70. A survey of the impact of interest groups abroad is found in Paul M. Collins, Jr. and Lauren A. McCarthy, "Interest Group Litigation in Comparative Context," *Journal of Law and Courts* 5 (No. 1, Spring 2017), 55–80.

[58] Mark Walsh, "A 'view' from the courtroom: "Strong feelings" in the latest abortion case," *SCOTUSblog* (March 4, 2020), available at https://www.scotusblog.com/2020/03/a-view-from-the-courtroom-strong-feelings-in-the-latest-abortion-case/ (last retrieved April 19, 2020). See also, *June Medical Services LLC v. Russo*, No. 18–1323 (U.S. Jun. 29, 2020).

[59] Collins, Jr. and McCarthy, "Interest Group Litigation in Comparative Context," 64, 65 (Table 1), 72 (Table 2).

[60] Richard L. Pacelle, Jr., John M. Scheb II, Hemant K. Sharma, and David H. Scott, "Assessing the Influence of Amicus Curiae Briefs on the Roberts Court," *Social Science Quarterly* 99 (No. 4, 2018), 1254–55.

[61] Ibid., 1254.

[62] This is the working definition adopted by Paul Collins and other political scientists. Paul M. Collins, Jr., *Friends of the Supreme Court: Interest Groups and Judicial Decision Makers* (New York: Oxford University Press, 2008), 19. See also Matt Grossmann, *The Not-So-Special Interests: Interest Groups, Public Representation, and American Governance* (Stanford, Calif.: Stanford University Press, 2012), 1, 81 (listing the number of interest groups and identifying types of advocacy interests).

[63] Clyde Brown and Herbert Waltzer, "Virtual Sources: Organized Interests and Democratization by the Web," *The Social Science Journal* 41 (2004), 543–58.

[64] See, e.g., Nancy Scherer, *Scoring Points: Politicians, Activists, and the Lower Federal Court Appointment Process* (Stanford, Calif.: Stanford University Press, 2005).

[65] Collins, *Friends of the Supreme Court*, 24–25. See also Nelson Lund, "The Second Amendment, Heller, and Originalist Jurisprudence," *U.C.L.A. Law Review* 56 (2009), 1343–76; Brian Doherty, "How the Second Amendment Was Restored: The Inside Story of How a Gang of Libertarian Lawyers Made Constitutional History," available at http://reason.com/archives/2008/11/18/how-the-second-amendment-was-r (last retrieved May 28, 2014); Stephen L. Wasby, *Race Relations Litigation in an Age of Complexity* (Charlottesville: University of Virginia Press, 1995); and *District of Columbia v. Heller*, 554 U.S. 570 (2008). Notably, while scholars are divided on the issue of what motivates organizations to litigate, using the courts may yield desirable organizational outcomes due to consensus building and the accumulation of an evidentiary record, neither of which is easily found in legislative or executive venues. See Aaron J. Ley, "The Costs and Benefits of American Policy-Making Venues," *Law and Society Review* 48 (2014), 91–125.

[66] Susan E. Lawrence, *The Poor in Court: The Legal Services Program and Supreme Court Decision Making* (Princeton, N.J.: Princeton University Press, 1990), 123–47.

[67] Pacelle, Jr., Scheb II, Sharma and Scott, "Assessing the Influence of Amicus Curiae Briefs on the Roberts Court," 1262.

[68] Scott A. Comparato, *Amici Curiae and Strategic Behavior in State Supreme Courts*, 6, 44.

[69] The Supreme Court of Ohio, "2020 Rules of Practice," Rule 16.06. ("An amicus curiae may file a brief urging affirmance or reversal, and leave to file an amicus brief is not required."), 94.

[70] Rule 37, Rules of the Supreme Court of the United States (Adopted April 19, 2019; Effective July 1, 2019), available at www.supremecourtus.gov (last retrieved April 20, 2020).

[71] Lee Epstein, "Exploring the Participation of Organized Interests in State Court Litigation," *Political Research Quarterly* 47 (1994), 335–52; Joseph D. Kearney and Thomas W. Merrill, "The Influence of Amicus Curiae Briefs on the Supreme Court," *University of Pennsylvania Law Review* (January, 2000), 743–855.

[72] "Brief of Amici Curiae American Psychological Association, American Psychiatric Association, American Academy of Psychiatry and the Law, Florida Psychological Association, National Association of Social Workers, and National Association of Social Workers Florida Chapter in Support of Petitioner (No. 12–10882)," available at www.americanbar.org (last retrieved May 29, 2014). See also *Hall v. Florida*, 572 U.S. 701 (2014).

[73] See, e.g., Collins, *Friends of the Supreme Court*, 4–10; Comparato, *Amici Curiae and Strategic Behavior in State Supreme Courts*, 23–43; and Paul M. Collins, Jr., and Wendy L. Martinek, "Friends of the Circuits: Interest Group Influence on Decision Making in the U.S. Courts of Appeals," *Social Science Quarterly* 91 (2010), 397–414; Pacelle, Jr., Scheb II, Sharma, and Scott, "Assessing the Influence of Amicus Curiae Briefs on the Roberts Court," 1253–1266; and, Jenna Becker Kane, "Informational Need, Institutional Capacity, and Court

Receptivity: Interest Groups and Amicus Curiae in State High Courts," *Political Research Quarterly* 71 (2018), 881–894.

74   Pacelle, Scheb II, Sharma, and Scott, "Assessing the Influence of Amicus Curiae Briefs on the Roberts Court," 1262.

75   See, e.g., Ryan C. Black and Christina L. Boyd, "US Supreme Court Agenda Setting and the Role of Litigant Status," *Journal of Law, Economics, and Organization* 28 (2012), 286–312; Barbara L. Graham, "Explaining Supreme Court Policymaking in Civil Rights: The Influence of the Solicitor General, 1953–2002," *The Policy Studies Journal* 31 (2003), 253–71. The seminal study of the "haves" and "have-nots" in litigation is found in Marc Galanter, "Why the 'Haves' Come Out Ahead: Speculations on the Limits of Legal Change," *Law and Society Review* 9 (1974), 96–160.

76   Paul Brace and Melinda Gann Hall, " 'Haves' Versus 'Have Nots' in State Supreme Courts: Allocating Docket Space and Wins in Power Asymmetric Cases," *Law & Society Review* 35 (2001), 393–417.

77   Charles R. Epp, *The Rights Revolution: Lawyers, Activists, and Supreme Courts in Comparative Perspective* (Chicago: University of Chicago Press, 1998); Thomas F. Burke, *Lawyers, Lawsuits, and Legal Rights: The Battle Over Litigation in American Society* (Berkeley: University of California Press, 2002).

Trial Courts: The Criminal Justice System

In July 1995, in Houston, Texas, Duane Buck murdered his ex-girlfriend and her friend because he thought they were in a new relationship. At the time of his arrest, police discovered murder weapons in his car and two witnesses confirmed he pulled the trigger. Regardless, he laughed about what he had done, even stating to a cop that "[t]he bitch deserved what she got."[1] After his conviction, at his capital sentencing proceeding a jury had to decide if he deserved the death penalty. Under Texas law, the death penalty is an appropriate sentence if there is evidence beyond a reasonable doubt that Buck was likely to remain dangerous. On that issue, Buck's court-appointed lawyer called an expert witness, Dr. Walter Quijano, a clinical psychologist, to testify on his client's behalf even though he knew that Buck's race, which was African-American, factored into the doctor's analysis of the risk of future violence. Thus, although Quijano testified that Buck probably would not engage in violent conduct, he also suggested that there was a statistical probability that Buck would act violently because he was a person of color. Accordingly, the jury sentenced Buck to death.[2]

After multiple appeals in state and federal court that upheld Buck's conviction, Buck eventually convinced a federal district court to review whether Buck's Sixth Amendment right to effective assistance of counsel was violated because his attorney allowed Dr. Quijano to testify about whether Buck's race might influence the likelihood that he would remain dangerous. The lower court denied Buck's appeal, reasoning that the expert psychologist's testimony only had a minimal effect on the jury's sentencing decision, and that judgment was upheld on appeal. Still, and over two decades later, in *Buck v. Davis* (2017), the Supreme Court reversed the decision. In a 6:2 ruling, Chief Justice John Roberts' Opinion for the Court held that the lower federal courts had not correctly applied the standards laid down in *Strickland v. Washington* (1984) for determining whether a defendant's right to effective counsel was violated, and thus prejudiced the outcome of the trial. After noting that "No competent defense attorney would introduce evidence" that his client's race would affect the likelihood of future violence, the Court reasoned that even if the expert had referred to Buck's race only two times during his testimony, the source of that evidence—a medical expert holding a doctorate and who had conducted similar analyses in about 70 other court cases—prejudiced the defendant in the jury's mind because "the impact of that evidence cannot be measured simply by how much air time it received at trial or how many pages it occupies in the record." That is, "Some toxins can be deadly in small doses." As a result, Buck's defense counsel's performance was deemed to be ineffective under the *Strickland* precedent and the Sixth Amendment.[3]

The Supreme Court's application of *Strickland* illustrates that decisions made by trial counsel must force the prosecution's case to "survive the crucible of meaningful adversarial testing."[4] Adversarial justice assumes that the facts underlying crimes are discovered by advocates locked in trials supervised by impartial judges. In *Buck*, the Court found that Buck's court-appointed counsel's decision to use Dr. Quijano as an expert witness failed to meet the minimum standards for legal representation. By knowing Dr. Quijano would introduce race as a factor in his statistical analysis about whether Buck would likely remain dangerous in the future—a critical issue determining if Buck would be spared the death penalty—Buck's counsel ran afoul of a constitutional norm obliging counsel to act competently in order to ensure a fair trial. As one judge once put it: while "a criminal trial is not a game in which the participants are expected to enter the ring with a near match in skills, [it also is not] a sacrifice of unarmed prisoners to gladiators."[5]

Buck's counsel's performance illustrates other problems in the criminal justice system. Chief among the criticisms are that: (1) the "adversary system is broken"; (2) "the jury system is not working properly"; (3) "the amount of justice meted out depends on the amount of money a person has"; (4) "there is a disparate and unequal treatment of the races"; and, (5) "lawyers are greedy and judges are insensitive."[6] These criticisms are fueled by shrinking government budgets, exploding incarceration rates, and harsh sentencing practices.[7]

In addition, media coverage and commentary on high-profile cases often tend to misinform and only reinforce popular misconceptions about the adversary process. While classic movies, such as *Inherit the Wind* (1960) and *To Kill a Mockingbird* (1962), as well as television dramas like *Law and Order* (1990–2010) or *Bluff City Law* (2019), portray lawyers and the legal system in a generally positive way, they ironically reinforce the myth that most lawsuits wind up in a courtroom.[8]

In fact, the reality is that an overwhelming majority of lawsuits never go to trial and instead are decided by plea bargains (in criminal cases) or negotiated settlements (in civil cases).

This chapter explores the myths and realities of the adversarial trial process by, first, outlining the purposes and characteristics of trials. It then turns to the key stages and issues in the criminal justice system by analyzing: (1) prosecutorial discretion; (2) plea bargaining; (3) the jury's role in criminal trials; and, (4) the politics of post-trial sentencing.

THE ADVERSARIAL PROCESS

In criminal prosecutions, offenders are sanctioned with fines, imprisonment, or an array of intermediate sanctions (home confinement, community service, intensive-supervision probation) and, sometimes, the death penalty. In contrast, civil lawsuits are over private behavior that causes harm and may lead to the responsible party paying for financial damages (see Chapter Eight for a full discussion of adversarial justice in civil cases).

Criminal and civil litigation have distinct purposes, but they are interrelated, and both are based on the adversary process. Although criminal defendants are subject to governmental prosecution, injured litigants may also sue for civil damages in a separate lawsuit. A drunk driver, for example, may be criminally prosecuted but may also face civil liability if he or she has caused serious personal injuries in an automobile accident. Yet important differences remain between criminal and civil trial processes: (1) criminal prosecutions involve public prosecutors and public defenders or private defense counsel, whereas in civil suits private parties—plaintiffs and defendants—are typically the central actors; (2) while there is a presumption of innocence in criminal trials, it is usually absent in civil actions; and, (3) the burden of proof in criminal prosecutions is to establish the defendant's "guilt" "beyond a reasonable doubt," whereas in civil suits defendants are held "liable" under the less rigorous "preponderance of the evidence" standard.

Notwithstanding these differences, criminal and civil litigation share the same adversarial premise: the underlying facts are determined by procedural rules of court and public trials before juries (and sometimes by judges, alone). Lawyers have substantial discretion to engage in "fact finding" before trial and presenting the facts they discover to the jury as evidence introduced and contested during various stages of the trial process (see Figure 7.1). The trial process may prove to be unpredictable, but it is often contentious.[9]

Figure 7.1   The Stages of Trial and the Presentation of Evidence

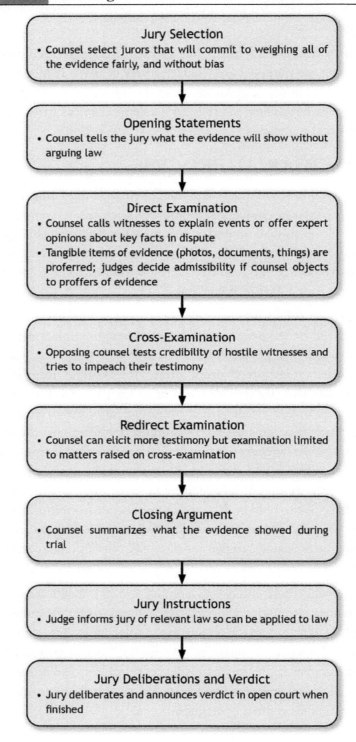

Jury Selection
- Counsel select jurors that will commit to weighing all of the evidence fairly, and without bias

Opening Statements
- Counsel tells the jury what the evidence will show without arguing law

Direct Examination
- Counsel calls witnesses to explain events or offer expert opinions about key facts in dispute
- Tangible items of evidence (photos, documents, things) are proferred; judges decide admissibility if counsel objects to proffers of evidence

Cross-Examination
- Opposing counsel tests credibility of hostile witnesses and tries to impeach their testimony

Redirect Examination
- Counsel can elicit more testimony but examination limited to matters raised on cross-examination

Closing Argument
- Counsel summarizes what the evidence showed during trial

Jury Instructions
- Judge informs jury of relevant law so can be applied to law

Jury Deliberations and Verdict
- Jury deliberates and announces verdict in open court when finished

"Truth" or "Fight" Theory?

Social scientists and legal scholars have long denounced the adversarial system for obscuring rather than revealing "the truth." Judge Jerome Frank famously contrasted the "fight" versus "truth" theory of the adversary process, and it remains a seminal critique. According to Judge Frank, adversary trials are similar to "private out-of-court brawls." Because "the lawyer aims at victory, at winning in the fight, not at aiding the court to discover the facts," the truth often remains a mystery and becomes distorted when partisan attorneys coach witnesses or fail to disclose incriminating evidence. In the adversary system, attorneys "fight it out" as surrogates for their clients' interests. That, argued Frank, makes the trial process unfair for a variety of reasons, including: (1) the truth is often overlooked because judges have limited roles and are inhibited from taking proactive steps to find it; (2) crucial evidence is lost because of the incompetence of attorneys or because clients cannot afford to hire first-rate counsel and other investigative staff or expert witnesses; and, (3) judges and juries depend too much on prosecutors and private attorneys to uncover, present and contest relevant evidence.[10]

Defenders of the adversarial system respond that the clash of opposing interests is the best procedural method for achieving fairness and uncovering the truth because attorneys are duty bound to protect their clients' interests. Without legal representation, critical facts surrounding crimes or disputes might remain undiscovered, the government might operate unjustly, and individuals may be wrongfully convicted or suffer financial losses. Persons may be wrongfully convicted or suffer substantial financial losses without the aggressive efforts of attorneys. Partisan advocacy also protects significant constitutional values, such as the basic right to be heard in public forums, and the right of criminal defendants to confront their accusers.[11]

Adversarial or Inquisitorial Justice?

The **adversarial model** of criminal justice in common law countries, like the United States and the United Kingdom, pits prosecutors against public defenders or private attorneys in a trial ending with a judge and/or jury verdict. The trial process is constrained by rules of evidence, and judges play a passive role—merely calling "balls and strikes but not playing the game itself." By contrast, in civil law jurisdictions, such as those in most of Europe, the judge operates under the **inquisitorial model** and is proactive, conducting extensive nonpartisan pretrial investigations of the facts—sometimes with the help of a prosecutor. Once the evidence is compiled, it is put into a full written record—called a "dossier"—to which the defendant has access. At trial, typically a panel of three judges adjudicates the case and has the responsibility of deciding all questions of fact and law; hence, there is far less reliance on the advocacy of lawyers, as in the common law adversarial system. In short, the difference between the two systems has been put this way: "As opposed to duel-like adversarial proceedings, adjudication in the inquisitorial tradition contemplates a definitive judicial inquiry revealing the truth and achieving accurate verdicts."[12]

Scholars debate the comparative strengths and weaknesses of adversarial and inquisitorial systems (see Table 7.1). Political scientist Robert Kagan, for one, argues that inquisitorial systems are reasonable alternatives to adversarial justice. In Germany, for example, criminal trials are tightly supervised by a panel of judges who do not use complex pretrial procedures or juries to determine a defendant's guilt. Instead, an extensive record of pretrial evidence is compiled by prosecutors, investigating judges, and the police, and defendants are given full access to it before trial. **Plea bargains**, or agreements between prosecutors and defendants that allow the accused to plead guilty in exchange for a more lenient sentence, are constructed under strict guidelines. Plea bargaining results in fewer trials, as in the United States. If there is a trial, it tends to be short and closely managed by judges who actively question witnesses and the defendant (who typically testifies first without counsel), unlike in the United States. Moreover, because identical procedures are in place in inquisitorial systems for civil litigation, Kagan concludes that there is more streamlined adjudication in Germany and elsewhere in noncriminal cases.[13]

Table 7.1	Trial Court Differences in Adversarial and Inquisitorial Legal Systems	
Legal System Characteristics	**Adversary Legal System**	**Inquisitorial Legal System**
Type of Law	• Common law • Judge-made law	• Civil law • Code-based law
Judiciary	• Nonprofessional; nonbureaucratic • No specially trained judges • Judges enter career as "amateurs," often from private practice • Judges are independent and not directly supervised during career • More political, less objective in decision making	• Professional; bureaucratic • Specially trained "career" judges • Judges enter career as civil servants, within bureaucracy • Judges are supervised by senior judges during career • More objective, less political in decision making
Legal Profession	• Not separated from judiciary • Individual attorneys have substantial discretion in controlling litigation • Individual attorneys are zealous advocates for clients' interest	• Autonomous from judiciary • Individual attorneys have less discretion in controlling litigation • Individual attorneys are not zealous advocates for clients' interest
Trial Processes	• Single judge in charge of case, and attorneys find facts through pretrial discovery processes and manage litigation up to trial • Trial record is built at trial, in single event, and judge does not find facts in pretrial investigations • Judges are neutral arbiters and less collaborative in trying to resolve disputes • Generalist courts are common • Lay juries often participate in final outcome • Costs of litigation mostly assumed by litigants	• Several judges determine facts, manage litigation, and collaborate in decision; in significant cases, sit in panels • Trial records are built over time through series of judge-led investigations • Judges are proactive problem solvers in collaborative effort to resolve disputes • Specialized courts are common Lay juries rarely participate in final outcome • Costs of litigation mostly assumed by government

Source: Charles H. Koch, Jr., "Globalization, Courts, and Judicial Power: The Advantages of Civil Law Judicial Design as the Model for Emerging Legal Systems," *Indiana Journal of Global Legal Studies* 11 (Winter, 2004), 139–60.

Notably, the structure, operation, and norms of adversary justice are "deeply rooted in the American system of government and in American political culture."[14] But that is not to say that certain features of inquisitorial justice are completely absent in the United States. There is a growing acceptance of "therapeutic jurisprudence" in state trial courts (as discussed in Chapter One), along with the managerial role judges play in civil cases and increasingly "alternative dispute resolution" procedures (discussed in Chapter Eight). So, too, as some scholars emphasize, "no system is entirely adversarial or inquisitorial" in practice, which explains why some European countries have incorporated common law procedures into their civil law systems.[15]

The "Crime Control" and "Due Process" Models of Criminal Justice

Within the adversarial system, criminologist Herbert L. Packer has described the tensions between a "crime control" and a "due process" mind-set or model of criminal procedure. The models "represent an attempt to abstract two separate value systems that compete for priority in the operation of the criminal justice system." On the one hand, the **crime control model**—associated with the thinking of police and prosecutors—presumes guilt and favors the swift prosecution of offenders with "assembly-line" efficiency, particularly during the early stages of apprehension and by the use of pretrial hearings and plea bargains (instead of trials) to determine guilt. On the other hand, the **due process model** operates like "an obstacle course" that slows down the efficacy of criminal prosecutions because it places a premium on achieving fairness through the imposition of formal rules—such as the *Miranda* warnings about the right to remain silent, the **exclusionary rule**, and other evidentiary rules—in order to preserve the presumption of innocence. As a result, police investigations and criminal prosecutions are presumed to be fraught with error and, thus, the due process model insists that the factual questions underlying guilt or innocence must be structured by "bright line rules" that safeguard defendants' rights.[16]

In fact, the crime control and due process models, which are always in tension, necessarily "co-exist in a fragile peace," as highlighted in *Missouri v. Seibert* (2004).[17] In *Seibert*, the police used a "two-stage interrogation" in order to get a murder conviction of a mother who contributed to the death of a mentally ill teenager that was asleep in the family's trailer home. The two-stage interrogation practice is controversial because it is designed to circumvent *Miranda v. Arizona* (1966)—the landmark ruling requiring police to give suspects warnings of their constitutional rights to remain silent and obtain legal counsel during custodial interrogations. Under a two-stage interrogation, the police first get a confession without giving the Miranda warnings. Once a confession is secured, the police then read the suspect the Miranda rights and resume questioning once the suspect signs a waiver of those rights. At that point, the suspect is prompted to confess again, and that second "Mirandized" confession is used to convict the defendant. But, in *Seibert*, the Court held that this practice violates the Fifth Amendment's prohibition against self-incrimination. Hence, the mother's confession was inadmissible in court. Writing for the Court, Justice David Souter reaffirmed the due process values of deterring police misconduct under *Miranda*.[18] By interposing a procedural rule against the admission of such confessions at trial, Justice Souter enforced the due process model's presumption of "the fallibility of actors and thus [the importance of] formalized procedures and protections" that are guaranteed in the Bill of Rights.[19]

The *Miranda* and *Seibert* rulings are examples of the kind of due process guarantees afforded criminal suspects. In other cases, however, the Court has ruled that the prosecution's evidence may be admitted because of overriding interests in preserving public order and repressing crime. In sum, the dynamics of the crime control and due process models underscore not only the clash of opposing interests, but also competing views of adversarial justice and rival political ideologies. They are further illustrated by examining in greater detail (in the next sections) the methods by which criminal suspects are prosecuted. Table 7.2 denotes constitutional protections in criminal cases, an important element of due process modeling.

Table 7.2	Constitutional Protections in Criminal Cases
Source in Bill of Rights	**Scope of Constitutional Right**
Fourth Amendment	• Prohibition of "Unreasonable" Searches and Seizures • Requirement of Warrant Based on "Probable Cause"
Fifth Amendment	• Grand Jury Indictment in Capital Cases • Prohibition of "Double Jeopardy" Attaching in "Same Offenses" • Testimonial Privilege Against Self-Incrimination • Right to Due Process (Notice and Opportunity to Be Heard)
Sixth Amendment	• Right to Speedy and Public Trial • Right to Impartial Jury • Right to Be Informed of Charges • Right to Confront Accusers • Right to Compulsory Process to Secure Witnesses • Right to "Assistance" of Counsel
Eighth Amendment	• Prohibition Against "Excessive" Bails or Fines • Prohibition Against "Cruel and Unusual" Punishments
Fourteenth Amendment	• Prohibition Against Deprivation of "Privileges or Immunities" of U.S. Citizens • Right to "Equal Protection" of the Laws • Right to "Due Process" (Notice and Opportunity to Be Heard)

Source: Legal Information Institute, "U.S. Constitution," available at https://www.law.cornell.edu/constitution (last retrieved April 21, 2020).

CRIMINAL LAW AND THE JUSTICE SYSTEM

Criminal law defines culpability by defining the intent (*mens rea*, or "guilty mind") and conduct (*actus reus*, or "criminal act") of offenders. The law's substantive content is put into effect by procedural rules governing the criminal justice system, which are designed to establish guilt or innocence while striking a balance between the competing interests of ensuring public safety and safeguarding individual rights. Whether the criminal justice system delivers on that promise remains controversial, however. As Chief Justice William H. Taft observed in 1905, a "jurist from Mars" would not be able to find in the United States a criminal code that successfully balances the interests between public safety and individual rights if the alien came to Earth to find it. In fact, critics routinely lament that the criminal justice system operates as a speedy plea-bargaining "machine" that is largely hidden and removed from the public.[20] The system's strengths and weaknesses are discussed next in the context of the operation of the criminal trial and appeal process.

The Criminal Trial and Appeal Process

In criminal cases, the government must prove its accusations "beyond a reasonable doubt," a rigorous standard of proof. Prosecutors must prove that the accused committed a crime, without receiving help from the defendant or the judge. If the prosecutor cannot satisfy its burden of proof, the defendant cannot be convicted even though there might be some evidence that a crime was in fact committed. As Judge Benjamin Cardozo once famously said: "The prisoner is to go free because the constable has blundered." In other words, as Justice William Brennan reminds us, the **reasonable doubt standard** is "a prime instrument for reducing the risk of convictions resting on factual error" because it "provides concrete substance for the presumption of innocence."[21]

Criminal trials begin after the investigation and arrest of defendants accused of misdemeanors or felonies. **Misdemeanors,** such as petty theft or disorderly conduct, are less serious acts that are punished by minor fines, incarceration for up to one year, or both. **Felonies,** such as manslaughter or rape, are more serious offenses and punished by higher fines, incarceration of one year or more, or both. Certain offenses, such as premeditated murder or the killing of a police officer during the commission of a felony, may result in the death penalty in federal and military prosecutions, as well as in twenty-eight states; however, in the remaining states (plus the District of Columbia) and in over one hundred other countries, capital punishment has been abolished (or not used under a gubnatorial moratoria) and therefore is not a prosecutorial option.[22]

Although police have responsibility for investigating and arresting criminal suspects, federal U.S. Attorneys or state prosecutors must choose whether to charge suspects with a crime. If a suspect is charged, the prosecutor determines whether a conviction is best secured by a plea bargain or going to trial. If there is a trial, the jury (and/or a judge) decides the defendant's guilt or innocence. If not acquitted, defendants are sentenced in accordance with the law, usually according to state or federal sentencing guidelines. Moreover, there are informal norms that are a part of the *courtroom workgroup*—the prosecutor, defense counsel, and judge—that explain the operation and "political realm of the courthouse" and variations in sentencing patterns in many criminal cases.[23]

The prosecutor, the jury, and the judge wield enormous influence. The different roles they play are best explained by exploring the critical stages of the trial process, including: (1) the discretion prosecutors have in charging defendants from the time of arrest to formal arraignment; (2) the influence prosecutors have in striking plea bargains; (3) the democratic role citizens play as jurors in criminal trials, and, (4) the underlying politics of the post-trial sentencing process.

Figure 7.2 shows the main stages in the criminal trial and appeal process.

Figure 7.2	The Criminal Trial and Appeal Process

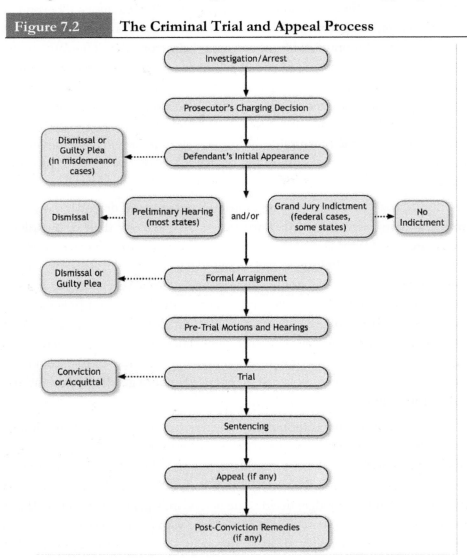

PROSECUTORIAL DISCRETION: FROM ARREST TO FORMAL ARRAIGNMENT

Since the 1980s, the U.S. political system generally has become more conservative, so legislation was enacted to control crime but also sharply limit the rights of criminal defendants. New federal laws increasingly sanctioned preventive detention (allowing judges to deny bail to dangerous criminals), expanded the death penalty, and imposed harsher penalties under mandatory sentencing guidelines in an effort to stop judges from showing leniency to offenders in individualized judgments that created sentencing disparities and racial bias. Those trends have continued in the twenty-first century, though in recent years they show signs of accepting less punitive criminal justice alternatives.[24]

In this light, due in part to shrinking budgets and the high cost of operating prisons, the federal government and a growing number of states have launched "Smart on Crime" initiatives—reforms aimed at eliminating long prison sentences for low-level and nonviolent offenders, creating rehabilitation options and other programs that permit more individualized treatment or make easier the transition from prison into communities. Indeed, at the federal level, President Donald Trump signed into law The First Step Act, a bipartisan effort that substantially reformed the nation's prison and sentencing laws by, among other things, reducing mandatory minimum sentences for some drug-related crimes and increasing "good time" served for most federal prisoners.[25] Nevertheless, the criminal justice system remains fundamentally punitive. It is within this "get tough" legal framework that prosecutors retain virtually unfettered discretion to place offenders into the criminal justice system and thereafter manipulate their case dispositions. It is no exaggeration to say, as Justice Robert Jackson observed, that prosecutors retain "more control over life, liberty, and reputation than any other person in America."[26]

Whereas U.S. Attorneys are appointed by the president and confirmed by the Senate, in all but four states (Alaska, Connecticut, District of Columbia, and New Jersey), state prosecutors are elected.[27] Although federal prosecutors occasionally litigate civil cases, the nation's U.S. Attorneys primarily investigate and enforce violations of federal criminal law. Of those prosecutions, the largest percentages involve immigration, drugs, violent crime, and white-collar crimes. Nearly seventy thousand federal prosecutions are brought annually in federal district courts against approximately one hundred thousand defendants that result in roughly seventy thousand convictions (a 91 percent conviction rate).[28]

Over two thousand state prosecutors' offices handle nearly three million felony prosecutions. State courts adjudicate about 93 percent of all felony convictions, with the largest proportion of cases involving methamphetamine production (71 percent), child exploitation involving the internet (58 percent), or elder abuse (55 percent) offenses. As on the federal level, few state prosecutions actually go to trial: jury verdicts accounted for less than three percent of all felony dispositions, and over 80 percent of state felony convictions result from guilty pleas. 69 percent of those types of convictions lead to incarceration in state prisons or local jails; of the remainder, 27 percent are placed on probation, and 4 percent receive sentences that include fines, restitution, treatment, community service, or other sanctions (such as periodic drug testing). While the exact number is not known, some reports estimate that state courts also adjudicate about 10.5 million misdemeanor offenses, which constitute over 90 percent of state prosecutors' nonfelony caseloads.[29]

Prosecutors are ethically bound to seek justice first and not to act solely in the interest of securing a conviction.[30] State and federal prosecutors have discretion over a wide scope of investigative and pretrial activities, including: (1) conducting criminal investigations; (2) initiating and executing arrest or search warrants; (3) subpoenaing witnesses and compelling testimony at preliminary proceedings and trial; (4) convening grand juries and securing indictments in serious cases; (5) formally charging criminal defendants at arraignment and placing them on trial; (6) negotiating and obtaining plea bargain agreements in lieu of trial; (7) supporting or contesting postconviction sentencing dispositions, including issuing recommendations about enhancing penalties, the length of incarceration, whether to seek the death penalty, and (in the states) structuring the terms of probation and the conditions for parole; and, (8) making appellate litigation decisions. Exercising these powers places prosecutors at the forefront of determining whether an individual's liberty is won or lost and, in some cases, whether offenders live or die.[31]

Prosecutorial discretion comes into play at several preliminary stages in the adversarial process, specifically during: (1) the defendant's initial appearance in court; (2) the preliminary hearing or grand jury indictment stage, and, (3) formal arraignment. These trial processes and the various issues they raise in criminal procedure are discussed next.

Initial Appearance

After the police investigate a crime, an arrest may be made based on **probable cause** (a reasonable assessment of facts indicating illegal activity) that the accused committed a crime. Once the prosecutor reviews the arrest and authorizes that charges be filed, a complaint is filed in court, and thereafter the accused is brought into court to answer charges at an **initial appearance hearing**. Typically, defendants briefly appear before a magistrate or judge, ordinarily within forty-eight hours of arrest, and are informed of their rights and the charges they face.[32] Defendants accused of misdemeanor crimes often plead guilty at this stage and are sentenced immediately. Usually in felony cases, the complaint will be replaced by an **indictment** or **information** (formal documents listing the charges and facts after subsequent proceedings, discussed below), and indigents are informed about the right to court-appointed counsel. If bail for release is also set, in many states a monetary bond of usually 10 percent is posted in order to ensure a defendant's presence at trial; if there is a failure to appear at trial, the full bond amount is forfeited, and an arrest warrant is issued.

Notably, though, there is a growing movement to reform the cash-bond bail system and some states, including California, have replaced it with a new one that allows judges to assess the risk suspects pose to the community while also giving them the discretion to keep those that they deem to be more dangerous behind bars indefinitely with preventative detention. While supporters of reform argue that cash-bond systems are racially discriminatory because suspects are kept in jail based on their ability to pay, defenders of the status quo counter that risk assessment and preventative detention techniques are just as discriminatory since they give too much power to judges to determine which suspects are too dangerous to release before trial, thus keeping them in jail for an indefinite period before they are convicted of anything. Still, despite these concerns, at least twenty states, including Ohio, New Jersey, New Mexico and Kentucky, are exploring bail reform or have begun to effectuate reforms that have adopted non-cash bond alternatives, such as risk assessment, citation in lieu of detention, or the elimination of bond schedules.[33]

Preliminary Hearings and Grand Jury Indictments

After the initial appearance, the prosecutor formally charges the accused with a crime, either by "information" or by "grand jury indictment." The flexibility of using either procedure in the states was established in *Hurtado v. California* (1884).[34] In jurisdictions where preliminary hearings are used, an "information form," stating the charges and evidence against the defendant, is filed by the prosecutor. In other jurisdictions, a grand jury approves the prosecutor's initial charges with an indictment. A few jurisdictions use both types of methods.[35]

A **preliminary hearing** is held to determine whether there is probable cause to charge the accused and resembles a "mini-trial" in which witnesses may testify and an official transcript is created. Ordinarily, only the prosecution presents evidence because it has the legal burden of proving probable cause to hold—or "bind over"—the defendant for trial. The defendant is not similarly obligated, and, hence, the preliminary hearing gives defense counsel the advantage of hearing the prosecution's theory of the case before going to trial. Even so, defendants have the right to waive a preliminary hearing and often do, especially when prosecutors offer a plea bargain.[36]

In some states and in federal prosecutions (as required by the Fifth Amendment), **grand juries** may either approve an indictment—often called a "true bill"—or decline to do so—a "no bill" against the accused. Most states reserve the option to use grand juries, but only a few require it to begin felony cases. In many states, grand juries perform other special functions, like inspecting prison or jail facilities and hearing evidence of political corruption.[37]

Historically, the grand jury's purpose was to prevent arbitrary charges. Under the prosecutor's direction, grand juries have the power to subpoena witnesses, provide immunity, compel the production of evidence, and, if probable cause exists, indict the accused. The size of grand juries varies widely in the states (ranging from five to twenty-three, for example), as does the number of votes needed to indict. Grand juries in federal prosecutions typically range in size from sixteen to twenty-three participants, and likewise hear the prosecution's evidence in a secret, nonadversarial proceeding. In most jurisdictions, prosecutors are not obliged to present exculpatory evidence that the suspect did not commit the crime; they only present inculpatory proof that they did. Also, defendants do not have the right to be represented by counsel, witnesses are not cross-examined, and the prosecution's evidence generally is not rebutted; unless called as a witness, defendants do not testify in their own defense. While grand juries retain the right to issue subpoenas to witnesses and ask them questions, those prerogatives are not frequently exercised. Furthermore, while some jurisdictions allow for "citizen presentments to the grand jury"—that is, a procedure that permits a citizen to petition the court to get access to grand jury proceedings in cases when a citizen believes that the prosecutor is abusing their duties by action or inaction—there are few checks on prosecutorial authority in the grand jury process. Moreover, only in rare instances do judges intervene to review allegations of grand jury misconduct.[38] Consequently, an old saw is that "prosecutors can get a grand jury to indict a ham sandwich"—a joke that speaks volumes about the prosecutor's sway over grand juries.[39]

Still, preliminary hearings and grand jury proceedings ensure that prosecutorial discretion is not completely unfettered. With preliminary hearings, judges initially assess the reasonableness of believing a defendant is guilty of a crime, whereas, in grand jury jurisdictions, citizens make a similar determination. In any event, a prosecutor's recommendations about how to proceed hold great weight, particularly in determining whether to continue the prosecution, plea bargain, or dismiss a case. For this reason, legal experts often characterize these pretrial proceedings as "prosecutorial in nature" and "an informal, accusatory threshold to the criminal process."[40]

Formal Arraignment

After a preliminary hearing or a grand jury proceeding, defendants are formally charged and arraigned. Arraignment signals that the prosecution intends to pursue a case to trial, and defendants are formally charged and asked to enter a plea. If a defendant pleads guilty, it is usually on the advice of counsel. Defendants may make three types of guilty pleas: (1) a guilty plea; (2) a plea of ***nolo contendere*** (a "no contest" plea, admitting only that the government probably has enough evidence to convict); or, (3) if a jurisdiction permits, a so-called an **Alford plea** (sometimes called a "best interests" plea because it lets defendants plead guilty while protesting their innocence, sometimes so that they may "cap" their maximum sentence). The federal courts and over three-quarters of the states permit *nolo* pleas, and all states except only a few allow *Alford* pleas.[41] While all three pleas hold the defendant criminally responsible, *nolo* and *Alford* pleas were approved in *North Carolina v. Alford* (1970), which explained that "an individual accused of a crime may voluntarily, knowingly, and understandingly consent to the imposition of a prison sentence even if he is unwilling or unable to admit his participation in the acts constituting the crime." In short, an admission of guilt is not a constitutional requirement and runs against the presumption of innocence.[42]

In most states and federal prosecutions, defendants may also make an insanity plea as a defense. Such pleas absolve mentally ill defendants of criminal responsibility and usually result in commitments to a mental institution. Not surprisingly, high-profile insanity cases—such as those involving James E. Holmes, who murdered a dozen people inside a sold-out Aurora, Colorado, movie theater in 2013—have made the insanity defense controversial and unpopular. Legislative reforms have generally made it more difficult to use mental illness as an excuse.[43] Consequently, insanity pleas are limited, and defendants must prove their mental illness should be considered a mitigating factor during sentencing. Still, the Supreme Court's ruling in *Clark v. Arizona* (2006) gave wide latitude in determining the basis for permitting insanity pleas. Under the so-called M'Naghten rule, in force in about seventeen states and in the federal courts, an accused is not criminally responsible if a "defect of reason, from [a] disease of the mind," results in the inability to understand his or her actions because of a lack of cognitive capacity, or the defect prevents distinguishing right from wrong. Eleven states apply some variation of M'Naghten's cognitive or moral incapacity standard. Another test—the "volitional incapacity" or "irresistible-impulse test"—asks whether a mental disease or defect has prevented the accused from controlling actions even when there is cognizance of an act's wrongfulness; about fourteen states use some variant of this test. Three states combine the M'Naghten two-prong standard (cognitive and moral incapacity) with a volitional test, and one state has a "product-of-mental-illness" test, simply inquiring if a person's actions were the product of a mental disease or defect. Idaho, Kansas, Montana, and Utah have abolished the insanity defense, but generally permit some evidence that bears on whether the defendant acted with intent to commit a crime. Notably, in a 6:3 ruling, in *Kahler v. Kansas* (2020) the Supreme Court held that a Kansas' failure to permit a mentally challenged defendant to raise an insanity defense is constitutional because "due process imposes no single canonical formulation of legal insanity." In that respect, the fact that the state lets defendants introduce evidence that there was no intention to kill meets constitutional standards even though it is not, *per se*, a process that accepts using a so-called insanity defense. While the effect of the ruling is unclear, it creates the possibility that more states will follow Kansas' lead in abolishing the insanity defense.[44]

If a defendant pleads not guilty, then a trial date is set, and counsels continue to engage in discovery of information through an exchange of pretrial **motions** (written or oral applications to a court or judge to obtain a rule or order). In the overwhelming majority of cases, however, defendants agree to a plea bargain on the advice of counsel.

PLEA BARGAINING

Although the adversarial system presumes that a defendant's guilt or innocence emerges after a jury trial, in reality, very few state and federal criminal cases actually go to trial. In many cases involving murder or rape, defendants nevertheless tend to opt for a trial, since they have little to lose in insisting on a trial. In most cases, though, a negotiated guilty plea is the better option because it provides leniency and allows prosecutors to secure convictions expeditiously. Although not unproblematic, because defendants waive their constitutional rights to a trial, the "mutuality of advantage" of plea bargaining was upheld in *Brady v. United States* (1972).[45]

In federal district courts, judicial workload statistics show that nearly 90 percent of convictions result from a guilty plea, and only two percent come from a bench or jury trial.[46] Similarly, as Table 7.3 shows, 94 percent of all convictions in state felony cases are due to guilty pleas.

Table 7.3	Criminal Convictions Resulting from Trials and Pleas in State Felony Cases		
Type of Offense	**Bench Trial**	**Jury Trial**	**Guilty Plea**
All offenses	2%	4%	94%
Violent Offenses	2%	36%	61%
• Murder/Non-negligent Manslaughter	2	10	88
• Sexual Assault	3	13	84
→ Rape	2	8	91
→ Other Sexual Assault	2	9	89
• Robbery	3	5	92
• Aggravated Assault	2	5	93
• Miscellaneous Violent	2%	8%	90%
All Violent Cases			
Property Offenses	2%	4%	94%
• Burglary	2	3	95
• Larceny	—	4	96
• Motor Vehicle Theft	2	3	95
• Fraud/Forgery	2%	3%	95%
All Property Offenses			
Drug Offenses	1%	1%	98%
• Possession	2	3	94
• Trafficking	2%	3%	96%
All Drug Offenses			
Weapons Offenses	2%	5%	93%
Miscellaneous Nonviolent Offenses	1%	3%	97%

Note: Data may not sum to total due to rounding.

Source: Sean Rosenmerkel and Matthew Durose, *Felony Sentences in State Courts, 2006—Statistical Tables*, available at https://www.bjs.gov/content/pub/pdf/fssc06st.pdf (last retrieved April 22, 2020).

Plea bargaining remains controversial because the agreements result from a variety of institutional, political, and legal considerations that have little to do with discovering guilt or innocence. For critics, the criminal justice system gives too much authority to prosecutors to make deals; that is, the "[S]ubstantive criminal law. . .now penalizes so much conduct, so severely, and so many times over that it serves simply to delegate power to prosecutors, transforming them into administrators of an unwritten criminal law that consists only of [their own] discretionary decisions to charge certain offenses or to offer certain deals." In this respect, plea bargaining "operates 'outside the law's shadow,' " governed instead only by brute prosecutorial power that is exercised in ways 'not usually written down anywhere.' "[47] In addition, the respective interests of the judge, prosecution, and defense counsel, and the need to reach speedy results due to caseload constraints and limited judicial resources, combine to promote the use of plea bargains, even if mistakes happen. After observing that "96 percent, the great majority of [defendants who strike a deal] are probably guilty," a Texas trial judge acknowledged that there is a "downside" to plea bargaining:

> [There might be] mistakes. . . made by a prosecutor who over-evaluates his or her case, a defense attorney who does not do their case, or a judge who is lazy and doesn't supervise the case. There can be mistakes made in plea bargains; mistakes are also made during jury trials. The whole purpose of plea bargaining is for the prosecutor to assess what this case is worth, and then offer just a little bit less than what a jury would probably come back with, in order to move that case and dispose of the case at that time.[48]

As the crime control model suggests, judges' interests in moving cases off their dockets overrides the due process value of having a jury trial and avoiding mistakes that inevitably occur. As legal historian George Fisher put it: "In place of a noble clash for truth, plea bargaining gives us a skulking truce. Opposing lawyers shrink from battle, and the jury's empty box signals the [criminal justice] system's disappointment."[49]

Such criticisms are especially relevant in considering the wide scope of discretion prosecutors have in successfully negotiating pleas as appointed or elected officials. Prosecutors have been accused of seeking higher conviction rates or launching high-power investigations—such as Kenneth Starr's independent counsel investigation of President Bill Clinton's involvement in an Arkansas Whitewater real estate deal, the Paula Jones sexual harassment civil lawsuit, and the Monica Lewinsky extramarital affair—to advance their careers.[50] Such denunciations are based on the fact that prosecutors have great leeway in charging defendants with an array of crimes that allow convicted offenders to get reduced or favorable sentences at the expense of victims' rights. Only a few states require prosecutors to inform or consult victims about plea bargains. The only judicial oversight that exists is when a deal is approved by a judge, who makes inquiries about whether the defendant voluntarily pleaded guilty without prosecutorial coercion or threats.[51] The issues of judicial oversight, and whether defendants voluntarily plead guilty on the basis of advice they receive from their attorneys, have been addressed by the Supreme Court and other foreign jurisdictions that use plea bargaining practices (see "Contemporary Controversies over Courts: Plea Bargaining, the Right to Counsel, and Global Trends").

Contemporary Controversies over Courts: Plea Bargaining, the Right to Counsel, and Global Trends

A recurring criticism of plea bargaining is that defendants enter into agreements without being fully informed of the terms and implications of the deals negotiated with prosecutors. Defense counsel may not properly advise the accused on whether it is better to plead guilty or to run the risk of going to trial. In 2012, those concerns were addressed in two watershed rulings where a bare majority of the Supreme Court held that the accused has a Sixth Amendment right to effective counsel with respect to plea bargains. In both cases, Justice Anthony Kennedy wrote for the majority, and Chief Justice John Roberts and Justices Antonin Scalia, Clarence Thomas, and Samuel Alito dissented.

In *Missouri v. Frye*, the defendant was not told by defense counsel of two plea offers by the prosecution that would have resulted in a misdemeanor instead of a felony conviction that would have yielded significantly less jail time if accepted. Accordingly, the Court held that "the constitutional right to counsel extends to the negotiation and consideration of plea offers that lapse or are rejected," though defendants must show that prejudice resulted due to ineffective counsel, based on the "reasonable probability they would have accepted [an] earlier plea offer had they been afforded effective counsel" and "a reasonable probability the plea would have been entered without the prosecution canceling it or the trial court refusing to accept it." The companion case, *Lafler v. Cooper*, involved a defendant's attorney reporting a favorable plea offer but recommending its rejection, which resulted in a trial and a harsher sentence than would have been obtained by the plea bargain. In such circumstances, Justice Kennedy held that "a defendant must show that but for the ineffective advice of counsel there is a reasonable probability that the plea offer would have been presented to the court"; that a judge would have accepted it; and, that the sentence under the offer's terms would have been less severe than under the imposed sentence.

Although *Frye*'s and *Lafler*'s long-term effect remains uncertain, there is little doubt that each case underscores Justice Kennedy's observation that American criminal justice "is for the most part a system of pleas, not a system of trials." Within that reality, though, the rulings arguably impose new and far-reaching responsibilities on trial courts to inquire, and to ensure, that defense counsel meet their constitutional obligation to render effective assistance when negotiating and striking plea bargain deals. Since discharging that duty runs the risk of judicial meddling into plea bargaining practices that would otherwise be of no concern to the courts, in both cases dissenting Justice Scalia complained that the rulings invited "a whole new field of constitutionalized criminal procedure: plea-bargaining law."

In recent decades, the U.S. practice has migrated and, with some differences, been adopted in some European countries and elsewhere. Plea bargaining has been assimilated in global jurisdictions that have long avoided or have been reluctant to use it. For example, once known as a "land without plea bargaining," since the 1970s, Germany has used the practice (*Absprachen*) in response to heavy caseloads and long trials in criminal cases. As in the United States, bargains are negotiated before and during trials. Yet German defendants only "confess" to crimes (rather than agreeing to "guilty pleas") in order to have shorter trials. Unlike in the United States, German defense counsel have access to the "written dossier" containing the full pretrial investigation, and therefore the prosecution and defense are on more equal terms during plea negotiations. In addition, German judges actively participate in the negotiations, whereas U.S. judges simply approve plea bargains negotiated by prosecutors and defense attorneys.

Italy's 1989 criminal code also adopted another version of plea bargaining (*patteggiamento*). Prosecutors and defense counsel may request "sentence bargains" that reduce a sentence by up to one-third in minor cases if the sentence would not exceed five years of imprisonment. Such agreements, however, are not strictly considered a "guilty plea," and Italian judges retain the power to enforce the original sentence. In addition, if prosecutors reject a proposed agreement, at the trial's end the defendant's counsel may ask the judge to nevertheless impose a reduced sentence after examining why the prosecution refused to agree to the deal.

In 1999, France adopted still another version of plea bargaining (*composition*). Prosecutors may offer to divert cases from the standard criminal trial process in exchange for defendants' confessing and agreeing to certain conditions, such as paying a fine or doing community service. As in Germany, *composition* does not strictly establish guilt; and, if the defendant fulfills the agreed-to conditions, the case may be completely dismissed. In short, *composition* does not aim at punishing offenders in the same way that guilty pleas do in the United States.

Regardless of the country, plea bargaining remains controversial for a number of reasons. Notably, the deals struck result from a variety of factors and interests that are unrelated to the defendants' guilt or innocence. Prosecutors and judges, who often confront burdensome caseloads and have limited resources, use plea bargains to reduce their workload or dockets and avoid time-consuming and costly trials. Moreover, plea bargains invariably have an element of coercion and originate in secrecy. As a result, using them runs the risk that innocent persons are wrongly convicted. Furthermore, defendants must relinquish their constitutional rights against self-incrimination and to a public jury trial, and they lose the right to confront their accusers. In addition, the presumption of innocence is, of course, forfeited. In sum, plea bargaining remains controversial because prosecutors are vested with virtually unbridled discretion to obtain convictions and to determine punishments, with little judicial oversight and at the cost of sacrificing individuals' constitutional rights.

Sources: *Missouri v. Frye*, 566 U.S. 134 (2012); *Lafler v. Cooper*, 566 U.S. 156 (2012); George Fisher, *Plea Bargaining's Triumph: A History of Plea Bargaining in America* (Stanford, Calif.: Stanford University Press, 2003); Mary Vogel, *Coercion to Compromise: Plea Bargaining, the Courts, and the Making of Political Authority* (New York: Oxford University Press, 2007); Stephen Thaman, *World Plea Bargaining: Consensual Procedures and the Avoidance of the Full Criminal Trial* (Durham, N.C.: Carolina Academic Press, 2010); and Stephanos Bibas, *The Machinery of Criminal Justice* (New York: Oxford University Press, 2012). Portions of the box have been reprinted with permission David M. O'Brien and Gordon Silverstein, *Constitutional Law and Politics: Civil Rights and Civil Liberties (Vol. 2)*, 11th ed. (New York: W.W. Norton, 2020), as well as earlier editions solely authored by the late David M. O'Brien.

THE JURY'S ROLE

In the event a plea cannot be negotiated before trial, the prosecution and defense must prepare the evidence they plan to use at trial by filing pretrial motions, such as a motion to dismiss or to suppress evidence. In criminal litigation, the prosecution is not under any constitutional obligation to share all that it learns from its investigation—except if it pertains to "exculpatory" evidence that the accused is innocent.[52] Hence, the defendant's right to collect critical facts (such as witness statements and forensic lab results) is usually determined by how the **rules**

of discovery are applied, though they vary around the country. Some prosecutors favor a policy of liberal discovery as a plea bargaining strategy, while others do not, and what is shared may be negotiated in pretrial motion hearings. In any event, the limited scope of criminal discovery tends to work in favor of the prosecution because it initially controls whether evidence is withheld or disclosed.

Once the prosecution and defense counsel complete discovery, the trial is held—which is conducted in front of a jury or held by a judge in a "bench trial" (if the defendant consents). Although most cases are resolved through plea bargaining, it is estimated that state courts perform nearly 149,000 jury trials annually. The rate of federal jury trials is far less, only at about 1,700 per year.[53]

The Democratic Politics of Citizen Juries

Historically, a counterweight to the prosecutor is the defendant's right to have a trial by an impartial **petit jury** drawn from the place where the crime occurred. Rooted in Article III, Section 2, the Sixth Amendment for criminal cases, and the Seventh Amendment for civil cases (if a dispute exceeds more than $20), the right to a jury trial is both an expression of democratic participation and a bulwark against oppressive government across the globe (see "In Comparative Perspective: The Evolution of the Common Law Jury Across the Globe"). In the United States, the jury trial was originally conceived as a right attaching only to federal criminal prosecutions, but the right to a jury trial was extended to the states in *Duncan v. Louisiana* (1968).[54]

The democratic role juries play is significant because they represent the community and have the flexibility to acquit, convict, or force a mistrial. Akin to "morality plays," trials historically determined whether the accused should be acquitted or punished in accordance with communal judgments on the circumstances of the crime and the defendant's fault. As one scholar put it, "The jury is generally a better representative of the community than a judge and is the more appropriate source for the normative assessments that the legislature has left to the trial decision maker."[55]

Over time, the jury's role has evolved, and how well it performs its function has been influenced by several factors: (1) what kinds of criminal cases juries are permitted to adjudicate; (2) whether it is possible to select a jury that fairly represents the community and is free from bias; (3) whether twelve-person juries or smaller juries are appropriate; (4) whether jury verdicts must be unanimous; and, (5) whether the jury has the authority to nullify the law and acquit defendants in complex cases, which may also apply to "hung" juries.

In Comparative Perspective: The Evolution of the Common Law Jury Across the Globe

The notion of a "common law jury"—which brings together lay persons in the community to deliver criminal or civil justice after a trial—has a longstanding history but continues to evolve across the globe. Its foundation, which represents the ideal principles of democratic participation, impartiality, and fairness in deciding the litigation fate of disputants in criminal and civil matters, is nonetheless a continuing source of controversy and resistance. Critics, for example, have often complained that common law juries cannot perform their function very well, typically because they are unrepresentative of the community, or that it is difficult, if not impossible, for lay persons to deliver rational or just verdicts due to the complexity of the law and the operation of the legal system. Except for the United States and some parts of Canada, the criticisms have had a powerful effect over time since civil jury trials in many parts of the world have disappeared; and, in criminal cases, the use of trials has diminished. Even so, roughly fifty countries still value having criminal jury trials, including the United States, England and Wales, Northern Ireland, Canada, New Zealand; and, they are used in some parts of legal systems found in Africa, Asia, the Mediterranean, the South Pacific, South America and the Caribbean.

In his famous work studying American democracy, in *Democracy in America* Alexis de Tocqueville observed that the jury's development in the United States can be traced to its English common law roots; but remains distinct because its political character is non-aristocratic and closely linked to the twin notions of popular sovereignty and the right to vote (all legally registered voters could serve as jurors). Historically, jury trials in England emerged after Norman Conquest in 1066. Under Norman practice, local residents were placed under an oath to tell the truth, but their primary function was to be only a source of information about local happenings and those who lived in the community. In time, jurors assumed the role of adjudicators of criminal and civil disputes and, by the eighteenth century, had to recuse themselves if they had any personal knowledge or connection to the case at hand. By 1367, in exercising that role unanimous verdicts in civil and criminal cases were mandated. And, in *Bushell's Case* (1670), the English courts established that jurors had independent authority to determine the facts and, relatedly, render verdicts without having to explain or justify their decisions-a vital principle of jury independence. Today, civil jury trials are infrequent because judges have the discretion to refuse them, and there is only a qualified right to request them in defamation, fraud, malicious prosecution, and false imprisonment cases. Similarly, only the most serious criminal prosecutions are heard by jury trial; instead, most criminal cases are disposed of by a panel of three lay magistrates in English magistrate courts.

Not surprisingly, some of the characteristics underlying the English conception of a jury were incorporated into the United States; though, its evolution and application in civil and criminal matters remains distinct, in part because of the unique circumstances surrounding the American Revolution and its aftermath. In general, the importance of having juries is registered by the understanding that it was a personal freedom that limited arbitrary government, an idea that greatly influenced state constitutional development and the framers' decision to guarantying it explicitly in the U.S. Constitution and the Bill of Rights. In addition, juries are infused into the common law adversarial model of justice in civil and criminal cases, where the truth is, in theory, uncovered by an opposing clash of interests vying for a court victory. Other values, such as democratic participation in governance and principles of federalism, transparency and impartiality, remain significant elements of the U.S. legal system and reflected in both jury selection (*voir dire*) and jury decision-making practices. Although, today, a majority of cases are either settled by negotiation (civil cases) or resolved by plea bargains (criminal cases), juries in the United States continue to play an important symbolic role, simply because they manifest the exercise of individual liberty in a democratic society and representative constitutional republic.

Juries are significant in legal systems in other parts of the world as well, and many were affected by British colonization. In Scotland, the modern iteration of the civil jury trial emerged from England in the early nineteenth century. Under that model, the decisions of twelve person juries were once required to be unanimous, but that practice has yielded to verdicts reached by majority that have a choice of two options (finding liability or not). Civil juries were abolished in the lower civil courts (Sheriff Courts) in 1980; and, in theory, they are available in the higher civil court (Court of Session), especially in personal injury and defamation actions. In practice, few civil jury trials are held because parties can opt to have a bench trial by either establishing "special cause" or by consent. In contrast, Scottish criminal trials are less influenced by English common law history; rather, its origins can be traced back to Nordic governance practices that became widespread in Scotland in the eleventh and twelfth centuries. Most criminal cases are resolved in the courts of first instance, namely the district court, the Sheriff Court, or the High Court of Justiciary. Whereas district courts hear minor criminal cases under a summary procedure (without a jury) held by one or more lay justices of the peace, Sheriff Courts, which have a varying number of sheriffs (appointed by legal practitioners) vested with adjudicatory powers (in accordance with the volume of caseload in different sheriffdoms) have the authority to resolve more serious criminal prosecutions by using either a summary procedure or a solemn procedure (with a jury). High Courts, on the other hand, operate as a final appellate court and consist of roughly twenty-five judges that always decide cases under the solemn procedure of using one judge sitting with a jury. Moreover, Scottish criminal trial juries cannot result in hung trials; and they are empowered to convict or acquit through a bare majority vote of eight to seven, though forepersons cannot be asked about the size of the majority. Another unusual characteristic of Scottish criminal jury trials is that they can result in three different verdicts: guilty, not guilty, and "not proven" (which has the same effect as an acquittal because the government has not conclusively proven the defendant's guilt). Despite the criticism that the "not proven" verdict option is illogical in light of the availability of the "not guilty" disposition, the three verdict system is fully ingrained within the Scottish system. Indeed, there is some empirical evidence showing that the "not proven" verdict is a preferred option in many Scottish criminal prosecutions.

Beyond the United States and Scotland, the template of the English common law jury was spread to other countries through colonization or indirect means. In the aftermath of the French Revolution and through subsequent Napoleonic conquests, the English model was inserted into the Napoleonic Code of 1809 and thus in legal systems of parts of Europe, including Switzerland, parts of Germany, Belgium, Austria, Greece, Russia, Spain and Portugal. Through British colonization, it was directly adopted in colonies in Africa, Asia and the Caribbean. Over time, the influence of English law has remained persistent, although it is not unusual that some countries have adopted revisions to the common law jury model by treating it more like a right instead of an entrenched bureaucratic procedure; or, incorporating elements of inquisitorial practice or other forms of indigenous dispute resolution into their respective legal systems; or, in other countries, to abolish jury trials altogether for political or cultural reasons. In still other foreign jurisdictions, such as Spain and Russia, juries were reintroduced to adjudicate criminal cases.

In sum, perhaps the most consistent trend in the evolution of the common jury trial is the diversity of its scope and application among nations, both in terms of how representative they are as the voice and conscience of a community, and by how they operate procedurally or substantively to administer justice in civil or criminal matters in adversarial, inquisitorial or mixed legal systems.

Sources: Neal Vidmar, ed., *World Jury Systems* (New York: Oxford University Press, 2000) (Chapters 1 to 3, 7, 11 and 13); Alexis de Tocqueville, *Democracy in America* (translated by G. Lawrence, ed. J.P. Mayer)(New York: Harper Row, 1966). See also, Suja A. Thomas, *The Missing American Jury* (New York: Cambridge University Press, 2016) Leonard W. Levy, *The Palladium of Justice: Origins of Trial by Jury* (Chicago: Ivan R. Dee, 1999); and Richard Terrill, *World Criminal Justice Systems: A Comparative Survey*, 8th ed. (Cincinnati, Ohio: Anderson, 2012).

The Types of Criminal Cases Juries Can Hear

The Supreme Court has established that the accused is entitled as a fundamental right to a jury trial in all serious, but not "petty" criminal cases—cases in which defendants face possible imprisonment of six months or more.[56] Still, in *Lewis v. United States* (1996),[57] the Court held that a jury trial is not required when a defendant is prosecuted in a single proceeding for multiple petty offenses— offenses that each carry a maximum of six or fewer months—even though the aggregate prison term exceeds six months. In federal courts, the right to a jury pertains only to those cases involving the Fifth Amendment's grand jury indictment clause, so they are not needed for some petty crimes. Also, it is not required for contempt proceedings, *habeas corpus* petitions, and some civil and administrative proceedings involving disbarment of attorneys and immigrant deportations, as well as military court martials.[58]

Selecting an Impartial Jury from a Cross-Section of the Community

In *Taylor v. Louisiana* (1975),[59] the Supreme Court established that the Sixth Amendment requires petit juries composed from a fair cross-section of the community in order to ensure impartiality. The difficulties of selecting an impartial jury, though, implicate Sixth Amendment as well as Fourteenth Amendment equal protection rights. Under these provisions, defendants may allege that the jury selection process is fraught with unfair racial, gender, and economic bias.[60] While the federal Jury Selection and Service Act (1968) imposed a requirement of random selection of jury venires, in most jurisdictions members of the jury panel are drawn from voting registration lists. Voting lists, however, are unlikely to produce a random supply of citizens because younger voters and minorities are largely underrepresented, along with the fact that many people who are more affluent, educated, and older tend not to register to vote. Consequently, many voting districts also draw prospective jurors from motor vehicle registration lists. Regardless of the method used, jury pools often remain depleted because citizens avoid jury service by claiming occupational exemptions (e.g., clergy, doctors, and lawyers), or they simply do not respond to appear for jury service.[61]

The problem of constructing a representative jury is compounded by the tactics of lawyers in trying select the most favorable jury that benefits their clients' legal interests. Lawyers try to influence jury selection and socialize prospective jurors through a ***voir dire*** selection process. Opposing counsel (and sometimes the judge) question potential jurors individually or in a group (sitting in the jury box) about whether they can fairly evaluate the evidence in spite of their personal biases. As part of the *voir dire* process, jurors are questioned and may be excused from serving if the lawyers exercise either a **challenge for cause** or a **peremptory challenge** (limited in number but based on any grounds). *Challenges for cause* are unlimited in number and based on responses to questions from prospective jurors that suggest they may not fairly weigh the evidence.[62]

The *voir dire* process has been criticized because it is discriminatory. In response, the Court has prohibited the discriminatory use of peremptory challenges if they are based on race, gender, or ethnic origin.[63] But the prosecutor's choices are evaluated on "facially neutral" grounds; that is, defendants must prove the prosecutor was acting with "purposeful discrimination" in excluding certain classes of persons from the jury panel once the trial court initially accepts the prosecutor's race-neutral explanations. Some critics argue that the standard ironically facilitates discrimination by encouraging courts to accept *any* rationale for exclusion that the prosecutor can create on a pretext, or "after the fact," if it appears to be "neutral."[64] Notably, prosecutors are given the same right to challenge the defendant's peremptory strikes on discriminatory grounds as well. Even so, challenges to the *voir dire* process often centers on prosecutorial action, and the principle established in *Batson v. Kentucky* (1986)—that prosecutors are banned under the Fourteenth Amendment's due process clause from excluding potential black jurors for racial reasons in order to secure an all-white jury—is a recurring issue, especially in capital punishment cases. In *Flowers v. Mississippi* (2019), for example, in a 7:2 decision the Supreme Court reversed a murder conviction and death sentence because the local prosecutor, who was white, used peremptory challenges to remove forty one of forty two possible black jurors in a total of six trials. Justice Brett Kavanaugh's Opinion for the Court explained that those facts, along with a cumulative "history from Flowers' six trials" of prosecutorial questioning and jury selection decisions exhibiting a clear discriminatory intent, is a simple application of "enforc[ing] and reinforce[ing]" the *Batson* precedent and "applying it to the extraordinary facts" of the case. Notwithstanding *Flowers* and *Batson*, a survey of the relevant jurisprudence in this area suggests that, in general, minority defendants routinely face sometimes daunting obstacles in trying to get more diverse and representative juries in their communities.[65]

The difficulties of jury selection also manifest themselves in the context of whether citizens are fully qualified to serve as jurors in a trial setting, something that does not happen very often. In response, many jurisdictions use written "jury questionnaires" to supply detailed information about the qualifications of jurors in advance of oral *voir dire* questioning. In essence, the questionnaires seek to determine if a juror is qualified, and eligible, to serve before they are called into court. In some high-profile instances, the questionnaires have been criticized because they may be too detailed or invasive, and difficult to manage. A juror who was chosen but later dismissed in the O.J. Simpson murder trial, for example, revealed that the questionnaire was seventy-nine pages long and had twenty-eight parts, with 294 questions. Also, jurors were asked questions that seemed irrelevant to the case, such as "Do you believe it is immoral or wrong to do an amniocentesis to determine whether a fetus has a genetic defect?" or "Have you ever provided a urine sample to be analyzed for any purpose?" Moreover, Judge Jackie Glass, who presided over O.J. Simpson's subsequent robbery and kidnapping trial (to recover allegedly stolen memorabilia), released the jury's questionnaires, which, as in the first unrelated trial, suggested that it is difficult to manage, or understand the value of, information that is compiled from 116 questions that were asked to each juror in a nearly thirty page document.[66]

Jury Size and Unanimity of Jury Verdicts

Traditionally, the size of the common law jury was twelve, and jury verdicts in criminal trials were required to be unanimous.[67] In the 1960s, however, several states and the federal courts began to push for jury reform in an attempt to save costs and, in general, thereafter the Supreme Court has permitted states to reduce jury sizes and let juries render non-unanimous verdicts.[68] To illustrate, *Williams v. Florida* (1970)[69] held that states could use six-person juries in felony (except capital punishment) cases, reasoning that there was little difference between twelve- and six-person jury verdicts. Subsequently, *Johnson v. Louisiana* (1972) and *Apodaca v. Oregon* (1972)[70] adopted that rationale in holding that unanimous and nonunanimous verdicts were "functionally equivalent," thereby approving nonunanimous, supermajority verdicts in criminal cases. In *Johnson*, the Court upheld Louisiana's law letting juries convict on the basis of nine (out of twelve) juror votes; and, in *Apodaca*, an Oregon law was similarly authorized the convictions of two defendants by votes of eleven to one, and ten to two. Notably, *Apodaca* and its companion case, *Johnson*, concluded that the Sixth Amendment only afforded defendants in federal, but not state court, a right to a unanimous jury verdict. Furthermore, in *Ballew v. Georgia* (1978) and *Burch v. Louisiana* (1979),[71] the Court drew another line in ruling that a Georgia law allowing convictions by a unanimous five-person criminal juries is unconstitutional (in *Ballew*), and that convictions from six-member jury verdicts in Louisiana had to be unanimous (in *Burch*). By 2019, only two states, Louisiana and Oregon, permitted non-unanimous verdicts for serious crimes; though, in *Ramos v. Louisiana* (2020),[72] in a 6:3 decision reversing the murder conviction of Evangelisto Ramos by a vote of ten to two in Louisiana, the Supreme Court declared that the Sixth Amendment guarantees a unanimous jury verdict in both federal *and* state criminal trials, thus overruling *Apodaca* in the process (see Chapter Nine for a discussion of *stare decisis*, or precedent, and the legal standards that courts and judges use to overturn it).

Subsequent research on the impact on jury size on decision-making is mixed. While some studies find that there is little difference between larger or smaller juries in respect to mistrial rates, other research shows that size matters because it affects trial outcomes and jurors' behavior. The latter findings are consistent with a concept in the law literature—Condorcet's Jury Theorem, which posits that jury decision-making in a group leads to better decisions than an individual would make—though some studies find that the theorem does not hold under certain conditions, like the presence of strategic voting, among other things. Even so, as opposed to six-member panels, larger juries are inherently advantageous because they may: (1) have more minority representation; (2) recall more evidence; (3) spend more time in deliberations; and, (4) recall more information during deliberations. In addition, as *Ballew* recognized, a jury with fewer than six members "promotes inaccurate and possibly biased decision-making,. . .causes untoward differences in verdicts, and. . .prevents juries from truly representing their communities."[73] While several states permit smaller juries for misdemeanor prosecutions, even before *Ramos*, virtually all states required unanimous verdicts regardless of their size.[74]

The Problem of Jury Nullification and Hung Juries

Although the Sixth and Seventh Amendments guarantee the right to a jury in criminal and civil actions, juries do not have a right to "nullify," or independently disregard, the verdict. Still, at the country's founding, the practice was for juries to decide the law as well as the facts. As the judges and lawyers became more professionalized, there was increasing pressure to counter the democratic impulses of juries. As a result, in *Sparf & Hansen v. United States* (1895), the Court held the jury's proper role is to apply the law (as determined by the judge) to the facts found after hearing the evidence at trial.[75]

Juries nonetheless still occasionally engage in nullification. A jury may acquit because it perceives a law to be unjust, as in assisted-suicide prosecutions of seniors who intentionally kill their terminally ill partner. Juries also may exonerate a defendant if the application of a law appears unfair. In addition, juries may disregard the law if they find prosecutorial or illegal police misconduct. In short, jury nullification "allows juries unreviewable discretion in refusing to apply the law to a particular person."[76]

Jury nullification, moreover, may occur if a single juror refuses to apply the law and causes a "hung" or "deadlocked jury" that forces a mistrial. While the rate of jury nullification remains unclear, a National Center for State Courts report found that 2.5 percent of federal criminal trials result in hung juries, and in state prosecutions the average rate is 6.2 percent. The reasons juries do not reach a verdict vary but appear due to: 1) the poor quality of the evidence; 2) the contentiousness of deliberations; and, 3) the perception of unfairness of a law. Other studies conclude that nullification is a response to jurors' perception of unlawful government behavior.[77]

Proposals to Reform the Jury Process

Whether juries are neutral and competent fact finders that can apply the law correctly has led to calls for reform. At trial, juries hear evidence and determine what the facts of the case are before they render a verdict based on the law. A jury's understanding of the "law", however, is conveyed by the judge near the end of the case through "jury instructions"—which in certain cases can be complex statements of legal principles about different facets of the case, including the elements of a crimes, or the availability of different legal defenses—and which can be very confusing for many jurors. This problem, as well as others that are a part of the jury deliberation process, has prompted numerous studies that have proposed different types of reform, including (1) permitting jurors to take notes during trials; (2) allowing jurors to ask witnesses questions during trial; (3) giving jurors "pre-instructions," or giving them a brief overview of the case before jury selection begins; (4) requiring "plain English" jury instructions; (5) facilitating posttrial meetings between the judge, jurors, and lawyers; and, (6) increasing jury size in complex cases. In response, several states, including Ohio, Massachusetts, Arizona, and New York, have enacted changes which have expanded the master voting list, increased juror pay, or created publications that detail jurors' rights and responsibilities. Other states have taken similar steps to improve jury procedures by, among other things, upgrading court technologies, abolishing occupational and status exemptions from jury service, or expediting qualification and summoning processes in order to expand jury pools.[78]

After receiving jury instructions and listening to opposing counsels' closing arguments, a jury's most important task is determining the defendant's guilt or innocence. If there is a reasonable doubt, the jury acquits. If a jury votes to convict, then the next stage is sentencing the defendant.

THE POLITICS OF THE POST-TRIAL SENTENCING PROCESS

After a defendant's conviction, the sentencing process begins. Those convicted are sentenced in accordance with one or more of the following punishment purposes: incapacitation, retribution, deterrence, and rehabilitation. Principally through incarceration, **incapacitation** makes it impossible for offenders to commit crimes in the future. **Retribution** is designed to exact revenge and to give offenders their "just deserts." **Deterrence** purports to eliminate or reduce crime by creating a fear of legal punishment while serving the community by putting offenders in jail or prison so they may not commit other crimes. **Rehabilitation** aims at treating offenders and subsequently reintroducing them into society—usually through some type of counseling or vocational training—and does not punish all offenders who commit the same crime equally, which critics argue diminishes its legitimacy as a penal policy.[79]

Sentencing policies have evolved with the growth of the modern prison system. In the colonial era, communities used retribution and deterrence to maintain social control. Imprisonment was not a popular option, so fines, corporal punishments and shaming were the most prevalent punishments. Shaming and painful punishments often included flogging, physical mutilation (cutting off ears or nails), and spending time in the stocks, along with staging mock executions. Branding or being dunked in water and similar punishments were ordinarily reserved for repeat or the most dangerous offenders.[80]

By the nineteenth century, Enlightenment rationalism led to an emphasis on deterrence and incapacitation, which in turn led to more professionalized police and a growing prison system. After 1870, prison overcrowding, though, gave rise to **indeterminate sentencing**—sentences imposed by judges after considering a broad range of minimum and maximum punishments to sanction offenders. Typically, a parole board had the power to release an offender and also revoke the terms of parole if the conditions for release were violated. Incarceration and the imposition of fines became predominant sanctions. Although determinate sentencing practices grew, rehabilitation largely remained the basis for penal policy throughout the nineteenth and much of the twentieth century.[81]

By the mid 1970s, rehabilitation gave way to a policy of **determinate sentencing** that returned to a combination of retribution and deterrence rationales. Mandatory minimum sentencing, "truth in sentencing," sentencing guidelines, and intermediate sanctions became the norm (see Table 7.4). Determinate sentencing aims to punish offenders with fixed sentences that reduce the discretionary power of judicial and parole officers to deviate from a prescribed range of punishments. The shift in sentencing policy from indeterminate to determinate practices registers the ideological struggle between the underlying philosophies of the "crime control" and "due process" models of criminal procedure and, in practice, shifted discretion in sentencing from judges and juries to prosecutors.[82]

Table 7.4	Sentencing Typologies and Practices
Sentencing Type/Practice	**Main Characteristics**
Indeterminate Sentencing	• Judge imposes sentence within range of minimum and maximum penalties set by legislature, but parole boards determine actual length of time served • Prevalent as a sentencing policy up until the 1970s, but its use has been substantially diminished in the federal government and the states • Actual release dates affected by inmate behavior with "good time" allowances being earned by participation in prison-based education and treatment programs • Many states use hybrid indeterminate/determinate sentencing practices
Determinate Sentencing	• Fixed prison terms imposed by legislature that may be reduced by good-time or earned-time credits; punishment severity is fixed by judges at sentencing, so length of imprisonment reasonably known based on estimate of good-time credit reduction • Typically sets a release date, with no independent review by parole board, but postincarceration supervision possible as part of sentence • Determinate sentencing practices include "truth-in-sentencing," mandatory minimum sentencing, sentencing guidelines (presumptive or voluntary), and intermediate sanctions (as a supplement to sentencing guidelines) • Increasingly prevalent in the federal government and in about half of the states since the 1980s
Truth in Sentencing	• Requires offenders to serve a substantial portion of their prison sentence (typically between 50% and 85%, or 100% of the minimum, depending upon class and degree of offense) • Parole eligibility and good-time credits are restricted or eliminated
Mandatory Minimum Sentencing	• Requires offenders, especially violent criminals, to serve minimum sentence before becoming eligible for parole • Can be used in indeterminate or determinate systems; yet, in determinate systems, the minimum time must be served

	before being eligible for release with the approval of a parole board • Typically target habitual offenders and often apply to violent, drug, sex offense, weapons, and driving under the influence of alcohol crimes
Sentencing Guidelines	• Requires or recommends that judges impose sentences in accordance with fixed penalties often promulgated by sentencing commissions • Guidelines determine the sentence by considering the offender's criminal history and the severity of the crime • Judicial discretion in imposing sentences is restricted, and "upward" or "downward" departures from the guidelines are disfavored • Parole restricted or eliminated; roughly half the states have guidelines with some parole-board prison-release discretion (other half does not)
Presumptive Sentencing Guidelines	• Sentencing guidelines are considered presumptively correct, and judges cannot depart from them absent legally permissible reasons that are explained on the record • Guidelines may require appellate review of departures by trial judge
Voluntary Sentencing Guidelines	• Sentencing guidelines are advisory (recommendations) only, based on past sentencing practices, and judges have discretion and can depart from the guidelines • Can be used in indeterminate and determinate systems
Intermediate Sanctions	• Noncustodial sanctions, used to supplement guidelines for sentencing • Examples include home confinement, community service, residential treatment (health, drug illness), victim restitution, and intensive-supervision probation (day reporting)

Sources: Kevin R. Reitz, "The 'Traditional' Indeterminate Sentencing Model," in *The Oxford Handbook of Sentencing and Corrections*, edited by Joan Petersilia and Kevin R. Reitz (New York: Oxford University Press, 2012), 270–98; U.S. Department of Justice, Bureau of Justice Assistance, *1996 National Survey of State Sentencing Structures* (Monograph, NCJ 169270, September 1998), available at https://www.ncjrs.gov/pdffiles/169270.pdf (last retrieved April 23, 2020).

The Growth of Determinate Sentencing

"Both before and since the American colonies became a nation," Justice Hugo Black wrote in *Williams v. New York* (1949), "courts in this country and in England practiced a policy under which a sentencing judge could exercise a wide discretion in the sources and types of evidence used to assist him in determining the kind and extent of punishment to be imposed within limits fixed by law." *Williams* held that a New York state trial judge acted appropriately in using information from a probation department's presentence report when sentencing a convicted murderer to death, instead of following the jury's recommendation of life imprisonment. The scope of the trial court's discretion under indeterminate sentencing, Justice Black acknowledged, is vast, and the "practice of probation" confirmed that "reformation and rehabilitation of offenders have become important goals of criminal jurisprudence." Hence, a trial court could rely upon witnesses' statements in the presentence report describing the defendant as a "menace to society" and having "a morbid sexuality," when concluding he should be executed. The defendant's due process rights were not violated because a judge could "consider information about the convicted person's past life, health, habits, conduct, and mental and moral propensities. . .even though [it was] obtained outside the courtroom from persons whom a defendant has not been permitted to confront or cross-examine."[83]

Justice Black's defense of indeterminate sentencing was subsequently attacked by the left and right. Early reformers, such as Harvard Law School professor Alan Dershowitz, argued for **presumptive sentences**—punishments that presumptively fix sentences by using ranges that base punishment on the seriousness of the offense and an offender's prior criminal history. These reform ideas were applied in few states with the adoption in the late 1970s of voluntary sentencing guidelines that typically used fixed sentences and abolished parole, though allowed early release based on good-time credits.[84]

In the 1980s, growing political dissatisfaction with indeterminate sentencing produced even more reforms. And in the next two decades, the federal government and all states established **mandatory minimum sentences** and, to a lesser degree, ***truth-in-sentencing*** laws (requiring certain offenders to serve most of their sentences), ***two- and three-strikes laws*** (providing for minimum sentences or life imprisonment after a second or third conviction), and ***life-without-possibility-of-parole laws***. At the same time, some states, such as Minnesota (1980), Pennsylvania (1982), Washington (1983), and Florida (1983), started using **presumptive sentencing guidelines** (see Figure 7.3). Working from the assumption that guidelines reduced cost and sentence disparities, sentencing guidelines were distinct because they were created by sentencing commissions (agencies in the executive branch, as opposed to the legislature) and relied on quantitative measurements to mete out criminal sanctions; and, significantly, they were legally binding, and not advisory or voluntary, which meant that judges had to apply them. The presumptive sentencing guideline format was later adopted by the federal government in the Sentencing Reform Act of 1984.[85]

The federal Sentencing Reform Act established an independent sentencing commission—the U.S. Sentencing Commission—which had several responsibilities: (1) to create presumptive federal sentencing guidelines; (2) to advise Congress on sentencing policy; (3) to generate federal sentencing statistics; and, (4) to provide education, training, and research material for judicial staff on how to implement the guidelines. The federal guidelines construct penalty ranges in grid boxes based on the offense's severity and the defendant's criminal history. Judges must almost mechanically determine whether certain sentencing factors are present or absent in each case, and the sentence is based on mathematical equations that add or subtract points within fixed guideline ranges. Furthermore, judges generally must impose guideline-specified sentences unless, in atypical cases, an upward or downward departure is warranted because of a narrowly defined set of aggravating or mitigating circumstances. If judges depart from the guidelines, the reasons for their decisions must be given and are subject to appellate review. Finally, parole was abolished, and the possibility of early release diminished.[86]

| Figure 7.3 | Minnesota's Presumptive Sentencing Grid |

4.A. Sentencing Guidelines Grid

Presumptive sentence lengths are in months. Italicized numbers within the grid denote the discretionary range within which a court may sentence without the sentence being deemed a departure. Offenders with stayed felony sentences may be subject to local confinement.

		CRIMINAL HISTORY SCORE						
SEVERITY LEVEL OF CONVICTION OFFENSE (Example offenses listed in italics)		0	1	2	3	4	5	6 or more
Murder, 2nd Degree (Intentional; Drive-By-Shootings)	11	306 261-367	326 278-391	346 295-415	366 312-439	386 329-463	406 346-480[2]	426 363-480[2]
Murder, 2nd Degree (Unintentional) Murder, 3rd Degree (Depraved Mind)	10	150 128-180	165 141-198	180 153-216	195 166-234	210 179-252	225 192-270	240 204-288
Murder, 3rd Degree (Controlled Substances) Assault, 1st Degree	9	86 74-103	98 84-117	110 94-132	122 104-146	134 114-160	146 125-175	158 135-189
Agg. Robbery, 1st Degree Burglary, 1st Degree (w/ Weapon or Assault)	8	48 41-57	58 50-69	68 58-81	78 67-93	88 75-105	98 84-117	108 92-129
Felony DWI Financial Exploitation of a Vulnerable Adult	7	36	42	48	54 46-64	60 51-72	66 57-79	72 62-84[2,3]
Assault, 2nd Degree Burglary, 1st Degree (Occupied Dwelling)	6	21	27	33	39 34-46	45 39-54	51 44-61	57 49-68
Residential Burglary Simple Robbery	5	18	23	28	33 29-39	38 33-45	43 37-51	48 41-57
Nonresidential Burglary	4	12[1]	15	18	21	24 21-28	27 23-32	30 26-36
Theft Crimes (Over $5,000)	3	12[1]	13	15	17	19 17-22	21 18-25	23 20-27
Theft Crimes ($5,000 or less) Check Forgery ($251-$2,500)	2	12[1]	12[1]	13	15	17	19	21 18-25
Assault, 4th Degree Fleeing a Peace Officer	1	12[1]	12[1]	12[1]	13	15	17	19 17-22

[1] 12[1]=One year and one day

☐ Presumptive commitment to state imprisonment. First-degree murder has a mandatory life sentence and is excluded from the Guidelines under Minn. Stat. § 609.185. See section 2.E. for policies regarding those sentences controlled by law.

▨ Presumptive stayed sentence; at the discretion of the court, up to one year of confinement and other non-jail sanctions can be imposed as conditions of probation. However, certain offenses in the shaded area of the Grid always carry a presumptive commitment to state prison. See sections 2.C and 2.E.

[2] Minn. Stat. § 244.09 requires that the Guidelines provide a range for sentences that are presumptive commitment to state imprisonment of 15% lower and 20% higher than the fixed duration displayed, provided that the minimum sentence is not less than one year and one day and the maximum sentence is not more than the statutory maximum. See section 2.C.1-2.

[3] The stat. max. for Financial Exploitation of Vulnerable Adult is 240 months; the standard range of 20% higher than the fixed duration applies at CHS 6 or more. (The range is 62-86.)

Source: Minnesota Sentencing Guidelines Commission, "2019 Sentencing Guidelines and Commentary (Standard Grid)" available at https://mn.gov/sentencing-guidelines/guidelines/currentguidelines.jsp (last retrieved July 1, 2020).

Sentencing reform caused about a third of the states to eliminate parole release and all others to end it for some categories of offenders. In addition to the federal government, several states moved to sentencing guidelines, and all states adopted mandatory-minimum laws for drug and violent crimes and for recidivist offenders, often triggering lengthy incarceration periods. Significantly, the political popularity of using determinate sentencing laws coincided with decreasing crime rates, but also a dramatic spike in prison populations over the past several decades.[87]

In the United States there are over two million persons in federal and state prisons; and, in terms of international rates, the level of imprisonment in the United States represents a ratio of 655 prisoners per 100,000 residents, the highest in the world, with El Salvador (618), Rwanda (464), Russia (383) and Brazil (333) close behind. Mass incarceration, as well, has a disproportionate impact on certain segments of the population: people of color constitute almost forty percent of U.S. population, but almost seventy percent of who is in prison.[88] Some estimates also show that the rate of imprisonment for black males is almost six times greater than for white males; and, in state prisons, a greater proportion of Hispanics and African-Americans that are convicted of a violent crime serve time as compared to whites. As one researcher put it, these trends show that "the term 'mass' is a bit of a monomer because it turns out that incarceration rates are—and have always been—a lot more 'mass' for some groups of people than they are for others."[89] By other estimates, U.S. incarcerations constitute more than one-fifth of the world's prison and jail populations—a rate that far exceeds that of other Western democracies. Such incarceration trends, though stabilizing somewhat due to some changes in policy and programmatic reform, have led to the criticism that sentencing policies are too punitive—and too costly, with expenditures growing from $6 billion in 1982 to over $68 billion in 2006, an increase of over 660 percent.[90]

Budget uncertainties, along with the reform of federal drug laws, has increasingly put the viability of sentencing guidelines into question, especially in light of a series of landmark Supreme Court "sentence-enhancement" rulings.[91] Beginning with *Apprendi v. New Jersey* (2000),[92] the Court established that the aggravating circumstances of a crime, or sentencing-enhancing "facts" that increase a defendant's punishment, must be determined by a jury instead of by judges in order to protect the defendant's Sixth Amendment right to a jury trial. The *Apprendi* principle was then applied in subsequent rulings. In *Blakely v. Washington* (2004),[93] the Court invalidated Washington's Sentencing Reform Act because it allowed the trial judge to increase the length of a defendant's sentence on the basis of facts not admitted by the defendant or determined by the jury. In writing for a bare majority, Justice Antonin Scalia held that the right to a jury trial was violated when the trial judge found that the defendant acted with "deliberate cruelty" (a "fact") in kidnapping his wife, and thereupon increased the sentence by more than three years. He concluded that the Sixth Amendment safeguards the right of a jury to ascertain all essential facts that may be considered when sentencing a defendant.

Shortly thereafter, *United States v. Booker* (2005)[94] struck down part of the U.S. Sentencing Guidelines and rendered them advisory. In this respect, the federal sentencing guidelines were transformed into merely recommendations for district court judges in sentencing—but, significantly, judges have the discretion to impose sentences that go beyond the guidelines in certain "enhancement" cases that permit harsher punishments under certain facts and circumstances (e.g., if the defendant has prior convictions, is a repeat offender, or uses a weapon). Still, in three post-*Booker* rulings, *Rita v. United States* (2007), *Gall v. United States* (2007) and *Kimbrough v. United States* (2007), the Supreme Court signaled that while district court judges must consult the guidelines, they still enjoy the flexibility and discretion to deviate from them and impose less harsh sentences in accordance with law and the facts of the case.[95]

For some critics, and in part because of that flexibility, *Booker* has increased sentence disparity among federal judges at the expense of eliminating sentence uniformity; and, empirical research by the U.S. Sentencing Commission reports that male African-American offenders get longer sentences than similarly situated white ones; and, female offenders received shorter sentences than white males. Significantly, the Commission's research found that African-American male offenders were less likely than white male offenders to be given a downward departure in sentencing; and, if they did get one, their sentences were longer as compared to white male offenders that received a downward departure. Even so, other studies have suggested that *Booker's* impact on federal sentencing remains largely unclear.[96]

Blakely, as well, prompted a number of states to enact new sentencing laws and prosecutors to change their charging and plea bargaining practices.[97] Subsequent Court rulings have also revisited the issue of whether a jury must weigh in on the facts in cases resulting in sentences increasing those beyond the mandatory minimum. *Alleyne v. United States* (2013),[98] for example, held that defendants have a right to have a jury decide facts that would raise a mandatory minimum punishment. In *Alleyne*, the Court reasoned that there was no constitutional difference between laws using mandatory minimums or those using maximum punishment standards to increase the severity of the sentence: hence, any fact that increases the punishment beyond the mandatory minimum must be put before a jury. Since mandatory-minimum laws are widely used in federal and state courts, *Alleyne* remains part of the ongoing assessment of the constitutionality of sentencing laws.

In sum, the politics of sentencing policy registers the ideological struggle over allowing judges and parole boards the discretion to individualize punishments or, conversely, fixing punishments under determinate sentencing criteria. In recent years, the Court has expanded judicial discretion in accord with an accused's Sixth Amendment right to a fair jury trial. Still, reforms are likely to continue as correctional budgets shrink and the cost of incarcerating inmates under strict determinate sentencing standards continues to increase. Lastly, the issue of racial disparity in sentencing practices has gained renewed intensity and interest, in large part due to the onset of large scale national protests that developed in the wake of the police killings of George Floyd and many other African-Americans in the spring and summer of 2020. As a result, many states and localities are trying to turn those protests into actionable reform that range from adopting racial impact statements (providing information about possible disparities relating to proposed sentencing laws before enactment and implementation) to others that rely more on community investment and resources as an informal means of social control that is thought to help reduce racial violence and contact with law enforcement officers.[99]

Post-Trial Motions and Appeals

After conviction and sentencing, the defendant may file several post-trial motions, including "motions for a new trial" and "motions for judgment of acquittal," which set aside the jury's verdict under certain circumstances, or "motions to vacate" or correct sentences fraught with some type of procedural or clerical error. If post-trial motions are denied, then the defendant has other procedural litigation options, such as filing appeals that claim the trial court committed a legal error, or once incarcerated filing a *habeas corpus* petition.

Chapter Summary

The myths and realities of the common law adversarial trial process, along with criticisms and in comparison with inquisitorial models of justice in civil law countries, are examined. The common law adversarial tradition has tensions between the "crime control" and "due process" models of criminal justice. Thereafter, the criminal justice trial and appeal process is discussed, focusing on the nature and scope of prosecutorial discretion, plea bargaining, the jury's role in criminal trials, and the politics of post-trial sentencing. An recurring theme is that prosecutors have virtually unrestrained discretion in filing charges and plea bargaining. The plea bargaining process promotes caseload efficiency but invites criticisms that it is actually coercive and secretive, thus requiring defendants to forfeit their constitutional rights. If the accused pleads not guilty and a plea bargain is not reached, then the defendant stands trial.

At trial, the government must prove guilt beyond a reasonable doubt. Juries play a significant and democratic role within the judicial system in determining guilt or innocence of the accused; but the role they play is controversial in meting out justice, and jury reform proposals are examined. Thereafter, the politics of sentencing policies that permit either greater or reduced judicial discretion under indeterminate and determinate sentencing practices—based on the punishment goals of incapacitation, rehabilitation, retribution, and deterrence—are analyzed. Whereas indeterminate sentencing sets a minimum and maximum range of punishments and allows for prison release through policies of parole and probation, determinate sentencing prescribes fixed minimum and maximum penalties. Recent Supreme Court rulings, however, have imposed new constitutional requirements that affect sentencing policies in the federal courts and in the states. Those rulings have coincided with a growing movement to reduce correctional populations and expenses and to diminish racial disparities in sentencing practices and policies.

Key Questions for Review and Critical Analysis

1. Do you think it is realistic for elected prosecutors to make achieving "justice" a priority over seeking a conviction when plea bargaining with criminal defendants?

2. Critics claim that the common law adversarial system "hides" the truth. Is the criticism accurate, or is "fighting" for the truth through opposing counsel the best way to achieve it? What role should the judge play in seeking out the truth of what happened in a criminal prosecution?

3. Do criminal defendants have a realistic opportunity to assert their innocence in a criminal justice system dominated by the prevalence of plea bargains?

4. Are juries incapable of understanding complex criminal prosecutions? Should they be allowed to ask questions, take notes, or otherwise be active participants in the trial process?

5. What are the strengths and weaknesses of indeterminate and determinate sentencing practices? Does it matter whether prosecutors or judges and juries have greater discretion in sentencing? In what ways would you reform the sentencing process?

6. Why do criminal justice system reform initiatives, such as "Smart on Crime" proposals, or national legislation, such as The First Step Act, receive bipartisan political support? Do such reforms satisfactorily address ongoing issues of racial sentencing disparities?

Web Links

1. National District Attorneys Association (https://ndaa.org/)

    *   A national group offering information, training, and advocacy resources for prosecutors relating to sentencing practices, gang cases, animal cruelty, and gun violence.

2. National Association of Criminal Defense Lawyers (https://www.nacdl.org/)

    *   A national organization supporting criminal defense attorneys and providing information on topics such as indigents' legal defense, the death penalty, searches and seizures, and human rights issues.

3. National Institute of Justice (https://www.nij.gov/Pages/welcome.aspx)

    *   An U.S. Department of Justice agency that works towards understanding crime and justice issues through science.

4. U.S. Bureau of Justice Statistics (https://www.bjs.gov/)

    *   A U.S. Department of Justice agency that collects, analyzes and distributes information and statistics about the criminal justice system at all government levels.

5. Center for Jury Studies (www.ncsc-jurystudies.org)

    *   A project of the National Center for State Courts providing information and community outreach resources for performing jury service.

6. The Sentencing Project (www.sentencingproject.org/template/index.cfm)

    *   Comprehensive website providing information about criminal sentencing practices and reforms.

Selected Readings

Alexander, Michelle. *The New Jim Crow: Mass Incarceration in the Age of Colorblindness.* New York: Free Press, 2020 (Tenth Anniversary Edition).

Barkow, Rachel Elise. *Prisoners of Politics: Breaking the Cycle of Mass Incarceration.* Cambridge: Belknap Press of Harvard University Press, 2019.

Bharara, Preet. *Doing Justice: A Prosecutor's Thoughts on Crime, Punishment and the Rule of Law.* London: Bloomsbury Publishing, 2019.

Braithwaite, John. *Restorative Justice and Responsive Regulation.* New York: Oxford University Press, 2002.

Chiao, Vincent. *Criminal Law in the Age of The Administrative State.* New York: Oxford University Press, 2019.

Bibas, Stephanos. *The Machinery of Criminal Justice.* New York: Oxford University Press, 2012.

Blom-Cooper, Louis. *Unreasoned Verdict: The Jury's Out.* Oxford, U.K.: Hart Publishing, 2019.

Dagan, David and Stephen Teles. *Prison Break: Why Conservatives Turned Against Mass Incarceration.* New York: Oxford University Press, 2016.

De Vos, Christian, Sara Kendall and Carsten Stahn, eds. *Contested Justice: The Politics and Practice of International Criminal Court Interventions.* Cambridge, U.K.: Cambridge University Press, 2015.

Edkins, Vanessa A. and Allison D. Redlich, eds. *A System of Pleas: Social Science's Contributions to the Real Legal System.* New York: Oxford University Press, 2019.

Feeley, Malcolm M. *The Process Is the Punishment: Handling Cases in a Lower Criminal Court.* New York: Russell Sage Foundation, 1992.

Fisher, George. *Plea Bargaining's Triumph: A History of Plea Bargaining in America.* Stanford, Calif.: Stanford University Press, 2003.

Frank, Jerome. *Courts on Trial: Myth and Reality in American Justice.* Princeton, N.J.: Princeton University Press, 1949.

Frase, Richard S. *Just Sentencing: Principles and Procedures or a Workable System.* New York: Oxford University Press, 2013.

Gastil, Gohn, E. Pierre Deess, Philip J. Weiser, and Cindy Simmons. *The Jury and Democracy: How Jury Deliberation Promotes Civic Engagement and Political Participation.* New York: Oxford University Press, 2010.

Gould, Jon B. and May Pagni Barak. *Capital Defense: Inside the Lives of American's Death Penalty Lawyers.* New York: New York University Press, 2019.

Hafemeister, Thomas L. *Criminal Trials and Mental Disorders.* New York: New York University Press, 2019.

Harding, David J., Jeffrey D. Morenoff, and Jessica J.B. Wyse. *On the Outside: Prisoner Reentry and Reintegration.* Chicago: University of Chicago Press, 2019.

Hoskins, Zachary. *Beyond Punishment?: A Normative Account of Collateral Legal Consequences of Conviction.* New York: Oxford University Press, 2019.

Howard, Marc Morje. *Unusually Cruel: Prisons, Punishment, and the Real American Exceptionalism.* New York: Oxford University Press, 2017.

Jonakait, Randolph N. *The American Jury System.* New Haven, Conn.: Yale University Press, 2003.

Kagan, Robert A. *Adversarial Legalism: the American Way of Law.* 2nd ed. Cambridge, MA.: Harvard University Press, 2019.

Kage, Rieko. *Who Judges?: Designing Jury Systems in Japan, East Asia, and Europe.* Cambridge, U.K.: Cambridge University Press, 2017.

Kessler, Amalia D. *Inventing American Exceptionalism: The Origins of the American Adversarial Legal Culture, 1800–1877.* New Haven: Yale University Press, 2017.

Langbein, John H. *The Origins of Adversary Criminal Trial.* New York: Oxford University Press, 2003.

Luna, Erik, and Marianne L. Wade, eds. *The Prosecutor in Transnational Perspective.* New York: Oxford University Press, 2012.

Packer, Herbert L. *The Limits of the Criminal Sanction.* Stanford, Calif.: Stanford University Press, 1968.

Reitz, Kevin R. ed. *American Exceptionalism in Crime and Punishment.* New York: Oxford University Press, 2018.

Schoenfeld, Heather. *Building the Prison State: Race and the Politics of Mass Incarceration.* Chicago: University of Chicago Press, 2018.

Scott-Hayward, Christine and Henry F. Fradella, eds. *Punishing Poverty: How Bail and Pretrial Detention Fuel Inequalities in the Criminal Justice System.* Oakland, CA.: University of California Press, 2019.

Smith, Alisa and Sean Maddan, eds. *The Lower Criminal Courts.* New York: Routledge, 2019.

Stith, Kate, and Jose A. Cabranes. *Fear of Judging: Sentencing Guidelines in the Federal Courts.* Chicago: University of Chicago Press, 1998.

Tonry, Michael. Ed. *American Sentencing: What Happens and Why?* Chicago: University of Chicago Press, 2019.

Vidmar, Neil and Valerie P. Hans. *American Juries: The Verdict.* Amherst, N.Y.: Prometheus Books, 2007.

Vogel, Mary E. *Coercion to Compromise: Plea Bargaining, the Courts, and the Making of Political Authority.* New York: Oxford University Press, 2001.

Whitman, James Q. *Harsh Justice: Criminal Punishment and the Widening Divide Between America and Europe.* New York: Oxford University Press, 2004.

Endnotes

1   See *Buck v. Stephens*, No. H–04–3965, 2014 WL 11310152, at *1 (S.D. Tex. Aug. 29, 2014).

2   *Buck v. Davis*, 137 S. Ct. 759 (2017), 768–769.

3   Ibid., 775–778. See also *Strickland v. Washington*, 466 U.S. 668 (1984); Amy Howe, "Opinion Analysis: Court-condemns use of race-based testimony in sentencing," *SCOTUSblog* (February 22, 2017), available at http://www.scotusblog.com/2017/02/opinion-analysis-court-condemns-use-race-based-testimony-sentencing/ (last retrieved April 21, 2020); and, Anonymous Note, "Buck v. Davis," *Harvard Law Review* 131 (2017), 263–272.

4   *United States v. Cronic*, 466 U.S. 648, 653–657 (1984).

5   *U.S. v. Twomey*, 510 F.2d 634 (7th Cir. 1975), 640 (Wyzanski, J.).

6   Judge J. Thomas Greene, "Some Current Causes of Popular Dissatisfaction With the Administration of Justice," *Federal Rules Decision* 198 (November 3, 2000), 566.

7   John D. King, "Procedural Justice, Collateral Consequences, and the Adjudication of Misdemeanors in the United States," in *The Prosecutor in Transnational Perspective*, eds. Erik Luna and Marianne L. Wade (New York: Oxford University Press, 2012), 20, 23. See also National Association of State Budget Officers, "State Spending for Corrections: Long-Term Trends and Recent Criminal Justice Policy Reforms (Issue Brief: September 11, 2013)," available at https://higherlogicdownload.s3.amazonaws.com/NASBO/0f09ced0-449d-4c11-b787-10505cd90bb9/UploadedImages/Issue%20Briefs%20/State%20Spending%20for%20 Corrections.pdf (last retrieved April 21, 2020); Alison Lawrence, *Trends in Sentencing and Corrections: State Legislation* (Washington, D.C.: National Conference of State Legislatures, 2013); and the *Smart on Crime Coalition, Smart on Crime: Recommendations for the Administration and Congress* (Washington, D.C.: The Constitution Project, 2011), available at https://constitutionproject.org/wp-content/uploads/2014/10/SmartOnCrime_Complete. pdf (last retrieved April 21, 2020).

8   Stewart Macaulay, "Images of Law in Everyday Life: The Lessons of School, Entertainment, and Spectator Sports," *Law and Society Review* 21 (1987), 185–216; and Carrie Menkel-Meadow, "Can They Do That? Legal Ethics in Popular Culture, of Characters and Acts," *UCLA Law Review* 48 (2001), 1305–37. See also Stephanie Francis Ward, "The 25 Greatest Legal TV Shows," *ABA Journal* (August 1, 2009), available at www. abajournal.com/magazine/article/the_25_greatest_legal_tv_shows/ (last retrieved April 21, 2020); Richard Brust, "The 25 Greatest Legal Movies," *ABA Journal* (August 1, 2008), available at www.abajournal.com/ magazine/article/the_25_greatest_legal_movies/ (last retrieved April 21, 2020).

9   Robert A. Kagan, *Adversarial Legalism: The American Way of Law* (Cambridge, Mass.: Harvard University Press, 2001).

10   Judge Frank's analysis of his "fight" theory is found in Chapter Six of Jerome Frank, *Courts on Trial: Myth and Reality in American Justice* (Princeton, N.J.: Princeton University Press, 1949), 80, 85.

11   See Gerald Walpin, "America's Adversarial and Jury Systems: More Likely to Do Justice," *Harvard Journal of Law and Public Policy* (Winter, 2003), 175–85.

12   Erik Luna and Marianne L. Wade, "Adversarial and Inquisitorial Systems-Distinctive Aspects and Convergent Trends," in *The Prosecutor in Transnational Perspective*, eds. Erik Luna and Marianne L. Wade (New York: Oxford University Press, 2012), 177, 180. See also ibid., 178–79. Also, criminal inquisitorial trials begin with a statement from the defendant, and thereafter, the presiding judge conducts questioning and calls witnesses, while the attorneys remain mostly passive (only suggesting lines of inquiry). Jury panels then render a verdict, and oftentimes two-thirds of the vote is needed to convict; and generally juries are not permitted to stalemate. After the conviction, the sentence is pronounced by an adjudicative panel of judges. Randolph N. Jonakait, *The American Jury System* (New Haven, Conn.: Yale University Press, 2003), 177–78.

13   Kagan, *Adversarial Legalism*, 4, 86–89, 104–25.

14   Ibid., 230.

15   Luna and Wade, "Adversarial and Inquisitorial Systems-Distinctive Aspects and Convergent Trends," 181–82.

16   Herbert L. Packer, *The Limits of the Criminal Sanction* (Stanford, Calif.: Stanford University Press, 1968), 153, 158–63.

17   *Missouri v. Seibert*, 542 U.S. 600 (2004). The quote is found in King, "Procedural Justice, Collateral Consequences, and the Adjudication of Misdemeanors in the United States," 22.

18   *Weeks v. U.S.*, 232 U.S. 383 (1914) (as applied to federal prosecutions); *Mapp v. Ohio*, 367 U.S. 643 (1961) (as applied to state prosecutions).

19   King, "Procedural Justice, Collateral Consequences, and the Adjudication of Misdemeanors in the United States," 22.

20   Stephanos Bibas, *The Machinery of Criminal Justice* (New York: Oxford University Press, 2012). The Taft commencement remarks were delivered at Yale Law School and are found in Erik Luna and Marianne L. Wade, "Preface," in The Prosecutor in Transnational Perspective, eds. Erik Luna and Marianne L. Wade (New York: Oxford University Press, 2012), xiii. For a similar criticism of the punitive approach that overemphasizes the efficiency of plea bargains from a historical perspective, see William J. Stuntz, *The Collapse of American Criminal Justice* (Cambridge, Mass.: Belknap Press of Harvard University Press, 2011).

21   *In re Winship*, 397 U.S. 358 (1970), 363. See also *People v. Defore*, 150 N.E. 585 (1926), 587. See also William Burnham, *Introduction to the Law and Legal System of the United States*, 5th ed. (St. Paul, Minn.: West Publishing Group, 2011), chap. 8.

22   Death Penalty Information Center, "State by State," available at https://deathpenaltyinfo.org/state-and-federal-info/state-by-state (last retrieved April 27, 2020); Death Penalty Information Center, "Death Penalty Information Center 2019 Year-End Report," available at https://deathpenaltyinfo.org/facts-and-research/dpic-reports/dpic-year-end-reports/the-death-penalty-in-2019-year-end-report (last retrieved April 27, 2020). See, generally, James Q. Whitman, *Harsh Justice: Criminal Punishment and the Widening Divide Between America and Europe* (New York: Oxford University Press, 2004).

23   James L. Croyle, "Measuring and Explaining Disparities in Felony Sentences: Courtroom Work Group Factors and Race, Sex, and Socioeconomic Influences on Sentence Severity," *Political Behavior* 5 (1983), 135–53; Peter F. Nardulli, James Eisenstein, and Roy B. Flemming, *The Tenor of Justice: Criminal Courts and the Guilty Plea Process* (Urbana: University of Illinois Press, 1988), 7. See also James Eisenstein and Herbert Jacob, *Felony Justice: An Organizational Analysis of Criminal Courts* (Lanham, Md.: University Press of America, 1991).

24   The Sentencing Project, "Top Trends in Criminal Justice Reform, 2019 (January 17, 2020)," https://www.sentencingproject.org/publications/top-trends-in-state-criminal-justice-reform-2019/ (last retrieved June 30, 2020). On the recent history and likely future of sentencing trends and reforms, see Michael Tonry, "Sentencing in America, 1975–2025," *Crime and Justice* 42 (2013), 141–98.

25   Jamiles Lartey, "Trump Signs Bipartisan Criminal Justice Overhaul First Step Act Into Law," *N.Y. Times* (December 21, 2018), available at https://www.theguardian.com/us-news/2018/dec/21/trump-prison-reform-first-step-act-signed-law (last retrieved April 21, 2020). See also, U.S. Department of Justice, Smart on Crime: Reforming the Criminal Justice System for the 21st Century (August 2013), available at www.justice.gov/ag/smart-on-crime.pdf (last retrieved April 21, 2020).

26   Quoted in Kenneth Culp Davis, *Discretionary Justice: A Preliminary Inquiry* (Baton Rouge: Louisiana State University Press, 1969), 190. See William J. Stuntz, *The Collapse of American Criminal Justice* (Cambridge, Mass.: Belknap Press, 2011), 245 (observing that Americans still "live in a more punitive country. . . than at any time in American history" in spite of falling crime rates and being in a safer country than before the 1970s and 1980s); Angela J. Davis, *Arbitrary Justice: The Power of the American Prosecutor* (New York: Oxford University Press, 2007), 22 (observing that the charging decision "pulls" offenders "into the criminal justice system" and "firmly entrenches him there, and maintains control over crucial decisions that will determine his fate").

27   Steven W. Perry and Duren Banks, *Prosecutors in State Courts, 2007—Statistical Tables*, available at https://www.bjs.gov/content/pub/pdf/psc07st.pdf (last retrieved April 22, 2020). See also Michael J. Ellis, "The Origins of the Elected Prosecutor," *Yale Law Journal* 121 (2012), 1528, 1529 (observing that historically all prosecutors were appointed officials but that the states started to elect prosecutors between 1832 and 1860).

28 U.S. Department of Justice, Executive Office for United States Attorneys, *United States Attorneys' Annual Statistical Report, Fiscal Year 2018*, available from https://www.justice.gov/usao/page/file/1199336/download (last retrieved April 22, 2020).

29 National Association of Criminal Defense Lawyers, *Minor Crimes, Massive Waste: The Terrible Toll of America's Broken Misdemeanor Courts* (Washington, D.C.: National Association of Criminal Defense Lawyers, 2009). See also Sean Rosenmerkel, Matthew Durose, and Donald Farole, Jr., *Felony Sentences in State Courts, 2006—Statistical Tables*, available from https://www.bjs.gov/content/pub/pdf/fssc06st.pdf (last retrieved April 22, 2020); Steven W. Perry and Duren Banks, *Prosecutors in State Courts, 2007* (December 2011, NCJ 234211), available from https://www.bjs.gov/content/pub/pdf/psc07st.pdf (last retrieved June 30, 2020); and, Steven W. Perry, Prosecutors in State Courts, 2005 (July 2006, NCJ 213799), available at https://www.bjs.gov/content/pub/pdf/psc05.pdf (last retrieved April 22, 2020).

30 Sanford C. Gordon and Gregory A. Huber, "The Political Economy of Prosecution," *Annual Review of Law and Social Science* 5 (2009), 135, 140–41. See also *Berger v. U.S.*, 295 U.S. 78 (1935).

31 Sanford C. Gordon and Gregory A. Huber, "Citizen Oversight and the Electoral Incentives of Criminal Prosecutors," *American Journal of Political Science* (April 2002), 334.

32 See *County of Riverside v. McLaughlin*, 500 U.S. 44 (1991); *Gerstein v. Pugh*, 420 U.S. 103 (1975).

33 For an overview of monetary bail practices and reform trends in the states, see Alison M. Smith, "U.S. Constitutional Limits on State Money—Bail Practices for Criminal Defendants," Congressional Research Service Report (R45533, February 26, 2019)(Washington, D.C.: Congressional Research Service, 2019). A survey of national trends in implementing bail reform is found in Ohio Sentencing Commission, *Ad Hoc Committee on Bail and Pretrial Services: Report and Recommendations* (March 2017), available at https://www.supremecourt.ohio.gov/Boards/Sentencing/Materials/2017/March/finalAdHocBailReport.pdf (last retrieved April 22, 2020). See also Jeremy B. White, "California Ended Cash Bail. Why Are So Many Reformers Unhappy About It?," *PoliticoMagazine* (August 29, 2018), available at https://www.politico.com/magazine/story/2018/08/29/california-abolish-cash-bail-reformers-unhappy-219618 (last retrieved April 22, 2020); and, Jonathan Witmer-Rich, *Cuyahoga County Bail Task Force: Report and Recommendations* (March 16, 2018), available at https://university.pretrial.org/HigherLogic/System/DownloadDocumentFile.ashx?DocumentFileKey=1a9e6280-dcf9-cf0e-3fe6-554af1258d29&forceDialog=0f (last retrieved April 22, 2020).

34 Niki Kuckes, "Retelling Grand Jury History," in *Grand Jury 2.0: Modern Perspectives on the Grand Jury*, ed. Roger Anthony Fairfax, Jr. (Durham, N.C.: Carolina Academic Press, 2011), 131. See *Hurtado v. California*, 110 U.S. 516 (1884).

35 U.S. Department of Justice, Bureau of Justice Statistics, *State Court Organization, 2004* (Table 38: Grand Juries: Composition and Functions), 213–17, available from www.bjs.gov/content/pub/pdf/sco04.pdf (last retrieved April 22, 2020). See also U.S. Department of Justice, Bureau of Justice Statistics, *State Court Organization, 1998* (Table 43, "Grand Juries: Composition and Functions"), 283–85, available from www.bjs.gov/content/pub/pdf/sco98.pdf (last retrieved April 22, 2020).

36 Kuckes, "Retelling Grand Jury History," 148. See also Burnham, *Introduction to the Law and Legal System of the United States.*

37 U.S. Department of Justice, Bureau of Justice Statistics, State Court Organization, 2004, 215–17. See also U.S. Department of Justice, Bureau of Justice Statistics, State Court Organization, 1998, 283–85.

38 Kuckes, "Retelling Grand Jury History." 128–29. Kuckes states that the Supreme Court's ruling in *Costello v. United States*, 350 U.S. 359 (1956), is the basis for "modern grand jury procedure" because it held that such proceedings are not governed by evidentiary rules or judicial oversight. Ibid., 132. For information about state and federal grand juries, see, generally, Greg Hurley, "The Modern Grand Jury (an article in Trends in State Courts (2014)," available from https://ncsc.contentdm.oclc.org/digital/collection/juries/id/281/ (last retrieved July 1, 2020).

39 The joke is retold in court cases. See, e.g., *People v. Dukes*, 592 N.Y.S. 2d 220, 223 (Sup. Ct. 1992) ("In this case, the prosecutor served the grand jury the proverbial 'ham sandwich' and told them, in effect, to take it or leave it.") Whether grand juries serve a meaningful screening function is "mixed and murky." Andrew D. Leipold, "Prosecutorial Charging Practices and Grand Jury Screening: Some Empirical Observations," in *Grand Jury 2.0: Modern Perspectives on the Grand Jury*, ed. Roger Anthony Fairfax, Jr. (Durham, N.C.: Carolina Academic Press, 2011), 211. See also ibid., 215 n. 2. Some states, like New York and Colorado, have tried to reform the grand jury process to give the defendants additional protections. Erin L. Crites, Jon B. Gould, and Colleen E. Shepard, *Evaluating Grand Jury Reform in Two States: The Case for Reform* (A Report Prepared for the National

Association of Criminal Defense Lawyers, November 2011) (Washington, D.C.: National Association of Criminal Defense Lawyers, 2011).

40   Kuckes, "Retelling Grand Jury History," 125.

41   Bibas, The Machinery of Criminal Justice, 61–62. Under the Federal Rules of Criminal Procedure, federal judges also have discretion to accept or reject Alford pleas. Jacqueline E. Ross, "The Entrenched Position of Plea Bargaining in United States Legal Practice," in *World Plea Bargaining: Consensual Procedures and the Avoidance of the Full Criminal Trial*, ed. Stephen C. Thaman (Durham, N.C.: Carolina Academic Press, 2010), 112.

42   Jenia I. Turner, *Plea Bargaining Across Borders: Criminal Procedure* (New York: Aspen Publishers, 2009), 29. See also *North Carolina v. Alford*, 400 U.S. 25, 37 (1970). Under the Federal Rules of Criminal Procedure, federal judges also have discretion to accept or reject Alford pleas. Ross, "The Entrenched Position of Plea Bargaining in United States Legal Practice," 112.

43   Associated Press, "Legal Experts Say Insanity Plea Unpopular With Jurors," Akron Beacon Journal (April 11, 2005), B4. See also Jack Healy, "Suspect in Colorado Killings Enters Insanity Plea" (June 4, 2013), available at www.nytimes.com (last retrieved April 22, 2020).

44   *Kahler v. Kansas*, 140 S.Ct. 1021 (2020); and, Amy Howe, "Opinion Analysis: Majority upholds Kansas scheme for mentally ill defendants," *SCOTUSblog* (March 23, 2020), available at https://www.scotusblog.com/2020/03/opinion-analysis-majority-upholds-kansas-scheme-for-mentally-ill-defendants/ (last retrieved April 22, 2020). See also, *Clark v. Arizona*, 548 U.S. 735 (2006) (J. Souter's majority opinion). A summary of state laws governing insanity pleas, and the different types of insanity verdicts that are used, is found in U.S. Department of Justice, Bureau of Justice Statistics, *State Court Organization 2004* (Table 35), available at www.bjs.gov/content/pub/pdf/sco04.pdf (last retrieved April 22, 2020).

45   *Brady v. United States*, 397 U.S. 742 (1972).

46   Mark Motivans, U.S. Department of Justice, Bureau of Justice Statistics, *Federal Justice Statistics, 2015–2016* (January 2019, NCJ 25177) (Table 6), available at https://www.bjs.gov/content/pub/pdf/fjs1516.pdf (last retrieved April 22, 2020).

47   As quoted in Andrew Manuel Crespo, "The Hidden Law of Plea Bargaining," *Columbia Law Review* 118 (2018): 1303, 1304–1305 (some internal quotation marks omitted; see also nn. 7 and 8 for other sources of quotation).

48   Public Broadcasting System, "Frontline: Interview With Judge Michael McSpadden (December 16, 2003)", available at www.pbs.org/wgbh/pages/frontline/shows/plea/interviews/mcspadden.html (last retrieved April 22, 2020).

49   George Fisher, *Plea Bargaining's Triumph: A History of Plea Bargaining in America* (Stanford, Calif.: Stanford University Press, 2003), 1.

50   Ellis, "The Origins of the Elected Prosecutor," 1528, 1532. See also Angela J. Davis, Arbitrary Justice: *The Power of the American Prosecutor* (New York: Oxford University Press, 2007); Angela J. Davis, "The American Prosecutor: Independence, Power, and the Threat of Tyranny," *Iowa Law Review* 86 (2001), 393–465.

51   Turner, *Pleading Bargaining Across Borders*, 1, 23–24, 38–41.

52   *Brady v. Maryland*, 373 U.S. 83 (1963).

53   Gregory E. Mize, Paula Hannaford-Agor, and Nicole L. Waters, *The State-of-the-States Survey of Jury Improvement Efforts: A Compendium Report* (April 2007) (Williamsburg, Va.: National Center for State Courts, 2007), 7, available at http://www.ncsc-jurystudies.org/~/media/Microsites/Files/CJS/SOS/SOS CompendiumFinal.ashx (last retrieved April 22, 2020); Administrative Office of U.S. Courts, "U.S. District Courts-Criminal Defendants Disposed Of, By Type of Disposition and Offense, During 12-Month Period Ending March 31, 2018." (Table D-4), available at https://www.uscourts.gov/statistics/table/d-4/federal-judicial-caseload-statistics/2019/03/31 (last retrieved April 22, 2020).

54   *Duncan v. Louisiana*, 391 U.S. 145, 156 (1968) (White, J.).

55   Bibas, *The Machinery of Criminal Justice*, 5.

56   See *Duncan v. Louisiana*, 391 U.S. 145 (1968) (making the right to a jury trial in all non-petty cases applicable to the states); and *Baldwin v. New York*, 399 U.S. 66 (1970) (defining "non-petty" cases as those carrying a potential sentence of six months or more imprisonment).

57   *Lewis v. United States*, 518 U.S. 322 (1995).

58 David M. O'Brien and Gordon Silverstein, *Constitutional Law and Politics: Civil Rights and Civil Liberties (Vol. 2)*, 11th ed. (New York: W.W. Norton, 2020), 1129.

59 *Taylor v. Louisiana*, 419 U.S. 522 (1975).

60 See, e.g., David Cole, *No Equal Justice: Race and Class in the American Criminal Justice System* (New York: New Press, 1999).

61 Shari Seidman Diamond and Andrea Ryken, "The Modern American Jury: A One Hundred Year Journey," *Judicature* 96 (2013), 315, 317–18. A summary of juror qualifications, source lists, and exemptions relating to juror service in the states is found in U.S. Department of Justice, Bureau of Justice Statistics, *State Court Organization 2004* (Tables 39, 40), available at https://www.bjs.gov/content/pub/pdf/sco04.pdf (last retrieved April 23, 2020). See also Richard Seltzer, "The Vanishing Juror: Why Are There Not Enough Available Jurors?" *The Justice System Journal* 20 (1999), 203–18.

62 Randolph N. Jonakait, *The American Jury System* (New Haven, Conn.: Yale University Press, 2003), 130, 128–55.

63 *Batson v. Kentucky*, 476 U.S. 79 (1986) (race); *J.E.B. v. Alabama*, 511 U.S. 127 (1997) (gender) *Hernandez v. New York*, 500 U.S. 352 (1999) (ethnic origin).

64 See, e.g., William E. Martin and Peter N. Thompson, "Judicial Toleration of Racial Bias in the Minnesota Justice System," *Hamline Law Review* (Winter, 2002), 235, 263–69.

65 O'Brien and Silverstein, *Constitutional Law and Politics* (Volume Two), 1130–31. See also *Flowers v. Mississippi*, 139 S. Ct. 2228 (2019); *Batson v. Kentucky*, 476 U.S. 79 (1986).

66 Deliberations: A Publication of the American Society of Trial Consultants, "Learning Voir Dire From the O.J. Trial" (October 8, 2008), available at https://jurylaw.typepad.com/deliberations/2008/10/oj-questionnaires.html (last retrieved April 23, 2020); and, Jonakait, *The American Jury System*, 153.

67 Alice Guerra, Barbara Luppi, and Francesco Parisi, "Accuracy of Verdicts under Different Jury Sizes and Voting Rules (February 25, 2020)," available at SSRN: https://papers-ssrn-com.proxy.library.kent.edu/sol3/papers.cfm?abstract_id=3432392 (citing *Thompson v. Utah*, 170 U.S. 343 [1898] as the leading case), 1.

68 Ibid., 2.

69 *Williams v. Florida*, 399 U.S. 78, 102 (1970). Williams reversed the twelve-member jury requirement established seventy years earlier in *Thompson v. Utah*, 170 U.S. 343 (1898). Jonakait, *The American Jury System*, 88.

70 *Johnson v. Louisiana*, 406 U.S. 356 (1972); *Apodaca v. Oregon*, 406 U.S. 404 (1972).

71 *Burch v. Louisiana*, 441 U.S. 130 (1979); *Ballew v. Georgia*, 435 U.S. 223 (1978).

72 *Ramos v. Louisiana*, 140 S.Ct. 1390 (2020).

73 *Ballew v. Georgia*, 435 U.S. 223, 239 (1978). The research studying the impact of jury size on jury decision making is summarized in Guerra, Luppi and Parisi, "Accuracy of Verdicts under Different Jury Sizes and Voting Rules" (February 25, 2020), 3–4 (also summarizing Condorcet's Jury Theorem); Jonakait, *The American Jury System*, 90; Diamond and Ryken, "The Modern American Jury," 319 n. 38.

74 National Center for State Courts, "Trial Juries: Size and Verdict Rules" (from State Court Organization as part of the Court Statistics Project), available at http://data.ncsc.org/QvAJAXZfc/opendoc.htm?document=Public%20App/SCO.qvw&host=QVS@qlikviewisa&anonymous=true (last retrieved July 1, 2020).

75 *Sparf & Hansen v. United States*, 156 U.S. 51 (1895). See also Jonakait, *The American Jury System*, 245–47; and Clay S. Conrad, *Jury Nullification: The Evolution of a Doctrine* (Washington, D.C.: Cato Institute, 2014).

76 Jonakait, *The American Jury System*, 252.

77 Aaron McKnight, "Jury Nullification as a Tool to Balance the Demands of Law and Justice," *Brigham Young University Law Review* 2013 (2013), 1103–32. See also Paula L. Hannaford-Agor and Valerie P. Hans, "Nullification at Work? A Glimpse From the National Center for State Courts Study of Hung Juries," *Chicago-Kent Law Review* 78 (2003), 1249–77. The 2002 NCSC Report is found at Paula L. Hannaford-Agor, Valerie P. Hans, Nicole L. Mott, and G. Thomas Munsterman, "Are Hung Juries a Problem? (September 30, 2002)," available at https://www.ncjrs.gov/pdffiles1/nij/grants/199372.pdf (last retrieved August 20, 2020).

78 See Mize, Hannaford-Agor, Waters, *The State-of-the-States Survey of Jury Improvement Efforts*, 1–88; James P. Levine and Steven Zeidman, "The Miracle of Jury Reform in New York," *Judicature* (January/February 2005), 178–84; Gregory E. Mize and Christopher J. Connelly, "Jury Trial Innovations: Charting a Rising Tide," *Court*

Review (Spring, 2004), 4–10; Lynne Forster Lee and Irwin A. Horowitz, "The Effects of Jury-Aid Innovations on Juror Performance in Complex Civil Trials," *Judicature* (January/February 2003), 184–90.

79 On the collapse of the rehabilitative ideal, see Kate Stith and Jose A. Cabranes, *Fear of Judging: Sentencing Guidelines in the Federal Courts* (Chicago: University of Chicago Press, 1998), 29–37. Richard Frase adds "moral education" as another punishment goal, which "reinforce[s] societal norms that guide and restrain behavior even when. . . the chances of detection and punishment are slight—the sentence sends a message to the offender and the public that the punished behavior was wrong, and the severity of the sentence shows how wrong it was." Richard S. Frase, *Just Sentencing: Principles and Procedures for a Workable System* (New York: Oxford University Press, 2013), 8. For a comparison of different types and punishment philosophies, see Maria J. Patterson, Angela R. Gover, and Maren Trochmann, "Victim Rights and Retribution," in *Routledge Handbook of Corrections in the United States* eds. O. Hayden Griffin III and Vanessa H. Woodward (New York: Routledge, 2018), 21–22.

80 Bibas, *The Machinery of Criminal Justice*, 9–10; Samuel Walker, *Popular Justice: A History of American Criminal Justice*, 2nd ed. (New York: Oxford University Press, 1998), 32–46. Today, shaming punishments are limited to less serious offenders, such as shoplifting, littering, and traffic violations, and a growing trend is to apply them to drunk driving violations, such as in Ohio. Lauren C. Porter, "Trying Something Old: The Impact of Shame Sanctioning on Drunk Driving and Alcohol-Related Traffic Safety," *Law and Social Inquiry* 38 (2013), 863–91.

81 Walker, *Popular Justice*, 80–81, 100–104, 119–20. See also Bibas, *The Machinery of Criminal Justice*, 13–15.

82 Pauline K. Brennan and Julie Garman, "Incapacitation and Sentencing," in *Routledge Handbook of Corrections in the United States*, 26.

83 *Williams v. New York*, 337 U.S. 241, 245 (1949).

84 U.S. Department of Justice, Bureau of Justice Assistance, *National Assessment of Structured Sentencing* (Monograph, 1996), available at www.ncjrs.gov/pdffiles/strsent.pdf (last retrieved April 23, 2020), 6–17.

85 The Sentencing Reform Act of 1984, 18 U.S.C. Section 3551 et seq. See also U.S. Department of Justice, *National Assessment of Structured Sentencing*, 17, 20–21 (Table 3.1, "Sentencing Practices in the United States, as of February 1994"); U.S. Department of Justice, Bureau of Justice Assistance, *1996 National Survey of State Sentencing Structures* (Monograph, NCJ 169270, September 1998), available at www.ncjrs.gov/pdffiles/169270.pdf (last retrieved April 23, 2020); and Kate Stith, "Principles, Pragmatism, and Politics: The Evolution of Washington State's Sentencing Guidelines," *Law and Contemporary Problems* 76 (2013), 105, 106 (discussing national sentencing reform movement goals).

86 See Stith and Cabranes, *Fear of Judging*, 82–85.

87 Tonry, "Sentencing in America, 1975–2025," 143–44.

88 The Sentencing Project, "Criminal Justice Facts," available at https://www.sentencingproject.org/criminal-justice-facts/ (last retrieved April 23, 2020); and, The Sentencing Project, "Trends in U.S. Corrections," available at https://www.sentencingproject.org/wp-content/uploads/2016/01/Trends-in-US-Corrections.pdf (last retrieved April 23, 2020) (showing U.S. trends between 1925–2017, and reporting international rates of incarceration, per 100,000 residents).

89 Travis C. Pratt, "Massive Incarceration," in *Routledge Handbook of Corrections in the United States*, 254. See also, U.S. Department of Justice, Bureau of Justice Assistance, *Prisoners in 2017* (Monograph, NCJ 252156, April 2019), available at https://www.bjs.gov/content/pub/pdf/p17.pdf (last retrieved April 23, 2020).

90 Todd R. Clear and Natasha A. Frost, *The Punishment Imperative: The Rise and Failure of Mass Incarceration in America* (New York: New York University Press, 2014), 17–20, 73–75, 80–81. See also Bert Useem and Anne Morrison Piehl, *Prison State: The Challenge of Mass Incarceration* (New York: Cambridge University Press, 2008), 40. See also, The Sentencing Project, "Criminal Justice Facts" (reporting that mass incarceration trends have stabilized, due to declining crime rates but also changes in sentencing policies and practices on the federal and state level).

91 Rachel E. Barkow, "Sentencing Guidelines at the Crossroads of Politics and Expertise," *University of Pennsylvania Law Review* 160 (2012), 1599–630.

92 *Apprendi v. New Jersey*, 530 U.S. 466 (2000).

93 *Blakely v. Washington*, 542 U.S. 296 (2004).

94 *United States v. Booker*, 543 U.S. 220 (2005).

95 *Rita v. United States*, 551 U.S. 338 (2007); *Gall v. United States*, 552 U.S. 38 (2007); and, *Kimbrough v. United States*, 552 U.S. 85 (2007). See also, Joshua B. Fischman and Max M. Schanzenbach, "Racial Disparities

Under the Federal Sentencing Guidelines: The Role of Judicial Discretion and Mandatory Minimums," *Journal of Empirical Legal Studies* 9 (2012), 729, 730; and, Stith, "Principles, Pragmatism, and Politics: The Evolution of Washington State's Sentencing Guidelines," 121.

96 For a survey of some post-Booker criticisms and research, see Joshua M. Devine, "Booker Disparity and Data-Driven Sentencing," *Hastings Law Journal* 69 (April, 2018): 771–833; United States Sentencing Commission, *Demographic Differences in Sentencing: An Update to the 2012 Booker Report*, available at https://www.ussc.gov/sites/default/files/pdf/research-and-publications/research-publications/2017/20171114_Demographics.pdf (last retrieved April 23, 2020), 20; United States Sentencing Commission, *Report on the Continuing Impact of United States v. Booker on Federal Sentencing* (Washington, D.C.: Government Printing Office, 2012) (reporting mixed findings about influence of federal guidelines and impact on judicial decision-making across federal courts in light of Booker); Joshua B. Fischman and Max M. Schanzenbach, "Racial Disparities Under the Federal Sentencing Guidelines: The Role of Judicial Discretion and Mandatory Minimums," *Journal of Empirical Legal Studies* 9 (2012), 729–64 (surveying conflicting studies examining Booker's impact on racial disparities but finding that disparities under the guidelines are not attributable to judicial discretion); D. Michael Fisher, "Still in Balance? Federal District Court Discretion and Appellate Review Six Years After Booker," *Duquesne Law Review* 49 (2011), 641, 642 (observing federal courts "continue to encounter some confusion and inconsistency in sentencing"). One sentencing law expert speculated that the unpopularity of the federal guidelines before Booker would mean that judges expand the use of their sentencing discretion under the advisory guidelines. Richard S. Frase, "The Apprendi-Blakely Cases: Sentencing Reform Counter-Revolution?" *Criminology and Public Policy* 6 (2007), 403–31.

97 Frase, "The Apprendi-Blakely Cases: Sentencing Reform Counter-Revolution?" 403, 425–28. See also Stith, "Principles, Pragmatism, and Politics: The Evolution of Washington State's Sentencing Guidelines," 121–22 (reporting that Washington State followed Kansas's lead in "Blakely-izing" its guidelines); Frase, *Just Sentencing: Principles and Procedures for a Workable System*, 6–7.

98 *Alleyne v. United States*, 570 U.S. 99 (2013).

99 The Sentencing Project, "State Advocacy News: From Protest to Policy, (June 12, 2020), available at https://www.sentencingproject.org/news/state-advocacy-news-protest-policy/ (last retrieved July 2, 2020). See also, Nicole D. Porter, *State of Sentencing 2012: Developments in Policy and Practice* (Washington, D.C.: The Sentencing Project, 2013) (detailing efforts by states to reduce prison populations while controlling correctional costs through various legislative reform, including relaxing mandatory minimums; abolishing the death penalty; reducing postconviction sentences through modifications; easing penalties for low-level, nonviolent offenders; authorizing the use of graduated sanctions; diminishing the impact of collateral sanctions; and instituting parole and probation revocation reforms); Roger A. Fairfax, Jr., "The 'Smart on Crime' Prosecutor," *Georgetown Journal of Legal Ethics* 25 (2012), 905–12 (surveying "Smart on Crime" initiatives that advocate or implement crime justice policies that allow prosecutors to reduce recidivism, increase successful reentry into the community, and the like); and Lawrence, *Trends in Sentencing and Corrections: State Legislation* (analyzing the growing trend by states to engage in "justice reinvestment" processes that determines trends driving prison populations and their underlying cost, with an eye toward policy development arresting those trends, including expanding the use of graduated [nonprison] sanctions, improving release and reentry programs, and modifying sentencing laws).

CHAPTER 8

Trial Courts: The Civil Justice System

For decades, vaginal or pelvic mesh products have been approved by the U.S. Food and Drug Administration (FDA) as safe medical devices that help patients correct conditions of pelvic organ prolapse and stress urinary incontinence in women. The synthetic net-like devices are inserted through the vagina instead of being implanted into the abdomen by traditional surgery. They are designed to provide support for a sagging bladder, uterus or other organs that have slipped out of their normal position causing, among other things, lower back pain, urine leakage, bladder infections, and difficulties in having bowel movements or sexual intercourse. According to the Cleveland Clinic, more than one-third of women in the United States suffer from some sort of pelvic area prolapse and about eleven percent require surgery, thus making the transvaginal mesh procedure a relatively common medical option that received full FDA-approval since the 1990s.[1]

In April 2019, however, the FDA ordered two medical device companies, Boston Scientific and Coloplast, to stop selling vaginal meshes after the FDA reclassified them in 2006 as a high risk device that required more proof by manufacturers that they were not a threat to public safety. Notably, the FDA's 2006 action was taken after its original decision to approve the meshes as a 510(k) device, a regulatory step that permitted manufacturers to put them into the marketplace sooner after merely showing that they were not substantially different than other devices on that were already on the market. Because vaginal meshes were similar to other synthetic products that were used to fix hernias and other conditions before they were first introduced into the market, manufacturers vying to sell vaginal meshes did not have to bear the high cost and expense of demonstrating the product's safety or effectiveness by conducting rigorous medical research or studies. Despite FDA-approval, many women suffered what the agency calls "serious adverse events" as a result of vaginal mesh implantation, including the perforation of organs, scarring, bleeding, nerve damage, emotional trauma, additional surgeries and, sometimes, death. For critics, the lax FDA approval and post-market supervision process was responsible for at least 100,000 victims suing in state and federal courts in class action lawsuits that have been filed against several medical device companies. Recent data shows that those businesses have paid out a total of eight billion dollars in settlement money to injured patients, thus making the ongoing vaginal mesh saga one of the largest, and perhaps most egregious, "mass tort cases" in U.S. legal history in terms of the number of claims filed, how many corporations were sued, and how much has been paid out to settle the lawsuits.[2]

Significantly, class action tort litigation and other related corporate legal problems are ingrained in the litigious American legal landscape. Shortly before the FDA's decision to pull vaginal meshes off the market, two major drug companies, Bayer AG and Johnson & Johnson, resolved over 25,000 claims with a 775 million settlement to patients who were harmed by taking Xarelto, a blood thinner, because it allegedly causes dangerous excessive bleeding. In addition, in 2019, analogous mass tort litigation was started in cases involving hearing loss injuries suffered by military veterans that used allegedly defective earplugs sold by GM in combat, as well as by victims hurt in the devasting 2018 "Camp" wildfire in California that was caused by a utility company's failure to maintain its electrical transmission lines safely. Moreover, in other recent lawsuits British Petroleum paid almost $8 billion to victims who were harmed by the Deepwater Horizon oil spill in the Gulf of Mexico; and, victims of Toyota Motor Corporation's sudden-acceleration design defect in some of the cars it produced reached negotiated settlements totaling $1.1 billion. For those cases alone, lawyers collected roughly $227 million in attorneys' fees and costs.[3]

While the vaginal mesh litigation and many others like it create a firestorm of criticism, it also invites the condemnation of lawyers and the American justice system. For example, research conducted by the New York Times showed that while the average settlement payment to victims of the vaginal mesh litigation was $60,000, much of what the injured clients received was far less after the lawyers representing them were paid under contingency fee agreements that not only reimbursed attorneys for their expenses, but also let them take fees as a hefty percentage of settlement funds, which routinely go as high as forty to forty-five percent.[4] As a result, beneath the public indignation and political rhetoric are persistent and long-standing allegations that lawyers routinely abuse the adversary system by manipulating legal rules to their advantage. While the perception that the legal process remains deeply flawed is not new, it is commonly, but perhaps unfairly, shared by many American citizens. In research conducted by the American Bar Association, respondents complained that lawyers are greedy and manipulative, charge too much for their services, and do not act diligently on cases that get bogged down in court with protracted delays. A typical refrain is that lawyers are susceptible to political influences, and that their insider knowledge of the law and government allows them to "play the system." Another ABA study of several major metropolitan areas likewise found evidence that public distrust of lawyers is rooted in deeply-held beliefs that the judicial process is fraught with racial bias and ethnic discrimination.[5]

This chapter examines adversarial civil litigation and its related criticisms at the trial stage. It then turns to the politics of tort reform movements, a persistent theme of the American civil justice system. The last section considers how civil litigation is affected by alternative methods of dispute resolution that critics of the civil justice system claim are necessary because of the high cost of commencing, and receiving adequate justice, through civil lawsuits.

ADVERSARIAL CIVIL JUSTICE

Noncriminal disputes are the focus of civil actions filed in either federal or state courts. Civil lawsuits are directed at making injured parties "whole" with monetary awards, or by compelling parties to take corrective nonmonetary actions. Put differently, civil litigation can be thought of as "the investment of scarce resources to achieve a future result. . .[that] include[s] recovering money (plaintiffs) or avoiding paying money (defendants), stopping something from happening or causing some act to be carried out."[6] When civil actions are brought, pretrial and trial procedures are used to resolve a wide range of issues pertaining to civil liability, including conflicts over tort liability, compensating injured parties as a result of defective products, or breaches of contract. Other common civil actions relate to issues of divorce and child custody, for example, and calculating the equitable distribution of estate property.

Civil litigation is distinct from the criminal trial process because it is governed by **civil procedure**—a complex body of formal rules by which courts conduct trials to resolve private disputes. Historically, understanding the rules of civil procedure was complicated by federal and state courts having different sets of rules, a consequence of our judicial federalism. Procedural reform was at first accomplished with the Rules Enabling Act and the 1938 Federal Rules of Civil Procedure, which not only unified federal procedural rules but also became widely adopted by states' courts after the mid-twentieth century. Today, federal judicial practice is controlled by the Federal Rules of Civil Procedure, whereas most state courts have increasingly adopted their own rules or a variation of the federal rules.[7] In theory, the rules enable access to the justice system and permit courts to settle civil disputes through the disclosure of relevant information by the opposing parties.[8] Still, compliance with the rules of civil procedure is inherently complicated and an expensive process that not only requires legal expertise but also raises questions about whether the goals of civil justice can ever be reasonably obtained. In theory, the civil litigation process is designed to achieve timely and fair resolution of private disputes in an efficient manner. Thus, in practice, if lawyers or judges apply procedural rules in a way that undermines those goals by unnecessarily increasing delay or the cost to secure them, then it is more likely that litigants will become dissatisfied and conclude that they did not receive justice or their proverbial "day in court." (See Table 8.1).

Table 8.1	Civil Justice and Procedure: Goals, Tensions, and Challenges
Underlying Civil Justice Goals	**Standards of Goal Achievement**
Accuracy of Case Outcomes	• Truth Ascertainment
Efficiency in Securing Case Outcomes	• Time to Disposition
Access to Civil Justice System	• Reasonable Litigation Costs • Availability of Legal Representation • Transparency and Simplicity of Rules and Court Procedures
Substantive Justice	• Accurate Fact-Finding • Correct Law Application • Attainment of Equitable Fairness
Procedural Justice	• Perceptions of Satisfaction with Dispute Resolution Process

Source: Carrie J. Menkel-Meadow and Bryant G. Garth, "Civil Procedure and Courts," in *The Oxford Handbook of Empirical Legal Research*, eds. Peter Cane and Herbert M. Kritzer (New York: Oxford University Press, 2010), 679, 680–81.

A "Litigation Explosion"?

Litigant perceptions of how they are treated in the civil justice system are important because the complexity of civil litigation is often criticized as too expensive, elitist, capricious, and unfair. Such perceptions, in turn, help generate myths about civil litigation that perpetuate false or misleading portrayals of the system itself. For example, in the 1990s a widely sensationalized McDonald's "hot coffee" case—which led to a jury awarding the plaintiff (an elderly woman) nearly $3 million after spilling hot coffee on her lap in her car—led to editorials characterizing the jury's decision an "absurd judgment [that] is a stunning illustration of what is wrong with America's civil justice system." In reality, in *Liebeck v. McDonald's Restaurants* (1994), the injured seventy-nine-year-old widowed grandmother, who was in the passenger seat and initially went into shock after the spill, received third-degree burns on her thighs, buttocks, and groin-area genitals (over 16 percent of her body, with 6 percent third degree). In a products liability suit, she sued because the coffee was served at a temperature of 180 to 190 degrees (home coffee machines brew at 158 to 168 degrees), causing permanent scarring and necessitating skin grafts that left her partially disabled for up to two years. She went to court only after McDonald's refused to compensate her for far less than what she ultimately received from the jury ($160,000 compensatory and $2.7 million punitive damages), which took into account her personal responsibility and was later reduced to about $500,000.[9]

In other highly publicized civil cases, an animal rights group filed a lawsuit against a nature photographer on assignment in Indonesia for violating U.S. copyright law after a monkey took a "selfie" with his camera, claiming that the monkey, and not the photographer, owned the picture; rebellious teens have sued their parents or prom dates when they are disciplined or jilted; and obese persons have sued fast-food restaurants for serving supersized French fries.[10] In large part because of extensive media coverage, such civil actions are frequently attacked as being abusive because they are characterized as frivolous lawsuits brought by "shyster" trial lawyers that are only interested in profiting from large legal fees.[11] Accordingly, a common perception is that lawyers litigate too frequently and spend most of their time preparing court papers, writing briefs, and prolonging trials, which needlessly drives up costs.[12]

Although some of the criticisms are valid, many are not. For one thing, attorneys are ethically obliged not to bring meritless lawsuits, and judges are empowered to discipline them for breaching that duty.[13] Also, while some high-stakes civil litigation involves great expense and produces large monetary awards, studies have shown that going to trial in most disputes is quite rare. For example, a classic empirical study of 1,649 federal and state civil cases found that most disputes are typically settled without litigation. Moreover, if formal litigation is necessary, most cases involve modest stakes ($10,000 or less) and relatively minimal time or cost. While there is some pretrial activity, attorneys in fact spend the bulk of their time, which amounts to thirty hours for each side in "ordinary" cases, working towards a negotiated settlement by talking to their clients, gathering facts, and doing some legal research.[14] (see Figure 8.1). More recent studies examining the cost of civil litigation report similar findings. One, for example, by the National Center for State Courts showed that the most time-intensive, and costly, aspects of suing in court are engaging in discovery (the process of gathering facts through pleadings and motions) and actually going to trial. Consequently, there is relatively little time and cost expended in performing the routine work-up of many civil cases, such as evaluating a case on its merits, preparing motions, and trying to get a settlement.[15]

| Figure 8.1 | Average Lawyer Time Spent in Ordinary Civil Lawsuits |

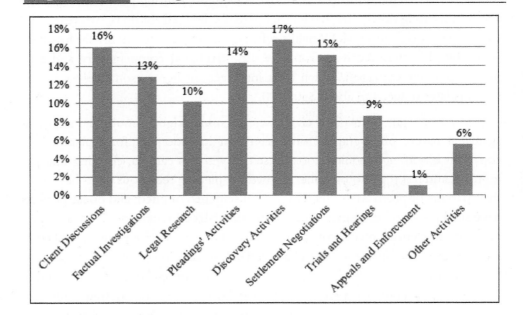

Note: Percentages do not equal 100% due to rounding.

Source: David M. Trubeck, Austin Sarat, William L.F. Felstiner, Herbert M. Kritzer, and Joel B. Grossman, "The Cost of Ordinary Litigation," *UCLA Law Review* 31 (1983): 72, 91 (Table 3).

Regardless, a different picture is painted by the research conducted by business industry organizations that may have ulterior political motivations for portraying trial attorneys in a bad light. For example, the U.S. Chamber of Commerce insists that the costs and compensation attributed to the U.S. tort system is extraordinarily high, representing $429 billion, or 2.3 percent of the nation's gross domestic product.[16] In some ways, such findings correspond to other research that implies that engaging in civil litigation—particularly when it relates to the time-intensive cost of using the discovery process to prepare cases for trial—can be cost prohibitive to many citizens with modest or less than modest means, such as *pro se* (unrepresented by paid counsel) litigants. Still, those within the legal system may also express frustration at the civil justice system for any number of reasons. For instance, in citing to research by the Federal Judicial Center, which found that the mean cost of civil litigation in federal courts for plaintiffs and defendants is between $15,000 to $20,000, a federal district court judge remarked at an academic symposium that "the average middle-class American family is not prepared to spend $20,000 on litigation—when they are earning $50,000 or less. . .[thus,] people are priced out of the litigation market." Notably, the same judge acknowledged that the litigation expenses for those at the "high end of the spectrum" are also highly disproportionate to the expenses incurred by most others; and, in his words, are sometimes "staggering" because they can range up to a million dollars or more in certain types of cases.[17]

As these comments and research findings suggest, in considering the impact of civil litigation and its consequences it is important to separate fact from fiction in trying to identify what may be responsible for shaping the perception that America is a litigious society. In this light, there is little doubt that civil litigation can be time consuming and expensive, especially for certain types of litigants that cannot afford legal representation or do not have the resources to sue. And while it is also true that civil filings have steadily increased since the 1960s, there is support for the argument that the trend has resulted from a "liability explosion" (an expansion of legislation that provided more court access and litigation alternatives) rather than a "litigation explosion" (the unnecessary filing of frivolous lawsuits by over-aggressive lawyers interested only in profiting from a case). Thus, the increase in filings may not necessarily convincing proof that there has been an ongoing pattern of lawyer misfeasance or the development of a "litigation explosion." In fact, as suggested above by the academic research, empirical studies indicate there is little evidence to show that citizens litigate too much, or that lawyers are abusing the legal system in resolving disputes.[18] Indeed, some scholars go so far as to argue that engaging in civil litigation produces valuable social goods, such as promoting democratic participation, initiating positive social change, and facilitating equality before the law as well as government transparency and accountability.[19]

Moreover, the political debate over tort reform (discussed later in this chapter) is but one manifestation of the confusion created by conflating litigation and liability trends. The distinction between the two becomes clearer upon learning that there have been several transformations in recent decades concerning the way in which civil disputes are resolved. With few exceptions, the rate of civil trials has been in sharp decline since the 1980s, a phenomenon that arose because judges and attorneys have increasingly used pretrial hearings and procedural rules to reach negotiated settlements. That in turn has led to a profound shift away from formal trials and has diminished the role juries play in civil disputes.[20] At the same time, litigating civil cases invariably involves spending time and money; so, the prospect of incurring expenses and the possibility of encountering unpredictable delays in getting successful outcomes have caused litigants to seek achieving justice through alternative methods of dispute resolution that do not always require the involvement of courts or lawyers. In short, in many ways civil justice has become increasingly privatized which, in turn, means that getting legal relief is not always achieved with the help of lawyers, or through formal litigation commenced in courts.

Types of Civil Cases

Roughly 15 million civil cases are annually filed in the state courts, a figure far exceeding the number in the federal courts. The federal judiciary has slightly more than 286,000 annual civil filings. Still, together, these figures underscore that roughly 70 percent of judicial business involves civil cases.[21] State caseloads predominantly consist of personal injury, debt collection, landlord-tenant, divorce, mortgage, tax, business regulation, and ordinary will and trust, or probate, lawsuits. Of these cases, while contract disputes are often a predominate aspect of the civil docket, it is not unusual for a court to spend its time litigating contentious issues of family law—divorces, paternity, child custody, and visitation cases—along with resolving probate and small claims cases that consume much of the court's limited resources. Notably, the adjudication of tort cases, such as automobile, medical malpractice, products liability or premises liability disputes, only account for a small proportion of the state civil docket (see Figure 8.2).[22]

| Figure 8.2 | Types of Civil Cases in State Courts |

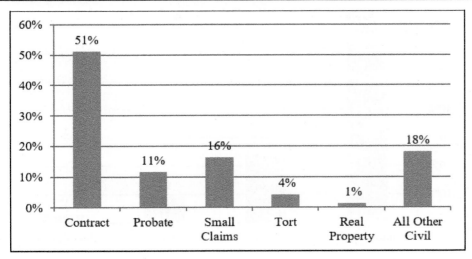

Note: Caseload composition is reflecting data from 22 states. "All Other civil" cases include mental health, civil appeals, habeas corpus, writs, and other miscellaneous civil cases.

Source: National Center for State Courts, "Contract Cases Dominate Civil Caseloads, 2015." In *Examining the Work of State Courts: An Overview of 2015 State Court Caseloads*, 6. https://ncsc.contentdm. oclc.org/digital/collection/ctadmin/id/2177/ (last retrieved on July 2, 2020).

While federal courts adjudicate many of the same types of cases state courts handle, a large majority consists of "statutory actions"—lawsuits over interpreting, applying, and enforcing federal laws. As one study demonstrated, federal laws include fee-shifting and award of damage-enhancement provisions that give incentives to counsel and clients to litigate in the capacity of "private attorneys general." As a result, they represent a large proportion of private civil actions enforcing federal laws.[23] In general, though, the composition of the federal civil docket include antitrust, banking, bankruptcy, civil rights, civil forfeiture, consumer, environmental, immigration, labor, securities, and Social Security cases, among scores of others (see Figure 8.3). Significantly, over almost twenty percent of statutory actions involve prisoner petitions, which typically involve inmate rights, *habeas corpus* claims, or motions to vacate a sentence on constitutional grounds. Less prevalent are adjudication of civil rights (voting and other types of discrimination lawsuits involving employment, housing, or disabilities), labor, intellectual property, and social security cases, to name a few. Moreover, in contrast to state lawsuits, tort cases, such as defective products (product liability) cases, comprise almost a quarter of federal civil litigation.[24]

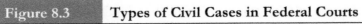

Figure 8.3   **Types of Civil Cases in Federal Courts**

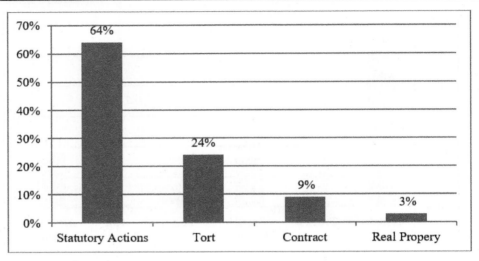

Source: Administrative Office of U.S. Courts, "U.S. District Courts-Civil Cases Commenced, by Basis of Jurisdiction and Nature of Suit, During the 12-Month Period Ending March 31, 2017 and 2018", http://www.uscourts.gov (last retrieved on April 23, 2020).

The Parties to Civil Actions

The civil justice system attempts to resolve legal actions that typically involve resolving disputes between private citizens, or between citizens and government, or parties to the litigation. Ordinarily, the party bringing a civil lawsuit is the **plaintiff,** and those defending against civil claims are known as **defendants**. This terminology is substantively different from how parties are understood in the criminal justice system, since prosecutors represent the government in criminal actions instituted against criminal suspects. Even so, as in criminal justice cases, where prosecutors hold enormous power in enforcing the penal code, the litigation status of persons filing civil actions is closely related to the influence they wield in civil lawsuits. In adversarial civil combat, "repeat players," or parties with greater resources and more extensive litigation experience, have an advantage over "one-shotters," or parties with fewer capabilities and limited experience in the courts.[25] Insurance companies, public prosecutors, and banking entities are typical repeat players, whereas citizens bringing a personal injury lawsuit as a result of an automobile crash or a divorce case are usually one-shotters.

Since they routinely litigate as a cost of doing business or as a part of government regulation, repeat players use to their benefit their longstanding institutional memory and substantial litigation expertise.[26] By contrast, one-shotters are usually less interested in establishing or overturning precedents and, instead, are more concerned about winning damage awards. On a one-time basis, for instance, a spouse may seek a divorce and an acceptable settlement of marital property and custody or visitation of children. Research demonstrates that the litigation "haves" usually prevail over the "have-nots" at the trial level, simply because they enjoy strategic and resource advantages in litigation.[27] The interplay between litigant status and legal representation reinforces the same dynamics: lawyers representing one-shotters tend to be nonelitist in their legal training and reputation, whereas counsel for repeat players enjoy higher professional status and specialized skills, which, of course, improves their chances of favorable results for their clients.[28]

Class Action Lawsuits

Although better-resourced and more seasoned repeat players enjoy many advantages, disadvantaged "have-nots" may improve their chances of successful litigation by using class action lawsuits and other legal resources that are mobilized by lawyers' rights-advocacy organizations.[29] *Class action* lawsuits—lawsuits that can aggregate civil claims among different litigants in either state or federal courts—originally were designed to provide greater court access to plaintiffs sharing similar claims who might not otherwise sue because of the complexity of the process or the high cost of doing so. Beginning in the 1970s, class actions increasingly were used to hold big business accountable in a variety of legal contexts, including consumer protection, environmental, antitrust, and securities fraud litigation. As legal scholar Robert Kagan explains, in addition to giving "entrepreneurial American lawyers potentially large fees," class actions are effective tools "to threaten companies with potentially enormous money damages" that would "deter them from engaging in fraudulent, unfair, or hazardous business practices."[30]

Still, class actions are politically controversial because they have also resulted in "mass tort actions" and other civil claims seeking high damage awards. They have also been scrutinized, in recent times, by the Supreme Court, which, for some, is committed to restricting their use and availability in the legal system (see the box, Contemporary Controversies over Courts: The Roberts Court and Class Action Lawsuits, discussed later in this chapter). Regardless, defenders of class actions, like former liberal Supreme Court Justice William O. Douglas, argue that they are "one of the few legal remedies the small claimant has against those who command the status quo." Critics, like the conservative U.S. Chamber of Commerce, oppose them because they are neither a deterrent to unlawful conduct and, in fact, are counterproductive since they threaten to "impose litigation costs and force settlement regardless of a company's choices, thereby deterring lawful, productive conduct."[31] Apart from the political debate, commencing and maintaining a class action invariably create complex logistical management problems for lawyers, clients, and the judiciary. When a large number of broadly dispersed individual claims are consolidated—as with the vaginal mesh litigation discussed at the outset of the chapter, or the BP Deepwater Horizon oil spill[32]— the sheer size of a class action and whether it appropriately addresses all individuals' claims in a common fashion present special case management problems for the judiciary. Because of that, under the direction of the Judicial Panel on Multidistrict Litigation (JPMDL, discussed in Chapter Three), cases pending in multiple federal district courts may be consolidated and transferred to a single federal district court. Subsequent court rulings have entrenched JPMDL procedures into mass tort lawsuits, thus transforming them into "quasi-class actions," giving district courts authority to rule on pretrial issues of class certification (the court order certifying that the class action can proceed if certain prerequisites are met), pretrial discovery, "global" settlements (involving thousands of plaintiffs in complex tort cases), and attorneys' fees.[33] As a result, the nature of a class action suit and the JPMDL process enable many mass tort lawsuits to be resolved through the use of settlement funds, which are then distributed as compensation to individual claimants (see Table 8.2).[34]

Table 8.2	Examples of Mass Tort Litigation and Settlement Funds
Mass Tort Controversy	**Nature of Mass Tort Litigation**
Opioid Epidemic (2010s)	Class actions against opioid manufacturers and distributors for causing drug addiction and other health problems, with many of the lawsuits consolidated into federal court, e.g. "Opiate MDL 2804"
Valsartan (2010s)	Mass litigation against drug companies for producing drug designed to reduce risks associated with hypertension and congestive heart failure but instead manufactured it with ingredients that are known carcinogens
Talcum Powder (2010s)	Mass tort claims filed against drug companies for manufacturing baby powder and other products that include asbestos, a known carcinogen
Monsanto Roundup (2010s)	Mass litigation filed against pesticide makers in manufacturing the popular weed-killer "Roundup" because its active ingredient, glyphosate, is suspected of causing cancer
Hernia/Vaginal Mesh (2010s)	Class actions filed against medical device companies that produce synthetic meshes that are designed to treat prolapse and urinary problems but instead fail after implantation and cause multiple types of debilitating personal injuries
BP Deepwater Horizon (2010s)	A class of persons sought compensation against an oil company for an oil spill that was caused by an explosion of an oil rig in the Gulf of Mexico
Vioxx and "Fen-Phen" (2000s)	Class actions seeking compensation against manufacturers of a nonsteroidal anti-inflammatory drug (Vioxx) that treated arthritis and menstrual pain; and against the manufacturers of "fen-phen" (fenfluramine/phentermine), a drug designed to help with weight loss
9/11 Victims (2000s)	Congress authorized the September 11th Victim Compensation Fund to provide no-fault administrative compensation in lieu of tort litigation related to claims arising from terrorist attacks
Silicone Breast Implants (1990s)	Class actions seeking compensation against manufacturers of silicone gel breast implants
Hemophilia/AIDS (1990s)	Class actions seeking compensation against "blood solid" drug manufacturers that led to HIV infections from blood transfusions

Sources: Alert Communications, "Top 5 Mass Torts to Watch for in 2019," available at https://blog.alertcommunications.com/top-5-mass-torts-to-watch-in-2019 (last retrieved April 23, 2020); Julie Isaacson, "Terrorism and Mass Toxic Torts: An Examination of the James Zadroga 9/11 Health and Compensation Act," *Fordham Environmental Law Review* 25 (2014), 509–51; Richard A. Nagareda, *Mass Torts in a World of Settlement* (Chicago: University Press of Chicago, 2007); Barry F. McNeil and Beth L. Fancsal, "Mass Torts and Class Actions: Facing Increasing Scrutiny," *Federal Rules Decisions* 167 (Updated August 5, 1996), 483–522.

Third-Party Litigation Funding

The criticism that civil justice is driven by self-interest and lawyer manipulation is underscored by a growing trend in civil litigation, namely the rise of ***third-party litigation funding***—the practice of allowing an independent third party (such as a bank, an insurance company, a hedge fund, or some other individual or entity) with no direct connection to the claims of a lawsuit to fund a civil litigant in exchange for receiving a share of the damages ultimately awarded. Yet, they are not loans because if the plaintiff who is under contract to pay the funder loses, then there is no obligation to repay the funder. In contrast, if the defendant is the funded party, the funder agrees to receive a predetermined amount from the defendant, akin to an insurance premium; and, if the defendant wins, the funder may get additional money if the contract so stipulates. As a multi-billion dollar industry, it has domestic and international applications, and it is commonly used in arbitrations, commercial actions, complex corporate disputes, and personal injury tort claims.[35]

In spite of the criticism surrounding it, the practice of third party litigation funding is based purely on a business model: financing litigation costs is an economic decision that seeks an appropriate return on investment in litigation.[36] In this respect, the negotiated settlement operates less like an official adjudication (that ends the litigation) and instead more like a market transaction that balances what the case is worth on its merits against the risks taken on between parties having unequal financial resources.[37] A typical arrangement stipulates that the private funder pays lawyers' fees and other costs in exchange for receiving between 20 and 50 percent of the damages awarded if the litigation is successful. While gaining prominence in Europe, Canada, and Australia, such third-party litigation financing is "still in its infancy but steadily growing" in the United States, making it "one of the most significant developments in civil litigation today [because] it represents a potential sea change in the character and policy implications."[38] Yet, despite its growing significance, the practice of third-party financing is largely unregulated. As a result, there has been a corresponding interest in the academic and legal community to create regulations and legal constraints that will subject third party funders to more governmental and judicial oversight.[39]

The ethical prohibitions of *champerty* and *maintenance* (disallowing agreements between litigants and nonlitigants to split litigation proceeds) prevent attorneys from sharing fees with nonattorneys. Thus, in theory there are several ethical and institutional barriers that counter the widespread adoption of third-party funding of civil litigation. Still, *champerty* restrictions are unevenly enforced in the states, and may be circumvented if private funders make a funding arrangement with the client who is suing (instead of with an attorney). Indeed, only a small minority of states still apply champerty and maintenance laws because the majority of states have either abolished them or have interpreted them loosely, thus permitting the practice of third-party financing to grow in the United States.[40]

Supporters of third-party funding contend that it increases access to courts for those who cannot afford the high cost of litigation. An infrequent one-shotter litigant or a small or growing business, for example, may join with a well-financed private funder to equalize the litigation playing field. Or a multinational company may use such funding as a means to offset or shift some litigation costs. Either way, third-party funding is analogous to other legal practices, such as contingency fees (discussed in the next section).[41] For critics, however, the investment practice exponentially creates the risk of lawsuit abuse. Allowing independent third parties, whose sole interest is maximizing profits, may also encourage frivolous lawsuits, violates professional ethics-related conflicts of interest, and permits nonlawyers to engage in the "unauthorized practice of law."[42]

Burden of Proof, Legal Remedies, and Damages

In civil litigation, claimants must prove that a defendant's liability (or legal responsibility) is established by a **preponderance of the evidence**. The preponderance standard is distinct from the "beyond a reasonable doubt" standard of legal proof that is used in criminal law. In criminal cases, the prosecutor must show that there is no reasonable doubt that a criminal suspect committed a crime. But, under the preponderance standard used in civil cases, the judge or jury merely weighs the evidence in terms of whether the plaintiff's allegations are probably more true than not. Sometimes this is expressed in percentage terms: there must be at least a 51 percent certainty that the defendant is liable for harmful consequences. In some civil cases, a higher standard, a "clear and convincing evidence" level of proof, is used because the consequences of imposing liability are more serious, as in cases involving the termination of parental rights and civil commitment. Under the **clear and convincing standard**, the proof must show a greater certainty (beyond mere probability) that the allegations are true. Through the use of percentages, the clear and convincing standard might roughly require a 75 percent certainty that the facts happened as alleged.[43]

In practical terms, the civil lawsuit is designed to secure a court order granting a party relief in terms of specific **legal remedies** after a defendant's liability is proven. In most civil cases, courts award monetary damages. In general, damages consist of compensatory, punitive, or nominal awards. **Compensatory damages** attempt to put injured parties back into the positions they were in before the harm. Not all suffered harms may be fully compensable, however, depending upon the facts of the case and what is established as a matter of causation and proof. For example, in a contract dispute, the recovery of lost profits because of a breach of contract may put the plaintiff in the same position had a breach not occurred due to the defendant's conduct. Yet, in a tort case, the money a plaintiff recovers for the cost of medical bills and lost income as a result of the injury may fully compensate for economic injuries, but not non-economic injuries, such as pain and suffering caused by the tort. By contrast, **punitive damages** aim to punish defendants but also deter them from future violations of the law. Yet these are awarded in only limited factual circumstances in situations where the defendant's conduct is egregious and warrant an award beyond mere compensation. **Nominal damages** symbolically deliver a positive outcome in cases involving no harm, and juries may opt to award a nominal sum in certain instances. Beyond monetary damages, a court may issue an **injunction** (a decree compelling the defendant to perform or to stop doing a specific act) or a **declaratory judgment** (clarifying the rights that the law affords). In general, nonmonetary relief is granted either in the interest of fairness and equity or on a statutory basis that clarifies the legal rights or duties in a specific legal context.[44]

CIVIL LAWSUITS: THE TRIAL AND APPEAL PROCESS

The civil trial process is similar, but distinct from, how cases are managed and adjudicated in the criminal adversarial system. Unlike the criminal justice system, the litigants in civil cases are not contesting a person's moral culpability, or guilt, in allegedly violating the federal or state penal code. Thus, in civil cases there is no assignment of criminal responsibility that leads to official punishment, such as incarceration, incurring a fine, or imposing capital punishment. Instead, the civil justice system is designed to allocate legal responsibility, or liability, among defendants that are being accused of causing harm to a plaintiff's (the person bring a civil action) personal or property interests. Therefore, civil actions often seek monetary damages or some other type of legal relief, such as an injunction, that prevents or stops a defendant from causing harm. Notably, since civil and criminal legal actions are distinct and separate from each other, it is possible for a defendant to be sued for damages in a civil lawsuit while also being prosecuted for engaging in criminal conduct in separate proceedings (the criminal case against O.J. Simpson and the civil action brought against him later for allegedly committing the wrongful deaths of his wife, Nicole Brown Simpson, and her friend, Ronald Goldman, is a good illustration).[45]

The civil trial process begins after an injury creates a grievance that causes the plaintiff to assert a legal claim against the allegedly responsible party. If the defendant denies liability, then the claim becomes a legal dispute that is brought into court for resolution. In this respect, there are different meanings, and legal implications, to what are considered to be "grievances," "legal claims" or "legal disputes" (see "Contemporary Controversies over Courts: The Dispute Pyramid"). While legal disputes may be dropped or resolved at any time after the civil action is commenced, those that go to trial involve a process of narrowing the legal issues through pleadings and motions—a series of rule-based, pretrial activities that allow parties to gather relevant information for trial preparation. During the pretrial stage, pretrial conferences are held with the parties and the judge in an ongoing effort to clarify the facts and legal issues of the case with an eye toward reaching a negotiated settlement. If a settlement is not reached, a trial is held, and the judge (if it is a bench trial) or the jury decides the case and renders a final judgment that can be enforced or appealed in a subsequent proceeding. The civil trial and appeal process is diagrammed in Figure 8.4.

Contemporary Controversies over Courts: The Dispute Pyramid

Scholars have long recognized that citizens who decide to litigate undergo an incremental decision-making process of "naming, blaming, and claiming" before they file a lawsuit. "Naming" is recognizing an injury; "blaming" is identifying who is responsible for the injury; and "claiming" is the pursuit of a claim against an allegedly responsible party. Identifying injuries and making claims against culpable parties is a complex sociopsychological, cultural, economic, and institutional process because litigants must make several choices among a range of options before deciding to sue, including whether to incur the time and expense of enlisting the help of lawyers or courts. Accordingly, going through the decision-making process to litigate often has the effect of discouraging citizens from pursuing their claims through formal legal action.

Individuals with *grievances*, or beliefs of perceived injuries or entitlements, assign blame and may elect to assert a *legal claim* against those who are thought to be responsible. The injury or entitlement may be real or not; and whether it is acted upon further depends upon the individual's perception or beliefs. Some claims may be brought to the offending party for relief while others are dropped for a variety of reasons (indifference, lack of knowledge about what to do next, or the reluctance to spend time or money in pursuing grievances further). If additional action is taken, a *legal dispute* emerges once the legal claim for relief is rejected by the offending party. Thereafter, the legal dispute may be handled in different ways, again depending upon another set of contingencies or circumstances: A person may opt to do nothing further, or to consult with a lawyer, or to file a formal legal action (with or without a lawyer's help). For those filing a lawsuit, a settlement or trial may occur, and, thereafter, an appeal may be filed if the losing party deems it is worth it to do so after weighing several alternatives.

The dispute pyramid (see graphic below) registers the significance of acting upon grievances, claims, and disputes in the judicial process in varying social and legal surroundings. Within the context of tort litigation (civil actions claiming monetary damages for wrongful acts), researchers have used the dispute pyramid to rebut the criticism that the civil justice system is being abused by lawyers and litigants who file groundless lawsuits in order to get a financial windfall from deep-pocket corporations or insurance companies. Such criticisms are highly relevant and generate contentious political and public policy arguments that weigh the merits of tort reform, including capping jury awards of punitive damages in medical malpractice lawsuits, or limiting the number of class action lawsuits that are filed for product liability claims.

In the realm of tort cases, for example, a review of the dispute pyramid shows how difficult it is to transform tort-based grievances into actionable legal claims and disputes that are handled by attorneys and courts. At the bottom of the pyramid rests a large number of grievances, which result from allegedly wrongful acts or events, such as the manufacture and use of a defective product that causes a real or perceived injury. While some grievances may be pursued further, many others are dropped for a variety of reasons. If more action is taken, those with grievances name their injury and assign blame by notifying the offending party of a legal claim. Those claims reside in the next layer above grievances in the dispute pyramid. Notably, claims may be satisfied in whole or in part, typically by fixing the problem or paying compensation without having to consult a lawyer or file a lawsuit. Thus, only a narrow set of claims are transformed into legal disputes once claims for relief are rejected (at the top of the pyramid). Yet many disputes may be abandoned, and only a few may be formally adjudicated by lawyers who file lawsuits and engage in the settlement, trial, or appeal process.

The true significance of the dispute pyramid is the principle that there is an increasing attrition of civil cases as cases move up the pyramid. Only a small proportion of grievances and claims become legal disputes requiring the formal action of lawyers or courts for resolution. In this respect, the pyramid suggests that the legal system may promise more than it can deliver in formally resolving disputes; and it provides evidence that critics may be overstating their case in making arguments that the United States is an overly litigious society in the tort reform debate (see The Politics of Tort and Civil Litigation Reform section and discussion in this Chapter).

Apart from tort reform, the dispute pyramid can also explain the litigation patterns of incarcerated prisoners asserting inmate administrative appeals and constitutional claims in federal courts. One study shows that despite many barriers California prisoners are more likely to file multiple grievances about inhumane prison conditions, but with little impact. Under federal law, prisoners must complete an internal three-stage administrative grievance process before filing a lawsuit raising constitutional issues, such as arguing that prison overcrowding or inadequate medical care violates the Eighth Amendment's cruel and unusual punishment ban. Other disincentives inhibit the filing of grievances in prisons: Prisoners may fear retaliation by prison officials, manifest self-blame in causing incarceration, or wish to avoid being stigmatized as a troublemaker.

Still, the study found that the prison environment mobilizes prisoners to name injuries, assign blame, and file claims in tens of thousands of cases because it is uniquely law-centric and tightly regulated within the prison environment (armed guards, strict control over movement, and disciplinary rules); but often prisoners do not get legal relief because a majority of complaints are resolved administratively, and they rarely reach the courts. Thus, as the dispute pyramid would predict, the mere presence of a large amount of perceived grievances does not mean they will become actionable legal disputes in courts because of administrative obstacles and underlying problems of prisoner vulnerability, self-blame, and stigma. Nonetheless, it is worth noting that the dispute pyramid cannot accurately predict all litigation outcomes. For example, in *Brown v. Plata* (2011), the U.S. Supreme Court ordered the release of thousands of California prisoners because allowing inhumane prison conditions was a violation of the Eighth Amendment's ban on unusual and cruel punishments.

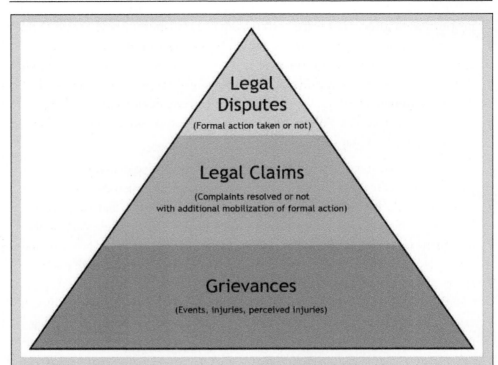

Sources: The two studies examined above are from Kitty Calavita and Valerie Jenness, "Inside the Pyramid of Disputes: Naming Problems and Filing Grievances in California Prisons" *Social Problems* 60 (2013): 50–80; and Marc Galanter, "Real World Torts: An Antidote to Anecdote," *Maryland Law Review* 55 (1996): 1094–160. See also, Richard E. Miller and Austin Sarat, "Grievances, Claims, and Disputes: Assessing the Adversary Culture," *Law and Society Review* 15 (1980–1981): 525–66; William L. F. Felstiner, Richard L. Abel, and Austin Sarat, "The Emergence and Transformation of Disputes: Naming, Blaming, and Claiming. . .," *Law and Society Review* 15 (1980–1981): 631–54; Galanter, Marc. "Reading the Landscape of Disputes: What We Know and Don't Know (and Think We Know) about Our Allegedly Contentious and Litigious Society." *UCLA Law Review* 31(1983), 4–72. Marc Galanter, "Access to Justice in a World of Expanding Social Capability," *Fordham Law Review* 38 (2010): 115–28; and *Brown v. Plata,* 563 U.S. 493 (2011).

Figure 8.4	The Civil Trial and Appeal Process

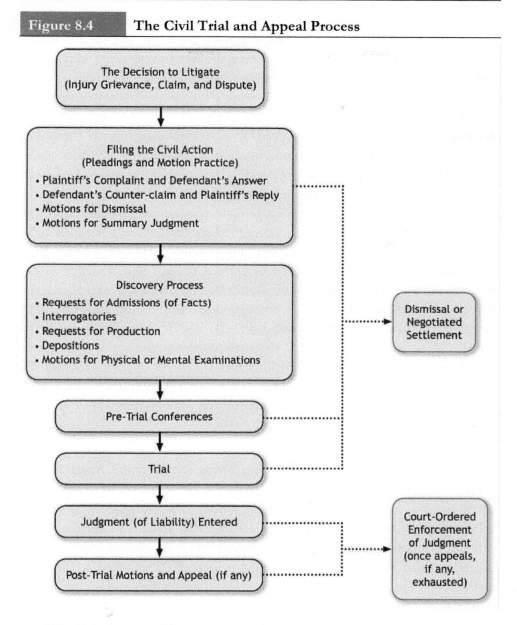

The Decision to Litigate

The decision to litigate and hire counsel is often a function of weighing a variety of factors that relate to deciding if the time, effort, and expense of filing a lawsuit is worthwhile. Scholars studying the intent to sue in the context of employment disputes have found that two factors—a person's personality (such as temperament, disposition, and interpersonal traits) and an individual's perceived notions of justice—are likely to affect the calculus about the wisdom of bringing a lawsuit.[46] Moreover, there are a number of practical and logistical disincentives to suing. Research has shown, in fact, that most injury victims are discouraged from filing claims because the experience of the injury itself, along with cultural and social norms that create the impression that it is better not to sue and rely, instead, upon alternative means to get over their injuries, indicates that most would-be litigants choose to "lump it," or not sue.[47] As some scholars observe, deciding to sue is probably influenced by a "complicated mix of community associations, social status, rights consciousness, knowledge of legal procedures, access to lawyers, procedural rules of court, and severity of physical and economic injury." The practical application of those factors and many others may create a general aversion to using the courts for personal reasons; or there may be a strong reluctance to sue due to ignorance about the legal process, or a personal lack a "consciousness of the law."[48] Moreover, unlike in criminal trials, persons below the poverty line are not constitutionally entitled to legal representation in civil lawsuits. An individual's wealth is significant because, with few exceptions, civil litigants cannot shift the costs of incurring legal fees to the opposing party; therefore, each side must pay its own counsel's fees. So, even though under the so-called American rule courts tend to award to the winning party "court costs," the losing party does not have to pay the attorney's fees of opposing counsel. The fact that litigants pay their own legal fees is not only a disincentive to sue, but it is also unusual because in most other countries the losers bear some or all of the costs of litigation, including legal fees.[49]

The financial constraints that shape the decision to litigate are a part of the historical evolution of norms and billing practices within the American legal profession. Since the 1950s, most litigation costs have been transferred onto the client instead of the attorney. Before World War II, professional norms encouraged lawyers to charge their clients by either fixed fee arrangements or offering clients a ***contingency fee agreement***—a billing practice that ties fees to obtaining a successful outcome. In the past, lawyers rarely kept track of their time, and in corporate practice, regular clients were billed at year's end on the basis of what the lawyers thought their services were worth. But in the latter half of the twentieth century, billing practices changed due to increased competition, the proliferation of lawyers, and the rise of large law firms. As a result, attorneys began to keep better track of their time by turning to the "billable hour" standard to keep revenues and profits consistently more reliable (discussed in Chapter Five). In contrast, contingency fees are more risky and perhaps less stable because lawyers do not generate any fee unless they win the lawsuit they commenced (and that fee is based upon a percentage, typically 33 and 1/3 percent, of the total recovery; plus the lawyer is entitled to reimbursable expenses of litigation that lawyers front in advance for clients, such as filing fees, the preparation of transcripts in depositions, or paying expert witnesses to testify and the like). Whereas defenders of contingency fees, such as trial lawyers, argue that they are necessary to allow clients with modest means to get access to courts and fair justice in lawsuits defended by deep pocket defendants, such as insurance companies, critics counter that they are reasons for tort lawyers, sometimes pejoratively labelled "ambulance chasers," to drive up insurance costs by filing meritless lawsuits in the hopes of getting a large jury award or negotiated settlement (the politics of the debate between the trial lawyer bar and the insurance or business industries are detailed in the Politics of Tort and Civil Litigation section later in this Chapter).

Although contingency fees are still a part of legal billing practices in certain civil cases, hourly billing remains the dominant form of compensation for most litigation.[50] However, if there is a contingency fee agreement, clients must still agree to file a formal complaint in court and, from the lawyer's perspective, the economics of legal practice and the likelihood that there will be a successful outcome weighs heavily in advising clients to sue or not. In this respect, lawyers are "portfolio managers" that professionally balance the risk of taking a case against the anticipated return if liability is imposed. As political scientist Herbert Kritzer explains,

> While virtually every contingency fee practitioner wants to find highly lucrative cases, such cases are relatively rare. Many cases presented to lawyers are not winnable, or they do not offer a prospect of even a moderately acceptable fee. The contingency fee practitioner seeks cases that offer a high probability of providing at least an acceptable return, hoping to find some fraction of cases that present the opportunity to generate a significant fee.[51]

At bottom, for lawyers the "portfolio of risks" that they confront in civil litigation is driven by economic self-interest and, not surprisingly, a substantial number of prospective clients are turned away or referred to other lawyers if the risks of suing are too great. As one legal practitioner put it, the cost-benefits of agreeing to take a lawsuit means, "in concrete terms, that individuals who suffer limited harms—though substantial harms from their perspective—are often unable to vindicate them through the legal system."[52] Still, the fact that lawyers may offer contingency fees to clients invariably fuels the national politics of tort reform debate because lawyers representing the "victim" in personal injury cases insist the contingency fee provides the "key to the courthouse." Defense lawyers aligned with business interests and the insurance industry, on the other hand, contend it is a "key to enormous and untold riches" for unscrupulous plaintiffs' lawyers.[53]

Finally, the decision to litigate also implicates the basic question of whether legal disputes are best resolved by means other than the adversary process. In addition to using "alternative dispute resolution" techniques (discussed in this Chapter's last section), only the most significant civil cases, arguably, should be litigated and subject to the time and expense of having full adversary trials. Under this view, shrinking judicial budgets and limited resources require courts to use a "case triage" management strategy to filter out the most serious disputes from those that could be handled in other less costly venues, such as an administrative or a nonadversarial problem-solving tribunal (see Chapter One and the discussion of therapeutic justice).[54]

Filing Civil Actions: Pleadings and Motion Practice

The adjudication of civil cases is a primarily a function of the application of statutes and, most importantly, procedural rules that are created by courts that give the judiciary the institutional capacity to manage, or process, disputes from the time the action is officially filed to the time a decree, or judgment, is formally issued in the plaintiff's or defendant's favor. The federal judiciary and all the state courts have procedural rules, or rules of court, that litigants and counsel use to commence and maintain a civil action in court until it ends. Like in the criminal justice context, using **pleadings**—formal documents that are filed in the lawsuit's beginning to notify each party of their respective claims and defenses—and engaging in **motion practice**—how each party file motions requesting legal relief for certain action, such as the admission of evidence or the disposition of the case—are integral to the operation of the civil justice system.[55] Significantly, how well the parties and counsel structure their case by the application of procedural rules has substantive implications for whether they are initially given access to the courts to present their legal arguments, gather evidence and, ultimately, if they should prevail, given the lawsuit's strengths, or merits.[56] Quite simply, the mastery or ineptitude of using the procedural rules to a party's advantage will often mean the difference between winning or losing in a court of law.

Civil lawsuits officially begin with the exchange of pleadings, which include the payment of a fee and the filing of a **complaint** asserting that the court has jurisdiction over the dispute. The complaint's main purpose is to identify the relevant parties and legal allegations underlying the conflict. A final requirement is to state what the parties seek in terms of legal remedies, which, in most civil cases, is monetary damages. Notably, complaints have to be filed within the applicable time period set by the jurisdiction's **statute-of-limitations** governing that type of civil dispute—the failure to do so will result in a case's dismissal, even if the underlying allegations or cause of action have legal merit. The reason why courts enforce statute-of-limitations provisions is to prevent claims from being tainted with old evidence or unreliable witness testimony that invariably results with the passage of time.[57]

Once a complaint is filed, the clerk of court issues a summons commanding the defendant to appear in court, and directs the defendant to respond, often within thirty days, to the plaintiff's allegations. If there is a legal basis to do so, defendants who are sued may file a **counter claim** that asserts a new allegation of legal wrongdoing based on the plaintiff's actions, and to which the original plaintiff responds by filing a **reply**. The original complaint filed by the plaintiff and a second counter claim filed by the defendant are separate actions to be resolved by the court, even though the facts mainly relate to the same issues of legal liability in one case. The same type of motion practice that governs the case disposition controls each claim and is defined by the governing procedural rules of court within its jurisdiction.

Notice Pleading vs. Fact Pleading

Civil pleadings and pretrial motion practices are premised on "notice pleading." The Supreme Court's ruling in *Conely v. Gibson* (1957) endorsed notice pleading by stating that "a complaint should not be dismissed for failure to state a claim unless it appears beyond doubt that the plaintiff can prove no set of facts in support of his claim which would entitle him to relief." In theory, it is designed to give the parties fair notice of the general facts and legal issues in dispute.[58] Yet, since notice pleading does not require the complaint to specify all the facts upon which the legal claim is based, it encourages the filing of numerous discovery motions in order to "uncover" any relevant fact in the case until the legal issues are no longer in dispute. Not only does this lead to frequent revisions to a complaint, but it also has the potential to turn the discovery process into protracted proceedings that increase litigation costs and delay trials. Consequently, critics assert that the federal courts should adopt rules that replace notice pleading with "fact-based" pleading—a reform that would require the parties to delineate specific facts in support of their legal claims at the earliest stages of the litigation. The movement toward fact-based pleading reform has grown in recent decades (it has been adopted in several states), and the Supreme Court has expressed a preference for fact-based pleading over notice pleading. Such developments have not only increased the likelihood that civil cases will end at the pretrial stage, but also have generated criticism that more rigorous pleading requirements are transforming civil procedure into a "process that favors simplicity over complexity, individual over collective actions, and settlement over adjudication." As a result, stricter pleading rules leads to a retrenchment or "containment of litigation to the point of derailing civil litigation and risking the erasure of substantive rights."[59]

Motions of Dismissal and Summary Judgment

After the complaint is filed, many jurisdictions permit either party to file a motion asking for dismissal of the case. Defendants, for example, may file a dismissal motion, arguing that the complaint fails "to state a claim upon which relief can be granted."[60] Alternatively, federal and many state courts permit either party to file a motion for summary judgment—a motion asserting that there is "no genuine issue as to any material fact and that the moving party is entitled to a judgment as a matter of law."[61] If granted, the court resolves the legal claims without further proceedings.

In the past two decades, the Supreme Court has indicated that summary judgment motions should be encouraged even though they displace jury trials.[62] *Bell Atlantic Corporation v. Twombly* (2007) and *Ashcroft v. Iqbal* (2009), for example, set new "heightened pleading" requirements that make it difficult to move a case past the pretrial stage and even to begin the process of discovery. *Twombly* established the rule that complaints in antitrust cases must include enough facts to create "plausible grounds" for asserting that a legal claim is true before going to trial. *Iqbal* expanded *Twombly*'s "plausibility" standard to all civil cases.[63] In light of these rulings, it is not surprising that federal caseload statistics indicate that summary judgment dispositions have dramatically risen, while the number of jury trials has sharply declined.[64] Of the roughly 325,000 thousand federal civil cases in 2019, less than 1 percent went to trial. More significantly, of the cases in which there was court action, 87 percent terminated before trial; whereas, in 1962 only 20 percent ended before trial; and, in 2002, nearly 70 percent of civil cases were disposed summarily. These trends suggest a "new era in which dispositions by summary judgment are a magnitude several times greater than the number of trials."[65] That "magnitude" is underscored by a recent study by the University of Denver's Institute for the Advancement of the American Legal System. It reported that the while the overall filing rate for motions for summary judgment across U.S. District Courts has slightly declined over the past ten years (from 17 percent to 14 percent in all cases), more than a third of cases (38 percent) were ended by summary judgment, which stood only behind negotiated settlement as the most efficient means to terminate a case in 45 percent of the time.[66]

Still, state courts are not obliged to follow the heightened pleading requirements adopted by federal courts, so the procedural rules that each state judiciary follows necessarily will dictate what type of impact they have in restricting access to trials or justice. One study shows, for example, that *Iqbal* and *Twombly's* plausibility standard has been reviewed by twelve state supreme courts; and, of those, only five have chosen to incorporate it within their civil rules of procedure, whereas another seven have opted to stay with the traditional notice standard. Also, notice-based pleadings continue to be followed in at least eighteen other state courts that have not yet considered the issue.[67]

The Discovery Process and Pretrial Conferences

The general burdens and costs of litigating civil claims are closely tied to the time and effort it takes for lawyers to gather key facts and evidence. As in the criminal justice system, discovery of facts is governed by procedural rules that control all aspects of pretrial activity.

There are five basic types of *discovery*: interrogatories, requests for production, requests for admissions, depositions, and motions for physical or mental examinations. With the exception of depositions and motions for production, during the discovery process, parties may only seek the information from parties in the case. Furthermore, though most court rules allow a broad scope of discovery, the information sought generally must be relevant to the legal issues at hand and not "privileged"—for example, the personal notes or "work product" of opposing counsel.[68]

Before 1990, the federal rules permitted discovery of "any matter, not privileged, which is relevant to the subject matter involved in the pending action."[69] The judiciary, however, has made it clear that discovery is not unlimited. Amendments to federal discovery practice have moved toward a system of mandatory disclosure for certain basic facts, such as revealing the names, addresses, and phone numbers of persons having discoverable information. Because they are mandatory, the scope of discovery has been narrowed, and discovery requests are now restricted to disclosing only facts "relevant to the claim or defense of any party." Only after good cause is demonstrated may a court order discovery for matters relevant to the subject matter of the case.[70]

State and federal litigants may still use generic discovery motions to uncover key facts and evidence. Two of the most common and cost-effective motions are a *motion to answer interrogatories*—a set of questions directed at the opposing party about the basic facts of the litigation event, such as learning the name and addresses of witnesses—and an accompanying *motion for production* (requiring the opposing party to produce, or give access to, tangible evidence, such as medical records, lost income statements, or photographs).[71] Another way to establish facts or legal issues that may not actually be in dispute is by filing a *request for admission* to the opposing party,[72] which requires the defendant to respond to allegations in the complaint.

Notably, in 2005, the federal rules of discovery were amended to obtain the disclosure and production of "electronically stored information" (ESI) that is stored in virtually any type of computing device. Using the federal rules to gather ESI information is often referred to as "e-discovery" and it encompasses a variety of digital formats ranging from individual emails to virtually anything, including meta-data, that is stored in computer databases or servers. Consequently, the rule change was controversial because traditionally the scope of discovery was limited to disclosing only relevant information; thus, in practical terms, the onset of e-discovery not only led to increased litigation costs, but it also allowed well-resourced litigants to gain an unfair advantage in preparing their case with electronic data or facts that less-affluent parties could not obtain. Thus, in 2015, the federal judiciary once again amended the rules to permit only the disclosure of information that is relevant to the parties' claims and defenses and proportional to the needs of the case.[73]

Depositions are an expensive but very effective discovery tool that solicits the sworn testimony of a party or a witness.[74] Not only do they offer a first glimpse of how witnesses and counsel may perform at trial, but they also preserve the statements as evidence that can confirm what was said if a witness has died prior to or is otherwise unavailable at trial. *Motions for physical or mental examinations* are also a significant discovery tool because they directly relate to establishing the basis for determining liability or damages.[75]

Pretrial Conferences

The pretrial conference purpose varies with the judge's discretion, the applicable rules of a court, the complexity of the case, and how interested the parties are in a negotiated settlement. For example, such conferences may: (1) establish a schedule for filing motions and setting deadlines; (2) allow for a ruling on pending motions in a coordinated and consolidated fashion, instead of on an *ad hoc* basis; (3) encourage settlement after discovery is completed; and, (4) help clarify issues relating to the presentation of evidence at trial. At a minimum, most trial courts use pretrial conferences to simplify the legal issues, identify the witnesses and expected evidence that will be used at trial, and explore the possibility of a negotiated settlement. Notably, the introduction of pretrial conferences has also expanded the "managerial" role of judges in supervising discovery and related settlement activities, as well as virtually causing jury trials to "vanish."[76]

Trial, Judgment, and Appeal

Whereas the Sixth Amendment affords criminal defendants the right to a "speedy and public trial" by an impartial jury, the Seventh Amendment guarantees civil litigants a jury trial only if the amount in controversy is more than twenty dollars. This limitation, however, applies only to federal litigation, and state courts are free to determine the amount in controversy for having a jury trial. In terms of how cases are tried, civil trials are generally conducted in the same way as criminal trials (see Figure 7.1, "The Stages of Trial and Presentation of Evidence," in Chapter Seven).

Even so, the role of civil juries is distinct from that of criminal cases and is often misunderstood.[77] One long-standing misperception is that civil juries are too quick to deliver "runaway verdicts." Critics contend that they result in: (1) a high number of jury awards favoring plaintiffs in tort cases; (2) high jury awards in malpractice and product liability cases; and, (3) disproportionate and arbitrary awards of punitive damages.[78] Yet empirical studies find that the rate of civil trials has steadily decreased over time and that juries render verdicts and damage awards that are, for the most part, modest; however, in some categories of tort cases, there are frequently large monetary awards.

To illustrate, in a Civil Justice Survey of State Courts (CJSSC) study of seventy-five of the most populous counties in the United States, researchers reported that the number of civil trials in tort, contract, and real property disputes fell by over 50 percent from 1992 to 2005. Among those types of cases, the majority of civil cases disposed of by trial involved tort claims (61%), whereas the rest were contract (33%) and real property issues (6%). Moreover, median damages awards from juries declined from a high in 1992 ($72,000) to a low in 2005 ($43,000)—a 40 percent decline. During that time period, the median damages in tort jury trials declined by 50 percent, from $71,000 to $33,000. These figures underscore the longstanding trend in federal and state courts toward the "vanishing trial" and diminishing damage awards, even in tort cases.[79] Indeed, some commentators go so far as to claim that trials are increasingly "obsolete," a phenomenon brought on by changes to the modern rules of civil procedure and their interpretation by courts that encourage settlement during the pretrial phase.[80]

In the CJSSC research, nonetheless, juries decided about 70 percent of all general civil trials, and plaintiffs won roughly six out of ten cases, with a median damage award of $28,000.[81] In contract cases, plaintiffs won 66 percent of the time and recovered a median damage award of $35,000. Among all state tort trials, the most prevalent type of case involved motor vehicles (35 percent) and medical malpractice (9 percent); and, juries resolved those cases about 90 percent of the time. Across all areas of tort liability, plaintiffs only prevailed slightly more than half the time (52 percent), and the median award was only $24,000. In less than 1 percent of all civil trials, plaintiffs won the most in animal attack cases, but in medical malpractice cases, plaintiffs only won about one of every five cases, though the median recovery is $400,000 (see Table 8.3).

After the trial, the next step is the enforcement of the judgment against the liable party, if there are no intervening posttrial motions that upset the verdict or if there is no appeal. For many civil litigants, though, the reality and procedural complexity of securing a favorable judgment, or in avoiding liability, is time-consuming, frustrating, and costly.

Table 8.3	Tort, Contract, and Real Property Trials and Median Final Awards to Plaintiffs		
	Percentage of Total Trials (Percentage via Jury Trial)	Percentage of Prevailing Plaintiffs	Median Final Award (in Dollars)
Tort Cases			
Motor Vehicle	35.0 (92.1)	64.3	15,000
Medical Malpractice	9.1 (98.7)	22.7	400,000
Premises Liability	6.9 (93.8)	38.4	98,000
Intentional Tort	2.7 (78.3)	51.6	38,000
Other or Unknown Tort	2.5 (71.6)	41.1	83,000
Conversion	1.4 (46.3)	48.3	27,000
Products Liability	1.3 (93.5)	—	567,000
• Asbestos	0.3 (95.5)	54.9	682,000
• Other	1.0 (92.7)	19.6	500,000
Slander/Libel	0.7 (64.2)	39.4	24,000
Professional Malpractice	0.6 (59.9)	39.2	129,000
Animal Attack	0.5 (80.6)	75.2	21,000
False Arrest, Imprisonment	0.2 (63.9)	15.5	259,000
Total Tort Trials (N = 16,397 Cases)	60.8% (90.0%)	51.6%	$24,000
Contract Cases			
Seller Plaintiff	10.7 (16.6)	74.6	27,000
Buyer Plaintiff	9.6 (44.1)	62.3	17,000
Fraud	4.1 (50.2)	59.1	75,000
Rental/Lease Agreement	2.2 (19.2)	62.5	35,000

Other Employment Dispute	2.1 (62.9)	50.9	45,000
Employment Discrimination	1.2 (91.2)	60.9	175,000
Mortgage Foreclosure	0.9 (3.5)	89.4	78,000
Other or Unknown Contract	0.9 (52.2)	59.3	30,000
Tortious Interference	0.6 (61.7)	60.3	169,000
Partnership Dispute	0.4 (32.3)	65.7	120,000
Subrogation	0.3 (7.4)	27.5	30,000
Total Contract Trials (N=8,917)	33.1% (36.0%)	65.6%	$35,000
Real Property Cases			
Title or Boundary Dispute	3.6% (15.0%)	NR	NR
Eminent Domain	2.0 (50.7%)	NR	NR
Other or Unknown Real Property	0.5 (9.0%)	NR	NR
Total Real Property Trials (N = 1,633)	6.1% (26.4%)	NR	NR

Legend: NR = Data Not Reported

Source: Lynn Langton and Thomas H. Cohen, *Civil Bench and Jury Trials in State Courts, 2005* ("Civil Justice Survey of State Courts") (October 2008, NCJ 223851), available at www.bjs.gov (last retrieved April 24, 2020). This study used data from 2005 and examined the nation's seventy-five most populous counties. "NR, Not Reported"

THE POLITICS OF TORT AND CIVIL LITIGATION REFORM

In its 2020 report, the conservative American Tort Reform Association (ATRA) listed nine judicial districts, and the New Jersey legislature, as most offensive "judicial hellholes, or forums "where judges systematically apply laws and court procedures in an unfair and unbalanced manner, generally against defendants in civil lawsuits."[82] At the top of the list was the Philadelphia Court of Common Pleas, a trial court that is "home to an astounding $8 billion product liability verdict in 2019," and where mass tort lawsuits abound, along with high jury awards and trial lawyer subsidies of television ads putting pressure on defendants to settle case. It is also characterized as "one of the preferred jurisdictions for asbestos litigation." The other hellholes—California, New York City, Louisiana, the City of St. Louis, Missouri, Georgia, St. Clair, Cook and Madison Counties, Illinois, Oklahoma, and the Minnesota Supreme Court/Twin Cities, Minnesota—are "known for allowing innovative lawsuits to proceed or for welcoming litigation tourism, and in all of them state leadership seems eager to expand civil liability at every given opportunity".[83]

In recent decades, the ATRA has campaigned for reforms, such as: (1) placing legislative caps on jury awards for punitive and noneconomic damages; (2) enacting asbestos litigation and other mass tort reform; (3) limiting the number of class action lawsuits filed in state and federal courts; and, (4) controlling attorneys' fees and imposing procedural sanctions on lawyers who bring frivolous lawsuits, among others.[84] Other proposals—which include restricting health care liability; ending abusive food industry, securities, and patent litigation; and preventing state attorneys from hiring contingency fee lawyers in suits targeting big business— have been the persistent focus of ATRA anti-tort reform efforts. The ATRA's advocacy is consistent with the lobbying activities seeking to achieve legislative policy changes since the 1970s that restricts the recovery of punitive damages, imposes caps on non-economic damages (e.g. pain and suffering awards), limits the range of defendants that can be sued under joint and several liability rules, and revises the collateral source rule, or the ban on introducing evidence that plaintiffs are receiving compensation from alternative sources, such as insurance contracts, for the claimed injury.[85]

Predictably, the liberal trial bar responds that "tort reform" is a misleading public relations ploy that paints corporations in a sympathetic light and would cut back on access to courts and fundamental rights. The American Association for Justice (AAJ), for example, contends that the architects of the "tort reform" disinformation campaign are only a few large corporations, such as Merck (Vioxx),

W.R. Grace (asbestos), Ford (Pinto), BP (Deepwater Horizon), and others, that in turn rely on the public policy and legal activities of the Civil Justice Reform Group (CJRG) and well-funded special interest groups, like the U.S. Chamber of Commerce's Institute for Legal Reform, the American Legislative Exchange Council, and academic thinktanks, such as the George Mason law school's Searle Civil Justice Institute. The AAJ's arguments are aligned with findings from empirical studies showing that certain factors, such as the level of incurred insurance liability losses and the number of tort cases filed, affect tort reform adaption; and that some political institutional factors, such as control of state government by the Republican party, leads to reform being enacted more quickly.[86]

Whether the anti-tort and civil justice reform movement is legitimately targeting the problems of civil litigation cost, delay, and litigiousness remains an unresolved question and the subject of ongoing academic debate. Notably, the debate is also infused with politics. As scholars Menkel-Meadow and Garth observe, "In the field of civil procedure, where there is a continuing demand for some procedural rule reform, empirical studies of how rules actually operate have, for the most part, been used in partisan ways to advocate for particular reforms in the interests of one or another legal or client constituency."[87] Still, empirical studies consistently show that civil trials are declining, procedural summary dispositions increasing, and plaintiffs rewarded with relatively modest success rates and damage awards in most areas of civil litigation.[88] Some researchers, moreover, argue that the way in which national and local news outlets selectively report "tort tales" (misleading accounts of jury verdicts) promotes the public perception that trial lawyers file frivolous lawsuits or that juries are out of control in delivering large damage awards.[89]

In short, reforming the civil justice system is politically contentious and hard fought. Also, reform proposals vary widely, and their enactment is uneven. Table 8.4 summarizes several tort reform objectives and the number of states in which they have been enacted. On the federal level, Congress regularly holds hearings on topics involving lawsuit abuse, class actions, and contingency fees.[90] In the last couple of decades, class action filings and certifications have been substantially restricted by the Private Securities Litigation Reform Act of 1995 and the Class Action Fairness Act of 2005. In addition, several Supreme Court justices have indicated strong support for these limitations and others involving class actions (For further discussion, see "Contemporary Controversies over Courts: The Roberts Court and Class Action Lawsuits").

Table 8.4	State Tort Reform Laws	
Type of Reform	**Tort Reform Objective**	**Number of States Adopting**
Class Action	Restrict class action filings	• 13
Punitive Damages	Restrict award of punitive damages (four states' reforms struck down as unconstitutional and none of those four have enacted additional reforms)	• 32
Noneconomic Damages	Restrict award of damages for "pain and suffering," emotional distress, loss of spousal companionship, and other intangible injuries (six states' reforms struck down as unconstitutional and of those six, only one has enacted additional reforms)	• 23
Product Liability	Restrict liability exposure for manufacturing defective products (three states' reforms struck down as unconstitutional and none of those three have enacted additional reforms)	• 21
Joint and Several Liability	Limit recovery of damages against multiple defendants collectively	• 40
Collateral Source Rule	Modify or abolish rule barring admission of evidence showing plaintiff's losses have been compensated from other sources, such as insurance or worker's compensation (two states' reforms struck down as unconstitutional and none of those two have enacted additional reforms)	• 24
Appeal Bond	Reduces amount of bond losing defendants have to post pending appeal (most states require bond amount of up to 150% of verdict)	• 42
Medical Malpractice	• Damage Award Limits/Caps • Limits or Sliding Fee Schedules on Attorneys' Fees • No "Junk Science" or Minimum Expert Witness Qualifications • Pretrial Alternative Dispute Resolution and Screening Panels	• 35 • 28 • 31 • 27 (ADR) • 17 (SP before trial)

Sources: American Tort Reform Association, "ATRA Tort Reform Record (July 2019)," available at http://www.atra.org/wp-content/uploads/2019/08/Tort-Reform-Record-7-12-19.pdf (last retrieved April 24, 2020); National Conference of State Legislatures, "Medical Liability/Medical Malpractice Laws" (updated August 15, 2011)," available at www.ncsl.org (last retrieved April 24, 2020).

Contemporary Controversies over Courts: The Roberts Court and Class Action Lawsuits

The Federal Rules of Civil Procedure (FRCP) provide for "class action" suits— suits filed by individuals for themselves and all others who have suffered the same injury. That enables individuals who have suffered small monetary damages to bring lawsuits they might not otherwise have brought because of the high cost of litigation. The FRCP also permit suits aimed at punishing businesses and corporations for defective and injurious products or practices with large damage awards. Specifically, Rule 23 provides that:

> one or more members of a class may sue or be sued as representative parties on behalf of all only if (1) the class is so numerous that joinder of all members is impracticable, (2) there are questions of law or fact common to the class, (3) the claims or defenses of the representative parties are typical of the claims or defenses of the class, and (4) the representative parties will fairly and adequately protect the interests of the class. . . .In any class action maintained under [this rule], the court shall direct to the members of the class the best notice practicable under the circumstances, including individual notice to all members who can be identified.

The scope of this rule, though, was limited in *Eisen v. Carlisle & Jacquelin*, 417 U.S. 156 (1974), which held that when a representative of a class action suit refuses to pay the cost of giving actual notice to all reasonably identifiable class members, federal courts are required to dismiss the suit; in *Eisen*, representatives had to notify 2.25 million class members at a cost of $225,000.

Federal courts generally tend to be more favorable to defendant businesses and corporations than state courts, which tend to be more favorable to consumers. Hence, businesses and corporations have tried to move such cases from state courts into federal courts. Large class actions brought in federal courts frequently are consolidated into multidistrict litigation. Due process requires those bringing a suit to send, publish, or broadcast a notice of the suit to all potential members of a class, permitting them to opt out of the suit. If a settlement is reached, the class must be given notice of the proposed details, and likewise notified of any awards that result from a judgment.

Class action lawsuits are used because of increased efficiency and lower costs of litigating other similar cases. They also avoid conflicting rulings on the same dispute from courts in different jurisdictions. In addition, they may force changes in the behavior of defendants by requiring them to pay large damage awards or to refund the cost of and replace defective and injurious products. As a result, automobile, drug, and tobacco companies, among others, have increasingly confronted expensive and lengthy class action litigation.

Not surprisingly, class actions have long been criticized by businesses and corporations, the U.S. Chamber of Commerce, and the Republican Party. One criticism is that they encourage frivolous and abusive suits, usually entail costly and protracted litigation and large attorneys' fees, and unfairly punish businesses, while class members often ultimately receive little or no benefits from the suits. Business groups have long lobbied for legislation making it easier to move class action suits from state to federal courts, making it harder to certify member classes, and limiting punitive damage awards. They also contend that trial lawyers file these suits in states and counties known to favor consumers. By contrast, consumer advocates, trial lawyers, and the U.S. Judicial Conference have opposed such changes. They counter that the federal courts are already overworked and ill-equipped to deal with such suits, as well as that consumers would be discouraged from bringing such suits.

The lobbying by business interests, nonetheless, paid off in 2005, when Congress passed and Republican president George W. Bush signed into law the Class Action Fairness Act (CAFA). That law moved from state to federal courts large, interstate class action lawsuits brought by consumers against businesses for fraud and faulty products. Under the CAFA, class action suits seeking $5 million or more remain in state courts only if the primary defendant and more than one-third of the plaintiffs are from the same state. Otherwise, if less than one-third of the plaintiffs are from the same state as the defendant and more than $5 million is sought, the case may be filed in a federal district court. The CAFA also limits attorneys' fees when plaintiffs only receive discount coupons on products instead of financial settlements and by linking the fees to the coupon's redemption rate or the actual hours spent working on the case.

In addition, President Bush appointed two members of the Supreme Court—Chief Justice John G. Roberts, Jr., and Justice Samuel Alito—who had records of opposing class action suits. After his 2016 election, President Donald Trump placed Justice Neil Gorsuch on the bench, a well-known conservative that had expressed hostility to class actions in securities' fraud cases. And, in turn, a bare majority of the Roberts Court has moved to limit such lawsuits in several rulings. In *AT&T Mobility v. Concepcion*, 563 U.S. 333 (2011), for example, consumers disputed the validity of a cell phone contract after they were charged $30 in sales tax after buying cellular phone service that they thought would be cost-free. As with many commercial transactions, the contract had a boilerplate mandatory binding arbitration clause, plus another that waived their right to sue in a class action. Still, a bare majority of the Supreme Court ruled that a state law that nullified the waiver in the event of unconscionable (i.e., unenforceable) contract was preempted by the Federal Arbitration Act (FAA), which meant that the consumers had to arbitrate and could not challenge the contract's enforceability in a federal class action. Similarly, in *American Express Company v. Italian Colors Restaurant*, 570 U.S. 228 (2013), the Court, in a 5:3 ruling, prevented a group of merchants from suing American Express for antitrust violations in a class action by strictly enforcing a class action waiver that was included in an arbitration agreement that was governed by the terms of the Federal Arbitration Act. In practical terms, this meant that the merchants had to file for arbitration though individual claims, even though the Court acknowledged that doing so would be cost prohibitive and exceed the amount of damages the merchants hoped to recover. In two subsequent rulings, *Epic Systems v. Lewis*, 138 S. Ct. 1612 (2018) and *Lamps Plus, Inc. v. Varela*, 139 S. Ct. 1407 (2019), the Roberts Court split 5:4 in holding that a mandatory arbitration agreement with a class action waiver under the Federal Arbitration Act prevented an employee for suing on a class-wide basis even though the health care software company may have violated the Fair Labor Standards Act in failing to give him overtime pay (*Epic Systems*); and, that an employee whose tax information was disclosed due to a data breach could not bring a class action against his employer because the arbitration agreement permitting it was ambiguous (*Lamps Plus*).

Moreover, in a widely watched case involving the largest "class action" suit ever, *Wal-Mart Stores, Inc. v. Dukes*, 564 U.S. 338 (2011), a bare majority of the Roberts Court overturned the certification (i.e. approval) of a nationwide class of some 1.5 million female employees of Walmart, who claimed that the company systematically discriminated against them in violation of the Civil Rights Act of 1964. Writing for the Court, Justice Antonin Scalia held that such a class was too large and inconsistent with the federal rules of civil procedure—specifically, Rule 23(a). Walmart has some 3,400 stores across the country (each with its own managers) and therefore was entitled to individual determinations of discrimination and employees' eligibility for back pay. In other words, Rule 23(a) requires showing a commonality that is shared by each member of the class and a single indivisible remedy that provides the same relief to each class member. The Roberts Court's four most liberal members—Justices Ruth Bader Ginsburg, Stephen Breyer, Sonia Sotomayor, and Elena Kagan—agreed that

Rule 23 permits class action suits seeking injunctions or declaratory judgments and does not generally allow claims solely for monetary payments, but otherwise dissented. In their view, the women's lawyers had presented enough evidence "that gender bias suffused Wal-Mart's company culture." Two years later, in rejecting the certification of Comcast cable television subscribers that were suing because of anti-trust violations in *Comcast Company v. Behrend*, 569 U.S. 27 (2013), the Court, in a 5:4 decision written by Justice Scalia and joined by Chief Justice Roberts and Justices Kennedy, Thomas and Alito, made it more difficult for courts to approve of class actions by requiring judges to grant certifications only if "the questions of law or fact common to class members predominate over any questions affecting only individual members" and the "trial court is satisfied, after a rigorous analysis, that the prerequisites" of Rule 23 are followed. In *Comcast*, the class action was thus disallowed because the claimants could not prove that damages could be measured on a class-wide basis.

A majority of the Roberts Court in a few cases has, nonetheless, upheld some class actions. In *Shady Grove Orthopedic Associates, P.A. v. Allstate Insurance Co.*, 559 U.S. 393 (2010), a badly divided Court held that Rule 23 preempted a New York law prohibiting class actions, thus permitting a defendant insurance company to be sued for not paying statutory interest penalties on overdue payments of insurance benefits owed under no-fault automobile insurance policies. Similarly, in *Smith v. Bayer Corporation*, 564 U.S. 299 (2011), a unanimous Court ruled that a lower federal court, after denying class certification, lacked the power to stop a state court from certifying a similar class against the same defendant in a subsequent proceeding. Also, in *Brown v. Plata*, 563 U.S. 493 (2011), Justice Kennedy joined with the four most liberal justices in upholding a class action suit against California prison officials for violating the Eighth Amendment because of prison overcrowding and the conditions of inmates, which required the state to release thousands of inmates and to improve the living conditions of California prisoners.

Besides federal court rulings, furthermore, an important "counter-weight" to Roberts Court rulings that impose new restrictions on the use of class actions are found in state courts, which can use their authority to interpret their respective state constitutions or laws in a fashion to expand access of courts or facilitate the recognition of personal liberties. A study by law professor Zachary Clopton (2018), for example, found that while thirteen state jurisdictions have endorsed *Dukes'* heightened evidentiary standards for class certifications, another six state courts have either expressly rejected them or have questioned their wisdom. Still, critics of the Roberts Courts' class action jurisprudence maintain that it, on balance, represents conservative judicial activism and, as such, increasingly is erasing the substantive rights of consumers and workers while protecting business interests.

Sources: J. Maria Glover, "All Balls and No Strikes: The Roberts Court's Anti-Worker Activism," *Journal of Dispute Resolution* 2019 (2019): 129–40; Zachary Clopton, "Procedural Retrenchment and the States," *California Law Review*, 106 (2018): 411, 434–435; Andrew Nolan, et al., "Judge Neil M. Gorsuch: His Jurisprudence and Potential Impact on the Supreme Court," *Congressional Research Service, March 8, 2017, R44778*, available at https://fas.org/sgp/crs/misc/R44778.pdf (last retrieved April 24, 2020); Robert H. Klonoff, "The Decline of Class Actions," *Washington University Law Review* 90 (2013), 72–830; Christopher P. Banks and John C. Blakeman, *The U.S. Supreme Court and New Federalism: From the Rehnquist to the Roberts Court* (Lanham, Md.: Rowman & Littlefield, 2012); Judith Resnick, "Fairness in Numbers: A Comment on *AT&T v. Concepcion, Wal-Mart v. Dukes,* and *Turner v. Rogers*," *Harvard Law Review* 125 (2011), 78–170.

ALTERNATIVE DISPUTE RESOLUTION

"We must move away from total reliance on the adversary contest for dispute resolution," declared Chief Justice Warren Burger in his 1984 annual state of the judiciary address. "For some disputes," he observed, "trials will be the only means, but for many claims, trials by the adversarial contest must in time go the way of the ancient trial by battle and blood. Our [adversarial] system," he concluded, "is too costly, too painful, too destructive, too inefficient, for a truly civilized people." Notably, the chief justice thought that judicial initiatives to change the federal rules of discovery were a step in the right direction. In other words, they would help counter the perception that lawyers were "hired guns" instead of "healers," an image created by the high cost of litigation, burgeoning caseloads, and the eagerness of attorneys to advertise their services as if they were selling "mustard, cosmetics, laxatives, or used cars."[91]

Chief Justice Burger, however, failed to stress that the alternative dispute resolution (ADR) movement had gained considerable traction in the 1980s after first emerging in the preceding decade. Prompted by his call to study the use of less costly and more efficient methods to resolve disputes at the Pound Conference on the "Causes of Popular Dissatisfaction With the Administration of Justice in 1976," the academic and legal communities began to adopt a variety of nonadversarial alternatives to achieve civil justice. These alternatives promised, among other things, that resolving disputes through non-judicial methods would be a better option because they would enhance access to justice by unburdening courts and therefore increase efficiency, cost savings, flexibility, and party satisfaction.[92] Notably, Chief Justice Burger's support for ADR was the backdrop for law professor Frank Sander's seminal lecture, delivered at the Pound Conference, suggesting that a "multi-door" courthouse be created, a reform that would allow clients to pick among a range of ADR options, including arbitration, mediation, and neutral third-party fact-finding, to resolve conflicts. This would be accomplished by creating a courthouse intake screening unit that would evaluate the dispute and try to resolve it by telephone conciliation or by supplying additional information. If the intake officers could not settle the case informally, then the litigants would be referred to the most appropriate "door" (e.g. arbitration, conciliation, mediation, or adjudication) for resolution within the courthouse. Using this structure, Sanders envisioned that the courthouse is the central location for not only diagnosing the nature of the disputes, but also providing a place for resolving them under one roof. The heightened academic interest in ADR ultimately pushed the ABA and the nation's law schools to incorporate ADR into their agendas and graduate school curricula.[93] Table 8.5 illustrates alternative dispute resolution and settlement practices.

Table 8.5	Alternative Dispute Resolution and Settlement Practices
Method	**Principal Elements**
Arbitration	• Quasi-formal adjudicatory process in which third-party neutral arbitrator evaluates competing positions and issues decision after adversary hearing conducted by attorneys representing each side under relaxed rules of evidence, with no witnesses; but documents can be submitted for arbitrator's review • Can be binding or nonbinding • Can be private or court-connected • Most often used in labor/management, construction contract, consumer protection, and medical malpractice disputes
Mediation	• Flexible, informal nonbinding process in which third-party neutral mediator facilitates communication between parties in confidential session in order to reach voluntary settlement • Mediator ordinarily does not issue opinion or finding of facts • Can be private or court-connected • Has wide applicability in general civil cases, but popular in labor/management and family law cases
Early Neutral Evaluation	• Informal, nonbinding process in which a third-party neutral, usually an experienced attorney with expertise in subject matter in dispute, evaluates each side's case in a confidential session with parties and counsel shortly after the lawsuit is filed and before discovery is completed

	• Designed to improve case planning and facilitate settlement prospects • Ordinarily court-connected • Has wide applicability in general civil cases
Summary Jury Trials	• Nonbinding, informal adjudicatory process, supervised by judge or magistrate, using nonbinding abbreviated trials by mock jurors chosen from the jury pool • Evidence presented to jury by counsel in summary form and usually witnesses are not called • Jury evaluates competing positions and issues advisory decision that is used to facilitate settlement in trial-ready cases • Court-connected • Has wide applicability in general civil cases
Mini-trials	• Flexible, informal nonbinding process in which each side presents, in front of a third-party neutral, its case in abbreviated form to settlement-authorized representatives of disputing parties, with relaxed rules of evidence and no witnesses • Its primary use is to facilitate settlement between company's senior executives • Can be private or court-connected • Most often used in complex business litigation
Settlement Conferences	• Judge- or magistrate-hosted conference, held pursuant to court rules, between opposing counsel in order to explore settlement options • Court-connected Has wide applicability in general civil cases
Online Dispute Resolution	• Informal, flexible, Internet-based online dispute resolution process, including arbitration, mediation, and other complaint-driven processes (e.g., escrow arrangements, complaint bulletin boards) • Ordinarily private, but method is still evolving and could expand to courts • Ordinarily used in business disputes between sellers and customers, or business-to-business disputes, relative to online transactions

Sources: Elizabeth Plapinger and Donna Stienstra, *ADR and Settlement in the Federal District Courts: A Sourcebook for Judges & Lawyers* (Washington, D.C.: Federal Judicial Center, 1996), 60–69; Henry H. Perritt, Jr., "Dispute Resolution in Cyberspace: Demand for New Forms of ADR," *Ohio State Journal on Dispute Resolution* 15 (2000), 675–703.

Over time, ADR has become an institutionalized element in the United States and in other legal systems throughout the world (see "In Comparative Perspective: The Global Expansion of ADR"). In the public sector, over 1,200 ADR programs have been established by or in conjunction with state courts as "court-connected" or closely related community initiatives that work with public officials. ADR's ubiquity is illustrated in several ways. Nearly twenty states, for example, have signed on to the Interstate Medical Licensure Compact, or legislation requiring physicians to participate in mediation or an alternative form of binding dispute resolution in conflicts relating to licensure requests by physicians seeking to practice medicine in multiple states in an attempt to increase health care access for patients in under-served or rural areas—those laws would thus impact how the disputes of roughly 726,000 physicians are resolved.[94] Furthermore, in Florida, nearly twenty-four thousand individuals have been trained as mediators to assist in administering at least one hundred different mediation programs.[95] In other states, ADR is seen as an attractive fiscal solution to cut costs and increase state revenues. In North Dakota, agricultural mediation services were expanded in order to help oil businesses resolve mineral rights disputes more efficiently, thus encouraging economic development; but, in Connecticut, a large spike in mortgage defaults prompted the state to provide homeowner mediation services with banks; and, in New Jersey, caps were placed on arbitration awards given to public safety workers as a means to save money.[96] Finally, many state courts have experimented with or adopted a wide variety of ADR tools, including mediation, early neutral evaluation, arbitration, settlement conferences, and summary jury trials, as part of their adjudication processes or by issuing ADR referrals to private entities.[97]

On the national level, Congress has supported the use of ADR in the federal courts by enacting the Civil Justice Reform Act of 1990 (CJRA) and the Alternative Dispute Resolution Act of 1998 (ADRA). Whereas the CJRA simply encouraged the use of ADR methods with the help of funding incentives, the CJRA mandated that trial courts provide ADR services to civil litigants. At least thirty-four districts authorize the use of at least two ADR methods. Typically, these districts allow mediation and early neutral evaluation, or arbitration and mediation, or sometimes all three methods. To be sure, districts vary considerably in how they use ADR. Whereas some districts allow mediation only, other districts vest power in the courts to use mediation, arbitration, early neutral evaluation, or settlement conferences. As well, several districts authorize other ADR methods, including summary jury trials and case evaluations (a quasi-arbitration method that is used in cases arising under state law, and using state tribunals). Another innovation is establishing mediation programs for *pro se* litigants. Furthermore, in a majority of districts the judge has the discretion to make an ADR referral, and most districts put the onus of paying for the fees of the third-party mediator on the parties.[98]

As in the state courts, ADR's impact is considerable in the federal judiciary. One study analyzing data from forty-nine federal district courts showed that roughly twenty-eight thousand cases were processed by using ADR programs, with mediation remaining the most popular choice. Similarly, ADR has gained a significant foothold in the federal executive branch, as Justice Department lawyers have turned to it in many cases. Also, it is widely adopted in the private sector because there are a plethora of fee-based companies offering ADR services, and a growing number of corporations have institutionalized arbitration, mediation, and other in-house grievance procedures as preferred methods to deal with workplace conflict. Some organizations, too, have established "conflict management systems" for handling employee and customer disputes. Finally, standardized provisions for binding arbitration (in lieu of pursuing court lawsuits) are now widely used in consumer goods, securities brokerage, construction, and employment contracts as well.[99]

The institutionalization of ADR does not mean it is immune from criticism and ongoing political debate, however. Proponents of ADR observe that the methods are advantageous because: (1) they give disputants more control over managing their personal conflict; (2) they protect individual privacy by using confidential sessions; and, (3) they reduce the time, cost, and delay associated with dispute adjudication. On the other hand, opponents counter that: (1) they are too cumbersome and slow; (2) they are prone to selecting third-party neutrals that are biased; and, (3) they remain unproven methods that do not considerably save time or cost in processing disputes. In criticizing summary trials, Judge Richard Posner adds another general objection. The benefits of privacy and confidentiality are outweighed by the cost of having the credibility of witnesses evaluated by the judge or jury in public proceedings that determine the facts underlying disputes.[100] A related criticism by law professor Owen Fiss argues that courts, as public institutions, must remain the primary venue for resolving legal disputes because they are in the best position to articulate public values and the law's meaning, a vital duty that courts must not relinquish to private entities or parties interested only in reaching settlements.[101]

ADR is also controversial as a political issue. The wide popularity of using arbitration in commercial transactions, for example, has come under sharp attack as the nation becomes more polarized and divided over the scope of consumer and worker rights in corporate industry. During the Obama administration, the

Consumer Financial Protection Bureau (CFPB) exercised its rulemaking authority under the 2010 Dodd-Frank Wall Street and Consumer Protection Act to prevent banks and credit card companies from banning class action lawsuits in mandatory arbitration agreements. The 2017 CFPB rule was promulgated, in part, after a CFPB study showed that consumers rarely filed individual arbitration actions even though millions of citizens were affected by arbitration clauses in credit card and checking account contracts. In response, banks and conservative special interest groups sued in federal court to stop the rule's enforcement and, after Trump's election, the Treasury Department released its own study in opposition to the Rule's findings and methodology. Thereafter, at Trump's urging, the Republican-controlled Congress reversed the CFPB rule under the Congressional Review Act, legislation that permits the reversal of federal regulations enacted in opposition to legislative prerogatives. As one regulatory expert observed, Congress' action prevented federal regulators in the future from adopting a similar authorization of class action lawsuits in subsequent rulemaking without congressional approval; and, that it was "revealing" that Congress acted so swiftly to negate a recently enacted rule that was issued by an independent agency (CFPB) that was, at the time, still under the leadership of Richard Cordray, an Obama appointee. Regardless, the politics surrounding the CFPB is part of a larger ideological battle that has been waged between conservatives and liberals in the Trump administration over the constitutionality of the CFPB's leadership structure and whether Presidents have the executive authority to remove its single director "at will"—a question that the Supreme Court answered in the affirmative, while also ruling that the CFPB can continue to exist as an independent agency in *Seila Law LLC v. Consumer Financial Protection Bureau*, a case decided by the Roberts Court at the end of its 2019–20 Term.[102]

In all likelihood, the debate over ADR will not lessen anytime soon. Still, it is clear that ADR has found acceptance in the legal culture and remains a viable choice for litigants. Although published reports and research often divide on the question of whether ADR is actually less costly and time-intensive than adversary trials, it appears that disputants often receive significant personal satisfaction from ADR procedures. However, the greatest danger to ADR may be not that it works, but rather that such methods become more like the traditional adversary method they are replacing. As one court watcher put it: "As lawyers have colonized the ADR field, they have made its processes more comfortable for them [and arbitrations] look more and more like trials," replete with formal rules, extensive discovery, and a variety of scheduling and case backlog problems.[103] If that trend continues, the promise that ADR remains less infused with formal legal processes and lawyering or courts will eventually evaporate.

In Comparative Perspective: The Global Expansion of ADR

Although most legal systems rely upon courts to resolve legal conflicts, a growing worldwide trend has been toward the adoption of "alternative dispute resolution" (ADR) methods. The movement to ADR is prompted by many of the same concerns that plague the administration of justice in the United States—high litigation costs and extensive delay, along with a general frustration that invoking the legal system will not yield tangible or fair results. Either in conjunction with or apart from the courts, ADR offers would-be litigants the flexible choice of using mediation, conciliation, arbitration, or other tools of conflict resolution to settle public or private disputes that threaten to disrupt the social peace. Its distinctly Anglo-Saxon origin has allowed ADR to become more readily infused into common law jurisdictions such as the United Kingdom, Canada, and Australia. Even so, other regions that are influenced by civil law or have hybrid legal systems, such as Indonesia, India, and Japan, have begun to incorporate ADR into their legal cultures to varying degrees.

In the United States, ADR was originally conceived as embracing a "multi-door" approach that let courts assist disputants' access to compulsory or nonmandatory ADR options. Once a lawsuit was filed, the judiciary referred parties to multiple ADR "doors" or pathways to resolve differences. Over time, the United States and other common law systems have increasingly adopted a "multi-option" response, which situates ADR services within or outside the formal court system, either before or after litigation has commenced. A hallmark of the multi-option approach is to encourage or require the parties to use ADR as a first option before going to court. In the United Kingdom, either on its own accord or if a party requests it, courts can leverage parties into using mediation by (1) issuing a "stay" upon the proceedings, which suspends court action until mediation is tried, or (2) issuing a cost-sanction order that makes litigants assume the costs of litigation if they unreasonably refuse to mediate. Similarly, in many Australian courts, disputants must file a "genuine steps" statement outlining the efforts they have taken to resolve conflicts before filing a suit. Such pre-action initiatives typically involve taking advantage of ADR services that are available outside of the legal system, another characteristic of the multi-door design. Moreover, as in the United Kingdom, the failure to comply will not nullify the action, but it will be taken into account when deciding who should bear litigation costs.

Formal and informal ADR methods are also being used as a flexible and multifaceted conflict resolution tool across a variety of civil law jurisdictions and mixed legal systems. In India and Indonesia, traditional forms of community mediation are still practiced, but increasingly they are supplemented or blended into other ADR mechanisms that are statutorily defined and available for use either in or out of court. Under the Legal Services Authorities Act of 1987, Indian disputants may reach judicial settlements under *Lok Adalat* (People's Court) procedures, a type of adjudication that was widely used in ancient India. *Lok Adalats* are different than regular Indian courts because their judges, acting as conciliators and without the constraint of formal procedural rules, can directly interact with the parties in an effort to persuade them to settle, using principles of fair play and simple justice. While Indian law also recognizes the binding effect of arbitration agreements and the use of conciliation or mediation in specialized areas of commercial trade or domestic affairs, *Lok Adalats* are responsible for resolving millions of minor civil and criminal cases. Likewise, while the Indonesian legal system embraces arbitration and other ADR methods, such as negotiation, conciliation, and receiving "expert judgment" (or a legal opinion by an arbitral body), it also has a steep tradition in settling private disputes and minor criminal cases through *Adat law* (customary law) mediation techniques. Used in rural and indigenous societies, *Adat* functionaries cajole parties to enter into "consent agreements," or "*musyawarah-mufakat*," that restore social peace and spiritual balance through receipt of statements of regret, acts of community service, or the payment of fines and compensation to victims.

A final characteristic of the growing global ADR movement is the proliferation of sophisticated administrative regulations and specialized "centres" that typically, but not exclusively, address arbitration cases. The United Nations Commission on International Trade Law (UNCITRAL) Model Law of 1985 and its 2006 amendments have become a major influence in regularizing domestic and international commercial arbitration standards across the globe, especially in civil law countries seeking to modernize their legal systems. The emergence of centers has had the same effect.

Sources: *Global Perspectives on ADR*, edited by Carlos Esplugues and Silvia Barona (Cambridge, U.K.: Intersentia, 2014); Bernadine Van Gramberg, *Managing Workplace Conflicts: Alternative Dispute Resolution in Australia* (Sydney, New South Wales, Australia: Federation Press, 2006); United Nations Commission on International Trade, "UNCITRAL Model Law on International Commercial Arbitration (1985), with amendments as adopted in 2006," available at http://www.uncitral.org/uncitral/en/uncitral_texts/arbitration/1985Model_arbitration.html (last retrieved April 24, 2020); Naoki, Idei, Japan Commercial Arbitration Association, "The Nuclear Damage Claim Dispute Resolution Center," *JCAA Newsletter* 28 (September 2012), available at https://www.yumpu.com/en/document/view/26661892/no28-september-2012-pdf (last retrieved July 3, 2020); and U.S.

Department of Justice, "September 11th Victim Compensation Fund," available at https://www.justice.gov/civil/vcf (last retrieved April 24, 2020).

Chapter Summary

The nature of the civil justice system is largely defined by rules of civil procedure. Civil litigation is complicated and arcane and has been criticized for fostering litigiousness, excessive cost, and delay. But there is little empirical evidence to support that view. Nearly 70 percent of trial cases involve civil litigation, typically resolving tort, contract, and real estate disputes. The status of civil litigants, whether they are "repeat players" with extensive resources and litigation experience or "one-shotters" who have less means and exposure to court processes, often helps repeat players to prevail in trial courts. In all civil actions, the parties in the litigation ask for legal remedies that usually involve monetary damages.

Once a civil lawsuit is filed, the trial and appeal process begins with the filing of the complaint and the receipt of an answer to the allegations and any relevant counterclaims. Cases move to the trial stage with the exchange of pleadings through pretrial motion practice that is premised on a theory of "notice pleading," or simply giving the opposing party just enough information to mount a legal defense. Still, a growing trend is the adoption of heightened, or more particularized, "fact-based" pleading. The movement toward fact-based pleading is significant because it increases the likelihood that the case will end through summary dispositions that have the effect of replacing jury trials. Key pretrial activities consist of filing discovery motions, such as interrogatories, requests for production, and requests to take depositions. In conjunction with the discovery process, pretrial conferences are used to clarify issues, set deadlines, and explore negotiated settlements. Cases that are not settled move to trial, final judgment, and appeal.

Whether the civil litigation system is broken or unfair has generated calls for tort and related civil justice reform, including the use of "alternative dispute resolution" (ADR) methods. The debate over reform is highly contentious and politicized. Conservative groups favor imposing caps on jury awards, limiting damage awards, and restricting class actions in order to protect business interests. By contrast, liberals and trial lawyers generally oppose those reforms because they would not keep large corporations accountable for their misfeasance and would deny victims access to courts. The politics surrounding civil litigation reforms has resulted in the enactment of state and federal reform legislation and Supreme Court decisions that restrict damages, attorneys' fees, and class actions. Moreover,

ADR services, which include arbitration, mediation, early neutral evaluation, summary jury trials, and other mechanisms that are used in or out of court, are widely available in the states and the federal government. There is a growing trend to adopt ADR around the world. But an unresolved question is whether ADR is sustainable in light of the criticism that it is not that much better than the much-maligned civil justice system it is designed to replace.

Key Questions for Review and Critical Analysis

1. A long-standing criticism of the civil justice system is that it is too costly, delay ridden, unfair, and inhibits access to the courts. The use of contingency fees has been widely accepted, though heavily criticized, as a means to facilitate court access. The rise of third-party litigation funding is not widely accepted and has been subject to criticisms. Should third-party funding of lawsuits be just as accepted as the contingency fee? Why or why not?

2. Heightened pleading requirements, such as substituting the "fact-based" pleading found in civil litigation complaints for the "notice-based" requirements, are politically controversial. But why is that so? What underlying values linked to civil justice are at risk with heightened pleading requirements?

3. What are the strengths and weaknesses of permitting class action lawsuits? Should they be further restricted and, if so, in what ways and why?

4. Is it a fair criticism to assert that the civil justice system must be reformed because "litigation costs too much," or that "justice delayed is justice denied"?

5. Which specific "alternative dispute resolution" (ADR) methods appear reasonable, and why? Also, has the use of ADR become too politicized in a national government that is characterized by polarization and intractable political divisions?

Web Links

1. Federal Rules of Practice and Procedure (www.uscourts.gov/RulesAnd Policies/rules.aspx)

   • The Administrative Office of the U.S. Courts provides information about the federal rulemaking process and access to the current rules of federal practice and procedure, pending and proposed amendments.

2.   American Tort Reform Association (www.atra.org/about/mission)

   •   A national organization devoted to enacting tort and civil justice reform. It provides information about current tort reform issues, plus legislative proposals and related research.

3.   American Association for Justice (www.justice.org)

   •   An association of trial lawyers that provides general news, resources, and research.

4.   American Arbitration Association (www.adr.org) and the International Centre for Dispute Resolution (www.icdr.org)

   •   The American Arbitration Association and its global counterpart provide information about rules and procedures, annual reports, forms, and educational research links.

Selected Readings

Bornstein, Brian H., Richard L. Wiener, Robert F. Schopp, and Steven L. Willborn, eds. *Civil Juries and Civil Justice: Psychological and Legal Perspectives*. New York: Springer, 2008.

Burch, Chamblee Elizabeth. *Mass Tort Deals: Backroom Bargaining in Multidistrict Litigation*. New York: Cambridge University Press, 2019.

Croley, Steven P. *Civil Justice Reconsidered: Toward a Less Costly, More Accessible Litigation System*. New York: New York University Press, 2017.

Daniels, Stephen and Joanne Martin. *Tort Reform, Plaintiffs' Lawyers, and Access to Justice*. Lawrence, KS.: University of Kansas Press, 2015.

Doherty, Joseph, Robert T. Reville, and Laura Zakaras, eds. *Confidentially, Transparency, and the U.S. Civil Justice System*. New York: Oxford University Press, 2012.

Engel, David M. *The Myth of the Litigious Society: Why We Don't Sue*. Chicago: University of Chicago Press, 2016.

Esplugues, Carlos, and Silvia Barona, eds. *Global Perspectives on ADR*. Cambridge, U.K.: Intersentia, 2014.

Farhang Sean. *Litigation State: Public Regulation and Private Lawsuits in the U.S.* Princeton, N.J.: Princeton University Press, 2010.

Haltom, William, and Michael McCann. *Distorting the Law: Politics, Media, and the Litigation Crisis*. Chicago: University of Chicago Press, 2004.

Hans, Valerie P. Business on *Trial: The Civil Jury and Corporate Responsibility*. New Haven, Conn.: Yale University Press, 2000.

Kagan, Robert A. *Adversarial Legalism: The American Way of Law*. Cambridge, Mass.: Harvard University Press, 2001.

Kritzer, Herbert M. *Let's Make a Deal: Understanding the Negotiation Process in Ordinary Litigation*. Madison: University of Wisconsin Press, 1991.

Kritzer, Herbert M. *Risks, Reputations, and Rewards*. Stanford, Calif.: Stanford University Press, 2004.

Kritzer, Herbert M., and Susan S. Silbey, eds. *In Litigation: Do the "Haves" Still Come Out Ahead?* Stanford, Calif.: Stanford Law and Politics, 2003.

Lahav, Alexandra D. *In Praise of Litigation*. New York: Oxford University Press, 2017.

McGarity, Thomas O. *The Preemption War: When Federal Bureaucracies Trump Local Juries*. New Haven, Conn.: Yale University Press, 2008.

Nagareda, Richard A. *Mass Torts in a World of Settlement*. Chicago: University Press of Chicago, 2007.

Redish, Martin H. *Wholesale Justice: Constitutional Democracy and the Problem of the Class Action Lawsuit*. Stanford, Calif.: Stanford Law Books, 2009.

Shapo, Marshall S. *An Injury Law Constitution*. New York: Oxford University Press, 2012.

Staszak, Sarah. *No Day in Court: Access to Justice and the Politics of Judicial Retrenchment*. New York: Oxford University Press, 2015.

Yeazell, Stephen C. *Lawsuits in a Market Economy: The Evolution of Civil Litigation*. Chicago: University of Chicago Press, 2018.

Endnotes

1   Cleveland Clinic, "Uterine Prolapse," available at https://my.clevelandclinic.org/health/diseases/16030-vaginal-and-uterine-prolapse (last retrieved April 23, 2020). See also, Drugwatcher, "Transvaginal Mesh Lawsuit Cases Updates 2020," https://www.drugwatcher.org/transvaginal-mesh/ (last retrieved April 23, 2020).

2   Matthew Goldstein, "As Pelvic Mesh Settlements Near $8 Billion, Women Question Lawyers' Fees," *N.Y. Times (February 1, 2019)*, available at https://www.nytimes.com/2019/02/01/business/pelvic-mesh-settlements-lawyers.html (last retrieved April 23, 2020); Editorial Board, "80,000 Deaths. 2 Million Injuries: It's Time for a Reckoning on Medical Devices," *N.Y. Times (May 4, 2019)*, available at https://www.nytimes.com/2019/05/04/opinion/sunday/medical-devices.html?searchResultPosition=1 (last retrieved April 23, 2020); Sheila Kaplan and Matthew Goldstein, "F.D.A. Halts U.S. Sales of Pelvic Mesh, Citing Safety Concerns for Women," *N.Y. Times (April 16, 2019)*, available at https://www.nytimes.com/2019/04/16/health/vaginal-

pelvic-mesh-fda.html?module=inline (last retrieved April 23, 2020); Drugwatcher, "Transvaginal Mesh Lawsuit Cases Updates 2019".

3   Tina Bellon, "J&J, Bayer Deny Liability But Settle 25,000 Xarelto Lawsuits for $775 Million," *Insurance Journal (March 26, 2019)*, available at https://www.insurancejournal.com/news/national/2019/03/26/521650. htm (last retrieved April 23, 2020); CBS News, "Veterans claim defective 3M earplugs caused hearing loss, ringing in ears: "It is torture," *CBS This Morning (March 12, 2019)*, available at https://www.cbsnews.com/ news/military-veterans-claim-defective-3m-earplugs-caused-hearing-loss/ (last retrieved April 23, 2020); Peter Eavis, "PG&E Says It Probably Caused the Fire That Destroyed Paradise, Calif.," *N.Y. Times (February 28, 2019)*, available at https://www.nytimes.com/2019/02/28/business/energy-environment/pge-camp-fire. html?searchResultPosition=1 (last retrieved April 23, 2020). See also, Michael A. Fletcher and Rebecca Robbins, "GM Offers Millions to Compensate Some Ignition Switch Victims, Families," *Washington Post* (June 30, 2014), available at www.washingtonpost.com (last retrieved April 23, 2020); Hilary Stout and Bill Vlasic, "G.M. Suits Will Proceed as One Case in New York," *New York Times* (June 9, 2014), available at www.nytimes. com (last retrieved April 23, 2020).

4   Goldstein, "As Pelvic Mesh Settlements Near $8 Billion, Women Question Lawyers' Fees" (reporting, as well, that some lawyer contracts allow for expense reimbursement of meals, hotels, and even private plan travel, along with to outside companies voluminous document reviews of patient medical records).

5   American Bar Association, Judicial Division Lawyers Conference, "Perceptions of Justice: A Dialogue on Race, Ethnicity, and the Courts (2006–2011): Summary Report," available at www.americanbar.org (last retrieved June 13, 2014); American Bar Association Section of Litigation, "Public Perceptions of Lawyers: Consumer Research Findings (April 2002)," available at www.cliffordlaw.com/abaillinoisstatedelegate/public perceptions1.pdf (last retrieved June 13, 2004), 4. See also American Bar Association, "Perceptions of the U.S. Legal System," available at www.abanet.org/media/perception/perceptions.pdf (last retrieved November 18, 2004) (Table 4), 115 (reporting that 74 percent of those surveyed thought lawyers were more committed to winning their cases than guaranteeing that justice was served; 73 percent believed lawyers spent too much time trying to get criminal defendants released on legal technicalities; and 69 percent asserted lawyers were more interested in making money than in representing clients).

6   David M. Trubeck, Austin Sarat, William L. F. Felstiner, Herbert M. Kritzer, and Joel B. Grossman, "The Cost of Ordinary Litigation," *UCLA Law Review* 31 (1983), 72, 76.

7   John B. Oakley, "A Fresh Look at the Federal Rules in State Court," *Nevada Law Journal* 3 (2003), 354, 355 (finding that "not only has the trend toward state conformity to the federal rules stopped accelerating—it has substantially reversed itself").

8   Arthur R. Miller, "Pleading and Pretrial Motions: What Would Judge Clark Do?" (Prepared for the 2010 Litigation Review Conference, May 10–11, 2010, Duke Law School, Revised April 12, 2010), available at www.uscourts.gov (last retrieved June 18, 2014), 1.

9   *Liebeck v. McDonald's Restaurants, P.T.S., Inc.*, No. D–202 CV–93–02419, 1995 WL 360309 (Bernalillo County, N.M. Dist. Ct. August 18, 1994). See also, Haltom William and Michael McCann, *Distorting the Law: Politics, Media, and the Litigation Crisis* (Chicago: University of Chicago Press, 2004), 186, 193, 208; Bonnie Bertram, "Storm Still Brews Over Scalding Coffee," *New York Times* (October 25, 2013), available at www. nytimes.com (last retrieved June 20, 2014) (reporting damages reduction and that a documentary about the case shown in 2013 still generated commentary that reiterated "their erroneous understanding of the case, [with] some [commentators] castigating Ms. Liebeck as foolish for driving with liquid she must have known would be hot").

10   Jason Slotkin, "Monkey Selfie' Lawsuit Ends With Settlement Between PETA, Photographer," *NPR* (September 12, 2017), available at https://www.npr.org/sections/thetwo-way/2017/09/12/550417823/-animal-rights-advocates-photographer-compromise-over-ownership-of-monkey-selfie (last retrieved April 23, 2020); Richard Brisbin and John Kilwein, *Real Law Stories: Inside the Judicial Process* (New York: Oxford University Press, 2010), 1; Laura Ly, "Student's Lawsuit Against Parents for Support Loses First Round in Court," *CNN Justice* (March 5, 2014), available at www.cnn.com (last retrieved June 20, 2014).

11   See, e.g., Walter K. Olson, *The Litigation Explosion: What Happened When America Unleashed the Lawsuit* (New York: Thomas Talley Books-Dutton, 1991); Walter K. Olson, *The Rule of Lawyers: How the New Litigation Elite Threatens America's Rule of Law* (New York: St. Martin's Press, 2003).

12   Trubeck, Sarat, Felstiner, Kritzer, and Grossman, "The Cost of Ordinary Litigation," 83–84.

13   Brisbin and Kilwein, *Real Law Stories: Inside the Judicial Process*, 15.

14 Trubeck, Sarat, Felstiner, Kritzer, and Grossman, "The Cost of Ordinary Litigation," 81–84 (examining 1,649 civil lawsuits and interviewing 1,812 lawyers who brought them). Other studies that involve far fewer respondent lawyers ($n = 202$) that handled automobile, premises liability, real estate, contract, employment, and malpractice cases find that the most time is spent on trials (if the case proceeds that far) and in engaging in discovery. Paula Hannaford-Agor and Nicole L. Waters, "Estimating the Cost of Civil Litigation," *Court Statistics Project (National Center for State Courts)* 20 (January 1, 2013), 1–7, available at https://ncsc.contentdm.oclc.org/digital/collection/civil/id/94/ (last retrieved July 2, 2020).

15 Paula Hannaford-Agor and Nicole L. Waters, "Estimating the Cost of Civil Litigation," *Court Statistics Project (National Center for State Courts)* 20 (January 1, 2013), 1–7, available at https://ncsc.contentdm.oclc.org/digital/collection/civil/id/94/ (last retrieved July 2, 2020).

16 U.S. Chamber of Commerce, Institute for Legal Reform, *Costs and Compensation of the U.S. Tort System (October 2018)*, available at https://www.instituteforlegalreform.com/uploads/sites/1/Tort_costs_paper_FINAL_WEB.pdf (last retrieved April 23, 2020).

17 Judge John G. Koeltl, a district court judge from the Southern District of New York, made these remarks at a symposium at the Cardozo School of Law in 2017. See Symposium, "Controlling the High Cost of Justice: Perspectives from the Federal Judiciary," *Cardozo Law Review* 40 (2018): 271, 279–280. Koeltl made his comments by referencing a 2009 Federal Judicial Center study by Emery G. Lee III & Thomas E. Willging, "Preliminary Report to the Judicial Conference Advisory Committee on Civil Rules," *Federal Judicial Center (October 2009)*, available at https://www.fjc.gov/sites/default/files/materials/08/CivilRulesSurvey2009.pdf (last retrieved April 23, 2020).

18 See, e.g., Mark Galanter, "Reading the Landscape of Disputes: What We Know and Don't Know (and Think We Know) About Our Allegedly Contentious and Litigious Society," *University of California Los Angeles Law Review* 31 (1983), 4–71. For the reasons underlying the expansion of liability, see Haltom and McCann, *Distorting the Law: Politics, Media, and the Litigation Crisis*, 36–38.

19 Alexandra D. Lahav, *In Praise of Litigation* (New York: Oxford University Press, 2017).

20 Marc Galanter, "The Vanishing Trial: An Examination of Trials and Related Matters in Federal and State Courts," *Journal of Empirical Legal Studies* 1 (2004), 459–570.

21 Brisbin and Kilwein, *Real Law Stories: Inside the Judicial Process*, 2. The composition and comparison of state and federal civil caseloads is found in National Center for State Courts, *Composition of Incoming Cases, All Trial Courts, 2016*, available at http://www.courtstatistics.org/~/media/Microsites/Files/CSP/National-Overview-2016/EWSC-2016-Overview-Page-4-Comp.ashx (last retrieved April 23, 2020); Administrative Office of the U.S. Courts, "Federal Judicial Caseload Statistics, 2019," available at https://www.uscourts.gov/statistics-reports/federal-judicial-caseload-statistics-2019 (last retrieved April 23, 2020).

22 National Center for State Courts, "Contract Cases Dominate Civil Caseloads, 2015." In *Examining the Work of State Courts: An Overview of 2015 State Court Caseloads*, 6. https://ncsc.contentdm.oclc.org/digital/collection/ctadmin/id/2177/ (last retrieved July 2, 2020); and, Brisbin and Kilwein, *Real Law Stories: Inside the Judicial Process*, 245 (reporting findings from an interview with a Michigan state trial judge).

23 Sean Farhang, *Litigation State: Public Regulation and Private Lawsuits in the U.S.* (Princeton, N.J.: Princeton University Press, 2010).

24 John Scalia, "Prisoner Petitions Filed in U.S. District Court, 2000, With Trends 1980–2000 (January 2002, NCJ 189430)," available at www.bjs.gov (last retrieved June 20, 2014).

25 Marc Galanter, "Why the 'Haves' Come Out Ahead: Speculations on the Limits of Legal Change," *Law and Society Review* 9 (1974), 95, 114–19.

26 Ibid., 97–104.

27 See, e.g., Paul Brace and Melinda Gann Hall, " 'Haves' Versus 'Have Nots' in State Supreme Courts: Allocating Docket Space and Wins in Power Asymmetric Cases," *Law and Society Review* 35 (2001), 393–417; Terence Dunworth and Joel Rogers, "Corporations in Court: Big Business Litigation in U.S. Federal Courts, 1971–1991," *Law and Social Inquiry* 21(1996), 497–592; C. K. Rowland and Bridget Jeffery Todd, "Where You Stand Depends on Who Sits: Platform Promises and Judicial Gatekeeping in the Federal District Courts," *Journal of Politics* 53 (1991), 175–85. See also Ryan C. Black and Christina L. Boyd, "US Supreme Court Agenda Setting and the Role of Litigant Status," *Journal of Law, Economics and Organization* 28 (2010), 286, 287 (concluding that most "merit stage" litigant status studies have "found that parties with greater levels of status are more likely to have judicial success").

[28]   Galanter, "Why the 'Haves' Come Out Ahead," 114–19.

[29]   Carrie J. Menkel-Meadow and Bryant G. Garth, "Civil Procedure and Courts," in *The Oxford Handbook of Empirical Legal Research*, edited by Peter Cane and Herbert M. Kritzer (New York: Oxford University Press, 2010), 679, 687; Brace and Hall, " 'Haves' Versus 'Have Nots' in State Supreme Courts: Allocating Docket Space and Wins in Power Asymmetric Cases," 393, 409; Charles R. Epp, *The Rights Revolution: Lawyers, Activists, and Supreme Courts in Comparative Perspective* (Chicago: University of Chicago Press, 1998).

[30]   Robert A. Kagan, *Adversarial Legalism: The American Way of Law* (Cambridge, Mass.: Harvard University Press, 2001), 120–21.

[31]   U.S. Chamber of Commerce, Institute for Legal Reform, *Unstable Foundation: Our Broken Class Action System and How to Fix It (October 2017),* available at https://www.instituteforlegalreform.com/uploads/sites/1/UnstableFoundation_Web_10242017.pdf (last retrieved April 23, 2020). The quote from Justice Douglas is found in J.D. Moore, "The Heightened Standard of Ascertainability: An Unnecessary Hurdle to Class Action Certification," *Penn State Law Review* 122 (2017): 247.

[32]   Richard A. Nagareda, *Mass Torts in a World of Settlement* (Chicago: University Press of Chicago, 2007), viii.

[33]   See Tammy B. Webb and Ina D. Chang, "Drawing the Line Between Class Action and Quasi-Class Action" (*ABA Section of Litigation, Mass Torts,* November 13, 2012), available at https://www.americanbar.org/groups/litigation/committees/mass-torts/articles/2012/fall2012-1112-drawing-the-line-class-action-quasi-class-action/ (last retrieved July 2, 2020). See also Tracey E. George and Margaret S. Williams, "Venue Shopping: The Judges of the U.S. Panel on Multidistrict Litigation," *Judicature* 97 (2014), 196–205.

[34]   The 9/11 settlement fund was relatively unique because it was a political response enacted only eleven days after the terrorist attacks, before any tort lawsuits were filed. Also, designed as a "preemptive" measure, roughly 97 percent of survivors of those killed chose the administrative settlement (coming out of public instead of private funds) over filing a tort lawsuit. Nagareda, *Mass Torts in a World of Settlement,* 102–6. Although unique, analogous settlement funds (though paid with private monies) have appeared in other disaster compensation cases (Boston Marathon bombing, Sandy Hook elementary school, Aurora, Colorado, and Virginia Tech mass shootings, and 1995 Oklahoma federal building bombing), that directly or indirectly implicate, but raise many unresolved questions about, the prospective or actual mass filings of tort lawsuits and their compensatory implications. See Ben Berkowitz, "Uncertainty Surrounds Compensation for Boston Bomb Victims," Reuters (April 17, 2013), available at www.reuters.com (last retrieved May 31, 2019).

[35]   Victoria Shannon Sahani, "Judging Third Party Funding," *U.C.L.A. Law Review,* 63 (2016): 388, 392–395.

[36]   Christopher Hodges, John Peysner, and Angus Nurse, "Litigation Funding: Status and Issues (Research Report, January 2012)," available at https://www.law.ox.ac.uk/sites/files/oxlaw/litigation_funding_here_1_0.pdf (last retrieved April 23, 2020).

[37]   Jonathan T. Molot. "Litigation Finance: A Market Solution to a Procedural Problem," *Georgetown Law Journal* 99 (2010): 65–115.

[38]   Maya Steinitz, "Whose Claim Is This Anyway? Third-Party Litigation Funding," *Minnesota Law Review* 95 (2011), 1268, 1270–71.

[39]   Sahani, "Judging Third Party Funding," 396–398.

[40]   James Batson, *Key Issues in Litigation Finance (a Bentham IMF publication presented at a 'Third Party Litigation conference, held in November 2018, by Georgetown Law School),* available at https://www.law.gwu.edu/sites/g/files/zaxdzs2351/f/downloads/bentham-imf-guide-to-key-issues-in-litigation-finance.pdf (last retrieved April 23, 2020); Samuel Issacharoff, "Litigation Funding and the Problem of Agency Cost in Representative Actions," *DePaul Law Review* 63 (2014), 561, 562–65. See also U.S. Chamber Institute for Legal Reform, *Selling Lawsuits, Buying Trouble: Third-Party Litigation Funding in the United States* (Washington, D.C.: U.S. Chamber Institute for Legal Reform, 2009), 1–2.

[41]   Steinitz, "Whose Claim Is This Anyway? Third-Party Litigation Funding," 1338 (suggesting that "litigation finance is an industry whose time has come"). See also Issacharoff, "Litigation Funding and the Problem of Agency Cost in Representative Actions."

[42]   U.S. Chamber Institute for Legal Reform, *Selling Lawsuits, Buying Trouble,* 1–12.

[43]   Geoffrey C. Hazard, Jr., John Leubsdorf, and Debra Lyn Bassett, *Civil Procedure,* 6th ed. (New York: Foundation Press, 2011), 442.

44 Kenneth S. Abraham, *The Forms and Functions of Tort Law*, 4th ed. (New York: Foundation, 2012), 241–59. See also Steven P. Croley, *Civil Justice Reconsidered: Toward a Less Costly, More Accessible Litigation System* (New York: New York University Press, 2017), 29–34; and, William M. Tabb and Rachel M. Janutis, *Remedies in a Nutshell*, 2nd ed. (St. Paul, Minn.: West, 2013).

45 In 1997, a jury in a civil wrongful death action assessed a 25 million dollar verdict of punitive damages against Simpson after a jury in his criminal prosecution in 1995 acquitted him of murder. B. Drummond Ayres, Jr., "Jury Decides Simpson Must Pay $25 Million in Punitive Award (February 11, 1997)," https://www.nytimes.com/1997/02/11/us/jury-decides-simpson-must-pay-25-million-in-punitive-award.html (last retrieved April 23, 2020).

46 Ashley Sturm and Lynn K. Bartels, "Personality and Perceived Justice as Predictors of the Decision to Litigate," *Psychology Journal* 8 (No. 4, 2011): 163–182.

47 David M. Engel, *The Myth of the Litigious Society: Why We Don't Sue* (Chicago: University of Chicago Press, 2016).

48 Brisbin and Kilwein, *Real Law Stories: Inside the Judicial Process*, 10, 15.

49 Herbert M. Kritzer, *Risks, Reputations, and Rewards* (Stanford, Calif.: Stanford University Press, 2004), 257.

50 See Robert E. Litan and Steven C. Salop, "Reforming the Lawyer-Client Relationship Through Alternative Billing Methods," *Judicature* (January/February 1994), 191–97.

51 Herbert M. Kritzer, "Contingency Fee Lawyers as Gatekeepers in the Civil Justice System," *Judicature* (July/August 1997), 22. This argument is expanded in Kritzer, *Risks, Reputations, and Rewards*.

52 Croley, *Civil Justice Reconsidered*, x.

53 U.S. Senate, Committee on the Judiciary, "Contingency Fee Abuses," 104th Cong., 1st sess., 1995. S. Hrg. 104–828 (November 7, 1995) (Washington, D.C.: U.S. Government Printing Office), 3, 37. For a conservative critique of contingency fees and their effect on the American legal system, see Lester Brickman, *Lawyer Barons: What Their Contingency Fees Really Cost America* (New York: Cambridge University Press, 2011).

54 Thomas M. Clarke and Victor E. Flango, "Case Triage for the 21st Century," in *Future Trends in State Courts 2011: A Special Focus on Access to Justice* (Williamsburg, Va.: National Center for State Courts, 2011), 146–50. See also Victor E. Flango, "Which Disputes Belong in Court?" in *Future Trends in State Courts 2010* (Williamsburg, Va.: National Center for State Courts, 2011), 11–17.

55 Cornell Law School, Legal Information Institute, "Pleading," available at https://www.law.cornell.edu/wex/pleading (last retrieved April 24, 2020); and Cornell Law School, Legal Information Institute, "Motion," available at https://www.law.cornell.edu/wex/motion (last retrieved April 24, 2020).

56 Susan L. Staszak, *No Day in Court: Access to Justice and the Politics of Judicial Retrenchment* (New York: Oxford University Press, 2015).

57 Croley, *Civil Justice Reconsidered*, 13.

58 Georgene M. Vairo, "*Wal-Mart Stores, Inc., v. Dukes*: The End of Class Actions?" in *Class Action Litigation 2012* (New York: Practicing Law Institute, 2012), 39, 48. See also, *Conely v. Gibson*, 355 U.S. 41, 45–46 (1957).

59 Margaret Woo, "The Disappearing Trial: Retrenchment of Litigation in North America," *IUS Gentium* 70 (2018): 145, 146; Stephen N. Subrin and Thomas O. Main, "The Fourth Era of American Civil Procedure," *University of Pennsylvania Law Review* 162 (2014): 1839–1895. See also, Alexander A. Reinert, "Screening Out Innovation: The Merits of Meritless Litigation," *Indiana Law Journal* 89 (2014), 1191, 1205–12; Rebecca Love Kourlis, Jordan M. Singer, and Natalie Knowlton, "Reinvigorating Pleadings," *Denver University Law Review* 87 (2010), 245, 265 n. 128; John B. Oakley and Arthur F. Coon, "The Federal Rules in State Courts: A Survey of State Court Systems of Civil Procedure," *Washington Law Review* 61 (1986), 1367–427.

60 Cornell University Law School, Legal Information Institute, Rule 12(b)(6), *Federal Rules of Civil Procedure*, available at https://www.law.cornell.edu/rules/frcp (last retrieved April 24, 2020).

61 Cornell University Law School, Legal Information Institute, Rule 56, *Federal Rules of Civil Procedure*, available at https://www.law.cornell.edu/rules/frcp (last retrieved April 24, 2020).

62 Vairo, "*Wal-Mart Stores, Inc., v. Dukes*: The End of Class Actions?" 47, citing *Celotex Corporation v. Catrett*, 477 U.S. 317 (1986), *Anderson v. Liberty Lobby, Inc.*, 477 U.S. 242 (1986), *Matsushita Electric Industrial Company v. Zenith Radio Corporation*, 475 U.S. 574 (1986). Notably, the "longstanding view" before these cases were decided indicated that the Rules of Civil Procedure were designed to eliminate "fact-pleading" (e.g., claim-specific pleading) and replace it with an increasing reliance on using the discovery process, and jury trials, to ascertain a civil case's "merit." Reinert, "Screening Out Innovation: The Merits of Meritless Litigation," 1206.

63 *Ashcroft v. Iqbal*, 556 U.S. 662, 684 (2009); *Bell Atlantic Corporation v. Twombly*, 550 U.S. 544, 555 (2007). See also Joanna C. Schwartz, "Gateways and Pathways in Civil Procedure," *UCLA Law Review* 60 (2013), 1652–708.

64 In 1962, for example, 5.5 percent of all federal cases were decided by jury trial. But in 2002, that percentage had dropped to only 1.2 percent. At the same time, between 1975 and 2000, summary judgment adjudications rose from 3.7 percent to 7.7 percent, respectively. Galanter, "The Vanishing Trial," 462–63 (Table 1), 483–84.

65 Galanter, "The Vanishing Trial," 484. See also ibid., 482 (reporting percentages of pretrial dispositions in 1962 and 2002). The percentages of jury trials and pretrial dispositions for 2019 are derived from Administrative Office of the U.S. Courts, "Table C-4, U.S. District Courts-Civil Cases Terminated, by Nature of Suit and Action Taken, During the 12-Month Period Ending June 30, 2019," available at www.uscourts.gov (last retrieved April 24, 2020).

66 Brittany K.T. Kauffman and Logan Cornett, University of Denver, The Institute for the Advancement of the American Legal System, *Efficiency in Motion: Summary Judgment in the U.S. District Courts (May 2018)*, available at https://iaals.du.edu/sites/default/files/documents/publications/efficiency_in_motion_summary_judgment.pdf (last retrieved April 24, 2020).

67 Danielle Lusardo Schantz, "Access to Justice: Impact of Twombly & Iqbal on State Court Systems," *Akron Law Review* 51 (2019), 951, 964–965.

68 See Cornell University Law School, Legal Information Institute, "Discovery," available at https://www.law.cornell.edu/wex/discovery (last retrieved April 24, 2020).

69 Christopher Frost, "The Sound and the Fury, or the Sound of Silence: Evaluating the Pre-Amendment Predications and Post-Amendment Effects of the Discovery Scope-Narrowing Language in the 2000 Amendments to the Federal Rules of Civil Procedure," *Georgia Law Review* 37 (2003), 1039, 1040.

70 Cornell University Law School, Legal Information Institute, Rule 26(b) (1), *Federal Rules of Civil Procedure*, available at https://www.law.cornell.edu/rules/frcp (last retrieved April 24, 2020).

71 See, e.g., Cornell University Law School, Legal Information Institute, Rule 33, *Federal Rules of Civil Procedure*, available at https://www.law.cornell.edu/rules/frcp (last retrieved April 24, 2020); and ibid., Rule 34, available at https://www.law.cornell.edu/rules/frcp (last retrieved April 24, 2020).

72 See, e.g., Cornell University Law School, Legal Information Institute, Rule 36, *Federal Rules of Civil Procedure*, available at www.law.cornell.edu/rules/frcp/rule_36 (last retrieved April 24, 2020).

73 Jeffrey S. Sutton and Derek A. Webb, "The 2015 Amendments to the Federal Rules of Civil Procedure and the 2017 Pilot Projects," *Judicature* 101 (No. 3, 2017): 12, 19; Josh Blane, "Drowning in Data: How the Federal Rules are Staying Afloat in a Flood of Information," *Rutgers Law Record*, 45 (2017–2018): 65, 73.

74 See, e.g., Cornell University Law School, Legal Information Institute, Rules 27–32, *Federal Rules of Civil Procedure*, available at https://www.law.cornell.edu/rules/frcp (last retrieved April 24, 2020).

75 See, e.g., Cornell University Law School, Legal Information Institute, Rule 35, Federal Rules of Civil Procedure, available at https://www.law.cornell.edu/rules/frcp (last retrieved April 24, 2020).

76 See Nagareda, *Mass Torts in a World of Settlement*, 7; Judith Resnik, "Managerial Judges," *Harvard Law Review* 96 (1982), 374–448. See also Hazard and Bassett, *Civil Procedure*, 391–94; Maurice Rosenberg, *The Pretrial Conference and Effective Justice: A Controlled Test in Personal Injury Litigation* (New York: Columbia University Press, 1964), 5–11.

77 See Paul D. Carrington, "The Seventh Amendment: Some Bicentennial Reflections," *University of Chicago Legal Forum* 1990 (1990), 33, 42–43.

78 See, e.g., Brian H. Bornstein and Timothy R. Robicheaux, "Crisis, What Crisis? Perception and Reality in Civil Justice," in *Civil Juries and Civil Justice: Psychological and Legal Perspectives*, edited by Brian H. Bornstein, Richard L. Wiener, Robert F. Schopp, and Steven L. Willborn (New York: Springer, 2008), 1–22.

79 Jeffrey Q. Smith and Grant R. Macqueen, "Trial Continue to Decline in Federal and State Courts," *Judiature*, 101 (2018): 26, 28; John H. Langbein, "The Disappearance of Civil Trial in the United States," *Yale Law Journal* 122 (2012), 522, 524 (reporting that, in 1940, federal civil trial rates were at 15.2 percent but, by 2002, the rate was 1.8 percent; and, in state courts, jury trials were less than 1 percent of all civil dispositions). See also Lynn Langton and Thomas H. Cohen, *Civil Bench and Jury Trials in State Courts, 2005* ("Civil Justice

Survey of State Courts") (October 2008, NCJ 223851), available at www.bjs.gov (last retrieved April 24, 2020), 10.

80 Jeffrey Q. Smith and Grant R. Macqueen, "Trials Continue to Decline in Federal and State Courts: Does it Matter?," *Judicature* 101 (2017): 26, 32.

81 Langton and Cohen, *Civil Bench and Jury Trials in State Courts, 2005*, 1.

82 American Tort Reform Association, *Judicial Hellholes* (Washington, D.C.: American Tort Reform Foundation 2019/2020), available at https://www.judicialhellholes.org/2019-2020/ (last retrieved April 24, 2020). See ibid., "About," available at https://www.judicialhellholes.org/about/ (last retrieved April 24, 2020)(defining "Judicial Hellholes").

83 American Tort Reform Association, *Judicial Hellholes 2019/2020*, 1.

84 See, e.g. American Tort Reform Association, "Issues," available at http://www.atra.org/issues/ (last retrieved May April 24, 2020).

85 Yiling Deng and George Zanjani, "What Drives Tort Reform Legislation?: An Analysis of State Court Decisions to Restrict Liability Torts," *The Journal of Risk and Insurance* 85 (2018): 959, 962–964; Ashley L. Taylor, Jr., "Walking a Tightrope: AG Enforcement Authority and Private Counsel Contingency Fee Arrangements," *State and Local Law News (American Bar Association's Section of State and Local Government Law)* 36 (Spring, 2013), available at www.americanbar.org (last retrieved July 1, 2014).

86 Deng and Zanjani, "What Drives Tort Reform Legislation?"; Mary H. Graffam, "The Web of Tort Reform," *Trial* 48 (December 2012), 15–19. See also American Association for Justice, *ALEC: Ghostwriting the Law for Corporate America* (Washington, D.C.: American Association for Justice, May 2010); American Association for Justice, *The Chamber Litigation Machine* (Washington, D.C.: American Association for Justice, October 2010).

87 A survey of the empirical literature is found in Menkel-Meadow and Garth, "Civil Procedure and Courts," in *The Oxford Handbook of Empirical Legal Research*, 679–704; and, ibid., 680 (remarking on the political nature of the academic debate).

88 See, e.g., Langton and Cohen, *Civil Bench and Jury Trials in State Courts, 2005*; and Galanter, "The Vanishing Trial," 459–570.

89 Herbert M. Kritzer and Robert E. Drechsel, "Local News of Civil Litigation: All the Litigation News That's Fit to Print or Broadcast," *Judicature* 96 (2012), 16–22; William Haltom and Michael McCann, *Distorting the Law: Politics, Media, and the Litigation Crisis* (Chicago: University of Chicago Press, 2004).

90 See, e.g., Kevin M. Lewis, "Tort and Litigation Reform in the 115th Congress," *Congressional Research Service (Legal Sidebar, April 15, 2018)*, available at https://digital.library.unt.edu/ark:/67531/metadc1157110/m2/1/high_res_d/LSB10118_2018Apr10.pdf (last retrieved April 24, 2020); U.S. House of Representatives, Subcommittee on the Constitution and Civil Justice of the Committee on the Judiciary, "Examination of Litigation Abuses," 113th Cong., 1st sess., 2013. Serial No. 113-8 (March 13, 2013) (Washington, D.C.: U.S. Government Printing Office, 2013); U.S. House of Representatives, Subcommittee on Intellectual Property, Competition, and the Internet of the Committee on the Judiciary, "Litigation as a Predatory Practice," 112th Cong., 2nd sess., 2012. Serial No. 112-79 (February 17, 2012) (Washington, D.C.: U.S. Government Printing Office, 2012); U.S. House of Representatives, Subcommittee on the Constitution of the Committee on the Judiciary, "Contingent Fees and Conflicts of Interest in State AG Enforcement of Federal Law," 112th Cong., 2nd sess., 2012. Serial No. 112-82 (February 2, 2012) (Washington, D.C.: U.S. Government Printing Office, 2012).

91 Chief Justice Burger's remarks are reported in "Mid-Year Meeting of the American Bar Association," *United States Law Week* 52 (February 28, 1984), 2471.

92 Orna Rabinovich-Einy and Ethan Katsh, "A New Relationship Between Public and Private Dispute Resolution: Lessons from Online Dispute Resolution," *Ohio State Journal of Dispute Resolution* 32 (2017): 695, 698. See also, Burger, "Mid-Year Meeting of the American Bar Association," *United States Law Week* 52 (February 28, 1984).

93 Jerome T. Barrett and Joseph P. Barrett, *A History of Alternative Dispute Resolution: The Story of a Political, Cultural, and Social Movement* (San Francisco: Jossey-Bass, 2004), 149–52, 182–83, 214. See also, Larry Ray & Anne L. Clare, "The Multi-Door Courthouse Idea: Building the Courthouse of the Future . . . Today," *Ohio State Journal of Dispute Resolution* 1 (1985): 7–54.

94   M. Katherine Kerbs, et al., "State Legislative Update," *Journal of Dispute Resolution* 2016 (2016): 444–439.

95   Thomas J. Stipanowich, "ADR and the 'Vanishing Trial': The Growth and Impact of 'Alternative Dispute Resolution,'" *Journal of Empirical Legal Studies* (November 2004), 843, 849–50.

96   Benjamin Angulo, Daniel J. Romine, and Matthew Schacht, "2011 State Legislative Update," *Journal of Dispute Resolution* 2011 (2011, Issue 2), 401–2.

97   See Howard W. Cummins, "Let Us Reason Together: The Role of Process in Effective Mediation," *Journal of the National Association of Administrative Law Judiciary* 33 (2013), 1–34; Paula Hannaford-Agor and Nicole Waters, "The Evolution of the Summary Jury Trial: A Flexible Tool to Meet a Variety of Needs," in *Future Trends in State Courts 2012* (Williamsburg, Va.: National Center for State Courts, 2012), 107–12.

98   Donna Stienstra, "ADR in the Federal District Courts: An Initial Report (Prepared for the Federal Judicial Center, November 16, 2011)," available at https://www.fjc.gov/sites/default/files/2012/ADR2011.pdf (last retrieved April 24, 2020).

99   Stipanowich, "ADR and the 'Vanishing Trial,'" 849–50, 866–67, 898–900; Stienstra, "ADR in the Federal District Courts: An Initial Report," 15 (Table 7); and, Rabinovich-Einy and Katsh, "A New Relationship Between Public and Private Dispute Resolution: Lessons from Online Dispute Resolution," 703.

100   Richard Posner, "The Summary Jury Trial and Other Methods of Alternative Dispute Resolution: Some Cautionary Observations," *University of Chicago Law Review* (1986), 356, 372–75; but see Thomas D. Lambros, "The Summary Jury Trial: An Effective Aid to Settlement," *Judicature* (July/August 1993), 6–8. The strengths and weaknesses of ADR are summarized from a practitioner's perspective in Edward J. Costello, Jr., "Whether and When to Use Alternative Dispute Resolution," in *Alternative Dispute Resolution: The Litigator's Handbook*, edited by Nancy F. Atlas, Stephen K. Huber, and E. Wendy Trachte-Huber (Chicago: American Bar Association, 2000), 35–58.

101   Owen M. Fiss, "Against Settlement," *Yale Law Journal* 93 (1984): 1073, 1085. See also, Thomas J. Stipanowich, "Arbitration: The 'New Litigation,'" *University of Illinois Law Review* (2010), 1, 6–8.

102   Amy Howe, "Opinion analysis: Court strikes down restrictions on removal of CFPB director but leaves bureau in place," *SCOTUSblog* (June 29, 2020), available at https://www.scotusblog.com/2020/06/opinion-analysis-court-strikes-down-restrictions-on-removal-of-cfpb-director-but-leaves-bureau-in-place/ (last retrieved July 3, 2020); and, *Seila Law LLC v. Consumer Financial Protection Bureau*, 140 S.Ct. 2183 (U.S. Jun. 29, 2020). See also, David Zaring, "Guidance and the Congressional Review Act," *The Regulatory Review (February 15, 2018)*, available at https://www.theregreview.org/2018/02/15/zaring-guidance-congressional-review-act/ (last retrieved April 24, 2020). See also, Deborah Greenspan, Fredric M. Brooks, and Jonathan Walton, "Recent Developments in Alternative Dispute Resolution," *Tort Trial and Insurance Practice Law Journal* 53 (No. 2, 2018): 199–225. The CFPB and Department of Treasury reports are found in CFPB, *Arbitration Study: Report to Congress, pursuant to the Dodd-Frank Wall Street Reform and Consumer Protection Act Section 1028(a)(March 2015)*, available at https://files.consumerfinance.gov/f/201503_cfpb_arbitration-study-report-to-congress-2015.pdf (last retrieved April 24, 2020); and, Department of Treasury, *Limiting Consumer Choice, Expanding Costly Litigation: An Analysis of the CFPB Arbitration Rule (October 23, 2017)*, available at https://www.treasury.gov/press-center/press-releases/Documents/10-23-17%20Analysis%20of%20CFPB%20arbitration%20rule.pdf (last retrieved April 24, 2020).

103   William C. Smith, "Much to Do About ADR," *American Bar Association Journal* (June 2000), 62–68.

PART IV

Judicial Policymaking

CHAPTER 9

The Appellate Court Process

After Donald Trump's presidential victory, Republican Senator Mitch McConnell (R-KY) reminded the American public that "elections have consequences." McConnell chose his words carefully. He remembered that President Barack Obama said the same thing to congressional Republicans in 2008 at a White House meeting involving the direction of his economic policy when the Democrats held the majority in Congress. But, in 2016, when the political tables turned and the Republicans captured both the White House and Congress, Senate Majority Leader McConnell gave the statement new meaning when he stopped Obama, in his last year in office, from filling a critical Supreme Court vacancy caused by Justice Scalia's unexpected death because he said that the American people should determine if Trump or Hillary Clinton should get to fill it after 2016 presidential contest. Throughout President Trump's first term, Democrats could do little to stop him from packing the federal courts with an unprecedented number of conservative lifetime judicial appointments. In May 2019, the irony of Obama's and McConnell's quip came full circle when an attendee at a local Chamber of Commerce luncheon asked McConnell if the American people or the Republican-controlled Senate would fill another Supreme Court vacancy should it arise in the 2020 presidential campaign. With a wry smile, McConnell replied, "Oh, we'd fill it."[1]

Senator McConnell's remarks illustrates the critical role appellate courts play in resolving disputes as legal change agents of public policy. Unlike President Obama, who did not prioritize placing nominees on the bench during his years in office, the Trump White House and McConnell appreciated the central significance of the third branch in the U.S. political system. In a 2018 speech, President Trump wondered why Obama did not work harder to fill judicial vacancies since judges "are the ones that judge all your disputes." As he realized, not filling those judicial vacancies "was like a big, beautiful present to all of us" when the Republicans took control of the federal government. So Trump was ecstatic to have a friendly Republican Senate confirm his nominees at an unprecedented pace. By June 2020, the Senate already confirmed fifty-three judges on the highly impactful federal appeals courts. As life-time appointments, appellate court judgeships are a highly valued political asset because they work in *de facto* "courts of last resort" for most federal litigants and, as such, are key policymakers that craft the nation's political, economic and social policies for years to come.[2]

In this light, the President's success in packing the federal appellate courts with his ideological preferences is a calculated political strategy that is designed to reconstitute the law through judicial policy-making. Although judges take an oath to uphold the U.S. Constitution, how they interpret the *doctrine of stare decisis*—the legal doctrine obliging judges to follow prior rules of law, or precedent—is critical to that effort. As President Trump and Senator McConnell knew well, fresh judicial appointments may coalesce into new coalitions of like-minded judges as they take their place on the bench. Trump's first Supreme Court nominee, Neil Gorsuch, a conservative advocate of originalism, replaced Justice Antonin Scalia. Likewise, in Trump's second year in office he picked Brett Kavanaugh, another conservative originalist, to be on the high court after Justice Anthony Kennedy's retirement. Once confirmed, they joined a bloc of three other conservatives, Chief Justice John Roberts and Justices Samuel Alito and Clarence Thomas on the Roberts Court. Not surprisingly, the new conservative coalition has started to issue rulings reversing longstanding precedents—among them *Janus v. American Federation of State, County, and Municipal Employees* (2018), a First Amendment case, decided 5:4, that overturned *Abood v. Detroit Board of Education* (1977), a forty-year old precedent that compelled workers to pay their "fair share" of union dues even though they were not part of the union; and, *Franchise Tax Board of California v. Hyatt* (2019), a 5:4 federalism case that reversed *Nevada v. Hall* (1979), a forty-year precedent permitting states to be sued in state court by individuals living in other states. For some court observers, those decisions as well as others signal that the Roberts Court is poised to transform other areas of controversial jurisprudence in upcoming Terms, including perhaps overturning *Roe v. Wade* (1973), the landmark precedent establishing abortion rights. Even Justice Stephen Breyer, who dissented (along with liberal Justices Ruth Bader Ginsburg, Sonia Sotomayor and Elena Kagan) in *Hyatt,* warned, "Today's decision can only cause one to wonder which cases the Court will overrule next."[3]

Accordingly, this chapter examines appellate courts' decision making and the corresponding influence on legal policy change. First, it outlines the appellate decision-making process and contrasts it with trial courts (see Figure 9.1). Four stages of the appeals process are highlighted: (1) agenda setting; (2) oral argument; (3) the judicial conference; and, (4) opinion writing. The Chapter, then, discusses how political scientists and legal scholars employ different research methods to explain the decision making of appellate court judges. The fact that appellate courts make, and do not simply declare, what the law is remains controversial, however. The concluding section, then, examines the principal rival interpretative methods used by appellate judges in statutory and constitutional cases in relation to the different ways appellate courts may forge legal and social policy change.

| Figure 9.1 | The Appellate Court Decision-Making Process |

Appeal Filed

- Clerk of Court determines if procedural requirements for filing appeal are met
- Dates for applicable summary dispositions, preliminary hearings, civil settlement or mediation conferences, legal brief submission, and oral argument (if any) are tentatively calendared

Legal Briefs Submitted and Bench Memos Prepared

- Parties file briefs summarizing legal arguments
- Third parties ("amicus curie") may file briefs with court's permission
- "Bench memos" with legal analysis prepared by law clerks in preparation for oral argument and conference deliberations

Oral Argument

- Opposing counsel present legal argument in front of judges during allotted time
- Judges ask questions from bench about strengths and weaknesses of case

Judicial Conference

- Judges discuss appeal's "merits" and cast preliminary votes to grant/deny relief
- Judges may assign duty of writing majority, concurring, or dissenting opinions

Drafting and Releasing Final Decision/Opinion

- Law clerks and judges write drafts of opinions and circulate them in chambers
- Final opinion is prepared and released to parties and public through clerk of court or public information office of court

THE APPELLATE COURT DECISION-MAKING PROCESS

State and federal appellate courts play a limited role in reviewing trial court decisions because the Constitution only guarantees "a fair trial, not a perfect one."[4] Studies confirm that only about 15 to 20 percent of trial court rulings are appealed annually and that most **appeals** are unsuccessful.[5] In addition, trial and appellate court behavior is largely indistinguishable from partisan affiliation, although there is evidence that Republican appointees tend to favor "upper-dogs," whereas Democratic appointees tend to support "lower-dogs."[6] Still, there are basic differences in the functions of trial and appellate courts, and their impact on law and society.

Trial court judges and juries primarily evaluate conflicting evidence and factual claims. As some court watchers observe, "Appellate law does not titillate the way that *Judge Judy* or the O.J. Simpson trial did," largely because "law's domain is staid, cerebral, and cabined in codes and cases."[7] Consequently, appellate judges approach the legal decision-making by ordinarily deferring to lower courts' findings of fact and they reverse trial court decisions only if the trial court's decision is "clearly erroneous." Appellate courts focus on questions of law and the interpretation of laws, as well as have (arguably) less discretion than trial courts, which have virtually unbounded discretion in applying laws (subject, of course, to appeals) and are generally the courts of first and last resort.[8]

Circuit Judge Richard A. Posner, therefore, argues that trial court opinions are less important sources of law than those of appellate courts.[9] Unlike trial courts, appellate courts render decisions that set precedents within a particular state or federal region.[10] Moreover, they decide cases in randomly assigned panels of three judges or *en banc* (when all judges in a circuit decide a case). Appeals courts are **collegial** (unlike trial courts) and work in small groups that often not only review the decision below but also may broadly affect social policy. Furthermore, research demonstrates that the ideological composition of federal circuit court panels produces distinctly liberal or conservative policy outcomes.[11]

In light of rising caseloads, appellate judges spend less time hearing oral arguments, and more time managing their staffs and writing opinions. Legal staff per judge in state appellate courts typically consists of two or three law clerks and staff attorneys, plus secretaries. The institutional arrangement of law clerks and staff in federal appeals courts is identical; but, as too in state courts, varies in accordance with the availability of judicial resources and the specific needs and idiosyncrasies of each court. The Chief Justice of the U.S. Supreme Court, for example, can hire up to five law clerks per Term, whereas Associate Justices can select four. Moreover, since the 1960s the Justices routinely select the top talent in a competitive applicant pool that ordinarily requires graduation from an elite law school as well as past clerkship experience in a district or circuit court. Moreover, in contrast to lower court judges, in general appellate judges must rely on their law clerks to do legal research and help write opinions; though standard duties also consist of helping judges determine what cases to hear and assisting them in oral argument preparation.[12]

The significance of the appellate courts is underscored by examining the critical stages of their decision-making process, including: (1) how they set their agenda; (2) the influence of oral argument; (3) the role judicial conferences play; and, (4) the saliency and utility of writing opinions. These appellate processes are discussed next.

Agenda Setting

In all appeals courts, the clerk of the court begins the process once the losing party at the trial level pays a fee and files notice of an appeal. Once an appeal is filed, the clerk assigns a docket number and puts the case on the court calendar. Typically, in federal appellate courts, the assignment of cases is done by the random selection of three-judge panels. Federal law gives each circuit the discretion to determine how to create their panels. In doing so, some circuits permit the chief judge to make panel assignments, whereas others let the clerk of court or circuit executive to make assignments, often by using computer programs.[13] In theory, random selection prevents courts and judges from picking the appeals they individually favor—for example, as some research has shown, random assignments would stop a chief judge from stacking panels with liberal judges that are likely to enforce Supreme Court school desegregation rulings in the South in the post-*Brown v. Board of Education* (1954) era.[14] Notably, however, a variety of factors, including scheduling conflicts among judges and the administrative problems that inherently are a part of docket management probably makes panel composition less random. In fact, one empirical study reported that several circuits—the D.C. Circuit, and the Second, Eighth and Ninth Circuits— have non-random panel assignments which, in turn, influences the ideological balance of panels and, presumably, case outcomes. Thus, in at least some circuits, there are fewer panels with either all Democratic or all Republican appointees that would be expected if the panels were truly random.[15] Regardless, and apart from panel assignment rules, the flow of appeals is controlled by the **clerk of court,** who serves as a kind of administrative "traffic cop" in communicating with counsel.[16]

After the preliminary case processing, staff attorneys and law clerks work on their assigned cases, along with continuing to screen appeals and determine whether they should receive plenary (full) consideration or summary disposition. Central staff attorneys, who are permanent staff, typically work for a court instead of specific judges, unlike law clerks. They also have diversified duties, including screening cases for jurisdictional defects, setting cases for oral argument or summary disposition (without oral argument), researching substantive motions, and writing memoranda on whether to grant or deny relief in discretionary cases.[17]

Studies of federal and state appeals courts show that the central staff significantly influences a court's agenda. In an analysis of three federal appeals courts, legal scholar Jonathan Matthew Cohen found that central staff was the touchstone for deciding which appeals received "full-dressed" treatment and whether cases were granted oral arguments or given summary disposition. Likewise, in a study of 151 state appellate courts, political scientists Roger Hanson, Carol Flango, and Randall Hansen found that central staff spent a significant portion of their time preparing legal memoranda for judges and advising them on whether an appeal should stay on the docket for further consideration. They also assist judges by providing legal analyses of cases granted full review. Both studies are consistent with other findings that concluded central staffs play an important role not only in dismissing cases, but also in reaching decisions on the merits.[18]

To a lesser degree, law clerks assigned to individual judges contribute to molding a court's agenda. Some researchers estimate that less than 3 percent of law clerks' time is spent handling procedural motions. Unless a court has discretionary authority, the rules governing the assignment of cases to panels, along with judicial norms controlling the screening process, substantially dictate the workload and the types of cases appellate courts decide.[19]

As in the trial courts, procedural rules and norms govern case selection in federal and state courts of last resort. For example, Rule 10, which guides the acceptance of *certiorari* (*cert.*) petitions in the Supreme Court, requires that appeal petitions must cite conflicting appellate court interpretations of important questions of federal law as one of the possible reasons to grant *cert.* The justices refer to these cases as involving so-called "deep splits"—questions on which several lower courts have disagreed and are unlikely to resolve without the Supreme Court's intervention.[20] Social scientists have established that a combination of political and legal factors affect appellate courts' case selection. Seminal research by political scientist S. Sidney Ulmer concluded that Supreme

Court justices' votes in deciding the merits of cases were strongly correlated with their initial votes to grant review. His key finding that justices vote to grant cases in accordance with their policy preferences is consistent with subsequent studies finding that judges act strategically in constructing their dockets. In other words, judges generally write their policy preferences into law when deciding what to decide, while also taking into account the preferences of other judges and the institutional context within which they operate.[21]

Strategic calculations in granting appeals also appear closely linked to a court's institutional and environmental situation. For example, political scientists Paul Brace and Melinda Gann Hall have shown that the availability of lawyers and the adequacy of resources (e.g., the number of clerks, central staff, and judges; salaries; docket size) significantly affect state supreme court agenda setting. In their words: "When lawyers are relatively plentiful and comparatively less costly, more have-nots [those with less money and legal resources to file lawsuits] reach state supreme courts, and they are more likely to win."[22] Likewise, other studies of the Supreme Court's agenda setting found a high correlation with the policy positions of the president, Congress, and public opinion.[23]

The agenda-setting stage is only the beginning of the appeals process, however. Once appeals are docketed and preliminarily screened, appellate courts may (though rarely) grant the litigants oral argument.

Oral Argument

In the early republic, attorneys in the United States built their reputations on persuasive oral arguments. Some orations, especially those of famous advocates like Daniel Webster and Luther Martin, spanned several hours or even days. The practice of oral advocacy derived from the English common law tradition of barristers presenting their cases in open court, a custom that still may result in lengthy oral arguments (typically spanning two days).[24] In U.S. appellate courts, however, the practice evolved differently and departed from that tradition. Indeed, rather than lengthy oral arguments, appellate lawyers now generally advance their arguments only in written **briefs**. For example, in addition to receiving information about a case from external sources, such as from the media or lower court opinions, Supreme Court justices gather a basic understanding about the facts and law of a case from several types of legal briefs, including briefs pertaining to *certiorari* petitions, briefs from the litigants, and **amicus curiae** briefs from interested third parties, or "friends of the court."[25] Still, at least for some judges, what is said by legal advocates in open court is significant even though less time is devoted to the practice of oral argument. As Justice Robert Jackson (who was famous for his oral advocacy) observed: "Over the years, the time allotted for [oral] hearing has been shortened, but its importance has not diminished. . . . The significance of the trend is that the shorter the time, the more precious is each minute."[26]

Regardless of their type, all appellate briefs identify the legal bases for the court accepting jurisdiction and to consider the merits of a case. Typically, they consist of a table of contents, a statement of the issues, and a summary of the argument. As Circuit Judge Frank Coffin once emphasized, the reputation of the attorney filing the brief and the identity of the lower court judge whose decision is appealed has a strong influence on whether staff counsel or law clerks recommend to grant or dismiss an appeal and whether appellate judges will take the time to read the brief thoroughly. In this regard, appellate briefs are directed to three audiences: the central staff attorneys, the panel of judges reviewing the case and their law clerks, and the judge who writes the court's opinion and his or her law clerks.[27]

If an appeal is granted oral argument, law clerks are usually assigned to write various memos explaining the case and its merits. Most judges require clerks to write a **bench memorandum**—a detailed memo that may be shared with other chambers and outlines the appeal's facts, legal issues, and legal authorities. Some judges describe bench memos as "road maps" to case specifics. Such memos are particularly valuable in allowing judges to prepare for oral argument because they do not present a one-sided view as to the legal merits of a cases, as legal briefs do; rather, their purpose is to give the judge an objective view of both sides of a legal argument while making a recommendation about how to decide the case.[28]

State and federal appellate courts typically use their discretion to grant oral arguments or limit their practice in accordance with statutory law and local court rules or practice. Across the states, different state appeals courts may require counsel or litigants to request an oral argument formally; or they may automatically allow (or disallow) it in all cases; or they may only grant it only as a matter of right in certain types of cases, such as death penalty, original proceedings, or judicial discipline cases. Likewise, Rule 34(2)(C) of the Federal Rules of Appellate Procedure gives federal appeals judges wide discretion to hear oral argument by permitting them to dispense with it if a panel (of three judges) unanimously concludes that it is unnecessary after a review of the legal briefs and trial record. Under its own rules, the Supreme Court, as well, hears oral arguments but they place different time and other specifications on how they are conducted.[29]

Regardless, all state and federal appellate courts place limits on the amount of time given to oral arguments. In state appeals courts, lawyers are typically afforded anywhere between ten to thirty minutes to present their arguments, depending upon the state and court in which they are held. The time restrictions are similar in federal courts. In the Supreme Court, litigants now generally have only thirty minutes per side to argue their cases even though, by contrast, lawyers at once time had unlimited time to present their case in the nineteenth century. Moreover, the shift away from oral arguments is most conspicuous in the federal circuit courts, which typically allocate only ten to fifteen minutes to oral advocacy.[30] There, the percentage of appeals decided without oral argument has sharply fallen since the mid-1980s, from a high of 56 percent (1985) to a low between 12 to 13 percent in recent years (2015, 2018) (see Table 9.1).

Table 9.1	Appeals Terminated After Oral Hearing in U.S. Courts of Appeals		
Year	Total Number of Appeals Terminated on Merits	Total Number of Appeals Terminated on Merits After Oral Hearing	Percentage of Appeals Terminated on Merits After Oral Hearing
1985	16,886	9,507	56%
1990	21,022	9,479	45%
1995	27,772	11,080	40%
2000	27,516	9,752	35%
2005	27,354	8,573	31%
2010	30,781	8,393	27%
2015	54,244	6,605	12%
2018	49,363	6,380	13%

Note: Data for the U.S. Court of Appeals for the Federal Circuit are unreported. Percentages are rounded off to the nearest whole number.

Sources: Administrative Office of the U.S. Courts, *Judicial Facts and Figures: Multi-Year Statistical Compilations of Federal Court Caseload through Fiscal Year 2004* (Compiled March 2005), available at https://www.uscourts.gov/statistics-reports/analysis-reports/judicial-facts-and-figures (last retrieved July 3, 2020), Table 1.8, (all years except 1985 and 2005). Data for 1985 are from Jonathan Matthew Cohen, *Inside Appellate Courts: The Impact of Court Organization on Judicial Decision Making in the United States Courts of Appeals* (Ann Arbor: University of Michigan Press, 2002), 62, Table 3; 2005–2018 data are at Table B-1, in Administrative Office of the U.S. Courts, "Federal Judicial Caseload Statistics," available at https://www.uscourts.gov/statistics/table/b-1/federal-judicial-caseload-statistics/2018/03/31 (last retrieved April 24, 2020).

The scarcity of oral arguments raises the question of their value or significance in explaining judicial behavior and case outcomes. While the findings are mixed, political and legal scholars observe that oral arguments play at least some role in four distinct aspects of judicial decision-making: (1) as information gathering tools for judges; (2) as a strategic factor that allows judges to evaluate how their colleagues may coalesce into voting or policy-making coalitions in accordance with their individual preferences; (3) as an element of persuasion in any given case; and, (4) as an important variable that helps scholars predict case outcomes.[31]

Judges actually serving on the bench reinforce what researchers have suggested in determining if oral arguments make a difference in making decisions. Although some judges—such as Justice Oliver Wendell Holmes, who used to take catnaps or write letters while on the bench, and Justice Clarence Thomas, who rarely asks questions during oral arguments (and who once quipped "[I]f I wanted to talk a lot, I would be on the other side of the bench" in explaining his silence)— do not get much out of oral arguments, others are different.[32] Justice Ruth Bader Ginsburg, for one, considers arguments not "an occasion. . .for grand speechmaking, but for an exchange of ideas about the case, a dialogue or discussion between knowledgeable counsel and judges who have done their homework, a 'hot bench,' as appellate advocates say." In addition, Justice Ginsburg characterizes oral arguments as the "last clear chance to convince the justices concerning points on which the decision may turn." Nor is she alone in that assessment. For Justice John M. Harlan II, oral argument was invaluable "in getting at the real heart of an issue and in finding out where the truth lies." In this respect, not only do oral arguments provide a forum for exchange and persuasion, but they also personalize the case and give judges information that they might otherwise overlook or was not presented in the briefs. Moreover, oral arguments are an opportunity for the justices to explore the logical extension of counsel's arguments by presenting hypotheticals. For all of these reasons, on balance, argument sessions remain significant and take place shortly before voting on the merits of cases in judicial conferences, the next stage of the appellate process.[33]

Judicial Conferences

As with oral arguments, judicial rules or procedures and institutional norms dictate the manner in which federal and state appeals courts use judicial conferences to manage their docket and decide cases. In this respect, all appellate courts have conferences that assist in the process of case disposition in different ways. The Supreme Court, for instance, has an opening conference in the week before the beginning of each term in October in order to dispose of petitions for review that were filed during the summer recess. In subsequent private conferences that are held after oral argument during the Term, the justices discuss appeals and cast preliminary votes on the merits of appeals. In accordance with governing norms and traditions, private conferences discussions are secret and not open to public until the information about what transpired in them are released in judicial opinions, off-the bench communications, or through their private papers after they have left the bench. The votes, too, are tentative because the justices may change their minds at any time prior to announcing the final judgment (see Figure 9.1). Moreover, and unlike in the past when the Supreme Court's caseload was much smaller, today's conferences primarily serve the purpose of learning the justices' alignments as there is little time for, as former Justice William O. Douglas once put it, "deliberation, reflection and mediation."[34] Indeed, most of the exchanges between the justices occur mostly in written communications in and between chambers, before and after conferences. Notably, with less conference time spent on deliberation, it is more difficult for the justices to achieve consensus and reach compromises on difficult or more hotly-contested cases which, in turn, contributes to justices writing a greater number of separate decisions and the Court issuing fewer institutional opinions that send clear signals about what the law is, or means, to litigants, lawyers, and the public. Even so, although judicial conferences in the Supreme Court and other appellate courts are now largely symbolic forums for collective deliberation and individual persuasion, they still remain significant venues that permit the justices to form strategic voting coalitions that help determine final decisions.[35]

Strategic Consensus Building and Opinion Assignment

The formal and informal institutional mechanisms underlying deliberation, voting, and opinion assignment impact consensus-building among the judges, not only on a case's merits but also as to its final outcome. Scholars have shown that the order of conference discussion and voting, along with how appellate courts assign the writing of majority opinions, shape individual judicial preferences and collective judicial policy-making.[36] Accordingly, judges may adopt different tactics during conferences to build or strengthen voting coalitions. The strategies vary with the court and its members. But, significantly, the ability to persuade a colleague is also dictated by institutional procedures and norms. As in the U.S. Supreme Court, most state courts of last resort stick to the tradition of discussing and voting on cases based on seniority—a practice based on the chief judge and then the most senior judge (followed by others based on their seniority) speaking and casting their votes. They do so either to permit the most senior judges to maximize their influence or, conversely, to shield junior members from the influence of their more seasoned colleagues.[37] Thus who speaks first-and the seniority they hold—may define another judge's strategy in casting a vote. Even so, some research demonstrates that judges speaking and voting last is also advantageous because it may determine the outcome in tied cases.[38] Apart from seniority-based rules, some state courts take a different approach and permit either a system of rotating order of votes (that allow for more equitable distribution of votes) or simultaneous voting by raising hands all at once (which diminishes any advantages for judges to condition their votes on the votes of others).[39]

After the initial votes are cast at conference, **opinion assignment**—or who writes the controlling opinion for the court—becomes a key part of judicial strategy and the bargaining and coalition-building process that ultimately yields a final opinion.[40] Who gets to write the majority opinion necessarily affects the size of the controlling decision on the case outcome along with whether the court's judgment ultimately reflects unanimity or discord among the judges in reaching it. The process by which opinions are assigned vary by court, though some studies indicate that using randomized procedures, such as mandatorily assigning an opinion by lot or through the clerk's office, helps lessen inter-personal influence among the court's membership; yet, randomized processes are not always effective in muting disagreement or conflict about case outcomes in appellate courts.[41] In contrast, courts using non-mandatory or discretionary opinion assignment processes typically vest more power in the chief justice or the most-senior judges in the majority coalition. For example, if the chief justice wields the authority to assign majority opinions, then she will have the strategic opportunity to shape the opinion's rationale and scope because the opinion writing could be assigned to herself or another justice who shares identical ideological views or policy goals. If the chief is not in the majority, the most senior justice in the majority has the opinion assignment power and likewise enjoys a similar strategic advantage.[42]

The institutional diversity of opinion assignment may be manifested in still other ways. In many appellate courts, such as in the Supreme Court, the practice of opinion assignment has historically varied with the chief justice's style of leadership and, sometimes, that style affects another norm that may let the justices at conference vote to "pass"—that is, not voting to affirm or reverse the lower court. One study found that passing was a strategy used by Chief Justice Warren Burger, and later by Chief Justice William Rehnquist, ostensibly to control opinion assignment in cases in which they did not know how a majority of the Court might vote. Both chief justices Burger and Rehnquist passed, in other words, when they were in doubt about whether they would be in the majority coalition. And both abstained from passing when they were sure that they would win or lose in cases decided on the merits. Such strategic behavior increased their capacity to set the Court's agenda and influence final outcomes.[43]

The dynamics of coalition building are not confined to the behavior of the chief justice, however. Although associate judges on the Supreme Court and other appeals courts may not hold opinion assignment power, they may still try to achieve their preferences by concurring (joining only the result, but not the rationale of the majority's opinion) or dissenting opinions. Such opinions exert pressure on judges in the majority because they undermine the legal weight attached to the majority's view and also expose a court's disagreements by "go[ing] public."[44] Still, because most cases are "easy" and result in unanimous or summary dispositions, individual threats to undercut the majority's opinion are only effective in cases that are the most significant or difficult to resolve. Regardless, the bargaining process remains fluid as drafts of opinions are freely circulated among the judges and their law clerks in chambers, thus making the opinion-writing stage very important to the appellate decision-making process.

Opinion Writing

"It will come out in the writing," observed Justice Ruth Bader Ginsburg, about the dynamics of the Supreme Court's decision making.[45] Justice Ginsburg's thoughts affirm that the final and most publicly accessible product of a court—namely, a written judicial opinion—comes from a variety of institutional processes that help define the law's scope and meaning. Yet the modern appellate practice of "reporting" bound volumes of printed judicial opinions historically evolved from the English common law practice of orally announcing legal judgments from the bench. At the Supreme Court, this was done in *seriatim*—that is, after each justice announced their decision, each opinion was reported with each author's name, followed by a short order afterwards summarizing the Court's ruling. In effect, there was no opinion of the court as a whole. By the early nineteenth century, both state and federal appeals courts required judges to generate written decisions in official print volumes—but, they generally retained the discretion to determine which opinions were to be designated for publication. Moreover, the *seriatim* norm was replaced by another convention of delivering a single "opinion for the court," with no separate opinions. Today, appellate opinions typically feature one opinion that represents the court's majority (the opinion for the court) or individual opinions that are written separately by justices who agree or disagree with the court's majority ruling; and they are disseminated in print and digital format, which has global implications for enhancing the individual and collective transparency of judicial work products.[46]

Notably, the modern origins of written judicial opinions and the law's development in appellate courts is shaped by lower court opinions, oral arguments, litigant and third (*amicus*) party briefs, case facts, legal precedent and the ideological preferences of judges.[47] A judicial opinion's clarity and to whom it is directed as an audience (the parties to the appeal, other judges and lawyers, interested legal stakeholders, or the public at large) is also a function of the strategic considerations underlying majority coalition-building on the court and the input from other internal actors, such as law clerks. Other factors that may affect a judicial opinion's content may include a court's workload, the political salience of a case, electoral pressures (for most state appeals judges), a judge's ethnicity, gender or race, past career positions (e.g. law professors or government experience), lifetime tenure (for many federal appeals judges), future career aspirations, opinion assignment rules, and the "freshman effect" (for new judges on a bench), among others. As some court watchers put it, judges certainly "do not start with a blank slate" when crafting judicial opinions.[48]

As former Justice Lewis Powell observed, one of the most important elements in opinion writing are the role law clerks play in appellate courts that are sometimes described as "small, independent law firms."[49] Indeed, some former clerks even claim that the Supreme Court has become "clerk driven." For that reason, it is not surprising that Justice Clarence Thomas characterized the significance of law clerks and the process of hiring law clerks as an ordeal that is similar to "selecting mates in a foxhole."[50] Law clerks not only typically write the first drafts of opinions but also take on other social tasks for their justices.[51] "The tasks of the clerks," as John P. Frank, who clerked for Justice Hugo Black, once put it, are "very much the product of the whims of their Justices." As he explained:

> In general, it is the job of the clerk to be the eyes and legs for his judge, finding and bringing in useful materials. This can involve an immense amount of work, depending upon how curious the Justice is. It is legend that Justice Brandeis once asked a clerk to look at every page of every volume in the United States Reports looking for a particular point. The clerks may also have semi-social duties, like those who visited with Holmes or took walks with [Justice] Stone or played tennis with [Justice] Black or superintended the circulation of the guests at the [Justice] Brandeis Sunday teas. All of this is in the spirit of an amiable relationship between a wise, elderly man and a young cub at the bar.[52]

A law clerk for Justice Powell echoed these sentiments, observing that the "ideal law clerk is both loyalist and critic—faithful to the judges' instructions, yet alert to any deficiencies of thought or expression."[53]

Law clerks earn the trust of their mentors by screening cases for review, conducting legal research, and writing draft opinions for in-chambers review. Of these duties, assisting in writing judicial opinions is the primary function. In state appellate courts, career law clerks spend roughly 65 percent of their time preparing opinions, and the same behavior appears in federal courts.[54] The give-and-take normally associated with drafting opinions occurs not only between law clerks and their justice or judge but also between judges in different chambers and their clerks. The "ambassadorial role" that clerks play in an informal "clerk network" consists of information gathering, lobbying, and even negotiating with other chambers.[55]

Regardless of the substantive content of judicial opinions and how they are created, it is significant to note that most appellate opinions are not the result of internal discord or conflict. Appellate courts, in fact, hand down unanimous opinions more often than not. Unanimity is generated because most cases are relatively easy to decide; that is, they involve appeals that do not present substantial legal conflict or *amicus* participation.[56] In "hard cases," though, or those involving thorny and vexing legal issues involving controversial social public policy issues, it is not unusual for judges to issue individual concurring or dissenting opinions (see Table 9.2). The mere threat to issue a concurrence or a dissent may influence coalition building and the drafting of majority opinions by forcing justices or judges in different chambers to rethink their positions, and even respond to points made by a concurring or dissenting opinion.[57]

Table 9.2	Types of Judicial Opinions
Type	**Characteristics**
Majority	An opinion supported by a majority of judges
Plurality	An opinion agreeing with the outcome but supported by less than a majority
Per Curiam	An opinion "by the court" but unsigned; the author/judge is not identified
Concurring	An opinion agreeing with the outcome but not the legal rationale
Dissenting	An opinion disagreeing with the outcome and/or its legal rationale
Concurring and Dissenting in part	An opinion that agrees, or disagrees, with the result or legal rationale in part

Concurrences and Dissents

In contrast to a majority opinion, a separately filed concurring or dissenting opinion may manifest either accord, institutional disobedience, or a combination of both.[58] Filing separate opinions is not the historical norm in many appellate courts. For example, under Chief Justice John Marshall's strong leadership in the formative years of the Supreme Court, unanimous opinions were deemed important to establishing the legitimacy of the federal judiciary—so the in *seriatim* practice of separate opinions, discussed earlier, was discouraged. But that tradition gradually broke down, and the decline of a "norm of consensus" has become a defining aspect of judicial behavior since the New Deal in the 1930s. The breakdown of that tradition has led to the contemporary appellate practice of writing an opinion for the court (reflecting the majority view) that may also include separate opinions authored by individual judges.[59]

With the rise of individual opinions, expressing an opposing viewpoint can be done in different ways by judges; nonetheless, such expressions have great utility.[60] In general, a concurring opinion indicates agreement with the case result and its legal rationale. But a discordant perspective may be communicated in a concurrence that agrees with the general result but disagrees with the majority opinion's legal rationale; or through a dissent that disagrees with the result *and* the legal basis for the majority opinion's conclusions. If there is not full agreement or disagreement with the court's ruling in a separate concurrence or dissent, judges may write an opinion that partially supports or rejects the majority opinion that is styled a "concurring and dissenting opinion, in part."

A concurrence or dissent's practicality is also apparent. Psychologists studying the impact of information and how it is shared amidst countervailing social pressures acknowledge that minority viewpoints remain unique and distinct opportunities for persuasion.[61] Internally, they force the majority to rethink or revise its position, which may improve the Court's final opinion. Certain dissents, also, are strategically designed to send a message to external actors, thus laying a foundation for an ultimate change in the law if the dissent subsequently commands a majority and later becomes the law in future litigation. As Chief Justice Charles Evans Hughes once said, a dissent in an appellate court is "an appeal to the brooding spirit of the law, to the intelligence of a future day, when a later decision may possibly correct the error into which the dissenting judge believes the court to have been betrayed."[62] Thus, the individual choice to dissent represents not only ideological and legal disagreement, but also strategic behavior, especially in highly salient or politically controversial cases.[63]

At times, a justice may read portions or summarize the main points of a dissent from the bench after the opinion of the Court has been handed down. Such oral dissents, as public statements, are unusual, however. When the Supreme Court announces a decision, ordinarily the majority author gives a short summary from the bench, and the justices in the minority remain silent. In this respect, the appellate norm is similar to European civil law practice in some countries in which dissenting opinions are rare or even barred. Still, when disagreement is particularly sharp in the Supreme Court, a justice may orally dissent from the bench in order to underscore "that the Court's opinion is not just wrong, but importantly and grievously misguided."[64] Besides highlighting sharp disagreements within a court, oral dissents also serve the purpose of being a call to action—they may alert Congress, the public, or other legal stakeholders that the majority opinion needs to be reversed with subsequent legislation that may eventually be enacted due to increased lobbying or advocacy by negatively affected groups or interests. In this respect, oral dissents "may spark a deliberative process that enhances public confidence in the legitimacy of the judicial process," simply because they are a "crucial tool in the ongoing dialogue between constitutional law and constitutional culture."[65]

Even though they have long been a part of Supreme Court history, such oral dissents remain infrequent. Between 1969 and 2008, 119 oral dissents were registered, which, on average, account for about three per term. Moreover, oral dissents are not confined to any particular type of case, though most often occur in only highly ideologically divisive rulings on controversies over abortion, school desegregation, flag burning, or death penalty, to name a few.[66] Sometimes, a justice may even read an angry concurrence (which actually dissents from parts of the opinion for the Court) from the bench—which Justice Antonin Scalia did in *Glossip v. Gross* (2015), a 5:4 decision authorizing the death penalty by legal injection using midazolam. In *Glossip*, Justice Scalia took the very unusual step of interjecting his comments *after* oral dissents delivered from Justices Sonia Sotomayor (who described the method of execution as being "drawn and quartered, slowly tortured to death, or actually burned at the stake") and Stephen Breyer (who explained why he and Justice Ruth Bader Ginsburg thought it was imperative for the full Court to decree the death penalty unconstitutional). Scalia also used the moment to lash out at both of his colleagues for voting to uphold same-sex marriage earlier in the Term by exclaiming "Unlike opposite sex marriage, the death penalty is approved by the constitution."[67] But, as one pundit observed after watching Justice Ginsburg read, for the first time in her career, two oral dissents in an abortion and a discrimination case, such public outbursts are relatively harmless as "an act of theater" that manifests strong disagreement with the majority's ruling.[68]

Unpublished Opinions

The growing practice of issuing separate concurring and dissenting opinions has been accompanied by the controversial emergence in federal appellate courts of "unpublished opinions" (which nonetheless remain available in the Federal Appendix and on some electronic databases, such as LexisNexis). Recent data shows that in the federal appellate courts, 88 percent of appeals were terminated without published opinions.[69] Because of rising caseloads, some courts now publish only those opinions that significantly contribute to development of the law. They may decide a published opinion is not justified because: (1) the appeal fails to raise an original or new legal question; (2) a published opinion explanation will not have an important impact on public policy; or, (3) the lower court's opinion can stand on its own. Arguably, the shift is justified on the grounds that it avoids cluttering the law with inconsistent and contradictory precedents that are, on balance, relatively inconsequential to the public. But critics (including some judges) counter that the practice erodes judicial accountability and public transparency. The debate over the propriety of unpublished opinions, moreover, extends to appellate state court practice since many state jurisdictions have procedural rules governing their citation as well.[70]

Once an appeal is decided, the parties are informed by an order affirming or reversing the lower court. Though the language of the order varies, courts may affirm, vacate, or reverse the lower court's ruling in its entirety, or affirm and overturn different portions of the lower court's ruling. Moreover, it is not unusual for courts to issue detailed instructions directing the lower court to correct the error it committed and for remedial action.

STUDYING JUDICIAL DECISION-MAKING

In his famous 1897 essay, "The Path of the Law," Oliver Wendell Holmes, Jr., declared that law is nothing more than "prophecies of what the courts will do in fact."[71] Holmes used the perspective of a "bad man"—who only would care about how the law would affect him negatively if the acted a certain way—to conclude that such men are only interested in predicting what the courts would do to him if he was punished for breaking it. In this regard, Holmes' "bad man" or prediction theory emphasized the law's practical effect; but it also presumed that the discovery of facts, and not the basic morality of whether to obey it, is the key to understanding judicial behavior. In his judicial opinions and other writings,

Holmes thus suggested that judges do not engage in legal reasoning by logical deduction in light of what universal first principles or legal texts command; rather, judicial reasoning is intuitive, so judges take into account their own experiences, along with the social and economic consequences of their actions, in deciding cases.[72]

In many respects Holmes' judicial philosophy is a forerunner to contemporary efforts to explain what influences or factors drive judicial outcomes. Today, scholars study judicial behavior, which is investigating what judges do and why they do it in a systematic, empirical, or theoretical framework, by examining the core issue of whether legal or political variables, or some combination thereof, explains judicial decision-making (see Table 9.3). In general, as political scientist James Gibson described it, the academic inquiry is directed at understanding why "judges' decisions are a function of what they prefer to do, tempered by what they think they ought to do, but constrained by what they perceive is feasible to do."[73] Consequently, three basic questions routinely frame judicial behavior analyses: (1) do judges decide cases solely on the basis of law or on their ideological predispositions?; (2) do institutional structures and norms play a significant role in explaining judicial decisions?; and, (3) are judges strategic actors in making decisions that take into account legal or institutional constraints in reaching their policy goals? These questions and others form the basis for other theories of judicial behavior that are not only grounded in political science, but also other disciplines, such as the legal academy, sociology, psychology, and economics.[74]

Table 9.3	Legal or Political Variables Used to Explain or Predict Judicial Decisions
Variable Categories	**What variable purports to explain or predict regarding judicial choices**
Personal Preferences	The impact of personal policy or ideological preferences of judges on judicial decision-making **Examples:** past judicial votes of judges and the background and social characteristics of judges (e.g., partisan affiliation; prior judicial, legal, or political employment; judge's age; judge's race; judge's gender; judge's income; judge's education)
Legal Factors	The impact "law" has on judicial decision-making **Examples:** past judicial opinions ("precedent" or "*stare decisis*")
Case Characteristics	The impact of specific case facts in judicial opinions on judicial decision-making **Examples:** "Aggravating" or "mitigating" factors in death penalty cases (e.g., killing a police officer during a robbery; whether the defendant is mentally disabled); the presence of certain factors in Fourth Amendment search or seizure cases (e.g., if the search is conducted with a search warrant at a private residence)
Institutional Arrangements	The impact of formal rules, organizational structures, and norms on judicial decision-making **Examples:** norms of consensus in writing judicial opinions; panel composition and size on appeals courts; methods governing judicial recruitment or retention (by partisan or nonpartisan elections or by executive appointment); presence or absence of an appellate court; the supply of lawyers in a jurisdiction; changing leadership styles of chief justice; judicial opinion assignment procedures; technological or staff changes affecting judicial operations
Environmental Characteristics	The impact of political, economic, or social environments on judicial decision-making **Examples:** electoral composition of legislative or executive branches; level of partisan electoral competition; level of budgetary support; urbanism

Sources: Lee Epstein, "Review Essay of Benjamin Alarie & Andrew J Green, Commitment and Cooperation on High Courts: A Cross-Country Examination of Institutional Constraints on Judges (Oxford: Oxford University Press, 2017)," *University of Toronto Law Journal* 69 (Spring, 2019), 275–293;

David M. O'Brien, "Institutional Norms and Supreme Court Opinions: On Reconsidering the Rise of Individual Opinions," in *Supreme Court Decision Making: New Institutionalist Approaches,* eds. Cornell W. Clayton and Howard Gillman (Chicago: University of Chicago Press, 1999), 91–113; Harold J. Spaeth and Jeffrey A. Segal, *Majority Rule or Minority Will: Adherence to Precedent on the U.S. Supreme Court* (Cambridge, U.K.: Cambridge University Press, 1999); Paul Brace and Melinda Gann Hall, "Integrated Models of Judicial Dissent," *Journal of Politics* (November 1993), 914–35.

The aim of these studies is to identify the underlying causes of judicial policymaking. Yet public law scholars across different academic disciplines sharply differ in their theoretical and methodological approaches to explaining judicial rulings. For example, researchers exploring normative theory might use historical analyses, the process of legal reasoning, and rival conceptions of judicial interpretation to study judicial politics. Studies in this area may rely upon legal doctrinal, historical, anecdotal evidence to support their findings, often through the application of discursive interpretations of the law, or qualitative methods. By contrast, while researchers taking an empirical or behavioral approach may acknowledge the merit of qualitative scholarship, they instead may insist that additional systematic and scientific rigor is needed to generate data, test hypotheses, and discover relationships between variables in judicial behavior research using quantitative methods. Not surprisingly, the fundamental disagreement over methodologies is essentially based on the sufficiency of proof needed to establish valid research findings: whereas empiricists argue interpretivist scholars over-rely upon subjective and unscientific reasons for judicial decision-making, interpretivists counter that not all understandings about judicial behavior are captured by falsifiable hypotheses and well-specified quantitative models.[75]

Some (but not all) of the principal rival theories of judicial politics are outlined below. Specifically, three predominant political science models of judicial behavior are discussed: (1) the attitudinal model; (2) new institutionalism; and, (3) strategic choice theory (see Figure 9.2). Thereafter, a fourth approach—a formalistic or normative theory of what may is often referred to as "traditional" legal reasoning to explain judicial behavior—is considered, along with the significance of interpreting constitutional law or statutes as part of the legal decision-making process.

| Figure 9.2 | Research Methodologies for Studying Judicial Politics |

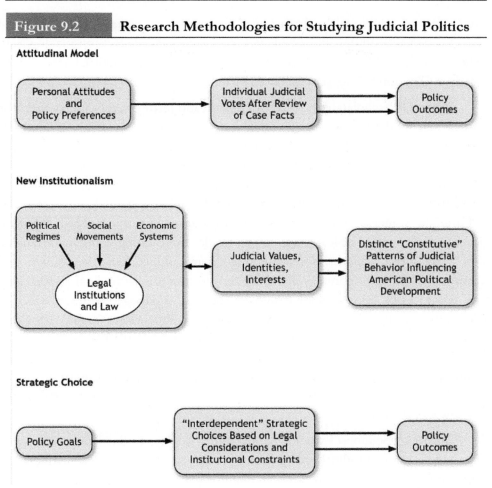

Attitudinal Model

New Institutionalism

Strategic Choice

The Attitudinal Model

C. Herman Pritchett's *The Roosevelt Court: A Study in Judicial Politics and Values, 1937–1947* (1948)[76] inspired scholars to seek "behavioral" explanations for judicial decisions. The so-called "behavioral revolution" of the 1940s and 1950s, led by Pritchett, Glendon Schubert, and S. Sidney Ulmer, stressed the "science" of politics and relied upon quantitative methods to explain individual judicial votes. In what he described as "bloc analysis" of the Supreme Court's nonunanimous opinions, Pritchett compiled data in descriptive tables to identify voting alignments among justices along ideological dimensions, which was innovative for the time. Subsequent judicial behaviorists have similarly de-emphasized the historical and institutional characteristics of courts and hypothesized that judicial votes are quantifiable expressions of individual policy preferences. Moreover, for behaviorists, the normative study of legal doctrine and the effect of traditional legal reasoning became less important than identifying how personal attitudes and ideologies influence judicial decision-making.[77] In short, Pritchett "blazed a trail" for subsequent generations of judicial behaviorists, such as Glendon Schubert and Harold Spaeth.[78]

Schubert's scholarship, along with Spaeth and Jeffrey Segal's updating of the attitudinal model in *The Supreme Court and the Attitudinal Model* (1993) and *The Supreme Court and the Attitudinal Model Revisited* (2002), represents the most rigorous (but controversial) attitudinal explanation for Supreme Court policymaking. In *Quantitative Analysis of Judicial Behavior* (1959), Schubert used scalogram analysis—a statistical method borrowed from psychological studies and also known as "Guttman scaling"—to test the theory that attitudes drive judicial behavior. Although the use of scales, which infer attitudes by counting votes and arranging them on ideological scales representing liberal and conservative values, was innovative, its shortcomings led Schubert to test the attitudinal model in a different way by using a factor analysis of the justices' votes in another book, *The Judicial Mind* (1965), in terms of two ideological dimensions (scales), "political liberalism" and "economic liberalism," in order to explain the justices' votes.[79] In *The Judicial Mind Revisited* (1974), Schubert applied these techniques and others not only to confirm his earlier findings but also to introduce **game theory**—a theory positing that Supreme Court justices make strategic choices to grant *certiorari* and set the Court's agenda.

Although Schubert's work generated much debate, it nonetheless established the basis for the attitudinal and strategic models that were later popularized.[80] The most complete analysis was done by political scientists Jeffrey Segal and Harold Spaeth in *The Supreme Court and the Attitudinal Model*.[81] In conjunction with *The Supreme Court Database*, an original set of Supreme Court cases created by Spaeth that identified and coded individual votes of justices, and other case-related information, dating back to 1791, the authors used the statistical method of logistical regression to argue that the **attitudinal model**—namely, that decisions of the Court are based on the ideological attitudes and policy preferences of the justices (and not their rival legal philosophies)—is the only empirically verifiable explanation for judicial policymaking. In other words, they maintain that Supreme Court decisions cannot be explained by the so-called **legal model**, which assumes that legal factors—such as precedent and the justices' legal philosophies—are the basis for judicial decisions. Instead, the attitudinal model stipulates "that personal policy preferences are the strongest influence, limited by the facts (stimuli) of the controversy at hand, on how a judge will rule on the merits of a case."[82]

According to Spaeth and Segal, the view that law determines judicial decision-making is mistaken because interpreting precedent and constitutional or statutory text is inherently subjective and may not be used as an independent variable—thus defeating attempts to test empirically the effects of a legal model. Hence, they contend that legal considerations have little impact on judicial decisions and that law is always "made" by judges, not "discovered." Their view is strengthened because the attitudinal model is capable of rigorous statistical testing. In other words, creating an empirically falsifiable model of law allows for a more accurate depiction of what judges actually do; and it avoids the problem of simply asserting that judicial decisions appropriately reflect the judges' sincere beliefs about what the law requires. Using observable data, such as justices' past votes, case facts, and the justices' ideologies (as constructed through newspaper editorials), and quantitative methods, they conclude that the justices' attitudes are the best predictors of case outcomes. In their words, former Chief Justice "Rehnquist votes the way he does because he is extremely conservative; [former Associate Justice Thurgood] Marshall voted the way he did because he is extremely liberal."[83] The same logic is applied to all political explanations of judicial outcomes in the Supreme Court, along with appellate decision making in other countries, such as Canada.[84]

The attitudinal model's success in explaining Supreme Court decisions is only matched by the critical responses to its validity. Critics, for example, have pointed out a number of inconsistencies in the model, including: (1) the attitudinal model does not adequately account for the role law plays in explaining judicial decision-making; (2) the political and legal factors affecting judicial decision-making cannot always be quantitatively reduced; and, (3) the attitudinal model unduly minimizes the significant role institutions and judicial strategies play in influencing judicial policymaking. Notably, Spaeth and Segal responded these criticisms and others in a revised edition, *The Supreme Court and the Attitudinal Model Revisited*; and they dismissed the objections because the detractors, in their words, are either "philosophically opposed," or lack "the requisite imagination," to adopt an empirical model which unequivocally is "[t]he dominant theory of judicial behavior in the field of political science."[85] Regardless, the debate over the attitudinal model is a significant illustration of the strengths and weaknesses of having alternative approaches to explaining judicial decision-making; and, it also prompted political scientists to develop alternative methodologies for explaining judicial behavior, as discussed next.

New Institutionalism

New institutionalism studies of courts are interdisciplinary, drawing on history, sociology, economics or political science. Inspired by the work of Martin Shapiro on the significance of "political jurisprudence" and that of Rogers Smith,[86] public law scholarship generally reflects two dominant strands: rational choice ("strategic") institutionalism and historical institutionalism. Drawing from economic theories and congressional studies, rational choice research focuses on the extent to which judges are strategic actors who try to achieve their policy goals by making rational choices that are constrained by other judges and participants in the judicial process. As in game theory, the application of rules and procedures within institutions structure the utility-maximizing and fixed choices of rational actors seeking to fulfill policy goals through strategic, interdependent action that may not always express one's "true" preferences. By contrast, historical institutionalism focuses on how judicial institutions are structured by their historical and political contexts, such as various interactions between groups, ideas, interests, or norms, which in turn explains the unique legal and political outcomes or positions of courts and judges. Although distinct, historical institutionalism resembles a third type of institutionalism found in political science—sociological institutionalism, which posits that cultural and societal procedures and practices, such as customs or conventions, contextually frame individual choices or collective action.[87]

New institutionalism stands in sharp contrast to the attitudinal model. But its basic premise—namely, that legal considerations affect judicial decisions—is not "new" and stems from traditional constitutional law analysis (e.g. legal reasoning) and, perhaps to a lesser degree, jurisprudence (see Chapter Two).[88] A principal objective of historical institutionalism is thus to connect, from an interpretative and historical perspective, normative conceptions of law and courts with the contemporary legal institutions and their political roles.[89] That is to say, judicial decision-making is contextualized within the framework of institutional arrangements and practices, such as the structure of courts, judicial norms, the makeup of law schools or bar associations, and the predominant legal culture, among others. In addition, its proponents maintain that the discovery of the institutional characteristics of judicial behavior offers a more nuanced and balanced view of the patterns of "purpose and meaning" that underlie American political development. Within a specific historical moment, for example, courts may have a distinct purpose or shared normative goal, such as the adherence to professional obligations or the need to sustain public legitimacy, that is infused with institutional structures or arrangements, and which necessarily transcend the achievement of personal goals through strategic rationality or calculations.[90]

The promise of new institutionalism is the wide net it casts and its broad scholarly focus. Unlike the attitudinal model, it seeks to explain judicial behavior by going beyond making predictions about how individual justices ideologically vote in cases. To illustrate, two anthologies edited by Howard Gillman and Cornell Clayton, *Supreme Court Decision-Making: New Institutionalist Approaches* (1999) and *The Supreme Court in American Politics: New Institutionalist Interpretations* (1999),[91] analyze how the Supreme Court's decision-making is affected by its own "internal" institutional norms, rules or practices, as well as the impact of "external" or extra-judicial forces. Whereas the *Supreme Court Decision-Making* investigates the effect of various institutional elements, such as judicial leadership styles, opinion assignment practices or judicial recruitment methods, *The Supreme Court in American Politics* traces the Court's historical development while examining the distinct legal, social, and political contexts defining the judiciary's operation in regards to political parties, interest groups, and larger societal issues of race, gender and capitalism, to name a few.[92]

Interpretative and normative public law scholarship suggests that the attitudinal model is an incomplete research methodology, mainly due to its narrow emphasis on explaining individual. preference-based judicial voting behavior in a dichotomous fashion. Put differently, not all public law scholars are convinced that judicial behavior can be reduced to quantifiable explanations of political influences and law's insignificant impact. Thus, the attitudinal preoccupation with explaining judicial votes behavior necessarily does not pay enough attention to the law's doctrinal or contextual development and how the law shapes normative legal policy outcomes. While historical new institutionalists accept that judges decide cases with their attitudes, preferences, or partisanship, they also observe that courts and judges draw their authority from, and use legal doctrines, to mold the political development of law and courts within broader societal structures and institutional arrangements, rules or practices. In this regard, new institutionalism is similar to other strands of law and politics research centered on legal mobilization and "cause lawyering"—where legal stakeholders, organized interests, and activist lawyers use the law and litigation to garner judicial support for policy goals—and "regime politics," an understanding of courts positing that legal ideas or doctrines, as influenced by organized activities, presidential appointments or legal-political arguments, are a foundation for comprehending judicial politics. In sum, the normative legal and political science literature asserts that judicial policy-making is a function of an interaction between law and politics and, therefore, cannot be not simply thought of as quantitative expressions of individual vote choice. Not surprisingly, critics of new institutionalism argue that its substantive claims and methodological approach are flawed because historical and interpretative findings are not subjected to rigorous empirical analysis and overestimate the role law plays as a constraint on the behavior of judges.[93]

Strategic Choice Theory

Although Glendon Schubert used game theory to explain Supreme Court decisions in some of his early work, political scientist Walter Murphy, in his classic *The Elements of Judicial Strategy* (1964), famously articulated that policy-minded Supreme Court justices construct a "grand strategy and particular strategies" to achieve their goals in dealing with colleagues and other nonjudicial political actors.[94] Subsequent research analyzed the role strategic considerations play in producing judicial outcomes, ostensibly reconciling the attitudinal and institutionalist assumptions that personal attitudes and legal considerations affect judicial decision-making. In addition, strategic or rational choice scholars tend to favor empirical methods. Thus, strategic choice theorists share the institutionalist belief that law matters, but in their use of quantitative methods, they share common ground with those who champion the attitudinal model.

Strategic choice theory maintains that judges base their decisions on strategic calculations that are tempered by legal factors and institutional constraints. Lee Epstein and Jack Knight, two leading scholars who proposed a strategic account of judicial behavior in *The Choices Justices Make* (1998), argued that "Justices may be primarily seekers of legal policy, but they are not unsophisticated actors who make decisions based merely on their ideological attitudes." Instead, they explain, "justices are strategic actors who realize that their ability to achieve their goals depends on a consideration of the preferences of other actors, of the choices they expect others to make, and of the institutional context in which they act."[95] Initially, *Choices* asserted that judges are primarily interested in maximizing policy goals; but its authors subsequently acknowledged that judges may seek a host of non-policy goals that relate to achieving job satisfaction, a good reputation, more leisure time, a better salary, or promotion, to name a few.[96]

Still, strategic-minded judges seek to achieve their goals only after weighing the risks and benefits of their actions. Judicial decision-making is thus interdependent because, in order to maximize their own policy preferences, judges choose courses of action that take into account the preferences of others, such as their judicial colleagues, elected officials and the public, in a given institutional context. That is to say, the interdependent decisions of goal-seeking judges are structured by a set of formal or informal rules, such as law, norms or conventions, that influence their choices in an institutional setting. As a result, judges are described as "sophisticated" decision makers: They may not be able to vote for their true or "sincere" preferences because such choices may not be the best ones to make under the circumstances. Thus judges vote in accordance with policy positions that best approximate their sincere choices because to do otherwise might compromise their chance to achieve their most preferred goals.[97]

Strategic choice theory has been applied to different areas of judicial behavior, ranging from how judges and courts operate internally to those exploring how they are affected by external environments.[98] For example, while some scholars have used it to study of judicial recruitment and the institutional relationship between courts and other political branches,[99] others have investigated the dynamics of coalition building and opinion writing. Two books, *The Choices Justices Make* and *Crafting Law on the Supreme Court: The Collegial Game*,[100] are illustrative. In *The Choices Judges Make*, Lee Epstein and Jack Knight used the private papers of justices and case analysis to highlight how decisions during the Burger Court (1969–1986) were achieved through an extensive process of strategic negotiations, bargaining, and compromise. Likewise, political scientists Forrest Maltzman, James Spriggs II, and Paul Wahlbeck in *Crafting Law on the Supreme Court* show that justices engage in a "collegial game" of strategic coalition building in opinion assignment and drafting opinions in order to maximize their policy preferences.

In general, strategic choice theory is distinctive in its attempt to reconcile some of the central themes that are a part of the attitudinal and new institutionalist perspectives. In this light, it tries to overcome the attitudinal model's insistence that judicial decisions are solely driven by political preferences while also acknowledging the impact that law and institutions have on judicial outcomes, a central claim of new institutionalists. Moreover, the recognition that judges are not only interested in maximizing their ideological or policy goals has spawned analogous interdisciplinary studies that argue for a "labor-market theory" of judicial behavior. That is, judges decide cases as participants in the labor market, weighing the costs and benefits of different outcomes based on a "judicial utility function," an economic term. In this theoretical account, rational judges take into account legal factors along with those of self-interest, including choices to avoid work, maximize leisure, earn promotion, avoid peer criticism, and build collegial relationships. Other considerations are time constraints, personal and work-related satisfaction (i.e., enjoying work while gaining reputation, power, and influence), and monetary benefits. Applying such categories across all levels of the federal judiciary, this line of empirical scholarship concludes that, to varying degrees, the ideological preferences and individual choices judges make in satisfying their professional and personal goals in a legal setting are a more "realistic" explanation of judicial behavior.[101]

Future Directions of Judicial Behavior Research

In the early twentieth century, public law scholarship was once characterized as "the last long-drawn-out gasp of a dying tradition." Today, the future of law and courts' research is much brighter, encompassing a wide range of theoretical and inter-disciplinary perspectives, along with a growing interest in using different and innovative datasets and methodologies that focus attention not only U.S. judicial institutions, but also comparative and international judging. The three models just outlined are certainly not the only ones political scientists employ to understand law and courts. For instance, political science public law behavioral research is now complemented, as well, by **empirical legal studies**, an initiative rooted in the legal academy that draws off of the insights of several academic disciplines—including political science, law, economics, criminology, finance, psychology, sociology, health care, and others—to study diverse topics in domestic and international legal studies. In a similar vein, political scientist Lawrence Baum has proposed an "audience-based" theory based on social psychology to explain judicial decision-making. Baum argues that judges are highly cognizant of "self-presentation," or how they are perceived by the internal and external audiences that matter to judges. These include judicial colleagues, the public, the media, politicians, other lawyers and bar associations, and the social groups or elites. Like Baum, still other scholars have explored the psychological motivations or incentives underlying judging including, among other things, the role a justice's personality traits play in affecting policy outcomes.[102] To be sure, C. Herman Pritchett's observation that law and courts scholars must embrace the old Chinese proverb to "Let a hundred flowers bloom" in undertaking prospective research goes a long way in explaining the significant inroads public law scholars have made in explaining judicial behavior in recent years.[103]

In addition, several developments in the field illustrate the direction of future judicial behavioral research. First, it is no longer simply confined to the realm of political scientists. As the empirical legal studies approach suggests, a greater diversity of social scientists from the academic disciplines of economics, psychology, history, and the law profession itself are making important quantitative and qualitative contributions to legal studies, and their work is grounded in the study of U.S. and international courts, such as the Germany or

Spanish Constitutional Courts, the Norwegian, French, German or Japanese Supreme Courts, Latin American courts, the European Court of Justice and the European Court of Human Rights, to name a few.[104] Second, the quality of collecting and using data for empirical analyses is greatly assisting law and courts' scholars to frame research designs exploring a diversity of judicial venues across jurisdictional, regional and international lines. These include, among others, the U.S. Supreme Court Database, the U.S. Court of Appeals Database, the State Supreme Court Data Project, and the National High Courts Judicial Database. And finally, these datasets, and many others, are the foundation for the emergence of different methodologies, such as matching methods, networking analyses, and event count statistical models, that frame new public law research in a variety of subject matter and legal issues in innovative ways.[105] Of course, the empirical orientation of judicial behavior research tends to favor quantitative methods; but, public law scholarship is also heavily influenced by traditional legal studies grounded in qualitative work, such as formalism, law and legal interpretation, discussed next.

Legal Formalism and Traditional Legal Reasoning

A longstanding tradition of legal interpretation, rooted in legal formalism, argues that "the law," and how legal principles are derived through legal reasoning, is the best explanation of judicial behavior. Formalists, sometimes referred to as "legalists,"[106] assert that the discovery of preexisting legal principles and their application to cases is the core of legal reasoning. In this regard, **traditional legal studies** emphasizes the creative interpretative choices of judges in deciding cases. As former D.C. Circuit Judge Harry Edwards once observed, "It is the law—and not the personal politics of individual judges—that controls decision making in most cases resolved by the courts of appeals." Later retreating somewhat from that view,[107] Edwards conceded his socialization and training in law school reinforced his belief that the judicial decision-making process is nothing more than "thinking like a lawyer"—in other words, legal conclusions are reached after the law is "found" and then applied to a case's facts in a rather formalistic, or mechanical fashion (discussed in Chapter Five). Blackstone's **declaratory theory of law** (discussed in Chapter One) exemplifies this approach in characterizing judicial interpretation as essentially value free and nondiscretionary decision-making process. But that theory has been largely debunked because judicial decision-making and the legal reasoning behind it is not so simple. As Seventh Circuit Judge Richard Posner explains, the law, in and of itself, "fail[s] to generate acceptable answers to all the legal questions that American judges are required to decide." As a result, judges frequently resort to relying upon other "sources of judgment," including their own personal views or policy preferences, which, in turn, "does not fit a legalist model of decision-making."[108]

Still, some judges and scholars, like former Chicago Law School dean Edward H. Levi, defend the traditional approach by arguing that legal reasoning inherently involves **reasoning by example or analogy**, or "reasoning from case to case."[109] Unlike the Blackstonian declaratory theory, reasoning by analogy ostensibly involves culling legal principles from past cases that are factually similar and applying them to new circumstances. Reasoning by example or analogy, Levi argued, occurs in three stages. First, judges recognize the similarity between a past case and the case under review. Next, the judge discovers a rule of law from the prior case. And, finally, judges apply the rule to the case at hand. Because the "rules arise out of a process which, while comparing fact situations, creates the rules and then applies them," for Levi the most crucial task of the judge is to determine the similarity or difference in facts between cases.[110]

Critics of the reasoning by example or analogy rationale, however, claim that carefully applying the facts to the law does not eliminate all judicial discretion. In fact, it may even encourage innovative judicial reasoning. For example, as Justice Benjamin Cardozo observed in his classic *The Nature of the Judicial Process*, judges often confront ambiguous cases and facts that invite making a judicial decision beyond what the "law" commands. "The rules and principles of case law," he explained, "have never been treated as final truths, but as working hypotheses, continually retested in those great laboratories of the law, the courts of justice." Cardozo thus understood that legal reasoning is a dynamic enterprise that sometimes inevitably entails subjective interpretation. As Cardozo put it, legal reasoning involves a "method of free decision" in which the "directive force of a principle" is fashioned by the judge through the combined use of community traditions and methods of philosophy, history, and sociology.[111]

The Law and Politics of Legal Precedent

A critical aspect of traditional legal reasoning is how courts and judges evaluate existing case law, or the binding legal precedents that are set in earlier cases. Under the common law, a precedent is defined as a prior ruling "that furnishes a basis for determining later cases involving similar facts or issues."[112] The manner in which judges weigh, and apply, legal precedents is infused within judicial politics and ongoing debates over controversial public policies. The intense deliberation among Supreme Court justices over the scope and application of criminal procedure precedent in *Ramos v. Louisiana* (2020) is illustrative. In *Ramos*, the Roberts Court overruled *Apodaca v. Oregon*'s (1972) longstanding Sixth

Amendment principle that let state governments convict offenders with non-unanimous jury verdicts even though unanimous verdicts is required for federal trials. In a 6:3 ruling, the Court held that both federal and state trials mandated unanimous jury verdicts; but the justices splintered into different blocs that crossed ideological lines in determining *Apodaca*'s precedential weight and if the law should change. While Justice Neil Gorsuch's majority opinion (and separate concurrences) decided that *Apodaca* must be overruled, the Court could not agree on the reasons why. In particular:

- Five Justices (Gorsuch, Ruth Bader Ginsburg, Steven Breyer, and in part by Sonia Sotomayor and Brett Kavanaugh) declared unanimous verdicts are required by federal and state courts, and that *Apodaca* was incorrectly decided, especially since Louisiana created the non-unanimous rule as part of its Jim Crow era racist past;

- Three Justices (Gorsuch, Ginsburg and Breyer) concluded *Apodaca* was not even a precedent that carried any binding effect; and,

- In separate concurrences, Justice Sotomayor classified *Apodaca* as at odds with different lines of precedent and had to be overruled because it was in a "universe of one" that was tainted by its racially-biased origins; and, Justice Brett Kavanaugh observed that while the Court has never established a consistent methodology to determine when it was appropriate to overrule precedent, it was warranted in *Ramos* because *Apodaca* was "grievously or egregiously wrong" and it has led to harmful "jurisprudential or real world consequences" that diminished any reliance upon it as a binding precedent.

- Justice Thomas, in a separate concurrence supporting the judgment, thought *Apodaca* is correct, but that Ramos deserved a unanimous jury verdict at the state level, but only because that right was given to him through the Fourteenth Amendment's privileges or immunities, rather than the due process, clause.

Furthermore, after observing that the doctrine of **stare decisis** "gets rough treatment in today's decision," dissenting Justices Samuel Alito, Chief Justice John Roberts and Justice Elena Kagan countered that *Apodaca* not only deserved respect as a binding precedent, but also that abandoning it ignores that Louisiana has heavily relied upon its non-unanimous verdict principle; and, reversing it will cause a "tsunami" of thrown out convictions under *Apodaca* non-unanimous rule that local prosecutors now will have to re-try in the criminal justice system.[113]

Ironically, the fractured analysis of the full Court in *Ramos* and its failure to shed consistent light on *Apodaca's* precedential weight does not offer much clarity to understanding the legal conditions, or the underlying justification, as to why precedent must change, a key tenet of the doctrine of *stare decisis*. Perhaps the only certainty is linked to the statement, as some scholars say, that "Nobody on the Court believes in absolute stare decisis."[114] An identical example, in *Webster v. Reproductive Health Services* (1989), shows the political implications of how the Justices view precedent is in the abortion context. In *Webster* (1989), a bare majority of the Supreme Court upheld several abortion restrictions enacted in the state of Missouri; but the justices nonetheless chose not to overturn *Roe v. Wade* (1973), the landmark abortion ruling. The ambiguous result, which endorsed state laws that undermined abortion rights while also supporting the continuity of *Roe's* basic meaning as a pro-abortion legal precedent, prompted Justice Antonin Scalia, a conservative justice and *Roe* critic, to conclude that not clearly reversing *Roe* judicially "preserves a chaos that is evident to anyone that can read and count. . .[and that] our retaining control, through *Roe*, of what I believe to be, and many of our citizens recognize to be, a political issue, continuously distorts the public perception of the role of this Court." As he lamented:[115]

> We can now look forward to at least another Term with carts full of mail from the public, and streets full of demonstrators, urging us—their unelected and life-tenured judges who have been awarded those extraordinary, undemocratic characteristics precisely in order that we might follow the law despite the popular will—to follow the popular will. Indeed, I expect we can look forward to even more of that than before, given our indecisive decision today.

Within a few years, though, two leading liberals—Justices William J. Brennan and Thurgood Marshall—were replaced by Justices David Souter and Clarence Thomas. So once again the Court appeared poised to overrule *Roe* in *Planned Parenthood of Southeastern Pennsylvania v. Casey* (1992), a case examining several abortion restriction enacted in the state of Pennsylvania.[116] But, in another five-to-four decision and an unusual joint opinion for the Court by Justices Sandra Day O'Connor, Souter, and Anthony Kennedy (which Justices John Paul Stevens and Harry Blackmun joined only in part), the Court upheld most of the abortion restrictions while also explicitly reaffirming "the essence of *Roe*." "Liberty finds no refuge in a jurisprudence of doubt," they observed, and the doctrine of *stare decisis* commanded respect for *Roe*. *Stare decisis*, in their words, required the Court to "take care to speak and act in ways that allow people to accept its decisions on the terms the Court claims for them, as grounded truly in principle, [and] not as compromises with social and political pressures having, as such, no bearing on the principled choices that the Court is obliged to make." To do anything less, the plurality continued, would damage the rule of law as well as the Court's legitimacy because citizens relied upon *Roe* and its underlying principle that women have the right to choose an abortion, at least within the first three months of their pregnancy. Significantly, this reasoning is at the core of Chief Justice Roberts' decision to cross party lines and apply *Whole Women's Health v. Hellerstedt* (2016), a controlling precedent that he disagreed with, to join the liberal bloc of Justices Ruth Bader Ginsburg, Steven Breyer, Sonia Sotomayor and Elena Kagan in nullifying a Louisiana law requiring that doctors performing abortions have admitting privileges at a nearby hospital in *June Medical Services v. Russo* (2020), another somewhat predictable 5:4 ruling (for a full discussion, see Chapter Ten).[117]

June Medical Services and *Casey* reminds us that even in "hard cases" the judiciary is generally inclined to adhere to precedent for several reasons. First, legal precedent promotes stability, certainty, and uniformity in the law. Second, adherence to precedent is a safeguard against arbitrary rulings and facilitates the development of the rule of law. Third, it reinforces the public perception that judicial decisions should be based on established legal principles. And, there are practical reasons for opting not to disturb long-standing precedents: doing so will encourage re-litigation of the legal meaning of "many settled construction of rules". For these reasons, some scholars contend that landmark rulings entrench "judicial regimes," or constitutional baselines that order public expectations and establish the boundaries for the exercise of governmental power.[118]

Ramos, Casey and *Webster* also underscore Justice William O. Douglas's observation that *stare decisis* is not "so fragile a thing as to bow before every wind," as well as that of Justice Louis Brandeis, who said that following precedent is "usually the wise policy, because in most matters it is more important that the applicable rule of law be settled than it be settled right."[119] Hence, the reversal of precedent is exceedingly rare in light of the total workload of policymaking appellate courts. According to estimates, for instance, the Supreme Court has overturned only 246 precedents in its entire history, which roughly translates to less than a handful or less of reversals per Term.[120] (See the Contemporary Controversies over Courts box on Precedent, Law and Courts for a full discussion).

Contemporary Controversies over Courts: Law, Precedent and Courts

Precedents remain central to English common law and the American judicial process. The respect courts hold for precedent originates from instrumental values that are internal and external to courts. The internal value of precedent lies in promoting non-arbitrary judicial decision-making. As Lord Patrick Devlin put it, adherence to precedent "primarily [is] a safeguard against arbitrary and autocratic decision-making." Judges and scholars also praise the external values, or reliance on precedent for promoting certainty, stability, and predictability in the law, as well as the legitimacy of judicial rulings. An early U.S. Supreme Court, *Ex parte Bollman*, 8 U.S. (4 Cranch) 75 (1807), emphasized that *stare decisis* ("let the prior decision stand") was critical for ensuring that legal rules are not "uncertain and fluctuating" or subject "to change with every change of times and circumstances." Still, few jurists are willing to defend adherence to precedent on intrinsic grounds. In his four-volume *Commentaries on the English Common Law* (1765–1769), Sir William Blackstone went so far as to contend that prior decisions which are later overturned were simply not law in the first place. Previous rulings deemed erroneous were misinterpretations or imperfect approximations (by human judges) are justly discarded because they were not in accord with "the laws of Nature and Nature's God" and therefore contrary to authoritative and controlling universal principles.

Courts and judges acknowledge precedents have vertical and horizontal dimensions that influence their binding effect. Vertical *stare decisis*—the application of precedents by lower courts—has been said to be an inflexible rule, permitting no exceptions. Thus lower courts (and attorneys) are expected to follow and abide by them when resolving actual factual disputes over competing interests; though it is not unusual for them to distinguish the cases they are reviewing based on their factual circumstance which, in turn narrows or broadens a precedent's application. They may also "cherry-pick" precedents, circle around and circumvent them, or misapply them (while denying they are doing so), and even depart from precedent in anticipation of eventually being overthrown by a higher court. Moreover, courts have considerable discretion in dealing with their own (individual and institutional) precedents—horizontal *stare decisis*. They may do so in a variety of creative and strategic ways, both in the short and long run. They may not only expressly but implicitly overrule, abandon or circumvent, precedents so as to render them no longer "good law;"

or undercut them by simply whittling them down to size, only then to reaffirm them subsequently.

Courts, too, reconsider their own prior rulings for any number of reasons, especially if they are deemed to be demonstrably wrong. In *Brown v. Board of Education*, 347 U.S. 483 (1954), the Supreme Court rejected the socio-psychological underpinnings of *Plessy v. Ferguson* 163 U.S. 537 (1896), the controlling precedent, by holding that the doctrine of "separate but equal" no longer supported or applied to racially-segregated public schools. Or, two precedents may come into such deep conflict that they may be said to be insufficiently distinguishable or reconcilable, so one of them must be abandoned. Additionally, appellate courts may misapply precedents that require the Supreme Court to resolve inter-circuit conflicts among two or more circuit courts of appeals. Or, precedents may prove so malleable under the pressures of technological and societal changes that they become not merely outdated but so unworkable that they cannot be salvaged, and therefore overruled. The application of the Fourth Amendment's bar against "unreasonable searches and seizure," for example, was initially held, in *Olmstead v. U.S.* (1928), not to apply to warrantless searches and seizures conducted by means of wiretaps. That precedent remained in force until it was reversed almost 40 years later, in *Katz v. U.S.* 389 U.S. 347 (1964), when the Court *expressly* overturned *Olmstead's* doctrine of "constitutionally protected areas" and substituted a new framework that declared the Fourth Amendment "protects people, not places," and turns on individual and society's "reasonable expectations of privacy." Even today, in cases such as *United States v. Jones*, 565 U.S. 945 (2012), the Court continues to wrestle with *Katz's* standard and application to the Fourth Amendment's protection against warrantless searches in regard to GPS devices and the new digital age. Finally, some precedents may not stand the test of time but yet, instead of being overturned, are simply abandoned, or no longer followed or applied, without an explicit judicial acknowledgement. Such is the case with *Buck v. Bell*, 274 U.S. 200 (1927), which held that the government may sterilize "feebleminded" men and women without violating their liberty under the due process of law; or, until it was formally overruled in *Trump v. Hawaii*, 138 S. Ct. 2392 (2018)(the Trump Administration's "travel ban" against immigrants' case), *Korematsu v. U.S.* 323 U.S. 214 (1944), the infamous ruling sanctioning the internment of Japanese-Americans during World War II.

It must also be borne in mind, finally, that courts and judges do not routinely overrule precedents. In historical perspective, the Supreme Court reversed itself on average about once each term. In the nineteenth century reversals were more infrequent, if only because there were fewer decisions to overturn. Notably, though, when the Court's composition changes dramatically in a short period of time, or a pivotal justice leaves the bench, the Court tends to overturn prior rulings. That occurred after Franklin D. Roosevelt's eight appointments and elevation of Justice Harlan F. Stone to the chief justiceship in the late 1930s and early 1940s. The Warren Court (1953–1969) was even more "activist" than the Roosevelt Court in reversing forty-five precedents. During Chief Justice Burger's tenure (1969–1986), the Court gradually became more conservative, particularly in the area of criminal procedure. As its composition changed, the Burger Court also continued reconsidering precedents—though typically liberal ones—reversing a total of fifty-two prior rulings. And, an unusually high number of reversals occurred during the first few terms of the Rehnquist Court (1986–2005) due to its changing composition and move into more conservative directions with a majority demonstrating its willingness to reconsider liberal precedents with which it disagreed. But the Rehnquist Court's initial rush to overrule liberal precedents diminished, however, as more moderate centrists came to command a majority due to Democratic President Bill Clinton's appointees. Whereas in the first seven terms of the Rehnquist Court, twenty-five precedents were abandoned, none was reversed in the 1993 term (Justice Ruth Bader Ginsburg's first term), and after Justice Stephen Breyer (1994–) joined the bench; as the Court's composition stabilized, only fourteen precedents were overturned in the following eleven terms. Under Chief Justice John Roberts (2005–), so far the Court has been less inclined to directly overrule prior decisions. Instead, the Roberts Court has been prone to simply narrow the continued application of precedents; or, strike down state laws but nevertheless uphold "as applied" virtually identical federal statutes, regardless of the obvious inconsistency and without squaring the two rulings. But, the recent additions of Justices Neil Gorsuch and Brett Kavanaugh, and the retirement of Anthony Kennedy as a pivotal swing vote in key controversial rulings, may lead to a spike in overrulings as a new conservative coalition, including the Chief Justice, Clarence Thomas and Samuel Alito, coalesces into a majority.

In sum, the precedential value of prior rulings, as Justice Jackson in half-jest quipped, "are [largely but not entirely] accepted only at their current valuation and have a mortality rate as high as their authors." Or, as Justice Samuel Alito more recently observed, "*Stare decisis* is like wine. If it's really new, you don't want to drink it, it has to age for a while. If it's really old, it is very valuable, or it has possibly turned to vinegar. There's this magical period in between. It [is] not difficult for a judge to make the *stare decisis* inquiry come out however the judge wants it [to] come out."

Sources: David M. O'Brien, based on a paper that was delivered before AJURIS, Associacao dos Juizes do Rio Grande do Sul, Porto Alegre, Brazil (November 28, 2017). See also, Lord Patrick Devlin, *The Judge* (Oxford: Oxford University Press, 1979); Richard Wasserstom, *The Judicial Decision* (Palto, CA: Stanford University Press, 1961); Sir William Blackstone, *Commentaries on the English Common Law*, 4 Vols. (Chicago: University of Chicago Press, 1979 [1965–1769]); Amy Coney Barrett, "Precedent and Jurisprudential Disagreement," 91 *Texas Law Review* 1711 (2013); Richard M. Re, "Narrowing Precedent in the Supreme Court," 114 *Columbia Law Review* 1861 (2014); David Skover, *The Judge: 26 Machiavellian Lessons* (New York: Oxford University Press, 2017); Justice Samuel Alito, Speech at the Federalist Society's Texas Chapter's Conference (September 21, 2015), as reported by Josh Blackman, "Justice Alito Reflects on his Tenth Anniversary on SCOTUS," available http://joshblackman.com/blog/2015/09/21/justice-alito-reflects-on-his-tenth-anniversary-on-scotus/; and, Robert H. Jackson, "The Task of Maintaining Our Liberties: The Role of the Judiciary," 39 *American Bar Association Journal* 962 (1953), at 962.

Yet, as the prior examples suggest, adhering to precedent is by no means automatic. In the words of Chief Justice William Rehnquist, "*Stare decisis* is not an inexorable command; rather, it is a principle of policy and not a mechanical formula of adherence to the latest decision."[121] A mix of legal and political factors permit appellate judges to make new policy by minimizing the force of precedent or, less often, entirely disregarding it. Judges may diminish the weight of precedents by "distinguishing," "questioning," or "limiting" them. Distinguishing cases avoids applying a precedent on the basis that the facts are different from those in the case under review. As *Casey* suggests, questioning a precedent permits courts to change the law without actually overturning a prior ruling. *Roe* is still on the books, but it does not carry the same weight as it once did because the Court threw out the so-called trimester approach to balancing the interests of women, the unborn, and governmental regulations. Moreover, the Court upheld restrictions on abortion that had been previously invalidated in earlier cases under *Roe*. In still other cases, appellate courts may choose to "limit" a precedent by confining its application in new cases to a very narrow set of circumstances, which, in turn, restricts it as a controlling legal principle.

Although such decisions permit judges to adjust the scope and application of a precedent in light of different facts, they shed little light on the specific legal criteria or political factors that lead to the reversal of precedents. Traditionally, *stare decisis* usually dictates that courts should not overturn past decisions unless there is a "special justification" to do so. Such reasons include a later court's conclusion that a precedent was wrongly decided in the first place, that a precedent's application has become unworkable in practice, or simply that changing law, facts, or circumstances have rendered a precedent obsolete or susceptible to misapplication. The highly discretionary nature of the analytical exercise, and perhaps the underlying wisdom, in determining if disrupting precedent is warranted is suggested by Justice Elena Kagan in *Kisor v. Wilkie* (2019), a case that wrestled with whether the Court should jettison over 75 years of settled law dictating that courts must defer to an administrative agency's interpretation of its own ambiguous rules in a case involving the recovery of veteran disability benefits. There, Kagan reiterated that, "Of course, it is good—and important—for our opinions to be right and well-reasoned. But that is not the test for overturning precedent." Put differently, there must be a firm basis in the law to reverse course and start afresh. Table 9.4 outlines some of the standards articulated by the Supreme Court to justify the reversal of precedent.[122]

| Table 9.4 | Factors the U.S. Supreme Court Considers in Deciding to Overturn Precedent |

Overruling Factor	Rationale

Is there is a "special justification" for overruling precedent?	Legal principles are based in law instead of personal judgments or feelings of justices in order to protect the "consistency of the principle." The underlying precedent, therefore, cannot be:
	
	• "Wrongly decided" or "badly reasoned"
	   ⇒ In relation to quality of legal reasoning
	• "Unworkable"
	   ⇒ In relation to workability of the rule it establishes
	• "Confusing" or "inconsistent"
	   ⇒ In relation to other analogous decisions

Is the precedent a "constitutional" or "statutory" case (of interpretation)?	• Cases interpreting the U.S. Constitution's meaning gives justices more flexibility to overturn precedents as the Supreme Court is the "final arbiter" of the document's meaning • Cases interpreting statutes enacted by the legislature are given more deference by the justices because courts cannot presume to know what the legislature meant in making laws
Is the underlying precedent contrary to justice or the social welfare?	Judges have the discretion to determine notions of justice and what the law's impact is on society
Has the underlying precedent produced a substantial reliance interest that prevents overruling it?	The existing law creates societal expectations that citizens can rely upon in understanding law's meaning and impact in terms of their daily lives
Did the court creating the precedent do so with one (unanimous) voice; or, did it create divisions in the court with dissenting voices?	The more unanimity amongst the justices creates a stronger precedent that carries substantial weight in future cases applying it
How old is the precedent?	The more time that passes allows the precedent to become more authoritative as a general legal principle; and, a "long line of precedents"—with each one reaffirming the rest over a long period of time—establishes more precedential weight
Have there been subsequent factual or legal developments from the time the precedent was decided that erode or alter its meaning and current application?	The factual and legal context in which the precedent was decided has changed over time and diminishes its authoritative and substantive weight as a legal principle

Sources: Christopher P. Banks, "Reversals of Precedent and Judicial Policy-Making: How Judicial Conceptions of Stare Decisis in the U.S. Supreme Court Influence Social Change," *Akron Law Review* 32 (1999): 233–258; Brandon J. Murrill, "The Supreme Court's Overruling of Constitutional Precedent," *Congressional Research Service (September 24, 2018, R45319)* (Washington, D.C.: Government Printing

Service, 2018); *Kisor v. Wilkie*, 139 S. Ct. 2400 (2019); *Janus v. American Federation of State, County and Municipal Employees, Council 31*, 138 S. Ct. 2448 (2018).

In addition, as Table 9.4 indicates, overturning a precedent significantly depends on whether it is a constitutional or statutory ruling. Supreme courts generally show more respect to precedents involving statutory interpretation because legislatures may override them by enacting new legislation, whereas the process of passing constitutional amendments to overturn a ruling is usually extremely difficult. Courts also are generally reluctant to reverse precedents involving economic interests because such interests are vested and may become more valuable over time. Moreover, if a precedent was handed down by a unanimous court, it is usually given greater respect than one established by a bare majority; indeed, the latter invites reconsideration because it was established by a single vote. Finally, courts are more likely to respect older precedents so as not to disturb the stability of the law and social expectations.[123]

Of course, reversals of precedents often result from changes in the composition of the bench. That is, when a court's membership rapidly changes and new majorities coalesce in a short period of time, "constitutional law will be in flux," at least "until the new judges have taken their positions on constitutional doctrine." Conversely, in periods of stable membership, known as **natural courts**, there are usually fewer reversals. In periods of constitutional flux, it is not unusual for judges to chastise publicly their new brethren for upsetting precedents in high-profile cases. In his last dissent, Justice Marshall, for example, accused the Court's majority of subverting *stare decisis* in overturning two recently decided cases that barred "victim impact statements" in sentencing hearings in death penalty cases. "Power, and not reason," he charged, is the "new currency of [the] Court's decision-making," and emphasized that "neither the law nor the facts supporting [the overturned precedents] underwent any change in the last four years. Only the personnel of [the] Court did."[124]

Some scholars go so far as to deny that *stare decisis* constrains courts from overturning past decisions. In one study, political scientists Thomas Hansford and James Spriggs concluded that the judiciary's respect for precedent depends on whether judges have ideological disagreements with the legal principles established in earlier cases. In their analysis of Supreme Court cases, they found that reversals of liberal precedents were more likely if the Court's composition changed and became more conservative, and conversely reversals of conservative precedents were more likely to be overturned when the composition of the bench became more liberal. They also found that legal norms and institutional constraints were key overruling factors as well. And in a subsequent analysis, they found that justices tend to interpret precedents in order to establish new legal policies that are aligned with their policy preferences.[125]

STATUTORY AND CONSTITUTIONAL INTERPRETATION

The formalistic or traditional approach of legal reasoning is supplemented by two distinct types of legal interpretation: statutory and constitutional interpretation. Each approach has an important impact on appellate court policymaking since the legal principles underlying their application by conservative and liberal judges factor into judicial outcomes and public policy. Accordingly, this section analyzes the different ways courts interpret **statutes**. In particular, the growing importance of the judicial politics of statutory construction is evaluated. The next and concluding section of the Chapter discusses the interplay between the various methods of constitutional interpretation and rival judicial philosophies.

Statutory Construction

"In my view today's opinion," dissenting Justice Antonin Scalia observed in *PGA Tour, Inc. v. Martin* (2001), "exercises a benevolent compassion that the law does not place it within our power to impose."[126] The main issue concerned whether the Americans with Disabilities Act (ADA) of 1990 should be interpreted to permit a disabled professional golfer, Casey Martin, to use a golf cart in a PGA competition. Writing for seven justices, Justice John Paul Stevens reasoned that the ADA's language and underlying legislative history showed that Martin, who suffered from a circulatory blood disease, was entitled to reasonable accommodations in order for him to have an equal chance to compete. Justice Scalia, joined by Justice Clarence Thomas, thought otherwise, claiming that the majority's interpretation of the statute "distorts the text of Title III, the structure of the ADA, and common sense."[127]

The issue before the Court, Justice Scalia maintained, was not whether Martin should have a disability accommodation, but rather whether Congress required the PGA to give him one on the basis of a common sensical reading of the statute. Although they disagreed on the outcome, both justices construed the ADA according to "the plain meaning" of the statute. What divided them was what to do afterward. For the late Justice Scalia, who embraced a textualist approach to statutory construction, the ADA plainly did not impose any legal obligation on the PGA to accommodate Martin's disability.

By contrast, for Justice John Paul Stevens, the text of the ADA was only the beginning and not the end of the analysis: the statute's total structure had to be considered, as well as its overall purpose and underlying legislative history. Though the interpretative approach Justice Stevens took might appear more compassionate (in the words of Justice Scalia, epitomizing a "decent, tolerant, and progressive judgment"), in his view it was actually more of an attempt to bring some objectivity to an otherwise vexing process of figuring out how to apply a statute in an entirely new context. Regardless, these competing viewpoints about how to interpret statutes registers a general disagreement about whether to engage in "strict" or "loose" construction of legislation. As with constitutional interpretation, discussed in the next section, legal scholars sometimes frame this debate as disagreements over judicial philosophies or theories rooted in "textualism (strict construction)" or "purposive" and/or "dynamic" interpretation (loose construction), among others. Apart from interpretative theories, judges may also analytically apply longstanding understandings of legal doctrine or principles, commonly referred to as "tools of statutory construction," to assist them in deriving the meaning of legislative language (see Table 9.5).[128]

Table 9.5	Interpretative Theories and Tools of Statutory Construction	
Theory/Tool	**Main Characteristics**	**Underlying Rationale or Application**
Textualism (Theory)	Judge construes plain meaning of statutory text in light of its overall structure and related parts	Formalistic approach uses statutory text to discover original intent of drafters and to show deference to the democratic policy choices of people's representatives in enacting statute
Purposive (Theory)	Judge ascertains legislative purpose or objective in enacting statute	Legislative purpose aids in finding meaning to vaguely worded statutes
Dynamic Statutory Interpretation (Theory)	Judge interprets statute in light of how the original meaning of the law has evolved over time due to changing facts and circumstances	Pragmatic and normative approach that assumes statutory meaning is not fixed in time and changes dynamically in response to how the statute ought to be applied to contemporary problems in their present societal, political, and legal context
Intentionalism (Theory)	Judge explores legislative intent at time law was made	Under Blackstone's theory, as faithful agents of legislature, judges must explore intent to implement the legislature's will by consulting "legislative history" (see below)
Public Choice (Theory)	Judge interprets statutes by understanding that legislators are political actors who bargain and negotiate with other legislators and special	Approach emphasizing that judges must defer to the "bargains" struck by legislators, and which were created by the realities and "public choices" inherent in the operation of the political process, unless they are

	interest groups in order to maximize their self-interest	unreasonable; or the statute commands the judge to act a certain way in interpreting the statute
Legislative History (Tool)	Judge looks to legislative history to help ascertain meaning or purpose of statute	Judges consult the underlying history behind the law's enactment as an aid to determine legislative purpose or intent "Legislative history" includes: • congressional committee reports • conference committee reports • floor debate statements or votes made by legislators
Canons of Statutory Construction (Tool)	Judge uses traditional "canons" of statutory interpretation as guide to aid in the process of interpreting statute or applying it	Canons are used as rules or guidelines to help ascertain statutory meaning or understand how statutes apply to the facts of legal dispute "Canons" include: • the expression of one thing is the exclusion of another • repeals by implication are disfavored • every word of a statute must be given significance • if the language is plain and unambiguous, it must be given effect

Sources: Robert A. Katzman, *Judging Statutes* (New York: Oxford University Press, 2014); Elizabeth Garrett, "Legislation and Statutory Interpretation," in *The Oxford Handbook of Law and Politics* (New York: Oxford University Press, 2010), 360–65; Richard A. Posner, *How Judges Think* (Cambridge, Mass.: Harvard University Press, 2008),191–203; Robert A. Katzmann, *Courts and Congress* (Washington, D.C.: Brookings Institution Press, 1997); William N. Eskridge, Jr., *Dynamic Statutory Interpretation* (Cambridge, Mass.: Harvard University Press, 1994).

For some legal scholars, the ambiguity of statutory language and the debate it causes reinforces the fact that "American courts have no intelligible, generally accepted, and consistently applied theory of statutory interpretation."[129] The sticking point in the *PGA Tour* case, as Justice Felix Frankfurter once observed about reading statutes, is making "the determination of the extent to which extraneous documentation and external circumstances may be allowed to infiltrate the text on the theory that they were a part of it, written in ink discernible to the judicial eye."[130] The judicial choice of deciding to stay only within context of what the law says in its language, or to go beyond those words to discover an overriding "intent" by the law's drafters, is, at bottom, a function of applying competing ideological philosophies and principles to reach case outcomes. Even so, there is probably little disagreement that all judges begin the process of statutory interpretation by reading the text. But what "the plain meaning" of words might be or mean may only be clear to some but not to others, especially if the law's context and purpose are not taken into account. Justice Stephen Breyer has illustrated the point by using the example of the sign that says, "No animals in the park." An "animal," he noted, could be interpreted to be a squirrel, a dog, or even an insect. In New York, for example, a resident who sees the sign outside of New York City's Central Park would probably think that the sign refers to "dogs"; but, if the sign is outside a parking lot in a city where many residents ride donkeys or elephants, the sign's words and their meaning might be different. Or, if the sign is in an English laboratory in a place where microbiologists put their test tubes, Londoners might think something else because in England people call insects "animals."[131] Consequently, ambiguous statutory language often compels non-textualist judges to look to extraneous sources and to the overall context of a statute in order to ascertain the legislature's "intent." Hence, judges and lawyers of that ilk use extralegal sources as "tools" to determine the meaning of a statute—these include consulting "legislative history," as well as statutory "canons," or judge-made rules that aid in interpreting statutes (see Table 9.5).

None of the theories or methods of statutory construction are free from criticism, however. The search for **legislative intent** might have the advantage of being contextual, but in the end, all judges—those committed to textualism or not—intuitively make choices about what sources to consult and whose intent controls. The interpretative process in this regard is further complicated because of the self-interest of legislators and the fact that popular assemblies are an aggregation of many legislators and multiple conflicting intents. To illustrate, in referring to the futility of using interpretative "canons" as a tool in statutory interpretation, former federal appeals court Judge Abner Mikva once observed: "When I was in Congress, the only 'canons' we talked about were the ones the

Pentagon bought that could not shoot straight."[132] His colleague on the D.C. Circuit, former Judge Harold Leventhal, likewise once quipped that using legislative history was like "looking over a crowd and picking out your friends."[133] An analogous point can be made in a how judges decide statutory interpretation issues in respect to the actions of federal or state agencies. In administrative law, agencies, which are delegated law-making powers by Congress (or state legislatures) to carry out a legislative purpose, are in the unenviable position to do that because they are tasked with interpreting overly broad statutory mandates to implement the controlling legislation that helps to define the agency's mission. The Federal Trade Commission, for instance, has the power to eliminate "unfair methods of competition," and the Securities and Exchange Commission has authority to establish a "fair and orderly market."[134] Hence, when federal regulations are created by agencies to carry out the legislative mandate are challenged in court, judges may simply defer to an agency's interpretation of a contested statute because it is difficult for the court to know the statute's actual meaning, or what the agencies were thinking about when they interpreted their legislative mandate. That precise issue, discussed earlier, divided the Supreme Court along ideological lines in *Kisor v. Wilkie* (2019) (discussed earlier), where the justices intensely debated the statutory construction issue of whether courts must defer to an administrative agency's interpretation of its own ambiguous rules in a case involving the recovery of veteran disability benefits. In sum, every method of statutory construction is value-laden and remains a function of judicial discretion that has political and real-life, practical implications for the litigating parties.

Constitutional Interpretation

Generally speaking, judges tend to use one of two broad methods of constitutional interpretation: **interpretivism** and **noninterpretivism**. Interpretivism emphasizes giving a strict construction to "the plain meaning" of textual language, while also considering its historical context and "the original understanding" of the application of constitutional provisions. Noninterpretivism also respects the text and historical context, but as well embraces contemporary interpretations and applications of what the words mean today. The use of one or the other does not automatically create an outcome that is associated with either a conservative or a liberal philosophy. Still, identifying the general methods judges use provides insight to their judicial philosophy and the general guidelines or principles on which they decide cases.

Interpretivism holds that judges should construe constitutions by analyzing the text in light of historical context. One variant is **"strict constructionism,"** which dictates that judges should examine the plain meaning of the words as they literally appear within the four corners of a document. Limiting interpretation to the text, arguably, best preserves and remains faithful to the original intent of the Framers. According to Edwin Meese III, President Ronald Reagan's attorney general, respecting the Framers' intent is the "proper role of the Supreme Court in our constitutional system." In his words:

> The intended role of the judiciary generally and the Supreme Court in particular was to serve as the "bulwarks of a limited constitution.". . . As the "faithful guardians of the Constitution," the judges were expected to resist any political effort to depart from the literal provisions of the Constitution. The text of the document and the original intention of those who framed it would be the judicial standard in giving effect to the Constitution.[135]

In theory, judges who rely on original intent tend to favor judicial restraint in the sense that they claim not to apply constitutional provisions beyond what the Framers might have intended; thus they do not "legislate from the bench" by interjecting their own values.[136]

Judges endorsing **"originalism"**—or the "original meaning" or "original understanding" of constitutional provisions—such as Justice Antonin Scalia, Judge Robert Bork, and Chief Justice William Rehnquist—take a slightly different view. In order to meet the objection that it is impossible to know what the Framers intended, they conclude it is better to derive a general understanding of what the Framers meant, as informed by historical context. "What I look for in the Constitution," in the words of Justice Scalia, "is precisely what I look for in a statute: the original meaning of the text, not what the original draftsmen intended."[137] Similarly, the shift in emphasis away from founding intent is articulated by some constitutional scholars who argue that originalism is best understood as an "original public meaning," a legal principle that purports to be a more objective and legitimate basis for judicial decision-making because it represents a general notion of judicial deference to the political branches or popular majority will. Still, critics observe that the latest academic incarnations of originalism is a pretext for judicial restraint and, actually, indistinguishable from legal realist conceptions of more "activist" judicial policy-making. Though imperfect, originalists steadfastly defend the method as a better alternative to **noninterpretivism**.[138]

Noninterpretivists celebrate what originalist judges scorn: a "living constitution" that adjusts to changing circumstances. Justice William Brennan Jr., along with Justice Thurgood Marshall, for example, voted against the death penalty not only because it was a "cruel and unusual" punishment under the Eighth Amendment, but also because it violated basic principles of human dignity that are an essential part of an evolving civilization. Likewise, Justice Anthony Kennedy's opinion in *Roper v. Simmons* (2005)[139] relied upon the "evolving standards of decency" to forbid the execution of juveniles convicted of murder. In other words, constitutional provisions must be interpreted in accord with contemporary principles, social science, pragmatism, moral philosophy, and basic human values. Although text and history begin the analysis, they are incomplete guides. Justice Brennan explained:

> We current justices read the Constitution in the only way that we can: as [twenty-first-]century Americans. We look to the history of the time of framing and to the intervening history of interpretation. But the ultimate question must be, [w]hat do the words of the text mean in our time? For the genius of the Constitution rests not in any static meaning it might have had in a world that is dead and gone, but in the adaptability of its great principles to cope with current problems and current needs.[140]

The debate over constitutional interpretation is ongoing. Scholars as well as judges have not reached any consensus about the best philosophy, sources, and methods of constitutional interpretation.[141] For further discussion, see "Contemporary Controversies over Courts: How Should Judges Interpret the U.S. Constitution?"

Contemporary Controversies over Courts: How Should Judges Interpret the U.S. Constitution?

Disagreement, on and off the bench, remains over how the Constitution should be interpreted. But that should not be surprising, for the Constitution is a legal and political document that does not say how it should be interpreted. Its "majestic generalities," as Justice Benjamin Cardozo put it, like the guarantees for "free speech," "due process," and "the equal protection of the law," invite rival interpretations and competing conceptions. They also must be applied in new, unforeseen ways in light of changing social, economic, and technological changes.

In response, some scholars and judges—notably, Judge Robert H. Bork and Justices Antonin Scalia and Clarence Thomas—have championed the position that constitutional interpretation should be confined to the text and "original intent" of the Framers or the "original public understanding" of constitutional provisions in order to limit judicial discretion and to reconcile judicial review with democratic governance. As the excerpts below indicate, they maintain that staying faithful to the plain intent of the words restrains judges from abusing their discretion in a democracy and respects the people's will as expressed in legislation.

Originalism: The Lesser Evil—Justice Antonin Scalia

The principal theoretical defect of non-originalism, in my view, is its incompatibility with the very principle that legitimizes judicial review of constitutionality. Nothing in the text of the Constitution confers upon the courts the power to inquire into, rather than passively assume, the constitutionality of federal statutes. . . .[Instead], originalism seems to me more compatible with the nature and purpose of a Constitution in a democratic system. A democratic society does not, by and large, need constitutional guarantees to insure that its laws will reflect "current values." Elections take care of that quite well. The purpose of constitutional guarantee. . .is precisely to prevent the law from reflecting certain changes in original values that the society adopting the Constitution thinks fundamentally undesirable. Or, more precisely, to require the society to devote to the subject the long and hard consideration required for a constitutional amendment before those particular values can be cast aside.

By contrast, Justices Thurgood Marshall and William J. Brennan, Jr., among others, have countered that the Constitution is a "living document" that embodies substantive values or a "constitutional morality" that guarantees protection for "human dignity" from the majoritarian forces of democracy. Still others, such as Justice Stephen Breyer, argue that judges have an obligation to decide cases in light of history, text, precedent, tradition, and, above all, the pragmatic consequences of what the effect of the ruling will be in advancing underlying democratic values.

The Constitution: A Living Document—Justice Thurgood Marshall

[The] meaning of the Constitution was [not] forever "fixed" at the Philadelphia Convention. Nor [is the] wisdom, foresight, and sense of justice exhibited by the framers particularly profound. [T]he government they devised was defective from the start, requiring several amendments, a civil war, and momentous social transformation to attain the system of constitutional government, and its respect for the individual freedoms and human rights, that we hold as fundamental today.

The men who gathered in Philadelphia in 1787 could not have. . .imagined. . .that the document they were drafting would one day be construed by a Supreme Court to which had been appointed a woman and the descendent of an African slave. "We the People" no longer enslave, but the credit does not belong to the framers. It belongs to those who refused to acquiesce [to] outdated notions of "liberty," "justice," and "equality" and [those] who strived to better [those ideas].

Constitutional Aspirations and Contemporary Ratification—Justice William J. Brennan, Jr.

The Constitution embodies the aspirations to social justice, brotherhood, and human dignity that brought this nation into being. . . .Its majestic generalities and ennobling pronouncements are both luminous and obscure. . . .

There are those who find legitimacy in fidelity to what they call "the intentions of the framers.". . .But in truth, it is little more than arrogance cloaked as humility. It is arrogant to pretend. . .we can gauge accurately the intent of the framers on [the] application of principle[s] to specific, contemporary questions. . .

It is the very purpose of a Constitution—and particularly of the Bill of Rights—to declare certain values transcendent, beyond the reach of temporary political majorities. . . .Faith in democracy is one thing, blind faith is quite another. Those who drafted our Constitution understood the difference. One cannot read the text without admitting that it embodies substantive value choices; it places certain values beyond the power of any legislature.

Constitutional Pragmatism—Justice Stephen Breyer

The original Constitution's primary objective. . .[was] furthering active liberty, as creating a form of government in which all citizens share the government's authority, participating in the creation of public policy. It understands the Constitution's structural complexity as responding to practical needs, for delegation, for nondestructive. . .public policies, and for protection of basic individual freedoms. . . .And it views the Constitution's democratic imperative as accommodating, even insisting upon, these practical needs.

Sources: Antonin Scalia, *A Matter of Interpretation: Federal Courts and the Law* (Princeton, N.J.: Princeton University Press, 1997); Thurgood Marshall, "The Constitution: A Living Document," in *Judges on Judging: Views From the Bench*, 4th ed., ed. David M. O'Brien (Washington, D.C.: CQ Press, 2013), 244–48; William J. Brennan, Jr., "The Constitution of the United States: Contemporary Ratification," delivered at the Text and Teaching Symposium, Georgetown University, October 12, 1985; and Stephen Breyer, *Active Liberty: Interpreting Our Democratic Constitution* (New York: Knopf, 2005).

Chapter Summary

Appellate courts, unlike trial courts, have the capacity to make legal and public policy, whereas lower courts generally impact only the parties involved in a lawsuit. A relatively small percentage of trial court decisions are appealed, and the overwhelming majority of appeals are unsuccessful.

In general, the appeals decision making process consists of agenda setting, oral arguments, judicial conferences, and issuing a judicial opinion. Case selection is governed by statutes, procedural rules, judicial norms, and a variety of legal and political factors. Oral advocacy has become less prevalent in deciding appeals. Instead, written legal briefs and internal research memoranda supplied by law clerks and central staff attorneys are the basis of most rulings. Still, oral arguments remain important because they allow for an exchange of critical information not in the briefs. Judicial conferences are significant forums for case management and coalition building among judges. An appellate court's final judgment is delivered in a written opinion. The collaborative and dynamic process of writing judicial opinions includes the key role law clerks now play in researching and drafting opinions for judges.

Political scientists and legal scholars study judicial policymaking with different research methodologies. Whereas attitudinal theory posits that judicial decisions are solely a function of judicial preferences, rational choice theory hypothesizes that judicial behavior is driven by strategic calculations of judges that take into account what other judges will do in deciding cases. New institutionalism studies use a variety of interdisciplinary approaches. In contrast, traditional legal studies focus on the deductive process of legal reasoning and use of applicable legal principles or precedents. The reasoned application of the doctrine of *stare decisis*, or precedent, is the subject of ongoing debate among courts, judges and scholars, especially in determining when it is appropriate for the law to change in controversial areas of legal and social policy.

Appellate courts establish the law and make policy in statutory and constitutional cases. Judges use various theories, among them intentionalism, textualism, and legislative history, to construe ambiguous statutory language. Constitutional interpretation does so as well but also may draw on more extralegal sources, like tradition, social science, and history. Both approaches involve reconciling the tension between preserving democratic values of majority rule and respect for individual and minority rights.

Key Questions for Review and Critical Analysis

1. If you were an attorney making an oral argument, how would you approach preparing for it? Would your preparation be different if you were arguing in a trial court? Do you think oral arguments in appellate courts significantly influence appeals courts' decisions? Why or why not?

2. Do law clerks have too much influence on appellate courts?

3. Among the various ways in which political scientists and legal scholars study appellate judicial behavior, which methodology do you think best captures the dynamics of the decision-making process? Do you think "the law" or a judge's personal attitudes and preferences are more important in judicial decision-making?

4. What are the legal standards that allow courts and judges to change existing precedent, and are those standards merely a function of who is on the court at a particular time period? If so, does the doctrine of *stare decisis* have any real meaning, or binding effect?

5. How important is it for a judge to consult sources such as "legislative history" in interpreting an ambiguous statute, or should they defer to the executive branch's interpretation, and why?

6. How does adopting interpretivism or non-interpretivism approach in constitutional interpretation affect case outcomes or the ideological direction of social policy, especially in controversial areas of public debate, such as free speech, religious freedom, same-sex marriage, affirmative action, or the death penalty?

Web Links

1. National Conference of Appellate Court Clerks (www.appellatecourtclerks. org/links.html)

    *   It contains a list of links to all U.S. state and federal appellate court websites. Appellate court websites have information relating to justices and appellate judges, opinions, argument schedules, order lists, and procedure.

2. SCOTUSblog (www.scotusblog.com)

    *   The leading website covering the U.S. Supreme Court's procedures, decisions, and opinions. It contains legal news and commentary, court statistics, videos, legal analyses, and links to current and past term judicial opinions.

3. Empirical Legal Studies Blog (https://www.elsblog.org/)

   - The blog's purpose is to advance interdisciplinary empirical legal research. The blog has legal news; commentary; links to government, academic, and bar association home pages; plus links to political science and law journals and widely used data sets (e.g., the Spaeth SCOTUS Database, the Interuniversity Consortium for Political and Social Research, the Lower Federal Court Confirmation Database, and the State Supreme Court Data Project).

4. National Center for State Courts, State Court Web Sites (https://www.ncsc. org/information-and-resources/browse-by-state/state-court-websites.aspx)

   - It provides structural and procedural information about all state appellate and trial courts, along with educational resources about its use and impact on the judicial process.

Selected Readings

Balkin, Jack. *Living Originalism*. Cambridge, Mass.: Belkap/Harvard University Press, 2011.

Baum, Lawrence. *Judges and Their Audiences: A Perspective on Judicial Behavior*. Princeton, N.J.: Princeton University Press, 2006.

Baum Lawrence and Neal Devins. *The Company They Keep: How Partisan Divisions Came to the Supreme Court*. New York: Oxford University Press, 2019.

Black, Ryan C., Ryan J. Owens, Justin Wedeking and Patrick C. Wohlfarth. *The Conscientious Justice: How Supreme Court Justices' Personalities Influence the Law, the High Court, and the Constitution*. New York: Cambridge University Press, 2020.

Black, Ryan C., Ryan J. Owens, Justin Wedeking and Patrick C. Wohlfarth. *U.S. Supreme Court Opinions and Their Audiences*. Cambridge, U.K.: Cambridge University Press, 2016.

Bork, Robert. *Tempting America: The Political Seduction of the Law*. New York: Free Press, 1990.

Breyer, Stephen. *Active Liberty: Interpreting Our Democratic Constitution*. New York: Knopf, 2005.

Calabresi, Steven, ed. *Originalism: A Quarter-Century of Debate*. Washington, D.C.: Regnery, 2007.

Cardozo, Benjamin N. *The Nature of the Judicial Process.* New Haven, Conn.: Yale University Press, 1921.

Clark, Thomas S. *The Supreme Court: An Analytic History of Constitutional Decision-making.* New York: Cambridge University Press, 2019.

Clayton, Cornell W., and Howard Gillman, eds. *Supreme Court Decision-Making: New Institutionalist Approaches.* Chicago: University of Chicago Press, 1999.

Cohen, Jonathan Matthew. *Inside Appellate Courts: The Impact of Court Organization on Judicial Decision Making in the United States Courts of Appeals.* Ann Arbor: University of Michigan Press, 2002.

Collins, Ronald K. L. and David M. Skover. *The Judge: 26 Machiavellian Lessons.* New York: Oxford University Press, 2017.

Cross, Frank B. *Decision-Making in the U.S. Court of Appeals.* Stanford, Calif.: Stanford University Press, 2007.

Epstein, Lee, and Jack Knight. *The Choices Justices Make.* Washington, D.C.: CQ Press, 1998.

Fallon, Richard H., Jr. *Law and Legitimacy in the Supreme Court.* Cambridge, MA.: The Belknap Press of Harvard University Press, 2018.

Geyh, Charles Gardner, ed. *What's Law Got to Do With It? What Judges Do, Why They Do It, and What's at Stake.* Stanford, Calif.: Stanford University Press, 2011.

Gillman, Howard, and Cornell Clayton, eds. *The Supreme Court in American Politics: New Institutionalist Interpretations.* Lawrence: University of Kansas Press, 1999.

Hall, Matthew. *What Justices Want: Goals and Personality on the U.S. Supreme Court* (New York: Cambridge University Press, 2018.

Hansford, Thomas G., and James F. Spriggs II. *The Politics of Precedent on the U.S. Supreme Court.* Princeton, N.J.: Princeton University Press, 2006.

Hettinger, Virginia A., Stephanie A. Lindquist, and Wendy L. Martinek. *Judging on a Collegial Court: Influences on Federal Appellate Decision-Making.* Charlottesville: University of Virginia Press, 2006.

Hitt, Matthew P. *Inconsistency and Indecision in the United States Supreme Court.* Ann Arbor, MI.: University of Michigan Press, 2019.

Katzmann, Robert. *Judging Statutes.* New York: Oxford University Press, 2014.

Lessig, Lawrence. *Fidelity & Constraint: How the Supreme Court Has Read the American Constitution.* New York: Oxford University Press, 2019.

Maltzman, Forrest, James F. Spriggs II, and Paul J. Wahlbeck. *Crafting Law on the Supreme Court: The Collegial Game.* Cambridge, Mass.: Cambridge University Press, 2000.

Murphy, Walter. *Elements of Judicial Strategy.* Chicago: University of Chicago Press, 1964.

O'Brien, David M. *Storm Center: The Supreme Court in American Politics.* 12th ed. New York: Norton, 2020.

Peppers, Todd C., and Artemus Ward, eds. *In Chambers: Stories of Supreme Court Law Clerks and Their Justices.* Charlottesville: University of Virginia Press, 2012.

Pritchett, C. Herman *The Roosevelt Court: A Study in Judicial Politics and Values, 1937–1947.* New York: MacMillan, 1948.

Scalia, Antonin, and Bryan A. Garner. *Reading Law: The Interpretation of Legal Texts.* St. Paul, Minn.: Thomson/West, 2012.

Segal, Jeffrey A., and Harold J. Spaeth. *The Supreme Court and the Attitudinal Model Revisited.* Cambridge, U.K.: Cambridge University Press, 2002.

Segall, Eric J. *Originalism as Faith.* New York: Cambridge University Press, 2018.

Spaeth, Harold J., and Jeffrey A. Segal. *Majority Rule or Minority Will: Adherence to Precedent on the U.S. Supreme Court.* Cambridge, U.K.: Cambridge University Press, 1999.

Strang, Lee J. *Originalism's Promise: A Natural Law Account of the American Constitution.* New York: Cambridge University Press, 2019.

Endnotes

[1]   Ted Barrett, "In reversal from 2016, McConnell says he would fill a potential Supreme Court vacancy in 2020," *CNNpolitics* (May 29, 2019), available at https://www.cnn.com/2019/05/28/politics/mitch-mcconnell-supreme-court-2020/index.html (last retrieved April 24, 2020). The "election have consequences" quotes are found in C-Span, "Senator Mitch McConnell Interview (December 16, 2016, Video)" available at https://www.c-span.org/video/?420609-1/senator-mitch-mcconnell-interview&start=624 (last retrieved April 24, 2020)(by McConnell); Michael Steele, "the SCOTUS nomination clearly demonstrates that elections have consequences," *The Hill (July 18, 2018)*, available at https://thehill.com/opinion/judiciary/396476-the-scotus-nomination-clearly-demonstrates-elections-have-consequences (last retrieved April 24, 2020); David Paul, "Eight Years Ago, Obama Told Republicans That Elections Have Consequence. They Hold the Whip Hand Now," *Huffpost (April 5, 2017)*, available at https://www.huffpost.com/entry/eight-years-ago-obama-told-republicans-that-elections_b_58e46f57e4b09dbd42f3dbc0 (last retrieved April 24, 2020)(by Obama).

[2]   Devan Cole and Ted Barrett, "Senate Confirms Trump's 200th Judicial Nominee," *CNN* (June 24, 2020), available at https://www.cnn.com/2020/06/24/politics/trump-200-judicial-appointments-cory-wilson/index.html (last retrieved June 24, 2020); Mark Joseph Stern, "While the House Impeaches, the Senate Will Confirm 13 More Trump Judges," *Slate* (December 18, 2019), available at https://slate.com/news-and-politics/2019/12/senate-impeachment-trump-judicial-nominees.html (last retrieved April 24, 2020); Priyanka Boghani, "How McConnell and the Senate Helped Trump in Setting Records in Appointing Judges," *PBS Frontline* (May 21, 2019), available at https://www.pbs.org/wgbh/frontline/article/how-mcconnell-and-the-

senate-helped-trump-set-records-in-appointing-judges/ (last retrieved April 24, 2020). See also, Christopher P. Banks, *Judicial Politics in the D.C. Circuit Court* (Baltimore: John Hopkins University Press, 1999 (examining U.S. Court of Appeals for the D.C. Circuit as a *de facto* "court of last resort").

3   *Franchise Tax Board of California v. Hyatt*, 139 S. Ct. 1485 (2019) (Breyer, J., dissenting). See also, Tony Mauro, "Staring Down 'Stare Decisis': How to Ask SCOTUS to Overturn Precedent," *National Law Journal (May 15, 2019)*, available at https://www.law.com/nationallawjournal/2019/05/15/staring-down-stare-decisis-how-to-ask-scotus-to-overturn-precedent/ (last retrieved April 24, 2020); Issac Chotiner, "A Supreme Court Reporter Defines the Threat to Abortion Rights (An Interview with former N.Y. Times legal reporter, Linda Greenhouse)," *New Yorker (May 14, 2019)*, available at https://www.newyorker.com/news/q-and-a/a-supreme-court-reporter-defines-the-threat-to-abortion-rights (last retrieved April 24, 2020). See generally, *Janus v. American Federation of State, County, and Municipal Employees*, 138 S. Ct. 2448 (2018); *Abood v. Detroit Board of Education*, 431 U.S. 209 (1977); *Franchise Tax Board of California v. Hyatt*; *Nevada v. Hall*, 440 U.S. 410 (1979); and, *Roe v. Wade*, 410 U.S. 113 (1973).

4   *Rose v. Clark*, 478 U.S. 570, 579 (1986).

5   See Donald J. Farole and Thomas H. Cohen, *Appeals of Civil Trials Concluded in 2005* (October 2011, NCJ 235187), available at https://www.bjs.gov/content/pub/pdf/actc05.pdf (last retrieved April 24, 2020); C. K. Rowland and Robert A. Carp, *Politics and Judgment in Federal District Courts* (Lawrence: University Press of Kansas, 1996), 8.

6   Rowland and Carp, *Politics and Judgment in Federal District Courts*, 24–57.

7   Ronald K. L. Collins and David M. Skover, *The Judge: 26 Machiavellian Lessons* (New York: Oxford University Press, 2017), 143.

8   Richard A. Posner, *The Federal Courts: Challenge and Reform* (Cambridge, Mass.: Harvard University Press, 1996), 340. For an explanation of appellate standards of review, see Jonathan Matthew Cohen, *Inside Appellate Courts: The Impact of Court Organization on Judicial Decision Making in the United States Courts of Appeals* (Ann Arbor: University of Michigan Press, 2002), 46–48.

9   Posner, *The Federal Courts*, 158.

10   J. Woodford Howard, Jr., *Courts of Appeals in the Federal Judicial System: A Study of the Second, Fifth, and District of Columbia Circuits* (Princeton, N.J.: Princeton University Press, 1981), xvii. See also Susan B. Haire, Stephanie A. Lindquist, and Donald R. Songer, "Appellate Court Supervision in the Federal Judiciary: A Hierarchical Perspective," *Law & Society Review* 37 (2003), 145.

11   Cass R. Sunstein, David Schkade, Lisa M. Ellman, and Andres Sawicki, *Are Judges Political? An Empirical Analysis of the Federal Judiciary* (Washington, D.C.: Brookings Institution Press, 2006), 11–12 (finding that a panel of three Democratic appointees issue liberal rulings 62 percent of the time, whereas a panel of three Republicans deliver liberal rulings 36 percent of the time). See also Cohen, *Inside Appellate Courts*, 12–13, 27–34, 171–74.

12   Posner, *The Federal Courts*, 158, 348–49; Adam Bonica, et al., "Legal Rasputins? Law Clerk Influence on Voting at the US Supreme Court," *Journal of Law, Economics, and Organization* 35 (2019): 1, 4–5. Allocations of legal staff for state appellate judges are found in Roger A. Hanson, Carol R. Flango, and Randall M. Hansen, *The Work of Appellate Court Legal Staff* (Williamsburg, Va.: National Center for State Courts, 2000), 20–22. For an overview of federal and U.S. Supreme Court law clerkships, see Todd Peppers, *Courtiers of the Marble Palace: The Rise and Influence of the Supreme Court* (Stanford, CA.: Stanford University Press, 2006).

13   Adam S. Chilton and Marin K. Levy, "Challenging the Randomness of Panel Assignment in the Federal Court of Appeals," *Cornell Law Review* 101 (2015): 1, 8–9.

14   This example is used in Todd C. Peppers, Katherine Vigilante and Christopher Zorn, "Random Chance or Loaded Dice: The Politics of Judicial Designation," *University of New Hampshire Law Review* 10 (2012): 69, 70, citing to research in Deborah J. Barrow and Thomas G. Walker's *A Court Divided: The Fifth Circuit Court of Appeals and the Politics of Judicial Reform* (New Haven: Yale University Press, 1988).

15   Chilton and Levy, "Challenging the Randomness of Panel Assignment in the Federal Court of Appeals," 1–56. See also,

16   See Hanson, Flango, and Hansen, *The Work of Appellate Court Legal Staff*, 8. Random panel selection is discussed in Cohen, *Inside Appellate Courts*, 72.

17   Hanson, Flango, and Hansen, *The Work of Appellate Court Legal Staff*, 19, 46–52, 54–55.

[18]   Mary Lou Stow and Harold J. Spaeth, "Centralized Research Staff: Is There a Monster in the Judicial Closet?" *Judicature* (December/January 1992), 216–21, 218–20. See also Hanson, Flango, and Hansen, *The Work of Appellate Court Legal Staff*, 54–55; Cohen, *Inside Appellate Courts*, 71.

[19]   Cohen, *Inside Appellate Courts*, 83–84. The time law clerks spend on procedural motions in state appeals courts is reported in Hanson, Flango, and Hansen, *The Work of Appellate Court Legal Staff*, 42.

[20]   Ruth Bader Ginsburg, "Workways of the Supreme Court," *Thomas Jefferson Law Review* 25 (Summer, 2003), 517, 522.

[21]   H. W. Perry, *Deciding to Decide: Agenda Setting in the United States Supreme Court* (Cambridge, Mass.: Harvard University Press, 1991), 272–77. See also S. Sidney Ulmer, "The Decision to Grant Certiorari as an Indicator to Decision 'On the Merits,' " *Polity* 4 (1972), 429–47.

[22]   Paul Brace and Melinda Gann Hall, " 'Haves' Versus 'Have Nots' in State Supreme Courts: Allocating Docket Space and Wins in Power Asymmetric Cases," *Law & Society Review* 35 (2001), 393, 409.

[23]   Jeff Yates, Andrew B. Whitford, and William Gillespie, "Agenda Setting, Issue Priorities and Organizational Maintenance: The U.S. Supreme Court, 1955 to 1994," *British Journal of Political Science* 35 (2005), 369–81.

[24]   Alan Paterson, *Final Judgment: The Last Law Lords and the Supreme Court* (Oxford, U.K.: Hart, 2013).

[25]   Timothy R. Johnson and Thomas K. Pryor, "Oral Arguments." In *The Routledge Handbook of Judicial Behavior* eds. Robert M. Howard and Kirk A. Randazzo (New York: Routledge, 2018), 222.

[26]   Robert H. Jackson, "Advocacy Before the United States Supreme Court," *Cornell Law Quarterly* (Fall, 1951), 2. For an analysis of the legal norms of written and oral advocacy in the United States and England, see Suzanne Ehrenberg, "Embracing the Writing-Centered Legal Process," *Iowa Law Review* (April 2004), 1159–99.

[27]   Frank M. Coffin, *On Appeal: Courts, Lawyering, and Judging* (New York: Norton, 1993), 107–8, 111–12.

[28]   Georgetown University Law Center (Writing Center), "The Bench Memorandum," available at https://www.law.georgetown.edu/wp-content/uploads/2018/07/The-Bench-Memorandum-Jessica-Klarfeld-2011.pdf (last retrieved April 24, 2020). See also, Cohen, *Inside Appellate Courts*, 91–92, 101–5. See also Howard, *Courts of Appeals in the Federal Judicial System*, 198.

[29]   U.S. Supreme Court, Rule 28, *Rules of the Supreme Court of the United States,* available at https://www.supremecourt.gov/ctrules/2019RulesoftheCourt.pdf (last retrieved April 24, 2020). See also, Legal Information Institute (Cornell Law School), "Federal Rules of Appellate Procedure, Rule 34. Oral Argument," available at https://www.law.cornell.edu/rules/frap/rule_34 (last retrieved April 24, 2020); National Center for State Courts, "Oral Arguments in Appellate Cases (Table 2.14)," available at http://data.ncsc.org/QvAJAXZfc/opendoc.htm?document=Public%20App/SCO.qvw&host=QVS@qlikviewisa&anonymous=true&bookmark=Document\BM127 (last retrieved April 24, 2020).

[30]   Michael Duvall, "When Is Oral Argument Important? A Judicial Clerk's View of the Debate," *Journal of Appellate Practice and Process* 9 (2007), 121, 122. See also, National Center for State Courts, "Oral Arguments in Appellate Cases (Table 2.14); Christine M. Venter, "The Case Against Oral Argument: The Effects of Confirmation Bias on the Outcome of Selected Cases in the Seventh Circuit Court of Appeals," *Legal Communication & Rhetoric* 14 (Fall, 2017), 45, 52–54 (observing that the Oklahoma Supreme Court rarely hears oral arguments; and, for the California Supreme Court, oral argument is granted in most cases but it is used as a means to "test" the soundness of a draft judicial opinion that was formulated from reading the legal briefs beforehand).

[31]   Johnson and Pryor, "Oral Arguments," 224.

[32]   Michael A. Fletcher & Kevin Merida, "Jurist Mum Come Oral Arguments; Reticence on Bench Perplexes Observers," *Washington Post* (Oct. 11, 2004), available at https://www.washingtonpost.com/archive/politics/2004/10/11/jurist-mum-come-oral-arguments/ad2f7ab4-991c-454a-a5a5-a34388fc15e8/?utm_term=.8a370131e600 (last retrieved April 24, 2020).

[33]   Ginsburg, "Workways of the Supreme Court," 522–25; John M. Harlan II, "What Part Does the Oral Argument Play in the Conduct of an Appeal?" *Cornell Law Quarterly* 41 (1955), 6. See also Timothy R. Johnson, *Oral Arguments and Decision Making on the United States Supreme Court* (Albany: State University of New York Press, 2004).

[34]   David M. O'Brien, *Storm Center: The Supreme Court in American Politics*, 12th ed. (New York: Norton, 2020), 258.

35 O'Brien, *Storm Center*, 260–66. The structural rules and institutional norms of state supreme courts relating to conference deliberations, votes and opinion assignments are analyzed in David A. Hughes, Teena Wilhelm and Richard L. Jr. Vining, "Deliberation Rules and Opinion Assignment Procedures in State Supreme Courts: A Replication," *Justice System Journal* 36 (2015): 395–410. For an analysis of the dynamics underlying shifting judicial preferences, see J. Woodford Howard, Jr., "On the Fluidity of Judicial Choice," *American Political Science Review* (March 1968), 43–56.

36 David A. Hughes, Teena Wilhelm, and Richard L. Vining Jr., "Deliberation Rules and Opinion Assignment Procedures in State Supreme Courts: A Replication" *Justice System Journal* 36 (2015), 395, 396.

37 Hughes, Wilhelm, and Vining Jr., "Deliberation Rules and Opinion Assignment Procedures in State Supreme Courts," 396.

38 Ginsburg, "Workways of the Supreme Court," 526.

39 Hughes, Wilhelm, and Vining Jr., "Deliberation Rules and Opinion Assignment Procedures in State Supreme Courts," 397.

40 Jeffery R. Lax and Charles M. Cameron, "Bargaining and Opinion Assignment on the U.S. Supreme Court," *Journal of Law, Economics and Organization* 23 (2007), 276–302.

41 Elisha Carol Savchak and Jennifer Barnes Bowie, "A Bottom-up Account of State Supreme Court Opinion Writing," *Justice System Journal* 37 (2016), 94, 101. See also, Hughes, Wilhelm, and Vining Jr., "Deliberation Rules and Opinion Assignment Procedures in State Supreme Courts," 399.

42 See Cliff Carrubba, Barry Friedman, Andrew D. Martin, and Georg Vanberg, "Who Controls the Content of Supreme Court Opinions?" *American Journal of Political Science* 56 (2012), 400–412 (finding that the median justice of the coalition of justices that sign the opinion is influential in determining the content of Supreme Court majority opinions after noting the alternative claim that opinion writers shape content); Forrest Maltzman and Paul J. Wahlbeck, "A Conditional Model of Opinion Assignment on the Supreme Court," *Political Research Quarterly* 57 (2004), 551–63. See, generally, Maltzman, Spriggs, and Wahlbeck, *Crafting Law on the Supreme Court.*

43 Timothy R. Johnson, James F. Spriggs II, and Paul J. Wahlbeck, "Passing and Strategic Voting on the U.S. Supreme Court," *Law & Society Review* (June 2005), 349–77.

44 Howard, *Courts of Appeals in the Federal Judicial System*, 208.

45 Ginsburg, "Workways of the Supreme Court," 526.

46 J. Lyn Entrikin, "Global Judicial Transparency Norms: A Peek Behind the Robes in a Whole New World-A Look at Global 'Democratizing' Trends in Judicial Opinion-Issues Practices," *Washington University Global Studies Law Review* 18 (2019), 55–159; and, M. Todd Henderson, "From Seriatim to Consensus and Back Again: A Theory of Dissent," *Supreme Court Review* 2007 (2007), 283–344.

47 A summary of some of the relevant political science research is found in Savchak and Bowie, "A Bottom-up Account of State Supreme Court Opinion Writing," 94.

48 Savchak and Bowie, "A Bottom-up Account of State Supreme Court Opinion Writing," 95. See generally, ibid., 94–105.

49 Lewis F. Powell, Jr., "What the Justices Are Saying," *American Bar Association Journal* 62 (1976), 1454.

50 Justice Thomas is quoted in Corey Ditslear and Lawrence Baum, "Selection of Law Clerks and Polarization in the U.S. Supreme Court," *Journal of Politics* (August 2001), 869, 883.

51 Normana Dorsen and Amelia Ames Newcomb, "John Marshall Harlan II, Associate Justice of the Supreme Court 1955–1971: Remembrances by His Law Clerks," *Journal of Supreme Court History* (July 2002), 138–75.

52 John P. Frank, *Marble Palace: The Supreme Court in American Life* (Westport, Conn.: Greenwood Press, 1958), 116.

53 John C. Jeffries, Jr., *Justice Lewis F. Powell, Jr.* (New York: Charles Scribner's Sons, 1994), 294. See also J. Harvie Wilkinson III, "Justice Lewis F. Powell, Jr.: A Personal View by a Former Clerk," in *In Chambers: Stories of Supreme Court Law Clerks and Their Justices*, edited by Todd C. Peppers and Artemus Ward (Charlottesville: University of Virginia Press, 2012), 342–49.

54 Hanson, Flango, and Hansen, *The Work of Appellate Court Legal Staff*, 39, 64–65. For a specific description of the various tasks law clerks perform, see Charles H. Sheldon, "Law Clerking With a State

Supreme Court: Views From the Perspective of the Personal Assistants to the Judges," *Justice System Journal* 6 (1981), 346, 352 (Table 1).

55   David M. O'Brien, "The Dynamics of the Judicial Process," in *Judges on Judging: Views From the Bench*, 5th ed. (Washington, D.C.: CQ Press, 2016), 64–65. The "ambassadorial role" is analyzed in Todd C. Peppers and Artemus Ward, "Introduction," in *In Chambers: Stories of Supreme Court Law Clerks and Their Justices,* eds. Todd C. Peppers and Artemus Ward (Charlottesville: University of Virginia Press, 2012), 7–8.

56   Pamela C. Corley, Amy Steigerwalt, and Artemus Ward, *The Puzzle of Unanimity: Consensus on the United States Supreme Court* (Palo Alto, Calif.: Stanford University Press, 2013). The percentages of unanimity on the Supreme Court and circuit courts are reported in Lee Epstein, William M. Landes, and Richard A. Posner, *The Behavior of Federal Judges: A Theoretical and Empirical Study of Rational Choice* (Cambridge, Mass.: Harvard University Press, 2013), 54–55.

57   See Lax and Cameron, "Bargaining and Opinion Assignment on the U.S. Supreme Court," 276–302.

58   See Paul J. Wahlbeck et al., "The Politics of Dissents and Concurrences on the U.S. Supreme Court," *American Political Quarterly* 27 (1999): 488–517; Pamela C. Corley, *Concurring Opinion Writing on the U.S. Supreme Court* (Albany: State University of New York Press, 2010).

59   David M. O'Brien, "Institutional Norms and Supreme Court Opinions: On Reconsidering the Rise of Individual Opinions," in *Supreme Court Decision-Making: New Institutionalist Approaches,* ed. Cornell W. Clayton and Howard Gillman (Chicago: University of Chicago Press, 1999), 113. See also, Entrikin, "Global Judicial Transparency Norms," 68–69; and, Lee Epstein et al., "The Norm of Consensus on the U.S. Supreme Court," *American Journal of Political Science* 45 (2001), 362, 362–63

60   See Paul J. Wahlbeck et al., "The Politics of Dissents and Concurrences on the U.S. Supreme Court," 488, 494.

61   Morgan L. W. Hazelton, Rachael K. Hinkle & James F. Spriggs II, "The Influence of Unique Information in Briefs on Supreme Court Opinion Content," *Justice System Journal* (DOI: 10.1080/0098261X.2019.1613202, published online June 3, 2019), 6 (citing studies).

62   The remark by Chief Justice Hughes is found in Ruth Bader Ginsburg, "The Role of Dissenting Opinions (October 21, 2007)," available at https://www.supremecourt.gov/publicinfo/speeches/sp_10-21-07.html (last retrieved April 24, 2020). See also Eva M. Guzman and Ed Duffy, "The Multiple Paths of Dissent: Roles of Dissenting Judges in the Judicial Process," *Judicature* 97 (2013), 105, 106 (observing that writing a dissent may "further the interests promoted by the rule of law").

63   Timothy R. Johnson, Ryan C. Black, and Eve M. Ringsmuth, "Hear Me Roar: What Provokes Supreme Court Justices to Dissent from the Bench?," *Minnesota Law Review* 93 (2003), 1560, 1569–70. See also, Wahlbeck et al., "The Politics of Dissents and Concurrences on the U.S. Supreme Court," 488, 494.

64   Ginsburg, "The Role of Dissenting Opinions."

65   Lani Guinier, "Demosprudence through Dissent," *Harvard Law Review* 122 (2008), 4, 14. See also, Christopher W. Schmidt and Carolyn Shapiro, "Oral Dissenting on the Supreme Court," *William & Mary Bill of Rights Journal* 19 (2010), 75, 78.

66   Jill Duffy and Elizabeth Lambert, "Dissents From the Bench: A Compilation of Oral Dissents by U.S. Supreme Court Justices," *Law Library Journal* 102 (2010), 7–37. See also, William D. Blake & Hans J. Hacker, "The Brooding Spirit of the Law: Supreme Court Justices Reading Dissents from the Bench," *Justice System Journal* 31 (2010), 1–25.

67   Irin Carmon, "Scalia protests gay marriage ruling again in unrelated case," *MSNBC* (June 29, 2015), http://www.msnbc.com/msnbc/scalia-protests-gay-marriage-ruling-again-unrelated-dissent (last retrieved April 24, 2020). See also, Sonja R. West, "The Supreme Court's Limited Public Forum," *Washington and Lee Law Review Online* 572 (2017), https://scholarlycommons.law.wlu.edu/wlulr-online/vol73/iss2/1 (last retrieved April 24, 2020); *Glossip v. Gross*, 576 U.S. 863 (2015)(death penalty); and *Obergefell v. Hodges*, 576 U.S. 644 (2015)(same-sex marriage).

68   Linda Greenhouse, "In Dissent, Ginsburg Finds Her Voice at the Supreme Court," *New York Times* (May 31, 2007), available at https://www.nytimes.com/2007/05/31/world/americas/31iht-court.4.5946972.html (last retrieved April 24, 2020). See also *Gonzales v. Carhart,* 550 U.S. 124 (2007) (partial birth abortion); *Burwell v. Hobby Lobby Stores, Inc.*, 573 U.S. 682 (2014) (religious discrimination).

69   Administrative Office of the U.S. Courts, "U.S. Courts of Appeals—Opinions and Orders Filed, by Type, in Cases Terminated on the Merits After Oral Hearing or Submission on Briefs During the 12-Month

Periods Ending June 30, 1990, and September 30, 1995 Through 2018 (Table 2.5)," available at https://www.uscourts.gov/statistics/table/25/judicial-facts-and-figures/2018/09/30 (last retrieved April 24, 2020). See also, Katrin Marquez, "Are Unpublished Opinions Inconsistent with the Right of Access?," *MFIA (Media Freedom & Information Access Clinic,* November 19, 2018), available at https://law.yale.edu/mfia/case-disclosed/are-unpublished-opinions-inconsistent-right-access (last retrieved April 24, 2020).

70   David Schanker and Theresa Owens, National Center for State Courts, "Citation of Unpublished Opinions in State Courts," in *Future Trends in State Courts* 2010/Appellate Reengineering 147–151, available at, https://ncsc.contentdm.oclc.org/digital/collection/appellate/id/196/rec/32 (last retrieved July 3, 2020). See also, Cohen, *Inside Appellate Courts,* 74.

71   Oliver Wendell Holmes, "The Path of the Law," *Harvard Law Review* 10 (1896), 43.

72   Richard A. Posner, *How Judges Think* (Cambridge, Mass.: Harvard University Press, 2008), 232.

73   James L. Gibson, "From Simplicity to Complexity: The Development of Theory in The Study of Judicial Behavior," *Political Behavior* 5 (1983), 7, 9. See also, Jeffrey A. Segal, "Judicial Behavior." In *The Oxford Handbook of Political Science.* Ed. Robert E. Goodin (New York: Oxford University Press, 2011), 276.

74   Lee Epstein, "Some Thoughts on the Study of Judicial Behavior," *William and Mary Law Review* 57 (2016), 2017, 2022.

75   The scholarly debate over the strengths and weaknesses of the attitudinal model registers the differences in methodological approaches used by some law and courts scholars. See, e.g., Symposium, "The Supreme Court and the Attitudinal Model," *Newsletter of the Law and Courts Section of the American Political Science Association* 4 (Spring, 1994), 1, 9–10 (comments by Rogers Smith, Jeffrey Segal and Harold Spaeth); Keith E. Whittington, "Once More Unto the Breach: PostBehavioralist Approaches to Judicial Politics," *Law & Social Inquiry* 25 (2000), 601–634. Also, the distinction between normative and empirical theory is discussed in John B. Gates, "Theory, Methods, and the New Institutionalism in Judicial Research," in *The American Courts: A Critical Assessment,* ed. John B. Gates and Charles A. Johnson (Washington, D.C.: CQ Press, 1990), 469–70.

76   C. Herman Pritchett, *The Roosevelt Court: A Study in Judicial Politics and Values, 1937–1947* (New York: Macmillan, 1948).

77   See Nancy Maveety, "The Study of Judicial Behavior and the Discipline of Political Science," in *The Pioneers of Judicial Behavior,* ed. Nancy Maveety (Ann Arbor: University of Michigan Press, 2003), 9–17. See also Pritchett, *The Roosevelt Court,* xiii; and, C. Herman Pritchett, "Public Law and Judicial Behavior," *Journal of Politics* 30 (1968): 480, 498.

78   Jeffrey A. Segal, "Glendon Schubert: The Judicial Mind," in *The Pioneers of Judicial Behavior,* ed. Nancy Maveety (Ann Arbor: University of Michigan Press, 2003), 80. See also Lawrence Baum, "C. Herman Pritchett: Innovator With an Ambiguous Legacy," in *The Pioneers of Judicial Behavior,* ed. Nancy Maveety (Ann Arbor: University of Michigan Press, 2003), 57–77.

79   Segal, "Glendon Schubert," 80. See also Glendon A. Schubert, *The Judicial Mind: The Attitudes and Ideologies of Supreme Court Justices, 1946–1963* (Evanston, Ill.: Northwestern University Press, 1965).

80   Segal, "Glendon Schubert," 78–100. See also Glendon Schubert, *The Judicial Mind Revisited: Psychometric Analysis of Supreme Court Ideology* (New York: Oxford University Press, 1974).

81   Jeffrey A. Segal and Harold J. Spaeth, *The Supreme Court and the Attitudinal Model* (New York: Cambridge University Press, 1993).

82   Jeffery A. Segal and Alan J. Champlin, "The Attitudinal Model." In *The Routledge Handbook of Judicial Behavior,* 17. See also, *The Supreme Court Database,* available at http://scdb.wustl.edu/ (last retrieved August 6, 2019); and, J. Mitchell Pickerill and Christopher Brough, "Law and Politics in Judicial and Supreme Court Decision-Making." In *The Routledge Handbook of Judicial Behavior* eds. Robert M. Howard and Kirk A. Randazzo (New York: Routledge, 2018), 36.

83   Segal and Spaeth, *The Supreme Court and the Attitudinal Model* (New York: Cambridge University Press, 1993), 65. See also, Segal, "Judicial Behavior," In *The Oxford Handbook of Political Science,* 276.

84   See, e.g., Emmett Macfarlane, *Governing From the Bench: The Supreme Court of Canada and the Judicial Role* (Vancouver: University of British Columbia Press, 2013) (finding that judicial role perceptions, along with attitudinal and strategic factors, explain judicial behavior on the Supreme Court of Canada).

85   The quotations are from Segal, "Judicial Behavior," In *The Oxford Handbook of Political Science,* 276 and Segal and Champlin, "The Attitudinal Model," In *The Routledge Handbook of Judicial Behavior,* 17. Segal and Spaeth revised their original book in Jeffrey A. Segal and Harold J. Spaeth, *The Supreme Court and the Attitudinal Model*

Revisited (Cambridge, U.K.: Cambridge University Press, 2002). Various criticisms and rebuttals from political scientists and legal scholars concerning the merits and application of the attitudinal model are found in "Symposium: The Supreme Court and the Attitudinal Model," *Newsletter of the Law and Courts Section of the American Political Science Association* 4 (Spring, 1994), 3–12; "Symposium on the Supreme Court and the Attitudinal Model Revisited," *Newsletter of the Law and Courts Section of the American Political Science Association* 13 (Summer, 2003), 10–38.

[86]   Rogers M. Smith, "Political Jurisprudence, the 'New Institutionalism,' and the Future of Public Law," *American Political Science Review* 86 (1988), 89–108. For an overview of the rise of new institutionalism in political science, see Rogers M. Smith, "Historical Institutionalism and the Study of Law," in *The Oxford Handbook of Law and Politics*, eds. Keith E. Whittington, R. Daniel Kelemen, and Gregory A. Caldeira (New York: Oxford University Press, 2010), 46–59. See also J. G. March and J. P. Olsen, "The New Institutionalism: Organizational Factors in Political Life," *American Political Science Review* 78 (1984), 734–49.

[87]   Thomas A. Koelble, "The New Institutionalism in Political Science and Sociology," *Comparative Politics*, 27 (1995), 231–243; Whittington, "Once More Unto the Breach: PostBehavioralist Approaches to Judicial Politics," 609–612.

[88]   Keith E. Whittington and R. Daniel Kelmen, "The Study of Law and Politics," in *The Oxford Handbook of Law and Politics*, eds. Keith E. Whittington, R. Daniel Kelemen, and Gregory A. Caldeira (New York: Oxford University Press, 2010), 3–15. See also, Pickerill and Brough, "Law and Politics in Judicial and Supreme Court Decision-Making." In *The Routledge Handbook of Judicial Behavior*, 35.

[89]   Cornell W. Clayton, "The Supreme Court and Political Jurisprudence: New and Old Institutionalisms," in *Supreme Court Decision-Making: New Institutionalist Approaches,* ed. Cornell W. Clayton and Howard Gillman (Chicago: University of Chicago Press, 1999), 15–41.

[90]   Clayton, "The Supreme Court and Political Jurisprudence," 35 ("patterns of purpose and meaning"); Rogers M. Smith, "Historical Institutionalism and Public Law," *Law and Courts Newsletter* (Summer, 1998), 6–7.

[91]   Cornell W. Clayton and Howard Gillman, eds., *Supreme Court Decision-Making: New Institutionalist Approaches* (Chicago: University of Chicago Press, 1999); Howard Gillman and Cornell Clayton, eds., *The Supreme Court in American Politics: New Institutionalist Interpretations* (Lawrence: University Press of Kansas, 1999).

[92]   See Whittington, "Once More Unto the Breach: PostBehavioralist Approaches to Judicial Politics," 602–603.

[93]   Pickerill and Brough, "Law and Politics in Judicial and Supreme Court Decision-Making." In *The Routledge Handbook of Judicial Behavior*, 35–41; Whittington, "Once More Unto the Breach: PostBehavioralist Approaches to Judicial Politics," 604–609. See also, Lee Epstein and Jack Knight, "The New Institutionalism, Part II," *Law and Courts Newsletter* (Spring, 1997), 4–9; Howard Gillman, "Placing Judicial Motives in Context: A Response to Lee Epstein and Jack Knight," *Law and Courts Newsletter* (Spring, 1997), 10–13.

[94]   Walter Murphy, *The Elements of Judicial Strategy* (Chicago: University of Chicago Press, 1964), 207. See also, Pritchett, "Public Law and Judicial Behavior," 505–06.

[95]   Lee Epstein and Jack Knight, "Toward a Strategic Revolution in Judicial Politics: A Look Back, A Look Ahead," *Political Research Quarterly* (September 2000), 625–61.

[96]   Lee Epstein and Jack Knight, "Strategic Accounts of Judging." In T*he Routledge Handbook of Judicial Behavior*, 48, 53–55. See also, Lee Epstein and Jack Knight, *The Choices Justices Make* (Washington, D.C.: CQ Press, 1998).

[97]   Epstein and Knight, "Strategic Accounts of Judging." In T*he Routledge Handbook of Judicial Behavior*, 48–49; Epstein and Knight, "The New Institutionalism, Part II," 4.

[98]   Epstein and Knight, "Strategic Accounts of Judging." In T*he Routledge Handbook of Judicial Behavior*, 50–53.

[99]   See, e.g., Jeffrey A. Segal, Chad Westerland, and Stephanie A. Lindquist, "Congress, the Supreme Court, and Judicial Review: Testing a Constitutional Separation of Powers Model," *American Journal of Political Science* 55 (2011), 89–104; Tom S. Clark, "The Separation of Powers, Court Curbing, and Judicial Legitimacy," *American Journal of Political Science* 53 (2009), 971–89; Jeffrey A. Segal, "Separation-of-Powers Games in the Positive Theory of Courts and Congress," *American Political Science Review* 91 (1997), 28–44; and David C. Nixon and J. David Haskin, "Judicial Recruitment Strategies: The Judge's Role in Influencing Party Control of the Appellate Courts," *American Politics Quarterly* 28 (2000), 458–89.

[100] Forrest Maltzman, James F. Spriggs II, and Paul J. Wahlbeck, *Crafting Law on the Supreme Court: The Collegial Game* (Cambridge, U.K.: Cambridge University Press, 2000); Epstein and Knight, *The Choices Justices Make.*

[101] Epstein, Landes, and Posner, *The Behavior of Federal Judges: A Theoretical and Empirical Study of Rational Choice* (Cambridge, MA.: Harvard University Press, 2013), 385–86. See Richard A. Posner, *How Judges Think* (Cambridge, MA.: Harvard University Press, 2008); Richard A. Posner, "What Do Judges Maximize? (The Same Thing Everybody Else Does)," *Supreme Court Economic Review* 3 (1993), 1–41. For an overview and criticisms of labor market theory, see Susan B. Haire and Rorie Spill Solberg, "Introduction: The Behavior of Federal Judges," *Judicature* 97 (2013), 70–71; Jeffrey A. Segal, Benjamin Woodson, and Joshua Johnson, "The Behavioral Economics Alternative: The Legal-Model Fiction in Epstein, Landes, and Posner's *The Behavior of Federal Judges," Judicature* 97 (2013), 75–81; Renee Cohn Jubelirer, "The Behavior of Federal Judges: The 'Careerist' in Robes," *Judicature* 97 (2013), 98–104; and Douglas H. Ginsburg, "The Behavior of Federal Judges: A View From the D.C. Circuit," *Judicature* 97 (2013), 109–12.

[102] Ryan C., Black, Owens, Ryan J., Justin Wedeking and Patrick C. Wohlfarth. *The Conscientious Justice: How Supreme Court Justices' Personalities Influence the Law, the High Court, and the Constitution.* (New York: Cambridge University Press, 2020); Matthew E.K. Hall, *What Justices Want: Goals and Personality on the U.S. Supreme Court* (New York: Cambridge University Press, 2019). See also, Lawrence Baum and Neal Devins. *The Company They Keep: How Partisan Divisions Came to the Supreme Court* (New York: Oxford University Press, 2019); Lawrence Baum, "Motivation and Judicial Behavior: Expanding the Scope of the Inquiry," in *The Psychology of Judicial Decision Making*, eds. David Klein and Gregory Mitchell (New York: Oxford University Press, 2010), 3; Laurence Baum, *The Puzzle of Judicial Behavior* (Ann Arbor: University of Michigan Press, 1997), 137. The audience-based theory is detailed in Laurence Baum, *Judges and Their Audiences: A Perspective on Judicial Behavior* (Princeton, N.J.: Princeton University Press, 2006). Other research using psychological orientations to judging is found in *The Psychology of Judicial Decision Making*, eds. David Klein and Gregory Mitchell (New York: Oxford University Press, 2010); Eileen Braman, *Law, Politics and Perception: How Policy Preferences Influence Legal Reasoning* (Charlottesville: University of Virginia Press, 2009).

[103] Pritchett's quote, and Felix S. Cohen's characterization of the dismal state of public law scholarship in 1935 are found in Pritchett, "Public Law and Judicial Behavior," 509 and 480, respectively. On the growth of legal empirical studies and its relationship to political science and law, see *What's Law Got To Do With It?: What Judges Do, Why They Do It, and What's At Stake* Ed. Charles Gardner Geyh (Stanford, CA.: Stanford University Press, 2011); Gregory C. Sisk, "The Quantitative Moment and the Qualitative Opportunity: Legal Studies of Judicial Decision Making," *Cornell Law Review* (2008), 873–900; Michael Heise, "The Past, Present, and Future of Empirical Legal Scholarship: Judicial Decision Making and the New Empiricism," *University of Illinois Law Review* (2002), 819–50. See also, Cornell University Law School, "The Society for Empirical Legal Studies, About Us," available at https://www.lawschool.cornell.edu/SELS/about.cfm (last retrieved September 2, 2019).

[104] For an overview of the future of judicial behavior research outlining these developments and others, see Lee Epstein, "Some Thoughts on the Study of Judicial Behavior"; and, Robert M. Howard and Kirk A. Randazzo, "Conclusion: Where Do We Go From Here?" In *The Routledge Handbook of Judicial Behavior*, 509–513.

[105] Epstein, "Some Thoughts on the Study of Judicial Behavior," 2037–38 (listing datasets and URLs); the University of South Carolina Judicial Research Initiative, available at http://artsandsciences.sc.edu/poli/juri/databases.htm (last retrieved April 24, 2020) (listing datasets); and, the blog at Cornell University Law School, "Empirical Legal Studies," available at https://www.elsblog.org/ (last retrieved April 24, 2020) (listing datasets).

[106] Posner, *How Judges Think*, 7–8. See, e.g., MacFarlane, *Governing From the Bench: The Supreme Court of Canada and the Judicial Role.*

[107] Harry T. Edwards, "The Judicial Function and the Elusive Goal of Principled Decisionmaking," *Wisconsin Law Review* (1991), 837, 838.

[108] Posner, *How Judges Think*, 9.

[109] Edward H. Levi, *An Introduction to Legal Reasoning* (Chicago: University of Chicago Press, 1949), 1.

[110] Levi, *An Introduction to Legal Reasoning*, 2, 4.

[111] Benjamin N. Cardozo, *The Nature of the Judicial Process* (New Haven, Conn.: Yale University Press, 1921), 16, 23, 28, 30–31.

[112] *Ramos v. Louisiana*, 140 S.Ct. 1390 (2020)(Alito, J., dissenting), 8.

[113] Amy Howe, "Opinion analysis: With debate over adherence to precedent, justices scrap nonunanimous jury rule," *SCOTUSblog (April 20, 2020)*, available at https://www.scotusblog.com/2020/04/opinion-analysis-with-debate-over-adherence-to-precedent-justices-scrap-nonunanimous-jury-rule/ (last retrieved April 25, 2020). See also, *Apodaca v. Oregon*, 406 U.S. 404 (1972).

[114] William Baude, "Precedent and Discretion" (January 15, 2020). For the *Supreme Court Review*, Forthcoming. Available at SSRN: https://ssrn-com.proxy.library.kent.edu/abstract=3517580 or http://dx.doi.org.proxy.library.kent.edu/10.2139/ssrn.351758 (last retrieved April 26, 2020), 4.

[115] *Webster v. Reproductive Health Services*, 492 U.S. 490 (1989), 535 (Scalia, J., concurring in part). See also *Roe v. Wade*, 410 U.S. 113 (1973).

[116] *Planned Parenthood of Southeastern Pennsylvania v. Casey*, 505 U.S. 833 (1992).

[117] *June Medical Services LLC v. Russo*, No. 18-1323 (U.S. Jun. 29, 2020); *Whole Woman's Health v. Hellerstedt*, 136 S.Ct. 2292 (2016). See also, *Planned Parenthood of Southeastern Pennsylvania v. Casey*, 846, 861, 866, 877–79.

[118] See, e.g., Mark J. Richards and Herbert M. Kritzer, "Jurisprudential Regimes in Supreme Court Decision Making," *American Political Science Review* 96 (2002), 305–20; Herbert M. Kritzer and Mark J. Richards, "Jurisprudential Regimes in Supreme Court Decision Making: The Lemon Regime and Establishment Clause Cases," *Law and Society Review* 37 (2003), 827–40; and Herbert M. Kritzer and Mark J. Richards, "The Influence of Law in the Supreme Court Search-and-Seizure Jurisprudence," *American Politics Research* 33 (2005), 33–55. The quote in the paragraph is found in *Kisor v. Wilkie*, 139 S. Ct. 2400 (2019)(Kagan, J., Opinion for the Court).

[119] *Burnett v. Coronado Oil and Gas Co.*, 285 U.S. 393, 406 (1932) (Brandeis, J., dissenting). See also William O. Douglas, "*Stare Decisis*," *Columbia Law Review* 49 (1949), 735.

[120] David M. O'Brien, *Constitutional Law and Politics: Civil Rights and Liberties (Volume Two)*, 11th ed. (New York: Norton, 2020), 142. See also Saul Brenner and Harold J. Spaeth, *Stare Indecisis: The Alteration of Precedent on the U.S. Supreme Court, 1946–1992* (Cambridge, U.K.: Cambridge University Press, 1995).

[121] *Payne v. Tennessee*, 501 U.S. 808 (1991), 828.

[122] See, e.g., *Dickerson v. United States*, 530 U.S. 428 (2000), 443 ("special justification"); and *Planned Parenthood of Southeastern Pennsylvania v. Casey*, 864, "special reason." For a general statement of *stare decisis* principles, see *Planned Parenthood of Southeastern Pennsylvania v. Casey*, 854; and *Kisor* (Kagan, J., Opinion for the Court).

[123] Cardozo, *The Nature of the Judicial Process*, 149; Robert C. Wigton, "What Does It Take to Overrule? An Analysis of Supreme Court Overrulings and the Doctrine of *Stare Decisis*," *Legal Studies Forum* 18 (1994), 3, 7–8; Christopher P. Banks, "Reversals of Precedent and Judicial Policy-Making: How Judicial Conceptions of *Stare Decisis* in the U.S. Supreme Court Influence Social Change," *University of Akron Law Review* 32 (1999), 233–58.

[124] *Payne v. Tennessee*, 501 U.S. 808 (1991), 844. See also Christopher P. Banks, "The Supreme Court and Precedent: An Analysis of Natural Courts and Reversal Trends," *Judicature* (February/March 1992), 264–68, Tables 3, 4, 5; Douglas, "*Stare Decisis*," 736–37.

[125] Thomas G. Hansford and James F. Spriggs II, *The Politics of Precedent on the U.S. Supreme Court* (Princeton, N.J.: Princeton University Press, 2008). See also James F. Spriggs II and Thomas G. Hansford, "Explaining the Overruling of U.S. Supreme Court Precedent," *Journal of Politics* (November 2001), 1091–111.

[126] *PGA Tour, Inc. v. Martin*, 532 U.S. 661, 691 (2001) (Scalia, J., dissenting).

[127] *PGA Tour*, 691.

[128] See John Paul Stevens, "The Shakespeare Canon of Statutory Construction," *University of Pennsylvania Law Review* 140 (1992), 1373–87.

[129] Henry M. Hart, Jr., and Albert M. Sacks, *The Legal Process*, eds. William N. Eskridge, Jr., and Philip P. Frickey (Westbury, N.Y.: Foundation Press, 1994), 1169.

[130] Felix Frankfurter, "Some Reflections on the Reading of Statutes," in *Judges on Judging: Views From the Bench*, 2nd ed., eds. David M. O'Brien (Washington, D.C.: CQ Press, 2003), 248.

[131] Stephen Breyer, "On the Uses of Legislative History in Interpreting Statutes," *Southern California Law Review* 65 (1992), 845, 848.

[132] Abner J. Mikva, "Reading and Writing Statutes," *University of Pittsburg Law Review* (1987), 627, 629.

[133] As quoted by Abner. J. Mikva, "Statutory Interpretation: Getting the Law to Be Less Common," *Ohio State Law Journal* 50 (1989), 979, 981.

[134] David M. O'Brien, "The Judiciary and Federal Regulation," in *Judges on Judging: Views From the Bench*, 2nd ed. (Washington, D.C.: CQ Press, 2004), 242.

[135] Edwin Meese III, "Speech Before the American Bar Association, July 9, 1985, Washington, D.C.," in *The Great Debate: Interpreting Our Written Constitution* (Washington, D.C.: The Federalist Society, 1986), 1.

[136] Daniel A. Farber and Suzanna Sherry, *Desperately Seeking Certainty: The Misguided Quest for Constitutional Foundations* (Chicago: University of Chicago Press, 2002), 11.

[137] Antonin Scalia, "Common-Law Courts in a Civil-Law System," in *A Matter of Interpretation: Federal Courts and the Law*, ed. Antonin Scalia (Princeton, N.J.: Princeton University Press, 1997), 38.

[138] William H. Rehnquist, "The Notion of a Living Constitution," *Texas Law Review* 54 (1976), 693, 699; Antonin Scalia, "Originalism: The Lesser Evil," *Cincinnati Law Review* 57 (1989), 849, 854–55, 862. See also, Jamal Greene, "On the Origins of Originalism," *Texas Law Review* 88 (2009), 1, 9 (noting a discernable "shift in preference among academic originalists in favor of original meaning rather than original intent"); and Eric J. Segall, *Originalism as Faith* (New York: Cambridge University Press, 2018) (criticizing originalism as a pretext for judges that decide cases based on their personal preferences).

[139] *Roper v. Simmons*, 543 U.S. 551 (2005).

[140] William J. Brennan, "The Constitution of the United States: Contemporary Ratification," in *Interpreting Law and Literature: A Hermeneutic Reader*, ed. Sanford Levinson and Steven Mailloux (Evanston, Ill.: Northwestern University Press, 1988), 17–18.

[141] Frank B. Cross, *The Failed Promise of Originalism* (Stanford, Calif.: Stanford Law Books, 2013), 1–22.

CHAPTER 10

The Scope and Limits of Judicial Power

In denouncing the infamous *Dred Scott v. Sandford* (1857) case—which declared African-Americans are an "inferior class of beings who had been subjugated by the dominant race" and cannot sue in federal courts as U.S. citizens—Abraham Lincoln observed that legal precedents help teach "the public how other similar cases will be decided".[1] Lincoln's thoughts are significant because state and federal appellate courts routinely shape the ideological direction of controversial public policies with decisions that legally bind future generations. In 2019, for example, the Kansas Supreme Court interpreted the Kansas Constitution as embracing natural rights that protect a woman's personal choice to abort an unborn fetus. Although Kansas joined a minority of other states giving state constitutional protections to abortion rights, Kansans are deeply divided over abortion's legality and, not surprisingly, Republicans controlling the Kansas legislature and other pro-life activists have vowed to reverse the court's 6:1 ruling through constitutional amendment. How the Kansas abortion legal saga unfolds, though, must also be placed in the context of how the U.S. Supreme Court interprets the U.S. Constitution and corresponding federal laws relating to a woman's right to choose under the landmark 1973 *Roe v. Wade* decision and its progeny, including *Planned Parenthood of Southeastern Pennsylvania v. Casey* (1992) and its "substantial obstacle" test. While *Roe* and *Casey* continue to remain viable precedents, their scope and application continue to infuse national and state politics in light of President Donald Trump's success in placing two conservative appointments, Neil Gorsuch and Brett Kavanaugh, on the Supreme Court—something that conservative activists hope might prove to be decisive in tipping the ideological balance on the Court in favor of rejecting abortion rights by either reversing *Roe* or eviscerating its precedential effect even further. Either way, as Lincoln foresaw, the Court's evolving abortion jurisprudence will clearly educate the public on what to expect from the law and state or federal courts in the future.[2]

503

The abortion cases, as well as countless others that help define the parameters of social public policies, remind us that courts are not the "least dangerous branch." Such was the argument made by Alexander Hamilton in defending the legitimacy of federal courts at our nation's founding. Hamilton's contention that judicial independence—the principle that courts are different from executive or legislative institutions because they have "neither force nor will, but merely judgment"—is still true, but clearly he did not anticipate the degree to which courts would expand their powers and shape the parameters of social policy in legal areas that were unknown to Americans in the eighteenth century.[3] Today, his conclusion that **judicial discretion** is relatively harmless, because it is checked by democratic politics and the judicial obligation to uphold the rule of law, seems almost quaint, if not naïve, because many court watchers would probably agree that courts are often at the forefront of proactive contemporary legal and cultural change.

For political reasons, then, it is not surprising that federal and state judges are routinely attacked for "legislating from the bench" and creating social public policies in hot-button areas of the law. Federal courts, such as the Supreme Court under the leadership of Chief Justice John Roberts, are lambasted across party lines for sanctioning same-sex marriages, not upholding voting rights, restricting criminal defendants' rights in capital punishment cases, or expanding presidential power to control the nation's borders. In the states, political opposition has led to reform proposals and new legislation seeking to diminish judicial influence over public policies supporting abortion rights, approving the business development of oil pipelines, increasing police authority over drunk driving, and requiring the political branches to subsidize public schools (see Table 10.1).

Table 10.1	Federal and State Court Policymaking
Federal Judicial Policymaking	**Legal Policy Effect**
Rucho v. Common Cause (2019)	Supreme Court ruled that courts cannot review claims of partisan redistricting because they are political questions that are more appropriately resolved by the political branches
Bucklew v. Precythe (2019); *Glossip v. Gross* (2015) and *Baze v. Rees* (2008)	Supreme Court declared that death penalty does not forbid a painless death because it only bans "cruel and unusual punishments" that "superadd" terror, pain, or disgrace and which creates a demonstrated risk of severe pain that is a substantial risk, as compared to known and available alternatives
Trump v. Hawaii (2018)	Supreme Court upheld "travel ban" executive order that restricted immigration to the United States by citizens from predominately Muslim-populated countries for national security reasons
Obergefell v. Hodges (2015)	Supreme Court ruled that states must license same-sex marriages under the Fourteenth Amendment's due process and equality principles
State Judicial Policymaking	**Legal Policy Effect**
Hodes & Nauer v. Schmidt (2019)	Kansas Supreme Court interpreted Kansas Constitution to embody a natural rights protection to a woman's right to choose to abort an unborn fetus
In re: Application No. OP–0003 (2019)	Nebraska Supreme Court upheld a state agency's decision to approve a XL Keystone oil pipeline route to Canada over the objections of Native American tribes, environmental groups and citizens
State v. Mitchell (2018)	Wisconsin Supreme Court ruled that police can perform blood draws to determine blood alcohol content of unconscious person suspected of drunk driving without a search warrant under the Fourth Amendment because implied consent was given by driving on state highways and drinking to a point demonstrating probable cause of intoxication
Gannon v. State (2014) and *Montoy v. State* (2005)	Kansas Supreme Court ruled public school financing formula creates wealth-based disparities and violates equality under state constitution

Accordingly, there are repeated calls on both sides of the aisle to increase legislative oversight over courts and judges. For example, congressional representatives have argued for the creation of an inspector general's office as a watchdog to keep judges in check and accountable. Other legislative solutions include diminishing court funding; stripping the courts of jurisdiction over abortion, health care, or death penalty cases; or, in addition to impeachment or altering the size of a court, expediting the removal of judges who are deemed to not exhibit "good behavior." Typically, reform proposals are highly politicized statements of policy preferences. In her unsuccessful run to become the Democratic nominee in the 2020 presidential election, for example, Elizabeth Warren announced a new judicial ethics plan that would prevent Supreme Court justices and other federal judges from taking advantage of stock transfers or ownership; and it would place restrictions on recusal practices or "extra-judicial" (off-the-bench) activities that reap large speaking fees and all-expenses' paid conference travel. Although Warren touted the plan as a way to increase judicial accountability and public transparency, she was quick to point out that the reforms are necessary, in part, to allow for investigations of alleged illicit behavior by Supreme Court Justice Brett Kavanaugh and two other conservative federal judges, Maryanne Trump Barry (President Trump's sister, Third Circuit) and Alex Kozinski (Ninth Circuit). As she argued, because no ethical rules were in place, 83 ethics complaints were dropped when Kavanaugh became a Supreme Court Justice; and, the ongoing investigations against Trump Barry (tax fraud involving her siblings) and Kozinski (sexual abuse against his law clerks and staff) abruptly ended when they both retired.[4]

This Chapter considers the scope and limitations of judicial power by examining the political struggles over the judiciary's independence and its policymaking. The first section provides an overview of judicial policymaking and whether judges engage in so-called "judicial activism" or "judicial restraint." It then illustrates how courts may become agents of political change in, for example, creating rulings on public school funding, capital punishment and abortion. Next, the impact of judicial policymaking is considered in light of the implementation of school desegregation policies and the corresponding struggle to recognize same-sex marriages. The Chapter concludes by considering the internal and external restraints on judicial power and whether courts are institutionally capable of forging major social change.

JUDICIAL POLICYMAKING

Although former Justice Benjamin Cardozo acknowledged that judges have discretion to make law, he nonetheless admonished that a judge "is not to innovate at pleasure" as "a knight-errant roaming at will in pursuit of his own ideal of beauty or of goodness."[5] Yet beauty is in the eye of the beholder. And critics often attack courts and their exercise of judicial review for the following interrelated reasons: (1) for making "unprincipled" decisions (those not based on established rules of law); (2) for making social policy decisions exceeding judicial capacity or competence; and, (3) for "legislating from the bench" and functioning as **counter majoritarian** institutions that are not directly accountable to the people.[6] These issues often become part of the debate involving the concepts of "judicial activism" and "judicial restraint," which is discussed next.

"Judicial Activism" and "Judicial Restraint"

Courts are often attacked for fashioning legal policy over a wide range of areas of law—from school desegregation to the rights of the criminally accused, abortion, freedom of speech and religion, and same-sex marriages, among others. When they deliver poor policy outcomes, critics typically accuse them of engaging in judicial activism or judicial restraint. Yet, the meaning of those terms fluctuates with the prevailing political climate and the axiomatic "whose Ox is gored" adage: that is, someone will win or lose depending upon how judges rule on cases in any given political time. Activist or restraint-oriented judicial behavior thus is highly situational and varies with several factors, including: (1) the partisan composition of courts (i.e. whether dominant political parties and executives help shape policymaking by influencing who is serving on the bench through the judicial selection process); (2) the identity (and ideological interests) of litigants making legal arguments in cases; and, (3) the types of cases that invoke social controversy and appear on a court's docket. In this respect, some scholars characterize activism (or restraint) as an "attitude, [or] a deliberate choice" by individual judges about how to interpret the law "best", which is nothing more than a value-laden exercise of discretion.[7]

Generally speaking, an activist court is linked to rulings that deviate or overturn precedents, or which support or upset legislation that results in creating major political controversies. In deciding cases, judges are said to "legislate from the bench" or engage in "result-oriented jurisprudence" because they are deciding cases based on something other than what the law says or commands. Among other things, this could mean that "activist" judges are interpreting the law, such as constitutions, in a way that is not explicitly authorized by the plain reading of the text; or, perhaps, they manipulate the law to define or create public policies that ordinarily is supposed to originate from legislative action and the normal operation of democratic politics.[8] By contrast, a judicially self-restrained court is thought of as adhering to precedent and the so-called "rule of law" by deferring to Congress or state legislatures, and not issuing rulings that puts the judiciary in the forefront of making social policy, a task ordinarily assigned to the legislature or executive.

Still, the perception of being an activist or a restraint-oriented court is built from a false premise that the judiciary is incapable of making neutral judgments that are squarely based upon the law. Often, but mistakenly, "conservative" courts are viewed as exemplifying judicial self-restraint whereas "liberal" courts are branded as "activist." But history, and contemporary examples, show that such labels are misleading. For example, during the era of Social Darwinism and laissez-faire ("the government that governs best, governs least") politics at the end of the nineteenth and early twentieth centuries, the Supreme Court decided *Lochner v. N.Y.* (1905), a ruling that safeguarded conservative business interests by creating out of whole constitutional cloth a "liberty of contract" in the Fourteenth Amendment's due process clause, while striking down a New York law designed to increase the health and safety of bakery workers that toiled in unsafe working environments by limiting the hours that they were allowed to work in a week. Moreover, to the disappointment of some of its allies, the liberal Roosevelt-New Deal Court of the 1930s–1940s favored judicial self-restraint in reviewing progressive federal and state legislation. Indeed, the term *judicial self-restraint* was coined in the 1930s by liberal critics of the then-conservative majority on the Supreme Court, which was striking down progressive legislation dealing with child labor, women's rights, and minimum wage/maximum hours laws.

Yet, thirty years later, conservatives attacked the liberal Warren Court (1953–1969) for forging a "due process revolution" that expanded protections for the right of the accused, and "the reapportionment revolution" that reinforced the democratic process by guarantying equal voting rights. Likewise, today, the Roberts Court (2005–present) is frequently criticized for its conservative activism in extending protection for gun rights and corporate business interests, along with diminishing voting rights and striking down campaign finance laws, among others. At times, such criticism is manifested by symbolic action, as when James Dannenberg, a retired Hawaii state judge, publicly tendered his letter of resignation from the Supreme Court Bar on the grounds that Chief Justice Roberts is leading a Court that is no different than the one ushering in the early twentieth century *Lochner* era because it shows a bias for corporate and insurance interests at the expense of laborers and, significantly, transforming the Court into "an 'errand boy' for the [Trump] administration that has little respect for the rule of law."[9]

Judicial activism and self-restraint, in other words, are "notoriously slippery" terms that both liberals and conservatives invoke to attack rulings and constitutional (or legal) interpretations with which they disagree. For this reason, whether a judge is engaging in activism or restraint is nothing more than a political criticism that registers a profound disagreement on how courts or judges ought to decide public and legal controversies that are being debated across the country and in the states. Fueling the political criticism is the fact that, as Justice Benjamin Cardozo once put it, "the majestic generalities" of the law, and constitutional provisions, are ambiguous "empty vessels into which [a justice or judge] can pour nearly anything he [or she] will [into]."[10] Even so, some scholars have tried to characterize activist or restraint-oriented judicial behavior in objective terms and, arguably, with some success. For instance, political scientist Bradley Canon created a useful framework for understanding "judicial activism" by assigning it certain "dimensions" (see Table 10.2). Even so, Canon's analysis is similar to the other research that cannot help but conclude that "activist" judicial behavior is, by any measure, invariably multidimensional and complex.[11]

Table 10.2	The Dimensions of Judicial Activism
Dimensions	**Standards Used to Define Activist Dimension**
Majoritarianism	The degree to which policies adopted through democratic processes are judicially negated
Interpretive Stability	The degree to which earlier court decisions, doctrines, or interpretations are altered
Interpretative Fidelity	The degree to which constitutional provisions are interpreted contrary to the clear intentions of their drafters or the clear implications of the language used
Substance/Democratic Process Distinction	The degree to which judicial decisions make substantive policy rather than affect the preservation of democratic political processes
Specificity of Policy	The degree to which a judicial decision establishes policy itself as opposed to leaving discretion to other agencies or individuals
Availability of an Alternate Policymaker	The degree to which a judicial decision supersedes serious consideration of the same problem by other governmental agencies

Source: Bradley C. Canon, "Defining the Dimensions of Judicial Activism," *Judicature* (December/ January 1983), 236, 239.

The debate over whether courts are "activist" is exemplified by two controversial topics of legal and social policy: state school-funding cases and federal court rulings on capital punishment and abortion. (In addition, it bears noting that criticisms of judicial activism are not confined to the United States. The expanding powers of courts elsewhere in the world, such as the European Court of Justice, are increasingly criticized as well. See "In Comparative Perspective: The European Court of Justice and the Globalization of Judicial Power.")

In Comparative Perspective: The European Court of Justice and the Globalization of Judicial Power

The Court of Justice of the European Union (also commonly known as the European Court of Justice, or ECJ) was created in 1952. Along with the Council of Ministers, the European Commission, the European Parliament, and later the Court of Auditors, the ECJ was established to promote economic integration in Western Europe. The ECJ's role is to create a uniform system of law—referred to once as European Community (EC) law and now as European Union (EU) law. Originally, only six countries—Belgium, France, West Germany, Italy, Luxembourg, and the Netherlands—participated, but other countries subsequently joined. In 1973, Denmark, Ireland, and Britain became members, followed by Greece in 1981, and Portugal and Spain in 1986. In 1995, Austria, Finland, and Sweden joined, bringing the total number in the EU to fifteen. The largest expansion occurred in 2004 with the addition of ten other Central and East European countries—Cyprus (Greek part), the Czech Republic, Estonia, Hungary, Latvia, Lithuania, Malta, Poland, Slovakia, and Slovenia—followed by Bulgaria and Romania in 2007, and Croatia in 2013— bringing the current membership to slightly less than thirty in light of Brexit. Today, it fundamental purpose is treaties' and secondary legislation enforcement. In exercising its powers, the ECJ is not only directly accessible to citizens, but it also adjudicates disputes between EU institutions and monitors compliance of national and EU laws, among other things. As a result, the ECJ may be one of the most influential supranational courts in the world.

The ECJ, located in Luxembourg, is composed of twenty-eight justices— one justice appointed from each country with the unanimous approval of all member states. The justices serve six-year staggered terms, and generally hear cases in panels of three, five, or thirteen, and occasionally as a whole court. They also vow not to consider national interests in rendering decisions. All decisions are unanimous, no dissenting opinions are issued, and even opinions announcing the decisions are not signed by individual justices.

Cases may be filed before the ECJ by other EU institutions, member states, or "directly affected" EU citizens. Most of the ECJ's caseload comes as reference (Article 177) cases from member states' national courts that ask for preliminary rulings on EU law that the ECJ has not yet determined. Since its inception, the ECJ's caseload has grown steadily. As a result, in 1998, a General Court (formerly the Court of First Instance) was created in order to ease the ECJ's workload and backlog of cases. There are also now a number of specialized courts, such as the Civil Service Tribunal. Still, the ECJ annually hands down about six hundred decisions.

The ECJ has been compared to the U.S. Supreme Court in the early nineteenth century under Chief Justice John Marshall, whose rulings striking down state taxes, trade barriers, and other regulations promoted an economic common market and solidified the Court's power of judicial review. Critics of the ECJ have complained that it has been too activist. Yet EU member states may overturn ECJ decisions, though only by unanimous consent of all member states.

During the 1960s and 1970s, the ECJ laid the groundwork for promoting the value of European integration. From the 1980s to the 2000s, the ECJ solidified not only its power of judicial review but also: (1) the supremacy of EU law over that of member states' legislation, in holding that national courts of the EU must always interpret their laws to be in conformity with EU laws; (2) the competence and superiority of EU institutions over areas, such as environmental protection and human rights, that the treaties were originally silent about; and, (3) it expanded the legal policy areas over which it has jurisdiction by expanding standing for private parties to sue on the basis of treaty provisions and acts of EU institutions requiring implementing legislation. The ECJ also ruled that national courts have the power to declare EU acts valid, but not invalid, within their countries. Moreover, the ECJ held that a national court must refuse to enforce a national law or statute that contravenes EU laws while questions concerning the compatibility of the national law and EU law are pending before the ECJ.

In addition, initially, EU law based on treaties contained few provisions for dealing with individual rights. Yet the ECJ's decisions on citizens' standing to sue when "directly affected" by EU law expanded its jurisdiction over member states and its power to strike down legislation contravening EU law. As a result, the ECJ not only promoted an economic common market, but also developed a human rights jurisprudence based on the doctrines of the "direct effect"—the direct effects doctrine—and the supremacy of EU law. For example, in *Judgment of 14. 5. 1974, J. Nord, Kohlen und BaustoffengroBhandlung v. Commission of the European Communities*, the ECJ invoked the European Convention for the Protection of Human Rights, in addition to the constitutions of member states, as sources for its recognition of fundamental rights.

Paralleling the U.S. Supreme Court's incorporation of guarantees of the Bill of Rights into the Fourteenth Amendment and their application to the states, the ECJ also "discovered" fundamental rights in the treaties of member states. The ECJ also requires member states' national courts to always interpret their own laws in conformity with EU laws—the so-called indirect effects doctrine. In addition, the ECJ has enforced human rights principles against not only member states but also corporations and private parties.

Observers and scholars disagree over how to explain the expansion of the ECJ's power of judicial review. Some consider the expansion of the ECJ's power as inevitable given its treatment of EU treaties as though they are a "higher law" constitution. Others argue that the ECJ's role has grown as part of the so-called trend toward the "globalization of judicial power" as a result of pressures for greater economic and legal integration. More specifically, four competing explanations for the expanding power of the ECJ have been advanced: (1) a legalist explanation; (2) a neorealist explanation; (3) a neofunctionalist explanation; and, (4) an intercourt competition explanation.

The legalist explanation for the ECJ's expanding power maintains that EU law, like other countries' constitutional law, has an inherent logic. That creates a kind of internal dynamic built on precedents and expanding the role of the ECJ along with member states' courts' compliance with the ECJ's decisions. In other words, the ECJ's rulings are authoritative because they have transformed the legal and political integration of Europe. Political scientist Martin Shapiro, among others, however, has criticized this legalist explanation as "constitutional law without politics," because the ECJ is presented "as a juristic concept; the written constitution (the treaty) as a sacred text; the professional commentary as a legal truth; the case law as the inevitable working out of the correct implications of the constitutional text; and the constitutional court (the ECJ) as the disembodied voice of right reason and constitutional teleology." In short, critics of the legalist explanation argue that it amounts to legal formalism. It omits the role of politicians, the member states, and other political forces in reinforcing the ECJ's decisions.

By contrast, neorealists argue that ECJ and national courts' decisions are shaped by EU member states' national self-interests in economic integration. They underscore that courts are subject to external political pressures and reprisals if they go too far and too fast. In the words of political scientists G. Garrett and Barry Weingast:

> Embedding a legal system in a broader political structure places direct constraints on the discretion of a court, even one with as much constitutional independence as the United States Supreme Court. . . .The reason is that political actors have a range of avenues through which they may alter or limit the role of courts. . . .The principal conclusion. . .is that the possibility of such a reaction drives a court that wishes to preserve its independence and legitimacy to remain in the arena of acceptable latitude.

Courts, of course, are constrained by external political pressures and their environment. But all political institutions are subject to political and legal constraints and restraints, so it remains unclear whether neorealists explain that much. Critics of the neorealist theory counter that it fails to demonstrate how national self-interests are constituted and influence the ECJ's decisions. Neorealists also have been criticized for neglecting political opposition to the ECJ's decisions promoting integration. In contrast to the legalist theory, the neorealist position appears to amount to "politics without constitutional law."

A third, neofunctionalist explanation emphasizes the self-interests of litigants, judges on national courts and the ECJ, and other EU institutions promoting integration as bases to reinforce the ECJ's role. That is, the ECJ and its rulings create structural incentives for entrenching its role through economic and legal integration. EU citizens receive new rights and ongoing justifications for pursuing their interests through litigation and EU integration. Also, national courts enhance their prestige by referring cases to the ECJ, and lawyers practicing EU law receive more business through the continuing expansion of EU law. In short, neofunctionalists, like the legalists, underscore the importance of the rule of law but, unlike the legalists, characterize the expansion of the ECJ's power in terms of a process of incremental legal integration that "upgrades common interests" of individuals and institutions in the EU.

Finally, a fourth explanation accentuates the ECJ's and national courts' intercourt competition in promoting legal integration, which thereby strengthens the ECJ's role. As a variant of the theory of bureaucratic politics, the intercourt competition theory posits that courts, like other bureaucracies, pursue their own interests within the constraints imposed by other political institutions.

Ultimately, each of these competing explanations go a long way toward explaining different aspects of the expansion of the ECJ's power and the EU's legal integration.

Sources: Mary L. Volcansek, *Comparative Judicial Politics* (Landham, MD.: Roman & Littlefield, 2019); Katalin Kelemen, *Judicial Dissent in European Constitutional Courts: A Comparative Perspective* (New York: Routledge, 2018), 102–103; G. Garrett and Barry Weingast, "Ideas, Interests, and Institutions: Constructing the ECs Internal Market," in *Ideas and Foreign Policy*, edited by J. Goldstein and R. Keohane (Ithaca, N.Y.: Cornell University Press, 1993), 173; A. M. Burley and W. Mattli, "Europe Before the Court," *International Organization* 47 (1993), 41; Gunner Beck, *The Legal Reasoning of the Court of Justice of the European Union* (Oxford, U.K.: Hart, 2013); and Mark Dawson, Bruno DeWitte, and Elise Muir, eds., *Judicial Activism at the European Court of Justice* (Cheltenham, U.K.: Edward Elgar, 2013). Portions of the box have been reprinted with permission from David M. O'Brien and Gordon Silverstein, *Constitutional Law and Politics: Struggles for Power and Governmental Accountability (Vol. 1)*, 11th ed. (New York: W.W. Norton, 2020); and David M. O'Brien and Gordon Silverstein, *Constitutional Law and Politics: Civil Rights and Civil Liberties (Vol. 2)*, 11th ed. (New York: W.W. Norton, 2020), as well as earlier editions solely authored by the late David M. O'Brien.

State Judicial Policymaking

In reflecting upon his time as State Solicitor of Ohio, conservative federal circuit Judge Jeffrey Sutton referred to state constitutions as a "meaningful source of rights protection, but not a one-size-fits-all source of rights protection."[12] From his vantage point, state courts of last resort, typically referred to as state supreme or "apex" courts, play an important, but limited, role in generating personal freedoms. In contrast, former liberal Justice William Brennan regarded state supreme courts as critical venues to protect substantive individual rights, especially when federal courts are reluctant to do so.[13] In spite of their differences, there is little doubt that state courts of last resort are highly significant agents of legal and social change. Not only do the affect how their federal counterparts construe federal rights that are similar to those in the states, state supreme courts also remain, by definition, the primary source of legal interpretation about what state constitutional rights mean in their own right, or when federal appellate courts decline to enforce rights' claims in a similar areas of law.[14]

Not surprisingly, studies of state supreme court policy-making illustrate they adjudicate cases across a wide diversity of politically controversial topics, such as those involving privacy rights, the death penalty, voting rights or same-sex marriage, to name a few.[15] For example, state supreme courts have influenced the enactment of new law and rights pertaining to criminal procedure (such as determining the scope and application of the so-called exclusionary rule that excludes at trial evidence of a defendant's guilt due to police misconduct), religious freedom, gun or property rights, and racial discrimination.[16] With these rulings, state courts must be mindful of the supremacy of the U.S. Constitution in certain areas of the law, as well as filling in the gaps with their own state constitutional provisions if need be. In this light, a longstanding debate is whether the right to education is a fundamental right in accordance with state constitutional equality principles. Thus, the next section addresses this issue and, in the process, illustrates the complex political dynamics that underscores how the dual system of federal and state courts work in unison, or against each other, in guarantying citizens an equitable and adequate public school system.

"Equal" and "Adequate" Public School Funding in the States

In ruling that racially separate educational facilities are unconstitutional, *Brown v. Board of Education* (1954) stressed that "education is perhaps the most important function of state and local governments. . .[because] it is the very foundation of good citizenship." As Chief Justice Earl Warren explained, "It is doubtful that any child may reasonably be expected to succeed in life if he is denied the opportunity of an education, [and] such an opportunity, where the state has undertaken to provide it, is a right which must be made available to all on equal terms."[17] The right was premised, of course, on the idea that the color of one's skin cannot deprive students of an equal opportunity to learn in public school classrooms under the Fourteenth Amendment. But *Brown's* mandate to integrate public schools emerged in the context of another equality problem that states increasingly confronted as they began to first create, and then maintain, a system of public education (which at that founding did not exist because schooling was done largely by the private sector). That is, by the mid-1960s, most state-run public school systems had adopted a "foundational program" system of funding that relied heavily on property taxes and some additional state monies to educate students. Although foundational systems were designed to lessen the effects of wealth disparities among school districts, they never achieved that goal in practice. Thus, in spite of the efforts by states to devise analogous equalization programs that would narrow the funding gap between the wealthiest and less affluent school districts, only those cities and localities with robust property tax bases could deliver more educational resources to students in comparison to those that could not. In light of this reality, by the 1970s state supreme courts began to review challenges to educational funding systems and test the scope of *Brown's* equality principle in school financing litigation.[18]

Initially, such challenges received a warm reception in a few state courts. In *Serrano v. Priest* (1971),[19] the Supreme Court of California struck down the state's system of public school funding because it deprived students of a "fundamental right" of education based on the Fourteenth Amendment's **Equal Protection Clause**. Specifically, the state over-relied on local property taxes to fund public schools, and that policy created disparities in expenditures that discriminated against the poor living in underfunded school districts. Likewise, in *Robinson v. Cahill* (1972) the New Jersey Supreme Court also nullified the state's financing scheme. But, unlike *Serrano*, the court reasoned that it did not satisfy the state constitution's obligation to provide for a "thorough and efficient" system of public education. Systems of state public educational funding were declared to be unconstitutional in a few other jurisdictions, including West Virginia and Connecticut.[20]

The momentum toward reforming state public school funding on the basis of the Fourteenth Amendment Equal Protection Clause was abruptly halted, however, by the Supreme Court's decision in *San Antonio Independent School District v. Rodriguez* (1973).[21] In a 5:4 ruling, the justices rejected the claim of Mexican American and African American students who argued they were denied an equal public education as compared to schools in wealthier districts because they lived in urban districts with a low property tax base. Instead, a bare majority of the Court reasoned that an equally funded education is not a "fundamental right" because the U.S. Constitution did not textually include any provision that mentioned education. Notably, the outcome probably would have been different if the Court did not use the **rational basis test** in its constitutional analysis—that is, whether the state had a rational, or reasonable, basis for funding public schools based on local tax rates and in maintaining local control over educational policy.[22] By using the rational basis test, and by not opting to apply a more rigorous "strict scrutiny" standard, such as the **compelling state interest test** (which requires government to show that it had a compelling interest and used a "narrowly tailored" law to funding schools in a particular way), the Court exercised judicial self-restraint in deferring to state and local governments' power to set educational policy, a traditional province of the states. In doing so, the Court shifted the burden to the states to develop their own solutions to the education funding problem on a state-by-state basis, an invitation they began to take up in the aftermath of the *Rodriguez* ruling.[23]

Rodriguez, thus, led to the onset of voluminous and protracted litigation in state courts, ostensibly because many state systems for financing public education had ongoing "extensive inequities" that allegedly violated constitutional principles. After 1989, forty-five states faced legal challenges to their education finance systems, and many were directly based on specific provisions that purportedly guaranteed educational rights in their state constitutions. In several early cases, also, state courts relied on the equal protection clauses in their state constitutions to invalidate inequitable school funding mechanisms. But they did not specify how to remedy the problem. In other states, some popular assemblies struggled to equalize resources but found it impracticable to do so. As a result, the initially favorable rulings for reforming public school funding systems in the 1970s gave way to a series of defeats in the 1980s. By 1989, fifteen state supreme courts had denied relief, whereas only seven others granted it.[24]

Nonetheless, reformers continued to bring litigation aimed at achieving equality in state financing for public schools on state constitutional grounds, but their legal arguments changed. In the next wave of educational funding lawsuits, litigants stressed that there must be an "adequacy" of educational resources instead of "equity." Whereas "equity lawsuits" pushed for the elimination of wealth disparities by equalizing the amount of resources distributed to all districts, "adequacy lawsuits" sought school reforms on the basis of demonstrable standards of academic performance. In doing so, state courts interpreted educational clauses in their state constitutions that guarantee a "high quality system of free schools," a "sound basic education," a "system of free common schools," a "thorough and efficient education," or an "adequate public education," as the basis for reforms. Such language, which is present in at least thirty-one state constitutions, reflects the longstanding notion that securing an education is the basis for reinforcing "republican civic virtues" that allow citizens to reach their full potential in society. As a pragmatic issue, though, the new approach meant all students must have a reasonable chance under the law to get an "adequate" public education, and whether they received one was measured by academic achievement that met performance standards.[25]

Although the state supreme courts in New Jersey, Washington, and West Virginia nullified state education financing systems on the basis of inadequacy, it was not until the Kentucky Supreme Court's ruling in *Rose v. Council for Better Education* (1989) that the adequacy reform movement in state courts reached its full potential.[26] After *Rose*, the shift from equity to adequacy challenges produced more victories, even though slightly more state courts upheld, rather than struck down, school funding systems. Indeed, one study found that there were twenty-three victories in the highest courts in states as opposed to fifteen defeats in lawsuits pressing for educational funding reforms.[27]

Regardless, *Rose* is a significant precedent that helped establish the principle that there must legal compliance with specific standards that determine if students are achieving an "efficient" education: whether, for example, they were taught effective oral and written communication skills or gained a sufficient understanding of government, the arts, or vocational skills. As opposed to equity cases, the standards reviewed by courts have become both a yardstick of educational quality and the basis for identifying if the state has met its obligation to provide an adequate education. In this respect, the standards-based approach in adequacy cases permits courts to evaluate "the substance of the education students are receiving in the classroom rather than on comparing the amount of funds that are available to each school district," thus making it easier for the judiciary to oversee whether the political branches are fulfilling their constitutional duties.[28] Significantly, the reliance on meeting specific educational standards as a measure of adequacy was, in part, developed from findings by various commissions and studies that were initiated by the federal government and states in the aftermath of *Rodriguez*. At the behest of President H.W. Bush and with the support of all state governors and many corporate leaders, for example, the 1989 National Education Summit created a template for policy reform that encouraged the states to establish definitive standards for educational progress across the nation. The statewide standards that emerged set the criteria for how well school districts were performing in delivering to students adequate grade-level academic content, teacher training, curricula, and instructional resources, such books, equipment or facilities.[29]

Accordingly, one education expert was quick to identify *Rose* as the "starting point in what has become a significant dialogue among the public, the courts, and the legislature on standards-based reform."[30] Of course, an important element of that dialogue is the political reality that budget-strapped state legislatures are often unwilling to address school funding issues by raising taxes or creating laws that help equalize the distribution of tax dollars to localities that need them. Framing the issue in terms of adequacy, and not just money, however, helped facilitate reform efforts and increased judicial receptivity to complaints that students were not receiving a fair or quality education.[31]

In the aftermath of *Rose*, many states had to defend their public school funding decisions in litigation, and the arguments made by legal advocates continue to evolve and inspire new legal rationales supporting educational reform. In *Gannon v. State* (2014), the Kansas Supreme Court reaffirmed the state's constitutional obligation to "make suitable provision for finance of the educational interests of the state," based on the convergence of equity and adequacy theories (see Table 10.1) In other instances, litigators with substantial experience in state school funding cases have used their skills to argue in federal court that students are entitled to a "public right to education" under the U.S. Constitution. In particular, in *Cook v. Raimondo,* a 2019 class action lawsuit, a cadre of high school, middle school, elementary school, and preschool students, and parents, alleged that certain states, such as Rhode Island, are "denying students a meaningful opportunity to obtain a basic education" that is required "to prepare them to be capable voters and jurors, to exercise effectively their right of free speech and other constitutional rights, to participate effectively and intelligently in our open political system and to function productively as civic participants."[32] Similarly, in a 2:1 ruling that has been granted *en banc* review, the Sixth Circuit Court of Appeals, in *Gary B. v. Whitmer* (2020) ruled that there is a fundamental right to a "basic minimum education" that guarantees an "access to literacy" as a Fourteenth Amendment right of substantive due process.[33] While *Gary B.* may not withstand *en banc* review, such federal lawsuits may help establish the foundation for the development of new jurisprudential inroads regarding the scope and application of constitutional educational rights in the future.

In this respect, the role that state supreme courts play in shaping local education financing and related educational policies is probably going to be affected by the ongoing status or evolution of federal law. To illustrate, the federal No Child Left Behind Act of 2001 (subsequently replaced by Congress in 2015 with the Every Student Succeeds Act) has prompted states revisit the question of whether their school systems meet academic performance standards. Subsequent federal initiatives, such as the Obama administration's Race to the Top Fund and the American Recovery and Reinvestment Act of 2009, similarly used competitive grants along with standards and assessments to create incentives for states to enact educational reform. In the states, state leaders also launched the Common Core State Standards Initiative, a performance-based reform designed to encourage states to develop a "common core" of knowledge and skills that all high school students should master before going to college or entering into a career. Notably, a growing number of states, including Oklahoma, have modified their "college and career ready" standards to include "citizenship ready" requirements, an approach that is analogous to the one taken in the *Cook* federal class action lawsuit commenced in Rhode Island.[34]

These legislative developments have not only become part of the litigation landscape, but they also raise a recurring issue about the propriety of judicial intervention in setting educational policy, a task traditionally assigned to the legislative and executive branches. Critics complain that interfering with democratic lawmaking responsibilities violates the constitutional principle of separation of powers and invites activist decisions that originate from courts that lack the capacity or competence to create, influence, or direct educational change or reform. Advocates counter that critics are missing the point: that is, detractors ignore that courts are only one part of a deliberative, political process that collectively produces beneficial policy outcomes that result from the judicial branch's application of its managerial and administrative expertise in resolving socio-economic disputes.[35] From either perspective, the debate over educational reform is likely to intensify because of the difficulties state governments have in meeting their responsibilities to guaranty an adequate education in light of the financial challenges not only once imposed by the Great Recession of 2008, but most especially recently by the 2020 Covid 19 pandemic. Both crises are stark reminders of the difficulties, and growing prospect, that many state and local governments will have to overcome significant obstacles in fulfilling their educational funding obligations under federal and state laws.[36]

The closely related issue of whether courts should, or in fact can, force state legislatures to enact reforms is also an open question. There is evidence that judicial intervention has prompted some legislatures to increase state spending or renew their commitment to correct the wealth imbalances between affluent and less-affluent districts; and, in some instances, those steps have led to a boost in student test achievement scores from low-income districts.[37] Moreover, a 2015 study by the National Bureau of Economic Research reported that in states where courts invalidated school financing systems that state legislatures generally increased spending and reduced the wealth disparities among low- and high-income districts; and, that K–12 low-income students completed at least one more year of education and, into adulthood, those students achieved a twenty-five percent increase in higher earnings and a twenty-percent reduction in adult poverty.[38] Even so, reform initiatives have not fared as well in states that are controlled by governors, state legislatures or even courts that strongly resist them for political reasons. In Alabama and Ohio, for example, both state supreme courts terminated judicial proceedings in public school funding suits because their legislatures declined to pass laws to remedy the constitutional violations, thus leaving reforms to be implemented haphazardly in the future, or in limbo. Likewise, in West Virginia, the legislature refused to comply with the state judiciary's remedial orders in the 1980s, only to have some narrow reforms take effect when new litigation challenges came to the courts in the mid-1990s. And, in Kansas, after the Kansas Supreme Court declared the state's financing system was unconstitutional, the Court has been engaged in a pitched political battle over reform with the governor and legislature that has spanned years, but which only has resulted in (so far) six judicial rulings that have yet to fully resolve the constitutional issues (see Chapter Three for a discussion of the Kansas litigation).[39]

Furthermore, state courts are likely to confront new questions about whether a basic purpose of state constitutional educational clauses-to prepare students to participate competently in civic affairs—is being achieved adequately in locals school districts across the nation. Reformers observe that at least thirty-four state supreme courts have acknowledged that preparation for civil participation is a primary aim of educational clauses; but no courts, as of yet, have formulated any judicial decrees to accomplish that objective. As the *Cook v. Raimondo* federal litigation suggests, some reformers argue that policy advocates and state courts must take the lead in fashioning legal remedies that guaranty students: (1) acquire civic knowledge (being exposed to a broad array of civics, history, world languages, social studies, economics and arts' curricula); (2) acquire civic skills (learning how to engage in voting, or civic debate over controversial political and social issues in the classroom, social media and Internet); (3) have access to civic experiences (engaging in in-class and extra-curricular service or experiential learning exercises involving, to name a few, school government, school newspapers or clubs, city councils, state legislatures, or courts); and (4) develop civic values (including, among others, learning about anti-bullying strategies or other norms that promote tolerance, inclusion, patriotism, civic responsibility, empathy, compassion or integrity).[40]

In sum, state supreme court decision-making is an integral element of setting and administering education policy; but, the enforcement of judicial decrees on the state level is contingent upon the responses and support of other political institutions.[41] Not surprisingly, given the institutional and political limitations that inherently a part of judicial policy-making, federal courts similarly play a controversial role as legal change agents for socio-economic and cultural reform, a topic discussed next.

Federal Judicial Policymaking

The *Dred Scott* controversy, referred to in this Chapter's introduction, amply illustrates the difficulty the Supreme Court faces when it resolves a legal dispute that interprets the U.S. Constitution in a way that purports to apply the law faithfully but has disastrous unintended consequences for the nation and its society. In a 7:2 ruling written by Chief Justice Roger Taney, *Dred Scott v. Sandford* (1857) declared that Dred Scott, a Missouri slave asking for his freedom because he temporarily lived in Illinois and in the Louisiana Territory (a free state and a territory where slavery was banned under the 1820 Missouri Compromise), could not sue in federal courts because he was not a U.S. citizen; and, that Congress lacked the authority to ban slavery in the territories, thus holding that the Missouri Compromise was an unconstitutional exercise of congressional power. Then-candidate Abraham Lincoln realized that the Supreme Court immediately (and dangerously) interjected itself into the national debate over slavery and, in effect, used its powers to affirm slavery at a time when Congress was trying to keep the peace between the North and the South with the Missouri Compromise. In his famous debates with Stephen Douglas, Lincoln argued that the decision was wrong, but also acknowledged the importance of following the rule of law and showing respect for Supreme Court precedents. Still, after he became President, he also said that the Court overstepped its authority because "if the policy of the government, upon vital questions affecting the whole people, is to be irrevocably fixed by the decisions of the Supreme Court, the instant they are made. . .the people will have ceased to be their own rulers, having to that extent practically resigned their government into the hands of that eminent tribunal."[42] Of course, the Supreme Court's decision was a key factor in the reasons why the country split apart and descended into a bloody and lengthy Civil War.

Lincoln's thoughts register that the Supreme Court's exercise of judicial review—as legitimized in *Marbury v. Madison* (1803), which empowers the Court to be the final arbiter of what the Constitution means at any given political time-is inherently controversial. As the late law professor Alexander Bickel explained, difficulties arise because the Court's rulings are always **counter-majoritarian** to the people's will whenever they strike down laws or executive action that they deem offensive to the Constitution.[43] Whether the Court is acting in accordance with Constitution's true meaning, or the people's will, is especially subject to fierce debate in volatile areas of social and legal policy, such as capital punishment or abortion. In regard to capital punishment, the Court's jurisprudence centers around the legal question of whether the death penalty is permissible in accordance with the Eighth Amendment's ban on "cruel and unusual" punishment. Abortion, on the other hand, considers whether women have the "liberty" of personal choice to abort a fetus under the Fourteenth Amendment's Due Process clause. In both instances, what the Court decides is literally the difference between life and death.

Capital Punishment

When Vicente Benavides Figueroa (Benavides) woke up on November 17, 1991, he did not know that he would be soon accused of, and later convicted of, raping a 21 month old toddler he was caring for on behalf of her mother who left to go to work as a nurse in a local hospital. He also did not realize that he would spend nearly 26 years on death row in a California prison for a crime he did not commit. Shortly after his release from prison as a victim of a wrongful conviction, Benavides filed a civil rights action in federal court for damages, alleging that a series of prosecutorial and medical errors led to a murder prosecution for the toddler's death, who was probably hit by a car after getting out of the apartment where she was staying with Benavides. After he and the toddler's mother got the child to a hospital, the doctors treated her injuries by repeatedly inserting an adult size catheter into her anus, and no one diagnosed her as being a victim of sexual abuse. After her condition worsened, the toddler succumbed and Benavides became the prime suspect after a forensic pathologist—who had been fired from at least four other jobs for gross forensic incompetent practices and erroneously reporting causes of death—concluded that the toddler's passing was caused by "blunt force penetrating injury of the anus," and that her fractured ribs and brain swelling was consistent with being squeezed and shaken during an alleged sexual assault. Although Benavides continued to assert his innocence, it was not until the San Francisco-based Habeas Corpus Resource Center agreed to represent him (who filed suit in 2002) and the California Supreme Court (in 2018) vacated the conviction on the grounds that Benavides, now 68 years old, was convicted because of false evidence and the misconduct or incompetence of the county's law enforcement officers, the District Attorney's office, and the county's Medical Examiner's office.[44]

Benavides' story is not that unusual in the United States, and it is indicative of trends found in the minority of countries from around the world that still retain capital punishment.[45] In 2018, at least five persons were exonerated from wrongful convictions in cases involving the misuse or threatened use of capital punishment; and, since 1989, over 2,600 individuals have been exonerated in the United States. Although exonerations involve violent crimes, they also resulted from the type of official misconduct and false allegations that characterize the Benavides case.[46] In terms of public support, the growing problem of fairly administering the death penalty coincides with Gallup Poll data showing, for the first time, that sixty percent of Americans think that life imprisonment without the possibility of parole is a better punishment alternative, a finding that represents a fifteen point shift away from endorsing the death penalty in recent years. Notably, the growing anti-capital punishment public sentiment is measured across partisan lines, though Democrats and Independents are more in favor of the shift away from using the death penalty than Republicans.[47]

In spite of these developments, the United States legal system has a longstanding history of supporting capital punishment, both in terms of constitutional principle and in practice. In colonial times, the first recorded executions occurred by shooting, and hanging was used for crimes ranging from espionage, theft, bestiality, rape, murder, piracy, adultery, slave revolt, burglary and witchcraft, among others.[48] While the Eighth Amendment bans "cruel and unusual punishment," the death penalty has been legally ratified under the U.S. Constitution since the nation's founding and its use has expanded over time. Empirical data shows that between 1608 to 2002, there have been a total of 15,269 executions; and, between 2008 and 2019, there have been 1,511 executions, with a majority being put to death by legal injection and electrocution; but death-by-firing squad is also an option for some states. From the founding to the present, the methods of putting convicted felons to death included those techniques, but also by "breaking by the wheel," being burned, "hung in chains," shot, or "gibbeted" (a form of hanging on a gibbet, or a projected arm or post, as symbolic "waring" or measure of public scorn), plus by public hanging or lethal gas. While most persons are put to death for committing murder in modern times, others throughout U.S. history have been executed or subject to the death penalty after being found guilty of rape, armed robbery, kidnapping, poisoning, arson, desertion, and, in theory, treason or espionage.[49] Throughout U.S. history, as well, there is substantial evidence in social science research showing that issues of racial, gender and income bias continues to affect the historical and contemporary debates over the legitimacy of the death penalty in the United States.[50]

For its part, the United States Supreme Court has consistently reaffirmed capital punishment in its jurisprudence and judicial policy-making. The issue of the death penalty's morality or how it is administered and whether it falls within the Eighth Amendment's ban on "cruel and unusual punishment" has been at the center of the Court's constitutional analysis. Specifically, the Eighth Amendment states, "Excessive bail shall not be required, nor excessive fines imposed, nor cruel and unusual punishments inflicted."[51] The scope this provision was considered in *Trop v. Dulles* (1958),[52] a case raising the issue of whether a federal law that denationalized an army deserter after a court-martial by military tribunal was a "penal" statute that punished the wrongdoer. In taking citizenship, a fundamental right, away by law, the Court observed that the law was indeed a form of punishment; and then it analyzed if the punishment complied with the Eighth Amendment. On the vital issue of whether a punishment is "excessive," the justices declared that "The basic concept underlying the Eighth Amendment is nothing less than the dignity of man." As such, the Amendment insures that the exercise of government power over individuals must occur "within the limits of civilized standards." Using these standards, the Court concluded that the loss of citizenship is an Eighth Amendment violation because it is a punishment that is inconsistent with "its meaning from the evolving standards of decency that mark the progress of a maturing society." Although the Court noted, ironically, that the death penalty could not be considered "cruel" because of its historical use and contemporary "wide" acceptance, the justices stressed that denationalization runs afoul of the Eighth Amendment because it represents "the total destruction of the individual's status in organized society" and, in fact, is "a form of punishment more primitive than torture, for it destroys for the individual the political existence that was centuries in the development."[53]

The *Trop* "evolving standards of decency" standard has been the controversial touchstone for subsequent rulings that reviewed a steady stream of challenges to capital punishment. In *Furman v. Georgia* (1972),[54] in a 5:4 *per curiam* opinion, the Supreme Court used it, in part, to strike down the death penalty. But, of the five-member plurality, three Justices (William Douglas, Potter Stewart, and Byron White), in separate opinions, determined it was unconstitutional because it was arbitrarily applied in practice; whereas, Justice William Brennan wrote separately to add that capital punishment is categorically (in all instances) unconstitutional because it violates human dignity; and, in agreeing with his colleague Brennan, Justice Thurgood Marshall observed that it is a morally unacceptable punishment to the people in the United States at "this time in their history." In contrast, the dissenters (Chief Justice Warren Burger and Justices Harry Blackmun, Lewis Powell, and William Rehnquist), opted to defer to the legislative judgment authorizing the death penalty's use and application.

Thereafter, in *Gregg v. Georgia* (1976),[55] the Supreme Court reversed itself amidst growing public sentiment in favor of capital punishment. In a 7:2 decision, the Court's plurality ruled that the death penalty is constitutional under the Eighth Amendment so long as it does not "involve the unnecessary and wanton infliction of pain," and it is not used as a punishment that is "grossly out of proportion to the severity of the crime." In addition, *Gregg* signaled to the states that capital punishment is constitutionally permissible under state law if a bifurcated trial is used to determine guilt and a sentence of death in separate proceedings. During those proceedings, the judge, or jury, as fact-finders must be guided by specific legal standards in sentencing a capital defendant, such as whether there were "aggravating" or "mitigating" circumstances in the case—those safeguards are necessary, the Court declared, to make the application of death sentences less arbitrary. In a companion case, *Woodson v. North Carolina* (1976), that was decided on the same day as *Gregg*, the Court also held that mandatory death sentences are unconstitutional, thus ensuring that defendants in capital sentencing proceedings will be afforded an individual assessment of whether the death penalty is warranted on a case-by-case basis.[56]

In the aftermath of *Gregg* and *Woodson* the federal government (including the U.S. military) and at least twenty-eight states authorize the death penalty; whereas, twenty-two states, plus the District of Columbia, have abolished it, and three states have in place a moratoria imposed by gubernatorial order.[57] In its year-end report, the Death Penalty Information Center finds that "[c]apital punishment continued to wither across the United States in 2019," citing that half of the states have either abolished or prohibit it; and most regions across the country have either abandoned it (e.g. New England) or has seen diminishing use, a trend coinciding with declining public support. At the end of 2019, Ohio joined other states in suspending the death penalty because the Republican leader of the Ohio House observed that it, like many other states, cannot buy the necessary drugs to carry out the sentences (much of Europe, which supplied death penalty drugs to the U.S., has stopped selling them); and, that the penalty itself is cost-prohibitive in light of the time and effort needed to litigate capital punishment court challenges. Ohio's action coincides with the federal government's efforts, under the direction of the Attorney General, William Barr, to resume federal executions after a sixteen-year hiatus, due to the rulings by lower federal courts to prevent them by injunction. Still, in total, roughly 2,600 inmates remain on death row, with almost half of them in three states, California, Texas and Florida.[58]

The problems associated with administering the death penalty, which include questions of morality and fairness (to offenders and victims alike), costs, claims of innocence, wrongful conviction exonerations, botched executions and inadequate legal representation, chronicle the underlying, and ongoing, political and societal divisions about its acceptability which, of course, is also a part of U.S. Supreme Court jurisprudence in the Roberts Court. In general, the justices remain deeply divided over the manner in which executions must be carried out in light of prevailing constitutional precedents, as well as over the related issue of whether the Court should be supportive of granting stays of executions that are routinely filed on behalf of death row inmates and their attorneys.[59] In *Bucklew v. Precythe* (2019),[60] the Court split 5:4 in rejecting Russell Bucklew's claim that executing him by legal injection by the use of a single drug, pentobarbital, was cruel and unusual punishment because he had a rare medical condition (cavernous hemangioma) that might cause blood-filled tumors in his neck and throat to burst and cause him excruciating pain through suffocation during the execution.

Drawing off two earlier cases, *Baze v. Rees* (2008)[61] and *Glossip v. Gross* (2015),[62] Justice Neil Gorsuch's Opinion for the Court in *Bucklew* declared that "the Eighth Amendment does not guarantee a prisoner a painless death—something that...isn't guaranteed to many people, including most victims of capital crimes." As such, only those punishments that "intensified the sentence of death with a (cruel) 'superadd[ition]' of 'terror, pain, or disgrace' " runs afoul of constitutional requirements. Furthermore, the Court reiterated the *Baze* and *Glossip* rule that capital offenders must prove there is an Eighth Amendment violation by showing: (1) the proposed method [of execution] entails a substantial risk of severe pain, and; (2) that there is a known, and available, alternative method of execution that reduces pain risk. As the Court reasoned, the two-part test is relevant to Bucklew's challenge because he did not argue that lethal injection, *per se*, was unconstitutional in all cases; but only that it was cruel and unusual only as it applied to him, since he stated that he was willing to die by an alternative method of injection, by using the drug nitrogen hypoxia, that he contended would probably lessen the pain.[63]

Notably, the dissent, led by liberal Justices Stephen Breyer, Ruth Bader Ginsburg, Elena Kagan and Sonia Sotomayor, protested against Gorsuch's suggestion that the Court should turn away similar method-of-execution challenges because they often serve as one of the "tools to interpose unjustified delay" in carrying out executions. In his dissent, Justice Breyer said the Court's ruling incurs "too high a constitutional price" because it unnecessarily "limit[s] constitutional protections for prisoners on death row."[64] In a separate dissent, Justice Sotomayor reminded Gorsuch that "[t]here are higher values than ensuring that executions run on time" since "[i]f a death sentence or the manner in which it is carried out violates the Constitution, that stain can never come out." Accordingly, she argued the Court's duty is to review all death penalty challenges faithfully because "[o]ur jurisprudence must remain one of vigilance and care, not one of dismissiveness."[65] To be sure, the death penalty debate will likely to continue across the country and in the nation's highest Court so long as the justices remain ideologically divided, something that is also true in the highly contentious area of abortion rights, a topic that is considered next.

Abortion

Before he was defeated by Democratic Attorney General Andy Beshear in the 2019 elections, former Republican Kentucky Governor Matt Bevin signed into law several anti-abortion laws supported by the Republican state legislature, including a "display and describe" ultrasound law. Under this type of "informed consent" law, Kentucky physicians were required to explain, in detail, ultrasound images to women that were about to have an abortion while listening to the fetus's heartbeat. As described by Steve Pitt, Governor Bevin's legal counsel, the law's objective was to educate "women who might have a lack of understanding of what's actually in the womb, that this is a real living human being there [and to hope that] they might change their mind." In early December 2019, the U.S. Supreme Court, without hearing the case's merits, affirmed the Kentucky law after it was challenged by the American Civil Liberties Union, who alleged that it violated the doctor's free speech rights under the First Amendment.[66]

The Kentucky ultrasound law's enactment highlights the growing political division in the states about whether to ban (or severely restrict), or to guaranty (or afford access to having) the right to abortion in the United States. The legislative policy trends across the nation are split between regional areas that reflect conservative and liberal views on abortion. In early 2020, nearly sixty new abortion bans, or restrictions, were enacted by conservative legislatures, mostly in the South and Midwest; whereas, thirty-six pro-abortion proposals were signed into law primarily in the Northeast and West. The intensity and conviction of the anti-abortion movement is highlighted by the introduction of legislative proposals in some conservative statehouses, including Mississippi, Ohio and Texas, designed to limit or end abortions as "non-essential" services related to the shut-downs and "shelter in place" actions taken by states as a result of the Coronavirus (Covid 19) pandemic. Such bills were denounced by pro-abortion advocates as politically-motivated responses that only had the effect of delaying medical care to the those who need it and unnecessarily jeopardizing women's health.[67] The polarization of the abortion issue across state lines is politically aligned with the larger national debate about the Supreme Court's role in abortion policy-making in light of President Donald Trump's 2016 election and his successful conservative transformation of the federal judiciary thereafter (see Chapter Four).

At the federal level, by using a "show vote" strategy to force Senators to reveal their policy positions on anti-abortion legislative proposals that had no chance of passing in a run-up to the November 2020 elections, Republican Senate Majority Leader Mitch McConnell (R-KY) ramped up political pressure to highlight conservative support for the "Pain-Capable Unborn Protection Act" (banning abortion at twenty weeks), and a second bill designed to make abortion providers "preserve the life and health" of any infant born after a failed abortion. McConnell defended his actions by saying, "Today, every senator will be able to take a clear moral stand. . .[and] have the chance to proceed to common sense legislation that would move our nation closer to the international mainstream with respect to defending innocent human life."[68]

The Republican policy machinations underscore the conservative anticipation that the Republican-held Senate confirmations of Trump's two Supreme Court appointments (Justices Neil Gorsuch and Brett Kavanaugh, who might coalesce with Chief Justice John Roberts and Justices Samuel Alito and Clarence Thomas) will be enough to achieve a longstanding objective to undercut seriously, or possibly reverse, *Roe v. Wade* (1973), the landmark ruling establishing an abortion right under the Fourteenth Amendment's due process clause. Still, as discussed shortly, *Roe* remains viable as a constitutional principle at the end of the Court's 2019–20 Term. Specifically, in *June Medical Services v. Russo* (2020), Chief Justice Roberts crossed party lines and sided with the Court's liberal bloc (Justices Ruth Bader Ginsburg, Steven Breyer, Sonia Sotomayor and Elena Kagan) to strike down a challenge to a Louisiana law requiring that doctors performing abortions have admitting privileges at a nearby hospital.[69]

Regardless, if the Supreme Court ultimately decides to reverse *Roe*, it will do so by disturbing a long line of precedents relating to the protection of the right to privacy. Although courts have long recognized protected privacy interests,[70] a constitutional right of privacy was not established until *Griswold v. Connecticut* (1965).[71] There, a physician and the director of the Planned Parenthood League of Connecticut were prosecuted for dispensing contraceptives to a married couple in violation of state law. In a 7:2 decision written by Justice William O. Douglas, the Court invalidated the state law and proclaimed a constitutional right to privacy based on the penumbras or shadows of several guarantees in the Bill of Rights. As Justice Douglas explained:

> Specific guarantees in the Bill of Rights have penumbras, formed by emanations from those guarantees that help give them life and substance. . . .Various guarantees create zones of privacy. The right of association contained in the penumbra of the First Amendment is one. . . .The Third Amendment in its prohibition against the quartering of soldiers "in any house" in time of peace without the consent of the owner is another facet of that privacy. The Fourth Amendment explicitly affirms the "right of the people to be secure in their persons, houses, papers, and effects, against unreasonable searches and seizures." The Fifth Amendment in its Self-Incrimination Clause enables the citizen to create a zone of privacy which government may not force him to surrender to his detriment. The Ninth Amendment provides: "The

enumeration in the Constitution, of certain rights, shall not be construed to deny or disparage others retained by the people."[72]

In dissent, Justices Hugo Black and Potter Stewart countered that the Court was acting like "a super-legislature" in proclaiming a right to privacy and exercising "unbounded judicial authority would make of this Court's members a day-to-day constitutional convention."[73]

Griswold had implications for other areas of privacy and reproductive rights as well. *Eisenstadt v. Baird* (1972)[74] held that *Griswold* and the Fourteenth Amendment justified striking down a Massachusetts law outlawing the use of contraceptives by unmarried persons. According to Justice William J. Brennan, "If the right to privacy means anything, it is the right of the *individual*, married or single, to be free from unwarranted governmental intrusion into matters so fundamentally affecting a person as the decision whether to bear or beget a child."[75] *Eisenstadt*, then, helped set the stage for the landmark ruling in *Roe v. Wade* (1973)[76] on abortion.[77]

In *Roe*, the Burger Court (1969–1986) struck down Texas's criminal abortion statute on the grounds that it violated a woman's fundamental right to privacy. Specifically, it compromised a pregnant mother's "liberty" interest to have an abortion under the Fourteenth Amendment's due process clause. In writing for the majority, and in using a strict scrutiny standard, Justice Harry Blackmun reasoned that government did not have a **compelling interest** in barring access to abortions. Instead, it had the power to regulate abortions more intensively as the pregnancy progressed to term. Under the so-called trimester approach, it was necessary to balance the interests of women and those of states in protecting the unborn. Women and their physicians retained a right to abort, at least in the first three months of the pregnancy. In the second trimester, up to the point of viability (at that time, between twenty-four and twenty-eight weeks—the time a fetus may live outside of the womb), states could regulate abortions in order to protect maternal health. After viability, or in the third and last stage of pregnancy, states had a compelling interest to preserve fetal life and could limit access to or even ban abortions, except when necessary to save a woman's life.

Roe ignited a firestorm of controversy, and a majority of states and the federal government rewrote their abortion laws. Some state jurisdictions tailored their legislation to conform to the Court's ruling, but many others either left their pre-*Roe* laws in place or began to restrict sharply the availability of abortions. Some laws narrowed or eliminated public funding for abortions, prohibited abortions in public hospitals, required spousal or parental (for a minor) informed consent before allowing abortions, required fetal lung and maturity tests, imposed mandatory waiting periods, and banned advertisements for abortion clinics.[78] In the decade after *Roe*, the Court evaluated some of these restrictions by deciding *Planned Parenthood v. Danforth* (1976),[79] which upheld a state requirement that a pregnant mother had to give written, informed consent, during the first twelve weeks of the pregnancy before having an abortion. And, in *Harris v. McRae* (1980),[80] the Court approved of the Hyde Amendment, which restricted federal Medicare reimbursements to only certain medically necessary abortions. As Justice Potter Stewart's Opinion for the Court in *Harris* reasoned, a woman's liberty under the Fifth Amendment's due process clause is not violated because "it does not confer an entitlement to such funds as may be necessary to realize all the advantages of that freedom."

Although the Supreme Court invalidated some abortion restrictions in the 1980s,[81] anti-*Roe* sentiments galvanized the Christian evangelical movement and helped frame Republican platforms during the Ronald Reagan presidency, as well as the subsequent administrations of George H. W. Bush and George W. Bush. In addition, abortion politics fueled battles over federal judicial appointments— most notably, in the Senate's defeat of President Reagan's 1987 nomination of Judge Robert Bork for a seat on the Supreme Court (for further discussion, see the section in Chapter Four titled, "The Battle Over Robert Bork's 1987 Nomination").[82] Afterward, President Reagan appointed Anthony Kennedy, a moderate Ninth Circuit appeals court judge, and he was easily confirmed by the Senate.[83] Ironically, Justice Kennedy would come to play a key role in voting to uphold *Roe* in subsequent cases seeking to overturn that precedent; and, his retirement in 2018, which led President Trump, who has expressed opposition to abortion by, perhaps, filling Kennedy's seat with conservative Brett Kavanaugh, sparked a fear among abortion supporters that *Roe* is likely to be overturned or severely diminished as a precedent during his tenure.[84]

The bench's changing composition and its shift to the right since the 1980s has led the Court to revisit *Roe* several times. Most significantly, with a slim majority and structured by an unusual joint opinion by Justices Sandra Day O'Connor, David Souter, and Kennedy, in *Planned Parenthood of Southeastern Pennsylvania v. Casey* (1992)[85] the Court reaffirmed *Roe*'s "essential holding" that women have a right to terminate a pregnancy up to the point of a fetus's viability; thereafter, the State may enact abortion regulations designed to protect its interest in the potentiality of human life, except where it is medically necessary to preserve the mother's life or health. Still, the Court replaced *Roe*'s key rationale—that abortion is a fundamental right under a right to privacy and trimester analysis— with a less rigorous "undue burden" test (discussed below). In creating the new standard, the Court acknowledged that a woman's freedom in choosing an abortion is not absolute; and, that the State has an interest in preserving the life of the unborn after the point of viability and as the pregnancy continues to term. As applied to the case facts in *Casey*, the Court used its new test to uphold several Pennsylvania anti-abortion restrictions, including a twenty-four hour waiting period, a parental consent requirement for minors seeking abortions, and reporting and disclosure requirements placed on abortion clinics and doctors. Yet, the justices nullified the state's requirement that spouses consent to abortions, finding it too burdensome because of, among other things, it might negatively impact the pregnant mother's decision-making in cases where there is sexual violence or abuse by husbands. In general, the ruling is highly salient because it changed the constitutional standards pertaining to abortion's legality; but it did not completely overturn *Roe* on the grounds that the Court thought that its institutional legitimacy would suffer if *Roe* was reversed under political pressure. Also, *Roe*'s central reasoning was upheld because the justices reasoned that the case is an important precedent that citizens must continue to rely upon in the area of personal autonomy jurisprudence (see the section in Chapter Nine, "The Law and Politics of Legal Precedent," for additional discussion of *Casey* and the doctrine of *stare decisis*).

With *Casey*, *Roe* has been considerably weakened as an abortion-friendly ruling because it is easier for anti-abortion states to enact laws that restrict the right to abortion under *Casey's* undue burden test. Under the undue burden test, anti-abortion laws are constitutional unless they have a purpose or effect that places a "substantial obstacle in the path of a woman seeking an abortion before the fetus attains viability." Although *Roe* remains the law of the land, *Casey* undermined it considerably since its effect is to allow for more and greater restrictions on the availability of abortions. Such restrictions have included, among others, putting stringent conditions upon the operation of abortion clinics; requiring that abortions are performed by licensed doctors; requiring mandatory waiting periods after a physician consultation before having an abortion; mandating an ultrasound imaging test and viewing the results before having an abortion; and, limiting the use of state Medicaid funds to pay for only medically necessary abortions. The effect of these restrictions, say some critics, is to erect high barriers to getting an abortion by, for example, preventing them from as early as zero weeks from a women's last menstrual cycle, with no exceptions for rape or incest, or to bar them before viability; and, there is a growing movement to prohibit abortions if a fetal heartbeat is detected though so-called "fetal heartbeat" legislation.[86] Table 10.3 is a summary of the types of state abortion laws that are a frequent source of constitutional litigation.

Table 10.3	Abortion Restrictions in the States
Major Provisions	**Legal Restrictions**
Refusals by Health Care Providers	Laws allowing individual health care providers to refuse to participate in an abortion • 45 states allow individual health care providers to refuse to participate in an abortion • 42 states allow institutions to refuse to perform abortions, 16 of which limit refusal to private or religious institutions
Gestational Limits	Laws prohibiting abortions except when necessary to protect the woman's life or health, after a specified point in pregnancy (e.g., fetal viability) • 43 states have such restrictions
Physician and Hospital Requirements	Laws requiring an abortion to be performed by a licensed physician • 40 states require an abortion to be performed by a licensed physician • 19 states require an abortion to be performed in a hospital after a specified point in the pregnancy • 17 states require the involvement of a second physician after a specified point
Parental Involvement in Minor's Decision to Have an Abortion	Laws requiring one or both parents to consent to the procedure • 37 states require some type of parental involvement in a minor's decision to have an abortion • 26 states require one or both parents to consent to the procedure • 11 require that one or both parents be notified
Waiting Periods	Laws requiring a woman to wait a specified period of time, usually 24 hours, between the time she receives counselling and the time the procedure is performed • 27 states have such restrictions, 14 of which have laws that effectively require the woman make two separate trips to the clinic to obtain the procedure

State-Mandated Counseling	Laws mandating that women be given counselling before an abortion • 18 states mandate that women be given counselling before an abortion that includes information on at least one of the following: the purported link between abortion and breast cancer (5 states), the ability of a fetus to feel pain (13 states) or long-term mental health consequences for the woman (8 states)
Partial-Birth Abortions	Laws prohibiting "partial-birth" abortion • 21 states ban the provision of "partial-birth" abortion; and of these states, 3 apply only to post-viability abortions
Public Funding of Abortions	Laws allowing states to use their own funds to pay for all or most medically necessary abortions for Medicaid enrolees in the state • 16 states use their own funds to pay for all or most medically necessary abortions for Medicaid enrolees in the state • 33 states and the District of Columbia prohibit the use of state funds except in those cases when federal funds are available: where the woman's life is in danger or the pregnancy is the result of rape or incest (contrary to federal requirements, South Dakota limits funding to cases of life endangerment only)
Private Insurance Coverage	Laws restricting coverage of abortion in private insurance plans (most limit coverage only to when the woman's life would be endangered if the pregnancy were carried to term) • 12 states have such laws • Most states allow the purchase of additional abortion coverage at an additional cost

Sources: Alan Guttmacher Institute, "An Overview of Abortion Laws" (as of April 27, 2020), available from https://www.guttmacher.org/state-policy/explore/overview-abortion-laws (last retrieved April 27, 2020); Alan Guttmacher Institute, "Bans on Specific Abortion Methods Used After the First Trimester" (as of April 1, 2020), available from https://www.guttmacher.org/state-policy/explore/bans-specific-abortion-methods-used-after-first-trimester (last retrieved April 27, 2020).

All told, *Casey* did not settle much as the abortion controversy today is just as hotly contested and politically explosive as it was when *Roe* was decided. As Yale law professor Jack Balkin observes, the Court's efforts to settle the question of abortion rights "has proved to be little more than wishful thinking."[87] A recurring issue, among others,[88] is the constitutionality of so-called "late-term" or "partial-birth" abortion bans that were enacted immediately after *Casey*.[89] In *Stenberg v. Carhart* (2000),[90] a bare majority of the Rehnquist Court struck down Nebraska's ban on partial-birth abortions because it did not contain a medical exception for the procedure to take place if the pregnant mother's health was in danger. Thereafter, Congress passed the Partial-Birth Abortion Ban Act, which also banned late-term abortions; and the Court's composition changed with the appointment of Chief Justice John Roberts and Justice Samuel Alito. Subsequently, in *Gonzales v. Carhart* (2007),[91] a slim majority of the nascent Roberts Court upheld the federal law even though it did not have a medical exception for allowing the procedure if a woman's health is endangered. Thus, the constitutionality of states' partial-birth abortion bans remain uncertain—until (and if) the Roberts Court decides to revisit the issue.[92]

Apart from the partial-birth abortion controversies, *June Medical Services v. Russo* (2020)[93] suggests that President Trump's new appointments, and the corresponding fervent effort to enact anti-abortion laws in the states, portend that the politics of abortion will continue to be a part of the Supreme Court's evolving constitutional jurisprudence. In *June Medical Services*, a 5:4 ruling, the Court struck down a Louisiana law requiring doctors performing abortions to have admitting privileges at a nearby hospital, a restriction that abortion supporters claimed unduly burdened the right to choose and abortion access. In siding with the liberals, Chief Justice Roberts cast the key vote in a separate concurrence that reasoned *Whole Woman's Health v. Hellerstedt* (2016),[94] an analogous case that invalidated an admitting privileges' law in Texas, dictated the result under the doctrine of *stare decisis*. Still, while abortion supporters praised the outcome, Roberts' concurrence (in only the result) argued that neither *Whole Woman's Health*, nor *Casey*, allows the Court to balance the burdens a restrictive abortion law has against its benefits-a principle embraced by the plurality in *June Medical Services* (Justices Ginsburg, Breyer, Sotomayor and Kagan) and one more accepting of abortion freedoms.[95] But for Roberts, *Casey* only requires a judicial evaluation of whether a law creates a substantial obstacle in the path of a woman seeking an abortion under a rational basis test, a legal standard that is more permissive in limiting abortion rights. In this respect, his concurrence can be interpreted as merely "plant[ing] a flag to mark the battlegrounds for future abortion fights" and laying the foundation for subsequent rulings that "will effectively sanction anti-abortion laws enacted to test interpretations of "substantial obstacle," target individuals seeking abortion and the doctors who provide that care, and increase litigation."[96] Consequently, the rejection of *Whole Woman's Health's* balancing of benefits and burdens (of anti-abortion laws) principle by Roberts and the conservative dissenters in *June Medical Services* (Justices Thomas, Alito, Gorsuch and Kavanaugh) makes it less likely that the Court will be more sensitive to protecting the right to choose based on the "real-world" impact of laws that negatively affect access to having an abortion, such as disrupting market prices, hospital policies and provider budgets; and implicitly, driving up the cost and severely restricting the availability of abortions for indigent women.[97] To be sure, the post-*Roe* and post-*Casey* rulings on abortion have generated a judicial impact on American politics and society that is an integral part of understanding judicial policymaking, a topic that is taken up next.

THE IMPACT OF JUDICIAL DECISIONS

Judicial decisions shape public policy and social relationships. They not only affect the parties to a lawsuit, but they also influence the choices of government officials and private entities who must, in turn, implement the legal rules or policies that their decisions create, affirm, or reverse. So, too, they may broadly affect the public at large and have an impact on whether their rulings invite political opposition or compliance and respect. In this light, scholars often claim that unpopular judicial rulings are the main driving force that inspires political reactions that diminish their public policy influence.[98]

But the popularity of judicial decisions is not the only measure of a case's impact, its public saliency, or effect over time. The concept of "judicial impact," in other words, is multifaceted, fluid, and complex.[99] The "cause and effect" of judicial rulings is largely dependent upon how they are perceived, implemented, and followed. Though courts may at times be at the forefront of dictating the parameters of social policy, as Alexander Hamilton astutely observed in *Federalist No. 78*, they always must rely on other institutional actors to translate their rulings into real-world practice.[100] It is precisely through such implementation and compliance that judicial rulings derive their meaning.[101] Still, courts cannot control whether their rulings will be administered properly or accepted as legitimate, and that fact makes it difficult to know whether courts and judges are truly making a difference in helping shape public policies. The terms scholars use to measure that effect are also easy to confuse with each other, which makes understanding judicial impact even harder. For example, "judicial compliance" (i.e. whether a court decision is obeyed or not) and "judicial implementation" (i.e. the extent to which courts, government agencies and the affected litigants enforce rulings) are analytically distinct terms and different from "judicial impact" (i.e. what all the effects of rulings are). Still, each concept, independently defined, helps to give us a better cumulative sense of the practical and public policy consequences of judicial decision-making.[102]

Although all judicial rulings have some effect on different subpopulations, groups, or citizens,[103] the extent to which judicial decisions are properly administered is far from certain and sometimes controversial. The Roberts Court's decision supporting "Obamacare" (the Patient Protection and Affordable Care Act, or ACA) in *National Federation of Independent Business v. Sebelius* (2012)[104] is illustrative. Though the ruling upheld the so-called "individual mandate"—the legal obligation to buy health insurance—the decision also made Medicaid expansion optional in the states. How Medicaid was made available in the states was ambiguous, though, because the federal government and state governments had to work together to create an insurance marketplace through "American Health Benefit Exchanges" (for individuals) and "Small Business Health Options Programs" (for small business owners) in order to comply with the Court's ruling. Each exchange provides buyers with information and access to the insurance coverage they must buy (or, at the time the ACA was upheld, face a tax penalty if they do not).

Although governing the exchanges is the responsibility of the states, the federal government must set them up if a state refuses to create them. After the ACA's enactment in 2010, and in light of the *Sebelius* ruling, the practical implementation of the exchanges and compliance with the law has varied considerably from state-to-state, with some states relying upon the federal government to run parts or all of their exchanges; but others have continued to resist the ACA and have done little to nothing in establishing health exchanges.[105] Besides these mandates, the legality of the exchanges and how they operate has been continuously challenged in the federal appeals courts, a trend that has been accelerated by the Trump Administration's opposition to the ACA and Congress' decision to render the ACA's individual mandate provision unenforceable through tax reform legislation in 2017 after several failures to "repeal and replace" the entirety of the health care act.[106] Moreover, in late 2019, the Fifth Circuit ruled that the individual mandate was unconstitutional, prompting the House of Representatives and a coalition of states with Democratic attorney generals to ask the Supreme Court to revisit the constitutionality of the law in light of Congress's action and the Fifth Circuit's decision. The Supreme Court has since granted review and is set to review the case shortly before the November 2020 elections.[107]

Accordingly, the Department of Health and Human Services (the agency responsible for implementing the law), as well as federal judges, state officials, insurance companies, small businesses, and citizens, are likely to continue to re-adjust their policies, behavior, and actions in an increasingly uncertain legal and volatile political environment in the years to come.

National Federation of Independent Business shows that a number of interrelated factors influence implementation of and compliance with judicial decisions and hence, their impact. Whether an appellate court speaks with one voice, or it is fragmented or split by dissents and separate opinions, affects the weight of a decision as a precedent and, therefore, compliance with it. In *National Federation of Independent Business*, the Supreme Court was bitterly divided on the result, 5:4, with the four conservative dissenters (Justices Antonin Scalia, Clarence Thomas, Samuel Alito and Anthony Kennedy) and other right-wing pundits and commentators chastising the decision by fellow conservative Chief Justice John Roberts to join the liberal bloc (Justices Ruth Bader Ginsburg, Stephen Breyer, Elena Kagan and Sonia Sotomayor) in upholding the ACA.[108] The nature of the dispute may make a difference as well, because controversial decisions are likely to provoke more hostility and opposition, especially in an era of hyper-polarization. It is highly significant that the ACA was enacted with only support from one party, the Democrats, and not one Republican signed on to it. Beginning with his presidential campaign and continuing throughout his first term, with few exceptions, President Trump has not eased up on his criticism of the health care act, and he, along with Republican party, has shown un unrelenting commitment to attack it at every turn, in both the halls of Congress and in the courts. Finally, the institutional prestige of the Court, along with the dynamics of the prevailing political climate and public opinion, is important too, and the latter may prove to be ultimately significant not only as a 2020 election year issue, but also in terms of whether the ACA remains law in subsequent years.

These elements and many other intangibles may hinder enforcement and compliance, especially when the Supreme Court is not in sync with prevailing public opinion. Although there are many high-profile examples of the implementation of and compliance with rulings of the Court—ranging from the enforcement of affirmative action policies, to the regulation of political campaign finances, to the display of religious monuments in public spaces, to the imposition of capital punishment—arguably, the best example of the difficulties courts may confront in achieving implementation and compliance with their rulings on major political controversies involves the politics of school desegregation following the

Warren Court's decision in *Brown v. Board of Education* (1954),[109] a topic considered next.

Brown v. Board of Education (1954) and School Desegregation Politics

After decades of racial segregation, which supporters argued was constitutionally permissible so long as whites and blacks had relatively equal facilities and public accommodations, the U.S. Supreme Court seemed to have ushered in a new era of race relations shortly after World War II with its landmark *Brown v. Board of Education* (1954)[110] ruling. Before then, and even afterwards until today, the issue of racial equality in American society has been a particularly persistent, thorny and contentious area of public policy, underscored by the existence of slavery and its repudiation during the Civil War, and registered by the ongoing struggle for civil rights in the aftermath of the emergence of Jim Crow laws in the South, and the Supreme Court's decisions in *Plessy v. Ferguson* (1896),[111] announcing the "separate by equal doctrine," and *Korematsu v. United States* (1944),[112] the ruling upholding President Franklin Delano Roosevelt's executive order to isolate Japanese-American citizens into internment camps following Pearl Harbor on December 7, 1941. Today, racial politics is still at the forefront of American culture and political division, as manifested by a growing list of racial violence episodes and societal disruptions in recent times, including the civil unrest unleashed by George Floyd's death at the hands of a white police officer during the Covid 19 pandemic, the events of Ferguson, Missouri, racially motivated mass killings, the emergence of the Black Lives Matter movement, immigration policy conflicts, and the resurgence of white nationalism in organized groups, and even in some governmental circles.[113]

In this context, the Supreme Court's leadership in putting the issue of racial justice on the American political agenda is not only historic, but also deeply problematic for the time it was issued and perhaps even for the future. In *Brown v. Board of Education* (1954), racial segregation in public schools was prohibited by implicitly ending (but not directly overruling) the so-called "separate but equal principle" of *Plessy v. Ferguson* (1896).[114] In a companion case, *Bolling v. Sharpe* (1954),[115] racial segregation in the District of Columbia's public schools was also invalidated on the basis of the Fifth Amendment's due process clause, a decision holding that the guarantee of equal protection applied against federal action as well as against state governments. The mandate in both cases, however, met with stiff resistance in many local communities, a problem that was compounded by the Court's failure to issue any remedial orders to implement its decree until a year later in *Brown v. Board of Education* (1955)(*Brown II*).[116] Even then, the only remedy offered was the justices' insipid pronouncement that desegregation in schools should commence "with all deliberate speed."

The Court's inability to enforce its own rulings transformed *Brown*'s mandate into little more than a "moral appeal and an invitation for delay."[117] Although a few states began to move toward desegregation even before the Court's rulings, *Brown II* invited defiance in the South instead of compliance. Immediately after *Brown*, white supremacist "citizen councils" were organized. Several state legislatures and school boards enacted numerous resolutions disputing *Brown* and condemning the Warren Court for its decision. In Congress, 101 senators and representatives issued the "Southern Manifesto," denouncing *Brown* as an unconstitutional exercise of judicial power. President Dwight Eisenhower reluctantly accepted *Brown* but refused to enforce it aggressively and defended the federal government's inaction, saying that "it is difficult through law and through force to change a man's heart."[118]

Mounting pressures of the civil rights movement and persistent litigation by the National Association for the Advancement of Colored People Legal Defense Fund forced the federal government to act more decisively in the early 1960s. In 1961, the U.S. Civil Rights Commission recommended that all school districts file desegregation plans with the federal government and to deny 50 percent of federal funds for education from segregated districts. Subsequently, Congress passed the Civil Rights Act of 1964, the landmark civil rights legislation that guaranteed prohibiting segregation in public accommodations and the workplace.[119] The Department of Justice then began suing school districts and forcing them to desegregate or lose millions of dollars in federal money.

Despite this progress, *Brown*'s enforcement remained uneven and piecemeal as the composition of the Supreme Court changed with President Nixon's four appointees and the momentum of the civil rights movement also began to fade in the late 1970s. The Burger Court (1969–1986) reacted to lower court rulings authorizing gerrymandered school district lines and compulsory busing of school children by issuing key rulings prohibiting *de jure* (state-sponsored) segregation in public schools but permitting *de facto* segregation (resulting from demographic changes in housing patterns), unless there was evidence of intentional discrimination.[120]

Although hundreds of lawsuits were filed in the 1970s and 1980s to press local school boards to integrate fully, courts confronted massive resistance to enforcing *Brown* in local communities, and the Burger Court generally upheld lower courts' micromanaging efforts to achieve integration. Without firm

Supreme Court guidance, the desegregation litigation remained controversial and arguably floundered in the lower federal courts. After 1986, when the most conservative member of the Burger Court—Justice William H. Rehnquist—was elevated by President Ronald Reagan to the chief justiceship, the Rehnquist Court (1986–2005) began revisiting the controversy over school desegregation. A majority of Rehnquist Court started disengaging the federal judiciary from the task of superintending local school boards in order to achieve integrated, or "unitary," school districts.

In *Missouri v. Jenkins* (1990),[121] the Rehnquist Court affirmed the power of federal judges to order a school board to levy taxes to implement desegregation plans. But, subsequently, as the Court's composition further changed and became more conservative, a majority of the Rehnquist Court moved further in the direction of getting lower federal courts out of the business of forcing compliance with *Brown*. In *Board of Education of Oklahoma City Public Schools v. Dowell* (1991),[122] and later in *Freeman v. Pitts* (1992),[123] the Rehnquist Court held that judicial supervision of segregated school districts could end if there was evidence that school boards had made reasonable efforts to comply with desegregation plans and, to the extent practicable, eliminated "the vestiges of past discrimination." As some political scientists observe, *Dowell* and *Freeman* heralded a "new course, not a dramatic reversal, pointing to a new period of litigation—a period not unlike that immediately after *Brown* but one in which lower courts gradually moved to relinquish, rather than assert, control over public schools."[124] In this light, the Roberts Court's ruling in *Parents Involved in Community Schools v. Seattle School District* (2007)[125] ruling is further evidence, for some, of the federal judiciary's retreat from *Brown*.

In *Parents Involved in Community Schools*, a group of white parents complained to the U.S. Supreme Court that voluntary school integration plans, which meant that children, who were assigned, without a court order, into certain public schools into Seattle, Washington and Louisville, Kentucky, at the exclusion of others, discriminated against them on equal protection grounds. In general, the plans were designed to give parents some choice about which schools their children could attend while, at the same time, create school districts with some racial balance, an objective that facilitates educational diversity in the student body. They did this, in part, by using "tiebreakers" that used racial classifications in determining the assignments to schools that were in popular demand. The Court, split 5:4, struck down the plans down because they were not specific enough in application to achieve a racial balance in public schools, which the Court held was not a legitimate compelling state interest. The Court's strict "color-blind" interpretation of the Constitution meant, in the words of Chief Justice John Roberts who wrote the Opinion for the Court and had the support of the conservative Justices (Antonin Scalia, Anthony Kennedy, Clarence Thomas and Samuel Alito), that "[t]he way to stop discrimination on the basis of race is to stop discriminating on the basis of race." For the dissenters, which included the liberal bloc of Justices Stephen Breyer, John Paul Stevens, Ruth Bader Ginsburg and David Souter, the Court's approach violated the purpose of *Brown*'s integration mandate. As Justice Stevens put it, "[t]here is a cruel irony" in the Court's reliance on *Brown* in reaching the case outcome, for "the history books do not tell stories of white children struggling to attend black schools." As such, earlier interpretations by the Court were more cognizant of the need to correct racial injustices and, thus, he concluded that "it is my firm conviction that no Member of the Court that I joined in 1975 would have agreed with today's decision."[126]

For critics, *Brown* and its aftermath underscore the inability of courts to force major social change.[127] The Supreme Court could not fully implement *Brown* without the sustained cooperation of the political branches and, in the end, without full public support. Although total compliance with *Brown* has never been achieved, the Court's policymaking did steer the country in the direction of significant public policy change toward ending racial discrimination in public schools and elsewhere. In this regard, *Brown* "dramatically and undeniably altered the course of American life."[128]

Nor is *Brown* an isolated case. *Lawrence v. Texas* (2003),[129] the Court's controversial ruling striking down laws criminalizing homosexual sodomy, and the jurisprudence from state and federal courts addressing the scope of gay (LGBTQ) rights, provoked similar responses and opposition. The reactions are considered in the next section in accordance with a model public law scholars use in evaluating the implementation, compliance, and impact of judicial rulings.

The Politics of LGBT Rights and Same-Sex Marriages

Political scientists Bradley Canon and Charles Johnson have analyzed the scope and application of judicial policymaking in terms of how different populations in the legal culture interpret, implement, and comply with judicial decisions.[130] They emphasize that judicial policies are not self-executing, and appellate courts must rely on other institutional actors—besides lower courts, state attorneys general, for example, and prosecutors, police, key agency officials, and municipal employees—to translate legal principles into actionable public policy.

Judicial impact is a function of implementation (how court decisions are implemented by government officials) and compliance (whether judicial policies are followed or not by those interpreting or implementing them) (see Figure 10.1). The underlying dynamics of implementation, compliance, and impact are not mutually exclusive or static. Rather, they are fluid and situational. Illustrative of the impact of the Court's watershed rulings in the area of gay rights, and ultimately those determining the constitutionality of same-sex marriage, is *Lawrence v. Texas* (2003),[131] which had important consequences for the development of due process and equality principles in American courts.

| Figure 10.1 | Judicial Compliance and Impact |

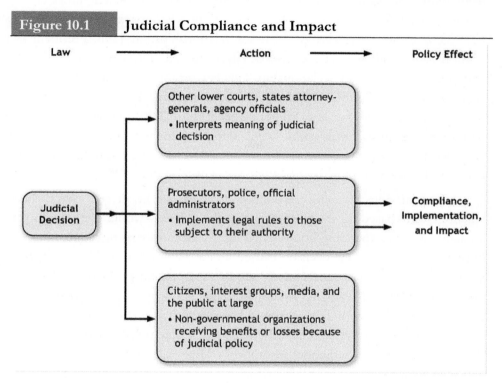

Before *Lawrence*, in *Bowers v. Hardwick* (1986),[132] a bare majority of the Burger Court (1969–1986) ruled there was no constitutional right under the Fourteenth Amendment to engage in consensual homosexual sodomy. But, by a 6:3 vote, *Lawrence* struck down Texas's anti-sodomy law and overturned *Bowers*. Writing for the Court, Justice Anthony Kennedy held that criminalizing homosexual conduct between consenting adults violates the Fourteenth Amendment and the right to privacy. Although *Bowers* emphasized that "for centuries there have been powerful voices to condemn homosexual conduct as immoral," Justice Kennedy highlighted the "emerging awareness" over the past fifty years that "liberty gives substantial protection to adult persons in deciding how to conduct their private lives in matters pertaining to sex." This "emerging recognition" is apparent not only in U.S. law, but also in foreign law. In Justice Kennedy's words, "Other nations. . .have taken action consistent with an affirmation of the protected right of homosexual adults to engage in intimate, consensual conduct." Consequently, he emphasized, the personal autonomy of homosexuals "has been accepted as an integral part of human freedom in many other countries."[133]

Although *Lawrence v. Texas* only nullified criminal bans on sodomy, advocates and critics of homosexual rights perceived it as opening the door for judicial recognition of same-sex marriages.[134] Still, there remained cross-cutting movements and countervailing pressures to reaffirm heterosexual marriage, along with recognizing the legality of same-sex relationships. In 1996, President Bill Clinton signed the federal Defense of Marriage Act (DOMA), which defined marriage as a heterosexual relationship. That law prompted a majority of states to enact similar laws, "junior DOMAs." At the same time, as *Lawrence* recognized, many states were moving in a different direction. In 2000, Vermont became the first state permitting homosexual "civil unions" (allowing same-sex couples to enjoy legal rights given in heterosexual marriages). And by 2001, half of the states had repealed their criminal laws banning consensual sodomy.[135]

Different constituencies responded to *Lawrence* in diverse ways. Their reactions were based on the possibility that the judiciary would continue to play an active role in expanding homosexual rights. Homosexual rights activists saw hope in *Lawrence*, but the decision caused an equally intense backlash, especially among religious and conservative groups. Significantly, *Lawrence* had the unintended effect of changing rights' discourse: anti-gay animus was no longer necessarily rooted in moral objections to homosexuality, as it was before *Lawrence*. Rather, arguments for restricting same-sex unions were refashioned to stress that they undermined the traditional institution of marriage and harmed children.[136] The new parameters of the political debate about gay rights thereby redefined the strategies, responses, and burdens of legislators and well-organized special interest groups for and against same-sex marriages.

Consequently, after *Lawrence*, the primary actors—lower courts, judges, and lawyers—began to adjudicate the basic question of whether the traditional conception of marriage should remain. With the state supreme court's ruling in *Goodridge v. Department of Health* (2003),[137] Massachusetts became the first state to validate same-sex marriages. At the time, only four other jurisdictions across the globe—Ontario, British Columbia, Belgium, and the Netherlands—had authorized gay marriages. In the United States, the ruling created a strong backlash among religious leaders and political opponents. In his 2004 State of the Union Address, President George W. Bush declared that a constitutional amendment preserving traditional marriage would be the "only alternative left" if "activist judges" continued to thwart the people's will. With public opinion polls showing little support for same-sex marriage, several states passed nonbinding resolutions demanding Congress enact such an amendment, but it did not garner enough votes in the House of Representatives to pass.[138]

Local officials, however, began issuing marriage licenses to gay and lesbian couples. Subsequently, the courts voided them in California, New Mexico, New York, and Oregon. In response, opponents of homosexual rights turned to the ballot box and pressured state legislatures to pass laws and constitutional amendments to bar same-sex marriages. By 2004, anti-gay marriage amendments to state constitutions had been enacted in thirteen states. Within five years of *Goodridge*, more than twenty-five states had enacted similar prohibitions; before *Goodridge*, only three states—Alaska, Nebraska, and Nevada—had constitutional bans on homosexual marriages.[139]

In light of these developments, the progress toward judicially sanctioned same-sex marriage remained uneven, though public opposition dramatically increased after 2006.[140] Yet, public opinion polls found increasing support for gay marriage or civil unions. Also, there was a growing recognition of "relationship equality policies" in a variety of progressive venues—by 2006, several hundred Fortune 500 companies gave their workers' health care plans for same-sex domestic partners, and by 2008, fifteen states enacted similar benefits for public employees. Several states enacted enhanced punishments for anti-gay "hate crimes," and many others passed antidiscrimination laws applying to sexual orientation. While the different signals emerging from the judiciary may have complicated reform efforts, *Lawrence* and *Goodridge* undeniably encouraged the national lesbian, gay, bisexual, and transsexual (LBGT, Lesbians, Gay, Bi-Sexual and Transgender) community to advance its political agenda.[141]

By 2009, the Connecticut, California, and Iowa Supreme Courts each interpreted their state constitutions to recognize same-sex marriage.[142] While the Connecticut ruling was accepted by the legislature and a majority of voters, the California and Iowa decisions generated a substantial political backlash that reverberated across the nation. Whereas California voters approved of a constitutional amendment banning same-sex marriage (Proposition 8), Iowa voters removed three justices from the state supreme court in the 2010 retention elections. Also, the remaining four Iowa justices were targeted for impeachment and salary cuts by some Republican legislators, though those efforts failed. These developments were accompanied by a sharp decline in public opinion polls supporting gay marriage and Maine's ratification of a constitutional amendment banning them. Legislative bills to legalize same-sex marriages also failed in New York and New Jersey.[143]

Subsequently, however, the Supreme Court handed down two rulings that significantly altered the legal and political landscape. *U.S. v. Windsor* (2013)[144] challenged the constitutionality of the federal DOMA law, and *Hollingsworth v. Perry* (2013)[145] contested California's antigay Proposition 8. In *Windsor,* in a 5:4 ruling, with Justice Kennedy joining his four liberal colleagues (Justices Ginsburg, Breyer, Sotomayor, and Kagan), the Court held that DOMA's Section 3, which defined marriage as only between heterosexuals, violated due process and equal protection because it discriminated against same-sex couples who were legally married in states that recognized those unions. In *Hollingsworth,* which was another closely divided decision, Chief Justice Roberts—but joined by only one conservative (Justice Scalia) and three liberals (Justices Ginsburg, Breyer, and Kagan)—ruled that supporters of Proposition 8, who intervened in the suit when state officials refused to defend the controversial initiative in the litigation, lacked standing to bring the suit in order to force its implementation. While the Court did not directly address the constitutionality of same-sex marriages, *Hollingsworth* left intact the lower federal court decisions declaring Proposition 8 unconstitutional. For some scholars, *Windsor* "alter[ed] the terms of the debate" over gay rights because same-sex couples could no longer be denied federal rights and benefits.[146]

The prognosticators turned out to be correct. In a landmark decision, the Supreme Court in *Obergefell v. Hodges* (2015) declared that same-sex couples have a fundamental right to marry under the Fourteenth Amendment's Due Process and Equal Protection clauses, thus invalidating the legal bans against same-sex marriage in Michigan, Kentucky, Ohio, and Tennessee. In a 5:4 ruling, Justice Anthony Kennedy's Opinion for the Court, joined by liberal Justices Ruth Bader Ginsburg, Stephen Breyer, Sonia Sotomayor and Elena Kagan, reasoned that same-sex couples cannot be denied their rights because of four principles and traditions that are inherent in the marriage relationship: (1) the preservation of individual autonomy; (2) the necessity to recognize a two-person union that goes beyond individual interests; (3) safeguarding children and families; and, (4) the preservation of social order. The dissent, consisting of separate opinions by Chief Justice John Roberts and Justices Antonin Scalia, Clarence Thomas, and Samuel Alito, countered by accusing the Court of judicial activism and usurping the democratic process by taking away the power of the states to outlaw same-sex marriages and preserve heterosexual unions. As the Chief Justice put it, "Five lawyers have closed the debate and enacted their own vision of marriage as a matter of constitutional law;" whereas, for Justice Thomas, the lack of judicial restraint only "exalts judges at the expense of the People," an approach that undercuts the Constitution's original meaning and natural rights.[147]

The internal division over *Obergefell's* constitutional meaning and its societal implications and impact has translated into ongoing litigation that tests the legal boundaries of religious freedom, LGBT rights, the allocation of government benefits or obligations, the legality of polygamist unions, and other related areas of public policy. To illustrate, in a 6:3 ruling in *Bostock v. Clayton County* (2020),[148] the Court held that gay, lesbian and transgender employees can sue their employers under Title VII of the Civil Rights Act of 1964 because they lost their livelihoods as a result of their sexual orientation, and not poor job performance. *Bostock*, which was consolidated with two other cases, involved the claims of two gay men that were fired from their jobs as skydiving instructors; and a transgender person's position as a funeral director was terminated. Those actions, the Court held, violated Title VII's federal prohibition of employment discrimination "because of. . .sex." In an Opinion for the Court that crossed party lines, Justice Neil Gorsuch reasoned that the "ordinary public meaning of the statute's language at the time of the law's adoption" yielded only one "straightforward rule": "If the employer intentionally relies in part on an individual employee's sex when deciding to discharge the employee—put differently, if changing the employee's sex would have yielded a different choice by the employer—a statutory violation has occurred." Two dissenters, Justices Samuel Alito and Clarence Thomas, flatly countered that "There is only one word for what the Court has done today: legislation"; whereas, Justice Brett Kavanaugh lamented that the Court disrespected the principle of separation of powers and usurped Congress's prerogative to make the nation's laws. As a result, "Instead of a hard-earned victory won through the democratic process, today's victory is brought about by judicial dictate—judges latching on to a novel form of living literalism to rewrite ordinary meaning and remake American law."[149]

The Supreme Court's resolution of the dispute is impactful because nearly five percent of adults in the United States are gay, lesbian, bisexual or transgender; and, according to an **amicus curiae** ("friend of the court") brief filed by 21 states and the District of Columbia, 42 percent of gay, lesbian and bisexual individuals, and 90 percent of transgender persons, have encountered discrimination, harassment, or mistreatment on the job because of their sexual orientation. Such victims, supporters say, suffer from being paid less and experiencing higher rates of unemployment, homelessness, and economic hardships, especially in states that do not have laws protecting against sexual orientation employment discrimination—all of which increases the demand for relief under states benefits programs. Still, as advocates of the employers argue, recognizing such rights will displace the religious or moral beliefs of those opposing LGBT rights in the states, and it will raise the cost of doing business while undercutting traditional values.[150]

Apart from employment discrimination cases, the legal recognition of same-sex marriage has spawned related lawsuits that try to strike a balance between the individual freedoms of those supporting or opposing LGBT rights in a business setting. In 2019, for example, a writ of *certiorari* was filed with the Supreme Court on behalf of florist who contested a civil judgment that she violated the State of Washington's anti-discrimination laws for refusing to sell flowers to a gay couple because it violated her religious beliefs. The case, and others that are likely to follow in the future, originate from the Supreme Court's decision in *Masterpiece Cakeshop, Ltd. v. Colorado Civil Rights Commission* (2018), which left open the legal question of whether businesses have a constitutional right of religious freedom to refuse to serve gay clientele after deciding that a Colorado civil rights agency showed bias against a bakeshop owner that would not sell a wedding cake to a gay couple for similar reasons.[151] In short, the politics of gay rights and the controversy over same-sex marriages engenders unceasing public debate and, at bottom, raises a concern in judicial politics about whether courts are the proper institutional venue to forge social change, especially when judicial outcomes may not always be in line with prevailing dominant political coalitions or public opinion (for further discussion, see the "Contemporary Controversies over Courts: Do Courts Forge Major Social Change?" box in this Chapter).

THE LIMITATIONS OF JUDICIAL POWER

As the capital punishment, abortion, school desegregation, and same-sex marriage controversies demonstrate, courts are often asked to be at the forefront political and social change, even though, at their core, they remain passive governmental institutions that can only respond to lawsuits brought to them by aggrieved litigants. While, in certain cases, they may opt to be agents of robust legal and social change, ordinarily they do so with decidedly mixed results, simply because the exercise of judicial power is always subject to a variety of internal and external constraints that limit the impact of their judicial policymaking. Some of the main internal constraints, and external restraints, on judicial authority are considered next.

Internal Constraints

A number of informal norms and professional factors temper the public policy effects of judicial policymaking. These "internal" constraints stem from the personal values of judges, shared conceptions of collegiality, and informal traditions defining proper judicial behavior. A fundamental maxim, for example, is the faithful adherence to the judicial oath. As Chief Justice John Marshall put it, the Constitution was thought of by the Framers as "a rule for the government of courts."[152] When they assume office, all judges vow to uphold the U.S. Constitution and the corresponding rule of law, a notion that registers the values of justice, accountability, the fair and impartial administration of the law.[153] Hence, they have a duty to follow what the founding document symbolically represents in discharging their official duties, notwithstanding their personal feelings about a case and its public policy implications.

As former Justice Benjamin Cardozo reasoned, similar conceptions of judicial philosophy and institutional deference to court-generated norms, procedures, and traditions also restrain judges from not "yield[ing] to spasmodic sentiment, [or] to vague and unregulated benevolence" in cases; instead, they resolve legal matters by "draw[ing]. . .inspiration from consecrated principles."[154] Put differently, the formal and informal obligation to obey the law and conform to judicial norms or practices impel judges to respect the meaning of duly enacted statutes, institutional rules, and legal precedent.[155]

Judges understand these restrictions and consider them seriously in judging. "Judges have to look in the mirror at least once a day, just like everyone else," federal appellate Judge Alex Kozinski once observed, and "they have to like what they see."[156] In this light, self-respect is another powerful constraint on judicial behavior because it forces judges to base their decisions on legal reasons that must withstand scrutiny from peers and the test of time. Self-respect thus works in tandem with the fear of being chastised by colleagues, either internally or by appellate judges who have the power to reverse lower court decisions. At a deeper psychological level, some scholars argue that judges are very attentive to their judicial reputations and how they are perceived by their elite social, legal and political networks. Consequently, judges deviating too far from the law or precedent may also damage professional reputations.[157]

External Restraints

Besides internal constraints, the structural politics of constitutionalism and the separation of powers principle operate as broad "external" limitations on judicial decision-making. Courts are subject to an array of checks imposed by legislatures, the executive branch, interest groups, and public opinion. In a study examining "court curbing"—whenever the legislature submits proposals or enacts laws designed to limit the impact of court rulings it disagrees with—political scientist

Tom Clark found that the external political environment influences the Court's behavior, simply because it fears losing public support, and its institutional legitimacy, if it does not act differently.[158] To illustrate further, a federal court of appeals judge perceived Congress's enactment of the Civil Rights Act of 1991 as check on his authority because it overturned several Supreme Court opinions relating to employment discrimination. Another example is the decision of California voters to oust at least three state supreme court justices in judicial elections because of their rulings on the death penalty.[159] In 2005, moreover, a group known as the South Dakota Judicial Accountability unsuccessfully pushed for a state constitutional amendment to eliminate immunity for state judges and permit citizens to sue and criminally prosecute judges who were considered to violate the law in their decisions. And, as a result of their rulings favoring same-sex marriage and abortion, Iowan lawmakers advanced proposals in 2019 to change how justices to Iowa Supreme Court, and judges to the state Court of Appeals, are elected to office by requiring that the dominant political party control of the nomination process in that state's judicial merit plan (see Chapter Four for a full discussion of state judicial election methods).[160] These and countless other illustrations highlight that federal and state judiciaries are pressured by, and perhaps ultimately accountable to, politicians and the public for their rulings, especially in controversial areas of public policy. Some of these external restraints are considered next.

Restraints Imposed by Legislatures

Legislatures have a variety of options that can be used to curb courts that stray too far. They may: (1) amend their constitutions to reverse unpopular judicial decisions; (2) change the court's size or jurisdiction by legislation; (3) enact legislation that "overturns" or "curbs" the power of courts due to unpopular judicial decisions; or, (4) simply ignore judicial rulings and not comply with them. They may also use other tactics to pressure courts, such as attempting to influence judicial appointments and reelection, or imposing term limits on judges. They also may reduce funding for courts or refuse to provide salary increases. In extreme instances of political retribution, legislatures may opt to initiate impeachment proceedings or, more commonly, at least threaten to use them against particular judges.

Still, constitutional amendments remain the most effective court-curbing method, although it is a cumbersome and lengthy process to implement. The protracted nature of the federal amendment process, which has thus far only yielded 27 amendments to the U.S. Constitution, is perhaps best exemplified by the Equal Rights Amendment (ERA), which was first approved by Congress in 1972 but not (technically) ratified until January 2020 (by Virginia's vote as the thirty-eighth state). Virginia's action resulted decades after 1982, the time Congress set as a deadline for ratification. Although enough states have voted in favor of the ERA, whether it goes into effect still remains uncertain because the Department of Justice has taken the legal position that the ratification deadline has expired; and a lawsuit has been filed by three states (Alabama, Louisiana and South Dakota) against the archivist in an attempt to block it from being appended to the U.S. Constitution.[161] On the state level, while constitutional amendments are far more frequent, the process of enacting them is no less cumbersome. Still, while they often times do not go into effect, amendments are routinely introduced in a variety of public policy areas, including those aiming to reverse or revise judicial decisions relating to hot-button topics such as abortion, flag burning, busing, and same-sex marriages; but only a small percentage have been ratified.[162]

Significantly, attempting to amend the constitution has the symbolic effect of representing the people's will while also reigning in courts that threaten to go too far ahead of prevailing public opinion in local or national political communities. In the aftermath of *Goodridge* (the same-sex ruling from the Massachusetts Supreme Court discussed earlier), one-half of the states put amendments on the ballots that would bar same-sex marriages, and none were rejected by the voters.[163] On the federal level, out of the tens of thousands of proposed constitutional amendments introduced in Congress, only six have overridden rulings of the Supreme Court, with the passage of the Eleventh, Thirteenth, Fourteenth, Sixteenth, Nineteenth, Twenty-Fourth, and Twenty-Sixth Amendments (Table 10.4).

Besides amending constitutions, legislatures may constrain courts by altering their size, changing their jurisdiction, or redrawing jurisdictional boundaries. In the 1970s, for example, the Nixon administration convinced conservatives in Congress to oppose the liberal direction of the Court of Appeals for the D.C. Circuit by taking away its authority to act as a de facto "state" supreme court in criminal appeals, principally because the D.C. Circuit was perceived to favor criminal defendants and the protection of their constitutional rights. Under the pretext of court reform, Congress thus enacted the "D.C. Circuit Crime Bill," legislation that removed criminal appeals from the docket and, in turn, replaced that jurisdiction with the power to hear federal agency appeals.[164]

Table 10.4	Amendments Overturning Unpopular U.S. Supreme Court Decisions	
Supreme Court Opinion	**Opinion's Impact**	**Constitutional Amendment(s) and Effect**
Chisholm v. Georgia, 2 U.S. 419 (1793)	Allowed citizens to sue state governments in federal courts	Eleventh Amendment (1795) provided sovereign immunity for states in lawsuits commenced in federal court by state citizens
Dred Scott v. Sandford, 60 U.S. 693 (1857)	Denied emancipated blacks full citizenship rights	Thirteenth (1865) and Fourteenth Amendments (1868) abolishing slavery and giving blacks full citizenship rights
Pollock v. Farmers' Loan and Trust Company, 157 U.S. 429 (1895)	Disallowed imposition of a federal income tax	Sixteenth Amendment (1913) enacted federal income tax
Minor v. Happersett, 88 U.S. 162 (1875)	Denied women the right to vote under state law	Nineteenth Amendment (1922) allowed women the right to vote in state and federal elections
Breedlove v. Suttles, 302 U.S. 277 (1937)	Permitted use of poll tax in elections under state law	Twenty-Fourth Amendment (1964) barred use of poll tax in state and federal elections
Oregon v. Mitchell, 400 U.S. 112 (1970)	Allowed Congress to lower the voting age to eighteen for federal, but not state, elections	Twenty-Sixth Amendment (1971) allowed voting age to be lowered to eighteen in state and federal elections

Source: David M. O'Brien, *Storm Center: The Supreme Court in American Politics*, 12th ed. (New York: Norton, 2020), 361–2.

Likewise, in the 1980s, the Fifth Circuit, which then spanned a number of southern states, was split in two, in part because federal judges in that region were sympathetic to black civil rights. A new circuit, the Eleventh, was created in an attempt to diminish and undercut the old Fifth Circuit's authority.[165] Circuit-splitting, or the process of reconfiguring judicial boundaries, remains a popular court-curbing tool in the new millennium as well because conservatives in

Congress have reignited legislation to divide the Ninth Circuit in late 2005, the nation's largest appellate court covering several western states. As in the cases of the D.C. and Fifth Circuits, splitting the Ninth is purportedly justified by claims that the division would streamline judicial operations; but studies have shown that the proposal is driven by potent political constituencies seeking to diminish the power of liberal California judges to decide cases favoring criminal defendants' rights and broadening environmental protection, and others that strike down the Pledge of Allegiance on the grounds of religious freedom.[166]

Apart from trying to change a court's jurisdiction for political reasons, attempts to reign in courts by statutory overrides are also an option but may not always succeed, especially if they threaten the power of courts to be the final arbiter of constitutional disputes. After the Court's ruling in *Employment Division, Department of Human Resources of Oregon v. Smith* (1990) (*Oregon*),[167] which had the effect of limiting the free exercise of religion, Congress enacted the Religious Freedom Restoration Act (RFRA), which reinstated the preexisting legal test governing religious freedom in prior cases. But, shortly thereafter, the Rehnquist Court (1986–2005) ruled in *City of Boerne v. Flores* (1997)[168] that Congress exceeded its authority in enacting the RFRA under the power to "enforce," by "appropriate legislation," the substantive provisions of the Fourteenth Amendment. The Court justified its ruling on the basis of judicial supremacy and its power to determine the scope and meaning of constitutional law. Thus *Boerne* is an example of the judiciary rebuffing a bold attempt by Congress to override a decision of the Court on constitutional law.

The historic struggles over legislative versus judicial supremacy underscore the political reality that courts and legislatures are engaged in an ongoing constitutional dialogue to set legal and public policy.[169] According to the Congressional Research Service, the Supreme Court has struck down an 75 congressional acts, and 299 state or local laws.[170] On the other hand, other studies find that Congress has overridden 275 Supreme Court statutory construction decisions.[171] Notably, this political dynamic is a natural function of a complex and fluid political process that also registers the pressures that interest groups and political parties exert on each other within the American constitutional framework.[172]

Finally, the political branches may limit judicial power by simply ignoring rulings from the judiciary. As passive institutions, courts have little power to enforce their own decisions. Perhaps the most famous example is President Andrew Jackson's refusal to abide by *Worcester v. Georgia* (1832),[173] a Supreme Court decision favoring the rights of Cherokee Indians over the sovereign rights of Georgia. President Jackson reportedly rebuked the Court by saying, "John Marshall made his decision—now let him enforce it!"[174] Such inter-branch tensions are conspicuous today in all state and federal courts. As discussed earlier, the Kansas Supreme Court's ruling embracing the right to abortion under natural rights theory has generated an intense political opposition from the right-leaning Kansas legislature, and the same type of partisan conflict has erupted in response to the high court's recognition of progressive rights in respect to public school financing cases. In Ohio, as well, the state supreme court ruled in *DeRolph v. Ohio* (1997)[175] that the method of funding public schools violated the state constitution by creating an unequal disparity between rich and poor school districts. Yet, that decision has never been enforced because of fierce legislative opposition and partisan changes in the court's composition.[176]

Restraints Imposed by the Executive Branch

While governors and the president, along with their subordinates (attorneys general, agency counsel, and cabinet officials) have limited authority to curb courts directly, a principal method of shaping the court's influence is through influencing judicial recruitment in the states and the federal appointment process (discussed in Chapter Four). In the states, the pervasive impact of state judicial elections diminishes executive control over the judiciary, although governors may still influence the composition of the bench by, for example, making recess appointments or by affecting the decisions about who serves on judicial nomination commissions. Likewise, presidents have not always been successful in entirely transforming the federal courts; but there have been exceptions. In the beginning of the republic, Presidents George Washington and John Adams were able to fill the bench with Federalist appointments; and President Franklin D. Roosevelt's long tenure in the Oval Office over four terms in the 1930s and 1940s gave him the unprecedented chance to fill eight vacancies on the Supreme Court.[177] These examples suggest that presidents serving at least two terms have a likelihood of greater success in packing the federal courts because they simply have more opportunities to fill vacancies with like-minded judges.

Besides appointments, presidents and governors may undermine judicial policymaking in subtle ways by using litigation to advance their own political agendas or, conversely, to resist certain unpopular rulings. Political support for the president's agenda may come from the use of a sympathetic judiciary that is allied with the many of the same litigation goals as the prevailing administration.[178] Similarly, government lawyers appointed by the president—most notably the solicitor general and the attorney general—have a significant influence as "repeat players" in the judicial and governmental process (as discussed in Chapter Eight). It is not an overstatement to say that the president, either directly or indirectly, controls litigation policy in the federal bureaucracy,[179] and thereby influences judicial decision-making over vast areas of law, ranging from abortion, affirmative action, the death penalty, and religious freedom, to environmental protection, consumer rights, and antitrust law, among others. State attorney generals, working on behalf of the states they represent, have a similar impact on state as well as national court systems.[180]

Restraints Imposed by Public Opinion

The judiciary is always accountable to the people. As legal historian Barry Friedman put it, "Ultimately, it is the people (and the people alone) who must decide what the Constitution means."[181] Thus, courts are sensitive to public opinion in the constitutional republic in different ways. Judges that are elected to office in the states are probably more cognizant of what the public thinks because it will most likely affect their chances to win or lose in judicial campaigns, or to remain in office once they are elected; but, federal judges with lifetime appointments, and which are constitutionally protected from having their salaries diminished, have more judicial independence and are less fearful of public opinion. For former Chief Justice William Rehnquist, competent and ethical judges are unlikely to be swayed in most ordinary cases by volatile or sometimes hostile "barometers of public opinion" or media pressures in any given case. Still, and even though they work in an "insulated atmosphere in their courthouse," judges still "go home at night and read the newspapers or watch the evening news on television" and "they talk to their family and friends about current events." In this respect, Rehnquist concludes that it is hard for judges to ignore the "tides of public opinion that lap at the courthouse door."[182]

Moreover, judges invariably are responsive to public views as part of the information they gather in deciding cases and making legal policy. And, as some scholars argue, judges "are subject to significant influences from the world around them," especially those which are related to their ongoing efforts to seek approval, or professional recognition, from those who are part of the judge's social, legal and political networks.[183] As well, public opinion may, at times, affect judicial behavior during times of political upheaval, such as partisan realignments, or during critical elections. In other moments in political or legal history, courts or judges may align their rulings with overarching concerns about the way the public may perceive its institutional legitimacy—such as when the Supreme Court, in *Planned Parenthood of Southeastern Pennsylvania v. Casey* (1992), refused to overrule the landmark abortion case of *Roe v. Wade* (1973) on the grounds, in part, that "The Court's power lies, rather, in its legitimacy, a product of substance and perception that shows itself in the people's acceptance of the Judiciary as fit to determine what the Nation's law means and to declare what it demands"; or, perhaps, when Chief Justice John Roberts, a conservative, joined his fellow liberal colleagues in upholding Obamacare, or the Affordable Care Act—the same controversial health care program that no Republican voted for during the Obama presidency. Many journalists, and some scholars, thought that Roberts crossed party lines to approve the health care act because he donned the role of public statesmen, ostensibly because he feared that the public would lose faith in the nation's highest court if it was seen as nothing more than a political, and not an impartial, legal institution.[184]

Regardless, although there is ongoing academic debate on the issue of whether the judiciary directly responds to mass public opinion, the predominate view is that courts tend to follow the election returns and to dispense justice in accordance with the policy preferences of dominant national coalitions. In this sense, courts are simply one element in an ongoing "constitutional dialogue" in American democratic politics.[185] Even so, scholars remain divided on the related question of whether courts are institutionally capable of creating major social change (For further discussion, see "Contemporary Controversies over Courts: Do Courts Forge Major Social Change?").

Contemporary Controversies over Courts: Do Courts Forge Major Social Change?

In one of his annual reports on the state of the federal judiciary, former Chief Justice William H. Rehnquist focused "on the recently mounting criticism of judges for engaging in what is often referred to as 'judicial activism,'" though he also emphasized that "criticism of judges and judicial decisions is as old as our republic." The Marshall Court (1801–1835) was sharply criticized, and as the chief justice noted, it took a generation for the Court's reputation to recover after its infamous ruling on slavery in *Dred Scott v. Sandford*, 19 How. (60 U.S.) 393 (1857). The Court's invalidation of early New Deal and other progressive legislation culminated in President Franklin D. Roosevelt's court-packing plan and the "constitutional crisis" of 1937. Over sixty years ago, the landmark school desegregation decision, *Brown v. Board of Education*, 347 U.S. 483 (1954), sparked massive resistance and a long-running controversy over the implementation of its mandate. More recently, cases such as *Goodridge v.*

Department of Health, 798 N.E.2d 941 (Mass. 2003), and other decisions such as *Obergefell v. Hodges*, 576 U.S. 644 (2015), register the role state and federal supreme courts have played in advancing gay rights and same-sex marriage, and they also have produced significant political and social backlash.

Along with the issue of same-sex marriage, judicial rulings on abortion, health care, immigration, and religious freedom have intensified contemporary controversies over the role of courts. Sometimes, judicial outcomes even generate sharp disagreements within courts and amongst colleagues. In 2013, Justice Ruth Bader Ginsburg, one of the Court's leading liberals, said in an interview with a *New York Times* reporter that the Roberts Court is "one of the most activist courts in history." She explained that she made a "mistake" in joining an earlier opinion that later helped the Court to strike down a key provision of the Voting Rights Act of 1965 in *Shelby County v. Holder*, 570 U.S. 529 (2013). She characterized, *Shelby County* as a ruling that is "stunning in terms of activism." Such high-profile criticisms fuel the debate about whether the judiciary is an "activist" body that disregards the rule of law; an "imperial" institution in overturning federal, state, and local laws; leading a "vital national seminar" that engages the country in a constitutional dialogue within a pluralistic political system; one that is usually "behind the times" and reinforcing the dominant national coalition; or, finally, a "hollow hope" in terms of ensuring minority rights and bringing about major social changes.

"Imperial Judiciary"?

Whereas liberals criticize a conservative Court for invalidating progressive legislation before 1937, afterward conservatives turned the table and attacked courts during the last fifty years for "activist" liberal rulings on individual rights, due process, and the equal protection of the law. In a very influential article in *Public Interest*, "Towards an Imperial Judiciary?," Harvard University sociologist Nathan Glazer argued that "American courts, the most powerful in the world. . .are now far more powerful than ever before. . . .And courts, through interpretation of the Constitution and the laws, now reach into the lives of the people, against the will of the people, deeper than they had in American history."

Subsequently, conservative scholars, jurists, and politicians expanded and advanced Glazer's argument in two different directions. On the one hand, many conservatives contending that we have "an imperial judiciary" follow Judge Robert Bork in claiming that courts have forged major social changes with their rulings on desegregation, abortion, affirmative action, school prayer, the rights of the accused, and equal protection for women and gay persons.

Justice Neil Gorsuch, presently serving on the U.S. Supreme Court, made a similar argument when he accused liberals in a provocative 2005 *National Review* article ("Liberals'N'Lawsuits) of supporting "an overweening addiction to the courtroom as the place to debate social policy," which he concluded "is bad for the country and bad for the judiciary." From their conservative perspective, unelected judges have increasingly functioned antidemocratically, and their rulings are countermajoritarian in thwarting popular opinion. Moreover, in light of the Court's and federal judiciary's move in more conservative directions since the 1980s, even some liberal scholars agree and have lamented recent conservative "judicial activism" and the judiciary's antidemocratic role.

On the other hand, some conservatives and scholars argue that the judiciary lacks the resources and managerial expertise to forge significant social change in, for example, overseeing the supervision of public school desegregation, improving the conditions of prisons, and reforming law enforcement policies. In short, courts lack not only the legitimacy but also the institutional capacity, expertise, and resources to bring about coherent social change.

A "Vital National Seminar," "Behind the Times," or a "Hollow Hope"?

By contrast, writing in the 1960s at the height of massive resistance to *Brown v. Board of Education*, Yale law school professor Eugene V. Rostow countered conservative criticisms of the judiciary by arguing that the Court engages the country in a "vital national seminar" over constitutional values. In his words, "The Supreme Court is, among other things, an educational body, and the Justices are inevitably teachers in a vital national seminar." Rostow emphasized that

> the process of forming public opinion in the United States is a continuous one with many participants—Congress, the President, the press, political parties, scholars, pressure groups, and so on. . . .The reciprocal relation between the Court and the community in the formulation of policy may be a paradox to those who believe that there is something undemocratic in the power of judicial review. But the work of the Court can have, and when wisely exercised does have, the effect not of inhibiting but of releasing and encouraging the dominantly democratic forces of American life.

Other scholars, such as historian Louis Fisher, add that the Court's rulings, along with those of state and federal judiciaries, engage other political branches and the country in an ongoing constitutional dialogue over the direction of law and public policy. They underscore the often neglected but important role of state legislatures, Congress, the executive branch, and other political institutions and organizations within a pluralistic political system in determining the direction of law and social change. Similarly, in his 2017 *Judicial Politics in Polarized Times* study of four "polarizing" areas of social policy (abortion, LGBT rights, affirmative action and gun rights), political scientist Thomas Keck found that courts have a substantial influence in all areas (except for, more modestly, gun rights), a finding that must be understood in the relationship courts have to other ingrained aspects of the institutional policy process.

Yet, Yale University political scientist Robert Dahl took a different direction in alleging that the Supreme Court is generally in tune with the dominant national political coalition, and hence it is not as countermajoritarian as conservatives claim. "By itself," he concluded, "the Court is almost powerless to affect the course of national policy." On the basis of an examination of the Court's invalidation of congressional legislation, Dahl found that Congress ultimately prevailed 70 percent of the time. Congress was able to do so by reenacting legislation and because of changes in the composition and direction of the Court. In other words, on major issues of public policy, Congress is likely to prevail or at least temper the impact of the Court's rulings.

However, the Court forges public policy not only when invalidating federal legislation but also when overturning state and local laws, and Dahl failed to consider that important fact. The continuing controversies over decisions invalidating state and local laws on abortion, school prayer, and gay rights are a measure of how the Court's striking down state and local laws may elevate issues to the national political agenda.

Nonetheless, a number of scholars have recently followed Dahl in maintaining that, contrary to conservatives who charge that we have an "imperial judiciary," the Court largely reinforces the policy preferences of dominant national political coalitions rather than forging major social change. Legal scholar Jeffrey Rosen, in his book *The Most Democratic Branch: How the Courts Serve America* (2006), claims the Supreme Court is most successful when it crafts constitutional principles that are supported by a majority of the people. In this respect, it is plausible that the Court usually only reaches out to bring "outliers" into line with an emerging or the dominant national consensus. Still other research, such as the work from law school professor Michael J. Klarman, similarly contends that the Court has not brought about major social changes.

Instead of forging "counter majoritarian revolutions" with its rulings on civil rights and liberties, the Court has largely followed social changes in tune with an emerging national consensus. He writes that

> the modern Court's individual rights jurisprudence can be usefully distilled into two general categories. First,. . .frequently. . .the [court seizes] upon a dominant national consensus and impos[es] it on resisting local outliers. Cases illustrating this pattern include Griswold v. Connecticut, 381 U.S. 479 (1965). . . .Second,. . .the Court intervenes. . .where the nation is narrowly divided—racial segregation in 1954, the death penalty in 1972, abortion in 1973, affirmative action in 1978, and. . .sexual orientation in 1986. On these occasions, the justices seem, whether consciously or not, to be endeavoring to predict the future.

In *From the Closet to the Altar* (2013), Klarman strikes an identical tone in conceding that "gay marriage litigation has undeniably advanced the cause of gay rights," but also that "dramatic social change does not happen until the people begin contemplating and discussing it." Klarman's views, of course, predate the Supreme Court's stunning landmark ruling in favor of same-sex marriage in *Obergefell v. Hodges* (2015).

Regardless, still other scholars, such as Gerald N. Rosenberg, in his book *The Hollow Hope: Can Courts Bring About Social Change?*, go even further in claiming that "courts can *almost never* be effective producers of significant social reform." *Brown*'s failure to achieve widespread desegregation in the following decades, for instance, remains instructive, Rosenberg contended, in developing a model of judicial policymaking based on two opposing theories of judicial power. On the one hand, a *"constrained court"* theory posits that three institutional factors limit judicial policymaking: "the limited nature of constitutional rights," "the lack of judicial independence," and "the judiciary's lack of powers of implementation." On the other hand, a *"dynamic court theory"* emphasizes the judiciary's freedom "from electoral constraints and [other] institutional arrangements that stymie change" and thus enable the courts to take on issues that other political institutions might not or cannot. But neither theory is completely satisfactory, according to Rosenberg, because only occasionally the Court brings about social change. The Court may do so when the three institutional restraints identified with the constrained court theory are absent and at least one of the following conditions exists to support judicial policymaking when other political institutions and actors offer either (1) incentives; or, (2) costs to induce compliance; or, (3) "when judicial decisions can be implemented by the market"; or (4) when the Court's ruling serves as "a shield, cover, or excuse, for persons crucial to implementation who are *willing to act.*" On the basis of the resistance to *Brown*'s mandate, Rosenberg concluded that "*Brown* and its progeny stand for the proposition that courts are impotent to produce significant social reform." Likewise, in regard to the negative backlash same-sex marriage litigation generated in the states and across the country, Rosenberg reasoned that "there is no reason why the constraints and conditions that limit federal courts from producing significant social reform should not apply to state courts as well." In sum, conservatives' charges of "an imperial judiciary" are sometimes exaggerated, whereas liberals may be misguided in looking to the courts to bring about major social changes.

Sources: Chief Justice William H. Rehnquist, "2004 Year-End Report on the Federal Judiciary" (January 1, 2005), available at www.supremecourt.gov/publicinfo/year-end/2004year-endreport.pdf (last retrieved April 27, 2020); Adam Liptak, "Court Is 'One of Most Activist,' Ginsburg Says, Vowing to Stay," *New York Times* (August 24, 2013), available at www.nytimes.com (last retrieved April 27, 2020); William E. Leuchtenburg, *The Supreme Court Reborn: The Constitutional Revolution in the Age of Roosevelt* (New York: Oxford University Press, 1995); Nathan Glazer, "Towards an Imperial Judiciary?" *The Public Interest* 104 (1975), 106; Robert H. Bork, *The Tempting of America: The Political Seduction of the Law* (New York: Free Press, 1990); Donald L. Horowitz, *The Courts and Social Policy* (Washington, D.C.: The Brookings Institution, 1977); Eugene V. Rostow, *The Sovereign Prerogative: The Supreme Court and the Quest for Law* (New Haven, CT.: Yale University Press, 1962), 167; Louis Fisher, *Constitutional Dialogues: Interpretation as Political Process* (Princeton, N.J.: Princeton University Press, 1988); Robert Dahl, "Decision-Making in a Democracy: The Supreme Court as a National Policy-Maker," *Journal of Public Law* 6 (1957), 279, 293; Neil Gorsuch, "Liberals'N'Lawsuits," *National Review* (February 7, 2005); Jeffrey Rosen, *The Most Democratic Branch: How the Courts Serve America* (New York: Oxford University Press, 2006); Michael J. Klarman, *From the Closet to the Altar: Courts, Backlash, and the Struggle for Same-Sex Marriage* (New York: Oxford University Press, 2013); Gerald N. Rosenberg, *The Hollow Hope: Can Courts Bring About Social Change?* 2nd ed. (Chicago: University of Chicago Press, 2008), 35–36, 340; and Robert J. Hume, *Courthouse Democracy and Minority Rights: Same-Sex Marriage in the States* (New York: Oxford University Press, 2013); Thomas M. Keck, *Judicial Politics in Polarized Times* (Chicago: University of Chicago Press, 2014).

CONCLUDING THOUGHTS

A legal expert once said that "the judiciary is the beating heart of the modern legal system."[186] In this light, this book has shown that what courts do in interpreting and applying law is integral to maintaining societal stability and peace through the process of dispute resolution. A corollary principle is that judicial resolution of specific disputes is the exercise of governance power that reinforces political obedience, social norms, notions of morality and justice, and public respect for the law and courts. Yet it also highlights that courts, as government institutions, face a number on ongoing challenges that broadly affect their public legitimacy as well as their specific capacity to administer justice fairly. Recent findings from the National Center of State Courts' "State of the State Courts" survey (NCSC Survey) suggest that an initial challenge is one of perception: whereas registered voters have a declining confidence in state and federal court systems in comparison to past years, by a two to one margin those having direct experience with courts report that they are satisfied with the judiciary's procedural fairness and the general capacity to gain access to courts: that is, "it was easy for [respondents] to locate the people, places, and services they needed."[187]

Still, while courts are rated more favorably that other government institutions, the NCSC survey intimated that public attitudes about courts are negatively impacted by the dysfunctional hyper-partisanship that has increasingly characterizes the nation's political system, thus causing public trust in government, and in courts, to decline steeply. While the survey's findings remained fairly consistent across demographic and ideological groups, the lowest confidence levels were aligned with younger and not ideologically resolute voters (under fifty years old and Independents). Apart from public trust perceptions, the survey addressed how well judicial operations meet the needs of clientele in terms of providing access to justice and legal services. In regard to state courts, which handle the bulk of the nation's legal business, a majority of survey respondents (fifty percent of more) agreed that they performed their core mission well, including that they are fair and impartial; but slightly under fifty percent thought they supplied equal justice. In addition, fifty-five percent perceived state courts as political institutions, and another forty-four percent characterized them as "intimidating". Moreover, only thirty-six percent thought state courts were "innovative"; forty-two percent believed they were "efficient"; and fifty-three percent agreed that they are not "doing enough to empower regular people to navigate the court system without an attorney."[188]

These findings echo two basic themes that are found in the reform scholarship in the legal academy and political science community.[189] The first is that courts must be cognizant, and responsive, to criticisms questioning their institutional capacity to deliver justice equally, efficiently, and impartially in criminal and civil cases. There must be continuous efforts by courts to strengthen community outreach programs and build effective judicial infrastructures that take advantage of new technologies so that the citizenry can be educated about the vital mission and role courts and judges play in the twenty-first century. Recurring issues relating to affordability, impartiality and fairness infect the criminal justice system's operation including, to name a few, the arbitrary exercise of prosecutorial discretion, the coercive effect of plea bargaining, the high cost and limited availability of legal representation for indigent defendants, the disproportionate imposition of costs, fees and fines on less violent offenders, and the myriad related problems caused by mass incarceration or determinate sentencing policies. Clear-eyed and (increasingly) bi-partisan solutions, such as local efforts to ease the deleterious impact of "pay as you go" fee structures or, at the federal level, the enactment of the First Step Act, are actions that align with the types of reform that is appropriately lauded by the American Bar Association and the National Center for State Courts (see Chapter Seven for a full discussion). Notably, the same type of criticisms of the civil justice system—which are based on the lack of affordability and access to legal representation and courts in the procedural administration of civil lawsuits, including of the problems of the "Civil Gideon" justice gap—are the target of identical reform efforts designed to expand legal aid for *pro se* litigants through *pro bono* work, or to supply litigants with less costly and non-judicial alternative dispute resolution methods (see Chapters Five, Six and Eight).

Apart from initiatives to improve court processes for litigants enmeshed in the adversarial system of justice, a second theme—to mitigate the negative influence politics has on the composition, operation, and decision-making of the judiciary—is just as important because it implicates broader underlying principles of legal systems in western democracies, such as maintaining respect for the rule of law, increasing public accountability, securing representation, and enhancing the public legitimacy of courts. Many of these issues focus on the need to preserve judicial independence and prevent the public from concluding that courts are simply the minions of, and are no different from, political representatives or institutions. As suggested in Chapter Four, reform efforts must concentrate on proposals to de-politicize the judicial selection process, and to explore solutions at the state level that seek to refine merit selection systems or to deflate the role money plays in fueling unchecked special interest group advocacy; and, at the federal level, taking steps to diminish the hardball politics of confirmation politics through bi-partisanship solutions and political compromise. In sum, while the judiciary may indeed be the "heartbeat" that drives the legal system, the general health of law and courts, and democracy itself, is substantially determined by the way a politically independent judiciary, and its judges, are positively shaped by the bi-partisanship compromises and civility that represent the underlying, and prevailing, norms of the domestic (and international) political environment.

Chapter Summary

Appellate courts are agents of legal and political change. Under the principle of judicial federalism, judicial policy is made by state and federal appellate courts. Judicial policymaking is controversial because critics assert that judges engage in "judicial activism" or "result-oriented" jurisprudence in forging social policy, as with imposing restrictions on public school funding, for example, or issuing rulings on abortion rights, capital punishment, and same-sex marriages.

The concept of "judicial impact" is complex. Since courts are not "self-starters," the enforcement of their rulings depends on the responses of government officials and private entities and, ultimately, public opinion. The impact of major judicial policymaking is exemplified by the controversies over school desegregation in the aftermath of *Brown v. Board of Education* (1954) and the struggle to win legal recognition for same-sex marriages after *Lawrence v. Texas* (2003) and *Goodridge v. Department of Health* (2003). The fruits of such political and legal contests, at times, produce landmark rulings, such as *Obergefell v. Hodges* (2015), which established a fundamental right to same-sex marriage. Still, the judiciary cannot fully implement its policies without the sustained cooperation of other political branches and public support.

There are internal constraints and external restraints on judicial power. Internally, judges are mindful of judicial norms, principles of judicial philosophy, and informal traditions of collegiality and professional reputation that define proper judicial behavior and influence judicial decision-making. Externally, the judiciary is subject to various checks by legislatures, the executive branch, interest groups, and, ultimately, public opinion. What the courts accomplish as proactive agents of legal and social change, however, is a highly debatable topic among many social scientists and legal academics. The predominant view, though, is that courts remain a significant player in an interactive, dynamic and fluid political environment that places a premium on following dominant national political coalitions and the election returns.

Key Questions for Review and Critical Analysis

1. Is it true that, as Alexander Bickel once said, courts are "counter-majoritarian" institutions? Why or why not?

2. Explain and contrast the concepts of "judicial self-restraint" and "judicial activism." What contrasting examples would you give, and why?

3. What will happen if certain landmark rulings in controversial areas of social policy, such as those favoring abortion and same-sex marriage, are reversed by the U.S. Supreme Court in the near future? Will state supreme courts respond to "re-establish" those rights and, if so, what are the likely political consequences in the American legal system?

4. What are the different ways that courts make a discernible "impact" on legal and social policy? Are certain areas of public policy more likely to make such an impact? If so, why? If not, why not?

5. What are the most effective "internal" constraints or "external" restraints on judicial power?

6. Can and should courts attempt to forge social change? In what areas has the judiciary appeared to try to do so? Do you believe that courts are effective agents of major social, legal and political change in the American political system?

Web Links

1. Constitutional Law Reporter (https://constitutionallawreporter.com/)

    - A legal blog addressing a variety of topics relating to the U.S. Constitution, including judicial biographies, cases, the Supreme Court, amendments, and chronological history.

2. Brennan Center for Justice (www.brennancenter.org/)

    - A liberal organization focusing on the advocacy of policy issues relating to democracy, including election, criminal rights, personal freedoms and structural constitutional reform.

3. Judicial Watch (www.judicialwatch.org)

    - A conservative organization that strives to provide transparency to legal and judicial developments through public outreach, litigation, and educational projects.

4. American Civil Liberties Union (ACLU) (www.aclu.org)

    - A liberal organization devoted to individual rights and progressive reforms through litigation, public outreach, and educational activities.

5. Washington Legal Foundation (www.wlf.org)

    - A conservative public interest law and policy center engaged in litigation, public outreach, and educational activities.

Selected Readings

Bartels, Brandon L. and Christopher D. Johnston. *Curbing the Court: Why the Public Constrains Judicial Independence* New York: Cambridge University Press, 2020.

Canon, Bradley C., and Charles A. Johnson. *Judicial Policies: Implementation and Impact*. 2nd ed. Washington, D.C.: CQ Press, 1998.

Devins, Neal and Lawrence Baum. *The Company They Keep: How Partisan Divisions Came to the Supreme Court*. New York: Oxford University Press, 2019.

Frank, Nathaniel. *Awakening: How Gays and Lesbians Brought Marriage Equality to America*. Cambridge: Harvard University Press, 2017.

Friedman, Barry. *The Will of the People: How Public Opinion Has Influenced the Supreme Court and Shaped the Meaning of the Constitution*. New York: Farrar, Straus and Giroux, 2009.

Gould, Jon and Maya Pagni Barak, *Capital Defense: Inside the Lives of America's Death Penalty Lawyers*. New York: New York University Press, 2019.

Hume, Robert J. *Courthouse Democracy and Minority Rights: Same-Sex Marriage in the States*. New York: Oxford University Press, 2013.

Keck, Thomas M. *Judicial Politics in Polarized Times*. Chicago: University of Chicago Press, 2014.

Keck, Thomas M. *The Most Activist Supreme Court in History: The Road to Modern Judicial Conservatism*. Chicago: University of Chicago Press, 2004.

Klarman, Michael J. *From the Closet to the Altar: Courts, Backlash, and the Struggle for Same-Sex Marriage*. New York: Oxford University Press, 2013.

Mezey, Susan Gluck. *Beyond Marriage: Continuing Battles for LGBT Rights*. Lanham, MD.: Roman & Littlefield, 2017.

Rebell, Michael A. *Flunking Democracy: Schools, Courts, and Civil Participation*. Chicago: University of Chicago Press, 2018.

Rollins, Joe. *Legally Straight: Sexuality, Childhood, and the Cultural Value of Marriage*. New York: New York University Press, 2018.

Rosenberg, Gerald N. *The Hollow Hope: Can Courts Bring About Social Change?* 2nd ed. Chicago: University of Chicago Press, 2008.

Sanger, Carol. *About Abortion: Terminating Pregnancy in Twenty-First Century America*. Cambridge, MA.: Harvard University Press, 2017.

Sigalet, Geoffrey, Grégoire Webber, Rosalind Dixon, eds. *Constitutional Dialogue: Rights, Democracy, Institutions*. New York: Cambridge University Press, 2019.

Sommer, Udi and Aliza Forman-Rabinovici. *Producing Reproductive Rights: Determining Abortion Policy Worldwide*. New York: Cambridge University Press, 2019.

Stone, Geoffrey R. and David A. Strauss. *Democracy and Equality: The Enduring Constitutional Vision of the Warren Court.* New York: Oxford University Press, 2020.

Sutton, Jeffrey S. *Imperfect Solutions: States and the Making of American Constitutional Law.* New York: Oxford University Press, 2018.

Tate, C. Neal, and Torbjorn Vallinder, eds. *The Global Expansion of Judicial Power.* New York: New York University Press, 1995.

West, Martin R., and Paul E. Peterson, eds. *School Money Trials: The Legal Pursuit of Educational Adequacy.* Washington, D.C.: Brookings Institution Press, 2007.

Whittington, Keith E. *Repugnant Laws: Judicial Review of Acts of Congress from the Founding to the Present.* Lawrence, KS.: University Press of Kansas, 2019.

Ziegler, Mary. *Beyond Abortion: Roe v. Wade and the Battle for Privacy.* Cambridge: Harvard University Press, 2018.

Endnotes

[1]   Abraham Lincoln, "Speech on the *Dred Scott* Decision in Springfield, Illinois (1857)." In *American Political Thought: A Norton Anthology* 2nd ed., eds. Issac Kramnick and Theodore J. Lowi (New York: W.W. Norton 2018), 567. See also *Dred Scott v. Sandford,* 60 U.S. 393 (1857).

[2]   Jonathan Shorman and Lara Korte, "Right to abortion protected by Kansas Constitution, state Supreme Court rules (April 26, 2019)," *The Wichita Eagle,* available at https://www.kansas.com/news/politics-government/article229693509.html (last retrieved April 26, 2020). The Kansas Supreme Court ruling is reported in *Hodes & Nauser v. Schmidt,* 440 P.3d 461 (2019). See also, *Roe v. Wade,* 410 U.S. 113 (1973); *Planned Parenthood of Southeastern Pennsylvania v. Casey,* 505 U.S. 833 (1992).

[3]   Alexander Hamilton, "Federalist No. 78," in *The Federalist Papers,* ed. Clinton Rossiter (New York: Mentor, 1961), 465.

[4]   Ryan Wangman, "Elizabeth Warren proposes tougher judicial ethics rules that would allow new investigations into Brett Kavanaugh and President Trump's sister," *Boston Globe* (October 7, 2019), available at https://www.bostonglobe.com/news/politics/2019/10/07/elizabeth-warren-proposes-tougher-judicial-ethics-rules-that-would-allow-new-investigations-into-brett-kavanaugh-and-president-trump-sister/ZGUzKR eLz4f6oVmY3mylbN/story.html (last retrieved April 26, 2020); Elizabeth Warren, "Restoring Trust in an Impartial and Ethical Judiciary," *Elizabeth Warren,* available at https://elizabethwarren.com/plans/restore-trust (last retrieved April 26, 2020). Republicans, too, have made identical reform proposals. In 2011, Congressman Jim Sensenbrenner (R-WI) and Senator Chuck Grassley (R-IA) sponsored legislative proposals to create an Inspector General to monitor "waste, fraud and abuse with the federal judiciary." Chuck Grassley, "Grassley, Sensenbrenner Work to Bring Transparency, Accountability to Federal Judiciary (February 15, 2011)," available at https://www.grassley.senate.gov/news/news-releases/grassley-sensenbrenner-work-bring-transparency-accountability-federal-judiciary (last retrieved July 4, 2020); Jay L. Jackson, "The Siege on State Courts," *ABA Journal* 99 (2013), 54–61 (reporting several states use chastisement, salary cuts, and removal from office as measures to retaliate against unpopular state judge opinions). See also Ruth Marcus, "Booting the Bench," *Washington Post* (April 11, 2005), A19. See also Pamela A. MacLean, *The National Journal* (May 5, 2005), available at www.law.com (last retrieved May 27, 2005).

[5]   Benjamin Cardozo, *The Nature of the Judicial Process* (New Haven, Conn.: Yale University Press, 1921), 141.

[6]   See, e.g., Herbert Weschler, "Toward Neutral Principles of Constitutional Law," *Harvard Law Review* 73 (1959), 1–35.

7   See Luis Roberto Barroso and Aline Osorio, "Democracy, Political Crisis, and Constitutional Jurisdiction: The Leading Role of the Brazilian Supreme Court." In *Judicial Power: How Constitutional Courts Affect Political Transformations*. ed. Christine Landfried (New York: Cambridge University Press, 2019): 164, 181 (arguing "activism" is a specific and proactive choice that tries to expand the judiciary's role); and, Jack M. Balkin, "Why Liberals and Conservatives Flipped on Judicial Restraint: Judicial Review in the Cycles of Constitutional Time (draft-7/19/2019)" SSRN, available at http://dx.doi.org/10.2139/ssrn.3423135 (last retrieved April 27, 2020), 5, 7, 19, 31, 35 (describing the exercise of judicial review is manifested in a shift in judicial attitudes in a specific political time).

8   Luis Roberto Barroso and Aline Osorio, "Democracy, Political Crisis, and Constitutional Jurisdiction: The Leading Role of the Brazilian Supreme Court," 164; Malcolm Langford, "Judicial Politics and Social Rights." In *The Future of Economic and Social Rights* (New York: Cambridge University Press, 2019), 69 (characterizing activist courts as "push[ing] the bounds of legal text). See Stephanie A. Lindquist and Frank B. Cross, *Measuring Judicial Activism* (New York: Oxford University Press, 2008), 39; and Wayne Justice, "The Two Faces of Judicial Activism." In *Judges on Judging: Views From the Bench*, 4th ed., edited by David M. O'Brien (Thousand Oaks, Calif.: CQ Press, 2013), 44.

9   Dahlia Lithwick, "Former Judge Resigns From the Supreme Court Bar," *Slate* (March 13, 2020), available at https://slate.com/news-and-politics/2020/03/judge-james-dannenberg-supreme-court-bar-roberts-letter.html (last retrieved April 27, 2020). See also, Adam Liptak, "Court Under Roberts Is Most Conservative in Decades," *New York Times* (July 24, 2010), available at www.nytimes.com (last retrieved July 25, 2010); Lee Epstein, William M. Landes, and Richard A. Posner, "How Business Fares in the Supreme Court," *Minnesota Law Review* 97 (2013), 1431–72; Lindquist and Cross, *Measuring Judicial Activism*, 1–9; *Lochner v. N.Y.*, 198 U.S. 45 (1905). Notably, the *Lochner* decision is now often used by critics of court action by claiming that the court producing the ruling is engaging in *Lochnerizing*, or judicial activism, if the "right" outcome is not reached.

10   Learned Hand, "Sources of Tolerance," *University of Pennsylvania Law Review* 79 (1930), 1, 11–12. See also Keenan D. Kmiec, "The Origin and Current Meanings of 'Judicial Activism,' " *California Law Review* 92 (October 2004), 1441, 1463–77 (analyzing activism and judicial role); and Frank H. Easterbrook, "Do Liberals and Conservatives Differ in Judicial Activism?" *Colorado Law Review* 73 (Fall, 2002), 140 (labeling *activism* as a "notoriously slippery" term).

11   Lindquist and Cross, *Measuring Judicial Activism*, 33 (listing studies in Table 1). Lindquist and Cross also conclude in an empirical study that "judicial activism [is] best viewed as a multidimensional concept." Ibid., 133.

12   Jeffrey S. Sutton, *Imperfect Solutions: States and the Making of American Constitutional Law* (New York: Oxford University Press, 2018), ix.

13   William J. Brennan, Jr., "State Constitutions and the Protection of Individual Rights," *Harvard Law Review* 90 (January 1977): 489–504.

14   Sutton, *Imperfect Solutions*, 1–2.

15   See generally, Melinda Gann Hall, "Decision Making in State Courts." In *Routledge Handbook of Judicial Behavior* eds. Robert M. Howard and Kirk A. Randazzo (New York: Routledge, 2018), 301–320.

16   See generally, Sutton, *Imperfect Solutions* (discussing these and other areas of contentious social and legal policy in state courts).

17   *Brown v. Board of Education*, 347 U.S. 483 (1954), 493.

18   Sutton, *Imperfect Solutions*, 27–31.

19   *Serrano v. Priest*, 487 P.2d 1241 (1971).

20   Michael A. Rebell, *Flunking Democracy: Schools, Courts, and Civil Participation* (Chicago: University of Chicago Press, 2018), 51. See also, *Robinson v. Cahill*, 303 A.2d 273 (N.J. 1973); *Horton v. Meskill*, 376 A.2d 359 (Conn. 1977); and, *Pauley v. Kelly*, 255 S.E.2d 859 (W.Va. 1979).

21   *San Antonio Independent School District v. Rodriguez*, 411 U.S. 1 (1973).

22   *San Antonio Independent School District*, 24, 31, 33, 40. Notably, some scholars have challenged this interpretation by asserting there is a recognizable federal right to an adequate education in the U.S. Constitution. See Barry Friedman and Sara Solow, "The Federal Right to an Adequate Education," *George Washington Law Review* 81 (2013), 92–155.

23 Sutton, *Imperfect Solutions*, 36–37. See also, Michael A. Rebell, "The Right to Education in the American State Courts." In *The Future of Economic and Social Rights*. ed. Katharine G. Young (New York: Cambridge University Press, 2019), 138.

24 Rebell, "The Right to Education in the American State Courts," 141. See also, Rebell, *Flunking Democracy*, 51; Michael A. Rebell, "Educational Adequacy, Democracy, and the Courts," in *Achieving High Educational Standards for All: Conference Summary (2002)*, available at https://www.govinfo.gov/content/pkg/ERIC-ED465845/pdf/ERIC-ED465845.pdf (last retrieved April 27, 2020), 226–27.

25 Most research characterizes school finance reform in terms of three "waves" of judicial rulings. The first began in the late 1960s in which plaintiffs relied upon the U.S. Constitution's Equal Protection Clause to argue that funding schemes were discriminatory. After the Supreme Court's *Rodriguez* (1973) decision, the second wave concentrated on relying upon state equal protection clauses and the inequities caused by property-based funding mechanisms. After *Rose* (1989), plaintiffs in the third wave based their claims on education clauses in state constitutions. Richard Briffault, "Adding Adequacy to Equity." In *School Money Trials: The Legal Pursuit of Educational Adequacy*, edited by Martin R. West and Paul E. Peterson (Washington, D.C.: Brookings Institution Press, 2007), 25. See also Rebell, "The Right to Education in the American State Courts," 141; and, Rebell, *Flunking Democracy*, 55.

26 Rebell, "Educational Adequacy, Democracy, and the Courts," 229–34. Other scholars observe that *Rose v. Council for Better Education*, 790 S.W.2d 186 (1989), along with *Helena Elementary School District No. 1 v. State*, 769 P.2d 684 (Mont. 1989), and *Edgewood Independent School District v. Kirby*, 777 S.W.2d 391 (Tex. 1989), made adequacy, instead of equity, the predominant theory underlying plaintiffs' victories. The "adequacy" case trilogy was a spark to the reform movement because six years had passed after the last plaintiffs' victory, and the highest courts in several states upheld their state school finance systems. William E. Thro, "Judicial Humility: The Enduring Legacy of *Rose v. Council for Better Education*," *Kentucky Law Journal* 98 (2009–2010), 717–38.

27 Rebell, "The Right to Education in the American State Courts," 141. As a result, scholars generally acknowledge that the shift to adequacy had a significant impact on generating more plaintiff victories than in the past. Briffault, "Adding Adequacy to Equity," 26.

28 Rebell, "The Right to Education in the American State Courts," 145.

29 Ibid.

30 Ibid., 235.

31 Ibid., 140–146.

32 The Center for Educational Equity (Teacher's College, Columbia University), "Cook v. Raimondo: The Case to Establish a Right to Education Under the U.S. Constitution," available at http://www.cookvraimondo.info/ (last retrieved November 21, 2019). In *Gannon*, the court declared the adequacy element is met when the funding system for grades K–12 is structurally and reasonably calculated to meet the standards set out in the Kentucky Supreme Court's *Rose* ruling, as codified in Kansas law; and the equity component is met through Gannon's creation of a "new test" that obliges the legislature to give "school districts. . . reasonably equal access to substantially similar educational opportunity through similar tax effort." Gordon L. Self, "Analysis of the Kansas Supreme Court's Opinion in *Gannon v. State*, Case No. 109, 335 (March 7, 2014)," *Office of Revisor of Statutes, Legislature of the State of Kansas*, available at www.ksrevisor.org/rpts/gannon_v_state_analysis.pdf (last retrieved November 21, 2019). See also Joshua E. Weishart, "Transcending Equality Versus Adequacy," *Stanford Law Review* 66 (2014), 477–544; Thro, "Judicial Humility: The Enduring Legacy of *Rose v. Council for Better Education*," 719 n. 7 (listing nearly forty states addressing school funding issues through litigation); and *Gannon v. State*, 298 *Kansas* 1107 (Kan. 2014).

33 *Gary B. v. Whitmer*, 957 F.3d 616 (2020). *Garb B.*, however, is being revisited as per the Sixth Circuit's decision to grant *en banc* review. See *Gary B. v. Whitmer*, 958 F.3d 1216 (2020). See also, Ruthann Robson, "Sixth Circuit Recognizes Fundamental Right to Literacy," *Constitutional Law Prof Blog* (April 26, 2020), available at https://lawprofessors.typepad.com/conlaw/2020/04/sixth-circuit-recognizes-fundamental-right-to-literacy-.html (last retrieved April 27, 2020).

34 Rebell, *Flunking Democracy*, 55. See also, National Conference of State Legislatures, "Common Core State Standards (May 1, 2014)," available at www.ncsl.org/research/education/common-core-state-standards.aspx#1 (last retrieved April 27, 2020). U.S. Department of Education, "Race to the Top Fund," available at https://www2.ed.gov/programs/racetothetop/index.html (last retrieved April 27, 2020).

35 Rebell, "The Right to Education in the American State Courts," 152–157.

36   Jessica Dickler, "College Enrollment Likely to Drop as Schools Consider Staying Closed Until 2021," *CNBC* (April 27, 2020), available https://www.chronicle.com/article/How-Will-the-Pandemic-Change/248474 (last retrieved April 27, 2020); Michael A. Rebell, "Safeguarding the Right to a Sound Basic Education in Times of Fiscal Constraint," *Albany Law Review* 75 (2012), 1855–976. See also National Conference of State Legislatures, "Promises Versus Challenges Related to Implementing the Common Core Standards," available at   www.ncsl.org/research/education/common-core-state-standards-promises-vs-challenges.aspx   (last retrieved April 27, 2020) (identifying cost, along with the effect of federal legislation and general unknown policy consequences, as a few of the problems that will impede implementing the core standards).

37   Rebell, "The Right to Education in the American State Courts," 149–150.

38   C. Kirabo Jackson, et al., " The Effects of School Spending on Educational and Economic Outcomes: Evidence From School Finance Reforms," *National Bureau of Economic Research* (Working Paper No 20847, January 2015, available from https://www.nber.org/papers/w20847 (last retrieved April 27, 2020). See also, Rebell, "The Right to Education in the American State Courts," 151.

39   Special to the Gazette, "Supreme Court Rules School Finance Adequacy Not Quite Met: One Year to Make Adjustments." *The Emporia Gazette* (June 25, 2018), available at http://www.emporiagazette.com/area_news/article_fff9d44e-788f-11e8-ac8f-6f3e7f614f0c.html (last retrieved on April 27, 2020). See also, Rebell, "The Right to Education in the American State Courts," 151 (discussing the Ohio and West Virginia cases). The Alabama and Ohio cases are *Ex Parte Governor Fob James*, 836 So.2d 813 (Ala. 2002) and *State v. Lewis*, 789 N.E.2d 195 (Ohio 2003).

40   Rebell, *Flunking Democracy*, 124–127, 134–138.

41   Sutton, *Imperfect Solutions*, 34–41; Rebell, "The Right to Education in the American State Courts," 149–157; Christopher Berry and Charles Wysong, "Making Courts Matter: Politics and the Implementation of State Supreme Court Decisions," *University of Chicago Law Review* 79 (2012), 1–27.

42   Abraham Lincoln, "Speech on the *Dred Scott* Decision in Springfield, Illinois (1857)." In *American Political Thought: A Norton Anthology* 2nd ed., eds. Issac Kramnick and Theodore J. Lowi (New York: W.W. Norton 2018), 567; ibid, "First Inaugural Address," 584. See also *Dred Scott v. Sandford*, 60 U.S. 393 (1857).

43   Alexander M. Bickel, *The Least Dangerous Branch: The Supreme Court at the Bar of Politics* (Indianapolis: Bobbs-Merrill, 1962), 16–18. See also, Barry Friedman, *The Will of the People: How Public Opinion Has Influenced the Supreme Court and Shaped the Meaning of the Constitution* (New York: Farrar, Straus and Giroux, 2009), 259. There are many historical and contemporary examples of controversial, and sometimes, infamous Supreme Court decision-making. See, e.g., *Bradwell v. Illinois*, 83 U.S. 130 (1873) (upheld an Illinois law barring women from the legal profession because it was in the "nature of things"); *Plessy v. Ferguson*, 163 U.S. 537 (1896) (upheld a Louisiana law implementing the "separate but equal" doctrine and refusing to let an African American sit in a railway car with white persons); *Buck v. Bell*, 274 U.S. 200 (1927) (upheld Virginia's compulsory sterilization law of "feeble-minded" persons); *West Virginia State Board of Education v. Barnette*, 319 U.S. 624 (1943) (struck down a West Virginia law requiring a compulsory American flag salute in public school classrooms); *Korematsu v. United States*, 323 U.S. 214 (1944) (ratified President Franklin Delano Roosevelt's order to place Japanese Americans into internment camps during World War II); *Texas v. Johnson*, 491 U.S. 397 (1989) (struck down Texas's law prohibiting the burning of the American flag); *Bush v. Gore*, 531 U.S. 98 (2000) (stopped the state-wide manual recount of disputed Florida ballots in the 2000 presidential race, which had the effect of determining the victor instead of allowing the democratic process to do so); *National Federation of Independent Business v. Sebelius* 567 U.S. 519 (2013) (upheld a federal law that required citizens buy health insurance or face a tax penalty); and, *Trump v. Hawaii*, 138 S. Ct. 2392 (2018)(upheld President Donald Trump's order to implement a U.S. "travel ban" against foreign nationals from predominately Muslim-populated countries).

44   *Figueroa v. Kerns County, et al.*, "Complaint for Damages" (U.S. District Court, Eastern District of California, filed April 19, 2019), available at https://www.courthousenews.com/wp-content/uploads/2019/05/False-conviction.pdf (last retrieved April 27, 2020). See also, Innocence Project (Staff), "Vicente Benavides Freed After 25 Years on California's Death Row" (April 19, 2018), available at https://www.innocenceproject.org/vicente-benavides-to-be-freed-after-25-years-on-californias-death-row/ (last retrieved April 27, 2020).

45   Death Penalty Information Center, "Policy Issues (International)," available https://deathpenaltyinfo.org/policy-issues/international (last retrieved April 27, 2020) (reporting that more than seventy percent of the world's countries have abolished the death penalty in law or practice). See also, Jon B. Gould and Maya Pagni Barak, *Capital Defense: Inside the Lives of America's Death Penalty Lawyers* (New York: New York University Press,

2019), 3 (observing that the U.S. is arguably the only "developed, democratic" country, besides Japan, still retaining the death penalty).

[46] The National Registry of Exonerations, "Exonerations," available at https://www.law.umich.edu/special/exoneration/Pages/browse.aspx (last retrieved April 27, 2020). See also, ibid., "Exonerations in 2018 (April 9, 2019)," available at https://www.law.umich.edu/special/exoneration/Documents/Exonerations%20in%202018.pdf (last retrieved on April 27, 2020).

[47] Death Penalty Information Center, "Gallup Poll-For the First Time, Majority of Americans Prefer a Life Sentence To Capital Punishment (November 25, 2019)" available at https://deathpenaltyinfo.org/news/gallup-poll-for-first-time-majority-of-americans-prefer-life-sentence-to-capital-punishment (last retrieved on April 27, 2020).

[48] Death Penalty Information Center, "Executions in the U.S. 1608–2002: The Espy File," available at https://deathpenaltyinfo.org/executions/executions-overview/executions-in-the-u-s-1608-2002-the-espy-file (last retrieved April 27, 2020).

[49] Ibid. See also, Death Penalty Information Center, "Crimes Punishable By Death," available at https://deathpenaltyinfo.org/facts-and-research/crimes-punishable-by-death (last retrieved April 27, 2020); Death Penalty Information Center, "Methods of Execution," available at https://deathpenaltyinfo.org/executions/methods-of-execution (last retrieved April 27, 2020).

[50] Gould and Barak, *Capital Defense*, 107 n. 3 (reporting findings from such research indicating that the death penalty is more often applied against if there are black defendants, white victims (both male and female) and poor defendants). See also, Jon B. Gould and Kenneth Sebastian Leon, "A Culture that is Hard to Defend: Extralegal Factors in Death Penalty Cases," *Journal of Criminal Law & Criminology* 107 (2017): 643–686; Kim Masters Evans, *Capital Punishment* (Farmington Mill, MI.: Gale, 2019), 79–92 (compiling multiple government reports with statistics supporting racial bias and non-racial bias findings involving capital punishment and jury selection); Roger Hood and Carolyn Hoyle, *The Death Penalty: A Worldwide Perspective* 5th ed (New York: Oxford University Press, 2015), 371–380 (reporting studies with mixed results on issue of racial bias and gender discrimination relative to capital punishment).

[51] U.S. CONSTITUTION, Amendment VIII.

[52] *Trop v. Dulles*, 356 U.S. 86 (1958).

[53] Ibid., 98–101.

[54] *Furman v. Georgia*, 408 U.S. 238 (1972). Justice Marshall's quote is found on ibid., 360.

[55] 428 U.S. 153 (1976).

[56] *Woodson v. North Carolina*, 428 U.S. 280 (1976). See also, Michael A. Foster, "Federal Capital Punishment: Recent Developments," *Congressional Research Service (Legal Sidebar, Updated November 22, 2019)*, available at https://crsreports.congress.gov/product/pdf/LSB/LSB10357 (last retrieved on April 27, 2020).

[57] The states with the death penalty are Alabama, Arizona, Arkansas, California, Florida, Georgia, Idaho, Indiana, Kansas, Kentucky, Louisiana, Mississippi, Missouri, Montana, Nebraska, Nevada, North Carolina, Ohio, Oklahoma, Oregon, Pennsylvania, South Carolina, South Dakota, Tennessee, Texas, Utah, Virginia and Wyoming. The abolitionist states are Alaska, Colorado, Connecticut, Delaware, Hawaii, Illinois, Iowa, Maine, Maryland, Massachusetts, Michigan, Minnesota, New Hampshire, New Jersey, New Mexico, New York, North Dakota, Rhode Island, Vermont, Washington, West Virginia and Wisconsin. The remaining states, California, Colorado, Oregon and Pennsylvania, have a moratorium on the death penalty. Death Penalty Information Center, "State by State," available at https://deathpenaltyinfo.org/state-and-federal-info/state-by-state (last retrieved April 27, 2020); Death Penalty Information Center, "Death Penalty Information Center 2019 Year-End Report," available at https://deathpenaltyinfo.org/facts-and-research/dpic-reports/dpic-year-end-reports/the-death-penalty-in-2019-year-end-report (last retrieved April 27, 2020).

[58] Death Penalty Information Center, "Death Row," available at https://deathpenaltyinfo.org/death-row/overview (last retrieved January 2, 2020); Death Penalty Information Center, "Death Penalty Information Center 2019 Year-End Report". See also, Anna Staver, "Householder says legislature may dump Ohio's death penalty law" (December 19, 2019), available at https://www.dispatch.com/news/20191219/householder-says-legislature-may-dump-ohiorsquos-death-penalty-law (last retrieved April 27, 2020).

[59] Death Penalty Information Center, "Death Penalty Information Center 2019 Year-End Report"; Amy Howe, "Opinion analysis: Divided court rejects lethal-injection challenge by inmate with rare medical condition," *Scotusblog* (April 1, 2019), available at https://www.scotusblog.com/2019/04/opinion-analysis-

divided-court-rejects-lethal-injection-challenge-by-inmate-with-rare-medical-condition/ (last retrieved April 27, 2020).

60   *Bucklew v. Precythe*, 139 S. Ct. 1112 (2019).

61   *Baze v. Rees*, 553 U.S. 35 (2008).

62   *Glossip v. Gross*, 576 U.S. 863 (2015).

63   *Bucklew*, 1123–27(J. Gorsuch, Op. for Court).

64   *Bucklew*, 1145 (J. Breyer, dissenting op.). See also, ibid., 1134 (J. Gorsuch, Op. for Court).

65   *Bucklew*, 1148 (J. Sotomayor, dissenting op.).

66   Mark Sherman, "Ky. Ultrasound Law Stays in Place,' *Associated Press* (December 9, 2019), available at https://apnews.com/d36c289f1d5692fea014e5996f19de7a (last retrieved April 27, 2020). The Sixth Circuit's ruling, in *EMW Women's Surgical Center v. Meier*, 920 F.3d 421 (6th Cir. 2019), was affirmed by the Supreme Court's denial of *certiorari*. See Amy Howe, "Justices turn down opioid lawsuit, challenge to ultrasound law" (December 9, 2019), available at https://www.scotusblog.com/2019/12/justices-turn-down-opioid-lawsuit-challenge-to-ultrasound-law/ (last retrieved April 27, 2020).

67   Caroline Kelly, "Mississippi, Texas and Ohio Move to Limit Abortion as Part of Coronavirus Response," *CNN* (March 25, 2020), https://www.cnn.com/2020/03/25/politics/coronavirus-abortion-texas-ohio/index.html (last retrieved April 27, 2020).

68   Savannah Behrmann, "Two Longstanding Abortion-Related Measures Fail in the U.S. Senate," *USA Today* (February 25, 2020), available at https://www.usatoday.com/story/news/politics/2020/02/25/two-abortions-measures-fail-senate/4872454002/ (last retrieved April 27, 2020).

69   *June Medical Services LLC v. Russo*, 140 S.Ct. 2103 (U.S. Jun. 29, 2020). See also *Roe v. Wade*, 410 U.S. 113 (1973); Elizabeth Nash, et al., "State Policy Trends 2019: A Wave of Abortion Bans, But Some States Are Fighting Back,' *Guttmacher Institute* (December 2019, Policy Analysis, December 10, 2019), available https://www.guttmacher.org/article/2019/12/state-policy-trends-2019-wave-abortion-bans-some-states-are-fighting-back (last retrieved April 27, 2020).

70   In *Boyd v. United States*, 116 U.S. 616 (1886), the Supreme Court recognized privacy rights in the Fourth and Fifth Amendments in a search and seizure case. Thereafter, state courts began to recognize privacy, and by 1960, the right to privacy was recognized in over thirty states. David M. O'Brien and Gordon Silverstein, *Constitutional Law and Politics: Civil Rights and Civil Liberties* (Volume 2), 11th ed. (New York: Norton, 2020), 1228–30. By the mid-twentieth century, the Supreme Court also extended the right under the Fourteenth Amendment's due process clause to protect against governmental interference in areas of child rearing and, later, to reproductive rights and marriage interests. In *Pierce v. Society of Sisters*, 268 U.S. 510 (1925), the Court struck down a state law requiring parents to send their children to public instead of private schools because it restricted parental freedom to rear and educate offspring. Although *Buck v. Bell*, 274 U.S. 200 (1927), upheld a Virginia law authorizing the compulsory sterilization of mentally challenged individuals, in *Skinner v. Oklahoma*, 316 U.S. 535 (1942), the Court nullified a state law allowing for the sterilization of "habitual criminals." Several years later, interracial marriages were legally sanctioned by the reversal of a state miscegenation law in *Loving v. Virginia*, 388 U.S. 1 (1967).

71   *Griswold v. Connecticut*, 381 U.S. 479 (1965).

72   Ibid., 484.

73   Ibid., 520 (Black, J. dissenting).

74   *Eisenstadt v. Baird*, 405 U.S. 438 (1972).

75   Ibid., 453 (Brennan, J.).

76   *Roe v. Wade*, 410 U.S. 113 (1973).

77   The movement to liberalize abortion laws prior to *Roe*, ironically, was a return to earlier pre-Civil War jurisprudence. By the mid-nineteenth century, most states permitted abortions until the first movement of the fetus, or "quickening"; and in jurisdictions criminalizing it, abortions were generally minor offenses. The growing pressure of the medical profession and antiabortionists induced states to ratchet up penalties and enforcement. By 1910, all states except Kentucky made abortions a felony, and a majority authorized them when it was necessary to save the mother's life. Still, in the 1960s and 1970s, the trend had begun to reverse itself as a minority of states condoned abortions in other circumstances, such as when the pregnancy was the result of a rape or incest, or when there was a likelihood of fetal abnormality. Four jurisdictions—Hawaii, Alaska, New York, and Washington—went so far as to abolish criminal penalties for abortions performed in

the early stages of pregnancy. Barbara Hinkson Craig and David M. O'Brien, *Abortion and American Politics* (Chatham, N.J.: Chatham House Publishers, 1993), 9–10.

[78] O'Brien and Silverstein, *Constitutional Law and Politics: Civil Rights and Civil Liberties* (Volume 2), 1234–35.

[79] 428 U.S. 52 (1976).

[80] 448 U.S. 297, 318 (J. Stewart Op. for Court).

[81] These included mandatory waiting periods, hospitalization requirements for second and third trimester abortions, physician reporting requirements for post-viability abortions, among others. Katherine Kubak, Shelby Martin, Natasha Mighell, Madison Winey and Rachel Wofford, "Abortion," *Georgetown Journal of Gender and the Law* 20 (2019): 265, 269 (citing cases).

[82] Bork, who was widely regarded as the new "swing vote" in replacing Justice Lewis Powell, generated intense interest group and media coverage because Bork had not only publicly denounced *Roe* but also intimated that he would vote to overturn it. As a result, Bork and the abortion issue polarized the nation. In the end, the pro-choice groups mobilized faster and better than their conservative counterparts, and they were instrumental in defeating Bork's claim to the bench.

[83] Jack M. Balkin, "*Roe v. Wade*: An Engine of Controversy," in *What Roe v. Wade Should Have Said: The Nation's Top Legal Experts Rewrite America's Most Controversial Decision*, edited by Jack M. Balkin (New York: New York University Press, 2005), 11–13.

[84] Katie Reilly, "Here's What Could Happen to Roe v. Wade and Abortion Rights After Justice Kennedy's Retirement," *Time* (June 28, 2018), available at https://time.com/5325124/justice-anthony-kennedy-supreme-court-roe-v-wade-overturned/ (last retrieved April 27, 2020); Dylan Matthews, "America under Brett Kavanaugh," *Vox* (October 5, 2018), available at https://www.vox.com/2018/7/11/17555974/brett-kavanaugh-anthony-kennedy-supreme-court-transform (last retrieved April 27, 2020).

[85] *Planned Parenthood of Southeastern Pennsylvania v. Casey*, 505 U.S. 833 (1992).

[86] Baskt, Laura. "Constitutionally Unconstitutional: When State Legislatures Pass Laws Contrary to Supreme Court Precedents" *U.C. Davis Law Review Online* 53 (2019): 63, 78; Claire Sweetman, "State Abortion Bans: The Future of Roe v. Wade," *Denver Law Review Forum* 97 (2019): 215, 217–18; Katherine Kubak, Shelby Martin, Natasha Mighell, Madison Winey and Rachel Wofford, "Abortion," 266.

[87] Balkin, "*Roe v. Wade*: An Engine of Controversy," 17.

[88] For example, a majority of states compel minors to notify their parents or obtain their consent before having an abortion. The Alan Guttmacher Institute, "Parental Involvement in Minors' Abortions" (as of April 1, 2020), available at https://www.guttmacher.org/state-policy/explore/parental-involvement-minors-abortions (last retrieved April 27, 2020). In *Ayotte v. Planned Parenthood of Northern New England*, 546 U.S. 320 (2006), a unanimous Roberts Court returned the case to the lower courts to reconsider whether New Hampshire's law, which barred abortions for minors until forty-eight hours after a parent was notified, was appropriate because the law did not have a medical emergency exception to protect the pregnant teen's health. The Court suggested that the entire law should be invalidated, however, if it did not have a medical exception.

[89] Alan Guttmacher Institute, "Bans on Specific Abortion Methods Used After the First Trimester" (as of April 1, 2020), available from https://www.guttmacher.org/state-policy/explore/bans-specific-abortion-methods-used-after-first-trimester (last retrieved April 27, 2020).

[90] 530 U.S. 914 (2000).

[91] 550 U.S. 124 (2007).

[92] See Alan Guttmacher Institute, "Bans on Specific Abortion Methods Used After the First Trimester" (as of January 1, 2020).

[93] *June Medical Services LLC v. Russo*, 140 S.Ct. 2103 (U.S. Jun. 29, 2020).

[94] 136 S.Ct. 2292 (2016).

[95] *June Medical Services LLC v. Russo* (CJ Roberts, concurring in the result). See also, *Whole Woman's Health v. Hellerstedt*, 136 S.Ct. 2292, 2309 (2016) (J. Breyer, Op. for Court) (articulating the benefits and burden standard); and, *Planned Parenthood of Southeastern Pennsylvania v. Casey*, 505 U.S. 833 (1992). As some commentators note, *Hellerstedt* stressed that the *Casey* undue burden test, as applied, requires courts to "consider the burdens a law imposes on abortion access together with the benefits those law confer," which, as applied to the Texas law, placed a substantial obstacle in the path of women seeking abortions. Mary Ziegler, "The

New Negative Rights: Abortion Funding and Constitutional Law after Whole Woman's Health v. Hellerstedt." *Nebraska Law Review* 96 (2018): 577–623.

96   Gretchen Borchelt, "Symposium: *June Medical Services v. Russo:* When a 'win' is not a win," *SCOTUSblog* (June 30, 2020), available at https://www.scotusblog.com/2020/06/symposium-june-medical-services-v-russo-when-a-win-is-not-a-win/ (last retrieved June 30, 2020).

97   See Ziegler, "The New Negative Rights: Abortion Funding and Constitutional Law after Whole Woman's Health v. Hellerstedt," 577, 619.

98   Thomas M. Keck, "Beyond Backlash: Assessing the Impact of Judicial Decisions on LGBT Rights," *Law & Society Review* 43 (2009), 151, 152.

99   Wheeler concludes that judicial impact research presents a number of methodological, theoretical and topical challenges. Darren A. Wheeler, "Methodological, Theoretical and Topical Challenges in Judicial Implementation and Impact Studies," *Indiana Journal of Political Science* 13 (2011), 18–26.

100   Alexander Hamilton, "Federalist No. 78," in *The Federalist Papers*, ed. Clinton Rossiter (New York: Mentor, 1961), 465.

101   Wheeler, "Methodological, Theoretical and Topical Challenges in Judicial Implementation and Impact Studies," 18.

102   Ibid., 19.

103   See Bradley C. Canon and Charles A. Johnson, *Judicial Policies: Implementation and Impact*, 2nd ed. (Washington, D.C.: CQ Press, 1999), 2–3.

104   567 U.S. 519 (2012).

105   One health insurance authority reports that in 2020 there are 13 state-based exchanges, 6 federally supported exchanges, 6 state-partnership exchanges, and 26 federally facilitated exchanges. Louise Norris, "States vary considerably in terms of how they manage their insurance markets and health insurance exchanges" (November 18, 2019), *HealthInsurance.org*, available at https://www.healthinsurance.org/state-health-insurance-exchanges/ (last retrieved April 27, 2020).

106   With the Tax Cuts and Jobs Act of 2017, Congress established that the penalty for not buying health insurance would be zero, essentially nullifying in, even though the remainder of the ACA was left undisturbed. Amy Howe, "House, blue states ask justices to uphold Affordable Care Act," *Scotusblog* (January 3, 2020), available at https://www.scotusblog.com/2020/01/house-blue-states-ask-justices-to-uphold-affordable-care-act/#more-291055 (last retrieved April 27, 2020). See also Daniel Béland, Philip Rocco and Alex Waddan. "Obamacare in the Trump Era: Where are we Now, and Where are we Going?," *Political Quarterly* 89 (4, October–December 2018): 687–94; Christopher P. Banks, "Of White Whales, Obamacare, and the Robert's Court: The Republican Attempts to Harpoon Obama's Presidential Legacy," *Political Science and Politics* 50 (1, January 2017): 40–43.

107   Sheryl Gay Stolberg, "Trump Administration Asks Supreme Court to Strike Down Affordable Care Act," *New York Times* (June 26, 2020), available https://www.nytimes.com/2020/06/26/us/politics/obamacare-trump-administration-supreme-court.html (last retrieved July 4, 2020). See also, Howe, "House, blue states ask justices to uphold Affordable Care Act," *Scotusblog* (January 3, 2020). See also, SCOTUSblog, "Texas v. California," available at https://www.scotusblog.com/case-files/cases/texas-v-california/ (last retrieved April 27, 2020).

108   Banks, "Of White Whales, Obamacare, and the Robert's Court: The Republican Attempts to Harpoon Obama's Presidential Legacy," 40.

109   *Brown v. Board of Education*, 347 U.S. 483 (1954).

110   347 U.S. 483 (1954).

111   163 U.S. 537 (1896).

112   *Korematsu v. U.S.*, 323 U.S. 214 (1944).

113   See Dylan Scott, "2 Public Health Crises Have Collided in the Protests Over George Floyd's Death," *Vox* (June 1, 2020), available at https://www.vox.com/2020/6/1/21276957/george-floyd-protests-coronavirus-police-brutality-racism (last retrieved July 4, 2020); Jon Meacham, "The Power of a President's Words," *Time Magazine* 194 (6, August 19, 2019), 29–30.

114   *Plessy*, 163 U.S. 537 (1896).

115   *Bolling v. Sharpe*, 347 U.S. 497 (1954).

[116] *Brown v. Board of Education*, 349 U.S. 294 (1955), (Brown II).

[117] O'Brien and Silverstein, *Constitutional Law and Politics: Civil Rights and Civil Liberties*, 1380.

[118] As quoted in Michael J. Klarman, *From Jim Crow to Civil Rights: The Supreme Court and the Struggle for Racial Equality* (New York: Oxford University Press, 2004), 324. See also Klarman, *From Jim Crow to Civil Rights*, 320, 344–45.

[119] Klarman, *From Jim Crow to Civil Rights*, 362–63.

[120] *Swann v. Charlotte-Mecklenberg Board of Education*, 402 U.S. 1 (1971); *Milliken v. Bradley*, 418 U.S. 717 (1974).

[121] *Missouri v. Jenkins*, 495 U.S. 33 (1990).

[122] *Board of Education of Oklahoma City Public Schools v. Dowell*, 498 U.S. 237 (1991).

[123] *Freeman v. Pitts*, 503 U.S. 467 (1992).

[124] O'Brien and Silverstein, *Constitutional Law and Politics: Civil Rights and Civil Liberties*, 1385.

[125] *Parents Involved in Community Schools v. Seattle School District No. 1*, 551 U.S. 701 (2007).

[126] Ibid., 798–99, 803 (J. Stevens, dissenting). See also, ibid., 748 (C.J. Roberts, Opinion for the Court).

[127] See, e.g., Gerald N. Rosenberg, *The Hollow Hope: Can Courts Bring About Social Change?* (Chicago: University of Chicago Press, 1991).

[128] David M. O'Brien, *Storm Center: The Supreme Court in American Politics*, 11th ed. (New York: Norton, 2020), 334.

[129] *Lawrence v. Texas*, 539 U.S. 558 (2003).

[130] Bradley C. Canon and Charles A. Johnson, *Judicial Policies: Implementation and Impact*, 2nd ed. (Washington, D.C.: CQ Press, 1998).

[131] *Lawrence v. Texas*, 539 U.S. 558 (2003).

[132] *Bowers v. Hardwick*, 478 U.S. 186 (1986).

[133] See, e.g., *Lawrence*, 539 U.S. 558, 571–72, 576–77 (J. Kennedy, Opinion for the Court").

[134] In the words of dissenting Justice Antonin Scalia, *Lawrence* "leaves on pretty shaky grounds state laws limiting marriage to opposite-sex couples." *Lawrence*, 601 (Scalia, J. dissenting).

[135] See William N. Eskridge, Jr., *Equality Practice: Civil Unions and the Future of Gay Rights* (New York: Routledge, 2002), 16–82. Also, before *Lawrence*, two state appellate courts, in Vermont and Hawaii, and a lower court in Alaska extended some legal protections to homosexual relationships. *Baehr v. Lewin*, 852 P.2d 44 (Haw. 1993); *Brause v. Bureau of Vital Statistics*, 1998 WL 88743 (Alaska Sup.Ct 1998); *Baker v. Vermont*, 744 A.2d 864 (Vermont 1999). In both Hawaii and Alaska, however, the popular assembly subsequently amended their constitutions to limit marriage to opposite-sex couples. Jason Pierceson, *Same-Sex Marriage: The Road to the Supreme Court and Beyond* (Lanham, Md.: Rowman and Littlefield, 2014), 93–103.

[136] Frederick Liu and Stephen Macedo, "The Federal Marriage Amendment and the Strange Evolution of the Conservative Case Against Gay Marriage," *PS: Political Science & Politics* (April 2005), 211–15.

[137] *Goodridge v. Department of Health*, 798 N.E.2d 941 (Mass. 2003). Shortly after *Goodridge*, the state senate drafted a "civil unions" bill and forwarded to the court for an advisory opinion about whether those arrangements complied with *Goodridge*. The justices rejected civil unions because they reduced gays and lesbians to "second-class citizens." This allowed Massachusetts to begin granting marriage licenses. Michael J. Klarman, *From the Closet to the Altar: Courts, Backlash, and the Struggle for Same-Sex Marriage* (New York: Oxford University Press, 2013), 91–92. See also *Opinions of the Justices to the Senate*, 802 N.E.2d 565 (2004).

[138] Klarman, *From the Closet to the Altar*, 90–105.

[139] Klarman, *From the Closet to the Altar*, 105–6. See also Kavan Peterson, "Same-Sex Unions—A Constitutional Race," available at http://www.stateline.org/live/ViewPage.action?siteNodeId=136&languageId=1&contentId=20695 (last retrieved August 20, 2020).

[140] In 2006–2007, the Georgia, Maryland, New Jersey, New York, and Washington state supreme courts ruled against same-sex marriages under their state constitutions, whereas, in 2008–2009, Connecticut, California, and Iowa state supreme courts ruled in favor of it under their state constitutions. Moreover, though New Jersey's high court did not find same-sex marriage to be a "fundamental right," it held that denying same-sex state benefits was an equal protection violation. Pierceson, *Same-Sex Marriage*, 126–31, 151–59; Klarman, *From the Closet to the Altar*, 116 n. 142, 120–32.

[141] Patrick J. Egan and Kenneth Sherrill, "Marriage and the Shifting Priorities of a New Generation of Lesbians and Gays," *PS: Political Science & Politics* (April 2005), 229–32. See also Pierceson, *Same-Sex Marriage*, 151 (noting that "relationship equality policies" increased without help from the courts); Klarman, *From the Closet to the Altar*, 119 (surveying growing trend of public support for, and recognition of, same-sex legal rights and benefits).

[142] *Kerrigan v. Commissioner of Public Health*, 957 A.2d 407 (Conn. 2008); *In re Marriage Cases*, 183 P.3d 384 (Calif. 2008); *Varnum v. Brien*, 763 N.W.2d 862 (Iowa 2009).

[143] Klarman, *From the Closet to the Altar*, 143–55; Pierceson, *Same-Sex Marriage*, 126–33, 154–60; see also Miranda Blue, "Iowa Republicans Threaten to Cut Salaries of Judges Who Backed Marriage Equality (April 24, 2013)," available at www.rightwingwatch.org (last retrieved July 28, 2014).

[144] *U.S. v. Windsor*, 570 U.S. 744 (2013).

[145] *Hollingsworth v. Perry*, 570 U.S. 693 (2013).

[146] Pierceson, *Same-Sex Marriage*, 243.

[147] See Robert Barnes, "Appeals Court Upholds Bans on Same-Sex Marriage for First Time," *Washington Post* (November 6, 2014), available at www.washingtonpost.com (last retrieved November 10, 2014). See also Pierceson, *Same-Sex Marriage*, 248 (observing that the "right to travel," as part of the Supreme Court's Fourteenth Amendment privileges or immunities clause, is part of new litigation pressing for interstate recognition of same-sex marriages). See also, *Obergefell v. Hodges*, 576 U.S. 644 (2015); ibid., 2612 (C.J. Roberts, dissenting); ibid., 2631 (J. Thomas, dissenting).

[148] *Bostock v. Clayton County*, 140 S.Ct. 1731 (2020).

[149] Ibid., (J. Kavanaugh, dissenting), 146; ibid., (J. Alito, dissenting, joined by J. Thomas), 38; and, ibid., (J. Gorsuch, 13).

[150] Loren AliKhan, "Symposium: A trio of cases, a lot at stake," *Scotusblog* (September 9, 2019), available at https://www.scotusblog.com/2019/09/symposium-a-trio-of-cases-a-lot-at-stake/ (last retrieved April 27, 2020). See also, Amy Howe, "Argument analysis: Justices divided on federal protections for LGBT employees (UPDATED)," *Scotusblog* (October 8, 2019), available at https://www.scotusblog.com/2019/10/argument-analysis-justices-divided-on-federal-protections-for-lgbt-employees/ (last retrieved April 27, 2020).

[151] Jack Phillips, "Third Discrimination Suit Filed Against Masterpiece Cakeshop," *4CBS Denver* (June 6, 2019), available at https://denver.cbslocal.com/2019/06/06/discrimination-lawsuit-lakewood-jack-phillips-masterpiece-cakeshop/ (last retrieved April 27, 2020). See also, *Arlene's Flowers Inc. v. Washington*, *Scotusblog (Pending Petition)*, available at https://www.scotusblog.com/case-files/cases/arlenes-flowers-inc-v-washington-2/ (last retrieved April 27, 2020); and, *Masterpiece Cakeshop, Ltd. v. Colorado Civil Rights Commission*, 138 S. Ct. 1719 (2018).

[152] *Marbury v. Madison*, 5 U.S. 137 (1803), 180.

[153] World Justice Project, "The Rule of Law," available at https://worldjusticeproject.org/about-us/overview/what-rule-law (last retrieved April 27, 2020).

[154] Cardozo, *The Nature of the Judicial Process*, 141.

[155] Henry J. Abraham, *The Judicial Process*, 7th ed. (New York: Oxford University Press, 1998), 359–60.

[156] Alex Kozinski, "What I Ate for Breakfast and Other Mysteries of Judicial Decision-Making," *Loyola of Los Angeles Law Review* 26 (Summer, 1993), 993, 994.

[157] Ibid., 994–95. See also, Neal Devins and Lawrence Baum. *The Company They Keep: How Partisan Divisions Came to the Supreme Court* (New York: Oxford University Press, 2019) (arguing judges seek approval from elite social, legal and political networks).

[158] Tom S. Clark, *The Limits of Judicial Independence* (New York: Cambridge University Press, 2012).

[159] Kozinski, "What I Ate for Breakfast and Other Mysteries of Judicial Decision-Making," 995–96. Eskridge reports that the Civil Rights Act of 1991 overrode a total of twelve Supreme Court rulings. William N. Eskridge, Jr., "Overriding Supreme Court Statutory Interpretation Decisions," *Yale Law Journal* 101 (November 1991), 331, 332 n. 4 (listing cases).

[160] Marissa Endicott, "Iowa's Supreme Court Protected Gay Marriage and Abortion Rights—and Republican Lawmakers Are Out for Payback," *Mother Jones* (April 8, 2019), available at https://www.motherjones.com/politics/2019/04/iowas-supreme-court-protected-gay-marriage-and-abortion-rights-and-republican-lawmakers-are-out-for-payback/ (last retrieved April 27, 2020). See also, Associated Press, "Judges

in S.D. May Lose Lawsuit Immunity," *New York Times* (November 14, 2005), available at www.nytimes.com (last retrieved November 15, 2005).

161 Bill Chappell, "Virginia Ratifies The Equal Rights Amendment, Decades After The Deadline," *NPR (Politics)*(January 15, 2020), available at https://www.npr.org/2020/01/15/796754345/virginia-ratifies-the-equal-rights-amendment-decades-after-deadline (last retrieved April 27, 2020).

162 Ballotpedia, "Amending State Constitutions," available at https://ballotpedia.org/Amending_state_constitutions (last retrieved April 27, 2020).

163 See Graziella Romeo, "The Recognition of Same-Sex Couples' Rights in the US Between Counter-Majoritarian Principle and Ideological Approaches: A State Level Perspective," in *Same-Sex Couples' Before National, Supranational and International Jurisdictions*, eds. Daniele Gall, Luca Paladini, and Pietro Pustorino (Berlin/Heidelberg: Springer, 2014), 21. See also Klarman, *From the Closet to the Altar*, 107–9.

164 Christopher P. Banks, *Judicial Politics in the D.C. Circuit Court* (Baltimore: John Hopkins University Press, 1999), 26–32.

165 Deborah J. Barrow and Thomas G. Walker, *A Court Divided: The Fifth Circuit Court of Appeals and the Politics of Judicial Reform* (New Haven, Conn.: Yale University Press, 1988), 68.

166 Christopher P. Banks, "The Politics of Court Reform in the U.S. Courts of Appeals," *Judicature* 84 (2000), 34–43.

167 *Employment Division, Department of Human Resources of Oregon v. Smith*, 494 U.S. 872 (1990).

168 *City of Boerne v. Flores*, 521 U.S. 507 (1997).

169 Pablo T. Spiller and Emerson H. Tiller, "Invitations to Override: Congressional Reversals of Supreme Court Decisions," *International Review of Law and Economics* 16 (1996), 503–21.

170 Congressional Research Service, *Constitution Annotated: Analysis and Interpretation of the U.S. Constitution* (Table of Laws Held Unconstitutional in Whole or in Part by the Supreme Court), available at https://constitution.congress.gov/resources/unconstitutional-laws/ (last retrieved January 22, 2020).

171 Matthew R. Christiansen and William N. Eskridge, Jr., "Congressional Overrides of Supreme Court Statutory Interpretation Decisions, 1967–2011," *Texas Law Review* 92 (2014), 1317–541. See also Eskridge, "Overriding Supreme Court Statutory Interpretation Decisions," 331–424.

172 See Jeb Barnes, *Overruled? Legislative Overrides, Pluralism, and Contemporary Court-Congress Relations* (Stanford, Calif.: Stanford University Press, 2004).

173 *Worcester v. Georgia*, 31 U.S. 515 (1832).

174 Abraham, *The Judicial Process*, 370.

175 *DeRolph v. Ohio*, 677 N.E.2d 733 (Ohio 1997).

176 The Ohio Supreme Court, in fact, has terminated educational financing review because of the assembly's repeated failure to act to fix the constitutional violation. *State v. Lewis*, 789 N.E.2d 195 (Ohio 2003).

177 R. Shep Melnick, "The Courts, Jurisprudence, and the Executive Branch," in *The Executive Branch*, eds. Joel D. Aberbach and Mark A. Peterson (New York: Oxford University Press, 2005), 470.

178 Keith E. Whittington, " 'Interpose Your Friendly Hand': Political Supports for the Exercise of Judicial Review by the United States Supreme Court," *American Political Science Review* (November 2005), 583–96.

179 Melnick, "The Courts, Jurisprudence, and the Executive Branch," 476–79.

180 Paul Nolette. 2015. *Federalism on Trial: State Attorneys General and National Policymaking in Contemporary America*. Lawrence, KS: Kansas University Press.

181 Barry Friedman, *The Will of the People: How Public Opinion Has Influenced the Supreme Court and Shaped the Meaning of the Constitution* (New York: Farrar, Straus and Giroux, 2009), 367.

182 William H. Rehnquist, "Constitutional Law and Public Opinion," *Suffolk University Law Review* 20 (Winter, 1986): 751, 768.

183 Devins and Baum, *The Company They Keep: How Partisan Divisions Came to the Supreme Court*, 9. See also, Lawrence Baum, *Judges and Their Audiences* (Princeton: Princeton University Press, 2006); Kevin T. McGuire and James A. Stimson, "The Least Dangerous Branch Revisited: New Evidence on Supreme Court Responsiveness to Public Preferences," *Journal of Politics* (November 2004), 1018–35.

184 See Joseph Daniel Ura and Alison Higgins Merrill, "The Supreme Court and Public Opinion." In *The Oxford Handbook of U.S. Judicial Behavior*, edited by Lee Epstein and Stefanie A. Lindquist (New York: Oxford

University Press, 2017), 433; Banks, "Of White Whales, Obamacare, and the Robert's Court: The Republican Attempts to Harpoon Obama's Presidential Legacy".

[185] Louis Fisher, *Constitutional Dialogues: Interpretation as Political Process* (Princeton, N.J.: Princeton University Press, 1988). See also, Ura and Merrill, "The Supreme Court and Public Opinion," 446–47 (summarizing law and courts' literature on the issue of the mass public's influence on judicial behavior).

[186] Joe McIntyre, *The Judicial Function* (Singapore: Springer, 2019), 295.

[187] National Center for State Courts, "The State of State Courts: A 2019 NCSC Public Opinion Survey," available at https://www.ncsc.org/Topics/Court-Community/Public-Trust-and-Confidence/Resource-Guide/2019-State-of-State-Courts-Survey.aspx (last retrieved April 27, 2020), 1.

[188] Ibid., 2–4.

[189] See, e.g., American Bar Association, Commission on the Future of Legal Services, *Report on the Future of Legal Services in the United States* (2016), available at https://www.americanbar.org/content/dam/aba/images/abanews/2016FLSReport_FNL_WEB.pdf (last retrieved April 27, 2020); Christopher P. Banks, *The American Legal Profession: The Myths and Realities of Practicing Law* (Thousand Oaks, CA.: Sage/CQ Press, 2017) (ch. 1, 5).

Glossary

Administrative office of the courts: An administrative agency of the state judiciary that collects workload statistics, performs budgetary functions, handles personnel matters, and discharges miscellaneous functions that are related to the mission and operation of courts.

Adversarial (legal system): Legal institutions and legal practices within the legal system that are designed to find the truth through accusatorial methods. Evidence is gathered by the parties and lawyers and presented to a neutral fact-finder (either a judge or a jury) to resolve legal disputes. Common law jurisdictions use adversarial legal institutions, procedures, and practices.

Adversarial model: See *Adversarial legal system.*

Advisory opinion: An opinion or interpretation of law that does not have binding effect. The Supreme Court does not give advisory opinions, for example, on hypothetical disputes; it decides only actual cases or controversies.

Advocates: Lawyers who use their professional skills to advocate their clients' interests in trial court litigation.

Affirm: In an appellate court, to reach a decision that agrees with the result reached in a case by the lower court.

Affirmative action programs: Programs required by federal or state laws designed to remedy discriminatory practices by hiring minority-group persons and/or women.

***Alford* plea:** A plea of guilty in a criminal prosecution that lets defendants plead guilty while protesting their innocence.

Amicus curiae: A friend of the court, a person not a party to litigation, who volunteers or is invited by the court to give their view on a case.

Appeal: To take a case to a higher court for review. Generally, a party losing in a trial court may appeal once to an appellate court as a matter of right. If the party loses in the appellate court, appeal to a higher court is within the discretion of the higher court. Most appeals to the Supreme Court are within its discretion to deny or grant a hearing.

Appeal by permission: A discretionary appeal that appeals courts have the power to decide or not, even if there is an adverse trial court decision.

Appeal by right: A mandatory appeal that appeals courts must decide because the parties have a right to appeal an adverse trial court decision.

Appellate jurisdiction: A court's power to review appeals from trial courts.

Assigned counsel systems: A public defender system that lets judges appoint members of the local bar to represent clients as a public defender on a case-by-case basis.

Attitudinal model: A social science research methodology that asserts that appellate court decisions are solely based on the ideological attitudes and policy preferences of judges and not "the law."

Bench memorandum: An informal legal analysis written by appellate court law clerks that details an appeal's facts, legal issues, and legal authorities. The memo is often shared with other law clerks and judge's chambers during the appellate court decision-making process.

Bipartisan model (of judicial selection): A model of judicial selection that is used by Republican and Democratic presidents to appoint judges to federal courts. Typically, a judicial appointment is based on a candidate's professional qualifications in combination with patronage (to reward loyalty to a political party) or symbolic representation (to "represent" a specific race, gender, or ethnicity) criteria.

Blue slip: A Senate tradition in which a form on blue paper is sent by the chair of the Senate Judiciary Committee requesting if a senator from the nominee's home state approves or disapproves of the president's judicial appointment. An approval is signified by returning the blue slip; disapproval is signified by not returning the blue slip.

Brief: A document prepared by counsel to serve as the basis for an argument in court, setting out the facts and legal arguments in support of a case.

Career judiciary: A professional judiciary akin to civil service, based on competition examinations, requiring specialized education, and under strict supervision by higher courts; in contrast to U.S. judiciaries that are staffed by judges who are generalists by training and selected through a political process.

Case: A general term for an action, cause, suit, or controversy, at law or equity; a question contested before a court.

Casebook method: A method of legal instruction that allows students to learn legal principles by studying appellate opinions from a casebook that is devoted to a specific legal subject, such as contracts, torts, corporations, civil procedure, or criminal law.

Cert. pool: Since 1972, a majority of Supreme Court justices (except now for Justice Alito) have their clerks join in a *cert.* pool that screens and recommends which cases should be granted review. (See also *Certiorari*, writ of.)

Certiorari, writ of: A writ issued from the Supreme Court, at its discretion and at the request of a petitioner, to order a lower court to send the record of a case to the Court for its review.

Challenge for cause: A formal procedure that excuses a potential juror from jury service based on "cause," or a reason that establishes that the person cannot evaluate the evidence in a jury trial fairly due to personal bias.

Civil law: The body of law dealing with the private rights of individuals, as distinguished from criminal law.

Civil law system: A legal system that is based on codified law, or legal codes enacted by the legislature. Most European countries use civil law systems but they are also found in Asia, Latin America, South America, and parts of the Caribbean.

Civil procedure: A body of formal rules by which courts conduct trials to resolve private disputes.

Class action: A lawsuit brought by one person or group on behalf of all persons similarly situated.

Classic Democratic model (of judicial selection): A model of judicial selection that is used by Democratic presidents to appoint judges to federal courts. Typically, it rewards those who are faithful to the political party, and less attention is paid to achieving policy goals through the appointment. Sometimes, the president appoints judges as a "symbol" to represent a specific race, gender, or ethnicity.

Clear and convincing standard: A standard of legal proof in civil cases that requires the plaintiff to prove at trial a defendant's liability by a greater certainty, or beyond a mere probability, that the allegations are true.

Clerk of court: A public employee of a court who administers court operations, including record keeping, establishing court calendars, scheduling cases, and maintaining the flow of litigation between judges, attorneys, and the public.

Codification movement: See *Field Codes*.

Collegiality: A professional norm that characterizes the close interpersonal working relationships between groups of "colleagues," or appellate court judges, who decide appeals.

Common law: The collection of principles and rules, particularly from unwritten English law, that derive their authority from long-standing usage and custom or from courts recognizing and enforcing those customs.

Compelling (state) interest: A test used to uphold state action against First Amendment and equal protection challenges because of the serious need for government action (see *Strict scrutiny test*).

Compensatory damages: An award of money that attempts to put the injured parties in a civil lawsuit back to the position they were in before they suffered harm by the defendant's wrongdoing after liability is established.

Competitive private contract systems: A public defender system that allows lawyers, law firms, and legal nonprofit organizations to represent clients as a public defender through a competitive bidding process.

Complaint: A formal court document filed in civil cases that alleges the court's jurisdiction, the legal allegations of the legal dispute, and a statement of legal remedies or damages that the injured party is entitled to if liability and causation are established.

Compliance: A description of how a judicial opinion is followed or not by other officials or institutional actors who must interpret what the opinion means as law. (See *Implementation* and *Judicial impact*.)

Concurrent jurisdiction: The power of federal and state courts to decide the same type of case.

Contingency fee: An agreement between lawyers and clients in civil lawsuits that stipulates that legal fees are only paid as a percentage of the total amount of monetary damages recovered.

Contract: An agreement between two or more persons that creates a legal obligation to do or not do a particular thing. Often the law of contracts structure commercial transactions.

Corrective justice: A typology of justice that attempts to correct a legal wrong by imposing appropriate punishments or sanctions on those who break the law and cause harm to innocent parties.

Counter claim: A formal court document filed in civil cases that is filed by a defendant who raises new allegations against the plaintiff.

Countermajoritarian(ism): The power exercised by courts when overturning majoritarian preferences that are expressed in legislative enactments during the process of interpreting the Constitution's meaning.

Court unification movement: A reform movement to improve the judicial administration of state courts.

Crime control model: A model of criminal justice created by Herbert Packer that is associated with the swift prosecution of criminal defendants in an "assembly line" fashion, presuming that defendants are guilty as charged.

Criminal law: The body of law that deals with the enforcement of laws and the punishment of persons who, by breaking laws, commit crimes against the state.

Critical legal studies: An approach that critiques law and legal reasoning by arguing that judges use deductive reasoning and formal rules as a pretext to reach results that are based on personal preferences.

Critical race theory: A legal theory arguing that law and legal institutions are deeply ingrained with racism. Racism is socially constructed and manipulated by the dominant white legal, economic, and political power structure.

Customary law: Law based on social customs enforced by the community.

Declaratory judgment: A court pronouncement declaring a legal right or interpretation but not ordering a special action.

Declaratory theory of law: A legal theory or philosophy of legal positivism that holds that judges do not have the power or discretion to make law because they can only discover and declare the law.

De facto: In fact, in reality.

Defendant: In a civil action, the party denying or defending itself against charges brought by a plaintiff. In a criminal action, the person indicted for the commission of an offense.

De jure: As a result of law, as a result of official action.

Determinate sentencing: Sentences imposed by judges that are based on a combination of retribution and deterrence policies.

Deterrence: A punishment rationale in criminal cases that exacts a punishment on the basis that it will deter persons from committing crimes in the future.

Discovery rules, civil: The formal rules of civil procedure that govern the operation of civil cases.

Discretionary jurisdiction: Jurisdiction that a court may accept or reject in particular cases. The Supreme Court has discretionary jurisdiction in over 90 percent of the cases that come to it.

Distributive justice: A typology of justice that attempts to fix inequalities between legal parties by fairly distributing legal benefits and legal burdens to all members of society.

Docket: All cases filed in a court.

Due process: Fair and regular procedure. The Fifth and Fourteenth Amendments guarantee persons that they will not be deprived of life, liberty, or property by the government until fair and usual procedures have been followed.

Due process model: A model of criminal justice created by Herbert Packer that is associated with achieving fairness through the imposition of formal procedural rules, allowing criminal defendants to pass through an "obstacle course" that slows down the efficacy of criminal prosecutions, based on the presumption that defendants are innocent until proven guilty.

Empirical legal studies: A research methodology developed in the legal academy that uses statistical modeling and quantitative methods from the social sciences to explain judicial decision-making.

En banc: "In the bench." An appellate court ruling that is decided by all of its judges, not just a panel or group of three.

Equal Protection Clause: The guarantee that no person or class of persons shall be denied the same protection of the law in their lives, liberty, and property.

Equity: A special set of legal rules in common law legal systems that allow parties to get legal relief under circumstances in which the law, as applied, cannot adequately remedy an injustice under the facts of a legal case.

Exclusionary rule: This rule commands that evidence obtained in violation of the rights guaranteed by the Fourth and Fifth Amendments must be excluded at trial.

Ex parte: From, or on, only one side. Application to a court for some ruling or action on behalf of only one party.

Felony: An offense in criminal law that has a punishment of fines or incarceration of more than one year.

Field Codes: Five volumes of substantive and procedural codes law that were drafted in New York by David Dudley Field and other reformers between 1847 and 1865. As part of the "codification movement" in the United States, they were designed to simplify the common law and its pleadings, forms, and practices in the common law system.

Fight theory: A theory of the adversarial common law system developed by Judge Jerome Frank. The theory criticized the operation of the common law because lawyers representing parties are only interested in winning the legal case through adversarial combat, and not discovering the facts or truth underlying legal disputes.

Filibuster: A Senate procedure in which a senator can elect to continue to debate a president's judicial appointment, thus preventing the nomination from getting an up-or-down vote on confirmation by the full Senate.

Game theory: A social science theory that posits appellate judges make strategic choices to set a court's agenda and decide appeals.

General jurisdiction, court of: A court that has the power to decide a general set of legal issues, such as civil and criminal cases that are more serious in subject matter and possible legal consequences or punishments.

Grand jury: A jury of twelve to twenty-three persons that hears in private evidence for serving an indictment.

Habeas corpus: Literally, "you have the body"; a writ issued to inquire whether a person is lawfully imprisoned or detained. The writ demands that the persons holding the prisoner justify his detention or release him.

Implementation: A description of how officials and institutional actors interpret the meaning of judicial opinions when they implement them as statements of legal and public policy. (See *Compliance* and *Judicial impact*.)

Incapacitation: A punishment rationale that posits that removing an offender from society, primarily through incarceration, inherently protects the community from additional crimes being committed by that offender, thus promoting public safety.

Indeterminate sentencing: Sentences imposed by judges after considering a broad range of minimum and maximum punishments to sanction offenders.

Indictment: A formal charge of offenses based on evidence presented by a prosecutor from a grand jury.

***In forma pauperis*:** In the manner of a pauper, without liability for the costs of filing cases before a court.

Information: A written set of charges, similar to an indictment, filed by a prosecutor but without a grand jury's consideration of evidence.

Initial appearance hearing: A court proceeding in which those accused of a crime appear before a magistrate or judge generally within forty-eight hours of arrest for the purpose of being informed of the charges they face in a criminal prosecution.

Injunction: A court order prohibiting a person from performing a particular act.

Inquisitorial (legal system): Legal institutions and legal practices within the legal system are structured to find the truth by following specific legal procedures under a written code of law. It is nonaccusatorial. Civil law jurisdictions use inquisitorial legal institutions, procedures, and practices.

Inquisitorial model: See *Inquisitorial legal system*.

Interpretivism: A method of constitutional interpretation that gives strict construction to textual language in the context of its historical meaning.

Judgment: The official decision of a court.

Judicial accountability: A principle establishing that the judiciary is not "above the law" because it must be held accountable by majoritarian and democratic processes.

Judicial discretion: The capacity of judges to make legal decisions using judgment and reason.

Judicial federalism: The independence and interrelationship of federal and state courts.

Judicial impact: A description of how a judicial opinion, as law, affects the legal system, society, and public policy. (See *Compliance* and *Implementation*.)

Judicial independence: A principle establishing that the judiciary must be insulated from ordinary politics and the biases and pressures exerted upon courts by political institutions, such as the legislative or executive branches.

Judicial "merit" plans: A judicial selection method using a combination of appointment and elective mechanisms to staff state courts with judges that have "merit," or nonpolitical qualifications.

Judicial review: The power to review and strike down any legislation or other government action that is inconsistent with federal or state constitutions. The Supreme Court reviews government action only under the Constitution of the United States and federal laws.

Judicial self-restraint: A description of judicial behavior that asserts that courts or judges are constrained by law in using their authority to decide legal cases.

Jurisdiction: The power of a court to hear a case or controversy, which exists when the proper parties are present and when the point to be decided is among the issues authorized to be handled by a particular court.

Jus commune: The "law of the community," which is part of the basic codes found in civil law countries and adopted by some European states. It encompasses the civil code, the commercial code, the code of civil procedure, the penal code, and the code of criminal procedure.

Justiciability: A controversy in which a claim of right is asserted against another who has an interest in contesting it. Courts will consider only justiciable controversies, as distinguished from hypothetical disputes.

Legal model: A social science research methodology that stands in contrast to the attitudinal model. It asserts that appellate court decisions are based on legal factors, such as precedent and judicial legal philosophies.

Legal remedy: The specific legal relief that is granted by a court, jury, or agreement of the parties to a lawsuit that resolves a legal matter.

Legal system: A set of institutional structures, procedures, and rules for applying the law and giving it substantive content.

Legislative intent: The meaning judges give to written law in the course of deciding how to interpret ambiguous statutes enacted by the legislature.

Life-without-possibility-of-parole laws: Sentences that impose a penalty of life imprisonment without the possibility of parole. Used in states that have the death penalty or not; but, in part, they are designed to provide an alternative to the death penalty.

Limited jurisdiction, court of: A court that has the power to decide a narrow set of legal issues, such as traffic, minor civil, and less serious nonfelony criminal cases.

Magistrate judges: Judicial officers who serve in the U.S. district courts. They are appointed by district judges and decide almost all types of federal trial court cases except for felony criminal cases.

***Mandamus,* writ of:** "We command"; an order issued from a superior court directing a lower court or other government authority to perform a particular act.

Mandatory jurisdiction: Jurisdiction that a court must accept. The Supreme Court must decide cases coming under its appellate jurisdiction, though it may avoid giving them plenary consideration.

Mandatory-minimum sentences: Punishments in criminal law that require offenders to serve minimum sentences before becoming eligible for parole.

Mega-firms: Large, elite corporate law firms that deliver legal services domestically and across the globe.

Misdemeanors: Offenses that are punishable in criminal law that have a punishment of fines or incarceration of less than one year.

Missouri merit plan: A type of judicial selection method that Missouri adopted in 1940 and that uses appointment-elective mechanisms to staff state courts with judges who have "merit," or nonpolitical qualifications.

Mixed election: A method of judicial selection used in Michigan. Nonpartisan elections select trial and intermediate courts of appeals judges, but partisan nomination and nonpartisan elections select court of last resort judges.

Moot: Unsettled, undecided. A moot question is also one that is no longer material, or that has already been resolved, and has become hypothetical.

Motion: A written or oral application to a court or judge to obtain a rule or order.

Motion practice: The use of formal motions by a party to a lawsuit that ask the court to grant a specific type of request in that party's favor, such as a court decision to dismiss an action, or to exclude evidence, among others. They are often used in the pre-trial phase of litigation, such as the discovery process to gain and exchange information between opposing parties, and their operation is defined by the governing procedural rules of court.

Natural court: A period of stable membership in which there are fewer reversals.

Natural law: A legal philosophy that conceptualizes law in divine terms, or as God's law.

Natural rights: Rights based on the nature of man and independent of those rights secured by man-made, positive laws.

Negligence: The failure to do something that a reasonable person would do.

New institutionalism: An interdisciplinary social science research methodology that asserts judicial decision-making is the result of institutional arrangements, legal practices, and judicial norms that underlie American political development.

***Nolo contendere*:** A plea of guilty in a criminal prosecution that admits only that the government probably has enough evidence to convict the defendant.

Nominal damages: An minimal award of money in civil lawsuits that do not involve any substantial injury or loss to plaintiffs.

Noninterpretivism: An approach to constitutional interpretation that emphasizes text, history, and contemporary values to decide constitutional cases.

Nonpartisan election: A method of judicial selection used in the states. The judge's political affiliation does not appear on the ballot.

Opinion assignment: An appellate court norm that determines which judge will write the court's controlling opinion in an appeal. Assigning the responsibility to write opinions occurs during judicial conferences and is part of the coalition-building process during appellate court decision making.

Opinion for the Court: The opinion announcing the decision of a court.

Original jurisdiction: The jurisdiction of a court of first instance, or trial court. The Supreme Court has original jurisdiction under Article III of the Constitution.

Originalism: The "original meaning" or "original understanding" of constitutional provisions.

Panel: A group of appellate court judges that decides an appeal.

Partisan election: A method of judicial selection used in the states. The judge's political affiliation appears on the ballot.

***Per curiam*:** "By the court"; an unsigned opinion of the court.

Peremptory challenge: A formal procedure that excuses a potential juror from jury service for any reason in accordance with the prosecutor's discretion.

Petitioner: One who files a petition with a court seeking action or relief, including the plaintiff or appellant. When a *writ of certiorari* is granted by the Supreme Court, the party seeking review is called the petitioner, and the party responding is called the respondent.

Petit jury: A trial jury, traditionally a common law jury of twelve persons, but since 1970 the Supreme Court has permitted states to use juries composed of fewer than twelve persons.

Plaintiff: A party who commences a lawsuit in a civil case.

Plea bargaining: The process in which the accused and the prosecutor in a criminal case agree to a mutually acceptable disposition of a case without a trial.

Pleadings: Official court documents that are used in litigation and become part of the public record, often defining the cause of action (e.g. the complaint) and the required responses (e.g. reply), in accordance with the governing procedural rules of court.

Plenary consideration: Full consideration. When the Supreme Court grants a case review, it may give it full consideration, permitting the parties to submit briefs on the merits of the case and to present oral arguments, before the Court reaches its decision.

Plurality opinion: An opinion announcing the decision of the Court, but that has the support of less than a majority of the Court.

Political question: A question that courts refuse to decide because it is deemed to be essentially political in nature, or because its determination would involve an intrusion on the powers of the executive or legislature, or because courts could not provide a judicial remedy.

Preliminary hearing: A court proceeding in which those accused of a crime appear before a magistrate or judge to determine if there is probable cause to charge the accused with a crime and "bind over" the defendant for trial.

Preponderance of the evidence: A standard of legal proof in civil cases that requires the plaintiff to prove at trial a defendant's liability by "a preponderance of the evidence."

Presumptive sentences: See *Presumptive sentencing guidelines.*

Presumptive sentencing guidelines: Punishments in criminal law that fix the sentences of convicted defendants by using ranges that base the punishment on the offense's seriousness and an offender's prior criminal history. The guidelines are deemed presumptively correct, and judges cannot depart from them absent a legally permissible reason that is explained on the trial record.

Private law: A typology of law that defines legal relationships among the affairs of citizens in which private individuals resolve legal disputes.

Probable cause: Reasonable cause, having more evidence for, rather than against, when establishing the basis for obtaining a search warrant, for example.

Pro bono publico: Literally, "In the public good." It represents the ethical obligation of lawyers to represent clients for free, without the payment of legal fees.

***Pro se* filers:** Clients who represent themselves without the help of an attorney in legal cases.

Public defender programs: The way in which legal aid is provided to clients who are eligible to be appointed a lawyer in criminal cases because they cannot afford to pay for one.

Public law: A typology of law that defines legal relationships among governments and between governments and individuals.

Punitive damages: An award of money that goes beyond merely compensating injured parties for their actual losses in a civil lawsuit. They are designed to punish and deter defendants from committing egregious acts that cause substantial injuries to persons.

***Quo warranto,* writ of:** Literally, "By what authority." An order from a court challenging a person's legal right to hold a public or corporate office.

Rational basis test: A test used by appellate courts to uphold legislation if there is evidence of a rational basis for the law's enactment.

Reasonable doubt standard: A standard of legal proof in criminal cases that requires the government to prove at trial a defendant's guilt "beyond a reasonable doubt."

Reasoning by example or analogy: A legal reasoning technique that uses the analogy of past legal precedents as examples to derive legal principles that control how a new case is analyzed by judges and lawyers.

Rehabilitation: A punishment rationale in criminal cases that exacts a punishment on the basis of trying to rehabilitate offenders with the possibility of allowing them to assimilate into the community after their punishment has been served.

Reply: A formal court document filed in civil cases that answers the allegations of the plaintiff.

Republican ideological model (of judicial selection): A model of judicial selection that is used by Republican presidents to appoint judges to federal courts. Typically, a judicial appointment is based on achieving policy goals because the judgeship is a symbolic instrument of presidential power.

Respondent: The party that is compelled to answer the claims or questions posed in a court by a petitioner.

Retribution: A punishment rationale in criminal cases that exacts a punishment on the basis of revenge.

Ripeness: When a case is ready for adjudication and decision; the issues presented must not be hypothetical, and the parties must have exhausted other avenues of appeal.

Rules of discovery: See *Discovery rules, civil.*

Senatorial courtesy: The Senate tradition that the president consult with senators from the judicial nominee's home state before nomination.

Separation of powers: The division of the powers of the national government according to the three branches of government: the legislative, which is empowered to make laws; the executive, which is required to carry out the laws; and the judicial, which has the power to interpret and adjudicate disputes under the law.

Single-tier trial courts: A method of court organization in the states that gives trial courts general jurisdiction over a wide variety of civil and criminal cases.

Socialist law: Law derived from the political ideology of Marxism.

Standing: Having the appropriate characteristics to bring or participate in a case; in particular, having a personal interest and stake in the outcome.

***Stare decisis*:** "Let the decision stand." The principle of adherence to settled cases; the doctrine that principles of law established in earlier cases should be accepted as authoritative in similar subsequent cases.

State court administrator: A public employee who is in charge of running the state agency called the "administrative office of the courts." The administrator's duties include managing the agency and exercising oversight over the state judiciary.

Statute: A written law enacted by a legislature.

Statute of Limitations. The time period, established by statute, to commence a lawsuit. Unless there is an exception provided by statute or case precedent, persons seeking to begin a lawsuit must file it with a court in the time provided. An untimely filing will bar the person from seeking legal relief in court.

Strategic choice theory: A social science research methodology that asserts judicial decision-making is based upon the strategic choices of judges in the pursuit of policy goals after weighing the risks and benefits of their actions.

Strict constructionism: Dictates that judges should examine the plain meaning of the words as they literally appear within the four corners of a document.

Strict scrutiny test: A judicial standard of review that courts apply to constitutional law cases. It is used to discover whether government has a "compelling interest" and has used the "least restrictive means" in enacting legislation that is challenged as being a violation of constitutional rights and civil liberties.

Summary judgment: A motion asserting that there is "no genuine issue as to any material fact" and that the moving party in a civil lawsuit is entitled to a judgment as a matter of law and without the need for a jury trial.

Third-party litigation funding: A practice of allowing an independent third party with no direct connection to the claims of a lawsuit to fund a party in civil litigation in exchange for receiving a share of the damages ultimately awarded.

Three pillars: Written codes in civil law systems that broadly protect property, contract, and patriarchal family relationships. See *Civil law systems*.

Tort law: Affords remedies for private civil injuries.

Traditional legal studies: A research methodology in the legal academy that asserts that the "law" and the interpretative process of legal reasoning explains judicial decision-making.

Transactional lawyers: Lawyers that use their professional skills to complete business and legal transactions and generally do not engage in trial court litigation.

Trial administrators: See *Clerk of court*.

Truth-in-sentencing (laws): Sentences designed to make offenders serve their full, and not only a part, of their imposed legislative punishments in an effort to bring predictability and uniformity to the sentencing process. This is accomplished by replacing indeterminate with determinate sentencing, specifying how much actual time an offender will serve, and with little reduction in time served for good time or earned credits and/or no parole release allowed.

Two- and three-strikes laws: Sentences that enhance punishment on the commission of a second or third felony conviction, sometimes imposing mandatory life sentences or long imprisonments, in an effort to reduce offender recidivism through a deterrence punishment strategy.

Two-tier trial courts: A method of court organization in the states that splits trial courts into one or more sets of general and limited jurisdiction.

Voir dire: Literally, "to speak the truth." The formal process by which jurors are selected from the community to serve on civil or criminal trials.

Wall Street law firm: A type of private law practice developed in the 1890s by New York City attorney Paul D. Cravath. It uses a law office that is designed to be bureaucratically efficient and profitable.

Writ: An order commanding someone to perform or not perform acts specified in the order.

Legal Research Sources and Strategies

Most sources in legal research are found in public libraries, in law libraries, and on the Internet. Judicial opinions are accessed in "case reporters," or bound volumes of cases that are published and distributed by the Government Printing Office or West Publishing Corporation. Case reporters are indexed and arranged chronologically, by court and region. Electronic, or online, access to judicial opinions can be secured by home pages of courts (e.g., the U.S. Supreme Court's website is www.supremecourt.gov), Federal Court Finder (https://www.uscourts.gov/federal-court-finder/search), State Court Web sites (https://www.ncsc.org/Information-and-Resources/Browse-by-State/State-Court-Websites.aspx), or through generic legal research search engines, such as FindLaw (www.findlaw.com), or fee-based or academic online databases, such as Westlaw (or WestlawNext) (www.westlaw.com), LexisNexis (Lexis Advance, or LexisNexis Academic) (www.lexisnexis.com), and Bloomberg Law (www.bna.com/bloomberglaw).

A comprehensive law-related web journal, LLRX, provides online resources relating to court rules, legal forms, court dockets, and legal research (www.llrx.com). An annotated list of mobile apps for smartphones, tablets, and other mobile devices is found in the UCLA Law Library's "Mobile Applications for Law Students and Lawyers" (http://libguides.law.ucla.edu/content.php?pid=112286&sid=845584) (some apps are fee based, but others only require registration). Current and past U.S. Supreme Court merit briefs are accessible through the U.S. Supreme Court website (https://www.supremecourt.gov/meritsbriefs/briefsource.aspx).

Other free online legal research directories, portals, and blogs, some tailored to the U.S. Supreme Court and others to international or foreign law, include

- Cornell Law School's Legal Information Institute (www.law.cornell.edu);

- SCOTUSblog (www.scotusblog.com);

- Oyez (www.oyez.org);

- Library of Congress's "Guide to Law Online" (www.loc.gov/law/ help/guide.php) (this source has U.S. and foreign law links);

- American Society of International Law's "Electronic Resources Guide" (www.asil.org/resources/eresources) and "Electronic Information System for International Law" (www.eisil.org);

- New York University School of Law's "Guide to Foreign and International Legal Databases" (https://www.law.nyu.edu/ library/research/researchguides);

- Justia (www.justia.com);

- LPB Network, Law ProfessorBlogs.com (http://www.law professorblogs.com/)

- PrawfsBlawg (www.prawfsblawg.blogs.com)

- ABA Web 100 (https://www.abajournal.com/magazine/article/ best_legal_web_100_2018), including links to "best" law blogs, law podcasts, and Twitter accounts, among others.

- ABA Journal Blawg Directory (www.abajournal.com/blawgs);

- Feedspot "Top 100 Legal Blogs Every Lawyer and Law Student Must Follow in 2020" (https://blog.feedspot.com/legal_law_ blogs/), with links to Above The Law, the Volokh Conspiracy, Constitutional Law Reporter, European Law Blog, and Election Law Blog, among others.

For legal news, some free sites include Law.com (www.law.com), Jurist (www.jurist.org), and ABA Journal: Latest News (https://www.abajournal.com/ news). For empirical legal research, "Empirical Legal Studies" (https://www. elsblog.org/), with links to journals such as Journal of Empirical Legal Studies, Jurimetrics, Law & Society Inquiry, Law & Society Review, and research paper repositories, statistical programs, and databases, including SSRN (Social Science Research Network), STATA, Spaeth SCOTUS Database, State Supreme Court Data Project, the American Presidency Project, and Keith Poole NOMINATE Data, among others; or, Empirical SCOTUS, created by Adam Feldman (https:// empiricalscotus.com/tag/josh-blackmun/).

Helpful historical and research information on federal courts is found at the U.S. Courts (https://www.uscourts.gov/), including accessing court records (https://www.uscourts.gov/court-records), judicial statistics and reports (https://www.uscourts.gov/statistics-reports) and procedural rules and judicial policies (https://www.uscourts.gov/rules-policies); and, the Federal Judicial Center (www.fjc.gov), with especially helpful links to a biographical directory of Article III federal judges (https://www.fjc.gov/node/7946), plus other links to judicial salaries (https://www.fjc.gov/node/7441), diversity on the bench (https://www.fjc.gov/node/7491), and impeachments of federal judges (https://www.fjc.gov/node/7496). Analogous information on state courts is found on the National Center for State Courts website (https://www.ncsc.org/), with insightful references to annual reports on the Trends in State Courts (https://www.ncsc.org/trends), state court organization (https://www.ncsc.org/sco) and state court caseloads (http://www.courtstatistics.org/).

In short, there are plenty of ways to "get into" (i.e., discover) the law and related court information. The following provides a *legal research strategy* that gives you some guidelines or tips in analyzing a legal topic.

1. *Primary and secondary sources.* Generally, your task as a researcher is to discover *primary* and *secondary* legal authorities to support the legal argument or position (i.e., thesis statement) taken in your written legal analysis. *Primary authority* is the most persuasive source since it represents "official statements" from government sources as to what the law "is." Examples of primary authority include federal or state constitutions, statutes, case opinions (written by judges deciding specific legal disputes), and administrative regulations. Secondary authority, on the other hand, represents "secondary" perspectives about what the law says, or how the law may or should be interpreted. Secondary authority does *not* convey what the law actually "is." Examples of secondary authority include law review articles (written by law students or scholars), legal treatises (e.g., the Restatement of the Law of Contracts), legal annotations (e.g., *American Law Reports*), legal encyclopedias (e.g., *American Jurisprudence*), academic journal articles (in law or the social sciences, like *Judicature* or *American Political Science Review*), books, and legal newspapers (e.g., *Legal Times* or *National Law Journal*).

2. *The research strategy.* Below are some guidelines or tips that will help you devise an appropriate strategy if you are writing a college paper using legal and social science sources.

- *First*, begin your research early. Legal research takes (lots of) time! Start your legal research as soon as you receive the assignment.

- *Second*, consult secondary authorities *first* about how the "law" (or the legal topic) is interpreted, or what others say it means, as gleaned from a general perspective. Most times, you can accomplish this step by consulting legal encyclopedias, legal annotations, and/or legal (or nonlegal) newspapers. Once you are comfortable with the topic, review law reviews and, if relevant, peer-reviewed journal articles, such as *American Political Science Review*, *Law and Society Review*, *American Journal of Political Science*, *Political Research Quarterly*, and similar social science databases.

- *Third*, after you have a sense of the general legal issues, topics, or law involved in your assignment, explore *primary authority*, as described above. For example, if you are researching an issue regarding a Fourth Amendment case that challenges an allegedly illegal police search or seizure done without a warrant, then read what the courts say about the issue in their judicial opinions (see below).

- *Fourth*, generate a *balanced* perspective about what the law says by considering opposing viewpoints or criticisms about how the courts have ruled on the legal case or topic of interest. This can be done through analyzing "concurring" or "dissenting" opinions or, in regard to secondary sources, law reviews, legal or social science journals, and/or academic books.

- *Fifth*, try to be judicious in your research. It is very tempting to "over-research" a case or issue. Use common sense.

3. *Nonlegal and legal citation style.* As a rule of thumb, *any time* you take an idea or direct quotation from *any* kind of source, legal or otherwise, you *must* cite that source. Style manuals (*MLA Handbook*, *Chicago Manual of Style*, etc.) instruct you how to refer properly to nonlegal sources (and construct an appropriate list of "Works Cited" or "Bibliography"). Also, *usually* legal writing *mandates* correct citation form; but your instructor may not require it. If legal citation is necessary, the standard guide to legal citation form is *The Bluebook: A Uniform System of Citation* (19th ed.) (www.legal

bluebook.com), although some law schools and journals use the Association of Legal Writing Directors' *ALWD Guide to Legal Citation*, 5th ed. (www.alwd.org/publications/citation-manual/). Although many times legal research is done electronically, you may need to consult the print source if you need to cite a specific page. Not all electronic sources have corresponding print page references, but some do.

4. *Where to find legal cases.* Cases contain official and unofficial "citations" to a court opinion and include reference to the volume, page, and date of the case. *Official citations* are the formal citations of reported cases that are cited as precedents in judicial opinions or lawyers' briefs and memoranda. The official citation to a U.S. Supreme Court opinion is *Brown v. Board of Education*, 347 U.S. 483 (1954), which means it can be located in volume 347 of the *United States Reports*, at page 483. Yet the same case, *Brown*, can be located by accessing *unofficial citations*, or supplemental references to the same case, but using different reporters. Thus, *Brown* can also be found in volume 74, on page 686, of the *Supreme Court Reporter*, at 74 S. Ct. 686 (1954), or volume 98, page 873, of the *Lawyer's Edition*, at 98 L. Ed. 873 (1954), all in West's National Reporter System.

- *For federal courts:* U.S. Courts of Appeals cases are reported in West's *Federal Reporter* (*Buckley v. Valeo*, 519 F.2d 821 [D.C. Cir. 1975]), and U.S. District cases are found in West's *Federal Supplement* series (*Eaton v. Solon*, 598 F. Supp. 1505 [N.D. Ohio 1984]).

- *For state courts:* These are reported similarly, with the official citation naming the court issuing the opinion (e.g., Ohio Supreme Court) and the unofficial citation naming the region (*Pacific Reporter, South Western Reporter, Southern Reporter, North Eastern Reporter*). For example, the Ohio Supreme Court decided *DeRolph v. State of Ohio*, 93 Ohio St. 3d 628, 758 N.E.2d 1113 (2001). In researching state cases, it is helpful to review how state courts are organized because each state is different in terms of its trial and appellate court structure. A useful source is the National Center for State Courts, which has a listing of state court websites (www.ncsc.org) (see Chapter Three for discussion of state and federal courts' organization).

5. *Which cases should you cite?* When looking for cases to support your thesis statement or legal argument, consider the order of priority (or legal weight) of the cases that are consulted. Judicial opinions from "higher" appellate courts generally carry more legal weight, and hence are more persuasive. In general, use the following order of priority:

    1. Majority opinions for the U.S. Supreme Court

    2. Plurality opinions for the U.S. Supreme Court

    3. U.S. Court of Appeals opinions (previously known as Circuit Courts of Appeal; sometimes called "circuit courts")

    4. District Court opinions

    5. State Court opinions (only if there is an issue of state law presented in the case)

    Note that nonmajority opinions, like concurrences or dissents, should *not* be cited *as precedent* to support your argument (but they can be useful in *making an argument*).

6. *Shepard's Citations.* Shepard's Citations, or "Shepardizing," is an important research tool. It can be done manually, using print volumes, or, more commonly, through electronic sources such as LexisNexis (http://www.lexisnexis.com/documents/LawSchool Tutorials/20081015085048_large.pdf). Shepardizing will provide the most up-to-date version of the law (as compiled from primary authority), and it confirms if the case you are using as primary authority is still "good" law and has not been overturned or weakened by other courts by being treated differently. Also, it tells you how other courts have treated the case you are Shepardizing, which may be an important part of what you are trying to discover in your research. Moreover, it gives you references to other legal sources, including law reviews, which have analyzed the case you are researching.

Membership of the Supreme Court of the United States

Chief Justices	Appointing President	Dates of Service
Jay, John	Washington	1789–1795
Rutledge, John	Washington	1795–1795
Ellsworth, Oliver	Washington	1796–1800
Marshall, John	Adams, J.	1801–1835
Taney, Roger Brooke	Jackson	1836–1864
Chase, Salmon Portland	Lincoln	1864–1873
Waite, Morrison Remick	Grant	1874–1888
Fuller, Melville Weston	Cleveland	1888–1910
White, Edward Douglass	Taft	1910–1921
Taft, William Howard	Harding	1921–1930
Hughes, Charles Evans	Hoover	1930–1941
Stone, Harlan Fiske	Roosevelt, F.	1941–1946
Vinson, Frederick Moore	Truman	1946–1953
Warren, Earl	Eisenhower	1953–1969
Burger, Warren Earl	Nixon	1969–1986
Rehnquist, William Hubbs	Reagan	1986–2005
Roberts, John G., Jr.	Bush, G. W.	2005–
Associate Justices	**Appointing President**	**Dates of Service**
Rutledge, John	Washington	1790–1791
Cushing, William	Washington	1790–1810

Associate Justices	Appointing President	Dates of Service
Wilson, James	Washington	1789–1798
Blair, John, Jr.	Washington	1790–1796
Iredell, James	Washington	1790–1799
Johnson, Thomas	Washington	1792–1793
Paterson, William	Washington	1793–1806
Chase, Samuel	Washington	1796–1811
Washington, Bushrod	Adams, J.	1799–1829
Moore, Alfred	Adams, J.	1800–1804
Johnson, William	Jefferson	1804–1834
Livingston, Henry Brockholst	Jefferson	1807–1823
Todd, Thomas	Jefferson	1807–1826
Duvall, Gabriel	Madison	1811–1835
Story, Joseph	Madison	1812–1845
Thompson, Smith	Monroe	1823–1843
Trimble, Robert	Adams, J. Q.	1826–1828
McLean, John	Jackson	1830–1861
Baldwin, Henry	Jackson	1830–1844
Wayne, James Moore	Jackson	1835–1867
Barbour, Philip Pendleton	Jackson	1836–1841
Catron, John	Jackson	1837–1865
McKinley, John	Van Buren	1838–1852
Daniel, Peter Vivian	Van Buren	1842–1860
Nelson, Samuel	Tyler	1845–1872
Woodbury, Levi	Polk	1845–1851
Grier, Robert Cooper	Polk	1846–1870
Curtis, Benjamin Robbins	Fillmore	1851–1857
Campbell, John Archibald	Pierce	1853–1861
Clifford, Nathan	Buchanan	1858–1881
Swayne, Noah Haynes	Lincoln	1862–1881

Associate Justices	Appointing President	Dates of Service
Miller, Samuel Freeman	Lincoln	1862–1890
Davis, David	Lincoln	1862–1877
Field, Stephen Johnson	Lincoln	1863–1897
Strong, William	Grant	1870–1880
Bradley, Joseph P.	Grant	1870–1892
Hunt, Ward	Grant	1873–1882
Harlan, John Marshall	Hayes	1877–1911
Woods, William Burnham	Hayes	1881–1887
Matthews, Stanley	Garfield	1881–1889
Gray, Horace	Arthur	1882–1902
Blatchford, Samuel	Arthur	1882–1893
Lamar, Lucius Quintus C.	Cleveland	1888–1893
Brewer, David Josiah	Harrison	1890–1910
Brown, Henry Billings	Harrison	1891–1906
Shiras, George, Jr.	Harrison	1892–1903
Jackson, Howell Edmunds	Harrison	1893–1895
White, Edward Douglass	Cleveland	1894–1910
Peckham, Rufus Wheeler	Cleveland	1896–1909
McKenna, Joseph	McKinley	1898–1925
Holmes, Oliver Wendell	Roosevelt, T.	1902–1932
Day, William Rufus	Roosevelt, T.	1903–1922
Moody, William Henry	Roosevelt, T.	1906–1910
Lurton, Horace Harmon	Taft	1910–1914
Hughes, Charles Evans	Taft	1910–1916
Van Devanter, Willis	Taft	1911–1937
Lamar, Joseph Rucker	Taft	1911–1916
Pitney, Mahlon	Taft	1912–1922
McReynolds, James Clark	Wilson	1914–1941
Brandeis, Louis Dembitz	Wilson	1916–1939

Associate Justices	Appointing President	Dates of Service
Clarke, John Hessin	Wilson	1916–1922
Sutherland, George	Harding	1921–1938
Butler, Pierce	Harding	1923–1939
Sanford, Edward Terry	Harding	1923–1930
Stone, Harlan Fiske	Coolidge	1925–1941
Roberts, Owen Josephus	Hoover	1930–1945
Cardozo, Benjamin Nathan	Hoover	1932–1938
Black, Hugo Lafayette	Roosevelt, F.	1937–1971
Reed, Stanley Forman	Roosevelt, F.	1938–1957
Frankfurter, Felix	Roosevelt, F.	1939–1962
Douglas, William Orville	Roosevelt, F.	1939–1975
Murphy, Frank	Roosevelt, F.	1940–1949
Byrnes, James Francis	Roosevelt, F.	1941–1942
Jackson, Robert Houghwout	Roosevelt, F.	1941–1954
Rutledge, Wiley Blount	Roosevelt, F.	1943–1949
Burton, Harold Hitz	Truman	1945–1958
Clark, Thomas Campbell	Truman	1949–1967
Minton, Sherman	Truman	1949–1956
Harlan, John Marshall, II	Eisenhower	1955–1971
Brennan, William Joseph, Jr.	Eisenhower	1956–1990
Whittaker, Charles Evans	Eisenhower	1957–1962
Stewart, Potter	Eisenhower	1958–1981
White, Byron Raymond	Kennedy	1962–1993
Goldberg, Arthur Joseph	Kennedy	1962–1965
Fortas, Abe	Johnson, L.	1965–1969
Marshall, Thurgood	Johnson, L.	1967–1991
Blackmun, Harry A.	Nixon	1970–1994
Powell, Lewis Franklin, Jr.	Nixon	1972–1987
Rehnquist, William Hubbs	Nixon	1972–1986

Associate Justices	Appointing President	Dates of Service
Stevens, John Paul	Ford	1975–2010
O'Connor, Sandra Day	Reagan	1981–2006
Scalia, Antonin	Reagan	1986–2016
Kennedy, Anthony	Reagan	1988–2018
Souter, David H.	Bush, G. H. W.	1990–2009
Thomas, Clarence	Bush, G. H. W.	1991–
Ginsburg, Ruth Bader	Clinton	1993–
Breyer, Stephen G.	Clinton	1994–
Alito, Samuel, Jr.	Bush, G. W.	2006–
Sotomayor, Sonia	Obama	2009–
Kagan, Elena	Obama	2010–
Gorsuch, Neil M.	Trump	2017–
Kavanaugh, Brett M.	Trump	2018–

About the Authors

Christopher P. Banks is a professor at Kent State University. In 1980, he earned his BA in political science at the University of Connecticut, and in 1984, he graduated with his law degree from the University of Dayton School of Law. Before receiving his doctorate in American politics from the University of Virginia in 1995, he practiced law in civil and criminal litigation in Connecticut as well as being active in local and state politics. In Connecticut, he ran as a political candidate for state representative in 1988. After the election, he was appointed by Governor William O'Neill to serve as an administrative hearing officer for the Connecticut Commission on Human Rights and Opportunities. After graduating from the University of Virginia, he taught at the University of Akron for eleven years in the political science department while also serving as prelaw advisor. At Kent State University, he served as the department's graduate coordinator for its MA and PhD program, as well as an affiliate for the Center for Public Administration and Public Policy. He has served as the department's prelaw advisor and advisor to Pi Sigma Alpha, the Kent State chapter of the national honor society. He regularly teaches undergraduate and graduate courses in the judicial process, constitutional law, civil rights and liberties, law and society, terrorism, public administration, and American politics. He is the author of *Judicial Politics in the D.C. Circuit Court* (John Hopkins University Press, 1999) and *The American Legal Profession: The Myths & Realities of Practicing Law* (Sage/CQ Press, 2017); the co-author of *The U.S. Supreme Court and New Federalism: From the Rehnquist to the Roberts Court* (Rowman & Littlefield, 2012) and *Courts and Judicial Policymaking* (Prentice Hall, 2008); an editor of *Controversies in American Federalism and Public Policy* Routledge, 2018), as well as *The State and Federal Courts: A Complete Guide to History, Powers, and Controversy.* (ABC-CLIO, 2017), which received one of the ten of the Library Journal's Award for Best Reference Titles of 2017; and co-editor of *The Final Arbiter: The Consequences of* Bush v. Gore *for Law and Politics* (State University of New York Press, 2006), along with *Superintending Democracy: The Courts and the Political Process* (University of Akron Press, 2001). He has published numerous book chapters, book reviews, and journal articles on judicial behavior, law and politics, federalism, terrorism, and human rights in *PS: Political Science and Politics, Terrorism and Political Violence, Justice System Journal, Publius: The Journal of Federalism, Judicature, The International Journal of Human Rights, Public Integrity: A Journal of the American Society for Public Administration, Social Science Quarterly, Southeastern Political Review* (currently titled *Politics & Policy*), and *The Journal of Law & Politics*, among others.

David M. O'Brien is the late Leone Reaves and George W. Spicer Professor at the University of Virginia. He has been a judicial fellow and research associate at the Supreme Court of the United States; and held Fulbright teaching and research awards at Oxford University in England; at the University of Bologna in Italy; and in Japan; and was a visiting fellow at the Russell Sage Foundation in New York, and a visiting professor at Institut d'Études Politiques Université Lumière Lyon 2, France. He was a commissioner on the U.S.-Japan Conference on Cultural and Educational Interchange and the Japan-U.S. Friendship Commission. He is the author of numerous books and over one hundred journal articles and book chapters, including *Storm Center: The Supreme Court in American Politics* (11th ed., Norton, 2020), which received the American Bar Association's Silver Gavel Award; a two-volume casebook, *Constitutional Law and Politics* (11th ed., Norton, 2020); the annual *Supreme Court Watch* (Norton); *Animal Sacrifice & Religious Freedom:* Church of the Lukumi Babalu Aye v. City of Hialeah (University of Kansas Press, 2004); *To Dream of Dreams: Religious Freedom and Constitutional Politics in Postwar Japan* (University of Hawaii Press, 1996); and *Congress Shall Make No Law: The First Amendment, Unprotected Expression, and the U.S. Supreme Court* (Rowman & Littlefield, 2010), among other books. In addition, he has edited several books, including *Judges on Judging: Views From the Bench* (5th ed., CQ Press, 2016), and co-authored others, including *Government by the People* (22nd ed., Prentice Hall, 2008), *Courts and Judicial Policymaking* (Prentice-Hall, 2008), and *Judicial Independence in the Age of Democracy: Critical Perspectives From Around the World* (University of Virginia Press, 2001).

Index